Shopping for Pleasure

Shopping for Pleasure

WOMEN IN THE MAKING OF LONDON'S WEST END

· *ERIKA DIANE RAPPAPORT* ·

PRINCETON UNIVERSITY PRESS

PRINCETON AND OXFORD

Published by Princeton University Press, 41 William Street, Princeton, New Jersey 08540
In the United Kingdom: Princeton University Press,
3 Market Place, Woodstock, Oxfordshire OX20 1SY

Third printing, and first paperback printing, 2001
Paperback ISBN 0-691-04476-7

The Library of Congress has cataloged the cloth edition of this book as follows

Rappaport, Erika Diane, 1963–
Shopping for pleasure : women in the making of London's West End /
Erika Diane Rappaport.
p. cm.
Includes bibliographical references and index.
ISBN 0-691-04477-5 (cloth : alk. paper)
1. Consumer behavior—England—London—Sex differences—History.
2. Consumption (Economics)—England—London—Sex differences—History.
3. Women consumers—England—London—History.
4. Department stores—England—London—History.
5. West End (London, England)—Economic conditions. I. Title.
HF5415.33.E542L667 2000
658.8′342—dc21 99-28152

British Library Cataloging-in-Publication Data is available

This book has been composed in Adobe Caslon

Printed on acid-free paper. ∞

www.pup.princeton.edu

Printed in the United States of America

P

• FOR JORDAN •

• CONTENTS •

ILLUSTRATIONS

ACKNOWLEDGMENTS

THE INTELLECTUAL GUIDANCE and friendship of many individuals at several institutions have made the research and writing of this book a true pleasure. This project began as a doctoral dissertation at Rutgers University and in part is a product of its uniquely stimulating scholarly community. My greatest debt is to my adviser, John Gillis. John read, commented on, and discussed several drafts with tremendous care and enthusiasm. His advice and friendship at every stage have been absolutely invaluable. Victoria de Grazia initially provoked my interest in the history of consumer culture. Her extensive knowledge, incisive criticism, and personal warmth during the past decade have strengthened the arguments in both the dissertation and the book. I am also indebted to Bonnie Smith and Cora Kaplan for their reflections on the structure of the thesis. Special thanks must be given to Judy Walkowitz for her guidance during my first years at Rutgers and for introducing me to the pleasures of studying Victorian London. Her scholarship and teaching inspired me to write a dissertation on gender and urban history and pursue a career as a feminist historian. Long after we both left Rutgers, Judy graciously read and criticized parts of the revised manuscript. While at Rutgers, I had the opportunity to take courses from the late E. P. Thompson and from Leonore Davidoff. I hope my work reflects in small part their compassion for their historical subjects and their commitment to social history.

The women's history program at Rutgers provided an intellectually challenging and yet supportive environment. First and foremost, I would like to thank Maureen McCarthy and Tori Smith. Their friendship has sustained me from my very first day at Rutgers. Tori shared her own work on gender, representation, and Victorian culture and painstakingly read the dissertation and a final draft of this manuscript. Thanks also to Polly Beals, Joe Broderick, Joy Dixon, Sharla Fett, Gretchen Galbraith, Beth Rose, Scott Sandage, Pamela Walker, and Susan Whitney. I am tremendously grateful for their reflections on the thesis and for the pleasure of their company.

This project could not have been written without the financial support and inspiration I received while a student fellow at the Rutgers Center for Historical Analysis. Victoria de Grazia skillfully brought together an exceptionally strong and interdisciplinary group of scholars committed to studying consumer culture. While I greatly appreciate the help from everyone who listened to, read, and commented upon my work, I would especially like to thank Rachel Bowlby, Timothy Burke, Belinda Davis, Ellen Furlough, Ellen Garvey Gruber, Jennifer Jones, David Kuchta, and Kathy Peiss. Each offered detailed criticisms, but also shared his or her own ideas about the ways in which the concept of "consumer culture" has and has not illuminated key historical questions.

My colleagues at Florida International University were very helpful during the time I was in Miami. I owe particular thanks to Daniel Cohen, Mitchell Hart, Alison Isenberg, Joel Hoffmann, John Stuart, Mark Szuchman, and Victor Uribe for carefully reading and discussing sections of my manuscript. Alison and Mitch were especially careful readers whose comments helped me place my study of Victorian London into a broader context. My new colleagues at the University of California at Santa Barbara also deserve my gratitude for bringing me to such a beautiful and peaceful place to finish a book. They gave me the time and resources that I needed to complete this project.

Over the years, I have also been privileged to receive suggestions and comments from Peter Bailey, Leo Charney, Margot Finn, Susan Kingsley Kent, Deborah Epstein Nord, Maura O'Connor, Ellen Ross, Vanessa Schwartz, and Angela Woollacott. Two scholars deserve special mention for their guidance and friendship during the past several years. Lisa Tiersten tirelessly read every chapter of the manuscript and pushed me to think about the specificity of "English" consumer culture and urban development. Lisa's research on gender and urban consumer culture in late-nineteenth-century France also helped me to consider the role of politics in shaping consumer society. Geoffrey Crossick's vast knowledge of the history of retailing, the lower-middle classes, and Victorian London made his criticisms and interest in my work indispensable.

Several archivists and librarians lent me their time and assistance. Individuals at the British Library, the Guildhall Library, Westminster City Archives, the Fawcett Library, Glasgow University Business Records Center, Harrod's Department Store, Rutgers University, and the New York Public Library were especially helpful. Fred Redding was very accommodating, giving me free reign in Selfridge's archive and offering me dozens of cups of tea. The Interlibrary Loan departments at Florida International University and the University of California at Santa Barbara have retrieved hundreds of books and articles for me. This project received financial assistance from the Council for European Studies, Rutgers University Graduate School and Department of History, Florida International University, and the University of California at Santa Barbara.

Lastly, this book could not have been written without the enthusiasm and love of my family, especially my husband, Jordan Witt. Jordan showed unbounded patience and humor as we discussed every facet of this manuscript. His companionship in the United States and in England, editorial help and creative suggestions, friendship and love have made my work and my life a true pleasure.

A portion of chapter 1 appeared as " 'The Halls of Temptation': Gender, Politics, and the Construction of the Department Store in Late Victorian London," *Journal of British Studies* 35, no. 1 (January 1996): 58–83. A shortened version of chapter 2 appeared as " 'A Husband and His Wife's Dresses': Consumer Credit and the Debtor Family in England, 1864-1914," in *The Sex of Things: Gender and Consumption in Historical Perspective*, ed. Victoria de Grazia with Ellen Furlough (Berkeley: University of California Press, 1996), and part of chapter 5 appeared as " 'A New Era of Shopping': The Promotion of Women's Pleasure in London's West End, 1909-1914," in *Cinema and the Invention of Modern Life*, ed. by Leo Charney and Vanessa R. Schwartz (Berkeley: University of California Press, 1995).

Santa Barbara, California
July 1998

Figure 1. London's West End, 1893. *Kelly's Post Office Directory Map, 1893* (courtesy of the Guildhall Library, Corporation of London).

• INTRODUCTION •

"To Walk Alone in London"

Lucy Snowe, the heroine of Charlotte Brontë's novel *Villette* (1853), looked out of her hotel window on her first morning in London and thought, "Here was nothing formidable; I felt sure I might venture out alone." As Lucy stepped forth into the city's streets, her heart filled with "elation and pleasure." For this young single woman the idea of "walk[ing] alone in London seemed of itself an adventure." In contrast to Lucy's lonely and cloistered existence in the rest of the novel, on this trip "into the heart of city life" she enjoyed her solitude, her mobility, and her distanced perspective of the world around her. After purchasing "a little book—a piece of extravagance," Lucy climbed into the dome of St. Paul's Cathedral to achieve a bird's-eye view of "London, with its river, and its bridges, and its churches." She gloried in the spectacle of "antique Westminster and the green Temple Gardens" shining in the sun beneath the blue sky of early spring. Descending from this lofty height, Lucy continued her "wandering," experiencing an "ecstacy of freedom and enjoyment." "To do this, and to do it utterly alone," Lucy mused, "gave me, perhaps an irrational, but a real pleasure."[1]

A half century later, the artist Rose Barton expressed a similar passion for the metropolis by quoting this passage from *Villette* in the introduction to her book of London sketches, *Familiar London* (1904). Although much had changed since Brontë's day, as Barton walked in, wrote about, and painted London, she believed she was following in Brontë's footsteps. Barton assumed that Brontë's "wonderful description" through Lucy's eyes must have been a true rendering of her own "first impressions of London." Barton attempted to capture what she saw as the same "love" for "the Town" through colorful impressionistic paintings of London's people, its gardens, streets, sights, and shops.[2] Brontë and Barton lived during very different moments in London's history, yet both saw the metropolis as a sphere for female autonomy, pleasure, and creativity. Both novelist and painter imagined the city as a place to wander through, look at, and enjoy. During the half century that separated the lives of these two urban ramblers, many men and women came to see London in this way. This view of the city as a realm of individual freedom reflected London's transformation into a site of consumption and the new ideals of public and private and male and female that accompanied this change.

Like these works, *Shopping for Pleasure* embarks on an expedition through the Victorian and Edwardian metropolis. It explores how and why a solitary woman's urban journey could be described as an "ecstacy of freedom," as both an "irrational" and a "real pleasure." When Charlotte Brontë created Lucy Snowe in the 1850s, she invented a new type of urban character, a female rambler who consumed the city's sights and sounds, its goods and amusements. By the time that Barton wrote about and painted London, this coupling of bourgeois women and urban pleasure had fundamentally altered the English metropolis, especially key streets and institutions situated in London's West End (fig. 1). In this study, I examine how the West End came to be defined as an especially pleasurable place for bourgeois women. In particular, I explore how gender was central to the commercialization of England's capital city. In a sense, this book is also a history of the ambiguities of the public and private in the late-Victorian and Edwardian metropolis. Such uncertainties, I suggest, gave rise to untold anxieties and pleasures, new gender identities and relations between men and women.[3]

Though the West End had long been associated with wealth and amusement, after the middle years of the century it became a site of mass consumption, a shopping and entertainment center.[4] Like New York's Times Square, the late-Victorian and Edwardian West End may best be described as "an attraction," which was both "bounded and free, exploitive yet liberating, familiar yet exotic . . . [a] pleasure zone."[5] Witnessing the commercialization of the English metropolis, a *Saturday Review* correspondent professed in 1872 that London was becoming "a city of pleasure." "It was impossible," he wrote, "not to be struck by a certain brightness and glow in the Western parts of Town."[6] Several decades later, a suburban pleasure seeker from Streatham, Mrs. K. Davies, sent a letter to the *Evening News* in which she recalled the "delights" of "an occasional day's West End shopping." Miss E. Wilson of Crouch End similarly commented, "I delight, as every fashionable woman does, in taking a journey once every season to the West End, and thoroughly doing the sights."[7] Yet another suburbanite claimed to do all her purchasing there because "I for one prefer to do my shopping in the district I know from experience to be good—the West End."[8] The Edwardian business community held a similar conception of this neighborhood. An editorialist for *Modern Business* observed in 1908, "People shop in the magic West End because in some mysterious way they believe they get different or better goods there. . . . By years of suggestion [it] has created a special atmosphere."[9] As we will see, the creation of this "special atmosphere" involved new notions of bourgeois femininity, public space, and conceptions of modernity. Changes in retailing played a role in creating this "magic West End," but just as important were transformations in publishing, tourism, advertising, transportation, feminism, and family law, as well as in conceptions of pleasure, desire, and sexuality.

Many types of men and women inhabited, designed, and consumed in London between the 1850s and 1914. However, the West End shopper was invariably envisioned as a wealthy woman.[10] Indeed, her identity as a bourgeois woman rested on her yearning for this neighborhood. As Miss Wilson had put it, "every fashionable woman" was expected to enjoy shopping in the West End. The emergence of this desiring subject highlights but also reworks Michel Foucault's basic point about bourgeois society in this era. As he observed, the nineteenth century witnessed a multiplication of discourses about and sites of pleasure. For Foucault pleasure and power were inextricably linked, as pleasure came from both enforcing and evading power.[11] At the most fundamental level, my book analyzes the production and consumption of a set of discourses that constituted the city as a pleasurable arena during the latter half of the nineteenth century. Such discourses altered the way many Victorians viewed their city, produced new notions of desire, and rewrote gender ideals, producing a bourgeois femininity that was born within the public realm. I argue that public space and gender identities were, in essence, produced together. As the city became a pleasure zone, the shopper was designated as a pleasure seeker, defined by her longing for goods, sights, and public life. At times her desires were understood as sexual, but the Victorians also believed that shopping afforded many bodily and intellectual pleasures.

While the shopper was figured as an urban pleasure seeker, the other individuals who appear in this book achieved a place in public life by claiming to either stimulate or contain her pleasures. Retailers, journalists, jurists, politicians, feminists, reformers, and consumers built spaces and activities they hoped would appeal to wealthy ladies. As they constructed this commercial West End, these groups endlessly discussed and defined the shopper's needs and desires and their relationship to her morality and emancipation. They welcomed women into metropolitan culture by configuring public life as a pleasurable commodity and public women as natural consumers. While many decried the culture of shopping, critics never questioned the assumption that it was a "natural" feminine pastime. This conviction legitimized radically new aspects of urban social life, business practices, and even feminist politics.

As it does today, shopping in the nineteenth and early-twentieth centuries implied more than merely purchasing goods in a shop. As one recent theorist has remarked, it is not so much the "objects consumed that count in the act of consumption, but rather the unique sense of place."[12] Victorian shopping was similarly understood in spatial terms. Shopping meant a day "in Town," consuming space and time *outside* of the private home. A shopper might have lunch out, take a break for tea, and visit a club, museum, or the theater. Shopping also involved discussing, looking at, touching, buying, and rejecting commodities, especially luxury items such as fashions, furnishings, and other fancy goods.[13] The acquisition of commodities was considered enjoyable, but it was only one of the many pleasures of shopping. Although shopping was imagined as connected to a woman's domestic responsibilities, it was primarily conceived as a public pleasure.[14]

Shopping was never synonymous with buying nor was it simply the by-product of a growing network of retail facilities and the logical outcome of an economy geared toward mass production. According to one recent study, shopping emerged as a "discrete consumer activity" in the second half of the eighteenth century.[15] As mass production, distribution, and transportation developed during the nineteenth century, new groups began to shop in a host of new arenas. Novel definitions of femininity and public space associated with liberalism and the rise of an organized feminist movement as well as transformations in bourgeois family life also altered the understanding of shopping and shopping spaces.

In the second half of the century, female shoppers constantly traveled from their homes to the urban center, moving through both exterior and interior metropolitan spaces. The Victorian bourgeoisie was troubled and yet excited by this ambulatory crowd. They were intensely divided about the implications of shopping because shoppers blatantly disregarded the vision of society neatly divided into separate spheres.[16] During a period in which a family's respectability and social position depended upon the idea that the middle-class wife and daughter remain apart from the market, politics, and public space, the female shopper was an especially disruptive figure. Perhaps nothing was more revolting than the spectacle of a middle-class woman immersed in the filthy, fraudulent, and dangerous world of the urban marketplace. Nonetheless, the middle classes also needed the domestic angel to venture into the city's commercial culture. Especially after the 1870s, the expansion of mass production and the erection of tariffs abroad forced producers to "find" markets at home, in essence to manufacture shoppers. They did so in sites of consumption such as the West End.

If the city helped produce shoppers, it was also produced by consumers. As Henri Lefebvre observed, the city is "a space which is fashioned, shaped and invested by social activities during a finite historical period."[17] In *The Practice of Everyday Life*, Michel de Certeau has similarly explained that "space is a practiced place."[18] When Victorian women shopped, they imbued the urban center with meaning. Their consumption produced new attitudes about the city, while consumers contributed to the creation of new urban institutions. Shoppers were not free to design the city anew, however, since other images from both the past and the present conditioned their perspective.[19] Their ramble, nevertheless, did not always follow a prescribed tradition or path, nor did middle-class women experience the city solely as consumers.

Despite all the romantic, religious, legal, and scientific rhetoric extolling the virtues of the domesticated middle-class wife and mother, historians have charted her growing participation in public life. After midcentury, bourgeois women traveled through London's streets in search of employment, education, and amusement. They strolled in the city's parks, visited its museums, served in local government, and joined countless philanthropic, reform, and feminist organizations.[20] Middle-class women also authored numerous descriptions of the metropolis. As Deborah Nord has recently shown, quite a few female writers developed a distinctive vision of the Victorian city. Flora Tristan, Elizabeth Gaskell, Amy Levy, and dozens of others explored the city and participated in the culture of modernity.[21] Elizabeth Wilson has also analyzed women's complicated position in the modern metropolis. Wilson, for example, identified Lucy Snowe as an important departure from both the confined, chaperoned, home-centered, middle-class lady of Victorian domestic ideology and her alter ego, the denigrated prostitute.[22]

Though in *Shopping for Pleasure* I touch on the works of well-known authors such as Brontë, I consider these writers' part in a wider shift in popular representations of women and the city. Though novelists such as Brontë helped shape the new commercial city and consuming women, newspapers, women's magazines, guidebooks and the fin-de-siècle theater also invented a *flâneuse*, or urban woman who delighted in wandering through and writing about the commercial city. Many scholars have proposed that the urban rambler represented a peculiarly masculine perspective on the city and modernity.[23] Certainly, Brontë's London and that of other female writers I will be discussing was far less well known than that of the male writers—Charles Dickens, Gustave Doré, Henry Mayhew, G. A. Sala,

Henry James, George Gissing and Oscar Wilde—who haunted London's streets. Yet many middle- and upper-class women rambled in and wrote about the city as much if not more than did men of their class. These writers developed a popular mode of writing about female urban pleasure seekers and their city that drew upon but altered the literary tradition of the *flâneur*.[24] Thus, as writers and readers, workers and shoppers, middle-class women fashioned the late-Victorian and Edwardian West End as a shopping district, a tourist sight, an entertainment center, and an arena for female work and politics.

At first glance, this female London may appear to be an expression of pure fantasy. For much of this period, a woman's freedom to "walk alone" in the city was constrained by physical inconveniences and dangers as well as by social conventions that deemed it entirely improper for a bourgeois lady to roam alone out-of-doors. As Judith Walkowitz, Deborah Nord, and others have shown, any woman who strayed into the public spaces of the metropolis without the protective care of a chaperon could be perceived as a "public woman" or streetwalker. This was only one of the many restrictions placed on women who, for whatever reason, chose to venture into the streets of Victorian London. Not only were women constrained by the class and gender system, they also encountered very real limits on their mobility. The particularities of transportation, for example, enabled women to access the urban center yet the system also set up its own barriers. Married women's relation to the marketplace was also conditioned by the legal constraints placed on their property and their liability for debt. Moreover, the growth of commercial institutions and mass journalism spoke a good deal about the new woman in the city while also placing new constraints on female behaviors. In fact, emancipatory narratives did not remove the social rules that ordered Victorian men's and women's thoughts and activities; rather, they posed a new set of structures and ideals.

Shopping for Pleasure is thus not a social history of shopping, nor is it a straightforward narrative of London's wealthiest neighborhood. Rather, this study illuminates how the creation of the West End as a shopping center involved a reinterpretation of public life, the economy and consumption, and class and gender ideology. The West End was by no means the work of one class or one sex, nor can it be understood solely in terms of class and gender conflict. Its history is one of shifting alliances and confrontations between various segments of the urban middle classes, between those classes and older aristocratic elites, and between the middle classes and the working-class street folk who encroached upon their physical space and urban imagination. Like several recent studies, mine shows that the Victorian metropolis was the product of collaboration and conflict between different social groups attempting but not necessarily asserting mastery over the meanings and spaces of the city.[25]

In one respect, the West End was understood through opposition to other areas of the city, especially the East End. Scholars have often repeated, for example, that the Victorian imagination "juxtaposed a West End of glittering leisure and consumption and national spectacle to an East End of obscure density, indigence, sinister foreign aliens, and potential crime."[26] When Brontë wrote about London in the 1850s, however, she drew a distinction not between the East and West Ends, but between the hardworking, businesslike City of London and the pleasure-seeking, frivolous West End. As Lucy thought about the metropolis, she remarked to herself: "The City is getting its living—the West-end but enjoying its pleasures."[27] Though London's social and cultural life was far more complex than such dichotomies suggest, Lucy's preference for the City may be regarded as Brontë's memory of an earlier period when most commercial life and many important buildings and "sights" were not in the newer western half of London. It may also be seen as Brontë's distaste for the commercialization of the mid-Victorian West End.

London, of course, had long been a flourishing commercial center. As the seat of government, a port, and a financial, manufacturing, cultural, and social center, early-modern London was already a massive marketplace trading in goods, services, and amusements.[28] Prior to the mid-nineteenth century, most buying and selling took place in the oldest part of the metropolis, in the City of London, especially in the vicinity of St. Paul's Cathedral and Ludgate Hill. This area's narrow streets housed commercial warehouses, insurance companies, banks, and retail shops. Over time, demographic changes and a split between retailing and wholesaling physically and ideologically separated shopping from other forms of commerce. As this occurred, the City ceased to be the dominant shopping center and came to be perceived more or less as a masculine and serious preserve, a financial district. One observer even commented in 1863 that "ladies" had once bought fine silks and china in Cheapside, but "all this is changed." Now "business leaves no space for pleasure on the thronged pavements, [and] ladies have become a specialty."[29] By the 1860s, "ladies" shopped in the West End, especially in Regent Street, Oxford Street, Old and New Bond Streets, the Strand, Piccadilly, the Burlington Arcade, Leicester Square, and Tottenham Court Road. Collectively these streets became famous for having some of the most sumptuous boutiques, innovative stores, and pleasurable amusements in Europe.

In part the West End became known as London's premier shopping center because England's wealthiest and most powerful citizens had long made this neighborhood their home. As early as the sixteenth and seventeenth centuries, the aristocracy and gentry had started to migrate westward from the City to the West End despite the early Stuarts' attempts to limit urban growth in the area surrounding the Court.[30] Fleeing from plague, fire, pollution, and the threatening spectacle of the urban poor, the English elite set up house in the new squares and streets of Bloomsbury, Mayfair, and Belgravia. Peers, courtiers, and their friends and relatives stimulated commercial development with their prodigious appetite for consumer goods, services, and entertainments. As landlords, builders, residents, and consumers, aristocrats created what became the core neighborhoods of the West End.[31] Though middle-class speculative builders also shaped this area, its place names still bear witness to England's most powerful families. Grosvenor, Berkeley, Cavendish, and Portman Squares, for example, were monuments to the ruling order, while Regent Street and Regent's Park symbolized the power of the Hanoverian Court.

Regent Street, which the future George IV had laid out just after the Napoleonic Wars, signified royal power and prestige. And yet as it became the epicenter of the West End shopping district, it also housed a public form of aristocratic consumption and display. In the 1850s, the Frenchman Francis Wey wrote of Regent Street as "the only spot, outside the park, where Society people are certain to meet, as smart women would never dream of shopping elsewhere. The main artery of the West End therefore displays all the tempting treasures of the luxury trades." Wey called this shopping promenade a "precious observatory . . . [for] only here could you find the fashionable world so perfectly at home in the middle of the street."[32] The centuries-old link between this neighborhood and its aristocratic dwellers meant that "West End" was often seen as synonymous for Society, for those elite classes who lived, socialized, and shopped in this area of London.[33]

No street in the West End was ever the exclusive preserve of either the monarchy or the aristocracy, however. Especially as the middle classes gained wealth, power, and prestige in the nineteenth century, they began to assert their influence in this neighborhood. It is no coincidence that West End merchants and others began to court the middle classes in the second half of the century. During this period London's commercial and professional classes were richer "*per capita* and almost certainly more numerous than that in the provincial towns."[34] London's bourgeoisie may have been wealthier than its provincial counterparts, but by the 1860s West End merchants were also serving these "country cousins." Foreign and colonial tourists also spent a good deal of time and money in this neighborhood. This region thus became an international center catering to Britain's aristocracy and bourgeoisie as well as to wealthy colonials, Europeans, and Americans.

In many ways, the West End symbolized the protracted and uneven struggles between the monarchy, the aristocracy, and the commercial middle classes that dominated English political and social life during the eighteenth and nineteenth centuries.[35] Yet it also housed new types of commercial, political, and social formations. For example, Langham Place, which connected the northern part of Regent Street to Portland Place, was a center of the mid-Victorian women's movement. Nearby, Dover and Albemarle Streets, situated between Piccadilly and the residential area near Berkeley Square, became the heart of female clubland. After midcentury, mass commerce profoundly reshaped the West End's suburban landscape. Brompton Road, Kensington High Street, Westbourne Grove, and numerous other avenues in the western suburbs of London sported new department stores designed to appeal to a mass, heterogenous market.

Together, the shops, stately homes, clubhouses, spacious parks and squares, entertainments, and royal palaces lent the West End a unique prestige as the center of power, wealth, and pleasure in the empire. Overlapping and at times oppositional elite and mass cultures defined the West End. Throughout the modern period this territory exhibited a delicate balance between tradition and modernity. The West End never had any official or administrative meaning, however. Indeed, there was no single West End. Its contours shifted over time and depended upon the class, gender, and age of the perceiver, as well as the season and even the hour of the day that one visited this region. Like Bohemia, the West End was an imagined territory, whose frontiers crossed "back and forth between reality and fantasy."[36] This sense of the city structured an article on Regent Street published in the *Illustrated London News* in 1866. While describing the always elusive West End, the author commented that "Fashion has for more than an age been pushing its haunt further and further from the City—its cry has ever been 'Westward Ho!' " For this observer, social status and urban knowledge were intimately connected. Although the boundaries of the West End were somewhat "vague to persons living at a distance," this would-be geographer professed, " 'those to the manner born,' can draw the lines of demarcation with rigid accuracy."[37]

Though it was particularly linked with the upper classes, much of the eighteenth- and nineteenth-century West End was also devoted to masculine forms of consumption. Bond Street, "the best of all the London lounges," according to Henry Mayhew, had long been famous as a man's street.[38] Its apartments and hotels housed many well-known rakes, writers, and military men, such as James Boswell, Lord Nelson, and Lord Byron.[39] Its shops—hatters, tailors, and hairdressers—catered to this upper-class masculine clientele. Given the presence of such wealthy and dissolute masculinity, it is not surprising that such areas were also famous sexual marketplaces. Boswell captured this changeable and yet masculine view of the urban emporium:

> I have often amused myself with thinking how different a place London is to different people. . . . A politician thinks it merely as the seat of government . . . a grazier as a vast market for cattle; a mercantile man, as a place where a prodigious deal of business is done upon the "change"; a dramatic enthusiast, as a grand scene of theatrical entertainments; a man of pleasure as an assemblage of taverns, and the great emporium of ladies of easy virtue.[40]

If middle-class women were attracted to the aristocratic West End, the fact that the West End was also thought to be a "great emporium of ladies of easy virtue" meant that middle-class female shoppers were required to bring male relations, chaperons, or servants along on their shopping expeditions. More often than not, early-Victorian ladies waited in their carriages for the retailer to bring goods out to them.[41] However, by the time Lucy Snowe would walk alone in London, a confluence of social, economic, political, and cultural shifts occurred that encouraged middle-class women to step out of their carriages, to travel to, look at, and shop in the city on their own. As these women confronted a masculine and aristocratic West End, they reworked notions of gender, power, and the public sphere.

While there were multiple sources for such changes, quite a few recent studies have implied that department stores were responsible for this shift because they offered women a place in the public life of the city.[42] Though department stores did afford women access to the metropolis, the study of these institutions has often inadvertently accepted entrepreneurial rhetoric regarding gender ideals and notions of urban life. In this book, I focus on how and why stores presented themselves as safe, pleasurable, and emancipating places for urban women, while also exploring how such arguments fit within or challenged other aspects of bourgeois culture. In particular, this book illuminates how stores defined themselves as central to the project of civic improvement and women's emancipation and how different groups responded to such claims. In this effort, I focus on how other urban institutions paralleled, competed with, and engaged in a dialogue with department stores in constructing narratives about gender and public life.

While literary critics Rachel Bowlby and Thomas Richards have explored the relationship between gender, identity, and consumer culture, British historians have been somewhat slow to travel into similar territory. Bowlby and Richards were both informed by Guy Debord's view of modern consumption, as "a matter not of basic items bought for definite needs, but of visual fascination and remarkable sights of things."[43] Richards attributed the emergence of what he called "commodity culture" to the Great Exhibition of 1851 and the growth of the advertising industry and the illustrated press. Bowlby concentrated on the transformation of the literary marketplace, studying the place of consumption in the novels of Gissing, Dreiser, and Zola. While both captured an aspect of Victorian consumer culture, other studies have suggested that "modern" consumer culture did not emerge after 1851.

The Victorians clearly believed that they were building a modern world of mass production, distribution, and consumption. Recent scholarship, however, has shown that a complex world of goods was a distinct feature of early-modern society and culture. The vast majority of historical work on English consumer culture has located the emergence of a "consumer revolution" in the seventeenth and eighteenth centuries. Attention to this period is in part a result of the centrality of industrialization in English social and economic history. When Neil McKendrick, John Brewer, and J. H. Plumb published their seminal, if problematic, *The Birth of a Consumer Society: The Commercialization of Eighteenth-Century England*, they inspired a great deal of interest in the role of consumption in the transition to mass production and modern political systems.[44] More recently, the three-year project on consumption in early-modern Europe that Brewer directed at the Clark Library furthered the debate which *The Birth of Consumer Society* had in part instigated.[45] Though few agree on the nature or meaning of *consumer revolution*, many have intimated that aspects of a consumer society existed prior to the classic age of the Industrial Revolution. By contrast, there have been few comparable full-length studies of any aspect of consumption in nineteenth-century England.

Despite the relative neglect of historical studies of Victorian consumerism, there have been a number of detailed accounts of British retailing. Like those on the consumer revolution, however, many have been locked in a debate on the timing and nature of a *retailing revolution*.[46] Most argue that during the late-eighteenth and early-nineteenth centuries English shopkeeping expanded, rationalized, and became particularly innovative. While recent work has emphasized the persistence of older forms of retailing in the late-nineteenth century, fairs, annual markets, itinerant salesmen, and the use of verbal banter in buying and selling were slowly replaced by fixed shops and fixed prices and a greater emphasis on visual appeal to draw customers into the shop.[47]

The relationship between these transformations in retailing, consumer practices, and gender in the later half of nineteenth century has been acknowledged but not fully explored. In their monumental study of the early-nineteenth-century middle class, Leonore Davidoff and Catherine Hall have, for example, suggested that by studying production, distribution, and consumption as inextricably related processes, we may bring the household and gender into our understanding of middle-class culture.[48] They showed how the use and display of fashion and goods primarily within the home were essentially private activities that had public, particularly social, functions. In *Shopping for Pleasure*, I instead explore how the public face of consumption had both public and private meanings. Gender difference was still a central aspect of middle-class culture, as Davidoff and Hall have argued, but class and gender identities were often constructed within the commercial spaces of the late-nineteenth-century city, especially within London's West End.[49] In other words, gender was produced in public as well as the private spheres, and indeed it was central to the constitution of public life in metropolitan London.

More broadly, this study addresses recent debates about the nature of what has been called *consumer culture*, *consumer society*, *commodity culture*, or *commercial culture*. Scholars have employed these terms to describe the various processes by which commodities have acquired and produced meanings or value in modern or even postmodern capitalist societies.[50] Jean Baudrillard, for example, has defined consumption as "the virtual totality of all objects and messages constituted in a more or less coherent discourse."[51] While this definition points to the role of discourse in the study of consumption, I am not interested here in developing a general theory about the nature of consumer society, nor do I think that objects and their messages necessarily signify a "coherent" discourse. Frank Mort has observed in his recent study of masculinity, consumption, and social space in twentieth-century London that instead of searching for overarching theories or dating the rise of consumer society, we should examine how and why individuals were constructed as consumers within specific historical settings.[52] In a similar spirit, I focus on how gendered identities and physical spaces were constructed through narratives about consumption, whether they took the form of advertisements, newspaper editorials, social criticism, parliamentary legislation, or street protests. These narratives constituted the city and social identities, and were in essence what I see as consumer culture.

Some readers may assume that I am arguing that the West End's history demonstrates the demise of an authentic rational public sphere into an arena of irrational pleasures, or a pseudo-public of consumption. This view has been reiterated by critics from both the Left and the Right and most fully articulated by Jürgen Habermas in his *Structural Transformation of the Public Sphere*.[53] While a telling analysis of the fate of democratic politics in the twentieth century, Habermas's account of the decline of a liberal sphere of rational discourse into a mass-produced public of passive consumers does not adequately capture women's experience of the public, and it inadvertently positions women's presence in any manifestation of the public as a sign of its collapse and corruption. At the same time, those scholars who have championed consumer culture as emancipatory have often unintentionally reinforced the arguments of advertisers and entrepreneurs.[54] Both views raise questions about the role of consumption in the constitution of modern societies; however, I avoid relying on either position. Rather, I show how similar debates were at the heart of what constituted consumer culture in Victorian England.

This book implies, then, that our present attitudes about consumption or consumer culture, including that of historians, have in many ways replicated nineteenth-century notions of the individual and the masses, gender and commerce. When, for example, contemporary theorists argue that advertising, department stores, or the fashion industry seduce individuals, they often cast the consumer as a feminized victim of masculine (economic) aggression. This image of economic relationships as sexual maintains a binary opposition between an active male producer and a passive female consumer. It also obscures as much as it reveals about the cultural and social world of buying and selling in the nineteenth century. Yet the celebratory view of consumption not only overlooks the ways in which women have been subject to unique forms of oppression within consumer societies; it also adopts entrepreneurial narratives about individual freedom in the marketplace that have been prevalent both in the nineteenth and the twentieth centuries.

Class and gender contests were fought out through the construction of the female consumer as either a victim or an emancipated woman. These images were especially central to struggles over space, money, and identity in a rapidly expanding and fluctuating urban environment. Victoria de Grazia has suggested that instead of concluding that consumption was either emancipatory or oppressive for women, we need to explain how consumer culture constructed gender roles and power relations.[55] As part of this effort, *Shopping for Pleasure* explores the relationship, which Habermas implied, between consumption and shifting definitions of the public and the private. I examine the actors and motivations behind diverse conceptions of the commercial public and show how these views impacted men and women's daily lives, class and gender identities, and the history of particular businesses. This approach illuminates Joan Scott's argument that gender, society, and politics are mutually constitutive within specific historical contexts.[56] Through an analysis of particular events, spaces, and institutions, we may see how consumption, urbanization, and definitions of masculine and feminine overlapped and influenced one another in late-Victorian and Edwardian England.

Shopping for Pleasure begins in the years following Lucy Snowe's solitary journey and is organized as a shopper's expedition meandering in and out of some of the West End's main attractions. The chapters are roughly but not precisely chronological, with each concentrating on a different theme or location as it came to play in a given period. This journey begins in suburban Bayswater on the outskirts of the fashionable West End and explores the development of Whiteley's, one of England's first department stores. In this chapter, I consider how gender and commercial competition shaped the growth and meaning of large-scale retailing, suburban development, and gender identities between the 1860s and 1880s. In these years, local opposition to and subsequent acceptance of mass retailing involved a renegotiation of markets, bourgeois femininity, and urban space. By studying the conflicts between local shopkeepers, we begin to see how the idea of shopping as female leisure was embedded within larger political and economic arguments about urbanization and commercial culture.

The second chapter analyzes how this new leisure activity, visible in Bayswater and elsewhere, deepened tensions between credit traders and customers and husbands and wives. These anxieties were especially visible in the legal disputes between drapers and their customers over unpaid debts. I analyze the relationship between changing legal notions of family property and liabilities and individual disputes between creditors and female debtors to explain how urbanization and the relocation of urban markets influenced both family and market relations. Finally, this chapter also reveals how the persistent problems faced by credit traders contributed to the expansion of cash transactions that in turn aided the rise of the department store.

The following chapter picks up on the role of the emerging feminist movement in this history and documents the development of a feminist-inspired commercial culture in the West End. At the same time that the department stores were evolving, feminists and their allies shaped the gendered nature of the West End by building female-oriented clubs, restaurants, tea shops, and lavatories for shoppers. They hoped these institutions would provide an alternative to the mass market. However, while facilitating women's mobility in the public sphere, they also naturalized and expanded the conception of shopping as feminine activity.

Chapter 4 considers another aspect of the role of women as producers as well as consumers in the city. In particular it examines how women's magazines and a group of professional tour guides known as the Lady Guide Association characterized shopping as an urban leisure activity, akin to sight-seeing. By teaching middle-class readers how, where, and what to consume, women's journals and Lady Guides presented shopping as a form of female urban spectatorship. They also established the idea that seeing and being seen were central components of a "modern" woman's identity.

Chapter 5 returns to the department store to explore how this mass-market institution and new forms of publicity and advertising in the early-twentieth century helped construct shopping as a visual and public pleasure during the Edwardian period. The chapter recreates the advertising campaign and spectacular opening in 1909 of Selfridge's, an American-owned and -styled emporium in Oxford Street. This department store reconfigured London's commercial culture and raised concerns about American economic and cultural domination. This event particularly illuminates how Edwardian promotional culture altered class, gender, and national identities.

The final chapter focuses on the theater and expands the analysis of shopping as a form of female spectatorship. It looks first at the alliance that developed between the theater and commercial culture between the 1890s and the First World War. During this period, the West End stage acted like a store window, displaying the latest fashions and styles. This was particularly true of musical comedies, a new genre that was extremely popular during these years. Musical comedy audiences watched the latest fashions parade onstage while they also laughed at themselves and their role in the culture of consumption. In the plays' romantic and satirical treatments of consumption, we also see the emergence of shopping as part of a new heterosexual sensibility and culture in which the aim of a woman's consumption became her self-creation as a sexual object.

While the glamorous image of the shopper and shopping in musical comedy marks the end of this journey through London, the epilogue raises the question of other possible routes through the city. In particular, it looks at the militant Suffragette's window-smashing campaign in the West End in 1912 to consider the relationship between the commercial and political spheres in the early-twentieth century. This incident highlights the fluid nature of public space and identities, the multiple and often contradictory notions of female emancipation during this era, and the role feminists played in building and demolishing aspects of the English metropolis and notions of urban pleasure.

Although never exclusively a female or bourgeois arena, the late-Victorian and Edwardian West End was the locus of middle- and upper-class women's amusement, social life, and politics. *Shopping for Pleasure* attempts to illuminate this interplay between commerce, gender, and the city. It is both a social and economic history of the West End and a study of how ideals about gender and consumption structured the way people understood London. It contributes to an understanding of the structural shifts in late-nineteenth-century capitalism, to the transformations in bourgeois culture in relation to those changes, and, most directly, to the nature of women's role in that economy and culture.

• CHAPTER ONE •

"The Halls of Temptation": The Universal Provider and the Pleasures of Suburbia

On Guy Fawkes Day in 1876 an angry mob of retailers staged a charivari in the fashionable shopping promenade of Westbourne Grove in Bayswater. Their demonstration targeted William Whiteley, a linen draper who was rapidly expanding his shop into what would become London's first department store. According to the local newspaper, the recent addition of a meat and greengrocery department had made Mr. Whiteley "exceedingly distasteful" to the "provision dealers in the district." Bayswater's traders expressed their discontent through traditional forms of popular protest, using the neighborhood's streets as the venue for a raucous procession. The festivities began around noon as

> a grotesque and noisy cortège entered the thoroughfare [Westbourne Grove]. At its head was a vehicle, in which a gigantic Guy was propped up . . . vested in the conventional frock coat of a draper. . . . Conspicuous on the figure was a label with the words "Live and Let Live." . . . In one hand of the figure a piece of beef bore the label "5 1/2 d." and in the other was a handkerchief, with the ticket "2 1/2 d. all-linen."[1]

Dressed in the customary blue frocks of their trade and making "hideous" noises by banging cleavers against marrowbones, Bayswater's butchers finally disposed of Whiteley's effigy in a bonfire in nearby Portobello Road.

This spectacle involving one of England's most well known entrepreneurs, a noisy band of butchers, and the ostensibly neutral voice of the local newspaper editor provides a point of departure for an investigation of the commercial culture of the Victorian West End. This affair introduces many of the protagonists and the arenas—the department store, the shopping street, and the newspaper—that occupy a central place in this history. Finally, the charivari and the themes that emerge in its telling begin to reveal the social, cultural, and emotional world of London's trading classes.

The appearance of a charivari—or "rough music," as it was known in England—in late-Victorian suburban London is both striking and illuminating. In early-modern Europe, similar parades of boisterous young men mocked individuals who had in some way or other offended local morality. These events enforced community norms by censoring both public and private behaviors. Incidents of sexual misconduct, especially those involving women displaying aggressive or independent actions, frequently brought on this collective response. Female scolds, wife beaters, or couples in apparently mismatched unions might be chastised in this way. These protests might also be directed at any individual who, as E. P. Thompson described it, rode "rough-shod over local custom."[2] On Guy Fawkes Day, in particular, various "political, industrial or private grievances" could be settled through this elaborate form of street theater.[3] According to Robert Storch, Victorian Guy Fawkes demonstrations commonly targeted "unscrupulous tradesmen."[4] One contemporary believed, moreover, that butchers were particularly fond of celebrating the holiday by parading a local villain through the town.[5] The meaning of charivari and Guy Fawkes Day celebrations thus varied considerably. However, in suburban London in 1876 this holiday allowed a community of traders to vent their anxieties about an individual and the "modern" changes that he represented. Bayswater's unhappy retailers castigated William Whiteley for altering economic and gender norms, for reshaping the public and private spheres.

There is no question that Londoners regarded Whiteley as a renegade retailer. Between the 1860s and 1880s, Whiteley created a new persona as he built a new type of shop. He became known as the "Universal Provider"—a merchant who claimed to sell anything to anybody. By combining dissimilar goods in one business and offering cut-price goods for cash only, Whiteley had strayed far from the norms of the small independent shopkeeper.[6] Bayswater's traders perceived these innovations as a threat to their livelihood and their way of life. In a spirited letter titled "Wholesale Butchery in Bayswater" that was printed in the local paper, one of Whiteley's victims complained that he had watched a "startling succession of feats in the art of shutting up your neighbour's shop and driving him elsewhere, but this last daring and audacious feat—this vending of meat and greens as well as silk and satins—overtops them all."[7] As both this letter and Whiteley's effigy made clear, specialized shopkeepers believed that the move from dress goods to provisions was too great a leap. This promiscuous mingling of food and clothing bore little resemblance to more traditional organizations of craft production and distribution and seemed to spell the demise of the independent specialized trader. Although craft guilds had long since disappeared in England, the vestiges of trade-oriented identities and cultures lurked in popular memory and could be retrieved in times of economic and social crisis.[8] As late as the 1870s, small merchants could thus be horrified, if also amused, by the image of Whiteley with beef in one hand and linen in the other.

One should not, however, hastily conclude that Whiteley's effigy simply expressed an older trading community's rejection of newer forms of retailing. This assumption fits the diagnosis that a conservative or "backward" business culture contributed to the decline of the late-Victorian economy.[9] However, to cast these merchants as conservatives repudiating modernity is a simplistic reading of both the local and national economies. Many of Bayswater's traders were relative newcomers to the area and some were engaged in what were construed as modern trading practices. The charivari appeared in late-Victorian London at a moment when large-scale retailing and rapid urbanization became identified with shifting class and gender norms.

Bayswater's butchers picked up their cleavers and marrow bones to express their sense of insecurity in this competitive and fluctuating environment. They drew on older modes of social protest to regulate but not halt these changes. As we will see, they also invented new methods of protest that characterized mass retailing as dangerously reshaping bourgeois femininity. Traders who opposed Whiteley and the transformations he represented frequently avoided direct attacks such as the charivari and chose instead to charge Whiteley with the moral crime of unleashing uncontrollable female passions. It is no wonder, then, that he would become the subject of a charivari, a protest that could conveniently punish either a sexual or economic miscreant.

Between the 1860s and 1880s, the Universal Provider and the shopping district in an around Westbourne Grove symbolized the mass culture and economy that were becoming visible throughout the West End of London. During those years, transformations in retailing, catering, entertainment, publishing, and transportation produced public spaces that were identified with a new type of mass public. Large hotels and theaters, restaurants and department stores grew by selling diverse commodities and services to a clientele that could not be easily categorized. This mass market was not a synonym for either a working-class or a bourgeois public. Rather, it implied heterogeneity.

As Mary Poovey has explained, by the 1860s new technologies of representation along with material innovations "brought groups that had rarely mixed into physical proximity with each other and represented them as belonging to the same, increasingly undifferentiated whole."[10] Although society was also perceived as segregated by class, in certain locations it appeared as a mass aggregate. While Poovey emphasized how novel methods of quantification and social investigation represented this aggregate, others have observed that public transportation also constituted society in this way. In his work on public amenities in New York City, William Taylor pointed out that with the expansion of mass transit "the public" came to be perceived as a "mobile and embodied mass."[11] Taylor observed that in America the railway helped transform the political public into an embodied mass. This public was conceptualized as a mass market made up of, as Wolfgang Schivelbusch perceived it, "parcels" not unlike other goods circulating in the economy.[12]

There were in fact several competing notions of "the public" and "the masses" in mid- and late-Victorian London.[13] These constructs were both gendered and varied in meaning as particular groups attempted to legitimize their understanding of politics, urban space, and economic activities. At times the public was conceived as a male and political entity, but it equally could become a feminine body of consumers. While few understood how it would act, where it belonged, and what it wanted, virtually all agreed that the consuming public was primarily, if not wholly, a feminine entity. Between the 1860s and 1914, the shopping public also looked like a mobile crowd, a group of traveling suburban and provincial women who were defined by their presence outside of the domestic sphere. The mass press, large shops, and crowded shopping streets of the Victorian West End made this public manifest. Yet such entities could not have existed independent of the idea of this feminine public. The shopping public and London's commercial spaces were quite simply mutually constitutive. Throughout this book we will see many individuals and groups attempting to understand, perceive, and define the shopping public. This study traces how the emergence of this public was born at the intersection of social, economic, and cultural contests over new forms of retailing, communication, and urban space.

The shopping public was an integral part of urban and economic change in the late-nineteenth century, yet its feminine and amorphous nature challenged bourgeois gender ideology, which had long characterized public spaces and the more abstract public sphere as masculine. Not surprisingly, the implications of a female consuming crowd were fiercely contested. Shopkeepers, shoppers, social reformers, government officials, feminists, and journalists debated several related questions. To what extent did the presence of this crowd in London's streets spell social collapse or improvement? What type of pleasure did the city legitimately offer this public? What was the relationship between shopping, conceived as the public face of consumption, and what was perceived as the private sphere of the family and the self? Though the participants in and the terms of this discussion would shift over the course of the next fifty years, these questions would never entirely disappear. The attempt to find answers produced new social identities based upon notions of pleasure and consumption. Consumer practices such as shopping thus fashioned identities by disrupting and reconstituting social categories and their perceived relationship to public and private spaces.[14]

This chapter will explore these issues by focusing on particular individuals in a relatively bounded setting. No two stores or neighborhoods were identical, especially in a city as large and diverse as London. Still, the Victorians singled out Bayswater and its largest proprietor, William Whiteley, as pivotal to their city's history. After the middle decades of the nineteenth century, Bayswater became a thriving shopping district that rivaled more established West End centers.[15] Such western suburbs provided ideal conditions for the emergence of a new type of retailing and a new kind of shopping crowd. Though physically peripheral, suburban Bayswater was in many respects central to the creation of a new West End.

The shopkeepers, visitors, and writers who lived in and traveled to Victorian Bayswater would have agreed with Michel Foucault when he wrote, "The anxiety of our era has to do fundamentally with space."[16] During the second half of the nineteenth century, a rapidly altering urban landscape was profoundly influencing these traders' economic security and their social identities. Rowdy street demonstrators, politicians, shopkeepers, residents, and journalists both objected to and produced new spaces of consumption and consuming publics. The confrontations and solutions that appeared in this London suburb resonated throughout the city and across urban Britain.

"Young London": The Making of a Suburban Shopping Center

"Westbourne-Grove . . . [is] one of the most extraordinary thoroughfares in Young London," wrote the well-known journalist and man-about-town George Augustus Sala in 1879. Twenty years earlier, Sala had published the extremely

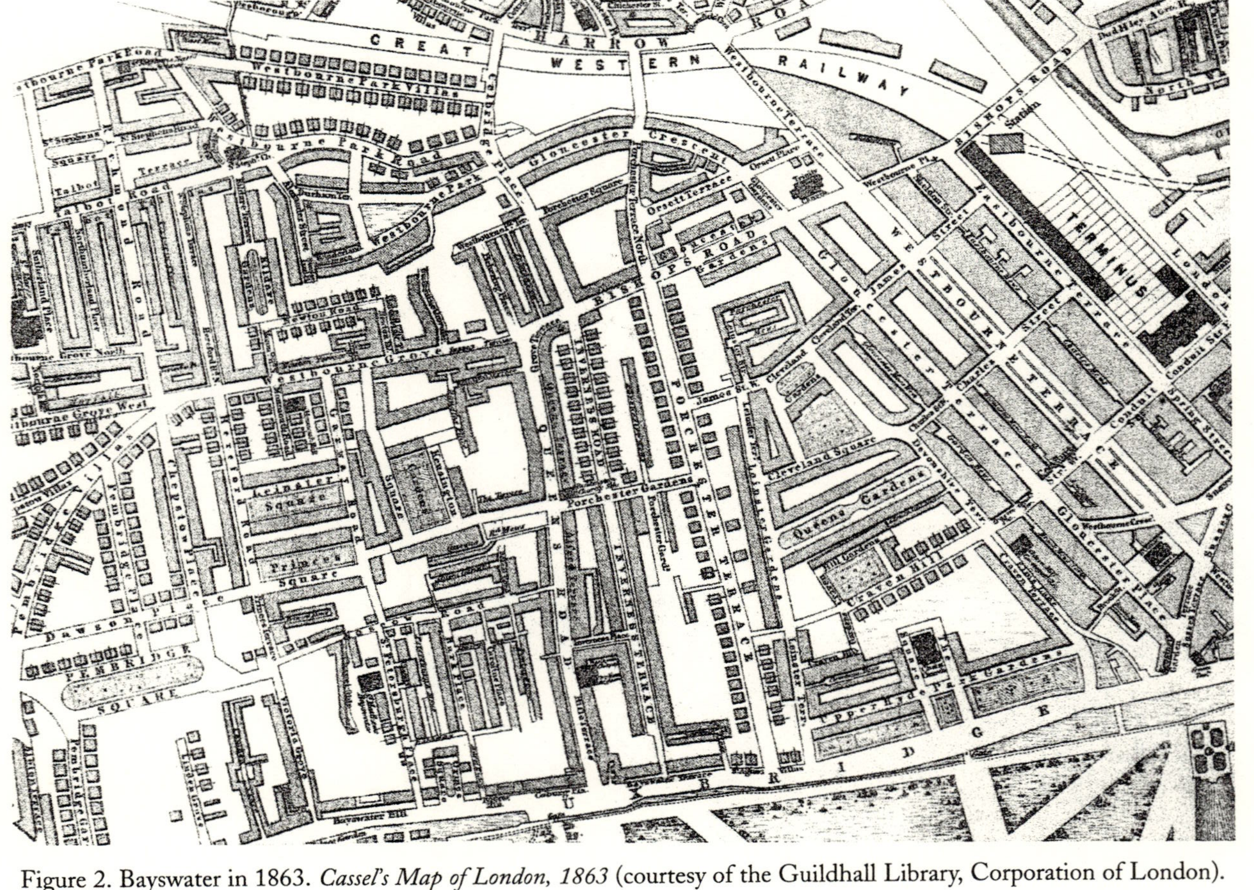

Figure 2. Bayswater in 1863. *Cassel's Map of London, 1863* (courtesy of the Guildhall Library, Corporation of London).

popular *Twice round the Clock, or The Hours of the Day and Night in London* (1859), an excavation of the social and commercial life of the mid-Victorian metropolis. In the late seventies, he was still fascinated with London's commercial culture, but he now turned his roving eye away from central London toward the city's newest western suburbs, or "Young London." Sala's exegesis of modernity began in "Westbourne-Grove and Thereabouts," a street he described as the "center of a new, prosperous, and refined district." Although Bayswater was situated at the northwest corner of the West End, Sala placed it at the heart of a new consumer-oriented city. He described it as the lustrous and affluent symbol of the powerful England that had appeared since the defeat of Napoleon and the crowning of Queen Victoria (fig. 2).

The shops that lined Westbourne Grove were central to Sala's reading of modern suburbia. He portrayed the Grove as "full of emporiums for the supply of almost every conceivable human want and wish; and all the creation, so to speak, of the day before yesterday." Although Sala paid tribute to the many shops that lined the street, he was most enraptured with "Wonderful Whiteley" or "The Westbournian Miscellany." Perhaps because Whiteley's occupied so many shops, when Sala strolled through the Grove all he could see was the Universal Provider and the "miscellany" that he sold.[17] Sala used Whiteley, Westbourne Grove, and Bayswater as metonyms for the growth of middle-class prosperity. The existence of stores like Whiteley's, he wrote, proved that "the world was pecuniarily richer than ever it was" and that "science, art, and free trade have brought luxury and comfort within the reach of the middle classes."[18] Bayswater's meteoric rise from a rural retreat to a thriving marketplace was a perfect symbol of the mid-Victorian ideals of progress, prosperity, and improvement.

A new relationship between the sexes also appeared in Young London. As Sala showered the region with praise, he could not restrain his obvious excitement at the sight of so many well-dressed and lovely women parading through the street. He wrote of Westbourne Grove as a sensual Eastern marketplace in which men delighted in looking at women who, in turn, enjoyed looking at goods. In this "open-air Bezesteen . . . sultana-valides from Lancaster gate, and khantoms from Porchester-terrace . . . Gulnare on her Arab steed, [and] Gulboyaz . . . from the bath, from the sweet waters of Asia" were all doing "a little shopping," while "John the footman change[d] into guardian of the harem." In this scene of oriental splendor, the male passerby and journalist became "a peeping-tom," and the "ladies of Westbourne-grove" became thousands of Lady Godivas, "enjoying the contents of the shop windows to the fullest extent."[19] Sala thus illustrated the erotic spectacle of a suburban marketplace by drawing upon what were hackneyed if pervasive images of the Orient. For Sala, a sensual, orientalized marketplace, commodified and objectified female shoppers, and a male observer were the representatives of modernity.

Quite a few residents rejected Sala's vision of their suburb, which equated modernity with eroticism, voyeurism, orientalism, and consumerism. Indeed, several letters in the local newspaper, criticized virtually every aspect of this "photograph of the locality." They rejected Sala's treatment of female shoppers and male loungers, his cataloging of commodities, and his uninhibited "panegyric about Mr. Whiteley's establishment."[20] These debates about suburban London centered upon the relationship between economic and urban change and shifting class and gender ideologies. Districts such as Bayswater raised the question of whether London's topography corresponded to its social geography. Residents, shopkeepers, local politicians, and journalists such as Sala saw Bayswater as something of an enigma. The wealthy middle classes built such neighborhoods to isolate themselves from their social inferiors, yet as soon as their houses went up another aspect of bourgeois life disrupted this fantasy. While suburbia may have reflected and reproduced social segregation, its commercial districts defied this development.[21]

Many of London's Victorian suburbs were at the crossroads of the public and private, both domestic havens and thriving marketplaces.[22] During the second half of the nineteenth century, several suburban streets evolved into flourishing retail centers with elegant small shops and monumental department stores. Parisian department stores first appeared along the new avenues being laid out in the center of the city by Baron Haussmann and Napoleon III.[23] Americans living in cities like New York, Boston, Philadelphia, and Chicago would also see mammoth commercial enterprises reshape their downtown districts during these years.[24] London's stores began a similar metamorphosis not only in the city center but in the new suburbs that inexorably expanded the boundaries of the nineteenth-century metropolis.[25] This distinction between center and suburb should not be overdrawn; however, West End residential districts such as Belgravia had once been understood as suburbs on the perimeter of London.[26] Nonetheless, many of the largest Victorian stores grew along streets such as Lisson Grove, Brixton Road, Kensington High Street, Brompton Road, and Westbourne Grove, the main traffic arteries of suburban London.[27]

When the novelist and journalist Walter Besant described late-Victorian suburbia, he invoked, as Sala had, images of prosperity, femininity, and commercialism. For Besant, suburbia's female inhabitants spelled commercial growth. "We must bear in mind," he remarked, that while the London suburb "may send up its tens of thousands every day to the city, there remain behind wives and families. For these an immense local trade arises; there spring up shops of every kind . . . the streets in the day-time are filled with women and children; and fortunes are made in local trade."[28] In this passage, Besant assumed that suburban shopping centers grew naturally and inevitably with a large, sedentary, and satisfied female population. While male suburbanites abandoned their neighborhoods each morning, their female relatives apparently remained at home, spending their day shopping in the local high street.

When Besant characterized the suburb as a female sphere, he echoed orthodox opinion regarding the gender divisions of bourgeois life. Numerous recollections portrayed suburbs as devoid of men during the daytime. For example, an autobiography written by a young woman who grew up outside of Manchester remembered that once the 9:18 train had left, her neighborhood became "exclusively female. You never saw a man on the hill roads unless it were the doctor or the plumber."[29] In such passages suburbia appeared as an extension of the private sphere, a safe haven in which women and children spent a quiet life of leisure.[30] In her study of gender and urban life, Elizabeth Wilson has argued that the most extreme example of confined femininity was the ubiquitous image of the middle-class wife and mother "in the prosperous suburbs of Bayswater or Edgbaston." Wilson implied that the suburban wife who was tightly constrained by rules of etiquette and the demands of a large household of children and domestics served as an antiurban foil in a range of different texts on the city.[31] Notwithstanding the entrenched nature of this portrait, when the middle classes moved their houses away from their places of work, wives and daughters did not remain isolated from the world of business, commerce, or public amusement.[32]

One of the key features of the late-Victorian suburban woman was her refusal to stay at home or even remain in her local high street. As early as the 1850s, she seemed to be in constant motion, ever traveling to and through the city center. In the late fifties, Sala believed that throngs of suburban ladies regularly invaded the West Strand, Piccadilly, and Oxford and Regent Streets.[33] Henry Mayhew likewise witnessed countless suburban mothers and daughters haunting Oxford Street in the 1860s.[34] In the early seventies, another journalist noted how "thousands of women in the West End" alternated "a day of visits with a day of shopping." These ladies evidently enjoyed "their sport" all over London. When tired of the "proper district of Regent-street, Bond-street, Oxford-street or Piccadilly," they even ventured into the older district of St. Paul's Churchyard in the City.[35]

Whether seeking business or pleasure, the suburban population became a traveling crowd that primarily experienced the city from the vantage point of a visitor. Suburban living had thus reoriented both men's and women's relationships to the metropolis. Observers were struck by the suburban woman's migrations because when she stepped into the city streets, she threatened her own reputation and her family's social position. Critics frequently castigated such a woman as a country bumpkin, tasteless fool, glutton, swindler, and fallen woman. Nevertheless, this ambulatory figure also excited those who could profit from, control, or at the very least direct her movements. Especially after the middle years of the century, numerous writers attempted to reconcile a mobile suburban femininity with London's ever-shifting commercial economy.

In one sense, Besant's portrait was a straightforward mapping of the ideology of separate spheres onto the suburban landscape. However, it also revealed some of the contradictions and inconsistencies inherent in bourgeois gender ideology.[36] Although he placed men and women in different social spaces, Besant also presupposed that women were at home in the public marketplace. As he moved from describing suburbia's women to its "immense local trade," Besant implied that women shoppers made "fortunes." In essence, Besant had acknowledged that commerce depended on its customers and that the public sphere of business arose from the private desires of women and children. Suburban economies therefore appeared subject to the whims and fancies of female consumers.

At the same time, suburban retailing insured that suburbia could never be an entirely female or middle-class sphere. High streets were inevitably filled with domestic servants, delivery boys, male shop assistants, shopkeepers, loungers, and shoppers.[37] In contrast to received wisdom, then, suburban districts were often as internally heterogeneous as any large urban area. Islington, Hackney, Clapham, and Brixton were quite unlike the western suburbs of Bayswater and Kensington, and even these areas, although sharing certain characteristics, were not identical. As F. M. L. Thompson so neatly put it: "The nineteenth-century suburban dream was a middle-class dream; the nineteenth-century suburban reality was a social patchwork."[38]

Late-Victorian suburbs such as Bayswater, therefore, both housed and disrupted Victorian class and gender ideology. Although reflecting, embodying, and producing social difference, such segregation was often more fantasy than fact. Suburban residents inevitably became mobile crowds, and suburban high streets were built upon the diversity this multitude represented. A mercurial entity, suburbia was as much a process as a place. Residents, local merchants, journalists, and government officials each attempted to control suburban change and, by extension, class and gender relations. As they did so, a desire for segregation confronted a newer integrative discourse. This clash between languages of social difference and cohesion shaped suburban London, as it did the central West End. Places like Bayswater represented the increasing power and stability of the middle classes as well as the tensions within that class and between the bourgeoisie and the rest of English society.[39]

The Bayswater that Sala visited in 1879 appeared to him to be the creation "of the day before yesterday," because within a few short decades a region with no streets, "only a few scattered cottages and windmills," and some market gardens devoted to the cultivation of dahlias and geraniums had become a fashionable and busy locale.[40] Between the 1830s and 1850s, this rural area just north of Kensington Palace Gardens began to feel the influx of migration. Bayswater, or Tyburnia as it was also known, was the name given to the area laying roughly between Westbourne Terrace in the east and Hereford Road in the west.[41] Part of the parish of Paddington, Bayswater was among the fastest growing areas of the metropolis. In 1801 this parish had only 1,881 inhabitants, but by 1861 its population had mushroomed to 75,784. Growth continued at a steady rate so that by 1891 Paddington housed nearly 118,000 residents.[42] Many of London's inner suburbs grew in like manner, contributing to the remarkable increases in the population of the metropolis during this period.[43] Such growth meant that by 1871 London had reached just over 3.25 million people, amounting to over 14 percent of the entire population of England and Wales.[44] Certain districts such as Bayswater were also "home" to a vast visiting population. Census figures alone, therefore, cannot convey the sheer size of the city or the nature of the urban crowd and its taste for goods.

Bayswater's explosive growth and fashionable reputation resulted from its proximity and accessibility to central London. Little over a mile from Park Lane in Mayfair, this neighborhood was also especially well served by public transportation. In 1829 George Shillibeer's famous omnibuses began to take residents from Paddington to the City four times a day. Other companies soon joined in so that by the late 1830s, over fifty vehicles traveled between Bayswater and the City. In 1846 a new route linked Paddington to Charing Cross, and by 1851 one could also ride directly to Tottenham Court Road. While the omnibus linked this western suburb to London's main business districts, the Great Western Railway opened Bayswater to the western counties of England when it built Paddington Station in 1838. The greatest change, however, came when the first Underground station was opened in 1863. Initially trains ran only from Bishop's Road to Farringdon Street, but the line was extended until the "Circle Line" was completed in 1884. By the early 1880s, Bayswater had become a major traffic center connecting long-distance and local trains with buses and cabs. It was a juncture between rural and urban Britain.[45]

Far from being an isolated and harmonious enclave, Bayswater increasingly embodied the social confusion present throughout the city. It included laborers' shacks and notorious slums as well as some of the most elegant houses in all of London.[46] By the 1870s, Bayswater had become a very popular address among the aristocracy, upper-middle classes, and former colonial administrators.[47] Within a few decades, its popularity and prosperity waned, and its social status dropped precipitously.[48] Yet even during its heyday, Bayswater was nicknamed "Asia Minor," because, as one author put it, it was inhabited by many "rich and cultured Orientals . . . who have come for pleasure, business, trade or education."[49] Sala's orientalized Bayswater drew on relatively common understandings of market exchange but it surely was also a reference to the area's large number of "rich and cultured Orientals."

Though a heterogenous crowd lived, worked, and traveled through Bayswater, estate agents, journalists, and developers promoted the district as one of the most fashionable, refined, and respectable neighborhoods in west London. *The Landlord's and Tenant's Guide*, for example, told prospective residents that Bayswater had "numerous wide and even roads . . . detached family mansions, stately gentlemen's residences, and villas, with large gardens and lawns in front and at the rear."[50] The author of a midcentury guidebook wrote that Bayswater's "fine squares, connected by spacious streets, and houses of great altitude, give a certain air of nobility to the district."[51] The *Paddington Times* emphasized its beautiful parks, rail links, elegant shops, and "magnificent" mansions and argued that it was "completely incorporated with the most fashionable districts in London."[52] These writers suppressed Bayswater's unsavory elements and publicized its many streets of terraced houses, acres of parkland, and numerous connections to the rest of metropolis. Such texts brought the image of this suburb into perfect conformity with the fantasies of the prosperous middle classes. A bourgeois family who moved to Bayswater could easily believe that they were far removed from the crime, disease, and poverty of the East End but still near to the urban center.[53]

The commercial development of Westbourne Grove, the area's main east-west artery, paralleled the rise and fall of the neighborhood. Residential street replaced rural grove, which in turn became a fashionable shopping promenade.[54] By all reports this transformation was extraordinarily rapid. A street with only a small chemist's nestled between comfortable homes in 1854 had become nearly unrecognizable six years later. By 1860, the Grove was lined with milliners, tailors, grocers, tobacconists, ironmongers, bakers, linen drapers, watchmakers, photographic artists, auctioneers, house agents, fishmongers, confectioners, butchers, and stationers.[55] The *Builder* praised this rapid development, remarking that "Westbourne-grove, only recently a double line of semi-detached villas . . . is now a thoroughfare of good shops."[56] In 1860 the *Building News* similarly assumed that Bayswater's commercial development was an unmitigated benefit, since residents need not "go into town" for the most expensive goods.[57] However, for another decade or so this claim of retail prosperity was more publicity than reality.

In the early sixties Westbourne Grove was most commonly known as Bankruptcy Avenue.[58] Blaming consumer conservatism for the travails of the suburban shopkeeper, trade manuals warned small shopkeepers against opening in such suburbs. *The Handy Book of Shopkeeping* cautioned: "There is a tendency among small capitalists to rush into new neighbourhoods, thinking to secure the connexion when it does come, low rents being a great attraction. . . . We have rarely found that the very early suburban shop succeeds. The few inhabitants prefer to supply themselves from established shops. . . . The suburban shopkeeper should confine himself to supplying the *necessities* of life."[59] In the early half of the nineteenth century, drapers were wary of opening in London's suburbs because, as one "old draper" explained, "They were not inhabited densely enough to give sufficient promise of adequate support."[60]

Such comments reflect an older conception of urban markets that still carried much weight in the 1860s. This view conceived of London's market as inelastic, immobile, and aristocratic. This idea informed an 1861 article that the *Building News* published about the avenues of Napoleon III's new Paris. The author believed that the expensive shops being built along the new avenues would fail because, as in London, customers would remain loyal to their local merchants. In London, he wrote, "the aristocracy but rarely shop further eastward than Wells-street or Berners-street" and building new shopping centers would not in itself draw customers further afield. As he explained, "A street and the business done in it is, or ought to be, fashioned in consideration of its particular neighborhood, and result generally from the necessities of the inhabitants."[61] By the late 1860s, Bayswater's shopping streets dramatically defied this perception of suburban markets and London's shoppers.[62]

Westbourne Grove's shops and shoppers became the linchpin of Sala's "Young London" series in the 1870s because they demonstrated a new view of markets and commercial growth. The Grove's success during the previous decade came to suggest that Londoners had insatiable consumer desires and that urban markets could change and grow with a speed and intensity heretofore thought to be impossible. Sala explained this view when he remarked that it typically "takes a hundred years at least . . . economic sages tell us, to attract custom to a new market," yet in just a few years Westbourne Grove had gone from a quiet country lane to an "astonishingly new and altogether marvelous street" of emporiums.[63] When Sala strolled through the Grove in the 1870s, it had shaken off its image as Bankruptcy Avenue. Dozens of elegant boutiques and grand commercial palaces displayed luxury goods such as jewelry, furs, watches and clocks, flowers, and decorative objects in their large plate-glass windows.[64] At the very center of this street stood Mr. William Whiteley, whom Sala obsequiously described as "perhaps one of the most remarkable traders of his time."[65]

The Spectacular Universal Provider

William Whiteley had been one of the many adventurous, or possibly foolish, shopkeepers who tried their luck in mid-Victorian Bayswater. After a seven-year apprenticeship with a provincial draper and several years working in various London shops, Whiteley opened his own enterprise in 1863. Aided by an errand boy and two female assistants—one of whom he eventually married—Whiteley began selling ribbons and other fancy goods in an unassuming and rather conventional shop.[66] By 1879 this store had become the magnificent emporium that Sala compared to Mr. Stewart's famous commercial palace in New York City and the "Parisian Warehouses" such as the Louvre and the Bon Marché.[67] A decade later, the author of *Modern London: The World's Metropolis, an Epitome of Results* remarked:

> It is a curious to reflect how inseparably Bayswater in general, and the streets around Westbourne Grove in particular, seem to be almost absorbed into one vast establishment, and to remember how well-nigh impossible it is for a thought of the district in question to enter the mind unaccompanied by some allusion to Whiteley's, that wonderful elysium of the London "shopper," the morning or afternoon resort, *par excellence* . . . the head-quarter's of the world-renowned "Universal Provider."[68]

As in Sala's description, this author identified Whiteley, Bayswater, and shopping with "modern London." This view was instrumental to the store's success, but it took years to solidify and was written by many retail experts, journalists, residents, and, of course, William Whiteley himself.

When it opened in 1863 Whiteley's shop was a very ordinary venture. Nevertheless, store histories have repeated two apocryphal tales about the shop's origins that have helped establish and maintain Whiteley's reputation as the spectacular Universal Provider. The first story recalls that Whiteley opened his new shop during the wedding celebrations held for the Prince of Wales and Princess Alexandra of Denmark. According to store legend, Whiteley wanted his shop to be associated with the festive mood that the wedding had brought to the city and with established images of authority and royal spectacle.[69] But even more importantly, Whiteley hoped that the crowds of tourists who came to London to see the new princess would find their way into his new shop.

Another tale relating the store's origins also helped establish its singularity and monumentality. This story implied that the department store Whiteley built in the late-nineteenth century was a direct descendent of the biggest and most famous mid-Victorian spectacle of all, the Great Exhibition. Throughout his life, Whiteley maintained that his inspiration had come from the many visits to the

Crystal Palace he had enjoyed as a young man. He described having been enchanted with the tantalizing way the Exhibition made goods available to the eye but ultimately unattainable.[70] Such anecdotes give Whiteley a tremendous degree of credit for not only building a unique institution but also conceiving of it as early as 1851. This history also fits perfectly with the commonly held view that the Great Exhibition had launched a new age.[71]

Whiteley's story of admiration for the Exhibition lends support to the view held by many contemporary scholars that exhibitions were a central facet of nineteenth-century capitalism and consumer culture. In 1851 the Great Exhibition displayed England's manufacturing prowess to the world. This palace of glass and iron also delighted its 6 million visitors by teaching them to enjoy looking at objects. As Thomas Richards has explained, the Exhibition transformed goods into signifiers, making "it possible to talk expressively and excessively about commodities."[72] In his consideration of consumerism, Walter Benjamin wrote that exhibitions "built up" commodities, "glorifying" their exchange value.[73] Commodities were thus "fetishized," as Marx described them in the 1860s. In such cathedrals they took on "metaphysical subtleties and theological niceties."[74]

Department stores and exhibition halls certainly share many similarities. In both locales, new glass and iron technology, special lighting, grandiose architecture, and the "overwhelming" and "chaotic display" of diverse products created a sense of "theatrical excess" intended to overwhelm if also delight the spectator.[75] Such parallels were also obvious to the Victorians. As we will see in chapter 4, mid-Victorian journalists often compared London's shop windows to exhibitions. The author of the 1866 article "Shop Windows," for example, made the connection explicit by asking, "After all, what are the Great Exhibitions but a sort of collective window display?"[76]

Although exhibitions clearly inspired traders and shoppers alike, they were not the only places that people learned to talk and think about commodities. Entrepreneurs such as Josiah Wedgwood and George Packwood, as well as their customers, had been talking "expressively and excessively about commodities" for nearly a hundred years before the Great Exhibition.[77] The Crystal Palace and the department store were thought of as special places even though the line between store, exhibition, street, and metropolis was a thin one. Arcades, dioramas, panoramas, bazaars, museums, theaters, zoos, and shop windows addressed the public as spectators, inviting people to look at goods and associate that looking with pleasure.[78] Indeed, Whiteley did not need to go to the Crystal Palace to see lavishly displayed goods. He would have had many examples in the shopping streets in which he lived and worked. Since the 1830s, many shops had adopted plate glass, luxurious interiors, and a host of other enticements to turn shopping into a captivating event.[79] Tony Bennett has argued that such institutions collectively constituted an "exhibitionary complex." Bourgeois society and its capitalist economy developed techniques and spaces for "the opening up of objects to more public contexts of inspection and visibility."[80] Within these spaces, objects and bodies once displayed in "enclosed and private domains" moved into "progressively more open and public arenas." This made both the goods and spectators part of the spectacle. According to Anne Friedberg, these institutions "extended 'the field of the visible' and turned visualized experience into commodity forms."[81] Such spaces produced consumption and consumers by creating certain modes of looking, desiring, and buying.

Neither Whiteley nor the Crystal Palace then single-handedly generated this culture of spectacle and consumption. There also was no absolute difference between department stores and more traditional shops, and there certainly was no single type of department store. Yet during the 1860s and 1870s, the idea of the department store and mass consuming public began to take shape in the streets of suburban London.[82] Instead of seeing this as a natural product of industrial change or the growth of mid-Victorian prosperity, the following sections will explore how contests over space and status, gender and pleasure gave birth to the perception of department store singularity and modernity. If Whiteley and his historians championed the store as an example of the age of improvement, a closer look illuminates a much more uneven and contentious history.

"When Ladies Go 'Shopping'"

Early department stores such as Whiteley's emerged within a culture that was profoundly equivocal about consumption and the urban crowd. Such ambivalence shaped the history of the department store because opponents charged Whiteley with having committed a variety of social and moral crimes, including turning ordinary suburban ladies into jezebels. While historians have noted how similar criticisms were leveled at French and American department stores during these years, these charges did not simply grow from the public nature of female shopping crowds or from long-standing associations between markets and excess. Rather, many enemies of the department store wanted to find a way to regulate market growth and protect their own financial and social status without denouncing the much-cherished ideals of free trade. One convenient way to do this was to suggest that the number of department stores had to be limited not because they fostered unfair competition but because they encouraged immoral female behaviors.

By the early 1870s, Whiteley's neighbors began to perceive that he was embarking on a new type of retailing in which diverse goods were being vended to a heterogenous urban crowd. They regarded this style of doing business as essentially immoral, threatening their trade and their values. Most troubling of all, they suggested, was that Whiteley's shop lured women into the city to engage in unhealthy pleasures.

The charivari in 1876 was only the most spectacular expression of resentment toward Whiteley and the principle of Universal Providing.[83] Although not consistently organized, retailers in Whiteley's shadow vented their frustration in the streets, in the press, and on local government committees. They were rarely as direct as the cleaver-wielding butchers. Instead of deploring the economic impact of large-scale trading on the retail community, they typically condemned the negative social and cultural consequences for consumers, especially female shoppers. They particularly "exposed" the almost pathological behaviors that such enterprises supposedly encouraged. Whiteley's enemies charged that by selling an array of commodities, services, and pleasures to a mixed shopping crowd, he had disorganized class, gender, moral, and aesthetic categories. By ignoring the cherished boundaries between public and private spheres, the Universal Provider denied the essential distinction between respectable and immoral women. Specialized shopkeepers thus deployed bourgeois gender ideology to defend their economic position against the threat of large-scale retailers.

If in November of 1876 William Whiteley stood in the doorway of his shop laughing as his effigy was paraded through Westbourne Grove, he more typically responded to these attacks by rejecting his competitors' negative depiction of the consuming woman. He legitimized his own institution by arguing that the shopper was a respectable, rational individual whose home was the public spaces of the metropolis. If his opponents portrayed shoppers as immoral and disorderly, Whiteley presented them as a sign of improvement. A debate about gender and consumption developed, then, from the social and economic struggle between retailers.

The Guy Fawkes Day demonstration culminated at least four years of rancorous dealings between Whiteley and his neighbors. During his first ten years, Whiteley had relentlessly acquired leases, renovated interiors, and opened up new departments. In 1872 he began selling entirely new types of commodities when he opened a house agency, a cleaning and dyeing service, and a small refreshment room.[84] The public attacks began with this latest "innovation." Opponents charged that Whiteley was selling more than just goods; he was now vending new identities. In the next decade many West End drapers would add dining facilities, reading and writing rooms, entertainments, lavatories, and a host of other amenities to their stores. Luxurious interiors and graceful exteriors may have made shopping comfortable and amusing, something apart from the everyday, but when amenities were first introduced in the early seventies, they sparked a great deal of anger and frustration. Even small lunchrooms aroused fears about the morality of consumption and the instability of urban class and gender identities.

The furor against Whiteley and the selling of conveniences first erupted in 1872 when Whiteley applied for a liquor license to serve wine and beer in his new refreshment room. At the general licensing meeting, the magistrates listened to Whiteley and his lawyer's arguments, they read an endorsing petition from several local religious and medical men, but in the end they refused Whiteley's application. Henry Walker, the liberal editor of the *Bayswater Chronicle*, championed this decision. The possibility of lady shoppers imbibing spirits in public violated this editor's, and presumably the magistrates', image of proper Victorian womanhood. Walker asserted that although "Mr. Whiteley may have a large number of ladies visiting his shops and spending hours in making their purchases . . . sherry and silks, or port and piques, need not of necessity go together when ladies go 'shopping.' " A confirmed liberal, Walker still maintained, "there is a point where enterprise should cease to be encouraged."[85] This point was reached when enterprise invited middle-class ladies to indulge too readily in public pleasures.

All those involved in the debate viewed shopping as an inherently female and amusing activity. The disagreement arose over whether this pleasure was healthy and profitable or socially and economically destructive.[86] At the licensing meeting, Mr. W. Wright argued the case against Whiteley by linking economic expansion with the decline of female morality. Wright first asserted that a person who "carried on the business of a linen draper, a hatter, a bootmaker, an upholsterer, and jeweller . . . had got enough irons in the fire." He then quickly shifted from questioning the legitimacy of large-scale retailing to doubting the morality of encouraging female intemperance. He posited that Mr. Whiteley must have not read the recent article in the *Saturday Review*, which warned that drinking was "on the increase amongst ladies," or he would not wish "to offer them a facility for indulging in that propensity." Assailing the character of Whiteley's customers still further, Wright implied that the provision of alcoholic beverages might transform "respectable" ladies into prostitutes and drunkards. Although he apologetically stated that he had no intention of "questioning the respectability of Mr. Whiteley or his customers," he felt that as many of the shoppers "might be ladies or females dressed to represent them . . . the place might be made a place of assignation." Therefore, Wright urged that "in the interest of morality the application would be refused." Wright argued that the sale of alcohol transformed a glorified linen draper's into a brothel filled with females "dressed to represent" ladies.[87]

Wright knew that women who drank in public were assumed to be prostitutes.[88] This assumption was underscored by a disquieting geographical correlation between the West End clothing and sexual markets.[89] The most fashionable West End shopping areas, such as Regent Street and the Burlington Arcade, were also the most well-known prostitute haunts in London. Even in Bayswater it was not at all clear what pleasures certain shops sold. For example, the owners of the innocent-sounding "Westbourne Grove Coffee and Dining Rooms," known to regulars as "The Drum and the Monkey," were convicted of running a "disorderly house" in March of 1872.[90] Brothels commonly disguised themselves as coffee-houses and temperance hotels so that when Whiteley's began to serve food and drink, residents could easily have been confused about what type of institution he was creating.[91] Whiteley's "innovation" therefore had raised concerns that this rapidly expanding, prosperous inner suburb would soon suffer from the ills as well as the benefits associated with urban life.

While opposing Whiteley, Wright raised the specter of the "Great Social Evil" because no other issue so directly touched upon the apprehension sparked by rapid urbanization, commercial growth, and women's place in this process. While the prostitute could symbolize the problems associated with urban life, she could also represent the fate of the individual-turned-commodity in a consumer society. As Walter Benjamin later wrote, "In the prostitution of the metropolis the woman herself becomes an article that is mass-produced."[92] The fallen woman could also, according to Amanda Anderson, personify the "predicaments of agency and uncertainties about the nature of selfhood, character, and society."[93] The shopper-turned-prostitute thus perfectly represented bourgeois angst that all those involved in market society were losing their agency, morality, independence, and reason.

Like other critics of market culture, Wright drew upon and furthered the perceived relationship between prostitution and women engaged in consumer activities. By collapsing the distinction between women buying and selling pleasure, Wright invoked the theme of Eliza Linton's notorious article "The Girl of the Period," published anonymously in 1868 in the *Saturday Review.* Linton had accused modern English girls, particularly those living in "Bayswater and Belgravia," of boldly imitating the ways of the prostitute. Dyeing their hair, painting their faces, and wearing the latest fashions, she warned, led to the use of "slang, bold talk, and fastness; to the love of pleasure and indifference to duty." To support these consumer desires such a young woman, Linton believed, would sell herself to a wealthy husband. Her marriage was then simply "the legal barter of herself for so much money."[94] Linton feared that young women's participation in an urban commercial culture of style and display encouraged sexual, moral, and social disorder. By entering the market as consumers, these girls ruined themselves in the public sphere and brought market relations into the sacred space of the private home.

The reactions to Whiteley's reflected specific local economic and political grievances and more general apprehension that urban commercial change had afforded women indulgent freedoms and improper powers. Critics contended that the "powerful fascination in shopping to most women" came from the "endless possibilities of indulgence which belonged to it." In the 1875 *Saturday Review* article "The Philosophy of Shopping," the author, probably Linton, wrote that in "its mystical feminine meaning, to shop is to pass so many hours in a shop on the mere chance of buying something. . . . [It] springs immediately from a taste for novel and various entertainment . . . [and] seems to be undertaken for the pure love of the occupation." This lengthy article concluded that the real pleasure associated with shopping came from the experience of being served. While shopping, "the dethroned mistress . . . trodden under foot in her own house," had the authority of "an Oriental potentate." Being patiently served by the "assiduous shopman" afforded "mothers and daughters" the opportunity to "luxuriate" in a deep and intense "sense of power."[95]

For others the problem with shopping was not that it granted women illegitimate powers, but that it represented the new, inauthentic, and vulgar suburban world that now ringed London. Although satirizing Linton's essay, the authors of the humor magazine *The Girl of the Period Miscellany* shared her belief that when "girls" participated in commercial culture, they acquired ugly, tasteless characteristics. In the sardonic essay, "Girls at the West End," Tyburnian girls were particularly lambasted for spending their days shopping and flirting in Westbourne Grove, lacking "*le style*," and possessing a certain "metropolitan provincialism."[96] This humorous essay played upon the same misgivings that surfaced with

Whiteley's lunchroom. In all of these portraits of shopping, young middle-class women appear to be out of their place, out of control, and willingly engaging in a sensuous and potentially sexual public culture. Disputes over large-scale retailing, then, were also debates about acceptable feminine spaces and behaviors outside the private home and family circle.

In order to gain acceptance from the local authorities and potential customers, Whiteley challenged these pervasive images of a passionate public sphere filled with disorderly women. He rejected the immoral associations attached to public amusements and attempted to create an acceptable public femininity. Charles Mills Roche, Whiteley's solicitor and a prominent local politician, argued for the license and the concept of Universal Providing by refusing to use the moral language established by his opposition. He first addressed the retailers' economic concerns. Roche professed that far from ruining the business of local traders, Whiteley had brought new wealth to the neighborhood. As he now occupied ten separate shops, and employed 622 individuals on the premises and another thousand out-of-doors, Roche stated that "Mr. Whiteley has been the making of Westbourne Grove." He then confidently asserted that drink was neither a physical nor social pleasure, but merely "a great public convenience."[97]

When questioned, Whiteley similarly defended large-scale retailing and cast himself as a benefit to the neighborhood, a provider of necessities, not a stimulator of desires. He pleaded that nearly a quarter of the four thousand customers who visited his establishment each day were country folk who stayed in his store from "ten o-clock in the morning until five o-clock in the afternoon." These provincial visitors, Whiteley asserted, had actually asked him "for a glass of wine and a biscuit." Whiteley thereby presented himself as merely responding to consumer demand, serving a public necessity. He defined drink as a "convenience," not as a luxury or indulgence to dispel the perception of moral danger with which it was associated. "There was not the shadow of foundation," Whiteley concluded, "that if he obtained a license his establishment would become a place of assignation." He further implied that the lunchroom would moralize the Grove, since female shoppers would not be forced to enter places of ill repute to have a drink or other refreshment. The magistrates refused to buy this argument, however. They resolutely denied the application with the suggestion that Mr. Whiteley "had enough to do in looking after his present establishment."[98]

As mentioned earlier, Henry Walker, the editor of the *Bayswater Chronicle*, fully supported this limitation on trade, but turned the event into a mediation on the morality and pleasures of shopping. After the license had been blocked, he quipped, "Shopping has sufficient charm in itself to prevent [customers] swooning."[99] An avowed proponent of women's emancipation, Walker nonetheless did not share Whiteley's image of women in public life. Instead, he sounded remarkably similar to the conservative moralist Eliza Linton, since Whiteley's thirsty shopper was something other than the productive, rational woman envisioned by early feminists. Whiteley's critics thus came from both ends of the political spectrum. Conservatives and liberals alike found fault with his large shop and the new women he apparently had created.

Although both groups shared assumptions about gender and consumption, established political antagonisms also came into play. In this parochial conflict, Whiteley found himself at odds with both sides of a heated national controversy between the Liberal government and the conservative drink trade.[100] Eighteen seventy-two was a particularly inauspicious moment to build a new site for the consumption of alcohol because Gladstone's government had just increased the regulation of this consumer pleasure. In response, publicans opposed the government and any proprietor who seemed to be threatening their trade. Even before Whiteley's application came before the general licensing meeting, one reporter for the *Paddington Times* had simply assumed that Whiteley wanted to turn a profit serving wine and beer to his hundreds of employees. This journalist voiced the concerns of the licensed victuallers when he concluded that "at the present time when restrictions of every description are being inflicted upon publicans, it is really a monstrous piece of audacity in a private individual, totally unconnected with the trade, applying for such a license."[101] Though the records for Whiteley's application no longer exist, similar cases induced the victuallers to fill meeting halls and submit opposing petitions to protect their monopoly.

The tremendous expansion of many kinds of eateries and refreshment rooms had also placed the publicans in an especially precarious position in the 1860s and 1870s. During this period, many art galleries, theaters, restaurants, and hotels opened in the West End with the desire to serve refreshments and entertainment to what their owners defined as a bourgeois, respectable crowd. When they applied for liquor licenses they put forth virtually identical arguments to those Whiteley had made in Bayswater. This similarity may have been the result of the format of the meetings, but it also illuminates the shared assumptions among certain segments of London's business community. More importantly, these episodes show how traders had begun to think and talk about their market in a new way within these legal settings. In their petitions traders reveal their understanding of the relationship between public space and the consuming public. Although these petitions were not necessarily accurate descriptions of that public, they paint a picture of retailers' *ideal public.*

In their applications, West End entrepreneurs repeatedly claimed to serve a respectable, mobile, middle-class, especially female public. When Sir Coutts Lindsay, the owner of the fashionable Grosvenor Gallery in Bond Street, petitioned the magistrates for a liquor license for his adjoining restaurant, he stated that in the three months since he had opened, "upwards of 100,000 persons [had] visited" the Gallery and that his restaurant had served between three and four hundred "upper and middle class" people daily. Lindsay attested that customers had "frequently informed" him that his restaurant "has supplied a want which has long been felt to exist in the West End, namely a place conducted on such principles and in such a manner as allows of its being visited for the purposes of refreshment by clergymen, ladies, and others by whom restaurants are considered objectionable." Even neighboring tradesman, he maintained, had called his restaurant "a confirmed boon . . . to the public visiting the West End."[102] This last claim was a bit of a stretch. Although Lindsay produced a supportive petition signed by dozens of "Inhabitants of New Bond Street and the Vicinity," sixteen local publicans submitted an opposing one in which they charged that "there is no public necessity for such a license, there being already several first class establishments of the same kind in Piccadilly and its vicinity."[103] Lindsay, like Whiteley before him, probably exaggerated his own novelty and the size of his market to win one of the few new licenses that London magistrates doled out each year. By stressing that he would create a safe, respectable haven for ladies and clergymen, Lindsay cast himself as a kind of entrepreneurial moral reformer. Morality and improvement, he implied, would radiate from the Gallery's restaurant to the whole of the West End.

When two female hoteliers in Bayswater applied for licenses in 1880, they too characterized their clients as respectable visitors seeking modest refreshment. Annie Bilton, the owner of the Leinster Hotel in Ossington Street, explained to the magistrates that she wanted a license because since the opening of the Metropolitan and District Railways, she housed "great numbers of visitors . . . who come up to town to visit the theaters or other places of public amusement." And these pleasure seekers, she argued, seldom retired without "the necessary luxury of spirituous liquors."[104] Bilton strengthened her request with a petition signed by many of her female customers and the several clubs that also used her premises for meetings. One of Bilton's competitors, a Miss Emma Shickle, simply stated that her patrons, "families of good position and great respectability," found it a great "inconvenience" to seek wine and spirits outside of her hotel in Bayswater Terrace.[105]

Mass caterers similarly contended that they served middle-class visitors who needed respectable public places in the urban center. For example, when James and Baptist Monico petitioned for a license to serve alcohol at Monico's Restaurant in Tichbourne Street, they described their neighborhood as "a place of great resort," thick with "persons visiting London" who would find their establishment "a great convenience" and a "great local improvement."[106] When Agostino and Stefano Gatti applied for a license for the Adelaide Gallery in the Strand, they explained that they had been serving light refreshment for some years, but that "lately in conformity with the wishes of the frequenters of the gallery" they had begun serving luncheon, dinner, and supper as well.[107] A nearby publican, Arthur Rake, opposed this petition with the ironic argument that Gatti's would be tempting "women to purchase spirits."[108]

In the political and economic climate of the 1870s and 1880s, publicans like Rake used the language of domesticity when confronting their rivals. Almost ancient conceptions of gluttony, luxury, intemperance, and abundance thus took on specific meanings.[109] The publicans developed an image of a ravenous and uncontrollable female consumer as a socially and legally acceptable method of restricting competition. Of course, they may have learned the political value of morality-based arguments from their own enemies, the temperance reformers. Nonetheless, the licensed victuallers implied that drink was a form of leisure and consumption that belonged in the male sphere. They did so not so much to keep women out of the public sphere, but to keep other men out of their trade.

In contrast, those who wished to serve the middle classes defended their right to do so by drawing upon the traditions of political economy and the catchphrases of mid-Victorian liberalism.[110] Lindsay and Whiteley, Bilton and Shickle, and the Monico and Gatti brothers all fashioned an amoral and progressive view of the economy and the consumer. Whiteley, like these other entrepreneurs, developed an understanding of the shopper as an individual who satisfied her needs, even her passions, in the marketplace. He suggested that by following their desires, shoppers stimulated the economy and benefited society and urban life. Because luxuries were seen by many as corrupting, however, these entrepreneurs often emphasized that they sold "necessities," although Bilton hedged a bit when stating she wanted to serve "necessary luxuries." By providing necessities, they each claimed to be "improving" their neighborhoods. Improvement meant various things: a growing market, harmonious social relations, and a morally elevated public sphere. Retailers, caterers, and hoteliers also invariably characterized themselves as innovators. Necessity, improvement, and innovation were thus the watchwords of these Victorian entrepreneurs.

Elements of the Angel in the House, the ideal of bourgeois womanhood, were also imbricated with their vision of economic woman. Just as this Angel could signify a virtuous middle-class home and society, she could also manifest a virtuous economy and city. This was a difficult argument to make, since the essential characteristic of the Victorian Angel was that she remained "in the house." Nevertheless, traders such as Whiteley identified their "houses" with respectable women and suggested that when they did so, they transformed the urban center into a chaste space. In a subtle way, then, domesticity and political economy competed and merged to develop a shopper who seemed both independent from the household and "at home" in the urban marketplace. Her liberty in the city and its shops also ideally enabled this shopping Angel to create a comfortable, pleasurable private realm. In this view the public and private were seen as overlapping and interconnected territories held together by a rational and moral female shopper. This image stood in opposition to the irrational and sensual shopper constructed by a range of different critics. These two views of the shopper circulated widely in the culture and were by no means restricted to local government committees.

The periodical, trade, and local presses relied upon similar images of the disorderly and rational shopper when reporting on the machinations of the Universal Provider. For example, the first issue of a national draper's trade journal began an article on Whiteley by describing his refreshment room as one of the many "new ideas" of this "enterprising man." Believing that the law of supply and demand would determine the value of the lunchroom, the editor wrote, "We offer no opinion on the absolute propriety of such an arrangement. Experience will soon show whether the innovation is acceptable to the visitors and advantageous to trade." His hope for its success was clear, however, for he believed that "[a] Day's Shopping is one of the most agreeable occupations a Lady can devise, but pleasure is toil without agreeable relaxation and rest." Although "wine may not be desirable," he felt sure that a "bun, ice or refreshing fruit beverage," if "attainable in the ladies' room," would enable the "varied attractions" of the dress, millinery, and other departments to be "better appreciated."[111]

This author believed that catering to women's bodily needs, albeit in a carefully regulated setting, stimulated trade without unleashing dangerous passions. To assuage lingering fears that food would lead to unregulated socializing between the sexes, the editor proposed a compromise. Women might have a bun or ice, but only if served in the "ladies' room." A letter from a "shop assistant" printed in the same issue of the journal, promised large, fashionable West End drapers such as Peter Robinson's, Marshall and Snelgrove's, and Swan and Edgar's that they would be "amply rewarded for their enterprise" if they established elaborate and comfortable ladies' rooms for their customers. "Many ladies," wrote this concerned employee,

> especially those who do not reside in town, are in the habit of devoting a day to "shopping. . . ." But sheer weariness, the necessity of rest, and the desire to arrange the toilet not infrequently shorten the visit. . . . The pastry cook's is the lady's resort, and the vendor of buns and ices gains little, while probably the draper or silk mercer loses much. I feel certain the ladies would be pleased if in each of these splendid establishments which adorn our large towns, there was a "Ladies Room," fitted with looking glasses and toilet appendages, and provided with neat and obliging female attendants.[112]

As Whiteley and others had done, this assistant wrote that such amenities were public conveniences, not devices creating new desires. He even quoted "a lady" who supposedly confided in him, "I always feel so much more disposed to be pleased with everything, when I have refreshed myself by washing my hands and arranging my bonnet."[113] Although obviously encouraging long-distance shopping, shopkeepers insisted that women already delighted in this activity. They naturalized shopping as a female, urban, commercial amusement and argued that its practitioners were the force behind their own expansion. New ideals of femininity and female public places developed, then, as part of the legitimation of a threateningly new form of retailing.

Critics, by contrast, played upon society's ambivalent attitude toward consumption and large-scale retailing by charging that abundant goods and opulent settings inevitably led to indulgence. The *Graphic* satirically labeled Whiteley's lunchroom as "an importation from Paris," which should be denounced as "dangerous in the highest degree." In removing the bodily discomfort associated with purchasing, it encouraged "excessive shopping" and thereby was "calculated to play all kinds of unpleasant things with the peace of families." Women already enjoyed shopping in drapers to such a degree that only hunger and fatigue could possibly limit this overwhelming desire. In traditional shops, "after having taken their pleasure among ten thousand pretty things . . . exertion induces . . . a return to their homes." But "under the new system . . . [in which] fatigue and restoration go hand in hand: there need be no flagging, so long as money or credit is available." At Whiteley's, shoppers

> acquire such things as soups, cutlets, omelettes, macaroni, fritters, and so forth, they revel in the accompaniments of cruets full of sherry or claret, or lilliputian bottles of champagne, what is the effect? They have not left the halls of temptation; the voice of the charmer still rings in their ears. . . . They return once more to the slaughter . . . [and] in the wild and reckless period that follows things are done in a financial way which would make the angels weep. . . . The afternoon's excitement has . . . all the attraction of a delightful dream, with a slight dash of an orgy, leaving a lingering pleasure even over repentance.[114]

Women's unrestrained consumer desires were imagined as insatiable appetites entirely depleting husbands' financial resources.

Self-restraint, prudence, even chastity, the main props of bourgeois womanhood, could seemingly be thrown off with a most unnerving sensuous abandon. This portrait of the seduced and gluttonous woman had as much to do with changing middle-class norms as it did with worries about female shopping orgies, however. She represented a class abandoning itself to consumer desires and giving new meanings to consumption. Although the author of the *Graphic* condemned women's lack of control and self-restraint, he also included a diatribe against men. "We all know," he stated, "that there is nothing less agreeable to a man than waiting at a linen draper's while a lady makes a purchase." With a lunchroom available, "he has an obvious recourse: he will lunch while the sweet operation is being performed. . . . Lunch is well known to intensify emotions. . . . Under the influence of . . . waiting, cheques are written for amounts which would never be figured in cold blood . . . weak men! They purchase a little temporary consolation at who shall say what cost?"[115] Whiteley's small luncheon room, not actually serving sherry, claret, or lilliputian bottles of champagne, inspired scenes of social collapse. Fears about commercial growth were thereby articulated through images of dissipation, disrupted family life, and disorderly women.

Of course, William Whiteley was virtually immune to such criticisms, whether they appeared as satire in the comic press or as a charivari in Bayswater's streets. Throughout the 1870s, the Universal Provider expanded into "nontraditional" trades, including stationery, household goods, and ironmongery. He started a house-building and decoration service, and in 1876 he opened hairdressing and small banking departments. As he moved into new areas, he acquired new enemies.[116] The most forceful and determined individual to step into Whiteley's path was James Flood, who, among other things, owned a house and estate agency that competed with Whiteley's. He also chaired the governing body that managed the Paddington Public Baths, which were next door to Whiteley's warehouse. Unlike the small butchers, grocers, and publicans who Whiteley drove to bankruptcy each year, Flood was a wealthy man and a prominent local politician. An active member of the vestry, he naturally hoped that this local body and the Metropolitan Board of Works would halt Whiteley's growth.[117]

Instead of calling shopping an indecent public pleasure, Flood followed the example of some liberal urban reformers and accused Whiteley of inconveniencing residents by obstructing and vulgarizing Bayswater's streets. He and his allies on the vestry constantly complained that Whiteley's vans, delivery trucks, and customers blocked the public thoroughfares. And yet in one especially telling moment in 1875, Flood reverted to gender-based arguments and asserted that Whiteley's male assistants had been spying on female bathers from the windows of the merchant's new warehouse.[118] When the matter came before the Metropolitan Board of Works, Whiteley won the day because his solicitor, Charles Roche, and the architect who had designed the warehouse were both members of the Board.[119] The following year, however, the vestry was able to force Whiteley to remove a flag he had hung across Westbourne Grove as a Christmas decoration. When the *Bayswater Chronicle* reported on this victory, Walker charged that Whiteley's flag inhibited the "liberties" of public thoroughfares and that such vulgarities, "typical of Broadway in New York," were inappropriate adornments for English streets. Walker patriotically defended English shopkeeping when he hailed the flag's removal as a national victory and asserted, "We don't want to Americanize the Grove."[120]

Walker, Flood, and several vestrymen may have resented Whiteley's spectacular shopkeeping, but they were not enemies of women's urban freedoms. As we will see in chapter 3, the vestry was in the midst of debating whether and how they should provide amenities for female residents, workers, and visitors. Feminist groups such as the Ladies Sanitary Association and individual feminists, including Emily Faithfull, supported Flood's vision of government-provided recreations and pleasures. In doing so, they began to articulate a critique of the commercial emancipation promoted by Whiteley and others.

As we have seen, Whiteley's critics came from diverse social and political groups. They included moralists like Linton, conservative publicans, upper-class magistrates, liberal journalists and politicians, feminists and shopkeepers. These commentators similarly painted the department store as the "halls of temptation." In their attacks, the department store was described as a threatening place that seduced women, encouraged shopping orgies, and introduced dangerous French, Oriental, and American influences into the heart of British bourgeois life. Marketplaces have been described in such terms in the past, but these images were developed by particular individuals for the specific purpose of market and moral control. Some used the spectacle of the sensuous bazaar to represent and contain the unruly nature of nineteenth-century capitalism, urban growth, and female independence. Others did so to promote an alternative vision of women's emancipation. Whiteley and his fellow merchants decried these portraits and championed the natural workings of an amoral market.

Large-scale retailers like the Universal Provider thus encouraged consumption by cleansing public amusements of their immoral image. They licensed consumer desires by theoretically separating the pleasures of shopping from other forms of physical desire and gender interactions. As this idea became more accepted by the late 1870s and 1880s, Whiteley's critics began to talk about department stores as bringing a delightful cosmopolitanism to suburban hinterlands, even suggesting that Whiteley's had single-handedly made Westbourne Grove into a cosmopolitan pleasure center. Together, the store, street, and shopping crowd were described as a glittering show, a symbol of prosperity and modernity. This is precisely the "Westbournia" that Sala witnessed in 1879 and that articles such as "Young London" also helped create. This narrative facilitated the expansion of the department store, London's commercial districts, and the production of new ideals of bourgeois femininity.

"Our Local Regent Street"

In the late seventies and the eighties, the local press began embracing Whiteley's vision of his store and the shopping crowd. The *Bayswater Chronicle* and other local papers began to publish blatant pieces of commercial propaganda which suggested that Whiteley's had given the Grove "quite a Bond Street air"[121] and helped it become "Our local Regent Street."[122] Only the day after Whiteley had been burned in effigy in Portobello Road, the *Paddington Times* proclaimed the new provision department as the quintessence of modernity, for "whatever part you go in this vast and varied establishment you see the realisation of organization and order."[123] Emile Zola would adopt precisely this same metaphor to describe his fictional Parisian department store in his novel of the same name, *The Ladies' Paradise.*[124] These authors saw the department store as a progressive, modern, and spectacular "sight" that had to be seen[125] (fig. 3).

This appreciation for the Universal Provider and his shoppers was in part the result of an increasingly competitive commercial environment in England during these years. Changes within London's retail and publishing industries encouraged Bayswater's residents, journalists, and politicians to look more kindly upon the spectacle of shopping. As we will see in later chapters, in the 1880s the press and large-scale retailers became allied as they sought to construct a mass consuming public. Despite its greater role as Pied Piper's flute, the press did not merely entice innocent shoppers and sightseers to the city. As multiauthored entities, newspapers also maintained the role of critic. Although advertisements and editorials championed a city devoted to consumption, the correspondence pages frequently denounced this picture of utopia. In a sense, newspapers were both advocate and adversary of the culture of consumption that was growing in London's West End.

The themes that structured the debate surrounding Whiteley's lunchroom, his liquor license, and the provision department were woven throughout the discourse on Bayswater's commercial culture in the 1880s. When discussing Whiteley's impact on the neighborhood, for example, some residents and journalists focused on the comfort, safety, morality, and pleasures of bourgeois women. Just as Whiteley had argued that women were safe and satisfied in his shop, others believed that middle-class ladies were content and secure in the shopping street. And just as Whiteley's competitors cast his shop as the "halls of temptation," critics of commercialization and urbanization conjured up images of an endan-

Figure 3. Whiteley's department store, ca. 1880s (courtesy of Hulton Getty Picture Collection).

gered and harassed female shopping crowd. The comfort or pleasure of the bourgeois shopper thus became the means by which individuals debated the impact of an ever-growing and increasingly commercial city.

If during the early 1870s the critical voice was the louder one, celebrations of consumerism grew stronger in the 1880s. Of course, many would still mourn the fate of communities living in the vicinity of the big stores. As one writer for the *Pall Mall Gazette* so dramatically stated it in 1887: "The Universal Provider has risen into fame upon the universal destruction of all his rivals. Little tradesmen have gone down by the score in order that he might establish in the place of a hundred little shops one mammoth emporium."[126] Bayswater's journalists rarely made such arguments after the late seventies. Instead they insisted that large stores stimulated rather than stole local custom. Journalists often still spoke to the concerns of the local shopkeeper and residents, but they identified the Universal Provider's success with that of everyone who lived and worked in Bayswater. Almost immediately after the Guy Fawkes Day protest, for example, the *Bayswater Chronicle* alleged that the outcry against "our U.P. had all but completely died away." The grocers and poulterers in the vicinity had found that they were doing more business "because Mr. Whiteley's 'Cheap Meat' sensation has drawn more people to Westbourne Grove, and made the place a better mart than ever." Walker even jokingly claimed to know "some other tradesmen in the Grove and elsewhere who would like their trade to be threatened." Another article called Whiteley's new Queen's Road (now Queensway) building "the Bayswater Sensation," since the road had "at once became a market, and has been thronged in the shopping hours ever since." Moreover, "the Bayswater tradesmen don't seem to mind it. They have learned to accept Whiteley as a fact. . . . 'Better for all of us,' said one of them, 'he makes Bayswater a grand market for all of us except the old-fashioned.' "[127]

Walker's seemingly unbridled enthusiasm during this period helped transform the once-hated "leviathan" into the popular "local U.P." Though he did not appreciate Whiteley's Christmas flag, even Walker admired the store's architecture. When Whiteley opened new premises along the Queen's Road in 1881, the *Bayswater Chronicle* praised this new "row of lofty and spacious edifices" as a "frontage certainly superior to that of any other retail house in the metropolis."[128] Former residents similarly remembered that Whiteley's had made Westbourne Grove into "one of the principal shopping thoroughfares in London."[129] Another recalled that in the early eighties, "shoppers were drawn from all over London, and one of the very first places that provincial visitors made for was Whiteley's."[130]

In the late 1870s, the local papers had introduced columns solely devoted to promoting the area's commercial culture. Every week, columnists such as "the Flâneur in the Grove" strolled through the street, telling readers about Bayswater's best florists, stationers, butchers, and drapers, and describing their beautiful window displays, quality stock, and good bargains. By leaving out the names of the shops, these articles avoided offending those who still associated advertising with vulgarity and lower-class business methods.[131]

These essays not only advertised Bayswater's commercial culture; they suggested that its elegant shops and shoppers demonstrated that this suburban district was now a cosmopolitan pleasure center. They turned the fact that Bayswater had been engulfed by London from a problem into an advantage. "Every year," claimed the *Bayswater Chronicle*, "Westbourne-grove attract[s] to itself business which was formerly wont to seek the West End Centres."[132] Another writer observed that "improvements in Westbourne Grove frontages which are now in vogue, are on the increase. Bayswater is getting to look less like a *faubourg* and more like a metropolitan centre."[133] By 1880, local journalists even contended that "Westbourne Grove as a shopping thoroughfare has now reached a pitch of unprecedented excellence. Both as a promenade, and a display of tasteful shop windows, it is now more inviting than ever."[134]

Embracing local commercial culture meant celebrating shopping as a legitimate, pleasurable, and fashionable social event. And this meant giving a special welcome to the crowds of women that occupied the neighborhood's streets. Instead of worrying that a luxurious environment would lead to moral ruin, the *Bayswater Chronicle* began to suggest, for example, that the mingling of different social groups was an innocent but cosmopolitan amusement:

> The Centre of social gravitation in Bayswater is undoubtedly the few hundred yards of roadway, familiarly known as "The Grove," . . . between 10 A.M. and 6 P.M. . . . Every class, every age . . . and almost every nationality contribute to the tide of life. . . . It is no doubt an exceedingly delightful and entertaining

> way of passing the afternoon and seeing the world and one's acquaintances, this gathering in clusters around displays of laces, feathers, jewelry, and what not, thrown before one's very feet as it were, and lavishly tempting the eye on every side. . . . London offers no more seductive allurements for this amusement than to be found in Westbourne Grove.[135]

Journalists in part developed this image of the heterogenous shopping crowd and the pleasures of shopping to demonstrate that Bayswater was a thriving and modern commercial district.

They also wrote about female shoppers as glittering objects and symbols of prosperity. Some journalists obviously described shoppers and shopping streets as beautiful, desirable, and fashionable in order to lure more shoppers to their neighborhood. This was an especially common strategy during the winter and summer sales, seasons when all women were thought to shop for bargains. For example, in January 1882 a correspondent wrote that in "Sale Season . . . that happy hunting time for the shopping sex," Bayswater truly earned "its gentle sobriquet of 'Woman's World.' "[136]

At first glance, such reverence for shopping and Bayswater's largest proprietor appears quite paradoxical. Those who had attacked Whiteley now heralded his emporium, while those who had not been driven out of business adopted his selling techniques and his arguments. This apparent change was in fact another response to the threat posed by the department store. Some Bayswater shopkeepers challenged the monster shops not with cleavers and marrow bones or with biting social commentary, but by sprucing up their interiors, offering special bargains, and paying more attention to window display. They adopted Whiteley's style and rhetoric to compete with the dozens of Universal Providers that had appeared throughout central and suburban London.[137]

In the late 1870s and 1880s, falling prices, a series of ruinous fires, and growing competition actually led to a decline in Whiteley's profits, which stagnated throughout the 1880s as other department stores appeared across the street and all over the West End.[138] Middle-class cooperatives, such as the Army and Navy Stores and the Civil Service Supply Association, also posed a challenge.[139] Bayswater's shopkeepers could thus hardly imagine that the Universal Provider was their only threat. They spoke of Whiteley's as "their own," to discourage customers from shopping in other neighborhoods.

The Universal Provider reacted to growing competition by expanding into new lines and indulging in new promotional techniques. While he avoided press advertising, in 1877 he began issuing the elaborately bound and illustrated *William Whiteley's Diary, Almanac, and Handbook of Useful Information.* Among other things, this annual diary republished extracts from newspaper articles that praised Whiteley for taking "charge of you from the cradle to the grave."[140] Such publicity helped legitimize shopping and department store methods just as overproduction and protectionism abroad made it harder for businessmen to sell their goods. While some manufacturers and retailers responded to the structural changes in the late-Victorian economy by aggressively advertising, many traders in wealthy areas fostered the image of consumption as a respectable and pleasurable female amusement.[141]

This culture of commercial pleasure was by no means hegemonic, however. In Bayswater, for example, some of its most outspoken critics were the wealthy residents who were supposed to enjoy its magnificent shops. They too identified department stores and shopping streets with urbanity and modernity, but they deplored this new culture, believing that it had transformed their idyllic home into a frenetic and crowded urban landscape. Although these reproaches challenged the artificiality of this commercial utopia, they also revealed an animosity toward outsiders, a fear of the crowd, and a sense of urban danger and vulnerability. These critics essentially argued that "Young London" was neither comfortable nor pleasurable.

As they saw it, the problem with this modern city was that it failed to accommodate bourgeois women. Many residents particularly decried the growing visibility of the working and lower-middle classes in their neighborhood's streets. Some objected to the fact that the Grove had become a popular meeting place for shop assistants, nannies, servants, and their male friends.[142] One "pedestrian" told of being pushed into the gutter by "maids" walking abreast "in full gossip," and insisted that "shop-staring" and "flirting" nurses deliberately ran their carriages against ladies dresses.[143] When two young servants were fined for driving their perambulators abreast, the magistrate asked them, "How are the people to pass if you girls are gaping after soldiers and policeman?"[144] The mere presence of working women and men in the streets was thought to obstruct the pleasures and freedoms of wealthy shoppers. One author countered these attacks by pointing out the similarities between workers and wealthier idlers:

> Why all this head-shaking and eye-rolling over the simple fact that from 8 to 9 in the evening, or a little later, Westbourne-grove is crowded with young shopmen and shopwomen who have just been released from the day's employ? I suspect these jealous and virtuous critics and censors of young people have plenty of leisure themselves, and may be seen taking their strolls in the same thoroughfare at a more luxurious hour of the day. . . . Why should not a young fellow be free to meet his comrades in the street—or his sweetheart either—after the shutters are shut?[145]

As this letter made clear, wealthy Tyburnia delighted in its promenade, but objected to others using the same spaces for virtually the same behaviors. Indeed, the affluent and poor struggled over the spaces and uses of the shopping street. David Scobey has shown in his study of New York City that the promenade allowed wealthy residents to consolidate their social status through subtle dramatizations of class position.[146] Bayswater's elite similarly saw their shopping streets as parade grounds in which they displayed wealth and position. However, in London, as in other large urban centers working people were also using these streets as "avenues for protest, celebration, and amusement."[147]

Wealthy residents were quick to condemn this working-class culture because it suggested that they could not fully control their neighborhood. This resentment became most pronounced in letters complaining about petty criminals wandering into Tyburnia. Virtually all of these portrayed shopping ladies as victims of beggars, street traders, petty thieves, and male pests. One "ratepayer," for example, recounted how female flower sellers "pursued" ladies into shops and "hustled" them off the sidewalk into the street, warning, "If the inhabitants wish to keep the Grove as the most noted shopping promenade in London, they will do well to keep it from undue obstruction and from becoming a street market."[148] Others reported harrowing tales of lady shoppers having their pockets picked and their purses snatched while they absentmindedly gazed into shop windows.[149] Some also told of women being harassed by strange men when they strolled in Bayswater's streets. For example, one "young Englishman" wrote a letter reporting that

> a lady friend of mine . . . on leaving a well-known trimming establishment . . . was saluted by a gentlemanly dressed man, aged about 55, who endeavored to attract her attention by touching the skirt of her dress twice with his walking stick, exclaiming at the same time, "How pretty, pretty!" The lady, taking no notice, crossed the road . . . stopped to purchase some flowers. . . . This fellow followed, and begged to be allowed to present her with a bouquet . . . assuring with spasmodic speeches that "he was dying to get to know her"; and even went so far, without the slightest encouragement, to ask her to meet him the same afternoon.[150]

The man turned out to be "respectably" married and a member of a church that stood only about a hundred yards from where the incident had occurred. In the absence of any legal remedy, the friend of the insulted lady hoped to shame her assailant by printing an account of the story in the local paper. Similar stories frequently appeared in the local paper as they did in the national press.

Shoppers, workers, and prostitutes, as public women, were commonly subjected to such insults. In 1880 Mark Twain even commented that in London, "If a lady unattended walks abroad in the streets . . . even at noonday she will be pretty likely to be accosted and insulted—and not by drunken sailors but by men who carry the look and wear the dress of a gentleman."[151] As Walkowitz has explained, accounts of sexual danger and harassment operated on many levels.[152] They were the product of bourgeois gender ideology, which cast all women in the street as streetwalkers. They were also reactions to the commercialization of urban life. As we saw with Whiteley's liquor license, the label given to shoppers and shop assistants as public women was central to the Victorian critique of consumerism.

And yet we should not presume that all Victorians saw shopping as a public activity or suburban streets as public places. Some shoppers clearly felt that the stores were intimately connected to the private domain. In his childhood recollections of Bayswater, Osbert Lancaster recalled that his "Victorian" cousin Jenny's "only excursion" was her "daily visit to Whiteley's." "No abbess," he wrote, "ever identified her life so closely with her convent, as did Cousin Jenny with that of Whiteley's Universal Stores." As closely as Cousin Jenny identified with Whiteley's, she evidently "deplored all innovation and expansion and had foreseen nothing but future disaster arising from each successive change, from the abandonment of oil-lamps in favor of gas to the introduction of a soda fountain." Nevertheless, "she would stoutly maintain in conversation with Great Aunt Bessie its manifest superiority to the Army and Navy Stores."[153] Cousin Jenny imagined Whiteley's as part of her domestic sphere and condemned those aspects which appealed to a wider public.

Others saw the stores as an unwelcome intrusion into their domestic retreat. Jane Ellen Panton, author of a number of household manuals and correspondent for the *Lady's Pictorial*, remembered the Westbourne Grove of her childhood "as a street of prim little houses . . . and our rage when the public house took its place and the big shops began to appear."[154] After she became an interior designer, Panton continued to criticize the "big" shops, but she nevertheless promoted her own vision of consumerism. Panton and Cousin Jenny both found fault with the big stores, but they certainly did not reject consumer culture per se. What they disliked was the too obvious signs of commercialism that had transformed their neighborhood from a leafy suburb into "Young London." They resented the very forces Sala had championed.

Although some women despaired at the commercialization of their neighborhood or felt vulnerable in shopping streets, others delighted in the urban freedoms that commercial culture seemed to offer. An "English Lady," for example, wrote that Twain's portrayal of sexual relations in London's streets was "simply and emphatically untrue." She encouraged the famous author to pay a visit to Bayswater and "observe 'ladies' who daily use our park and gardens for air and exercise, or who travel our streets some on pleasure, some on business bent."[155] The same sentiment appeared in a poem, "In Our Streets," which ended with the refrain:

> "Good Sir, you mistake me, I feel no alarm,
> No Arab or 'Toff' will offer me harm.
> In the hour of the glooming, and my dog's of no use,
> Yet the police take swell care, I need fear no abuse.
> So onward I go, on my quiet lone walk,
> Neither theft nor low rudeness e'er offers to balk;
> In our streets the women of Bayswater may,
> Walk safely at eve as they do in the day."[156]

These shoppers' opinions sounded nearly identical to the arguments made by Whiteley and fellow retailers during this period. Such poetry and letters promoted female freedom and commercial growth as signs of modernity. Others, however, were uncomfortable living in a world of strangers and were unhappy with the ideals of femininity that came with it. They simply would not endorse the belief that commercial growth spelled civic or female improvement. Instead, they saw a rapidly changing metropolis in which social hierarchies and class and gender differences had been torn asunder. And this, they maintained, led to female discomfort, not pleasure.

Bayswater's press and its residents thus held two visions of their shopping center. If some understood Whiteley's and Westbourne Grove as a utopian and pleasurable zone, others saw a hostile world of strangers. Both of these cities turned upon constructions of femininity. Both highlight how gender inflected the commercialization and urbanization of the suburban West End. Competing social and economic forces had created London's commercial culture and its diverse images of the public woman. Bayswater's business classes and its consumers were far from united in their opinions about this culture and economy or about what constituted proper bourgeois womanhood. Despite their differences, however, both critics and proponents of economic change furthered the understanding that shopping was a female activity. If men and women of all classes bought goods in a variety of retail environments, shopping was consistently gendered as a female pastime. This pleasure was tied to a vision of the urban landscape that identified consumption with modernity. This narrative was a product of the competition between drapers, grocers, butchers, and publicans; between these traders and London's magistrates; and between residents and visitors. As we will see, it was also the product of transformations in family property, the machinations of urban reformers and the feminist community, as well as alterations in the history of travel, communications, and entertainment.

In the following chapters, we will move from Bayswater to look at other narratives of female urban pleasure. The debate about the morality and pleasures of consumption was not settled by the 1880s, nor was it only a product of intense suburban growth. Anxieties associated with commercial culture and women's presence in the public spaces of the city became a constant force in London's history. Indeed, these concerns became more intense as the city become more commercialized. They entered into the history of female credit, sparked a perpetual debate about the safety of London's streets and commercial spaces for "respectable" women, and contributed to the development of "female-only" spaces and guides for urban women. Finally, they stimulated the growth of bigger, more dramatic, and more publicized retail ventures such as Gordon Selfridge's spectacular Edwardian store. The next chapter explores how debates about the morality of consumption dominated the relationship between traders and their customers and husbands and wives, and looks as well at the legal reforms governing marital property. In the home and the courtroom, as in the streets of Bayswater, men and women argued about the nature of women's relationship to goods, the pleasures of the purchase, and the implications of consuming in an urban center.

• CHAPTER TWO •

The Trials of Consumption: Marriage, Law, and Women's Credit

On August 5, 1892, Charles Portier, trading as "Mme Portier, dressmaker," brought an action in the City of London Court against Mr. and Mrs. Lewin to recover twenty pounds. Although all agreed that Portier had not been paid for the dresses he had made for Mrs. Lewin, both husband and wife denied responsibility for the bill. Mrs. Lewin pleaded that she owned no property and therefore could not be held liable for any debts. Mr. Lewin testified that he gave his wife a sufficient dress allowance beyond which he forbade her to spend. His attorney then argued that a husband was not legally accountable for his wife's debts "unless the wife had the direct authority of her husband to pledge his credit." The question of liability thus turned on proof that this privately bestowed authority had been granted. To settle this problem the court explored the couple's domestic arrangements, examining both their economic and emotional relationship. The judge investigated whether Mr. Lewin was aware of his wife's purchases when he asked whether "the fact that they are living together, eating and drinking at the same table is evidence that he sees the dresses on his wife?" Lewin, however, staunchly rejected this assumption, asserting "he never knew what dresses his wife wore or where they came from." Seemingly admiring Lewin's ignorance, the judge dismissed him from all financial responsibility and praised him for being one of the "few men of sense in this world . . . who don't care a farthing for what their wives wear." Although judgment was entered against the separate estate of Mrs. Lewin, recovering money from a married woman was a long, drawn-out, generally unsuccessful endeavor. Charles Portier probably never saw his twenty pounds. In addition to his financial loss, "Mme Portier" suffered further indignity when the judge insultingly called him "a man carrying on business as a woman."[1]

More than money was at stake in this courtroom. Throughout the second half of the nineteenth century, thousands of others found that their financial entanglements brought them before England's county courts each year.[2] In settling their debts they were debating the meaning of *family*, *property*, *consumption*, as well as the extent of wives' legal "agency," at a moment when these concepts were being disputed and dramatically reshaped.[3] Because the struggles around consumer debt involved confrontations within the home and between the home, the shop, and the courts, their history suggests that the family and the economy can hardly be regarded as separate spheres. As Leonore Davidoff and Catherine Hall have shown, the reproduction of the middle classes depended upon the linkages between these spheres.[4] Yet if gender ideals, the social organization of the family, and the economy could support one another, these same ideals and social arrangements could also undermine each other. Married women's debts raised just this fearful possibility.

Wives' debts, incurred through buying goods and services on credit, pointed out an irreconcilable conflict between bourgeois domestic ideology and the growth of an advanced capitalist economy. The increasing impersonality of the market, coinciding with the cultural prescription that purchasing was a female activity, collided with shifting definitions of property ownership to produce a volatile and problematic relationship between retailers and their customers and between husbands and wives. The social and cultural practices of buying and selling clashed with the laws that governed these activities. Put more concretely, wives shopped, but husbands generally paid for and legally owned the purchased goods. During the last decades of the nineteenth century, the legal system wrestled with this inconsistency while reforming both married women's property rights and creditor-debtor law. While a husband's liability for his wife's consumption steadily decreased after the 1860s, a wife's legal responsibility increased slowly and unevenly. Into the twentieth century, the responsibility for a wife's debts remained extremely unclear, and family discord and unpaid debts were frequently the result.

Whatever the precise locus of these financial and emotional conflicts, they ultimately turned upon a pervasive fear that the expanding consumer economy had unleashed female desires that could financially ruin both husbands and shopkeepers. Both parties looked to the legal system to protect their economic well-being from female consumption. Magistrates and the legislature, however, consistently privileged the interests of husbands over those of retailers. Regardless of the husband's social class or the amount of debt, the legal system buttressed his economic authority against the dangers of credit, advertising, large luxurious urban shops, and itinerant hawkers of finery. Legal authorities interpreted women's buying as inherently immoral, since it potentially conferred upon wives power over their husband's economic and social position. Common and statutory law responded to this fear by limiting men's liability for their wives' consumption. The specter of the naturally insatiable, extravagant woman thus motivated and remained embedded in legal reforms. By defining the female consumer as inherently uncreditworthy, these reforms in turn influenced retail and family history.

At the same time that wives' economic autonomy was officially discredited, the vague and inconsistent nature of the laws, the persistence of social practices, and the growing number of urban shopping centers created an opportunity for many wives to claim authority over their husbands' money even when no such authority legally existed. By examining individual court battles over familial debt between the 1860s and the early-twentieth century, it becomes quite clear that neither shoppers, shopkeepers, nor judges always understood or acted in accordance with the law. Women often disobeyed husbands, bought what they wanted, and sometimes cheated retailers out of extraordinary sums. When brought to court, they justified these acts by claiming status as the family's consumer and defining consumption as a rational and legitimate economic act.

As traders found themselves cheated out of vast sums of money, they increasingly shifted from informal to formal credit mechanisms and expanded their reliance upon cash transactions. The department stores, which were built upon lower prices and "ready money," were in some sense responding to the legal morass that surrounded selling to a "mass" market of married women. These stores institutionalized cash transactions, introducing a new relationship between buyer and seller, to extricate themselves from older trading practices that essentially protected wealthy shoppers at the storekeeper's expense. This chapter examines the laws and practices of credit purchasing and married women's debts to highlight some of the tensions surrounding buying and selling in the late-nineteenth century, to explore how women's shifting relationship to property influenced their position as buyers, and to consider how urban and retail change intersected with families' emotional and financial dynamics. Finally, the history of wives' credit exposes how anxieties revolving around female shoppers impacted the development of retailing and the legal position of both male and female consumers.

Credit: "The Shopkeeper's Temptation"

As the Lewins and "Mme Portier" discovered, credit purchasing was as much a "cultural transaction" as a simple financial exchange, in that it involved moral judgments about class, gender, consumer practices, and particular commodities.[5] In the late-nineteenth century but especially in the twentieth, standardized and relatively impersonal forms of credit such as the installment plan and credit card contributed to the expansion of consumer society by facilitating both the purchase and production of expensive consumer durables.[6] For most of the nineteenth century, however, consumer credit was still informal and based on personal trust and a financial and moral assessment of the buyer. From studies by Melanie Tebbutt, Paul Johnson, Ellen Ross, and others, we know that informal store credit and the pawn shop forged social relations and sustained working-class families during periods of economic distress.[7] That consumer credit also occupied a prominent role in the Victorian middle- and upper-class family economy has not been sufficiently emphasized.[8]

Buying on credit was a widespread if much criticized practice throughout the nineteenth century, as it had been earlier. Though it had always created financial problems for retailers, in the eighteenth century credit had also facilitated trade at a time when specie was in very short supply.[9] Although cash became more readily available in the nineteenth century, credit transactions remained extremely commonplace if still fraught with difficulties. In fact, they posed new problems in the second half of nineteenth century as the gender of shoppers, the types of goods, the location of markets, and the laws governing marital property changed. Just as all business relationships were growing more impersonal in the Victorian period, in large shopping districts such as London's West End relations between buyer and seller increasingly became fleeting contacts between strangers.[10]

The ever more spectacular transformation in late-nineteenth-century consumption—the advent of mass transportation, advertising, monumental architecture, store services, and lavish displays—encouraged women to consume more and to do so farther from their neighborhoods. The risks of offering informal store credit grew as the shopping population became a transient body of strangers. In order to limit its risks, the business community sought to regularize credit. Wholesalers turned to newspapers and trade papers to learn about the creditworthiness of their customers. Local newspapers could also be of some use to retailers since husbands sometimes printed notices in which they publicly renounced their wife's agency. The larger firms and multiples typically restricted the extension of credit and ultimately insisted upon cash, justifying this new practice by stressing the advantage of reduced prices.[11] These options were not readily available to many urban retailers, however, who were caught between the desire to sell to as many people as possible and the fear that doing so could lead to unpaid debts and business failure.

Traders such as milliners and drapers were placed in especially difficult circumstances. As they constantly bemoaned in their trade papers, they were finding it harder than ever to force men to pay for their wives' debts. Until the 1860s, the male head of household had been legally liable for most family debt. As the owner of the family's property, he was considered to have a legal duty to maintain his family and was assumed to have a direct knowledge of all familial consumption.[12] Since few married women possessed separate estates, they technically could not enter a contract of any kind, including purchasing on credit.[13] When they and other dependents bought goods, they traded on the basis of the householder's credit, essentially acting as his agent. In her study of wives' debt obligations prior to the 1860s, Margot Finn has argued that since the time of Henry VI, the common law had permitted wives to pledge their husbands' credit for goods deemed to be "necessaries."[14] This and other legal loopholes granted wives a greater degree of economic autonomy than the law of coverture implied. Though technically women became legal nonentities upon marriage, studies of the common law and equity courts are revealing a more varied picture of the legal position of wives. As we will see, however, legal reforms in the 1860s and 1870s began to close these loopholes and to attempt to limit wives' ability to pledge their husbands' credit.

The change in common law treatment of wives' agency was not so much a product of separate spheres ideology, which was so powerful during these years. Rather, it had to do with the shifting nature and location of shopping. Prior to the mid-nineteenth century, few wives would have wanted or been able to shop far from their homes. Most purchased goods in their local communities from traders they had known all their lives. Merchants typically brought their wares directly to the household and thus had at least a casual sense of the economic position of their customers. This hardly ensured that all bills were paid, but when shopkeepers sold their goods to wives on credit, they often knew the husbands with whom they were in fact trading. However, the idea of a wife acting as her husband's agent became more disconcerting for late-nineteenth-century retailers because they increasingly sold to women and, by extension, to men whom they did not know personally. The growth of new commodities and occasions for shopping, the relocation of markets, and the physical separation of workplace and home only added to the vagaries of an already confusing legal system.

For a variety of reasons, husbands' direct relationship to their family's consumption grew more distant. A shift in the cultural organization of gender and consumption had long castigated the male shopper as an effeminate and feeble creature. This is not to suggest that men did not buy goods. They certainly were deeply involved in a range of different consumer practices. However, too close involvement with domestic consumption, and especially with clothes shopping, exposed men to a good deal of ridicule in the nineteenth century.[15] The changing locus of paid employment meant that lower- and middle-class husbands were typically at work when itinerant tradesmen came to their homes to hawk their wares.[16] As shops' opening hours became progressively shorter, the time for either male or female workers to shop also came to be quite limited. At the same time, nonworking wives were traveling farther from home to do their shopping. As we saw in the last chapter, by the 1860s observers noticed thousands of suburban and provincial women regularly visiting the West End of London for a day's shopping.[17] Thus, the geography of Victorian production and consumption and cultural prescriptions about the gender of shoppers tended to work together to separate men from the day-to-day routines of domestic consumption.

Particularly when goods were bought on credit, women's long-distance shopping alarmed husbands, traditional retailers, and moralists. Husbands and moralists often claimed that easy credit, like lunchrooms in linen drapers, was among the traps that traders used to ensnare innocent female shoppers. In this view, easy credit aided in her conquest or seduction.[18] A sexualized image of buying and selling grew from the fragile and tense nature of both domestic and market relations. Though ideally separate spheres, domestic ideology encouraged women to take charge of familial consumption, an activity that urged them to travel to urban shopping centers. When these shoppers pledged their husbands' credit, they quite literally placed their spouses in a dependent economic position vis-à-vis the shopkeeper, in effect jeopardizing their husbands' economic and personal well-being. The female shopper inherently disrupted the supposedly separate spheres and the traditional balance of power between spouses and thus was often accused of a moral crime akin to adultery.

Retailers played the well-worn trope of the extravagant woman possessed of an insatiable appetite for all it was worth in their criticism of credit and other "immoral" trading practices. A writer in an early trade journal, the *Drapier and Clothier*, for example, warned that the "hundreds of hawkers vending tawdry and finery and vulgar ornaments to the wives of farm laborers and weavers" on credit empowered wives at their husbands' expense. "It would be fearful," the journal asserted, "to consider the number of persons in the country who have been imprisoned in respect of goods supplied to their wives during their absence from home."[19] Wealthy husbands in London's "metropolitan suburbs" were made to worry too, since it had become a common practice for London's retailers to send "false representations and puffs . . . during the period of the day when the male head of the family is most from home." Because wealthy women were "accustomed . . . to lives of purity, economy and domestic privacy, and truth," and were possessed of a "love of dress and great bargains," they "were far more easily ensnared by men than men are ensnared by each other."[20] Women's weakness for dress seemed the natural result of their seclusion in the private sphere and an inherent part of their femininity. They were of course most susceptible when their husbands were not around to keep them from succumbing to temptation. The sexualized effects of buying on credit were similarly conjured up in the homilies of magazines, household manuals, and fiction.[21] Legally excluded from most "honorable" means of making money, the female debtor was imagined as particularly vulnerable to male attentions. This image of the female debtor was not unlike that of the kleptomaniac or the prostitute. All three female types represented the social and moral collapse resulting from women's immersion in the mires of the economy.[22] Perhaps the debtor wife was the most frightening figure, however, for her consuming passions could destroy her entire family.

Prescriptive literature often treated a wife's credit purchases as a major source of infection in the home that weakened the husband's financial and moral strength.[23] Not surprisingly, credit, the "shopkeeper's temptation," was often the focus of the jeremiads of the middle-class moralist Samuel Smiles.[24] Responding in part to a pervasive sense in the 1860s and 1870s that the cost of living was rising, Smiles defended what he characterized as traditional notions of thrift and domestic economy.[25] He condemned all classes for living beyond their means in order to appear respectable and successful. This desire, he argued, led to ruin rather than prosperity by encouraging people to "spend their money before it is earned—run into debt at the grocer's, the baker's, the milliner's, and the butcher's . . . [to] entertain fashionable friends at the expense of the shop-keepers."[26] Smiles thus feared that credit disrupted what he hoped could be a direct relationship between actual and apparent income, between spending and social status. In a sense, Smiles was witnessing and deploring the same trends that Thorstein Veblen would see in the United States decades later. Smiles believed that credit purchasing encouraged conspicuous consumption, and this in turn unhinged fixed class identities. Though one can find similar anxieties in earlier periods, Smiles argued that the discrepancy between real and apparent wealth had grown especially large and would lead to dire social consequences.[27] He was particularly worried that women's passions, their "rage for dress and finery . . . [which] rivaled the corrupt and debauched age of Louis XV of France," would bankrupt both shopkeepers and husbands. "No woman," he asserted, "is justified in running into debt for a dress without her husband's knowledge and consent. If she do so, she is clothing herself at the expense of the draper." Husbands were cautioned that allowing wives to purchase on credit gave another person "power over your liberty."[28] The still common use of the debtors' prison underscored the reality of this threat.[29] However, Smiles believed buyers, not sellers, needed to be reformed. The solution was simple: "When pleasure tempts with its seductions, have the courage to say 'No' at once."[30]

Such warnings against consumer credit evidently fell on deaf ears, since so many of the commodities that filled the Victorians' homes and adorned their bodies were bought with its help. Throughout the century, credit allowed working-class families to make ends meet, while installment buying helped middle-class families on limited incomes set up households.[31] Credit also served the aristocracy, as evidenced by the fact that approximately 80 percent of all sales in the small, elite shops of metropolitan districts such as the West End were offered on credit.[32] Informal store credit was so prevalent and so irregular that studies of income levels alone tell us little about the nature of the growth of consumer society. It was quite possible for families to live well beyond their means and in many cases to do so with few legal repercussions. Of course, eventually debts had to be paid, but the long-term nature of most debts in the nineteenth century suggests that we need to be extremely careful when attempting to link the growth of consumption directly to income level.[33]

In the case of aristocrats, credit was clearly a vestige of an older client economy. Shopkeepers extended credit on the basis of aristocrats' social position, not on their financial solidity, while these customers viewed tradesmen more or less as retainers to be paid when and if it suited them. Many simply believed cash payment was a demeaning abrogation of their social privilege. For example, an exclusive London bootmaker testified, "A gentleman will perhaps come in and get a pair of boots and a couple of pairs of shoes, and I never see any more of him; and if I do find him out, when I press him for the money, he feels angry, because the sum is so small."[34] By definition, quality establishments extended credit. Lady Jeune, a prominent female journalist, wrote of shopping in the 1870s: "We dutifully followed in the steps of our forefathers, paying for the things we had at the end of the year, for no well-thought-of firm ever demanded or expected more than a yearly payment of their debts."[35] One Edwardian fashion designer found that it was nearly impossible to press her clients for payment, and recalled that "the richer people are the more difficult it is to get them to pay their bills."[36]

Many store owners fought back by charging high interest and printing warnings on their bills that they accepted only cash. At times, this worked. For example, Andrew and Company, ironmongers in Tottenham Court Road, clearly stated on their bills: "Our terms being strictly cash no goods can be left without money. NB:—The Proprietors particularly call attention to the above regulation, and trust that none of their respected patrons will consider their integrity in the slightest degree reflected upon by its being adhered to."[37] Evidently this message encouraged Horace Flower, Esq., to pay his bill of sixteen pounds immediately, though many tradesmen who sold goods and services to his family were not so lucky. A. Barrett and Sons, brush manufacturers, silversmiths, and jewelers, were forced to send this pleading letter to one of Flower's relatives, probably his son:

> We beg respectfully to again draw your attention to our account of *£10.9*, which has been standing on our books for some considerable time, and which has, we fear, escaped your notice. May we therefore ask you to kindly give the matter your *immediate attention* and forward us a remittance in settlement *per return* as we desire to balance our books.
>
> Thanking you in anticipation and awaiting your esteemed reply.[38]

The tone of these letters and bills reflects the deferential and sometimes quite delicate relationship between shopkeepers and their upper-middle- and upper-class patrons. Deference still occupied a central role in such relationships well into the twentieth century, placing even quite wealthy shopkeepers in an awkward position when their customers refused to pay their bills. Elite customers may have been poor credit risks, but their custom was difficult to refuse, since their patronage also contributed to business success. According to one draper, the "carriage custom" was not easily turned away, since he or she bestowed a "lustre" on the house they patronized. In a commercial economy in which credit was part aristocratic deference system, part modern financial incentive, shopkeepers walked a fine line. They relied on their customers for both payment and patronage, and too little of each could lead to bankruptcy.[39]

Middle-class women also tried to exploit this uncertainty. They too partook of society's ambivalent attitudes toward property and money that were inherent in commerce with the aristocracy. However, retailers' ambivalence about dealing with middle-class women resulted largely from their dependent legal status rather than from class privilege. If wives' authority to pledge their husbands' or their own credit was unclear prior to the 1860s, it became even more obscure in the following decades. Though someone like Smiles regarded credit as a temptation that shopkeepers used to beguile women, shopkeepers desperately hoped that legal reforms could contain the dangers involved in this seduction.

The Wife's Authority and Husband's Liability

Instead of smoothing out these difficulties between buyers and sellers, the legal system furthered anxieties about the transformation of distribution systems, women's appetites, and definitions of property. In the later decades of the nineteenth century, retailers sought to decrease their financial risks when selling to wives by reforming the laws governing married women's property rights and their liability for debt. Traders' interests initially coincided with that of liberal legal reformers and feminists who wanted married women to attain the same property rights and responsibilities as single women and men. Although compelled by quite different motivations, shopkeepers who traditionally sold to women, feminists, and reformers collaborated in their efforts to alter the economics of marriage. Married women's relationship to property was fundamentally rewritten during these years but not in the way that retailers had hoped. Judges and legislators thwarted shopkeepers' attempts to make wives responsible for their debts, violating a strict construction of laissez-faire ideology out of a reluctance to overturn conventional assumptions about class and gender roles. As the legal system persistently failed to meet what retailers believed were their needs, many shopkeepers eventually came to perceive women's emancipation as exacerbating their own precarious financial position.

In the 1860s, both the laws regulating credit and debt and those governing married women's property more or less concurred on the husband's liability for debts incurred by the wife. In the next decade, however, these laws grew more inconsistent. These inconsistencies were compounded when Parliament passed the Married Women's Property Act of 1870, its 1874 amendment, and the more sweeping 1882 act, which recognized married women as property owners without making them fully liable for the debts they incurred. The confusion was only heightened by the treatment of family debt in common law and by individual judges in the county and higher courts. These anomalies, however, put married women in an unusually strong position to avoid paying for what they purchased.

Part of the larger reformation of the antiquated legal system, the county courts had been established in 1846 to aid in the recovery of small debts.[40] However, the courts never worked in a straightforward way to oil the wheels of petty commerce. In 1857, the author of a book on the courts complained that they even operated "as a stagnation to trade in provincial districts."[41] A few years later, another critic maintained that "thousands of persons, sooner than risk the caprice, uncertainty, inefficacy, and expense of a county court, forego their claims . . . [hence] the public confidence has begun to cease."[42] The legal historian G. R. Rubin and others have explained such criticisms by documenting how judges' cultural and social prejudices often defeated the courts' original purpose.[43] Rubin argued that county court judges disliked their role as debt collectors, bore a great deal of animosity toward the small traders and traveling drapers who made up the majority of the plaintiffs, and believed that selling on credit, especially to women, was morally questionable. Though judges were prone to find against working-class debtors, they often sided with the husbands whose wives had pledged their credit, despite the straightforward nature of the original sale.[44] Judges' prejudices against small traders, as well as their attitudes toward gender, marriage, and consumption, influenced their decisions. The attitudes that had left Charles Portier a laughingstock in the City of London Court were rampant among both lower and higher court justices. County court practice and the changes in statute law were built upon the same images of threatened masculinity and frivolous femininity that permitted the Lewins to avoid paying their debt and that figured in the writings of Samuel Smiles.

Ironically, the courts worked to protect male control over the family purse by diminishing husbands' legal responsibility for wives' debts. This decline began with the 1864 precedent-setting case heard in the Court of Common Pleas. The decision allowed a husband to deny liability for his wife's debts if he could prove that the purchased goods were not "necessary" and that he had forbidden her to pledge his credit. *Jolly v. Rees* thus addressed the questions of whether a wife was a legal agent for her husband and whether and how he could revoke that agency.[45] The fashionable draper Jolly and Sons claimed they had sold goods to Mrs. Rees with the legitimate presumption that she had the authority to pledge her husband's credit. When payment time came, however, Mr. Rees, "a country gentleman," protested that he had explicitly forbidden his wife to act as his agent and that, therefore, he should not be liable for the debt.

After hearing the case, the justices concluded for the defendant. The decision stated that though it was often presumed that "a woman living with a man as his wife had his authority to pledge his credit," that man always had the right to revoke this agency without any public notice to retailers. To not permit a husband "this right" might lead to "domestic discords" and cause tradesmen to speculate "on enforcing payment for goods sold to a wife on such presumed authority." It was the court's "duty simply to say that a wife derived her authority from the husband's will, and that she had no right to pledge his credit from any presumption as his wife." The court decided that marriage gave women no inherent agency over their husband's property. The final authority over consumption was to belong to all men, but the decision specifically singled out those in "the lower ranks of life, where a man's labour compelled him to leave his house under the control of his wife." In this situation, "debts might be contracted which the husband never intended to contract." Therefore, the court found that "it was reasonable that he should have the power to regulate his expenditure."[46] These words remained the basis of the common law regarding familial debt responsibility until the mid-twentieth century. More or less explicitly, the court determined that women's agency with respect to family property was not an absolute right derived from marriage but a conditional one derived from the husband's authorization. In so ruling, the court reaffirmed the husband's authority over family expenditure. From then on, creditors had to presume that men could *privately* forbid their wives to pledge their credit—in sum, not buyers but creditors beware.

Whereas husbands' financial liability decreased, wives' liability increased very slowly and haltingly. The first Married Women's Property Act of 1870 bestowed women with only limited property rights and did not make them fully liable for their debts.[47] Mary Lyndon Shanley has argued that when it became law, the 1870 act was so far from the original intent of its feminist proponents that they did not know whether to treat it as a victory or defeat. The act removed only certain types of a wife's property from her husband's control. Instead of granting wives the same access to their property as they had prior to marriage, or as all men possessed, a married women's property was considered to belong to her "separate estate."[48] Originally a legal device developed in the early modern equity courts, the separate estate was a trust that had permitted wealthy families to keep a portion of a woman's property "protected" from her husband's creditors, thus guaranteeing the maternal property line.[49] In effect it prevented the wife too, through a device known as "restraint on anticipation," from disposing freely of her property or from charging it with debts. By adopting the conception of the separate estate, the 1870 act determined that a wife's property would frequently remain unavailable to creditors. She could be sued but was liable only for the amount of her estate at the time she entered the contract. Even then, a married woman could not be held personally liable, that is imprisoned, when she refused to pay her debts. A married woman's property, therefore, could be essentially marked off as outside of the market. According to Shanley, the 1870 act made a married woman, "less liable for her debts than other citizens were for theirs."[50] After describing the impact of this Act, the author of a legal textbook wrote in 1879: "The English law of conjugal property thus stands, at the present day, an unscientific mass of rules, exceptions, and exceptions to exceptions."[51]

One such exception had absolved husbands from responsibility for their wives' prenuptial debts even when, as in certain cases, he had acquired her property. This anomaly regarding prenuptial debts led to the passage in 1874 of an amendment to the 1870 act. Also known as the Creditors Bill, this act once again made husbands liable for their wives' prenuptial debts to the extent of the property they had acquired from the wife.[52] Husbands were, however, still technically responsible for debts determined by a court to be "necessaries." Debts for luxuries could be avoided if the husband pleaded, as Mr. Rees had, that he forbade his wife to incur them. What was necessary and what was a luxury depended upon the nature of the goods relative to the perceived social position of the couple. That status was often hard to determine, particularly when spouses came from different backgrounds and diverged in their conception of appropriate consumption. Categorizing commodities no doubt became all the harder as mass production and imperial expansion brought ever more unfamiliar products to market each year.

After the passage of the 1870 and 1874 acts, shopkeepers struggled with the legal nuances governing men and women's property rights and liabilities. Legal authorities such as Robert Malcolm Kerr could confidently write in 1876 that though "by marriage, the husband and wife are one person in law; that is the very being or legal existence of the woman is suspended during the marriage, or at least incorporated or consolidated into that of the husband. . . . A woman indeed may be agent for her husband; for that implies no separation from, but is rather a representation of her lord."[53] But few shopkeepers would have viewed marriage or a wife's agency as such a straightforward affair. They failed to see how spouses could be imagined as legally one person or as wives "representing" their lords in such a simplistic and direct way.

One might postulate that these discussions of women's economic agency corresponded to the debates about women's suffrage. In both areas, those involved were considering to what degree husbands and wives "represented" each other and, if so, in what context. Those who opposed married women's property reform and female suffrage maintained that husbands already represented wives in the political realm. Reformers seemed less sure about the degree to which wives represented husbands in the marketplace. If one assumes that the trade journals reflected general attitudes among the shopkeeping classes, then we may conclude that retailers were growing progressively more frustrated with this lack of clarity.[54] Drapers' journals were filled with letters and articles that debated the definition of necessaries and luxuries and discussed how to determine whether a woman's property was available if she failed to pay her bills. Ultimately, retailers found that they no longer knew whose credit they were trading upon when they sold to married women.

The drapers were particularly uneasy since they primarily sold to women and because clothing and related goods proved especially difficult to categorize.[55] Their papers religiously studied every legal development, fearing that the common law and Married Women's Property Acts had given couples free license to defraud them. In the seventies, the drapery trade watched county court judges routinely absolve husbands from liability for their wives' credit purchases.[56] "A dishonest couple," one trade journal complained, "might occupy a well-furnished house, appear to be in a respectable position and on the strength of that appearance the wife might order and obtain goods, and the husband when asked for payment, laugh at the credulity of the tradesman, and refer him to the County Court, where the Judge, armed with the precedent of 'Jolly v. Rees' . . . might support him in refusing to pay."[57] Retailers claimed that they sympathized with husbands whose "wives forgot their duty" and "the interests of the family," but hoped such an unfortunate man would afford them, "a quiet hint . . . that he preferred ready money transactions." Lacking this precaution, however, they wondered why traders should suffer financial harm from disobedient wives.[58]

An 1878 case involving a notorious demimondaine and a West End milliner might be characterized as a logical outcome of this legislative morass, notwithstanding the huge sums involved and its rogues' gallery of characters. The case involved Laura Bell, a former prostitute who, on her road to respectability, married Augustus Frederick Thistlethwayte, an army ensign who had inherited a considerable fortune. The couple constantly quarreled about money until Thistlethwayte warned tradesmen that his wife no longer had the authority to pledge his credit. Mrs. Thistlethwayte, nonetheless, continued to run up bills, which her husband refused to pay. Finally, a firm of West End milliners owned by Aaron Schwaebe but trading under the name Mme Rosalie sued Mr. Thistlethwayte for one thousand pounds for "bonnets and shawls and other feminine fripperies."[59]

Women's "natural" extravagance, the nature of luxury, and the limits of patriarchal authority became the questions argued in this case. Mrs. Thistlethwayte maintained that her dress allowance of five hundred pounds was far too low for her requirements and that her purchases were necessary for a woman in her social position. To test this claim the court sought to establish what "ladies of fashion" usually spent on their "feminine fripperies." When asked, Schwaebe tried to assert that such an amount was quite low but that he did know "several ladies of fashion who actually had as little as £500 pounds a year to spend on cutting a dash." Defending the husband, the attorney general exploited assumptions about women's extravagance by telling the jury that "Mrs. Thistlethwayte appears to have a passion for such wretched vanities, and it is most improper that her husband should be expected to meet the bills thus incurred." He then condemned Schwaebe for pandering to this "frivolous and shocking expenditure of money." The jury agreed with this moral conception of buying and selling and absolved Mr. Thistlethwayte from all responsibility.[60]

Given that these moral attitudes evidenced in court decisions had such profound economic repercussions, retailers were determined to shift the legal basis on which such decisions rested. For that reason, the drapery trade backed litigation in the Court of Appeal undertaken by the exclusive West End firm of Debenham and Freebody in their pursuit of over forty-three pounds from a Mr. Mellon, the manager of a large hotel in Bradford. Debenham and Freebody had lost their claim in a lower court on the defense, established in *Jolly v. Rees*, that Mellon had privately forbidden his wife to pledge his credit beyond her dress allowance. The trade hoped the Court of Appeal would overturn this precedent because it sacrificed their needs to the private arrangements between husband and wife.[61]

The Court of Appeal first sought to define the always ambiguous concept of *necessaries*. The justices sought to define *needs* in an expanding consumer society by attempting to resurrect some mythic correlation between class status and the level of commodity consumption.[62] Since English jurists had little knowledge of the material practices of everyday life, this proved quite complicated. Although a formidable legal thinker and proponent of strict economic liberalism, Lord Bramwell, somewhat vaguely stated that goods were necessary "not in the sense that she stood in need of them," but only in the sense "that they were such as the wife would require." While a couple is cohabiting, he suggested, "she may have authority to pledge his credit for articles of necessity, usually supplied on credit, or by weekly bills, as butchers' meat, or the like, where that is the convenient course. But here it is not so." Drawing a line between clothing and other commodities, Bramwell proved his ignorance of, or his distaste for, the nature of clothing retailing by stating, "There is neither general usage (that we are aware of) nor convenience in favor of having articles of dress on credit." It is unclear whether he was unaware of this practice or simply refusing to recognize it when he announced: "The Courts cannot take judicial cognizance of any practice of wives to pledge their husband's credit for such articles. . . . Why should she have such authority?" A husband, stated Bramwell, may say to his wife, "Go and pledge my credit to any extent your love of finery may prompt you to." However, it is the husband and not the law who possesses this "right." Summing up, the Lord Justice repeated, "It would be very mischievous if the law enabled a foolish woman and any tradesman eager for profit to combine together to impose serious liabilities on the husband contrary to his orders, without his knowledge and against his will. Consequently, this judgement must be affirmed."[63] The other two justices agreed and the lower court's decision stood.

This ruling had widespread reverberations. The drapery trade was outraged and protested that the decision was absolutely inconsistent with standard trade practice. For example, the editor of the *Warehousemen and Drapers' Trade Journal* wrote that "it was all very well to say that they [tradesmen] might conspire with wives to make husbands liable, but it is equally fair to retort that married people can now conspire together for the purpose of defrauding the tradesman." Moreover, he felt that the remedy put forth by the Lord Justice that shopkeepers should ask ladies "for their husband's authority before trusting them" was "absurdly impracticable."[64] A "County Court Judge" similarly wrote a letter to *The Times* in which he sided with the drapers, affirming that this law "had been and will continue to be exceedingly difficult" to apply, particularly since there was "a deeply rooted" impression among the parties involved that a wife had special agency with regard to pledging her husband's credit. Especially among the lower classes, "the wife is practically her husband's agent in almost all the daily affairs of life." It is she who "buys all articles of domestic consumption . . . appears for him, if any one does, in the county court, and agrees on his behalf to the monthly installment by which the debt shall be discharged." No amount of "judicial decisions would change this basic division of labor," as it was "incident to the conditions of rural labouring life." This judge, therefore, urged that the practice by "which one man parts with his goods and another receives them" via women must be taken into account.[65] In addition to ignoring the sexual division of labor that placed lower-class wives in charge of family purchasing, the decision failed to acknowledge the deferential relationship between elite shoppers and merchants, other critics argued. "Only the boldest of shopkeepers," claimed one writer, "would put to a lady of fashionable appearance the interrogatory: 'Does your husband know that you are shopping, and if so, does he approve of your engaging in that amusement? . . . Such conduct would soon drive away customers from any shop."[66] Given the state of the law, a *Daily Telegraph* editorialist quipped that retailers were lucky that "mankind" and "womankind" were "basically honest," that "husbands generally were a complaisant and forgiving race," and that few would "care to hold their wives up to public gaze as virtually repudiated agents in order to save themselves from monetary loss."[67] Whatever their specific grievances, all of these critics were arguing that this ruling dangerously disregarded the informal agency wives acquired as consumers and that someone other than traders should accept responsibility for this fact.

Unplacated, Debenham and Freebody was determined to take its case before an even higher court, the House of Lords. But the Lords, like the lower courts, stumbled over the complexities of defining "fripperies," female agency, and family relations. When hearing this case they considered the locus and meaning of women's shopping and the nature of the economic relationship implied by marriage. Queried by one lord as to whether a wife had a greater authority to pledge her husband's credit than a sister acting as a housekeeper, the appellants' attorney responded that wives did hold "greater authority than a servant or other relative." However, if "the husband found that his wife used her authority indiscreetly . . . he should give public notice of the revocation of that authority." But what if, the perspicacious Lord Watson asked, "the wife takes an express train and orders goods from a tradesman at a distance who has not had notice of the revocation. Would the husband be liable?" Mellon's attorney answered that a "woman travelling by express train to London to do her shopping would itself be notice that she was doing something improper."[68] The Lords agreed that long-distance shopping was disobedient behavior and that husbands should not be held liable for its consequences. Specifically referring to *Jolly v. Rees*, the Lord Chancellor affirmed that in the present case, "nothing had been done by the husband which would justify the assumption that he had given any authority to his wife to pledge his credit." Under no circumstances did Mrs. Mellon act as purchasing agent for her husband. He felt this was quite clear, since the couple lived in a hotel, "where all the usual necessaries of a household were supplied to them, and there was no domestic management at all." Marriage, the Lords had decided, "does not in itself imply an agency." Rather, it is the husband who "creates the agency."[69] With this ruling the Lords acknowledged that wives shopped, but they ensured that this activity would not give them greater access to family resources than that expressly countenanced by husbands.

The Lords' decision sparked a national discussion of the nature and propriety of women's shopping. An editorialist in *The Times* supported the decision and criticized Debenham and Freebody's business practices. "The very fact that their customer came from a distant town like Bradford should have put them on their guard," this writer confidently explained. He then admitted that it did seem "too much . . . to require a tradesman to question every unknown customer" about her marital arrangements and admitted the decision would probably lead to a "panic" among "West-end Milliners, who relied on credit trading." Though if this panic led to the expansion of the "ready-money system," this author felt it would ultimately be beneficial.[70] In response to this criticism, Debenham and Freebody defended the soundness of the transaction by explaining that they had extended Mrs. Mellon credit because they had enjoyed a long relationship with her mother, who had always promptly paid her bills. They also asserted that "although the husband resided at Bradford, which for all purposes of business is no further than Bayswater, we were perfectly acquainted with his position." The firm wished to relate these facts "because it is obvious that a very large proportion of the credit usually given to wives rests upon no firmer basis than that given in this case; and, as society is so constituted, we fail to see how it can be otherwise."[71] Debenham and Freebody thus believed that the legal restrictions on women's credit were inconsistent with their considerable freedom as consumers.

It is not surprising that this exchange between Debenham and Freebody, the House of Lords, and *The Times* erupted in 1880. As we have already seen, this was precisely the moment when stores like Debenham and Freebody's were introducing services and other amenities to encourage women such as Mrs. Mellon to shop alone all day if they felt so inclined. At the same time, a nexus of other institutions such as hotels, restaurants, clubs, and "express trains" also aided in the expansion of long-distance shopping. Clearly Mr. Mellon, the majority of the Lords, and *The Times* editorialist were not pleased with the "freedoms" that urban commercial culture appeared to afford to women. Among the most troubling of these was the liberty that shopping granted wives over their husband's money. When Debenham and Freebody defended their use of credit, they claimed that selling to a national market was not necessarily selling to strangers. The store was well acquainted with both Mrs. Mellon's mother and the economic position of her husband, despite the fact that the couple lived in Bradford. Two visions of the market are at play in this exchange in *The Times*. One imagined a crowd of strange women traveling to London's shopping districts to dissipate family monies. The other saw female consumers as legitimately moving goods and money between the shop and the home. Shopkeepers obviously recognized women as economic agents who, like many businessmen, sometimes pursued their activities far from their domestic abode. Many traders cared little for women's emancipation per se, but they wanted legal recognition of the wife's role as family consumer so that they would not suffer from what had come to be wives' anomalous legal status.

Yet through the 1880s legal innovations did not echo this desire. Early in 1880, before the final decision against Debenham and Freebody, Parliament debated another Married Women's Property Bill. At first many retailers supported the bill, once again hoping that if women were granted free use of their property, they could also be made to pay for their debts. Indeed, their expectations must have been raised by legislators who identified themselves as their advocates. For example, when John Hinde Palmer moved that the 1880 bill be read a second time in the House, he argued that "the Bill would tend to the advantage, not only of married women, but of tradesmen and society generally."[72] An editor of one draper's journal agreed, explaining to his readers that it could potentially "settle the vexed question as to the wife's authority and husband's liability." Unfortunately, this expert despondently wrote, this particular bill ignored the debts of wives who owned no property, and was "somewhat vague" on the extent to which credit could be pledged with reference to a woman's separate estate. Although this author recognized that many shopkeepers "longed" for some "provision to prevent that juggling between man and wife . . . the effect of which is to defraud creditors," he worried that if the bill passed, it would not address their needs.[73] By limiting married women's contractual rights, retailers complained that Parliament had the wronged husband and not the cheated trader in mind. The debates did indeed suggest that many members were more concerned with husbands' liabilities than creditors' losses. For example, Dr. Commins protested that he would not support the law because "there was no provision to protect the husband from the extravagance or dishonesty of his wife." He then explained his position by recalling the "vexatious litigations" in the county courts in which wives had attained a good deal of "power" over their husbands' money.[74]

When the more comprehensive Married Women's Property Act finally passed in June of 1882, it was applauded by feminists as " 'The Magna Carta' of Women's liberties."[75] Experts in the drapery trade also welcomed the new status of wives as property owners, believing that creditors too would benefit. An article on the act in the *Warehousemen and Drapers' Trade Journal*, for example, stated that "every contract entered into by a married woman shall be deemed to be for herself unless the contrary be shown." Yet this author was still worried, since wives were to be "legally looked upon as distinct persons," that it might be even harder to make husbands pay for their spouses' consumption.[76] When the new law was looked at closely, traders and feminists realized that because it preserved many of 1870 act's restrictions on married women's property, wives still lacked full contractual rights and responsibilities. Since restrained property could not be charged with debts and wives remained responsible only for debts equal to their separate property at the time they entered the contract, the question of wives' credit was as confused as ever.[77]

Retailers soon violently criticized the 1882 Act. A writer in *Warehousemen and Drapers' Trade Journal*, noted in a rather despondent way, "The legal position of husbands and wives is just now in a transition state, and hence the muddle." He warned shopkeepers to remain wary when extending credit to married women, since "ancient rules still cling to their new position."[78] Another similarly wrote, "It is well to be very cautious how goods are sold to married women with settlements."[79] Summing up the utter frustration the drapery trade felt in 1883, yet another author satirically commented, "It requires a strong imagination to grasp the idea of a time when paying, as well as purchasing, will be done by married women."[80] The discrepancy between the social and legal realities of women's purchasing and payment that was plaguing retailers thus was not removed when married women became property owners.

The Married Women's Property Acts together with the Lords' ruling on *Debenham v. Mellon* created widespread uncertainty about women's credit, which persisted for decades to come. Few shopkeepers understood the laws and most traded upon their misconceptions rather than the letter of the law. Especially after the 1882 act, many mistakenly assumed that they could hold women fully responsible for their debts. According to an 1890 editorial in the *Drapers' Record*, retailers erroneously believed that the 1882 act had "greatly enlarged the capacity of married women to contract." They had extended easy credit to married women only to discover later that they could not legally collect from these customers.[81]

It seems ironic that as married women became property owners they came to be regarded as less creditworthy. Yet restrictions on contractual rights and the degree of proof required to collect debts worked in this direction. Drapers' journals were filled with complaints from traders who had found it virtually impossible to collect debts from married women.[82] In 1890, the *Drapers' Record* printed this county court judge's explanation of the process to guide their readers: "In attempting to recover from a married woman certain matters have to be proved most conclusively . . . first, that the defendant had a separate estate; secondly, that she had it at the time the contract was entered into, and could bind it; and thirdly, that she intended to bind it."[83] When sued, women often pleaded "coverture," stating that they possessed no separate estate.[84] Even if they had such an estate and refused to pay, legally they could not be imprisoned.[85] By the early nineties, the *Drapers' Record* despondently commented, "The law relating to husband and wife is perhaps more difficult to understand than that relating to any other question."[86]

Shopkeepers interpreted their legal defeats in class and gender terms. Although many retailers had favored the reform of married women's property, they soon blamed their predicament on "the movement in favor of the so-called 'emancipation of women,'" and mourned the loss of a time when "in the eyes of the law husband and wife were one."[87] They felt especially cheated by a legal system that failed to recognize their needs. "If we are a nation of shopkeepers, is it not time that the Legislature should throw its aegis over the shopkeeper instead of over the social vultures who are ready enough to prey upon him," the *Drapers' Record* pleaded.[88] Shopkeepers felt squeezed between feminists and reformers who attempted to make women economic actors and conservative legislators who worked to maintain the status quo. Together these two forces had absolved husbands from many of their economic duties toward their spouses while placing wives in the liminal position of not being fully responsible for their commercial activities.

Although judges slowly began to find women liable for their debts, married women did not gain full contractual rights and liabilities until 1935.[89] The history of wives' credit is not a straightforward example of class struggle between an aristocratic legal system and middle-class retailers. Anti-trade bias within the legal system, fear of women's potential power as consumers, and Parliament's ignorance of shopping practices collectively aggravated tensions between buyers and sellers. Moreover, we cannot discount a certain emancipationist zeal on the part of the women themselves, who, in these legal loopholes, found a way to flout the authority of spouses, retailers, and, in certain measure, the legal system as well.

Consumption on Trial

In practice, many married women turned a real disability—their lack of full contractual rights—into an opportunity. When brought to court, wives consistently protested that they bought on credit because they disagreed with their husbands' limited perceptions of their material needs. Buying on credit in diverse stores, perhaps far from home, became a weapon that some wives used to circumvent the social and legal restrictions on their property rights. Both poor and wealthy women found that purchasing on credit gave them limited, if informal, access to property. Women whose husbands would not give them control over household or personal expenditure, who had no money of their own, or whose property was in some way restrained used their assigned role as consumers to gain a measure of economic control otherwise denied to them.

"A County Court summons," explained a satirist in 1867, "is not by any means a pleasant thing to find lying on one's breakfast table, amongst the ham and eggs!"[90] As this joke implied, debts and court summonses were a regular feature of English family life. Although many men paid their spouses' debts without complaint, disagreements over domestic expenditure commonly led to family quarrels, violence, divorce, or a county court summons.[91] Of course, husbands, wives, and children might all incur debts and fight about money, though most probably settled their disagreements before they were forced into court.[92] Whether financial difficulties contributed to familial estrangement or whether unhappy relationships encouraged economic problems, it is difficult to say. However, alienated couples often failed to pay their bills. One particularly harrowing example of this may be pieced together from the letters Maria Lydia Blane, "Minnie," sent to her mother in the late 1850s and early 1860s. Soon after Minnie arrived in India with her new husband, Captain Wood, an officer in the East India Company, disagreements and debts contributed to the breakdown of her marriage. High prices, Wood's neglect of family finances, and his habit of spending money sent by Minnie's mother had landed the couple deeply in debt. As Minnie explained to her mother in June 1860, "We are in debt, not from extravagance, but from allowing bills to stand month after month, year after year, and Archie [Captain Wood] just tossing them aside, and saying they may write again. The interest then rises frightfully."[93] Just before she was forced to leave her children and return to England, Minnie wrote, "Captain Wood allows me no regular allowance and the consequence is whenever I buy something there is an awful row. Bills flood in, he has not the money to pay, the tradespeople are abused, and it all ends up in the civil courts."[94] The civil court records tell countless stories of such desperate couples whose personal struggles turned into confrontations with merchants. After sending pleading letters and waiting patiently for their money, shopkeepers had little recourse but to turn to the courts to collect from these recalcitrant customers. Though the county courts handled only small debts, defined as less than fifty pounds after 1850 and one hundred pounds in 1902, similar problems plagued those families who found themselves sued in the higher courts.[95]

The tensions surrounding purchasing brought the economic and emotional life of these families into the public arena as county court and higher court judges were charged with sorting out the rights and liabilities of retailers and customers, and husbands and wives. Court decisions ultimately rested on the concept of extravagance, with each party involved articulating a different understanding of extravagant consumption. Throughout these years, the law continued to require husbands to pay for debts for goods determined to be "necessaries," that is, for those commodities deemed necessary to family maintenance.[96] Sued husbands therefore nearly always insisted they were the victims of an "extravagant" wife who had a passion for luxuries. Of course, as the legal expert for the *Lady* magazine explained, what was necessary always "varies with the rank and station of the parties, from the merest means of daily subsistence to comparatively luxurious living, which may include a carriage and jewellery of considerable value."[97]

Judges were required to consider several factors when deciding these cases. First, they had to evaluate the defendant's social class and then consider whether the commodities in question were necessary or extravagant at that social level. Secondly, the judge had to investigate the nature of the couple's marriage to explore whether the husband approved of his spouse's purchasing. Finally, the arrangement between shopkeeper and customer had to be assessed, since this would reveal whether or not the trader was aware of the credit status of his or her customers. Essentially, three relationships were investigated with each case: that between a customer's class and particular commodities; that between husband and wife; and that between buyer and seller. All three came into play each time a married woman walked into a shop.

The first issue to be settled, as the following case suggests, regarded the relation between the commodities bought and the family's social class. In June 1880, a Mr. Sharpe successfully avoided paying a £12 bill for a sealskin jacket his wife had bought from Whiteley's department store. Sharpe, who earned a very modest middle-class income of about £300 year as the Keeper of the Records at the Guildhall, argued that this jacket was an extravagant purchase for which he should not be held liable. Mrs. Sharpe, however, testified that she had warned her husband that if he did not supply her with the money for her winter things, she would purchase them without his consent. Sharpe denied hearing this threat and said he had assumed the new jacket had been part of her trousseau. Clearly, the Sharpes disagreed about what goods were necessary, leaving it to the court to decide this question. In this case the judge found that the jacket "may be perfectly 'suitable' . . . but it cannot be called necessary, and, if the husband is not generous enough or rich enough to indulge his wife in the luxury, she must go without."[98] Mr. Sharpe was absolved of this debt, and Whiteley's had to go without. The law, in recognizing that there was no absolute morality regarding consumption, rested on judges' determination of the social construction of needs. They determined that men were legally required to pay for women's needs but not their desires.[99]

In contrast to husbands, both retailers and wives could benefit by proving that even quite costly purchases were necessary, not extravagant. In 1896, for example, the Hallmanns' marital and economic problems resulted in their being sued in the Queen's Bench.[100] Vivian Floyd, a Savile Row court dressmaker, sued Edward Hallmann for £113, the cost of dresses and other goods that she had supplied to his wife in 1894. Floyd defended her reasoning behind extending credit to Mrs. Hallmann by claiming the goods were reasonably priced and appropriate for someone of her customer's status. She had also made careful inquiries before executing any orders, claiming to have known that Mrs. Hallmann was the daughter of a baronet and that Mr. Hallmann held "an exceptionally good position" as a clerk in a banking firm, for which he earned about £1,000 a year. Floyd thus felt assured that when she sold Mrs. Hallmann a plum-colored velvet gown for 20 guineas, some other less expensive dresses, and two silk blouses, she would eventually be paid.[101]

Attempting to establish whether such purchases were necessary, Justice Grantham asked Miss Floyd what she considered a fair amount for a husband with Mr. Hallmann's salary to "allow his wife to spend on her dresses?" Aware that if the purchases were considered extravagant she would lose her claim, Floyd suggested that two hundred a year was a very reasonable sum, but she also insisted that she could not possibly estimate that Mrs. Hallmann would exceed this amount.[102] The judge, however, expected this retailer to make inquiries into her customer's financial status and then to assess the appropriate level of expenditure relative to her family's position. He assumed that sellers should tell buyers when they had bought enough. Shopkeepers were thus expected, indeed legally encouraged, to make themselves aware of quite intimate family details. In essence, the law asked the market to intrude into the home.

When Mr. Hallmann was called to give evidence, he made his private life public in order to win the case. He presented himself as a long-suffering husband whose financial difficulties were worsened by an extravagant wife who acted as though "he were made of money." Although he had married the eldest daughter of Sir Digby Murray, Hallman complained that his wife had no money of her own. When they were first married, "they had moved in what is known as good society." However, he had not been able to support this lifestyle, and they had been forced to drop their former acquaintances. In 1892 they had had to give up their house in Park Street and move to a less expensive one in Sutton, Surrey, but "his wife's extravagance compelled him to move to a yet smaller one." His next step had been to advertise in the local Sutton paper that he would not be responsible for his wife's debts.[103] After Mrs. Hallmann found her credit "put an end to in Sutton," she moved on, without her husband's knowledge, to London to do her shopping. When the bills started flowing in, Hallman said that he had agreed to pay for some of her accounts, but when he received Miss Floyd's bill, he was astonished at the prices of certain items, especially infuriated that his wife had bought lace that cost 40 shillings a yard and buttons at over 7 shillings each. After he spoke to his wife about it, there had been "a scene," and he decided to place the matter in the hands of his solicitors rather than pay the bill.[104]

To win his case, Mr. Hallman had to prove that the goods in question were extravagant and that he was ignorant of these particular purchases. He consistently denied any knowledge of his wife's shopping and insisted that he had never seen the purchases in question, with the exception of the two blouses. When asked why he had not later sent these things back to the shop, he complained that his wife had locked them in her wardrobe. Under cross-examination, Mr. Hallmann insisted that he had "nothing to do with the ordering of the things, and he declined in any way to interfere with them." He concluded his testimony by saying that "if West-end tradespeople chose to supply things to married ladies on credit behind their husband's backs they must not find fault if the husband refused to pay for them."[105]

Like many couples, the Hallmans diverged in their attitudes toward expenditure. Mrs. Hallmann felt her husband could and should afford to give her more than the £60 to £90 a year he gave her to "dress herself."[106] Such disagreements were perhaps a result of the discrepancies in their class positions. With her aristocratic background, Mrs. Hallmann might very well have had different expectations from her husband. Although portrayed as irrationally given to overspending, she may have been trying to uphold the standards and acquaintances of her life before she married. She may have thought that a 20-guinea velvet gown was necessary to her station even if her husband thought such an item to be extravagant. Her motives were not relevant in the eyes of the law, however. When spouses disagreed about familial expenditure, the judges routinely sided with the husband. Accordingly, Miss Vivian Floyd lost her action.

Although a propertied wife could be sued and found liable for her "extravagant" purchases, it could be exceedingly difficult to force her to settle her debts. Burberry's discovered this when they tried to collect a debt from a Mr. and Mrs. Mayer. Mr. Mayer, a picture dealer with an income of between £4,000 and £5,000 a year, had married a Danish countess who owned a home and forty acres in her native country. Not long after Mrs. Mayer bought the goods in question, the couple divorced and neither party would pay the bill. According to Mrs. Mayer, the £156 debt was for "articles of ladies' wear, except two coats and a hat," which she said were presents for the "old man." After her marriage fell apart, Mrs. Mayer evidently lost interest in giving the "old man" presents and thus refused to pay for this bill. Mr. Mayer similarly disputed the bill because he claimed he had provided his wife with an ample allowance to run their household. In court, she argued that the £1,400 he gave her each year was both inadequate and irregular. When asked to support this charge, she detailed their housekeeping expenses, and then asserted that they were so great they left her only £300 a year for her dress. Mrs. Mayer maintained that since her allowance did not meet her expenses, her husband should pay this bill. The jury disagreed and found against her.[107] However, the firm had difficulty actually recovering their money, since her separate property was restrained from anticipation. As she could not alienate her property, she had little means of actually raising capital. Legal restrictions on married women's property as well as the couples' emotional and economic disagreements added up to a large loss for Burburry's.

If, however, plaintiffs could prove that the husband was aware of his spouse's consumption, he could usually be found liable for her bills. For example, in the 1891 case of *Jay v. Annesley*, this noted Regent Street firm sued Mrs. Annesley for a debt of 15 guineas. She was the object of the summons because Jay's knew she had her own property and paid her own bills. The plaintiff's counsel argued that she had ordered the "costume" and generally paid for orders with her own checks. But Mrs. Annesley used an interesting subterfuge. She maintained that in this particular instance her husband had accompanied her to the shop and exclaimed, "I will give you a present of a dress for Ascot!" Thus, in this case she had not pledged her credit. The judge absolved Mrs. Annesley from the debt because a husband's mere presence in the shop was always seen as a sign that he had willingly pledged his credit. In general, shopkeepers felt more comfortable extending credit to wives who brought their husbands shopping. But Jay's had misinterpreted the wife's economic position in this instance and lost their claim.[108]

Husbands who shopped with their wives were invariably made to pay for this pleasure. Clement Stanley, for example, was required to pay the 2-guinea bill for a coat his wife had bought from Thomas Wallis and Company of Holborn Circus. Although he tried the usual defense that shops should not give a wife credit without her husband's permission, the judge reminded Stanley that he had accompanied his wife on her expedition to the West End, explaining to the defendant, "If I went with my wife into a shop I should expect to have to pay for all she bought. . . . You have given yourself away by going shopping with your wife."[109] Following the logic of this argument, a husband could find it in his financial interest not to go shopping with his wife—that is, to forego the supervision that had been traditionally regarded as his right and his duty. In the nineteenth and early-twentieth centuries, then, men might have avoided shopping not only because of cultural and social norms, but also because of its potential financial and legal repercussions.

Designed to protect husbands who were unable to control their wives' consumption, the laws governing marital property and liability may actually have furthered the distance between men and the day-to-day provisioning of their families. Judges admonished husbands for shopping with wives and praised them, as in the case of Mr. Lewin, for not caring "a farthing for what their wives' wear." These cases suggest that we need to reconsider the legal context in which familial consumer practices were established. Moreover, they raise questions about Veblen's assertion that husbands considered that their wives' "conspicuous consumption" established their social position.[110] To the contrary, legislators, judges, and husbands perceived "excessive" consumption as potentially undoing that position. No legal authority ever suggested that wives should not buy goods for their families. However, they did try to limit the financial ramifications of that buying for husbands, but not for retailers. Ultimately, the legal treatment of wives' debts tended to fix shopping as a female practice that always involved financial risks for husbands and for retailers.

From the 1860s, at the very moment of the spectacular increase in the presence of female shoppers in the public spaces of the city, the law embodied the paradoxical nature of this activity. Women were the most prominent actors on the consumer scene, yet their financial liability was the legacy of a precapitalist order. Armed with an understanding of the cultural, social, and legal practices that governed buying and selling, certain women may have indirectly gained access to goods. To what extent women deliberately manipulated retailers, spouses, and judges deserves further study. These cases have suggested that spouses with troubled relationships as well as those from different class backgrounds—especially when the wife's position was higher than that of her husband—were especially likely to disagree about material needs and desires. While this was hardly a new situation in the nineteenth century, the opportunities to shop and the numbers of "luxurious" goods were expanding at a particularly rapid rate during this era. Shopkeepers were among the architects of this commercial culture, but they were also quite alarmed that legal loopholes had granted married people the opportunity to defraud them. At the same time, husbands and wives found their relationship to the economy was being fundamentally rewritten as the Married Women's Property Acts granted wives limited access to their property. Though social scientists frequently use the concept of the family as a unit of consumption, in some ways this might best be applied to families prior to the late-nineteenth century. At least for traders, families seemed little more than a loose association of individual consumers.

Ready Money, Married Women, and the Department Store

In 1885, William Whiteley explained his ready-money policy with this statement in the preface of his store's catalog:

> William Whiteley begs leave most respectfully to point out that the Goods are quoted at a very low rate of profit, for (Ready Money Exclusively, without Discount), and that in the calculation of price, no margin is allowed for Bad Debts, Advertising, Interest and Overdue Accounts, and other contingencies incidental to credit trade. The system of business being both to buy and sell for ready money, he is enabled to make his purchases on the most favorable terms, and in the best and cheapest markets in the world.[111]

Such epistles were common in Victorian department store catalogs and price lists. Whiteley used this deferential tone to convince customers to rethink the nature of shopping, to use cash instead of credit. This was arguably one of the greatest changes in nineteenth-century retailing. Of course, many stores did not abandon credit; and if the court records are any indication, even modern department stores like Whiteley's continued to sell on credit to some customers. Nevertheless, ready-money trading developed partly as a response to the legal entanglements that allowed married customers to avoid paying for their purchases.

The laws and practices governing wives' debts reinforced negative perceptions of the female shopper, but they also inspired the drapery trade to shift from credit to cash trading. Though this move was a reaction to the problems of selling to a mass market, it ultimately contributed to the development of mass retailing. Historians have often commented that department stores were successful because they insisted on cash, not credit, transactions.[112] As Whiteley explained to his skeptical customers, cash allowed him to buy and sell at lower prices than his competitors could. He did not tell them, however, how ready money allowed him to safely sell to total strangers. As one business manual put it, "The cash trader relies very much more than the credit trader on casual customers."[113] Given the legal developments and family histories this chapter has explored, it should come as no surprise that a ready-money policy developed in those urban trades which traditionally sold to female customers.[114] The benefits of cash trading soon manifested themselves, yet this development was prompted not by entrepreneurial foresight but by utter frustration.

Throughout these years, the drapery press constantly advised that a strict ready money policy was the only workable solution to the problems involved with selling to women.[115] This lamentation published in the *Warehousemen and Drapers' Trade Journal* in 1880 was typical: "Although much trade must be carried on upon credit . . . the law being what it is now declared by the highest court in the country, we can only suggest the encouragement of cash payments."[116] Even into the early-twentieth century, retail experts continued to warn shopkeepers that the "well-dressed but strange lady" who "crossed the threshold of the shop" could be a social pariah much like thieves and other criminals who deliberately attempted to "cheat shopkeepers."[117] A journalist for the *Retailer Trader* made light of the situation when he remarked how shopkeepers would "astound every fashionable dame with the question: 'Have you a private income: If so, what is it, and how much of it have you spent already?' "[118] But for most, selling to strange women was not a joking matter. "Appearances" were simply "superficial" when it came to female customers, warned the *Drapers' Record*. "True, the lady may be living with her husband in a fine house, and the marital relations of the pair may be absolutely felicitous," but this meant nothing. "The wife may be an extravagant woman who spends her month's allowance in a week; the husband may have absolutely forbidden her to pledge his credit. How can the poor dressmaker know this? It is idle to suggest that she should 'make inquiries.' Of whom?" For these drapers, a woman's "appearance" conveyed nothing about her ability or desire to pay. As they all too often discovered, outward appearance no longer represented social position or honest intentions. Retailers felt that because they knew little or nothing about a woman's private situation, they could not judge her credit. The privacy that the legal system ascribed to family relations only added to the sense of danger surrounding female customers. "Why," this author asked, should "secret proceedings" such as a man forbidding his spouse to pledge his credit "be recognized by the law? Out of consideration for the feelings of the husband and his family perhaps?

But what about the feelings of the trader and his family?" Given the public nature of consumption in a mass society, retailers demanded a way of knowing their public: "Publicity is the very thing required. . . . This could be effected by the publication in the *London Gazette*, or some other recognized organ, of all announcements affecting a wife's financial credit. The insertion of such notices in the ordinary press is of little use."[119] This plea for publicity went unheeded, however, as it violated Victorian gender and family ideals. With a tone of resignation, another *Drapers' Record* reporter simply wrote: "There seems to be no remedy unless, perhaps, it is to be found in an increasing determination . . . to refuse credit to any but well-known customers."[120]

Some heeded the experts' advice and sold their goods for cash only, but this development in itself added to the pressures felt by small traders. Merchants who sold to poor women who could not pay with cash or to wealthy women who would not pay with cash often deeply resented cash traders. Indeed, one of Whiteley's neighbors who had criticized his unstoppable growth had also taken exception to the way in which cash trading had allowed Whiteley to undersell his neighbors:

> I have for a considerable time been under the necessity of standing behind my counter when would-be ladies and gentlemen come into the shop, find fault with my goods and charges, and finally tell me they will go into Whiteley's. And they go, wearing the latest new fashionable dress purchased for ready cash at the above well-known establishment, whilst, their little bill with their small tradesmen has remained unpaid for 9 or 12 months.[121]

Although cash remained culturally suspect, even wealthy customers evidently flocked to the new stores for their lower prices. One "householder" responded to the above letter by professing that small traders were only getting what they deserved. At Whiteley's, he received "what I always knew I was entitled to . . . value for my ready money."[122] Although not everyone believed that Whiteley's offered the lowest prices, store owners attempted to convince customers that a cash business meant lower prices. Charles Digby Harrod, for example, explained in an interview with the *Chelsea Herald* that his "cash trade" allowed him to sell at or below the prices of even the co-operative stores.[123]

One wonders to what degree shopkeepers made such candid statements about the advantages of cash trading to reorient the shopping population's attitude toward actually handling money. It is also possible that comfortable lounges and lunchrooms may have helped offset the resentments that customers must have felt toward stores that would not lend them credit. Though there is still much to be known about the use of cash and credit in elite boutiques, department stores, and small local shops, this chapter has shown that despite the pleas of feminists, liberal legal reformers, and shopkeepers, many judges and legislators were extremely cautious about granting wives economic agency. Their moral assessment of shopping was not unlike that of those magistrates who failed to award traders such as Whiteley liquor licenses. Although many professed a belief that the law should be the foundation of a laissez-faire economy, jurists worked on a different set of assumptions when they mediated upon wives' economic practices. Many believed that their shopping, especially when done on credit, was inherently immoral and socially dangerous. It potentially created an almost adulterous alliance between shopkeepers and wives that stripped husbands of their property and, in the worst-case scenario, their personal liberty. While jurists could not limit wives' shopping, they tried to contain its financial ramifications for husbands. Yet the gap between the letter of the law and social practice was exceedingly wide. Many families clearly acted as though wives possessed agency over their husbands' property. This no doubt added to the complexities, dangers, and even pleasures of buying and selling in this era. It amplified tensions between husbands and wives, cash and credit traders, employers and employees, and, most directly, between buyers and sellers.

Marriage obviously altered a woman's relationship to the market and greatly shaped her shopping experiences.[124] While some wives were empowered with managing the family's expenditure, this was a power contingent on her individual relationship with her spouse and the particular nature of her property. Thus, especially in this period, we must refrain from making overly general statements about how women acquired control over family resources while shopping. While in practice this may have been the case, this was never a legal reality. This discrepancy between legal and social norms granted Victorian wives both freedoms and constraints when they went shopping. Although wives often could avoid paying for the goods they had bought, they could not escape feeling criminalized when they did so or facing dissension at home.

Like the first chapter, this study of family property and liabilities has argued that divisions within the trading community as well as the role of family conflict and negotiation shaped the history of English consumer society. Chapter 1 looked at the friction between large-scale retailers and independent shopkeepers, as well as between drapers and other trades; this discussion has illuminated the distinctions between cash and credit traders. While cash traders could comfortably sell to a mass market of women, credit traders were worried about such a prospect. Given the legal morass that credit traders found themselves in during these years, it is hardly surprising that they worried not about how to increase their market but how to ensure that they maintained a small and honest clientele.

This chapter has also touched upon the ambiguous and confusing relationship between the emerging feminist movement and the shopkeeping classes. At times feminists and retailers clearly shared an interest in granting women "agency" in the marketplace. For years both groups pushed the legal system to recognize the central role that women played in the English economy. Nonetheless, as retailers found that "women's emancipation"—that is, the reforms of married women's property—did not aid their position, trade papers came to denounce the women's movement. This history was also shaped, as we will see in the next chapter, by the direct competition between shopkeepers and feminists for bourgeois women's time and money.

• CHAPTER THREE •

"Resting Places for Women Wayfarers": Feminism and the Comforts of the Public Sphere

In 1912 the *Pall Mall Gazette* discovered a ubiquitous, fashionable, and seemingly necessary institution—the women's club. "Nearly every woman nowadays," the journal claimed, "has her club, where she lunches, plays bridge, entertains her friends, dines, and . . . 'puts up' . . . when house-cleaning, husband or children become too all-pervading." Echoing journalistic and literary sentiment of the period, clubs' ascendance was offered as proof that "the idea that a woman should, because of her womanhood, remain solely in the domestic circle . . . is a thing of the past." The piece happily concluded that clubs had "changed the face of life" for those women of the "middle-classes who live in the suburbs."[1] As this author suggests, in prewar England urban women's clubs had become socially acceptable symbols of female independence and emancipation. By this period, clubs were championed for having brought the suburban woman into the public sphere.

Such articles did not exaggerate the importance of this new aspect of bourgeois female London. Tens of thousands of women had joined clubs since the 1880s and a few daring individuals had done so as early as the 1860s. Edwardian women could choose among nearly forty different clubs, most of which were situated in the very heart of the West End shopping district. Although several were scattered in the western suburbs of Bayswater, Pimlico, Maida Vale, Earl's Court, and Chelsea, female clubland lay in the streets north of Piccadilly, south of Langham Place, west of Regent Street, and east of Park Lane. Close to London's most fashionable residential and commercial districts, this territory occupied the crossroads of the public and private West End.[2]

Like the men's clubs that dominated British politics and society, women's clubs were private institutions that played several public functions. At the most fundamental level, they provided comfortable, relaxing, and safe spaces for women who were alone in the city. A woman could quietly read the papers, write letters, play bridge, take lunch or afternoon tea. If she felt so inclined, she could socialize with friends or entertain colleagues. She could also listen to or take part in club debates, lectures, and concerts, and then spend the night in one of the club's bedrooms. Depending on the size of her pocketbook, the level of her education, and the nature of her politics and interests, a wealthy woman could find a club that suited her every need. For over a half century, roughly between the 1860s and the 1930s, thousands of women founded and joined clubs to satisfy their physical, economic, social, and political desires.[3]

London's female clubland grew at the intersection of the women's movement and the leisure industry.[4] The clubs were, in fact, the most fully documented and longest lasting aspect of what might be termed feminist commercial culture.[5] This culture also produced related urban institutions such as female lavatories, restaurants, and tea shops. Liberal feminists involved with the Langham Place Circle initiated the creation of these "resting places," but other feminist groups and even conservative political women contributed to their growth. As many have suggested, the nineteenth-century women's movement incorporated a diverse, even contradictory, set of basic assumptions and strategies. Opinions varied on such fundamental issues as the nature of gender difference and the sources of inequality.[6] Yet despite their disagreements, many feminists supported clubs and other female resting places because they assumed that comfort in the public spaces of the metropolis influenced one's relationship to the public sphere.

As early as the 1860s, but especially after the 1880s, feminists began to discuss how structural and demographic changes in the economy had produced a more fractured and alienating metropolis. The city seemed especially inhospitable because it lacked appropriate institutions for middle-class women. In their analysis of the modern metropolis, these feminists frequently characterized middle-class female workers, shoppers, and sightseers as lonely, hungry, and tired urban travelers. Though some pressured local government to solve this problem, others believed that enterprising women could themselves construct a comfortable female-oriented city. By comfort they meant several things: a sense of belonging in the city, an ability both to be alone and to find community with others, and a ready supply of nourishment and shelter. Armed with this multifaceted notion of comfort, feminists encouraged local government to build "resting places" or lavatories for ladies. They also invited bourgeois "ladies" to start, work in, and patronize "cozy" and "comfortable" urban "resorts" that offered "dainty" and yet "modern" amenities. Men might also enjoy these resorts, but feminists typically advised women to specialize in catering to ladies. This drive inspired the founding of an extraordinary variety of female-oriented "resting places" throughout the West End, including lavatories and female-owned and -managed restaurants, tea shops, dining rooms, and clubs.[7]

The women's club eventually became the most successful of these institutions, though it competed with many of London's profit-driven enterprises. By selling refreshment, entertainment, and temporary housing, clubs contested but also stimulated the growth of West End commercial culture. Clubs, stores, restaurants, hotels, and tea shops all vended space, services, and goods to women. Born during the same period, situated in the same neighborhood, and seeking the same public, these institutions addressed the middle-class woman as a consumer and urban traveler. They invited her to consume goods and services and to spend time outside of the domestic realm. While some feminists overtly criticized the mass commercial culture outside of the club, others encouraged any female involvement in the city, including shopping. They did so because they hoped that shopping would potentially reinforce female participation in politics, philanthropy, social work, and paid employment.

Social conservatives attacked women's clubs precisely because they too drew no line between women joining a club, shopping, and becoming politically active. They worried that clubs, like department stores and feminist organizations, persuaded women to reject their homes in favor of a frivolous, indulgent, and public lifestyle. These criticisms reflected the complex relationship between feminism and consumerism that had given birth to the clubs. Despite steady criticism, after the 1890s the club movement embarked on a period of steady expansion. By 1912 the *Pall Mall Gazette* could make the claim that "nearly every woman nowadays has her club" because clubs now dominated the West End landscape and popular imagination.

The clubs' physical presence in the urban center, the activities they sponsored, and the image they cultivated in the press transformed the gender system governing Victorian London. They were produced by and instigated "modern" ideals of middle-class femininity. The club movement highlights some of the inequalities that shaped the Victorian city and illuminates the connections between geography, gender, and power. Feminist commercial culture thus altered London's history and rewrote gender identities, reconfiguring dominant definitions of public and private.[8]

Pleasure in the Public Sphere

Women's clubs, ladies' lavatories, female dining rooms, and tea shops appeared amidst a wave of public and private efforts to improve London and satisfy the physical needs of an increasingly mobile population. Mid-Victorian Britons perceived their cities, especially London, as ugly, dirty, and uncomfortable.[9] People complained that the metropolis was congested, lacked architectural beauty, and was chaotically administered. Others focused on the scarcity and wretched quality of public catering. As James Winter has recently argued, however, these criticisms gave rise to a variety of reforms that sought to make London healthier, more comfortable, and more manageable.[10] As we saw in the first chapter, certain members of the business community professed that their establishments benefited and beautified neighborhoods, thereby "improving" London. We will see here that feminists often questioned this entrepreneurial narrative, and yet they too asserted that their institutions improved London and comforted women.[11] Throughout the latter half of the nineteenth century and into the twentieth century, entrepreneurs, reformers, and feminists erected similar structures and narratives in which they solidified their vision of gender and the metropolis, pleasure, and the public sphere.[12]

With drapers turning into Universal Providers and rural groves becoming shopping districts, the mid-Victorian period witnessed the growth of a public, commercial culture. In particular, West End consumer institutions were identified as serving rest and refreshment to a mobile crowd of pleasure seekers.[13] Especially in the 1870s, journalists, gourmands, and men-about-town frequently explained that such changes had transformed a drab and serious metropolis into "a city of pleasure." In 1872 the journalist Blanchard Jerrold concluded his famous pilgrimage through London with the illustrator Gustave Doré by writing: "We are now in the Music Hall and Refreshment Bar epoch: an epoch of much gilding and abundant looking glass. . . . It is a bright, gay, sparkling, dazzling time."[14] The same year, a *Saturday Review* columnist believed he detected "various indications that a change has of late been coming over the spirit of London. It is as busy and bustling as ever, as deeply engrossed in commerce and money-making; but it is also coming out as a city of pleasure." Pleasure meant consumption. "Everybody who makes money," the author asserted, "comes to London to spend it." London had usurped the title of capital of pleasure from war-ravished and revolutionary Paris, which, according to this author, was "clearly out of favour . . . [with] the throng of travellers and pleasure-seekers." The English metropolis, in contrast, offered abundant "opportunities for repose and refreshment" and was bursting with "a floating population of strangers . . . bent on pleasure during their stay in town." This journalist was of the opinion that "it was impossible not to be struck by a certain brightness and glow in the Western parts of Town."[15]

This dazzling urban culture had its roots in political, social, cultural, and technological changes underway in mid-Victorian Britain. War and revolution in Paris had temporarily boosted London's tourist industry, yet the Commune was not the only force driving pleasure seekers to London. Several decades of relative political stability and prosperity, developments in corporate law, such as the advent of limited liability, new building technologies, and greater facilities for transporting goods and people contributed to the expansion of commercialized leisure. At the same time, certain factions of the middle classes began to adopt a new attitude toward public amusement, as evangelical condemnations began to give way to a tentative acceptance of what came to be known as recreation.[16]

Feminists acknowledged the new leisure industries, but they often saw them as a source of growing gender inequality and female discomfort. Many surmised that the amusing culture that so excited male journalists offered little real pleasure to bourgeois women. They maintained that women did not enjoy this "city of pleasure" and that pleasure was not all that went on in this city. This assessment partly inspired the moral reform campaigns that were a notable aspect of feminism in both the United States and Britain. Feminists battled against intemperance and other forms of "vice," and most dramatically against what they saw as society's open acceptance of prostitution. Campaigns such as Josephine Butler's fight to repeal the Contagious Diseases Acts had heightened awareness of women's vulnerabilities in public spaces and sought to suppress "dangerous" male amusements. Yet feminists also promoted "respectable" amusements, businesses, and places.[17] As Foucault explained, the suppression and production of pleasure are, in essence, part of the same process.[18] When feminists and others condemned male leisure or commercial culture, they were not simply restraining pleasure. They were also exhibiting their own vision of the pleasurable city and the public sphere.

Feminists focused on male leisure not merely because of its association with prostitution, but also because sites of leisure were the foundation of the masculine public sphere in the Victorian era. Clubs, taverns, and other gathering places served the social, economic, and political needs of a resolutely masculine clientele.[19] They shaped men's identities and reinforced their dominance of politics, work, and education.[20] Like the countless voluntary associations that men joined in the nineteenth century, some clubs solidified class identities while others forged relations between men from different socioeconomic and religious backgrounds.[21] As G. A. Sala would famously jest, men's clubs were "a weapon used by savages to keep white women at a distance."[22] Historian Brian Harrison has further suggested that elite men's clubs formed the bastion of antisuffrage sentiment and activism in England. Influential and wealthy men raised money and formed alliances to fight the women's movement while dining and drinking together in their magnificent clubhouses. It should come as no surprise, Harrison pointed out, that feminists attempted to challenge this power by forming their own clubs.[23]

Designed as more than just sites of amusement and refreshment, women's clubs served as a point of access to the public sphere. Although women were excluded from many, though not all, aspects of the public sphere, nineteenth-century feminists successfully shifted its boundaries and meanings.[24] In a variety of locations, feminists debated the nature and location of this sphere, as well as its relationship to the organization of gender, class, and power.

Recent scholarship on the public sphere has maintained that we need to examine the many manifestations of the public which shaped nineteenth-century politics, commerce, class, gender, and national identities.[25] Most of these studies have reconfigured but been informed by Jürgen Habermas's notion of the public sphere as an ideal realm of rational discourse located between the private sphere of the family and the market and the formal institutions of the state. Habermas understood the public as a realm that emerged in the eighteenth century, in the "world of letters"—in the press, the coffeehouse, clubs, discussion societies, and salons—commonly associated with the Enlightenment. This theoretically but never actually egalitarian arena brought "private people" together as "a public."[26] Of course, as Habermas and his many critics have pointed out, women were often barred from this arena of "rational" discourse.[27] In his account, the entrance of women and "the unpropertied masses" into this sphere "led to an interlocking of state and society" that undermined the foundation of the public sphere and spelled its decline.[28]

Habermas's relatively linear history of rise and decline does not adequately capture the multiple formations of the public sphere that existed in nineteenth-century England. One complication, which several scholars have pointed to, is that many Victorians had a notion of the public quite unlike that described by Habermas.[29] Many middle-class Britons, for example, simply believed the "public sphere" was the world that lay physically outside of the home. It thus included the economy, the state, civil society, and public spaces such as the street and the park. In contrast to this view, Habermas wrote of the public as the space between the private world of the economy and the home and the public world of the state. As we will see, the nineteenth-century proponents of female lavatories and clubs held both views of the public. Indeed, they were rethinking the connections between the economy, state, civil society, and urban space and reconsidering the way in which gender acted as a boundary marking off and constructing these entities.

The remainder of this chapter will address the complex relationship between commercial culture and the formation of a feminist public sphere in the West End between the 1860s and 1914. During these years, a nexus of feminist journals, associations, and institutions grew in part as a critique of the divergence between male and female access to and experience of urban space. Its creators possessed both a liberal faith in the benefits of market forces and in the classical idealization of the polis. Indeed, they shared some of the same idealism in this construct that Habermas and Hannah Arendt would later express, even though they were not fully able to build and maintain this arena of feminist discourse and public opinion.[30]

At base, the builders of this feminist culture believed that by easing women's individual access to public space, they could create a powerful female public sphere. While not denying the importance of familial networks and domestic life, feminists anticipated women gaining membership to a public sphere of discourse and community, politics, education, and paid employment. Although Habermas and others have viewed this as a period in which the realm of commodity exchange was among those forces threatening the pristine public sphere, this was not the only view of the relationship between consumption and politics in the nineteenth century.[31] Some feminist entrepreneurs and activists perceived consumption as a possible route toward other aspects of the public sphere. The public sphere was thus a highly contested and ambiguous concept that was conceived as an abstract entity, a body of individuals, and a physical locale. It was constituted in a variety of discourses about consumption and urban life.

"Either Ladies Didn't Go Out or Ladies Didn't 'Go' "

In the 1870s, feminist, philanthropic, medical, and reform circles engaged in a curious discussion about gender, the public sphere, and the public body in considering the establishment of public lavatories for women. This question never garnered the same degree of attention among municipal reformers that William Taylor has shown it had in the United States. However, as in New York City, the idea of public conveniences did emerge with a new conception of "the public" as an embodied and mobile entity.[32] Those who wanted ladies' lavatories, or "resting places" as they were sometimes known, articulated a very literal understanding of female needs in urban space. They insisted that the ability to relieve oneself while away from home determined one's mobility in and access to public life. Their arguments were tied to broader feminist demands for work, education, and political rights, but they were also a backhanded criticism of London's commercial culture. Feminists and reformers urged local government to take up the cause of female conveniences because of a perceived need and because they distrusted the way retailers like Whiteley used such amenities to entice women into their stores.

The consideration of ladies' lavatories thus became important to the development of a feminist analysis of metropolitan commercial culture.

The *Woman's Gazette*, a feminist journal founded in 1875 by Louisa Hubbard "to represent the many branches of women's work," became one of the most vocal advocates of ladies' lavatories.[33] Along with groups such as the Society for the Promotion of the Employment of Women, established in 1859 by the Ladies of Langham Place, the journal's founders championed the expansion of paid employment for educated, single, middle-class women. They also supported the reform of married women's property rights, the growth of female-owned businesses, and the establishment of ladies' toilets and clubs. The fullest expression of the journal's view of toilets and the urban woman appeared in the 1870s with the publication of two articles entitled "Resting Places for Women Wayfarers." These pieces theorized that public lavatories were a necessary and natural product of urban growth and shifting gender norms. The first article began with a comment on the increasing pace of modern life: "The world is moving very fast, and social changes, which could almost be called social revolutions, take place with a speed and silence which prevent our even noticing them." One of the most remarkable of these social revolutions was, the author remarked,

> the extraordinary ease and cheapness with which locomotion is now effected by persons of both sexes and of all ranks, and one might add, of every age. People think nothing of running up constantly to London from the furthest corner of the Island, on pretexts which would hardly have served to move our forefathers more than once or twice in their lifetimes. . . . Ladies travel alone and unattended, for reasons which would, in the eyes of their grandmothers, hardly have justified a jaunt into the nearest market town.

This journalist welcomed ladies' participation in the new fast-paced urban culture but felt that mobility brought with it a new type of constraint. When away from home, women confronted a hitherto unfelt obstacle, a lack of places, so to speak, to go. While "men may and can . . . 'make themselves at home' anywhere," urban life was less hospitable to women: "However tired or wearied they may be they do not enter taverns for refreshment, or frequent clubs, while they feel the need for food and rest which are only thus to be obtained, even more than men."[34] This author noticed the imbalance in male and female urban amenities because women were traveling farther from their homes and because commuting men were being satisfied by an ever-expanding collection of clubs, pubs, and other amusing places.

Such complaints about the lack of public eateries for women may also be read as part of the reorganization of the rhythms of daily life among the middle and upper classes during the mid-nineteenth century. After the 1860s, the wealthier classes began to spend more time away from home each day. This led to a corresponding change in the nature and timing of meals. Breakfast stopped being a lengthy meal eaten around midmorning and became a quicker, early morning affair. The dinner hour was also moving progressively later to accommodate the longer day of the commuting householder. Lunch and afternoon tea were just being invented, in part, as a response to this new longer "public" day. Given that lunch became a significant and respectable meal only after midcentury, it should come as no surprise that in the 1870s writers were complaining that there were no places for ladies to dine in the middle of the day.[35] As we have already seen, and as the article on "resting places" made clear, both men and women were spending longer periods of time outside of their homes in the middle of the day. This meant that hunger and relief were public issues in a way they had not been before this period.

Of course, women who lived in the urban center or those with relatives and friends who owned homes quite near most West End businesses could easily move back and forth between domestic and commercial spaces. When they visited the capital they could be housed, fed, and entertained by relatives.[36] When the wealthy young Florence Sitwell traveled to London every summer, her daily round involved moving between domestic and commercial entertainments. During their visits, Florence and her brother had relative freedom to amuse themselves in the city. She also went on many shopping trips with her mother, aunt, and cousin. One passage in her diary particularly highlighted Florence's sense of freedom in the commercial areas of the city. On a Friday afternoon in 1877 Florence wrote that she and her cousin Grace "went to a shop or two, lost ourselves, and finally got home."[37] Several of the diaries of young women who were born and lived in central London betray a similar comfort in the commercial city. For example, Beryl Lee Booker remembered that as a child she delighted in her weekly trips to a sweetshop and toy store in Edgeware Road. Although her mother was one of the first Society women to open an amateur dress shop in Bond Street, it was Beryl's father who introduced her to London's commercial culture. On "wet days," for example, he would drive her to "Christie's sale-rooms, followed by a stroll in Covent Garden and back to Piccadilly by Long Acre, then given over to theatrical costumiers and carriage shops." If she were "lucky," however, her father would take her to "lunch at Princes."[38] In the 1880s, Marion Sambourne, the wife of the famous *Punch* cartoonist Linley Sambourne, evidently enjoyed shopping with her mother-in-law. The two women would often ride the "metro" to Westbourne Grove to shop at Whiteley's and visit relatives who lived nearby.[39] Marion, Florence, and Beryl enjoyed the West End because of their familiarity with its streets and a ready supply of familial companions. Their experiences were public, yet connected to the domestic realm.

In contrast to these women, those who lived far from London or who were lower on the social scale could find the city quite uncomfortable. Few modest middle-class families living outside of the capital could afford to keep a townhouse; and as the city itself expanded, women traveled relatively greater distances to work or to the shops. Until the 1880s, these female visitors could order respectable refreshments only in dark, musty pastry-cooks, confectioners, the back rooms of coffeehouses, or in Whiteley's still-small luncheon room.[40] Even wealthy women could return to their provincial homes after a long day shopping in London "famished and worn out."[41] Both middle-class and working women remembered that the lack of places to eat and relieve oneself was a serious check on their movements. The middle-class diarist Ursula Bloom explained that when she was a girl, "there were no public lavatories in England, and it was thought the height of indecency ever to desire anything of the sort." She went on to recall that "in London fashionable ladies went for a day's shopping with no hope of any relief for those faithful tides of nature until they returned home again. . . . The fact that the evening might easily be spoilt by the desires of nature was one of those hard facts which had to be accepted!"[42] Edith Hall, a working-class woman who was born in Middlesex in 1908, recalled that while walking with her mother along the Thames during the First World War, she asked, "There aren't many lavatories for ladies, are there?" Her mother matter-of-factly answered, "Well, we are more lucky now. . . . There didn't seem to be any at all when we were young. . . . Either ladies didn't go out or ladies didn't 'go.' "[43]

Feminists like Hubbard made this same link between toilets and women's physical freedoms in the city, conjuring up the same vision of the urban crowd that Whiteley had relied upon. Again, we encounter large crowds of women taking off from their suburban retreats, riding public transport, and invading the city. Feminists described women as ingesting and digesting bodies whose physical needs sometimes took precedence over other aspects of their being. However, unlike businessmen, feminists also looked upon this crowd as workers and citizens. A journalist in the *Gazette*, for example, was particularly worried that "the numbers of women, who, in pursuit of their various callings, or also, poor souls! sometimes in fruitless pursuit of the calling itself, have to traverse the great metropolis alone."[44] According to this author, the search for employment and commute to a job brought with it a new relationship to the metropolis. It led to a heightened recognition of bodily functions, of fatigue, hunger, and the desire for relief.[45]

One solution was for women to build resting places for other women. Hubbard's journal therefore endorsed any business that aided women workers. It offered financial advice to readers and actively promoted female-owned and -operated businesses.[46] In fact, the article "Resting Places for Women Wayfarers" was part discussion of urban women's needs and part advertisement for a new Oxford Street enterprise, the Vere Hall Rooms. Although she never explicitly mentioned toilets, the *Gazette*'s reporter admired these chambers for being "furnished as private rooms, with letter-paper and every convenience for writing and resting," and heralded them as "a great service to women wayfarers" and as a boon to lady shoppers in particular, for they could send their "parcels" there to be picked up "after a hard shopping campaign." When describing the Vere Hall Rooms, this writer therefore characterized shopping as part of women's increasingly mobile modern life.[47]

In addition to recommending such enterprises, the *Gazette* also propelled the public sector to create resting places for women wayfarers. In 1879 it joined forces with the Ladies Sanitary Association to induce London's vestries to build public lavatories for ladies. An affiliate of the National Association for the Promotion of Social Science and the Sanitary Institute of Great Britain, the LSA raised the issue by sending a letter to the vestries asking them to consider establishing water closets for women in the metropolis.[48] The most responsive to this call was none other then the obstreperous Paddington vestry. If in their dealings with Whiteley during these years the vestrymen appeared to be the enemy of urban women, in their consideration of lavatories they looked more like an advocate of women's emancipation. After the Paddington politicians asked their medical health officer, Dr. James Stevenson, to study the subject, the *Gazette* published a second article, "Resting Places for Women Wayfarers," to make it clear that the Paddington vestry "deserves the grateful acknowledgements of all who wish well women in their somewhat new position of English citizen."[49] By simply considering this issue, the vestry seemed to sanction women's emancipation. When one looks closely at Dr. Stevenson's report, this claim appears somewhat less hyperbolic than it might seem.

In his article "Report on the Necessity of Latrine Accommodation for Women in the Metropolis," Stevenson primarily focused on documenting the existence of the modern urban woman. He organized the report around three basic questions: Were ladies' lavatories necessary? Should the vestries supply them? And if so, what form should such provisions take? He addressed the first consideration by proving that many women spent a good portion of their time away from their homes. According to Stevenson, London's phenomenal recent population growth and the advent of "railways and steamboats" had "accelerated [the] rate of movement . . . in every sphere of human activity."[50] Although he admitted he could not compute "the number of women who daily pass along our streets," he calculated that a great number of female workers, shoppers, and students were among the "thousands of persons who used the variety of public conveyances on a daily basis." "As a consequence of all this material and mental advancement, and of the close relation between town and country in these days, the number of female workers is likely to increase."[51] Stevenson felt that urbanization and "material and mental advancement" had brought men and women out of the private household and that such trends would necessarily require a change in the nature of the city. "No one would think of proposing latrine accommodation for women in a town where most of the inhabitants are known to one another, and are within easy distance of their homes," he explained to the vestrymen. In London this was not the case. As Stevenson so artfully observed: "London is a populous wilderness, and nowhere is the sense of solitude at times more keenly felt." In other words, the bodily urge to relieve oneself amplified one's sense of publicness and solitude.

Stevenson then moved from an analysis of the urban crowd to a discussion of the traveling woman's body. Citing "abundant testimony from medical men," he argued that men and women have the same "physical necessities." They both "take food and drink . . . [and] get rid of what the system cannot appropriate." Male and female Londoners were simply consuming bodies, literally ingesting and using up resources, ultimately producing waste. From this point it was easy to argue that it was the vestry's job to deal with urban waste. Without such public conveniences, Stevenson explained that "some ladies go to restaurants and order refreshments which they do not require, and others to milliners' and confectioners' shops. It may safely be assumed that the money thus spent, even when it is only a few pence, cannot always be conveniently spared."[52] Stevenson did not oppose women's consumption per se. He even proposed that conveniences might include "a small shop for the sale exclusively of articles of feminine attire, or a cloak room or a tea room, or a room supplied with newspapers and writing materials." He did, however, believe that the bodily discomforts associated with urban life should not force women to become consumers. Stevenson challenged the link being forged between consumption and women's comfort in the city and urged that relief and spending should not be related activities.[53]

Stevenson thus had a progressive and egalitarian vision of women's role in urban life. In writing about latrine accommodation he argued against some of the most powerful assumptions of his profession. Stevenson did not see a fundamental difference between male and female bodies, nor did he believe that women should remain safely and comfortably within their private households. Though Stevenson believed in gender equality, he also maintained that architecture should reflect class hierarchies. In describing his proposed design for public toilets, Stevenson wrote that it was "imperative that the provision made should be of two kinds . . . for two classes," since "women of the middle class will not be willing to company, for however short a time, with a promiscuous crowd, even of their own sex." Wealthy women would no doubt pay a small fee for the privilege of white glazed tile and social exclusivity, while poorer women would be exempt from payment but find their accommodation decorated with dark glazed bricks.[54]

Dr. Stevenson's ambitious plans were not developed in Paddington or elsewhere in the West End during this period, even though prominent reform organizations and a private company were willing to build them. Though the reasons for this are unclear, a letter from Alfred Watkyns of the Châlet Company to the LSA provides one clue. Watkyns complained that although his company had built such amenities throughout England, "the feeling of distrust, and local factions, that are but too prominent at some of the Vestry Boards" obstructed their development in the metropolis.[55] Given Whiteley's treatment by the same vestry, Watkyn's analysis may have been accurate. This failure to establish public conveniences was not, as one recent historian has argued, due to the vestry's "incomprehension" or "inability" to see the necessity of women's bodily needs, nor was it their reliance on medical theory that suggested women did not need to urinate or defecate as frequently as men.[56] Notions of gender difference played a role, but they were intertwined with fears about the masses and urbanization. The most direct opposition to public conveniences came not from doctors or politicians but from residents. Into the late-nineteenth century sanitary reformers and government bodies repeatedly raised the issue of the inadequacy of public conveniences for women, especially after women joined the vestries in 1894.[57] For example, Mrs. Evans, a former poor law guardian and owner of a photographic shop who had been elected to the St. Martin-in-the-Fields' vestry, became a formidable champion of the cause during the late 1890s.[58]

At every turn, however, wealthy residents protested the installation of any sort of convenience in their midst.[59] Bayswater inhabitants, for example, fretted that such "German abominations" would lead to sexual disorder.[60] In 1891 the "residents of Upper Westbourne-park" and the Reverend J. R. Knowles similarly warned that "such spots" would become "disorderly centers" used by prostitutes.

"Ladies would especially be annoyed," he claimed, for they "would have to pass by the objectionable place every time they went to the railway station."[61] Knowles argued that public lavatories actually limited wealthy ladies' comfort in the city. Lavatories raised the same kind of antiurban sentiment and class and gender prejudices that Whiteley's luncheon room had inspired, since these amenities signified the presence of outsiders in West End neighborhoods. They symbolized the public quality of the streets in which all classes and sexes could potentially encounter one another. When residents opposed these conveniences, they turned to the tried and true arguments about "foreign" and "immoral" elements invading their homes and leading to sexual and social disorder. They believed that such services invited unruly strangers into their streets. Wealthy West End inhabitants wanted their neighborhoods to be private, elite spaces rather than sites of mass consumption and production.

Public toilets were thus at the very center of the debate about women and the city, public space, and the public sphere. Feminists and sanitary reformers had argued that women's relationship to the city was restricted by a lack of places that would accommodate their private needs. London's growth, mass transit, and economic changes had produced a female consuming body seeking satisfaction. Whether worker or shopper, this urban woman demanded comfort, nourishment, and relief outside of the domestic realm. Reformers like Stevenson and the writers and readers of journals such as the *Women's Gazette* authored a vision of the metropolis that would cater to this new public woman. If capitalists and feminists agreed that women needed comfortable havens in the urban frontier, they differed in their assessment of whether women should remain within feminine public places. The latter assumed that such urban homes allowed women to become active in the public spheres of education, employment, and politics. Entrepreneurs saw admission to the city as bringing female buyers into the marketplace. The tension between these two positions shaped the history of London's women's clubs more than of any other enterprise.

Female Clubland

In contrast to the fate of the public convenience, clubs played a large part in many women's lives and symbolized their increased visibility in the urban landscape. A few streets were so dominated by luxurious and wealthy all-female and mixed-sex clubhouses that journalists and others began to speak of a female clubland. This district was never as large, sumptuous, or influential as its male counterpart. However, as the most successful expression of feminist commercial culture, women's clubs transformed the history of the West End and its female inhabitants.

Clubwomen invariably maintained that their institutions served the urban woman, whether she was a typist, clerk, teacher, artist, journalist, philanthropist, social worker, civil servant, student, or shopper.[62] Although the percentage of women in the workforce did not change much during this period, the numbers of educated middle-class women workers were rising dramatically. This female class also began to fill positions in local government and privately funded philanthropies such as the Charity Organization Society. Paid employment, voluntary efforts, educational, political, and leisure pursuits worked together to make middle-class women a highly visible component of the urban crowd after the 1860s, but especially by the last decades of the century.[63]

Clubwomen were aware that a few department stores, restaurants, and even art galleries had been designated as havens for the female bourgeoisie.[64] As early as the 1850s and 1860s, some proprietors had opened female-only dining and retiring rooms in their restaurants to attract the middle classes. When, for example, Frederick Gordon opened Crosby Hall in 1868 he published a booklet in which he told women how much they would appreciate the female "Boudour and Retiring Rooms" he had built for them.[65] Trade journals such as the *Caterer* also believed that ladies were fast becoming part of the restaurant-dining community and that services such as "a separate room for women only, with lavatory, is appreciated when it has been adopted."[66] Making light of this social change, the journal's editor quipped: "Byron, we know, could not bear to see a lady eating: happily for hotel proprietors . . . this is not a Byronic Age."[67] Like Gordon, the catering mavericks Felix Spiers and Christopher Ponds introduced the restaurant habit to the male and female bourgeoisie in 1878, when they opened the Criterion Restaurant in Piccadilly. The East Room of the Criterion gained a reputation for being particularly pleasing to bourgeois women.[68] By the end of the century, the Criterion, Trocadero, and the Gaiety as well as the grand hotels such as the Savoy and the Ritz became the center of a new kind of heterosocial nightlife.[69]

Although the owners invented ways to cater to women as well as to men, feminists wanted to establish places where women could find pleasure and knowledge, be amused and enriched. As they became part of the catering and amusement industry, however, feminists became implicated in the construction of West End commercial culture. Clubs encouraged middle-class women to engage in long shopping campaigns and to indulge in a good deal of collective consumption, and to spend tidy sums, for example, on furnishing their clubs with the most up-to-date decor. All of these things made politics and urban life more palatable, but it also meant that feminists unwittingly reinforced the image of the West End as a sphere of entertainment and consumption.

As mentioned earlier, nothing so palpably represented masculine power and dominance of the public sphere as the clubhouses that lined Pall Mall, Piccadilly, and St. James's. When in 1885 the guidebook author Charles Pascoe described Pall Mall, he could not separate the street from its clubhouses and the men who gathered within them: "We are now coming to Pall Mall, one of the most splendid streets in London, deriving its splendour from its club-houses. It is the resort of all the most representative Englishmen." With "the most wealthy and influential political and social clubs in the world," Pall Mall symbolized masculine dominance of the nation and the empire.[70] Although men's clubs had developed from eighteenth-century coffeehouses, they were often described as among the modern aspects of the metropolis because their prestige, luxury, and popularity had grown dramatically in the second half of the nineteenth century.[71] In 1861, for example,

James Henry Leigh Hunt heralded the palatial men's clubs as one of the new features of West End social life. "Within these few years," he remarked, "half the private houses in Pall Mall have been converted into what may be called magnificent public-houses," in which men "can pass the day as well as eat and drink; in some they can sleep; in all they can dress, amuse themselves, concert political and other measures; in short, enjoy all the advantages of home and places of business without the ties of either." Hunt jokingly concluded his assessment of male clubland by surmising that this world left the lady "husbandless at home," wondering "whether female clubs will ever come up."[72] Hunt did not know, however, that a female club already existed in the West End. It too was a "public house" in which women could "enjoy all the advantages of home and places of business without the ties of either."

This club had been opened by Bessie Rayner Parkes, Barbara Leigh Smith Bodichon, Jessie Boucherett, Emily Faithfull, and other feminists who were loosely associated as the Langham Place Circle. Not only had this group published journals, started an employment registry and other female businesses, and worked to reform married women's property laws, they also launched the late-Victorian club movement. When the group moved to 19 Langham Place in 1860, their offices included a modest library and dining and club rooms. This club was one of the first venues where middle-class women could read, rest, and refresh themselves while in public. Noting this social function, the *Illustrated London News* welcomed this "centre where women might see reviews, magazines and papers" and urged support for what it assumed was "a place of rest and refreshment for ladies."[73] The club eventually became a more permanent institution known as the Berners Club. The Berners went through several forms during its lifetime, but by the early seventies its more than two hundred female members were governed by a council of notable men and women, including Barbara Bodichon, Frances Power Cobbe, and Thomas Huxley.[74]

An article published in the *Daily News* in 1871 argued that clubs began as an unconscious female protest against male urban privileges on the very same day that William Whiteley had opened his drapery shop in Bayswater. This author claimed that when the future Princess of Wales made her "triumphal procession through London" before her marriage in March of 1863, men's clubs opened their doors for the first time to female visitors wanting to view the parade. The princess's public appearance had thus inspired this female incursion into male space. Writing about women's move into clubland, the author remembered how "nothing was sacred from intrusion. The most privileged corners were invaded, and libraries where from time immemorial members have been permitted to sulk in silence, were full of animated groups who chatted and laughed and gave an uninvited grace to their somewhat gloomy grandeur." This event, he surmised, represented "a powerful though unconscious protest against being excluded from such establishments," concluding that "future historians will probably date the establishment of Ladies' Clubs from this occasion."[75]

This journalist then discussed the Berners Club in some detail without mentioning its feminist connections. With its "comfortable" furnishings, "good" and "moderately priced cooking," and "well-supplied" reading room, the Berners was described as a welcome retreat for "ladies who have experienced the discomfort of a long day in London with no resting-place but the shops, and no meal but such as it is furnished by the pastry cook; who have felt the want of a central meeting place."[76] This account situated female clubs within a commercial framework, but presented clubwomen as "unconscious" spectators yearning to see the princess. In this scenario, clubs satisfied female desires for urban comfort without reforming the gender order. They in fact achieved both comfort and social change.

When the feminist journalist and cofounder of the Berners Club, Frances Power Cobbe, wrote about women's clubs in 1871, she explained that these enterprises benefited single middle-class women who had no homes of their own and women who "live a little way out of town; and when they come into it for business or pleasure are perpetually driven to seek rest and refreshment in those miserable refuges of feminine distress, the confectioner's shops." She contrasted men's and women's urban amenities by complaining that while "young gentlemen entering their magnificent Pall Mall Clubs" dined in "a room fit to be a Temple of Eating," their "mothers and sisters, wearied and faint with their day's sightseeing and shopping," were forced to go "meekly to a greasy pastry cook's counter and munch patiently that horrid thing—a bonbon." Cobbe thus criticized the limited choice and poor quality of London's private and commercially provided amenities. She was particularly unhappy that shoppers treated drapers as urban refuges. While appealing for monetary support, Cobbe argued, "If the same generous men who lavish on their wives and daughters' dress, jewels, [and] horses . . . were awakened to the idea that a good club would probably contribute far more to their enjoyment, (and also, we may add, economise a vast amount of money expended *pour passer le temps* at such establishments as Messrs. Marshall and Snelgrove's), there is no doubt that needful sums would be forthcoming."[77] In other words, men could save money by supporting clubs since their wives would spend less time and money at stores like Marshall and Snelgrove's.

Cobbe admitted, however, that she was not simply recommending an alternative to the department store. She believed that inexpensive accommodations would help bring women more fully into the public sphere. "Women," she argued, needed places that both served "the wants of the body" and provided "facilities for improving their minds." Female clubs, she thought, would "rid [women] of their narrow political and ecclesiastical prejudices" by allowing them to read, meet friends, hear lectures, and thus come "to understand the great topics of public interest."[78] Although women might enter clubs as consumers, Cobbe assumed they would exit as citizens. She saw clubs as an intermediate territory between family and formal politics, as an institution that ideally supported women's participation in both realms.

Cobbe's friend and ally in the feminist struggle, Adelaide Drummond, similarly saw clubs as amusing yet political spaces. In her memoirs, she recalled discussing the suffrage and other political issues, enjoying afternoon tea and pleasant suppers at the mixed-sex club, the Albemarle. Although some of her friends looked upon clubwomen as "fast," Drummond eagerly joined soon after it opened in the midseventies. She appreciated having a central place in London to meet friends and make new acquaintances, especially since she lived in Hampstead, one of London's leafy northern suburbs.[79] When the feminist poet Amy Levy published her essay "Women and Club Life" in the *Woman's World*, a short-lived magazine edited by Oscar Wilde in the late 1880s, she too imagined clubs as magnets reversing the centrifugal pull of suburbia.[80] The modern woman, she believed, was streaming "from the high and dry region of the residential neighborhood . . . to those pleasant shores where the great stream of human life is dashing and flowing." Levy pictured the suburban woman as having been awakened by the "class-room and lecture-theatre, office and art-school, college and club-house . . . to the sense of the hundred and one possibilities of social intercourse."[81] Levy's clubwoman was educated and independent, and embraced her urban existence.

As Deborah Nord and Melvyn New have recently discussed, Levy found in London a muse, a protagonist, and a home. This was especially evident in the set of poems that was published as *A London Plane-Tree* (1889).[82] She wrote her essay on club life at approximately the same time as she had this volume. In both texts the city and not the home was seen as the center of the "stream of human life." In the essay, Levy implied that clubs allowed her to imagine the city in this way. Like Cobbe, Levy describes clubs as a refuge and haven. Such terms were more commonly used to construct the household as a private arena separated from the public world, but Levy employed them to express what she found in the public realm. "How many a valuable acquaintance has been improved, how many an important introduction obtained in that convenient neutral territory of club-land!" she remarked. "Here, at last is a haven or refuge, where we can write our letters and read the news, undisturbed by the importunities of a family circle."[83] Levy believed clubs were public havens that protected women from a hectic and disturbing family life. They enhanced nonfamilial associations and allowed for what Levy saw as a true form of privacy as well as for access to a new type of female community. Levy's admiration of club life lay in her belief that it provided an alternative female culture to that embedded in the domestic realm.[84]

Levy also assumed that shoppers would enjoy their clubs. She imagined that "the suburban high-school mistress, in town for a day's shopping or picture-seeing, exchanges here the discomfort of the pastry-cook or the costliness of the restaurant for the comforts of a quiet meal and a quiet read or chat in the cosy club precincts."[85] Away from the annoyances of the family and the pastry cook, women could read, chat, eat, and enjoy themselves. All educated women might appreciate clubs, but Levy finally conceded that "it is to the professional woman, when all is said, that the club offers the most substantial advantages. What woman engaged in art, in literature, in science, had not felt the drawbacks of her isolated position?"[86] Levy thus anticipated that these urban homes could help lonely women workers form meaningful relationships. Evidently Levy could not find this community, since shortly after she published this essay she ended her life. Levy's essay thus expressed some of the conflicts that middle-class women must have felt when they moved to the metropolis to pursue their careers. Levy's appreciation of clubs reflected both her loneliness and desire for companionship as much as her love of an urban existence.

Seeking both solitude and community, thousands of women like Levy joined the dozens of clubs that opened in the last years of the century. College graduates and "medical women," for example, associated at the Women's University Club in Maddox Street.[87] Those with a literary bent and proven reputation could also join the Writers' Club after it was established in 1891. Some of England's most well known female novelists, journalists, and academics formed this club after the masculine Author's Club refused to allow them to join. Such highly paid writers as Mrs. Stannard (who published as John Strange Winter), Lady Jeune, Frances Lowe, Mrs. Humphrey Ward, and Florence Routledge were evidently put off by Walter Besant's explanation that women should be excluded because they surely would not have the resources to pay the club's five guinea membership fee.[88] Although it was born as a protest, the Writers' became an important center of literary culture in the 1890s. Constance Smedley, who would become an instrumental figure in the English club movement, was first introduced to club life as a member of the Writers'. She later recalled that she and her "art-student friends" who were trying to make their livings as journalists, fashion designers, and illustrators enjoyed this "cozy spot" that provided them with a "dignified milieu where women could meet editors and other employers and discuss matters as men did in their professional clubs: above all, in surroundings that did not suggest poverty."[89] Smedley and her community made their club into a space where they could meet each other and their employers on neutral ground. For a group of young women struggling to make a living, the club proved an important site in which they could temporarily experience the luxuries of the wealthy.

Feminists founded and joined professionally oriented clubs like the Writers' and the Women's University Club, but these institutions were hardly their exclusive province. Perhaps these clubs' most distinguishing characteristic was that they brought educated women together from across the political and social spectrum.[90] At her club, for example, the antisuffragist Mrs. Humphrey Ward would have had regular contact with leading figures in the suffrage movement. Nonetheless, the feminist community wielded a good deal of influence in many of these professional clubs, as they did in the more overtly political clubs such as the Somerville, the Junior Denison, and the Pioneer.

The Somerville, founded in 1878 and named in honor of one of Cobbe's close friends, the astronomer Mary Somerville, was the oldest of these progressive clubs. Its first home was in Berners Street; according to one of its members, it was the "marching on of the soul of the Old Berners Club."[91] When it moved to Mortimer Street two years later, the feminist physician Elizabeth Blackwell remarked that this association proposed to "consider seriously all political and social questions." She supported the club because she felt it "will perform new and valuable work . . . by uniting all classes and shades of opinion . . . [and] by becoming a center for the serious study of all social questions."[92] According to a very sympathetic piece in the *Bayswater Chronicle* in 1880, the Somerville's initial backers were connected to the early women's colleges. The paper was so supportive of this progressive club because Henry Walker, the outspoken critic of the Universal Provider, was involved with its management.[93] Though Walker considered himself a progressive liberal, Sydney Webb remembered the Somerville as a meeting ground for Fabians and their sympathizers. His memory of the club reflected the same concept of the public sphere that Cobbe and Levy had held; he wrote that the Somerville had "supplied women 'hitherto impeded or narrowed' in their activity a place to 'have their interests awakened, and their energies called into a wider field.' "[94] Lecture and debate topics ranged from socialism to theosophy, vegetarianism, women's suffrage, children's health, the Direct Veto, and the Eight Hours' Bill.[95] In 1888, Mrs. Oscar Wilde delivered what a journalist for the *Lady* reported to be a "daintily-worded and most explicit lecture" on dress reform, entitled "Clothed and in Our Right Minds."[96]

Club culture was therefore progressive in the broadest sense. Debates and lectures dealt with up-to-date artistic, political, philosophical, and scientific subjects, and club members worked to solve some of the key social questions of the day. Like the Somerville, the mixed-sex club the Junior Denison also appealed to "persons interested in charitable and social subjects" and was closely affiliated with the Charity Organization Society.[97] Many of the members of the COS joined the Junior Denison to encounter like-minded individuals, but also because the club was conveniently situated in the same building as the Society.

Although the Junior Denison, Somerville, and Berners Clubs were quite well known in their day, the Pioneer Club had the most notorious and lasting "feminist" reputation.[98] The Pioneers ranked among England's most socially and politically active women, including "ardent suffragists" and "New Woman" novelists such as Sarah Grand, Mona Caird, and Olive Schreiner. According to a visiting American, the Pioneer's membership included many "women of title and position" as well as "others engaged in the profession." Since one of its objects was to "promote democracy and abolish class distinctions," the "names and titles of members were eschewed and members were designated by number only—so that '99' might be a duchess or a post-office clerk, as it happened."[99]

The club's radical image was also closely tied with that of its founder, Mrs. Massingberd. A wealthy widow, Massingberd spent much of her income and energies on the temperance movement, women's suffrage, and her own bid for a seat on the newly formed London County Council. Although defeated by what one historian has called "the combined forces of parsons, publicans, and the Primrose League," her liberal credentials could not have been more secure.[100] Her fame also came from what the *Illustrated London News* pejoratively explained in her obituary as an "unfortunate whim to wear her hair short, and a vest loose, 'morning' or evening 'swallow-tail' coat, and untrimmed soft felt hat, just like a man's."[101] Massingberd's "masculine" persona and her political and charitable activities added to the Pioneer's "advanced" reputation. Nearly every aspect of this institution contributed to this impression, however. Club walls displayed members' artwork, club members wore a silver ax as their insignia, and its debates and lectures were famous for discussing feminist, reform, social, and cultural questions. Many of the women who associated with the Langham Place Circle and later clubs like the Pioneer were involved in passionate friendships and often lived with one another, although it is not clear whether these were sexual relationships.[102] Further research would tell us whether or not these clubs contributed to the development of lesbian identities and culture during this period. What we may conclude, however, is that both proponents and critics of changing female roles believed the Pioneer was the cradle of the New Woman.[103]

As early as the 1860s, moralists and social observers were deeply troubled by women's clubs because they were identified with women like Cobbe, Drummond, Levy, and Massingberd. Clubs seemed to signify a full-scale attack on domesticity, male authority, and traditional gender identities. One critic, for example, warned that these enterprises would permit a woman to "escape from the conditions that surround her," provide a "safety-valve" from a "pious papa," or be used as "an enormous weapon against an overbearing fiancé."[104] The destruction of bourgeois domesticity also became the central theme of an anonymous 1874 *Saturday Review* article on female and mixed-sex clubs. Given the tone and themes of this piece, it is likely that its author was Eliza Lynn Linton. As she had in her famous article "The Girl of the Period," in this piece she bemoaned middle-class women's involvement in urban commercial culture. She denounced the proposal for a mixed-sex club because such a club would allow women to "receive their private letters, make appointments of which no one knows but themselves, eat their mutton chops, and discuss the affairs of Europe without fear of Mrs. Grundy or submission to the ordinary restraints of the drawing-room." She warned that a place where "pretty women and pleasant men are mixed up together" would lead to "flirting as surely as there is flirting now under more difficult conditions." She also stressed, however, that female clubs were as dangerous as the mixed-sex variety. Although these clubs had been represented as merely for "ladies who live in the country and want to come up to town for a day's shopping or an evening's amusement," she exposed them as another "manifestation showing the revolt against privacy and domesticity in which some of our women are engaged." Female clubs were another expression of "the love of dress, the passion for amusement, the frenzy for notoriety, for excitement, for change, which have possessed her [the modern woman] of late. . . . [They are] a dangerous experiment in which more is involved than appears on the surface."[105]

Twenty years later, Linton continued her attack on the clubs by presenting them as the home of the young, upper-class, unhappily married feminist of the 1890s. In *The New Woman in Haste and at Leisure*, a novel set in the Excelsior, a thinly veiled disguise for the Pioneer Club, Linton described clubs as "a nursery for man-haters and rebels, and the nucleus of the new order of feminine supremacy."[106] While she expanded upon all of the themes of her *Saturday Review* critique, her tone had become more strident by the 1890s, during this era of seemingly ubiquitous New Women and New Men. Mannish women, flirtatious girls, and listless, effeminate men were stock characters in club satire and social commentary. Clubs were clearly associated with what Elaine Showalter has described as the gender anarchy that pervaded fin de siècle culture.[107]

Contemporary jeremiads of consumerism, whether personified by department store magnates or fraudulent female shoppers, conjured up similar tales of a gender order turned upside down. Consumption, like feminism, bred dependent men and independent women and gnawed at the sanctity of the private sphere. For Linton and her fellow journalists at the *Saturday Review*, clubs and commercial enterprises thus occupied similar social realms. Both were new institutions making space for middle-class women in the public realm, and this in turn upset the "natural" social order. Linton's misgivings were in some ways well placed. When she complained that clubs were a manifestation of the New Woman's "love of dress, [and] the passion for amusement," she was arguing that clubs were promoting female consumerism. Rather than discount her tirade as mere hysteria, we must consider why she and others would indict clubs in this way.

"A Social Ark for Shoppers"

Political and social conservatives such as Linton viewed feminine clubland with suspicion precisely because they associated it with two despised facets of "modern" urban life, feminism and consumerism. Feminists started clubs because they felt that commercial culture and governmental efforts ignored urban women's physical and psychological needs. Despite their criticisms of consumerism, however, they were excited about the prospect of female shoppers finding a larger purpose in the public sphere. These feminists expressed angst about feminine frivolity and the fashion system but believed that shopping had a place in the modern woman's life. One need only recall Levy's portrait of the clubwoman as a "suburban high-school mistress, in town for a day's shopping or picture-seeing" to see how she could imagine a female identity defined by work and leisure, production and consumption. Some enthusiastically imagined shoppers as allies in the cause for women's emancipation, thereby becoming embroiled in a rivalry with capitalist entrepreneurs for the hearts and minds of the shopping public. By the Edwardian era, retailers claimed to emancipate women, and clubwomen professed to cater to shoppers. This competition ended not with winners and losers, but with a collection of analogous enterprises, institutions that were physically close and functionally similar.

Geography created the most rudimentary and perhaps significant bridge between shopland and clubland. Most clubs had settled in or were quite near Regent, Oxford, and Bond Streets. For example, Berners and Mortimer Streets, just north of the intersection between Regent and Oxford Streets, were preferred addresses for women's clubs because these streets were close to London's best shops and the feminist institutions founded by the Langham Place Circle. Hanover Square became another popular location, but the small elegant avenues in Mayfair just north of Piccadilly and east of Regent Street formed the heart of female clubland. Over half of all late-Victorian and Edwardian women's clubs inhabited mansions in Berkeley, Dover, Albemarle, Old Bond, Grafton, and Sackville Streets.

Geography was important to clubland's social acceptance, for it helped supporters describe clubwomen not as unfeminine, graceless, or fast creatures but as fashionable hostesses presiding over luxurious mansions. In the fin de siècle, female journalists favorably described clubs as advancing feminist and mainstream commercial culture. When, for example, the feminist *Englishwoman's Review* announced the opening of a new club at 25 Regent Street, it remarked that this club would be a particular "benefit" because of its "central position," which was "within easy distance of the chief shops, theatres, railways, etc."[108] In reporting upon the Somerville's move to 123 Oxford Street, the upper-class ladies' magazine the *Queen* pointed out that because the new clubhouse was "close to Oxford-circus, opposite Peter Robinson's, no halting place could better meet the wants of ladies."[109] Countless articles in both the fashion and the more overtly feminist press placed clubs within this commercial landscape. Characterizing clubs as adjuncts to other fashionable and feminine institutions no doubt attracted shoppers. This representation converted clubland from a feminist into a feminine space.

Journalists and clubwomen commonly designated clubs as "temporary homes" for urban shoppers.[110] Although this conception of clubs had existed since the 1860s, it became the dominant image in the 1880s and 1890s. By that period, new clubs appeared every few months, and older ones expanded and became more luxurious, adding such amenities as bedrooms for members visiting London "for a few day's shopping."[111] By building comfortable bedrooms, sumptuous lounging rooms, elegant dining rooms, and large concert halls, clubs were replicating the services provided by large hotels, restaurants, and theaters. Club advocates, nevertheless, consistently argued that their converted aristocratic mansions were more private and domestic than commercial institutions.

Still, the fin de siècle woman's club was becoming increasingly extravagant and leisure oriented, especially after membership-owned and -financed clubs started to give way to proprietary clubs.[112] The latter were commercial ventures supported by the capital of wealthy individuals rather than by the club's membership. The Tea and Shopping Club, founded in Hanover Square in the mid-1890s by a Mr. Oliver, was a typical example of such enterprises. Although it was renamed the more aristocratic-sounding Ladies' County Club, this institution was, according to one journalist, "a social ark for shoppers . . . [or] pied a terre . . . where members could rest after a pilgrimage through shopland, have parcels sent, meet their friends, and partake of that popular panacea—a cup of tea."[113] Whereas feminist clubs such as the Berners also served the needs of shoppers, the Ladies' County was solely intended as "a social ark for shoppers." Oliver's brother, Otho, admired this undertaking so much that he opened his own ladies' club, the Empress, in 1897. Managed by a committee of very highly placed ladies, including a princess and several countesses, the Empress quickly became one of the largest female clubs in London, with over twenty-seven hundred members. The Empress existed solely, as one writer explained, "for the convenience and comfort of members." Quoting W. S. Gilbert's famous line about the House of Lords, this author joked that "the Empress Club 'does nothing in particular, and it does it very well.' " Members must have found the Empress particularly comfortable, for it was lav-

THE MORNING ROOM, EMPRESS CLUB.

Figure 4. The morning room at the Empress Club. *Lady's Realm*, 1899 (by permission of the British Library, shelf mark pp. 6004og).

ishly furnished in what was then considered the most "smart and up to date" style.[114] Filled with plants, cut flowers, overstuffed easy chairs, and William Morris wallpaper, the Empress's expensive decor and, of course, its name signified luxury and loyalty. The bust of Queen Victoria at the top of the stairs and Union Jack pillow in the morning room left little doubt about the club's politics (fig. 4). When in 1900 the club moved into an even grander house in Dover Street, its seven floors included ninety bedrooms, reception rooms, "a handsome Louis XV drawing room, an oriental lounge, and a Georgian period dining room."[115]

Businesswomen also eagerly invested in clubland. For example, a Miss Cohen opened the Ladies' International Club in Old Bond Street after having already made her fortune as the proprietor of the Kettledrum Tea Rooms.[116] She originally intended to provide rest and refreshment for weary shoppers, but after a short time, she and a committee of ladies reestablished the Ladies' International as the Sandringham Club. Believing the Sandringham could approximate a "man's first-class club," Cohen and her associates hired a French chef and a "well-known club man" to select their wines.[117] The Sandringham introduced the gastronomic luxuries of masculine club life, satisfying female members and encouraging male guests to dine at the club.

The Sandringham and the other clubs that welcomed male visitors encouraged heterosocial as well as homosocial interaction. Although mixed-sex clubs had existed since the 1870s, by the late 1880s many single-sex clubs also appealed to the opposite sex on a limited basis.[118] Some of the newer or more radical men's clubs even admitted female visitors and members. In 1886, for example, the Cobden Club admitted Florence Nightingale and Richard Cobden's daughter, Mrs. Cobden Sickert, to its membership. The Bachelor's, Cavalry, New Vagabond, and even the Savages invited ladies into their masculine world in the early 1890s.[119] These clubs were becoming a central part of fin de siècle nightlife, in which men and women were dining and carousing together outside of the private home.

Clearly there was a difference between politically oriented clubs and those formed for entertainment and social purposes.[120] And yet this was a relatively superficial distinction. All clubs surrounded intellectual, cultural, and political pursuits in opulent decor and served the needs of women producing and consuming in the city center. In describing this dual project, one writer remarked in 1899 that the clubs welcomed both "the modern professional woman" and "the women of the leisured and wealthy class," who "call for lunch in the middle of a day of West End shopping, or to hear some of the most interesting people in England at the various club lectures and debates."[121] In the eyes of this and many writers, clubs were an adjunct to women's leisure, work, and politics. Even the extremely exclusive and fashionable Alexandra, Empress, and Grosvenor Crescent admitted women based either on their social status or their political and other public achievements.[122] Politics and pleasure were linked, albeit in varying proportions, in nearly all clubs. Clubs united different activities and types of people into a collective social body.

Fashion, furnishings, and consumption created a shared identity among the New Woman, the upper-class socialite, and the suburban shopper who made up the membership at many of the West End clubs. Journalists, as we have seen, encouraged readers to identify feminism with an elite, consumer-oriented femininity by endlessly and admiringly writing about decor and architecture. When Hilda Friedrichs described her visit to the Pioneer Club for the readers of the *Young Woman*, she began by explaining her trepidation that she would encounter the "newest of the New Women," the "loudest" of the "shrieking sisters," and "mannish-dressed man-haters." She quickly relaxed, however, once she realized that the club's interior was as luxurious and beautiful as many "London West End mansions."[123] Dora Jones, another of the magazine's writers, said much the same thing about the Pioneer, only adding that Lord Byron had once occupied this "fine old Adams house." A reporter for the *Lady* similarly was astonished that the Pioneer's debates took place "in one of the most aristocratic dwellings in Mayfair." She especially admired the "dignity of antique carving and gilding" blended "with the gay modernity of white paint and 'cozy corners.' "[124] At the Pioneer, feminism was evidently cushioned by luxurious furnishings (fig. 5).

After the 1880s, the mainstream women's press proclaimed clubs as socially acceptable, fashionable, "feminine" institutions. For example, in 1885 the *Lady* assured its readers that it was in the spirit of "womanly (not manly) independence" that the clubs were formed. While twenty years earlier the journal admitted that

AFTERNOON TEA

THE THURSDAY EVENING DEBATE

Figure 5. Feminist culture at the Pioneer Club, *Graphic*, April 1908 (by permission of the British Library, shelf mark LD 46).

"the promoters would probably have been tabooed by Society as 'fast' in the present day there is a distinction between being fast and being independent."[125] One of the *Queen's* reporters appreciated a new club for its lack of a " 'fast' or excessively 'strong-minded' element" and because "nothing in the associations or the circumstances of the ladies who are proposed for election which would debar them . . . from attending Her Majesty's Drawing-Rooms."[126] Clubwomen, like Whiteley's department store shoppers, were thus characterized as independent public individuals who were neither sexually nor socially disruptive. The women's press thus supplanted the inherently and explicitly threatening images of self-supporting, all-female urban institutions with a benign portrait of luxurious urban homes populated by apolitical and asexual ladies of fashion. According to the fin de siècle press, the clubwoman was modern but not daring. She enjoyed her autonomy in the public realm without being considered "fast" or even feminist.

The depiction of clubs as luxurious and cozy homes reflected, sanctioned, and advanced a shift in their nature. By the 1890s, but especially after the turn of the century, women's clubs were no longer necessarily liberal, feminist, or progressive. Indeed, some like the Empress were commercial institutions that also had become venues for the reconstruction of an increasingly diverse and troubled ruling class. England's elite women defended their power and position by forming associations such as the Primrose League and joining conservative imperialist clubs such as the Ladies' Army and Navy Club, the Ladies' Empire Club, or the "avowedly political" Ladies' Carlton Club.[127] The latter, for example, sought to unite "women of good social position . . . who are earnest supporters of the Unionist cause," "favored tariff reform," and wanted to "counteract socialism."[128] The Ladies' Army and Navy offered its over thirty-five hundred members the privileges befitting England's officer class, including a tent at Ascot, balls at the Ritz Hotel, and a famous all-female billiard room. The clubwomen who played games, smoked, dined, and politicked in their magnificent clubhouses were among the pillars of English society. They formed clubs to protect, not question, England's ruling class (fig. 6).[129]

Some women criticized the direction that the English club movement had taken, arguing that clubs were no longer significantly politically or socially engaged. The Canadian Margaret Polsen Murray complained that Englishwomen "enjoy their club in their own way, as a restful luncheon or tea-room, warmed up by an occasional lecture or discussion on a public question, its membership well fenced by society barriers."[130] A few years later, Annie Swan Smith, who published the journal *Woman at Home*, despaired that English women's clubs were poor imitations of their American counterparts. She felt that with but a few exceptions, they were "mere places of rendezvous, in which the real essence of club life created by unity of purpose and community of interest is conspicuous by its absence."[131] Smith and Murray found London's clubs disappointing because they did not fulfill Cobbe's dream of creating a collective community of women that would then aid women's entrance into the public sphere.

Yet what Smith and Murray had not understood was that the very idea of women forming clubs in the urban center was a sign of sweeping changes in

THE GENERAL DINING-ROOM

A QUIET GAME IN THE BILLIARD-ROOM

Figure 6. The Ladies' Army and Navy Club, *Graphic*, March 1908 (by permission of the British Library, shelf mark LD 46).

the organization of power in English society. Nothing represents this point more than a joke made in response to the Lyceum Club's opening in 1904. The Lyceum was the first club to establish itself within the boundaries of male clubland, opening in a Piccadilly mansion that had been occupied by the male Imperial Service Club. One reporter betrayed his anxiety that women had established an outpost in the public sphere by commenting that on the day the Lyceum opened men could be seen "from the windows of the eleven other clubs on Piccadilly . . . with shocked faces. . . . First Dover Street, now Piccadilly, what would the women conquer next?"[132] According to one of its historians, "Piccadilly was and still is a male street. . . . Its shops do not cater overmuch for ladies. But for men there is much. . . . The men of this country had walked along Piccadilly since the Empire had begun."[133] Whether or not this popular historian is correct in his assessment of Piccadilly, he captured the prevailing perception of the street at the time that the Lyceum Club opened. The members of the Lyceum had not simply moved into Piccadilly; they had migrated into a citadel of masculinity, the Imperial Service Club. Lyceum members were accomplished in the arts, science, and related professions. They traveled the world and advanced the cause of feminism. They literally inhabited male space and the more abstract masculine public sphere.

In the epilogue to her study of single middle-class women during this period, Martha Vicinus argued that clubs were not popular with many women because they were regarded as too public, as permitting unregulated socializing.[134] This view fails to consider, however, that middle- and upper-class women founded and joined clubs because they could forge new social ties and maintain old ones in a relatively exclusive environment. Married women with limited disposable income probably made the most use of their clubs. Living in small suburban houses, they could still entertain and socialize within their clubhouses.[135] These institutions never served the numbers of patrons that restaurants, tea shops, and department stores could accommodate. Intricate rules and hefty fees allowed clubs to maintain a degree of class distinction that mass entertainments seemed to deny.[136] Clubs thus reaffirmed class-based identities and contributed to the growth and status of a new female professional class.

When Linton railed against these dangerous modern experiments, she recognized that clubs promoted consumerism, feminism, and other facets of female public life. They produced class and gender identities within an urban, nondomestic setting. They remained an aspect of women's political culture—feminist and antifeminist alike—but were also a component of women's leisure. They grew from a feminist critique of a male-oriented city, but eventually became fashionable venues for socially ambitious women and wayward shoppers. And yet they asked women to combine shopping with other rational public activities such as debating the suffrage or tariff reform. Some clubs helped create a community of women, while others helped legitimize heterosocial amusement. They all made a place for women in the urban center. In doing so, they intrinsically disrupted traditional gender hierarchies and abetted the growth of consumerism.

"Shopland Is My Club"

As women's clubs reinforced West End commercial culture, they eventually became almost inseparable from that culture. During the fin de siècle, caterers and retailers became aware that wealthy women were spending significant amounts of time and a good deal of money in their clubs. Many saw in London's West End clubhouses the ideal female space. They believed that if they could unravel the clubs' appeal, they could understand and redirect women's desires. By 1912, when the *Pall Mall Gazette* proclaimed that nearly every modern woman had her club, women were faced not with a lack but with an abundance of public institutions catering to their private needs. Retailers and caterers, whether large or small, male or female, nearly fell over themselves to win over the shopping public and eventually urged women to abandon clubs in favor of department stores, tea shops, restaurants, and hotels. These entrepreneurs relied upon but then shifted the image of urban women and urban space that feminists had in part initiated.

Clubwomen believed they were providing an alternative to the shops, but drapers saw clubs as a complement to their businesses. The drapers' press, for example, charted the history of what they perceived as shoppers' resorts. For example, in 1894 the *Drapers' Record* noted the opening of the Tea and Shopping Club and jokingly proposed that by "providing for the comfort and convenience of ladies visiting the West End for shopping or other purposes," this club demonstrated that "woman came into a further square foot of her rights."[137] In other words, these retailers admired clubs as institutions that would guarantee women's right to shop. While this bit of trade press humor undermined the struggle for women's emancipation, it also points to the subtle way in which feminist discourses and institutions became embedded in mainstream commercial culture. Drapers aided female autonomy in the public realm when this independence would lead to the advancement of consumerism.

Just as the drapery press had admiringly followed the Universal Provider's history, it also scrutinized the conveniences that the female clubs sold to West End ladies. After clubs were no longer seen as socially daring, dangerous, or even feminist, shopkeepers used these luxurious and glamorous female institutions to lure women into their stores. Some, like Harrod's, Selfridge's, and Whiteley's included ladies' clubs and advertised that their stores freely offered clublike amenities. In 1905, for example, Harrod's announced that its "new ladies' club" was "undoubtedly the most handsome room of its kind in the world." Of course, it was an ideal "rendezvous . . . or resting place where the weary shopper may recuperate."[138] Gordon Selfridge borrowed from and then belittled women's clubs with a vengeance when he opened his new Oxford Street store in 1909. This monumental shop included female and male clubs whose decor, menus, and services were modeled after both English and American women's clubs.[139] Indeed, the Pioneer's "silence room" was nearly twenty years old when Selfridge introduced this "innovation." Memories were short, however, especially when Selfridge's advertisements were explicitly telling women to "give up" their clubs "in favour of Selfridges . . . since Selfridges gives you everything the Club does with lots of things it does not begin to do."[140] Selfridge incorporated the female club within the space and the meaning of the department store, thereby assimilating the women's club within its expansive domain.

As we will see in chapter 5, the mainstream press adopted many of Selfridge's arguments and his vision of the department store. Newspapers and magazines subverted clubs by explaining that shops freely provided a clublike atmosphere and amenities to all women. The *Pall Mall Gazette*, for example, reported on the war between clubs and shops in 1909 in an article entitled "Shopland Is My Club." This piece praised clubs for having encouraged "women's desire for comfort," but then sided with the shops for selling similar luxuries at affordable prices. "From the feminine standpoint," this article explained, "London is a veritable cradle of ease. Indeed, ever since the establishment of Ladies Clubs, women have refused to exist under any conditions other than those that minister to their comfort." The author credited women's clubs, then, for comforting women in the urban center and for "show[ing] what women really want, and what they count as essential to their comfort and their well-being." By looking to the clubs, shopkeepers "had begun to fully grasp . . . what irresistibly appeals to the fair sex." The Edwardian West End appeared so appealing to the fair sex that this author could write that "the whole of London's shopping centres, from Knightsbridge to Tottenham-court Road, has of late been transformed into a vast feminine club, run on a gigantic scale, that caters for a universal and unlimited membership."[141] By 1909, shopland and clubland were interchangeable territories of female pleasure, or so they now seemed. Female clubs had moved from being outposts in a hostile and barren urban frontier to symbolizing the commercial metropolis. And yet symbolic centrality did not guarantee long-term stability.

During this era, almost every imaginable West End business seemed to want to satisfy the female shopping public. The tea shop grew dramatically in the first years of the twentieth century largely because it successfully captured the shopping public. Many of these tearooms, especially those owned and managed by women, offered clublike conveniences in the heart of the West End. New Bond Street was a particularly popular location for female-owned and -managed tea shops.[142] The Ladies Tea Association, for example, opened its first "charming" shop there in the midnineties.[143] At about the same time, the female-managed Studio Afternoon Tea Rooms were established for "visitors from the country and other ladies who cannot afford the luxury of a club."[144] Down the street, Mrs. Robertson's tea shop served refreshments, but also allowed patrons use of a library, reading room, and "smoking balcony."[145] Nearby in Mortimer Street, a former Girton graduate opened "The Dorothy," a women's only restaurant, in 1888 to serve workers, students, and "weary" shoppers (fig. 7).[146]

The clubs' most significant rival, however, was not the female-owned tea or dining room, but the chains that quickly became a feature of everyday life in early-twentieth-century Britain. The Aërated Bread Company (known as the A.B.C.)

Figure 7. The Dorothy Restaurant, *Lady*, January 1889 (by permission of the British Library, shelf mark LD 51).

and Joseph Lyon's tea shops started in the 1880s and 1890s, but expanded at a phenomenal rate thereafter. Montague Gluckstein and Joseph Lyons began what is still a multinational corporation by opening a tea shop in Piccadilly in 1894. Within two years their company owned seventeen shops and by 1939 there were two hundred in London alone. By 1909, Lyons claimed to serve over 300,000 customers daily at his various shops and restaurants.[147] A similar story could be told about the American-born entrepreneur who began Fuller's confectionery shops with a small store in Regent Street in 1888.[148] Although tea shops also served men, those in the West End relied heavily upon the custom of the female shopping public. The *Bayswater Chronicle*, ever vigilant about the indulgences of shoppers, reported in 1899 that the recent increase in "the number of tea rooms that have been added in Westbourne Grove, Porchester Road and High-Street Kensington, are very strong evidence that shopping is an exhausting enterprise."[149]

In 1893, the *Queen* published a cartoon that caricatured the many pleasures of "Shopping." Though it satirized many shops and shoppers, it centered upon the tea shop. The caption read: "Perhaps the pleasantest part of shopping. Meeting one's brother and a friend and dropping in to a confectioner's for tea" (fig. 8).[150] Here the tea shop is certainly gratifying shoppers' appetites. Just as Eliza Linton's and William Whiteley's enemies had feared, commercial culture was becoming associated with a new type of heterosexual culture in which young men and women could flirt without fear of the watchful eye of the Victorian chaperon. Chapter 6 will focus on the development of heterosexual consumerism during this

Figure 8. Satire of shoppers and shopping, *Queen*, June 1893 (by permission of the British Library, shelf mark LD 45).

period, but here it is important to note that clubs were partly responsible for introducing the idea of public dining and a greater degree of informality between the sexes. Heterosocial amusement became most closely associated, however, with the restaurants and large hotels that became fashionable during the Edwardian period. Restaurant dining became a fashionable pastime after the Savoy Hotel opened in the Strand in 1889. Its owner choose Cesar Ritz as the main chef, since Lily Langtry advised him that "Ritz will attract the ladies." The hotel also established a rule that unescorted women were not permitted. Likewise, the Trocadero had a written code that excluded "strange ladies" from being admitted when they were alone or in pairs.[151] Of course, a male diner could invite any companion without trouble. Once prostitutes plied their trade less openly, the catering industry constructed their own vision of history, which asserted that the large, modern restaurant and hotel had emancipated women and introduced a new moral tone into public life. For example, a promotional booklet published in 1900 proudly if inaccurately claimed that "it seems scarcely credible that until the Savoy Restaurant was opened . . . there was not a single restaurant in all London where a man could take his wife or daughter."[152] A pamphlet printed in connection with the opening of Joseph Lyons's Trocadero Restaurant prefigured Foucault's formulation of repression and the production of desire. Lyons was venerated as the champion of "free trade in pleasure":

> My experience teaches me that restraints, checks, and grandmotherly legislation in connection with amusement have always encouraged vice and vicious pleasures; whereas free trade in pleasure has been of an enormous advantage, socially, intellectually, and morally, to the people at large. In this good, healthy want, Joseph Lyons and his friends have been spirited pioneers.[153]

The narrative that the mass market had initiated a modern notion of public life based on the "free trade in pleasure" quickly entered Edwardian popular culture and has become a truism of much recent historiography.[154] Yet restaurant and hotel proprietors, department store magnates, journalists, and clubwomen had been making much the same argument in slightly different forms since the 1860s.

Nonetheless, by 1900 quite a few observers believed that because they sold heterosocial pleasures, restaurants were leading to the decline of the single-sex club.[155] In 1906, a well-known gourmand wrote, "The restaurants have done more towards killing the clubs than any other species . . . [and] the gentler sex have indirectly assisted. . . . Ladies can and do dine at the restaurants to-day . . . and the man of gallantry gives his dinners where ladies can be part of the party."[156] In contrast to the leisure industry, class-specific and single-sex institutions increasingly appeared out of date, unfashionable, and simply boring. Even feminists no longer found clubs the thrilling institutions that they had once been. Although the suffragist Adelaide Drummond had so enjoyed her club in the 1870s, in 1909 she wrote that "the necessity for them, which existed at the time of their introduction has passed away." They met a particular need in later Victorian London, when "it was hardly possible for women to frequent restaurants; and no shops had tea-rooms, reading-rooms, and lounges."[157] This attitude, especially within the feminist community, contributed to the slow decline of female clubland during and after the First World War. Although some clubs like the Lyceum did quite well until the 1930s, most had trouble riding out hard times.[158] As the Lyceum went into liquidation in 1933, the receiver reported that its subscription had been too low to maintain its services and to pay the high charges for rent and rates. When its membership dropped during the Depression, the Lyceum could no longer raise funds to cover its debts.[159]

Despite its remarkable success, female clubland all but disappeared by the 1930s. The expansion of mass catering and entertainment, the declining financial position of the middle and upper classes, and the shifting nature of feminism contributed to its ultimate failure. Its demise was also a testament to the changing conceptions of and attitudes toward modernity. Although the clubs were once at the forefront of social change, by the early-twentieth century they represented the past. As heterosocial and cross-class interactions became the hallmark of modern urban life, single-sex institutions like clubs looked like a throwback from the age of separate spheres.

Women wayfarers, however, no longer lacked resting places in the city. Establishments that served their bodily needs were everywhere, and many were among England's most successful businesses. These enterprises had begun in the 1860s and 1870s when local government, philanthropic groups, feminist organizations, and entrepreneurs each tried to construct female public places. Though governmental efforts met with little success, the feminist community effectively built public spaces for the urban woman. Once established, however, they met with a good deal of competition from the department store, tea shop, hotel and restaurant. Feminists must take some of the blame for this development, since they encouraged women to shop and had frequently argued that clubs were the perfect shopper's resort. Department stores, hotels, and other mass caterers responded by advertising their manifest superiority to the club.

Urban women both gained and lost with this expansion of commercial "resting places." They certainly were no longer thwarted from exploring the metropolis because they could not find a place to eat or rest. Yet their public identities had in some ways narrowed. The numbers of women working and visiting London continued to grow, but the vision of shopping and the possibilities of public life became slightly more restricted. In the clubhouse, shoppers interacted with workers, listened to or participated in debates, and became involved in what Cobbe believed was a wider public sphere. In "Shopland Is My Club," female participation in public life and club culture was relegated to the sphere of consumption.

Entrepreneurs and advertisers did not single-handedly collapse the diverse meanings of public life that had existed in the late- nineteenth century, however. As we will see in later chapters, feminists and other progressives continued to find ways to expand and complicate its meaning. However, the feminist community unwittingly played a role in the construction of modern commercial culture and its gendered meanings. Neither feminists nor conservative critics ever challenged the perception of the urban shopping crowd as a feminine entity. Clubwomen also upheld class-based hierarchies and helped ensure that the West End would retain its exclusivity even as many aristocratic and bourgeois families could no longer afford to live there. This made clubs seem less progressive and modern than restaurants or department stores, which were championed as caterers to the millions.

• CHAPTER FOUR •

Metropolitan Journeys: Shopping, Traveling, and Reading the West End

> The Summer of 1895 was remarkable for the number of Americans who visited England; it was estimated that at least two hundred thousand were in London. . . . [T]ourists could be counted by scores along Piccadilly, thronging the shops in Oxford and Regent Streets, and wandering through the National Gallery, St. Paul's and Westminster . . . the women beautifully dressed consulting the inevitable Baedeker.[1]

THIS PORTRAIT of beautifully dressed American tourists gazing at a Baedeker-inflected metropolis, "thronging" the shops, and "wandering" through museums and other repositories of England's public memory could easily have described a summer afternoon in London of the 1990s. It was, however, the impression of Mary Krout, an American who published her memories of the English capital city in 1899 under the aptly chosen title *A Looker On in London*. Three urban types—the consumer, the writer, and the reader—populated Mary Krout's London. This chapter follows these three spectators as they travel through the late-Victorian and Edwardian metropolis, a city defined by looking and traveling, reading and writing, shopping and sightseeing. As the title of Krout's book implies, fin de siècle London was often understood as spectacle, marketplace, and commodity. Its shops, museums, and even its churches made it ripe for colonization by foreign consumers, especially female Americans. Tourists, like shoppers, sought "new" experiences, wanted to see "old" Europe, and wished to purchase "unique" objects. They were also a part of the urban spectacle. Even Krout described the "beautifully dressed" tourist as a site to be looked at and enjoyed.

Clubwomen had viewed these urban travelers not as spectators or spectacle but as speakers, writers, and readers. At the center of nearly every club was a reading room fully stocked with books, newspapers, feminist journals, and fashion periodicals. Many clubwomen made their living as writers and editors and were especially prominent in the feminist press and the "ladies' papers." Clubs aided this community of writers who, in turn promoted female-oriented metropolitan institutions.[2] As we have already seen, many of these journalists created a positive image of the women's club and similar venues. This effort was part of a wider move, as we will see in this chapter, to develop a new genre of urban literature directed at the female middle classes. At the same time that the clubs, department stores, restaurants, and other resting places appeared in the streets of the West End, women's magazines, guidebooks, and the daily papers offered female readers a way of imagining themselves enjoying and mastering this built environment.

Similar forces produced both this spectacular city and a new form of middle-class women's work. During the late 1880s and 1890s, a group of bourgeois women sought to professionalize their urban expertise by forming a business called the Lady Guide Association. This group's goal was to expand the employment opportunities for newly educated but unemployed middle-class women by hiring and training them as professional shoppers and urban guides. These Lady Guides would then navigate uneducated tourists and shoppers through modern London. After the 1880s, then, several new forms of urban guidance became available to bourgeois women. Each promised to make the commercial city intelligible and pleasurable.

During this period guidebooks and newspapers, works of fiction, history, and social science presented many, often contradictory visions of the metropolis. Judith Walkowitz has shown, for example, that by the mid-1880s the more visible political and physical presence of working men and all classes of women in the wealthy districts of the city had led to a proliferation of urban narratives in which class and gender could no longer be understood in a straightforward manner. Neat divisions between a dark, poor, and sinister East End and a glittering and wealthy West End gave way to more complex readings of the city. Walkowitz has argued, however, that the dominant narrative during this period was one of social crisis and class and gender conflict.[3] Indeed, in the 1880s West End complacency was quite literally shattered as the unemployed struck its plate-glass windows and demonstrated in its streets. One middle-class commentator, noting the encampment of unemployed men in the West End in October of 1886, captured the sense of crisis when he wrote, " 'The finest site in Europe,' had been turned into a 'foul camp of vagrants.' "[4] A few years earlier, Irish nationalists had set off bombs in the Local Government Board Offices, the Underground, Victoria Station, and even Scotland Yard.[5] The anxieties of the English populace eventually centered upon the frightening figure of Jack the Ripper stalking and mutilating East End prostitutes in the autumn of 1888. At the same time, the separate spheres of bourgeois gender ideology were being repeatedly crossed by feminists and dandies in London's streets and in the works of Wilde, Ibsen, Gissing, Stevenson, and the New Woman authors.[6]

Social investigations, newspaper exposés, novels, and personal forays into the slums of Victorian London forced the middle classes to see the problems of urban industrial society and to hear the "bitter cry of outcast London."[7] Journalists such as W. T. Stead publicized a metropolis that embodied class, gender, and racial difference, social decay, and urban crisis. As Walkowitz has shown, Stead's bifurcated image of urban women as either dangerous or endangered served to contain women's newfound independence. After reading Stead's exposés in the *Pall Mall Gazette*, for example, one woman remembered that "parents became conscious that they had not realized how wicked the world was, and here were their daughters going into the danger zones with a new independence."[8] Yet while parents were reading about "modern Babylon" in the daily papers, female readers also encountered tales in the pages of fashion magazines and feminist journals of dauntless heroines who safely and fashionably traveled alone in the city. While in certain texts London seemed to devour daughters, other facets of the media presented young women as at home in and even in control of the city. This was not just an alternative vision—rather, the dangerous and glamorous cities were intersecting and building each other.

Middle-class women played two roles in the glamorous metropolis. They acted the part of the voyeur who traveled in, gazed at, and wrote about the urban spectacle. They were also among the desirable objects on display in this marketplace. George Gissing presented both figures in several novels, but Nancy Lord, the heroine of *In the Year of Jubilee* (1894), best captured this duality. A resolutely modern girl, Nancy begged her old-fashioned father to allow her to celebrate the Queen's Jubilee, to "go about" London's "main streets—to see the people and the illuminations." She rejected her father's prohibitions and plunged herself into urban life, roaming the "imperial" West End, wandering London's "highways" as they "reeked and roared in celebration of Jubilee."[9] After abandoning her companions, her "sense of freedom soon overcame anxieties." Nancy thus participated in a festival of civic, national, imperial, and commodity culture. While walking London's streets, she celebrated Victoria's reign, England's hegemonic imperial status, and her own independence. Gissing's mixed feelings about the urban crowd, women's independence, and the spectacle soon rose to the surface, nevertheless, with this characterization of Nancy as she wanders the streets alone: "Nancy forgot her identity, lost sight of herself as an individual. She did not think, and her emotions differed little from those of any shop-girl let loose. The 'culture,' to which she laid claim, evanesced in this atmosphere of exhalations. Could she have seen her face, its look of vulgar abandonment would have horrified her."[10]

George Gissing and Mary Krout both dramatized the ambiguous position of the single urban woman during a period when dozens of outposts had been built in the name of her pleasure, comfort, safety, and improvement. This chapter will consider how this female figure and her city materialized in the mid- and late-Victorian women's press, especially in expensive "ladies' papers" such as the *Queen* and the *Lady*. These journals sought to normalize urban women's position by keeping them from making spectacles of themselves. Magazines and the Lady Guide Association promised to chaperon women through a pleasant, organized, and enticing urban realm. After the turn of the century, mass-produced shopping guides and women's pages in the large daily newspapers sold similar guidance at prices working- and lower-middle-class pleasure seekers could afford.[11]

Women's magazines and the Lady Guides invented an "authentic" London of churches, royal palaces, and other features of what might be labeled the "historical" city.[12] They also asked readers and visitors to purchase a "modern" London of restaurants, clubs, theaters, and department stores.[13] The historical and modern cities merged, however, into one compelling consumer-oriented experience. Tourists and shoppers alike wandered through, looked at, and purchased London's offerings. Yet while licensing female independence in the commercial city, these guides also managed the city and its inhabitants, rationalizing consumption and consumers. Magazines told ignorant and frightened female shoppers that by following prescribed routes, visiting the right places, and consuming the correct goods they could remake themselves as skilled consumers. They could learn to avoid the ruses of wily merchants and the attentions of male pests, and travel effortlessly through a metropolis that catered to their every want. Reading, looking, and shopping converged in this metropolitan journey. Shopping was written as urban exploration and visual pleasure, as consuming goods and experiencing an ideal London.[14] Ladies' magazines and Lady Guides rewrote women's urban vision and the vision of urban women. They created the *flâneuse,* a female urban stroller who was at home in the city, who enjoyed walking in and writing about the urban crowd and the city's shops. Her journey may be identified as one of "the new stories of the city" that, Judith Walkowitz has suggested, "competed, intersected with, appropriated, and revised the dominant imaginative mappings of London."[15] This narrative stimulated consumption, encouraged an urban sensibility, and supported bourgeois political and social ascendancy while it rewrote women's place in the social and cultural life of the metropolis.

The Women's Press and Consumer Culture

Like the department store, women's magazines were the product of and the showcase for the fruits of England's industrializing and free-trade economy. They were also sites of cultural production, generating class, gender, and national identities while selling goods and fashionable lifestyles. In contrast to the department store, however, the women's press was also a public forum in which concerns associated with consumerism and the tense social relations that accompanied modern urban life could find expression. In letters and editorials on shopping, kleptomania, and women's debts, for example, a mild critique of consumption emerged alongside its promotion. The women's press was then a commodity and advertisement, a venue for consumption and its criticism.

Recent scholarship has stressed the crucial role women's magazines played in constituting the female reader as a consumer.[16] Christopher Breward, for example, has written that the late-Victorian fashion press created and sustained an "intensified consumer literacy" among middle- and lower-middle-class women, acting as "detailed and comprehensive guide[s] to the range of fashionable goods available."[17] Journals did not treat consumption and femininity in precisely the same manner, however. The class level of the intended readership, for example, influenced editorial approaches to the topic of consumption. Women's papers kindled the flames of consumer desire, but they did not do so all in the same manner or in a straightforward fashion. Products of multiple authors and readers, they generated contradictory images of women and consumer culture. Advertising, fashion plates, fiction, and editorials projected a range of femininities in addition to that of consumer, and even that identity had many faces.[18] Whatever their differences from one another, however, magazines advanced the expansion of consumerism because they addressed the female reader as a consumer.[19] They all promised readers that buying and reading magazines could improve their "natural" femininity.

Women readers were trained, then, to browse deftly through magazines, the shops, and the urban realm.

In many ways, female periodicals grew from a set of circumstances similar to those which had given rise to the department store. Although journals that directly targeted the female reader appeared first in the eighteenth century, technological, economic, cultural, and social changes inspired a tremendous expansion of the genre during the second half of the nineteenth century. Scholars have estimated that somewhere between 50 and 120 new women's magazines were founded between 1880 and 1900.[20] As in newspaper and journal publishing generally, this growth was sparked by the removal of the advertisement and stamp duties in 1853 and 1855 and the taxes on paper and rags in 1860 and 1861. Compulsory education, the mechanization of paper making, type casting, and typesetting as well as the introduction of fast rotary presses and increased advertising revenue laid the foundation for a press that catered to the "millions."[21]

The *Queen* stood out as one of the success stories in this competitive world of female periodical publishing. Never the most widely read, it was the most prestigious of the women's papers.[22] In September of 1861 Samuel Beeton founded the journal with Frederick Greenwood's help as editor. Beeton and his wife, Isabella, had been extremely successful with their earlier publication, the *Englishwoman's Domestic Magazine*, a two-penny monthly that Cynthia White has labeled the "first 'cheap' magazine to be produced for women of the middle classes."[23] With the *EDM*'s notes on cookery, fashion, and household management—many of which were written by Isabella—its serialized fiction, and "Practical Dress Instructor," a forerunner of the paper dress pattern, its circulation peaked at about fifty thousand by 1860.[24] Flushed with his good fortune, Beeton launched the *Queen*, a sixpenny illustrated "class" weekly for ladies. Beeton announced in the prospectus that the magazine would be for "educated women what certain high-class journals are for men—recording and discussing from week to week whatever interests or amuses them." It would therefore include "a large number of original articles on the daily life of society . . . on books, music and the theatre . . . [on] amusements which ladies most pursue, at home and abroad . . . and on *la mode*."[25] Beeton believed that this mix of "news" and entertainment would appeal to a readership of comfortably well off middle- and upper-class "ladies."[26]

For all periodicals, however, there was always a gap between the intended audience and the actual readership. Price, layout, and content partly influenced a magazine's market. It was also quite common for domestic servants and dressmakers to read hand-me-down issues. Quite a few men also read such journals. For example, Charles Cavers, an elite Bond Street dressmaker, recalled that in the early- twentieth century he read the fashion press, including the *Lady* and *Vogue*, to see what his buyers were reading and wearing.[27] Readers would obviously have approached these texts differently. If some picked up the *Queen* to read about the world they inhabited, others would have seen a utopian realm far removed from their everyday experiences. All readers, nonetheless, would have been influenced by the way in which these texts presented consumption and femininity. At base, papers were directed at a female readership united by their supposedly natural inclination to consume goods, so that despite the many ways in which class differences appeared in these texts, gender was always fundamental and shaped by and through one's relationship to goods.

Like other ladies' papers, the *Queen* glorified women's role in the domestic sphere by cultivating an elite version of the Angel in the House. The first issue, for example, assured readers that "When we write for Women we write for Home." Greenwood explained, "We shall offend very few when we say that women have neither heart nor head for abstract political speculation. . . . Therefore our survey of foreign affairs, and of politics generally, will be recorded in a few notes."[28] That being said, the journal did report on public issues, including international, national, and feminist politics. The "Notes of the Week for Ladies," for example, reminded "ladies" that although they were not and should not become members of Parliament, "that is no reason why they should not take an interest in its proceedings," and applauded the attentive female spectators who frequented both houses of Parliament.[29] If its famous fashion plates and advertisements illustrated a corseted and crinolined female body, the *Queen* also followed this woman as she voyaged abroad, visited countless public amusements, and investigated the homes of Spitalfield's silk weavers.[30]

This mixture of domestic advice and public affairs did not initially prove profitable, however. Within a year, Beeton sold the magazine to Edward William Cox, a barrister who had already acquired more than a dozen "class" periodicals.[31] Greenwood went on to found and edit the *Pall Mall Gazette*, in which, before W. T. Stead took over as editor, he introduced the sensational exposés that became synonymous with the journal and the New Journalism.[32] After Greenwood's departure, Cox chose "a lady" editor. Although her identity remained anonymous, as was the common practice, Helen Lowe filled the post from 1862 until 1894. The daughter of the dean of Exeter, Lowe had published poetry and two anonymous travel books that narrated the adventures of "Unprotected Females" in Scandinavia and Italy. After she came onboard, Lowe continued to write this genre in serialized form, beginning a series in 1862 entitled "An Unprotected Female's Tour in Switzerland, or A Lady's Walk across the Sheideck and Wengern Alps."[33] Probably due to Lowe's influence, the image of the spunky female wanderer braving the elements was a regular feature of the journal. She spent more time traveling in the city, however, than she did abroad.

A tradition of anonymity makes it difficult to identify all of the *Queen*'s authors, though those we do know about were among the top-ranking names in Victorian and Edwardian journalism.[34] Edmund Yates, one of the pioneers of the new journalism, wrote as "the Lounger" for the *Illustrated Times*, "the Flâneur" in the *Morning Star*, and "Mrs. Seaton" in the *Queen*.[35] As "Jack Easel," Charles Locke Eastlake authored a series of twenty articles in the late sixties that were the basis of his immensely popular *Hints on Household Taste in Furniture, Upholstery and Other Details*. Mrs. M. E. Haweis, Dorothy Peel, Eliza Davis, and Mrs. Talbot Coke, and even Eliza Linton also contributed to the journal's fortunes. These authors helped the magazine gain what Peel called "great prestige," causing "Advertisers [to] humbly ask for space in the paper."[36]

The women's press was not unlike the women's clubs in that it served as a home of sorts for both progressive and conservative writers. Female authors were not as well paid as male journalists, and few became editors in their own right, but especially after the 1880s the magazines provided a source of income for educated women at time when few other options existed. Peel, who described herself as a Tory in favor of women's equality, eventually earned as much as eight hundred pounds a year as editor of the journal's household department.[37] Her colleague, Mary Haweis, was deeply involved in progressive politics. Haweis was an active clubwoman, worked for the franchise and the advancement of women, and held a salon with her husband, the Reverend Haweis, in their Welbeck Street home.[38] The women's papers aided the expansion of this diverse but growing female professional class. These women in turn clearly stimulated the expansion of the press.[39]

The *Queen*'s achievement excited others to launch similar periodicals during the latter part of the century. Thomas Gibson Bowles began the *Lady* in 1885, for "women of education," with the assertion that it would "cover the whole field of womanly action."[40] It included the same mixture of fashion advice, fiction, society gossip, household management, and female pastimes that the *Queen* had blended into a successful production. Bowles also added features on middle-class women's work and hired "a barrister" to write the "Law for Ladies" column. Readers could glean investment advice from "Spare Money" and parliamentary news in "From the Ladies Gallery." In 1886 the journal instituted a "Purchase Agency" that would shop for readers for a 5 percent commission.[41] One could also buy and sell old clothing through "*The Lady* Exchange and Sale Column" or find paid work through the journal's "Employment Column." In 1895 a new female editor, Rita Shell, transformed the journal from a "class" journal into a mass-market magazine. She increased the journal's circulation in part by dropping "public" topics such as parliamentary and legal news and adding more features on cooking, fashion, household management, and romance.[42]

During the same period, explicitly feminist periodicals such as the *Englishwoman*, edited by Ella Hepworth Dixon, also published news about women's work, politics, and consumption. Women's pages in the daily press similarly blended consumption and politics. The "Woman's World" column in the *St. James Gazette*, for example, covered all of these subjects in just one day in 1893: children's party dresses, children's yoke styles, a charitable sale run by the Princess of Wales and the duchess of Teck, crystallized party decorations, announcement of the 1894 Woman's Suffrage calendar, the annual report of the Women's Trade Union Association, and, finally, a recipe for German Chocolate Cake.[43] Politics were integrated into the everyday life of the middle-class woman, as the fight for the suffrage and search for a good chocolate cake recipe both belonged to the "woman's world."[44]

Though progressive politics were advertised in such mainstream journals, many women's magazines presented women's politics as naturally conservative, royalist, and imperialist. These journals sought their own legitimacy and a wide readership, in part, by allying themselves with the monarchy and the empire. Female periodicals even implied that improvements in middle-class women's employment, education, political rights, and consumption aided the project of empire building.[45] In constructing an elite feminine "English" identity, for example, Bowles guaranteed that "*The Lady* will be essentially English. It will be written in the English tongue; and the subjects to be dealt with will be treated from an English point of view, and with reference to the necessities of the English method of life, the English genius, and the English character, habits, and customs."[46] When the *Gentlewoman* was founded in 1890 its editor similarly declared that although it "knows no party politics . . . [it] is Royal, Loyal, and Constitutional."[47] The *Queen*'s title and its cover emblem illustrating Windsor Castle also marked it as royal and loyal. At times, then, these magazines blatantly asserted that women's public presence sustained English national traditions and imperial preeminence. These commodities, of course, also served as handmaidens to England's economy and consumer culture. Despite their many differences, virtually all these magazines relied upon and aided the growth of the advertising and fashion industries, while their layout and content constituted readers as consumers.

"The Best Exhibition in This Modern Babylon"

From its inception the *Queen* devoted a good deal of attention to London. In contrast to magazines directed toward a solidly middle- or lower-middle-class audience, the *Queen* spent relatively less time with "the minutiae of family relationships" than with the minutiae of the commercial metropolis.[48] In doing so, it addressed the reader as both a shopper and urban explorer whose territory was primarily, though not exclusively, the West End. In this text, shopping, traveling, and reading became "modern" activities that mapped class, gender, sexual, and national identities onto the spaces of Victorian London.

In its first issues in the 1860s, the *Queen* represented the city through the eyes of the *flâneur*, an observer and stroller whose home was the streets and arcades of the European metropolis, who made a living "botanizing on the asphalt."[49] As Raymond Williams and others have observed, the *flâneur* has most often been characterized as "a man walking, as if alone, in its [the modern city's] streets."[50] By the 1860s, however, one could no longer assume that modern stroller and writer was masculine. While many an English *flâneur* ventured to the East End of London and represented it as an unknown territory, a dark continent, a place of study and reform, in the 1860s the *Queen* turned this rambler westward and changed his sex. As a sightseeing tourist, browsing shopper, and magazine reader, this *flâneuse* charted a spectacular West End of commercial pleasures. She consumed London through what Anne Friedberg has identified as a commodified, mobilized, and ephemeral gaze.[51]

Feminist scholars have debated whether and how women could achieve a real or imagined position as *flâneuse*. Some have maintained that middle-class women's exclusion from public space meant that the literature and painting of modern life represented a wholly masculine perspective. Griselda Pollock, for example, has written that the *flâneur* symbolized "the privilege or freedom to move about the public arenas of the city observed but never interacting, consuming the sights through a controlling but rarely acknowledged gaze. The *flâneur* embodies the gaze of modernity which is both covetous and erotic." Like Williams, Pollock saw this figure as "an exclusively masculine type."[52] In Susan Buck-Morss's reading of Benjamin, the *flâneur* was also a masculine subject whose counterpart, the prostitute, was "the embodiment of objectivity, not subjectivity."[53] For these authors, modern urban relations were visual and sexual. Men gazed at women and women transformed themselves into objects to be looked at.[54] In this view, the *flâneuse* could not exist, not so much because she was literally barred from public life, but because when she went public she became the prostitute, a commodity, or object of the gaze.

Others, however, have shown that bourgeois women were "in public" and did actively construct a vision of modernity.[55] Moreover, their presence, as well as other economic, social, and cultural changes, destabilized the confident position of the *flâneur*. As Walkowitz writes, the scale and nature of urbanization turned the territory of the *flâneur* into "an unstable construct."[56] The forces that welcomed the bourgeois woman into the city thus threatened her male counterpart. Of course, the *flâneuse* was hardly a stable subject. As Deborah Nord has shown, quite a few middle- and upper-class women—including Elizabeth Gaskell, Flora Tristan, Beatrice Potter Webb, Margaret Harkness, and Amy Levy—adopted the persona of writer and urban observer. Their work was constrained, Nord writes, by their inability "to make themselves invisible and ignored," and by their consciousness of transgressing acceptable class and gender norms. Yet these authors placed a "female subject into a cultural and literary tradition that habitually relegate[d] her to the position of object, symbol, and marker."[57] When the *flâneuse* walked in and wrote about the Victorian streets, she stepped out of her proscribed role into male territory.

We have already seen that the history of the *flâneuse* was tied to the transformation of the commercial spaces of the metropolis. She appeared in the city's shopping streets, its clubs, restaurants, and department stores.[58] In some respects, these institutions and the *flâneuse* produced each other and were the consequence of similar economic, social, and cultural forces. The idea of the independent woman in the city emerged coterminous with, if not before, the department store, restaurant, or club. She took shape, for example, in Charlotte Brontë's peripatetic Lucy Snowe, who mastered London by achieving a bird's-eye view from the top of St. Paul's and then "wandered wither chance might lead," and "got into the heart of city life [and] saw and felt London at last."[59] Lucy's gaze was controlling, pleasurable, and mobile. She alternated between transporting her body through urban space and moving her gaze while remaining physically stationary. Lucy Snowe thus possessed the city through both a panoptic and panoramic gaze.[60] At the same time, women like Lucy also captured the attention of others. "Faces of Fortune," a columnist in Henry Mayhew's journal the *Shops and Companies of London* (1865), was both disgusted and delighted by the hordes of "pretty women of London" who "go out and see what is being worn." These women, however, in their "enraptured gazing, push[ed] and jostle[d] the philosopher most rudely, so that deep meditation" became "almost impossible." This *flâneur* then regained his countenance, concentration, and masculinity through his voyeuristic objectification of Oxford Street shoppers, commenting that "you may see more pretty faces in one hour than you would meet in any other country in a six months' voyage of discovery."[61] His voyeurism was thus in part a response to feeling "pushed" and "jostled" by the female crowd that had invaded his terrain.

William Whiteley had a somewhat different reaction to this female crowd. If "Faces of Fortune" achieved his masculinity by gazing lustfully at female shoppers, Whiteley did so by trying to take their, or at least their husband's, money. In 1863, the same year that Baudelaire published his famous essay "The Painter of Modern Life," the young Whiteley became a *flâneur* and roamed the streets of London in search of an appropriate location for his shop. Whiteley evidently settled upon Westbourne Grove after standing in the street one afternoon and counting a large number of prosperous female passersby.[62] Although he later claimed that he created this market, in some sense a market of wealthy women already wandered Bayswater's streets in the early 1860s. Whiteley characterized public women as consumers, not as the sexual objects that journalists like "Faces of Fortune" so desired. Whiteley's vision was nonetheless built upon notions of gender difference as he played the role of father/husband who protected and provided for these shoppers. He became the Universal Provider who built a home for urban women. William Whiteley, "Faces of Fortune," and Charlotte Brontë treated the *flâneuse* differently, but each reveals the very ambiguous relationship that these urban types had to the modern city and bourgeois culture.

Brontë's heroine most resembled the classic *flâneur*. Her London adventure came at a moment in which she was homeless and en route to France to find employment. Lucy Snowe was at home in the city precisely because, like the bohemian, she had no permanent place within bourgeois society.[63] She represents, then, the archetypal "*flâneur* . . . on the threshold, of the city as of the bourgeois class."[64] While her gaze attempts mastery and control of the city, her walking suggests her "lack" of a place.[65] Although Lucy Snowe stood on the periphery of bourgeois life, a very different vision of the *flâneuse* originated in the mid-Victorian women's magazine. The rest of this section will chart how the early issues of the *Queen* placed her at the center of the city and its bourgeois culture.

From its first issues in the 1860s, the *Queen* fashioned its readers as urban spectators and ramblers. It published numerous articles, probably written by male journalists, on London's shops, exhibitions, amusements, and streets. There were many ways the city could have been presented during this period, but the *Queen* most often described London as a great exhibition. This metaphor reflected the city's social, economic, and cultural geography, but it also drew upon older traditions in which London was conceived as the world's marketplace and the streets were seen as "democratic island[s]."[66] It also was a testament to the reflexive relationship between the Great Exhibition of 1851 and its 1862 sequel and the metropolis during these years.

During the 1860s, the *Queen* developed this metropolitan exhibition in many articles and editorials on London's topography, history, and public amusements.[67] These pieces delineated and circulated the meaning of the metropolis as a site of display that was theoretically free for anyone who sought to walk its streets. In 1861, for example, a two-part essay exploring the architectural and social history of Regent Street presented a panoramic vision of this delightful "lounge" through which "every variety of the human species passes and repasses along its broad and fair expanse."[68] The author of this series adopted the role of *flâneur,* explicitly expressing a "desire to lounge about the great thoroughfare in [an] aimless, wayward fashion. Glancing . . . at the triumphs of art and manufacture in the bright-coloured shop windows."[69] Two years later, the *Queen* again pictured this "roadway of Vanity Fair" as the "epitome of the world . . . [which was] better than any treatise on philosophy." In Regent Street, we are told that "each shop is a study," and again we hear that they represent, "the triumphs of art and manufacture."[70]

Not surprisingly, the 1862 International Exhibition garnered a great deal of the *Queen*'s attention. Numerous lengthy articles and detailed illustrations obsessively described the Exhibition halls' design and even published statistics on the feet of pipes, gutters, girders, and railings. Although architectural circles saw the South Kensington structure as one of the ugliest buildings in London, the magazine treated the exhibition spaces as a product of industrial genius, a symbol of the age of improvement.[71] The author of an 1866 article, "Shop Windows," published in the *Queen* simply regarded London's shops and its exhibitions as interchangeable, asking, "After all, what are the Great Exhibitions but a sort of collective window display?"[72] This upper-class women's magazine thus contributed to the development of what Tony Bennett had described as an "exhibitionary complex."[73]

In conceiving of the city as exhibition, the *Queen* viewed the West End as remarkably similar to the urban sketches of George Augustus Sala and the authors who published in Mayhew's *Shops and Companies of London.* Such "male" sketches provided an important model that female journalists followed. It is important to investigate briefly the common tropes and strategies these authors used to describe shops and shopping in these sketches, some of the most commonly cited sources on commercial London. Mid-Victorian journalists like Sala often emphasized how the aggregate of London's shop windows exhibited the products of a free trade and of an imperial and industrial economy.[74] Although the aristocracy patronized these shops, many journalists believed that London's emporiums, like the Great Exhibition, displayed bourgeois enterprise. Mayhew explained, for example, that his new journal was intended "not only [to] exalt work and manufacturing skill," but to "uphold the dignity of Trade itself," for English retailing was "the talk and marvel of Europe."[75] In one typical essay, West End shopping streets were said to be "bordered with gold, and bound on each side by glittering edges as rich as the jewels and precious ornaments fringing the costliest robe that ever a monarch wore." They were "the best exhibitions in this modern Babylon of ours . . . an endless source of pleasure . . . [an] ever-changing kaleidoscope of fancy and amusement."[76] Though described as jewels in a monarch's robe, the shops also had a democratic quality, since their windows could be freely enjoyed by anyone who chose to look. Another journalist similarly reported in the *Leisure Hour* in 1865 that "the shops of London in the aggregate constitute a museum which puts all others to scorn, and exhibit of a thousand things of general interest which are not to be found in the index of the cyclopedia."[77] Window shopping allowed one to read London as an encyclopedia, museum, or exhibition. It was not to be read as straightforward narrative, but as a "repository of knowledge."[78] In any order, though, London's shops represented capitalism and wealth. One oft-quoted author made this point by writing in 1864: "There are few people who have not been struck with the magnificence of the London shop-fronts. They form one of the most prominent indications of the grandeur and wealth of the metropolis."[79]

When writing about London's commercial culture, male journalists conveyed both their excitement about urban change and their ambivalence about their place in the city. G. A. Sala and his fellow male journalists constructed their "masculine" identities through their admiration of English productive skill, by ogling female shoppers, and by delineating between female shopping and male lounging. In typical fashion, one author who wrote about London's shops first had to tell his readers that he possessed a "horror of shopping. . . . My instincts in a manner react against it; and the result is that I rarely enter a shop." He dreaded "spending money over the counter," though his "lady friends" seemed to "take to shopping naturally, and really seem to revel in it."[80] Both sexes might look into shop windows, but only women were thought to want to go inside and buy something.

There were thus several spectators in such journalistic expeditions through the mid-Victorian West End. The *flâneur* gathered useful information about human psychology, bourgeois productivity, and retailing skill, while the female shopper became a desirable object who was seduced through her own consumerist gaze. And yet, while the shopper was seduced by goods, the *flâneur* had to protect himself from becoming overwhelmed by his desire for shoppers (fig. 9).[81] The *flâneur*'s opposition between rational and irrational, intellectual and sensual looking reflected the journalist's equivocal attitude toward consumption and vigilant maintenance of gender difference while he walked with women in the West End.

When wealthy women read such sketches they imagined themselves walking through the city, adopting the position of voyeur and thereby disrupting Victorian class and gender ideology. Nevertheless, their ramble also extolled bourgeois enterprise and maintained an image of women needing protection in the public realm. Indeed, female editors and journalists often placed themselves in the chaperon's role, ensuring that they would help readers have a safe and pleasurable journey through a respectable city. Female journalists, like their male counterparts, also displayed ambivalence toward the city and other ramblers. The *flâneuse* assuaged such feelings, however, by distancing herself from other urbanites, especially prostitutes, male workers, irrational wanderers, and ignorant shoppers.

If the prostitute was central to the *flâneur*'s pleasure, the *Queen* assumed that streetwalkers inhibited the pleasure and freedom of the *flâneuse*. Articles and edi-

Figure 9. "Christmas shopping in Regent Street," *Queen*, December 1893 (by permission of the British Library, shelf mark LD 45).

torials repeatedly called for the removal of "vice" from the theater, pleasure gardens, and other entertainments. Others directed readers toward safe and respectable areas of the city. In 1861 a column on public amusements, for example, observed that Cremorne Gardens were "now visited by ladies to whom the *demimonde* is quite unknown, and who indeed enter the pleasant grounds without necessarily coming into contact with that improper hemisphere."[82] Another happily noted that "the stage has improved," but still condemned some productions for "pandering to the lowest appetites of the lowest natures" and for "effacing the line between vice and virtue."[83] These articles simultaneously wrote about public amusements as dangerous and welcoming for elite women. They acknowledged the immoral trade that occurred in such settings but implied that reading the *Queen* would help "respectable" urban women avoid impropriety.[84]

Like male journalists, female authors often forged their autonomy in contrast to an ignorant or passive gaper. Among the journalists to do so was Lady Beatrice Violet Greville, who, in an 1880 essay "Shop-Windows," exhorted the English public to take up "that delightful amusement which the French call *flâneur*":

> In this busy and bustling city, where people seem scarcely to allow themselves time to breathe, much less to pursue that delightful amusement which the French call *flâneur* [*sic*], . . . few either care or dare to know its delights. Yet the student of human nature who walks about intent on seeing everything must inevitably discover a rich mine of wealth and solve one or two quaint psychological problems.[85]

Greville took readers with her as she walked through London's streets, looked in its shop windows, and contemplated the human behaviors that each window suggested. Like the writers of dozens of similar essays, she established an analogy between reading, walking, looking, and window shopping and turned author and reader each into a "student of human nature," able to "see everything" and "solve one or two quaint psychological problems." Reading shop windows while leisurely strolling through London afforded this *flâneuse*—as author and implied reader—the pleasure derived from comprehending humanity.

In "Shop-Windows," Greville opposed her own rational speculative gaze to that of a female shopper in front of a draper's window. In the middle of the essay, she condemns London's "merchant princes" for seducing women by stuffing the windows of their "huge palaces" with "lace trifles, gaudy ribbons, satins, delicate frills and confections and head dresses" and other "articles that sparkle and dangle and shine and attract." As she put it, the draper's window sings out to its victims: "Come and be dressed. . . . Come and put off your own individuality and put on the livery of your master, the despot of civilization—Fashion." Though the shopper's gaze was quite unlike the author's detached contemplative looking, the narrator, as if to stop her own seduction, hastily moves on. Then, quoting Hazlitt, she claims to have been "a silent spectator of the mighty scene of things, not an object of attention or curiosity in it; taking a thoughtful, anxious interest in what is passing, not feeling the slightest inclination to make or meddle in it."[86] "Shop-Windows" thus presented two modes of looking, one thoughtful and the other irrational, with the latter being associated with femininity and the fashion system. In Greville's essay, though, both of these lookers were female.

A frequent contributor to the women's press, Greville understood how hard it was for an urban woman to be "a silent spectator . . . not an object of attention or curiosity" in London's streets. In her memoirs she recalled her own discomfort while traveling alone through the West End. On these jaunts she remembered, "Men would often try to speak to one, but when they saw it was distasteful, generally gave it up."[87] This admission revealingly shows an ambivalent Greville acknowledging the threats to her freedom and proclaiming her own autonomy. As the author of "Shop-Windows," Greville constructed that autonomous persona in opposition to the uneducated, irrational, passionate shopper. Yet when she literally roamed London's streets, Greville could not avoid her own position as the object of a voyeuristic male gaze. She expressed, then, the dynamics of modern feminine identity as John Berger saw it; she is both the surveyor and the surveyed.[88]

By the time authors like Greville wrote about shopping and the urban center in the 1880s and 1890s, the West End was not the same place that it had been in the 1860s. New shopping centers such as Bayswater competed with older areas such as Regent and Bond Streets. Department stores, restaurants, clubs, and tea shops had joined smaller specialized shops and confectioners in the newer and older West End. A more complex and extensive system of public transport now brought a larger market of shoppers to the city; and, as Mary Krout had explained, many had come from as far afield as North America.

The fin de siècle West End and the women's press became both more diverse and more devoted to consumerism. As the city and urban crowd were being remade, the women's press was undergoing a similar transformation. By the mid-1880s, the *Queen* relied so heavily on advertising revenue that, according to Margaret Beetham, advertisements filled virtually half of its pages.[89] At the same time that the papers sought new ways to advocate consumerism, they also hired greater numbers of women journalists. Ironically, female writers made their way into the public sphere by selling a utopian commodified view of both the public and private spheres. Though, as Beetham explained, women's journals constructed the "female body out of commodities," they also represented that body as always on the move in the city.[90]

"Ballade of an Omnibus"

In the 1880s, journals like the *Queen* still described London as an exhibition, but they also presented it as a "real" feminine arena in which women wandered, worked, shopped, dined, and clubbed together. By and large, editors presumed that they were selling to a commuting, suburban, and provincial readership, basically the same women that William Whiteley and Frances Power Cobbe had hoped to serve. Since the expansion of the railway in the 1840s, W. H. Smith had instituted bookstalls in railway stations, making it his business to turn commuters into readers.[91] Newspaper and periodical publishers had likewise changed the form and content of their product for rapid superficial reading consistent with a less domestic lifestyle. Shorter articles and numerous illustrations became the hallmark of journals directed toward this traveling public. The act of reading as well as the nature of the reading public and its literature had altered with transformations in the nature of travel. The interplay between new lifestyles and new literature was not unidirectional, however. Women's magazines changed form to attract the attention of the commuting public, but they also attempted to turn female readers into riders.

Especially after the mid-1880s, magazines like the *Queen* and the *Lady* spent quite a bit of effort convincing women that they should ride London's trains, omnibuses, and Underground. This involved persuading readers that riding such conveyances was safe and respectable, that it was comfortable and easy, and that it could be a pleasurable and even poetic experience. It also required a challenge to the class prejudices that associated mass transport with the masses. Indeed, when retailers spoke of wealthy and aristocratic customers as "carriage trade," they were merely reiterating society's perception that there was a connection between class and conveyance. At the time that Dorothy Constance Peel started writing articles for Arnold Bennett's *Woman* in the 1890s, she remembered that "nice girls" from the suburbs were now going "about by themselves" and becoming "independent by the help of the train," but "grand ladies" still would have never ridden in an omnibus.[92] A lady's sexuality and her respectability, so closely linked with her social status, were also intertwined with how she traveled. Though times were changing, this was still an age when Society ladies and young women who ventured to the top of a 'bus or traveled alone in a hansom cab were thought to be "fast."[93]

Not only could she be considered "fast," but a woman who rode public transportation was also in danger of making a spectacle of herself. The *Saturday Review*, for example, continued its critique of the modern urban woman in 1881 with an article that lambasted female omnibus riders who were "going a-shopping" in the middle of the day. The author described these shoppers as "barbarians dressed in silk and sealskin" and as "the smiling cockatoo, all brown curls, fat cheeks, and velvet hat, who is going to buy things in Regent street." Somewhat bewildered, this writer wondered, "Who are they, these women, where do they come from? Have they husbands? Are there men in love with them? What are they like in the domestic circle, seeing they are so ill-bred, so rude, so incapable of common respect in public?"[94] The writer assumes female 'bus riders are shoppers, is disgusted by his/her proximity to this crowd of strangers, and clearly is worried by an inability to judge their character or social position. Outside of the domestic circle and dressed in silk and sealskin, these women assumed an anonymous identity. Such a view of the traveling woman as both ridiculous and dangerous competed, however, with the common belief that she placed herself in danger.

Throughout the second half of the century, the railway and other forms of public transport stirred anxieties about social mixing and the fast pace and disorder of modern life. According to Ben Singer, the illustrated and comic press in the United States popularized a frenetic and frightening portrait of public transport as symbolic of the chaotic nature of the modern urban environment.[95] In England as elsewhere, public transport was linked to the positive and negative sides of modernity. Trepidation about the changing nature of social relations and urbanization often focused on stories of assault and railway accidents. This was particularly true, according to Wolfgang Schivelbusch, after one brutal murder in a railway compartment in the 1860s. The private compartments common to British trains meant that travelers could be quite isolated. Railway companies made half-hearted attempts to provide female-only carriages, since female passengers were thought to be particularly vulnerable. The Board of Trade launched several investigations in which it considered but failed to do much about the security of the solitary female traveler.[96]

The ladies' papers considered the question of female safety in some detail, but nearly universally concluded that commuting was safe and respectable. When "A TRAVELLER" asked the *Lady* why English trains did not set aside "ladies only" compartments, the journal answered that this experiment had been tried in the early eighties, but had failed because women seemingly preferred to travel with men.[97] An 1887 leading article further proclaimed that "the risk which a woman incurs while travelling alone in England is almost infinitesimal. . . . At no period of our history has travelling been safer than it is now, and in no country perhaps is a woman more secure from insult."[98] The *Queen* dutifully reported assaults and robberies, but also asserted that "we conceive of the dangers of ladies travelling alone have been greatly overrated. . . . There is no doubt that a woman is much safer from assault or violence in a railway carriage than when walking alone on the street."[99] Moreover, the fashion press proposed that middle-class female travelers could avoid becoming the endangered heroines of Victorian melodrama. Armed with a consumer-oriented urban knowledge gained by reading magazines, one could evade the dangers and the discomforts associated with urban existence.

Women's journals tended to characterize public transport as a service that one should judge on the basis of efficiency, price, and comfort. Basically, these papers advocated that readers should make informed choices among a selection of possible products. Articles explored the pros and cons of London's tramways and omnibuses and the suburban and Underground railway systems. One editorialist, for example, complained in 1893 that waiting for or riding on London's suburban railways was a very uncomfortable experience.[100] A few months later, though, the journal reported that "ladies travelling alone" would find that carriage design was improving, and soon they could ride in complete comfort and privacy.[101] The journals condemned companies for not catering to women and championed those which provided "smooth," "well-lighted," and "luxurious" services.[102] The *Lady*'s "transport news" paid particular attention to developments that aided suburbanites' access to the West End. For example, it advised readers that a new omnibus route had opened between Baker Street Railway Station and Piccadilly Circus in 1888 and remarked that it would be "the greatest possible boon to the inhabitants of St. John's Wood, South and West Hampstead, Brondesbury, etc."[103] But a few years later, it still found that there was not enough affordable and efficient railway access from the western suburbs to Oxford Circus, the heart of shopper's London.[104]

Bourgeois women's comfort was understood in more than just physical terms. Indeed, it had as much to do with being able to distance oneself from the lower classes as it did with plush or warm waiting rooms. The women's press often exhorted transport companies to take note that women's pleasure and safety would increase if male working-class riders were better regulated. An editorialist in the *Queen* complained that overcrowded railway carriages compelled "ladies living in the country" to travel with "men in soiled garments, covered with clay or brick rubbish, or reeking with odours of stale fish."[105] This writer called upon transport companies to police the railway class system with vigilance so that respectable women could ride to and from London with comfort. In other words, women's comfort was understood as a kind of public privacy or distance from the smells and sights of working men. Their leisure or pleasure was premised upon a separation from the lower classes and the world of labor they inhabited.

If women did not want to travel with working men, they were thought to enjoy looking at them, albeit from a safe distance. The 'bus in particular provided a source of literary inspiration because of the way it allowed one to gaze upon humanity. Unlike the train, the omnibus moved riders slowly through the city streets, offering them a panoramic view of London's buildings and people. For example, Helen Hamilton's essay "Concerning the Bus" used these "democratic vehicles" as a vehicle to describe human diversity.[106]

The pleasure these riders derived from looking at and writing about the urban populous was matched by the satisfaction they gained from being able to "explore London thoroughly."[107] The *Lady*, for example, published a series called "London Locomotion" in 1891 so that women might feel more comfortable in omnibuses and trams and on the Underground, and visitors could become more intrepid as they sought out "the wonders and grandeur of the miles of buildings of London."[108] "London Locomotion" described the history of the public transport system and took readers on journeys through London's "chief thoroughfares."[109] The author noted that not only was it now respectable for women to travel around London, viewing its sights from the top of a 'bus, but by 1891 the "fair sex" had forced "the sterner sex . . . to take refuge inside!"[110] W. Pett Ridge similarly waxed eloquently about how London's new "beautiful" electric cars were among the improvements that allowed the "Londoner" to become better "acquainted with London," and even threatened to make him or her "patriotic," that is, proud of his or her capital.[111]

Amy Levy's poem "Ballade of an Omnibus," which she published as part of *A London Plane-Tree* (1889), is worth quoting in full because it brings together this sense that 'buses afforded their riders visual access to the city and its crowd. The poem begins with the quote, "To see my love suffices me" from *Ballades in Blue China*, Andrew Lang's poem that he published in the early 1880s, and then continues:

Some men to carriages aspire;
On some the costly hansoms wait;
Some seek a fly, on job or hire;
Some mount the trotting steed, elate,
I envy not the rich and great,
A wandering minstrel, poor and free,
I am contented with my fate—
An omnibus suffices me.

In winter days of rain and mire
I find within a corner strait;
The busmen know me and my lyre
From Brompton to the Bull-and-Gate.
When summer comes, I mount in state
The topmost summit, whence I see
Croesus look up, compassionate—
An omnibus suffices me.

I mark, troubled by desire,
Lucullus' phaeton and its freight
The scene whereof I cannot tire,

The human tale of love and hate,
The city pageant, early and late
Unfolds itself, rolls by, to be
A pleasure deep and delicate.
An omnibus suffices me.

Princess, your splendour you require,
I, my simplicity; agree
neither to rate lower nor higher.
An omnibus suffices me.[112]

The omnibus sufficed Levy because, like the women's club, it gave her access to her love, London. Watching and writing about the city pageant from this "democratic vehicle" afforded this wandering minstrel a deep and delicate pleasure.

The London Underground's poster campaign launched in 1908 similarly turned riding through London into an artistic subject. Many posters such as "The Way for All," "Always Warm and Bright," and for "Business or Pleasure" closely linked public transport with the idea of visual pleasure and urban access.[113] Londoners were asked to "travel into the heart of the shopping centres," and were told that there were "stations everywhere throughout our pleasuredome."[114] The Underground crowd was colorful, heterogeneous, and respectable, and middle-class women's comfort was depicted as a "milestone of progress."[115] One 1915 poster simply beckoned: "Look, Shop, Travel, Underground."[116] Female travelers in London's pleasure dome and shopping center came to symbolize progress and modernity. These posters solidified the perception of London that women's magazines and other promotional material were developing.

One might wonder why such campaigns and upper-class women's magazines spent so much time encouraging readers to patronize and enjoy public transportation. Female journalists and writers may have been, like Levy, using the 'bus and train as a vehicle to write about their sense of freedom in the city. But there might also have been commercial interests behind this attention. Though editors' motives went unrecorded, their preoccupation with transport coincided with their increasingly tight relationship with the advertising industry. It was not strictly necessary for readers to travel to London to buy the commodities that the journals advertised, but the magazines implied that the best products and the greatest pleasure could be had only in the West End. By cultivating readers as riders, the press encouraged a curiosity in a metropolitan lifestyle; this, in turn, necessitated the purchase of more magazines and more commodities.

"Madame's More Comprehensive Feminine Glance"

At the same time that female periodicals urged readers to travel to the city, they also started publishing detailed and specific guides to the city's shops, restaurants, clubs, and amusements. This development paralleled a shift we saw in the *Bayswater Chronicle* during this period. During the late-seventies and especially in the eighties, the wanderings of the urban stroller turned into "advertorials," or editorials that advertised specific places and products.[117] In female periodicals, the advertorial author typically presented herself as a *flâneuse* who possessed a discerning knowledge of goods, shops, streets, and neighborhoods. Readers were not asked to identify with this urban navigator but to need her services. There was an unstated implication that without the *flâneuse*, readers would wander the shops aimlessly, would lose themselves in the crowds, be consumed by commodities, and make a spectacle of themselves. The hopeless shopper and the educated *flâneuse* thus strolled arm in arm in the late-Victorian fashion press. Though magazines vowed that readers could become the latter, they also warned against being the former. In the end, readers learned that the rational consumption and looking the *flâneuse* embodied were a form of urban knowledge that could be gained only through reading and buying women's magazines.

Throughout these years, the ladies' papers published dozens of columns with names such as "A Day's Shopping," "Sketches from Oxford Street," and "Shopping Expeditions." These shopping narratives organized the city. They ordered and defined shoppers, shops, and streets, taking readers on a semiotic journey in which they essentially read the metropolis. These shopping narratives had the elements of what Michel de Certeau has defined as a travel story: "stories of journeys and actions . . . marked out by the 'citation' of the places that result from them or authorize them."[118] Rather than providing a map of the shopper's metropolis, these shopping narratives were "tours" in which the narrator became a metropolitan guide whose knowledge was contrasted to the ignorance of a country matron or helpless husband and, by implication, the reader. As de Certeau explained it, the map is a "totalizing stage" in which the narrator or producer has disappeared, while the tour follows the narrator as he or she makes sense or constructs places out of diverse spaces.[119]

Advertorials were always written as tours in which an educated guide/author wandered with an innocent rambler/reader. For example, the author of "Shopping in London," published in the *Lady* in the summer of 1888, identified herself as an expert who had "pioneered many a country cousin through her shopping and sightseeing." She promised the "hopelessly unpractical" ladies who "do not know much about London and have vague ideas with regard to its geography" that she would teach them to properly navigate the city, and thus become fashionable and modern. The essay began by satirizing a "Mrs. Greenwood," who "comes up from the Manor House, Cloverleigh," for "a nice long day's shopping." Mrs. Greenwood implored the author to join her because she claims to know nothing of the ways of the city. She demonstrates this by blathering on that she must visit her "lawyer in Lincoln's Inn Fields, then to Whiteley's and the Army and Navy Stores." She wants a bonnet from "that nice shop next to Swan and Edgar's, and there's one near Knightsbridge, . . . [and wants to] go to a shop somewhere near Cheapside and look at boys' suits." After which, "as everything in London is so close together," she hoped to visit the Academy, the theater, make a call in Hampstead and another in Kensington. Mrs. Greenwood's inability to map the city, to conceive proximity and distance, eventually leads to her complete loss of self-control. The poor woman loses "her head in the first large drapery shop she enters" and falls "in love with a mantle most becoming to a tall, graceful, plausible shop-girl, but utterly unsuited to adorn the stout, rather dumpy form of the Squire's wife." She becomes "hopeless to control, makes a dozen selections only to unmake them a minute later, loses her idea of colors altogether, and if let alone would choose something striking in moss-green, relieved with draperies of prawn-pink and bead embroidery, which would give the natives something to talk of for years if she wore it to church after her return."[120]

After painting this pathetic picture of the unskilled consumer wandering through a disorienting metropolis, the author instructed readers how to avoid becoming Mrs. Greenwoods. They learn where and how to shop and are especially warned against bringing one's spouse shopping. Husbands, we are told, make "the confusion" of shopping "worse confounded"; the "masculine mind is too uncompromising, and apt to stigmatise as waste of time this gratuitous acquirement of knowledge." While window shopping, "Monsieur only sees what is before him in the window," but "Madame's more comprehensive feminine glance has at once adapted the draperies and folds to her own requirements." According to this author, a husband's ignorance relegated his window shopping to mere staring, while "Madame's more comprehensive feminine glance" turned draperies into dresses. For women, controlled consumption came from wandering London's streets and studying its shop windows. "Many an idea," the author recalled, "have I acquired by a leisurely stroll through some of the best shopping streets." This solitary ramble did not separate women from their domestic lives. Rather, walking and shopping in the city enhanced the beauty of the domestic sphere. By gazing at Liberty's windows in Regent Street, for example, readers could obtain hints "of the very thing required to brighten up the drawing room."[121] With her "comprehensive feminine glance," Madame navigates the city to "brighten up" the domestic realm.

This comprehensive glance contrasted to the vacant staring of the country cousin and the shopping husband. These two characters often appeared as foils to the professional urban navigator and rational consumer. An early issue of the *Lady*, for example, published an exposé entitled "Shopping Husbands," describing these freaks of nature as "nervous amateurs" and "poor, confused, discomfited creature[s]." They shopped not because they liked the pursuit but because they were "selfish" individuals who treat their wives "as a child unfit to have the management of money."[122] It was simply seen as unnatural for a man to want to shop. "As a rule," one journalist explained, "men shop to get only the things they want. Even the effeminate masher-creature does not do quite as much of this as the ordinary woman, while the manly man does not do it at all."[123] The love of shopping served as a fundamental marker of gender difference. As one writer put it, "Shopping in London possesses an indescribable fascination" for all women from rich "fair *mondain*" to "the country cousin."[124]

Skill, however, was another matter. One journalist bluntly explained, "There are several types of the genus shopper . . . those who know their own minds and those who do not."[125] All women might like shopping, but women's magazines would have gone out of business if all women believed they were good shoppers and essentially knew "their own minds." Instead, they conceptualized shoppers through a series of binary oppositions—urban/rural, skilled/unskilled, rational/irrational—that were common to Victorian culture. These were not fixed categories, however. One had to study to acquire the "comprehensive feminine glance," and learn "what is worth seeing" from reading "the newspapers."[126] "Round the Shops," a regular series published in the *Housewife*, began, "Ladies are popularly supposed to be immensely fond of shopping . . . but shopping is nothing but a misery to the person who has little time and money, and no knowledge of where to go for what she wants." To help ignorant shoppers learn where to go and how to shop, one of the *Housewife's* reporters described what "she ha[d] seen" on her latest shopping trip.[127] Another "expert" maintained that she "obtained that knowledge very early in life," before she ever had been to London, by "studying her Mother's old map of London." Now, when shopping in "different quarters of London, the old map rises up before me." Her essays would then describe "Mother's old map of London," to her readers, since "a knowledge of London localities really is part of a polite education."[128] To become a good shopper then required education in urban geography as well as fashion sense.

Such articles guiding shoppers to and through the city were especially common in the late 1880s, at almost the exact moment of the Ripper hysteria. These shopping guides seemed almost deliberately designed to combat the image of London emerging from the media frenzy surrounding these murders. Instead of the city appearing as an extremely dangerous place for women, it was portrayed as both a safe and satisfying arena for female adventure. For example, between 1888 and 1889, the *Lady* published a dozen "Shopping Expeditions," which adopted an eyewitness mode of description and asked readers to follow the author into the city.[129] These trips took readers all over London, but Regent Street, Oxford Street, Bond Street, and Sloan Street were most often cited as the center of the shopper's metropolis. Occasionally suburban shopping districts, the City, and even the East End and South London were explored, but the southern part of the West End, the area of male clubland below Piccadilly, was never mentioned as a place to walk or shop.

While these narratives clearly benefited West End shops, they also worked against the idea of the department store. Rather than suggesting that women should buy everything under one roof, these expeditions implied that one needed to go to countless shops and walk all over the city to find the right goods. One adventure, for example, followed a shopping *flâneuse* through Piccadilly, Regent Street, and into Vere Street, where the author "had a peep at one of Marshall and Snelgrove's side windows, and saw that it was one mass of the loveliest crimson silks and plushes." She then walked north to Mmes Edmonds and Orr at 47 Wigmore Street because a friend asked her "to go and get some of their very special combination garments." After which she took a quick trip "into Donegal House to inspect Mrs. Ernest Hart's wonderful development of Irish industries" and "Messrs. Debenham and Freebody's 'Oriental Shop' . . . and marvelled much at the lovely things there displayed for presents." Finally, she "called at Mr.

Helbronner's, 300 Oxford Street, to have a peep at the lovely alter frontal he has just completed for St. James Church, near Worcester."[130] This trip, like so many others, implied that shopping was an individual act of urban navigation, of perceiving the sights and mastering the streets of the city.

These fictional shoppers explored an intensely feminine, commodity-filled urban marketplace that was well stocked with quality goods at fair prices.[131] They rarely encountered pushy crowds, unpleasant strangers, or nasty shopkeepers. They were never tired and never had sore feet. "Shopping Expedition IX," for example, published in the *Lady* just before Christmas in 1888, followed a Victorian matron throughout the West End in search of appropriate presents for her friends and relations. She began her Christmas shopping in New Bond Street, then went on to Berkeley Square, Bruton Street, Regent Street, and finally ended her expedition at Debenham and Freebody's in Wigmore Street. She bought and admired sweetmeats, bonnets, hats, cakes, cherries, silks, toys, fans, handkerchief sachets, curtains, cocoa, a tennis racket, and a tea cozy.

These shopping expeditions reworked older urban representations and clichés. Phrases such as " 'Sir,' said Dr. Johnson, 'let us take a walk down Fleet Street' " and " 'Madam,' say I, to my frivolous contemporary, 'let us take a walk down Sloan Street,' " were extraordinarily common.[132] The author of "A Day's Shopping" in the feminist journal the *Englishwoman* similarly wrote, "I am never tired of praising London. Does it not contain the concentrated essence of all good things . . . the best books, pictures, music, plays, lawyers, doctors, preaching, speaking, singing, teaching. . . . And are not our shops the best in all the world?" The beauty and diversity of London's shops, she wrote, served as a reminder "that London, beloved London is the market of the world."[133]

Instead of looking backward to famous eighteenth-century ramblers like James Boswell and Dr. Johnson, other narratives relied upon the metaphors of imperial exploration, social reform, and urban ethnography, which were becoming popular means to map late-Victorian London.[134] For example, one shopping trip took a respectable bourgeois matron into the netherworld of the shops near Moorgate Station. This intrepid shopper recalled, "I thought I must have descended to the lowest depths of Philistinism. 'Where will she want me to go next?' I mentally ask; 'to Curtain Road, or Barbican, or Mile End, or some of the places where people go about slumming.' "[135] When writers implied that areas such as Finsbury Pavement were only for the adventurous, the West End appeared all the more respectable, safe, and elite. Though these texts took readers slumming, they reinforced the difference between the wealthy West End and London's poorer regions.

The women's press frequently satirized the discourse and practices of social reformers. "Saturday Night in a West End Suburb," for example, caricatured the narratives of urban exploration:

> The Eastern Part of London has been searched for local colour, and the realistic life of the "other half" as carefully as if the scenes were laid out a thousand miles from civilization. The Rembrandt-like effects of light and shade, of colour and costume, belonging to this strange lower London, so foreign and so picturesque,

> have been minutely chronicled. We may expect soon to hear of personally conducted exploration tours to that other world, fenced off from the West-End by miles of thickly inhabited houses.

This city was simultaneously figured as a dark, uncivilized continent, a piece of art, a stage, and a tourist sight. We are told that from the top of a 'bus King's Road offered a spectacle thought to exist only in London's eastern half: "There is no need to tread the Deserted City streets to find local colour. . . . The West End can show scenes as exuberant in ruddy colour as the East." Because of the distance and perspective which the 'bus afforded, this ethnographer claimed to be far removed from the "jostling crowd of working-class women in rusty black, some carrying baskets, some string bags, and other armfuls of vegetables, obtained after much chaffering."[136] The 'bus offered a perspective to the female viewer that turned a working-class marketplace into an exotic spectacle.

As consumers, then, middle-class women occupied the voyeuristic position of the "English" masculine urban traveler. They went on "expeditions" in search of "local colour," "hunted" for bargains, and successfully completed "hard shopping campaigns." Most women, one article noted, enjoyed shopping in part because of the "love of the chase . . . and the element of chance."[137] This language drew upon those activities which defined upper-class masculine subjectivity: warfare, travel, exploration, hunting, and even gambling. Shopping, like these activities, constructed class and racial as well as gender differences.

Shopping narratives also created and reflected the social divisions that crisscrossed British society. Rather than presenting the city as divided along a straightforward east-west axis, these shopping expeditions implied that each street and shop could subtly signify social position. "Sloan Street," we are told, was for "the average middle-class woman who has a fair amount of money to spend, who lives in one of the smarter suburbs easily accessible, let us say, from Victoria, and who likes to have what is stylish and *chic*."[138] Dover Street, however, that "smart Petticoat Lane of the West End," was "the first great shopping rendezvous of the season." It was home to elite dressmakers, luxurious women's clubs, and shoppers as "intent upon seeing as being seen." The congregation of "Society" and "crowds of fair femininity . . . gliding alone in motors and carriages" was simply "not a sight to be missed."[139] Reading about shopping and this elite crowd no doubt stoked the anxieties of social climbers who were unfamiliar with the ways of Society. Here again, though, journals calmed uncertainty by bringing guidance to parvenus. At times journalists made this argument explicitly: "In these days of *nouvelles riches* such [fashion] information is doubly valuable because the lucky women who have suddenly come into money are chary of confessing their ignorance—and nowhere is the information safer than at Jay's."[140]

The point, of course, was that the distinctions between appropriate and inappropriate behaviors and commodities were extraordinarily subtle and changeable. This was especially true with regard to newer institutions and amusements such as restaurants. In addition to articles on shopping expeditions, journals like the *Lady* published guides to establishments that would cater to "ladies" as well as men. These articles were something like the modern restaurant review in that they described the food, decor, and services that each establishment provided; but they also commented on the respectability of each dining room. In 1888 the series "Where to Lunch When Shopping," recommended restaurants and promoted the very idea of having "lunch out." Its editor explained: "In the general advance of everything connected with the convenience and comfort of ladies visiting or residing in London, the most important item in a day's shopping—luncheon—has not been forgotten." The *Lady*'s readers would have no doubt which places they might patronize "without a thought of being considered 'fast.' "[141] The next year, "The Lady at Dinner" admired the drama of restaurants that, in contrast to the home, presented a spectacle of "light, life, colour and an endless change of scene and costume."[142]

Magazines thus bestowed the West End with its identity as a shopping and entertainment center and a tourist sight. Though women's magazines appropriated many modes of urban representation, portraying the city as labyrinth, tourist site, encyclopedia, or exhibition, each strategy implied that shopping gave one visual access and mastery of the urban scene. At the same time, magazines also stimulated new consumer-oriented anxieties. They instructed readers to travel perhaps far from home to be fashionable and modern, and told them that there were myriad, subtle, yet important differences between shops, streets, and neighborhoods, and that these distinctions might shift with the season and even the time of day. Missing appropriate cues could lead to a badly fitted dress or it could result in being mistaken as "fast" or even "fallen." The modern woman purchased more and more magazines so that she might chaperon herself through the late-Victorian city. Between the late 1880s and the early years of the new century, she could also hire a Lady Guide to take her to the fashionable and respectable West End. If she really knew her city, however, she might even find work as an urban guide.

The Lady Guides' London

In December of 1888 a meeting was held at the Royal Society of British Artists to discuss a new scheme for middle-class female employment.[143] This gathering launched the Lady Guide Association, an organization dedicated to refashioning public life in late-Victorian London. The group's stated goal was to hire unemployed but well-born women as travel agents, tour guides, chaperons, and professional shoppers. These "ladies" would then "guide" visitors on sightseeing and shopping trips through London. The Association's offices would also serve as a meeting or resting place, a club of sorts, for these ramblers during their hectic day in town. This organization of bourgeois women thus hoped to transform England's capital city into a comfortable, intelligible, profitable, and pleasurable arena for themselves and for others. This organization facilitated and embodied the transformation of the late-Victorian metropolis into a tourist site and shopping center, an arena for female work and leisure, and a symbol of liberal achievement.

Indeed, the Lady Guides participated in a heated debate about women's place in the commercial city. Their history reflects two tangled—even clashing—visions of urban women that we have seen emerging during the later part of the nineteenth century. At the same time there was a growing acceptance that bourgeois women could and should occupy the public streets and spaces of the metropolis, there was also a heightened sense of the dangers they faced when doing so. In one respect, the LGA was one of the many responses to the intense anxiety that characterized urban gender relations during these years. Although the connection was never made explicit, it is perhaps no coincidence that the Guides were formed only weeks after Jack the Ripper claimed his last victim. If the media representation of the Ripper murders cast the city as a dangerous place for women, the LGA and the shopping expeditions described above challenged this narrative by presenting London as a respectable, consumer-oriented pleasure center. Instead of attacking the source of crime, the Lady Guides challenged the image of the city as criminal. They portrayed urban women as neither dangerous nor endangered, but rather as respectable consumers. The LGA imagined no great divide between consumer and producer, however. They argued that the modern urban woman was also a worker whose job was to map the spaces and meanings of the metropolis. Their attitude toward the city was less a product of any feminist or socialist politics than an outgrowth of a liberal, commercial, and imperial sensibility. Of course, as Antoinette Burton has recently suggested, such positions were by no means mutually exclusive.[144]

The Association promoted itself by holding public lectures and by publishing booklets and their journal, *Progress: The Organ of the Lady Guide Association*. Brief supportive editorials also appeared in magazines such as the *Lady* and the *Queen*, in mainstream newspapers, and in guidebooks. In each of these locations, the LGA argued that it would benefit unemployed middle-class women, London's pleasure seekers, and the city itself. Although there is quite a bit of difference between journalistic urban guides and real Lady Guides, this organization's history brings to light some of the underlying tensions, motivations, and themes that appeared in the periodical press. One of the most compelling of which was that the Lady Guides' founder argued that a properly navigated London would help women become rational consumers and would teach foreigners, Americans, Europeans, and colonial subjects to feel England's cultural, economic, and political superiority. This nationalistic argument had been and continued to be present in the ladies' papers; the LGA used this argument, however, to justify its existence.

When lecturing to an audience of potential supporters, the LGA's founder and president, Miss Edith Davis, repeatedly emphasized London's symbolic potential, describing it as "the chief representative" of England and the "pride" of its "countrymen." She believed that London could serve as exhibition of Englishness and English national superiority. When foreigners visit London, she maintained, they feel "a sense of security, [and] . . . knowledge that they are in the midst of a nation avowedly the most liberal, free, honest and hospitable." She further asserted that "the wide-spread fame of the great Metropolis as a city of wonders has filled the heart of strangers with a longing to see and know, to feel themselves at home," and to understand "the glories under the rule and guardianship of the greatest Sovereign in the world."[145] The "city of wonders" conveyed what Davis believed were core facets of Englishness: monarchy, liberty, and hospitality.

Yet Davis admitted that this reading of the city was not an obvious one. In order to justify a need for the Guides she had to acknowledge that London was difficult to navigate and that its pleasures were not self-evident. Its size, complexity, and diversity, she suggested, often led to unrewarding and expensive visits. However, with a Guide's aid, strangers would "avoid the loss of time and money which occurs through not knowing the right omnibus, the right train, the correct cab fare, and the difference of prices in shopping in Bond Street, Westbourne Grove, or the City, and so on." They would also "be introduced to all the buildings, sights, picture galleries, entertainments (instructive and social), shops, &c."[146] Davis was arguing that if shopping and sightseeing were conducted efficiently, foreigners would understand that they were in the world's most "liberal" and "honest" nation. She also implied that showing strangers that London's commercial culture signified English national superiority was women's work.

While many argued that tourists and shoppers were frivolous and aimless creatures, Davis proposed that these consumers gained important political lessons during their urban rambles. This was an easy argument to make, since during the previous year advertisers, entrepreneurs, and government officials had turned London's streets into an exhibition of English imperial and commercial culture. The Queen's Jubilee celebration in 1887 had been a key moment in which commodity culture and imperial identity had merged.[147] Davis did not merely see London as a context for imperial display; she implied that its streets, shops, and historical sights were the very fabric of such spectacles.

If Davis recognized that strangers needed to be properly guided to see this spectacular city, she also felt they required a place where they could gratify their private needs. She spoke of the Association's Regent Street office, for example, as "a place of welcome to our foreign country sisters and brothers, their introduction, the passport to their freedom, the open sesame to their enjoyment."[148] Despite such hyperbole, the offices included not much more than a money exchange, a safe for clients' valuables, a lavatory, a small restaurant, and various reading and writing rooms.[149] The *Queen* reiterated Davis's views, calling these offices "a centre in the metropolis where all strangers and visitors shall call upon their arrival, make known their wants, ask advice, receive information upon any and every point, [and] find comfortable reception rooms where they can receive friends, tradespeople, and others."[150] The offices were thus central to the Association's vision of hospitality. It was not enough to guide visitors to London's comforts; one had to provide middle-class clients with a home away from home.

The LGA offices were part of the tremendous expansion of urban amenities that (as we saw in chapter 3) remade the late-Victorian West End. Along with various types of eateries, women's clubs, and shops, travel agencies such as American Express and the Great Eastern Railway Company's American Rendezvous began to sell urban guidance and domestic comforts to an increasingly mobile and even foreign bourgeoisie.[151] The LGA's offices were virtually indistinguishable from those of American Express or the American Rendezvous, but their exclusive use of female guides was a significant departure from the practices of their competitors. Some of the services the Guides performed were not available at American Express.

Lady Guides were hired as temporary housekeepers, chaperons, and hostesses. Davis emphasized that because they were "ladies by birth and education," her employees could act in any capacity where the "manners of a *lady*" were required. She noted, for example, that one of her Guides had recently helped "a young lady" entertain guests after a dinner party by providing "a little music" and "pleasant manners."[152] The *Queen* recommended that a suburban mother might hire a Lady Guide to watch her children so she might "enjoy a day's shopping and revel in the sales undisturbed by thoughts of her babies."[153] If she were unable to "revel in the sales," a Guide could do her shopping for her. Its shopping department was even staffed by, as one brochure explained, a Guide that had been "Certificated for Shopping."[154] In addition to asking for domestic help and urban guidance, then, one could hire a well-born but highly trained lady with fashion sense.

While other forces were telling women that shopping was a leisure activity, the Lady Guides defined it as women's work. This idea had been developing at least since the 1870s, when both fashion and feminist journals began to publish letters from women who either wanted to become or to hire a London commission agent. In one such letter a reader of the feminist paper the *Woman's Gazette* wrote, "I often wished I knew someone in London to whom I could write and ask to execute my orders," since relatives and friends frequently "complain[ed] of the time that is taken up by executing such requests from country cousins." Of course, one could write directly to the shops, but this woman explained that "ladies in the country do not always know what *are* the best shops for their purpose."[155] A similar letter from "A Londoner" bemoaned, "Everyone who lives in London knows what a nuisance it is to be continually bothered by one's friends and relations in the country to execute commissions for them."[156] Other letters also documented the woes of unemployed women and of annoyed Londoners and their country cousins.[157] Each resented the way in which an informal women's culture had become central to the nation's distribution system. These writers all recognized shopping as work for which one should be financially compensated. The LGA shared this conviction, hoping to professionalize what was more typically perceived as a female duty or pleasure.

The Guides focused on teaching bourgeois women the skills needed for professional employment in England's growing service sector. Davis made it perfectly clear from the outset that she would hire any well-born woman, whether married, single, or widowed, if she were properly educated and passed an examination in her particular area of expertise.[158] To those critics of middle-class female employment, she responded that guiding gave ladies "fair remuneration for fair work without usurping man's prerogative."[159] The *Graphic* likewise defended the Guides against critics who scoffed at "the idea of women guiding men! As if they were not doing so in thousands of cases, every hour of every day!"[160] Ironically, while it seemed acceptable that women could guide women and mixed parties all over the metropolis, Davis assured skeptics that she "allows no woman to occupy the place more fitted for a man. Thus, its Departments of Money Exchange, House Agency, accountant, and so forth have gentlemen for their direction."[161] While Davis felt women could and should have careers, she was not overturning all gender hierarchies. She did not offer her female employees the higher paid, more professional, and presumably higher status positions in the organization.

A fictional tale, "The Ladies Guide's Valentine," illustrated the nature of male resistance and attraction to this new type of woman worker. It also points to the way in which female guides derived their legitimacy from being contrasted with ignorant male and female visitors. Published in the February 1891 issue of the *Lady*, the story begins when a brother and sister, Hartley and Henrietta Grainger, have realized that although they have traveled to London together, they do not wish to visit the same city. Henrietta yearns to go "sightseeing" and Hartley wants to attend a series of scientific lectures. On the verge of tears, Henrietta finds she must "smother her girl-like longings 'for a good time' " after her brother tells her "in somewhat melancholy tones, 'I would not disappoint you for the world, but you might just as well ask your spaniel to conduct you over London. I am quite hopeless in these matters. I don't even remember where the Royal Academy is—somewhere in Kensington I suppose.' "[162] Henrietta responds to this admission of ignorance by asking if she might hire a Guide to help with their visit. Hartley agrees to accompany his sister and the Guide anywhere except to the very heart of commercial London, the "waxwork shows and—the milliner's."[163]

When Hartley finds that his sister has hired a Lady Guide, he cries out that such a figure must be "Monstrous!" and asks, "Who would wish to place a lady in such a position?" The Lady Guide, Miss Morrison, "sweetly" responds, "We cannot choose our work. . . . When a woman is left unprovided for, she has to do that for which she is best fitted."[164] Hartley's scientific bent persuades him to accept this Darwinian explanation of the rise of a new subspecies of female and agree to be guided by a woman. For several weeks, Dorthea Morrison guides the Grainger siblings through London, and because of her Cambridge degree and the fact that she is the niece of a famous professor, even introduces Hartley to London's scientific community.

The story thus constructs London as a sphere for female autonomy and independence while maintaining a clear sense of gender difference. The narrative initially sets up an opposition between a male London of science and rationality and a female London of consumption and, presumably, irrationality. Dorthea's scientific understanding undercuts this dichotomy; yet, by the end of the story gender difference reasserts itself in the form of heterosexual pleasure as Hartley and Dorthea fall in love. With the marriage that is assumed to conclude the story, we find that Dorthea's work and her sweet character have returned her to her proper class and her proper sphere. Although the tale is clearly intended to promote the LGA and its version of the New Woman worker, it also implied that such work was a temporary means by which appropriate class and gender norms might be preserved. Nonetheless, the story challenged bourgeois gender ideology by showing a respectable solitary woman working in the public spaces of the metropolis.

As this tale suggests, many observers assumed that although families went on trips together, they would not want to see or do the same things while away from home. One article amusingly noted that men are simply terrible guides, for "even when they are 'on duty' husbands have been known to express impatience if they are kept waiting outside or inside of shops, while brothers have a bad reputation for shirking their fraternal duties, reserving their attentions for other fellow's sisters." Female Guides, however, would "never grumble . . . even assist and encourage that delightfully long shopping, that delicious lingering over bargains, that hesitation between competitive shapes and colors, which so beautifully fill up women's thoughts when let loose in the happy hunting-grounds of Oxford Street, Regent Street and Piccadilly."[165] The Guides thus capitalized upon commonly held beliefs about gender and consumption. For most Victorians urban shopping, whether defined as work or leisure, belonged to the world of women. Its terrain, the "happy hunting-grounds of Oxford Street, Regent Street and Piccadilly," was not, however, an exclusively female or bourgeois world, and therefore could never be assumed to be an entirely safe or respectable place.

As we have seen, many areas of the West End contained both savory and unsavory characters and transactions. Even the most elite and aristocratic enterprises involved unregulated liaisons between buyers and sellers. Arthur Munby, notorious for his interest in Victorian working women, was fascinated by the mixture of respectable and unrespectable behavior in West End shops. He enjoyed flirting with shop girls, who he believed were also part-time prostitutes. In his notebooks, for example, he recalled being followed in Regent Street "by two shabby furtive looking girls, and importuned in the usual manner," but then he excitedly discovered that "they were not prostitutes—oh no! They were work girls, working at Mitchell's the artificial florist in Oxford Street: and when work is slack they turn out onto the streets for a living. Now Mitchell's is the fashionable shop where I went, with Ned Anderson . . . & Fanny Meredith and other bridesmaids, to buy wreaths and veils for Ned's Wedding."[166] This image of working women as selling more than flowers delighted male strollers like Munby while making all women vulnerable to male harassment and charges of solicitation when they walked West End shopping streets.[167]

Although some observers worried that the Lady Guides would suffer indignities while wandering through London, others welcomed them because they could make the city respectable. The *Spectator*, for example, admired the Guides because they could "meet single and unprotected young ladies at the stations, and deposit them in safe, clean, and respectable lodgings."[168] The *Daily Telegraph* explicitly commented that ladies who know "several foreign languages and have the topography and curiosities of London at their fingers' ends" will protect "ignorant and inquisitive strangers" from "the harpies who walk by day or the adventurers who prowl at night." She will lead clients "to fair-dealing merchants, and warn them off from the haunts of rogues. If we think of restaurants alone, there are places in the centre of London associated in minds of men about town with scenes of midnight dissipation. No honest man would like to see a lady enter such places, yet a stranger in London visiting them by daylight might not detect their objectionable character."[169]

The Lady Guides were thus understood as masters of the subtle distinctions between the respectable and unrespectable, the fashionable and unfashionable West End of the 1880s and 1890s. Profiting from the complexities of fin de siècle urban life, they became detectives able to read the "contested terrain" of the late-Victorian street.[170] The class and gender tensions that plagued the late-Victorian metropolis ironically opened a space for the LGA. Rather than reforming the behavior of urban men, they suggested that guidance and knowledge allowed women to maintain their respectability and avoid harassment. Instead of confronting the cultural, social, or economic conditions that made women vulnerable on city streets, the organization treated sexual harassment as a personal, indeed an intellectual question.

The Guides were not only a solution to these problems. Their existence also reflected the new belief that bourgeois women's independence in city streets was a welcome sign of modernity. During the 1880s, many commentators noted how the time-honored institution of the chaperon was a bit old-fashioned.[171] Margaret Fletcher, for example, remembered that it was during these years that "escorts were beginning to be thought unnecessary." Girls could, as she put it, "companion one another."[172] An 1882 article entitled "Walking Alone," published in the *Queen*, remarked that "although a generation ago it was not considered proper . . . for young ladies of good style and repute to walk the streets of London . . . at the present day a chaperon is the last thing desired of the modern girl, who loves liberty more than safety." According to this journalist, the modern girl relied on "her own courage and cleverness . . . to carry her out of dangers and difficulties of which her mother, when her age, was not supposed to know even existed." The modern girl was thus cognizant of the dangers that awaited her, but pretended, according to this author, to be "unconcerned" on "her lonely walks through the crowded West-end streets."[173] A view was developing that knowledge, confidence, and expertise could make the city a safe and pleasurable place for "modern" middle-class women and girls. This conviction, coupled with the lack of consensus on the chaperon issue, garnered support for the Guides. They could be accepted as modern chaperons perfectly suited for guiding modern girls. The *Daily Telegraph* told readers, for example, that "many a father anxious to allow his daughter freedom, but too old to follow them about and not liking to let them go alone, will welcome an active and judicious Lady Guide as the very thing long wanted."[174]

If the last decade of the nineteenth century gave birth to new ideas and reactions to women's independence, it also was a moment when a great many strangers—especially Americans—were coming to and shopping in London.[175] As early as the 1880s, American women were an acknowledged aspect of the West End consumer scene. In 1884 the *Standard*, for example, noted: "It is often remarked by our Transatlantic cousins that they can come to Europe to travel, enjoy good things and buy presents, for the same money that it would cost them to stay quietly at home."[176] Because England was a bargain for Americans, English retailers had come to believe that, as one trade journal commented, the American woman possessed a "national love of shopping."[177]

The Lady Guides served modern girls, American tourists, and female shoppers.[178] Many a "satisfied customer" pointed out that the Guides allowed them to see more of London than if they had only read their Baedeker. An American, for example, wrote, "The LG you furnished me with . . . has enabled me to see many more places and objects of interest in the four days, than I could have seen in twice the time with the aid of Guide Books Only."[179] A Mr. T. L. Chadwick explained that "both my wife and I are much obliged to you and the Lady Guide for the care and attention to my daughter." The countess of Aberdeen's children evidently "enjoyed their expedition to the Tower extremely," and a Pennsylvanian asserted that the Association "appeals to all travelled and un-travelled people alike."[180] Such apparently vocal support led one journalist for the *Queen* to comment in 1894 that "the lady guide has come to stay."[181]

Nevertheless, the Lady Guides disappeared by 1902.[182] A correspondent for the *Englishwoman* believed that despite the association's value,

> the public seems to prefer to lionise itself when it comes to London: to do its own shopping, to take its own tickets for concerts and theatres, to engage its own houses, rooms at hotels, or apartments, to meet itself at the railway stations. . . .
>
> Our country cousins will go to the wrong shops in blissful ignorance. . . . American cousins will rush unguided through England, missing the best things to be seen. . . . Our cousins German, as well as other foreigners, will murder our language, and get cheated for their pains.[183]

Although this journalist blamed the Guides' failure on consumers, it is not at all clear what led to their demise. The market of visitors seeking guidance certainly did not decrease. Davis may have lost interest in or could not raise enough capital to sustain the organization. Her staff may have accepted more stable, higher paying employment, which was increasingly available after the turn of the century. The likely explanation is that the business failed precisely because the services they had provided became so accepted and accessible. Guidebooks, businesses such as American Express, and even professional shoppers remained ever present features of urban commercial culture into the 1920s and 1930s and beyond.[184]

The LGA's importance, however, was not its successes or failures, but rather how it fit within the economic, cultural, and social transformations taking place in the late-Victorian metropolis. The growth of commercial culture and more diverse public identities for middle-class women meant that cities such as London became attractions. The LGA helped produce this attraction by constructing safe havens and exciting sights for shoppers and tourists. In doing so, they transformed both London and notions of proper gender roles. As modern consumer cultures colonized and reconfigured metropolitan landscapes across Europe and America, women were most frequently understood as passive consumers or objects of exchange. The Guides certainly constructed their female clients as shoppers. However, they did not see this identity as passive or women as objects necessarily consumed by male urban strollers. The Lady Guides argued that a commodified, indeed feminized, London symbolized liberal achievement and national superiority and that viewing the city was a modern, respectable amusement.

By the Edwardian period, several cheaply priced shopping guides further democratized the West End and served to replace the Lady Guide.[185] Some of these shopping guides attempted to distance themselves from the advertorial or advertisement by suggesting, as Edith Davis had, that "guides" pointed to shops or places because of their true value and not because the owners had paid the authors to "puff" them. For example, in the preface of the 1906 guidebook *Olivia's Shopping and How She Does It: A Prejudiced Guide to the London Shops*, the author directly challenged both the women's magazines and guidebooks for not meeting the needs of shoppers. "Shops should be criticised like pictures or plays," Olivia explained. "Instead they are merely boomed in advertisement. . . . Few women are at all impressed with the vapid flatteries of shops to be seen in ladies' papers, and simply ripe for a shop Baedeker which discriminates and chooses for them."[186] Baedeker's and other guidebooks met this challenge by devoting greater space to London's shops, shopping streets, restaurants, and entertainments.[187] By the fin de siècle, commercial guidance was as abundant as the goods that filled a department store window.

Cheaper forms of urban guidance even targeted the lower-middle- and working-class consumer. For only a penny the *A.B.C. Amusement Guide and Record* directed readers to London's museums, dramatic and musical events, shops, restaurants, and even women's clubs.[188] The West End could also now be purchased in the daily newspapers such as the *Pall Mall Gazette*, the *Evening News*, *Daily Chronicle*, and *Daily Mail*. Every week newspapers took lower-class readers wandering through West End streets in search of bargains or simply to enjoy the display of shop windows. For example, in May of 1907 the *Evening News* sponsored a contest for the "reader who maps out a model course of enjoyment which costs exactly £1."[189] The paper also described the pleasures of suburban shopping, which the editor wrote was now as enjoyable as "the happy hunting grounds of the West End."[190] The *Pall Mall Gazette* began a weekly series, "Shopping and Shopland," which promised to betray the "secrets of the smart" and show the masses how the wealthy navigated "the maze of West End shopping."[191] The paper also addressed the pleasure-seeking foreign tourist. In 1909 it began a new series "designed to guide the stranger in the social intricacies of London," to show the visitor "the London of the Londoner."[192]

The Edwardian press constituted a huge and growing readership as wanderers moving through the commodified spaces of the metropolis. A new era of publishers, advertisers, and entrepreneurs fully exploited the belief that readers could be transformed into a crowd of shoppers. As we turn to the American department store mogul Gordon Selfridge, we can see how his monumental store was literally built upon the vision of shopping and the urban woman that the clubwomen, the women's press, and Lady Guides had constructed during the previous half century. In 1909, when Selfridge opened his department store, Londoners also realized that their city was not as "English" as Edith Davis had confidently claimed. By this period, the center of the empire was colonized not only by foreign shoppers and sightseers, but also by foreign entrepreneurs. The linkages between consumption and Englishness that women's magazines and the Lady Guide Association had forged were torn asunder as a maverick draper from Chicago moved into Oxford Street.

• CHAPTER FIVE •

"A New Era of Shopping": An American Department Store in Edwardian London

"THOUSANDS OF WOMEN besiege the West," trumpeted a *Daily Express* headline on March 15, 1909. The *Standard* similarly proclaimed this day in early spring the beginning of "Woman's Week in London."[1] It was sale season, and as dozens of journalists cheerfully told their readers, the West End belonged to the women of Britain, the Empire, and foreign lands. This was no ordinary sale week, however, for it began with the spectacular opening of Gordon Selfridge's new "American" department store in Oxford Street and the sixty-year jubilee celebration of Harrod's in Knightsbridge. Never before had retail competition reached such heights, nor had it ever demanded such public attention.[2] London's shopkeepers went to extraordinary lengths to sell their wares in the spring of 1909, spending enormous sums on store decorations, special entertainments, and advertising. In turn, London's journalists covered the story with great enthusiasm and hyperbole. These efforts, a "lady correspondent" wrote, benefited women because they turned mere "shopping" into "a fine art." Advertising and opening ceremonies, she argued, expanded the very meaning of shopping: "From Times immemorial woman has shopped . . . [but] it is only since Monday that we have understood what the word really means."[3] Expressing a similar delight in novelty, a *Daily Express* reporter declared that Londoners were witnessing the dawning of a "new era of shopping."[4]

Despite such assertions, the West End had been associated with shopping, femininity, and modernity long before the 1909 opening of a new department store in Oxford Street. Decades of economic, social, and cultural transformation had produced this "new era of shopping." Yet Selfridge's London opening and rival celebrations in older English shops allowed Edwardians to reflect upon how commercial, class, and gender changes had remade their capital city during the previous decades. Though Londoners would have been familiar with grandiose commercial architecture, lavish interior decor, rationalized organization, store services, and publicity, they were not accustomed to the scale and intensity with which Selfridge constructed his commercial palace.[5] Nor had they encountered a retailer, especially a "foreigner," who talked about himself and his shop with such ardor and confidence. Even the Universal Provider had taken years to gain an international reputation. Both entrepreneurs had, however, inspired diverse reactions and ignited a vigorous rivalry within the West End business community. Like Whiteley before him, Gordon Selfridge compelled journalists, business experts, and consumers to rethink the value of mass consumption and publicity, the pleasures of the city, and the nature of bourgeois femininity.

As the "lady correspondent" had declared, shopping had been identified with women for some time, but the meaning of this activity was by no means stable. For much of the Victorian era, shopping had been seen as a wasteful, indulgent, immoral, and disorderly pastime. In the early 1870s, Londoners could easily imagine that William Whiteley had undermined the foundations of middle-class culture by disregarding the separation between different types of commodities, between men and women, and between "ladies" and "prostitutes." Whiteley's store was an extremely modest venture in comparison with Edwardian giants such as Selfridge's or Harrod's. It nonetheless had inspired fearful visions of "ruined" shopkeepers and "ruined" women. The economic and legal restrictions placed on married women during these years and the proximity of the feminist and retail communities also underscored the shopper's reputation as virago. To a certain extent, the image of the deranged and disorderly shopper remains with us today, but as we will see, this figure did not haunt Edwardians in the same way as she had in the past. If anything, she was characterized as more ridiculous than harmful.

Selfridge left nothing to chance, however. He and other entrepreneurs and journalists and, as we will see in the next chapter, theatrical impresarios assiduously worked to dispel the public's reservations about department stores and female shoppers. They built upon the ideas of earlier businessmen and women, reformers and feminists who had characterized shopping as a respectable female pleasure. Selfridge, like Whiteley, professed that shopping was pleasurable because of its public setting. He idealized this public sphere as a site of personal exploration, self-fulfillment, and independence. At the same time, he also characterized the department store as a comfortable resting place in which urban women's bodies could be satisfied, indulged, excited, and repaired. Shopping, he repeatedly stated, promised women access to a sensual and social metropolitan culture. While this understanding of gender, pleasure, and the department store was similar to that of William Whiteley, the growth of print advertising enabled Selfridge to enlist the mass media to his cause and to broadcast his message faster and farther than Whiteley could have imagined. Selfridge was thus able to adopt new forms of publicity to promote his vision of femininity, shopping, and the metropolis.

Gordon Selfridge garnered such attention because of his American background, his seemingly novel business methods, and his status as the most vocal entrepreneur of his generation. He audaciously claimed that he had single-handedly torn down the walls of conservative British shopkeeping and professed that his store was a "modern" public sphere devoted to the pleasure of ladies. Through the deft use of advertising and newspaper publicity, Selfridge argued that the department store had uniquely generated a new female urban culture. He represented the department store as emancipating women from the drab and hidebound world of Victorian commerce and gender ideals. The subtext, of course, was that an American businessman had liberated English women from old-fashioned English men. Liberation did not just bring pleasure; pleasure signified emancipation.

Selfridge's success came not from radical innovation, but from his careful deployment of already accepted ideas. He was particularly skilled at convincing others that he was ahead of his time. In other words, he persuaded the British public that he had introduced "a new era of shopping." Jackson Lears has recently observed in his study of American advertising that businessmen and advertisers did not " 'invent' the culture of abundance; they refashioned its conventions."[6] This chapter investigates one aspect of this refashioning. It charts how entrepreneurs, editors, and journalists wrote a compelling narrative about consumption, novelty, pleasure, and women and the city. In this story the department store became the agent of female emancipation and pleasure and the symbol of the modern metropolis.[7]

"London's American Phase"

Harry Gordon Selfridge, a middle-aged Wisconsin native, arrived in England in 1906 flushed with the confidence that Edwardian London contained all he needed to make his fortune. Somewhat ironically, this American viewed the English capital as the land of opportunity. His perception stemmed in part from the belief that there were fundamental differences between English and American retailing. Like many others, Selfridge presumed that English methods were "backward" in contrast to more "progressive" American approaches to selling. At the same time, he also cherished what he imagined were quintessential English values, most fundamental among these a persistent faith in the gospel of free trade. Finally, Selfridge was also mesmerized by the sheer size of London's domestic and transient population. Selfridge's assessment of London's retailers as old-fashioned and its shoppers as unsatisfied influenced the type of enterprise he would build and the way he would talk about it.

"Mile-a-Minute Harry," as he had been known, had been one of the leading "brokers" or creators of American consumer culture.[8] For over twenty-five years, he had participated in making an economy and culture geared toward the consumption of vast quantities of commodities. As the second in command of Marshall Field's department store in Chicago, Selfridge claimed responsibility for many of the famous emporium's innovations. He introduced the first restaurant and bargain basement and targeted children as consumers by starting a "children's day" and building an entire "children's floor." Selfridge claimed responsibility for having hired a famous window-display artist to design Marshall Field's spectacular show windows. He also believed in advertising, writing a good deal of Marshall Field's copy himself.[9] Like many of his contemporaries, Selfridge hoped that luxurious decor and architecture, amenities and entertainments, as well as extensive publicity would encourage patrons to reimagine the way they viewed shopping. In such colorful, light, and shimmering environments customers would see buying not as an economic act, but as a social and cultural event. Making shopping into entertainment also helped Marshall Field's to crush its competitors in what William Leach has described as the retail wars of the 1890s.[10]

After a long and profitable career in Chicago and with $2 million in the bank, Harry Gordon Selfridge came to London hoping to reap similar profits from the English middle classes. Selfridge choose England because of his professed affinity for its culture and especially its economic ideals, later confessing, "London is the capital of the only big Free Trade country in the world. I can buy merchandise there and put it on my counters more cheaply than anywhere else."[11] For some time, English retailers such as D. H. Evans had reminded "American and Colonial visitors" of the financial advantages of shopping in "Free Trade England rather than High Protection France."[12] Selfridge, like American shoppers, seems to have been enticed by this same promise of cheap goods. No doubt he was encouraged by the Liberal victory in the 1906 general election, which ensured that, for a time at least, England would cling to the free-trade principles that were being abandoned elsewhere. Selfridge had good reasons for believing that England offered cut-rate prices and an "immense" market of customers.[13]

Edwardian England, in fact, presented Selfridge with both a challenge and an opportunity. The crowning of a pleasure-loving king and the spectacular society that surrounded the court had injected new life into the luxury trades.[14] Yet Edward VII lent a glamorous and indulgent aura to an age otherwise marked by tremendous social, political, and economic upheaval. The Boer War had severely damaged British confidence overseas, while closer to home, Irish discontent, constitutional crisis, labor unrest, and the militant phase of the struggle for women's suffrage brought about what George Dangerfield famously called "the strange death of Liberal England."[15] In many respects, the social, economic, and political crises of the late 1880s appeared with new force in the first years of the new century.

Despite Selfridge's confidence in London's market, many Edwardians were still intensely poor. The social investigations of Rowntree, Maud Pember Reeves, and others revealed that a huge proportion of the population lived in dire destitution. A steady rise in prices after the midnineties meant that the poorer classes may have felt their penury even more severely. The Edwardian working classes lived in an inflationary era that made it extremely difficult to make ends meet. Workers also experienced a plateau in wage increases, sharp wage cuts, and severe unemployment.[16] The gap between rich and poor may have been wider than ever as a newly wealthy plutocracy was finding its way into the circles of power. While Edward VII and the tea magnate Sir Thomas Lipton went yachting together, many British could scarcely afford the types of goods that had made Lipton rich.[17]

Despite the dismal conditions of London's poor, businessmen like Selfridge often focused on the sheer size of the city's population when they considered its market for mass-produced commodities. The population of central London had continued its steady decline, but Greater London now swelled to well over 7 million people.[18] Motorcars and the motor bus were rapidly replacing horse-drawn transport, while the expansion and electrification of the underground railways, commuter railways, and electric tramways carried literally millions of suburbanites to and from the urban center each day.[19] As the "Tube" began to penetrate the West End, access to its shopping and entertainment centers dramatically increased. For example, after the Central Line opened in 1900 approximately 100,000 people a day rode some or part of the way from Shepherd's Bush to the Bank. With stations at Holland Park, Notting Hill Gate, Queen's Road (renamed Queensway in 1946), Lancaster Gate, Marble Arch, Bond Street, Oxford Circus, Tottenham Court Road, British Museum (closed in 1933), Chancery Lane, and Post Office (renamed St. Paul's in 1937), the Central Line could not have been better placed to serve the main West End shopping districts, especially Bayswater and the shops along Oxford Street.[20] The advent of such modes of transport was a necessary precondition for the type of mass market that Selfridge wished to entice to his store. "Electric cars," noted one retail expert in 1912, had improved trade by bringing shoppers to the main thoroughfares of towns and by affording "ladies opportunities of visiting drapers' shops without having to walk long distances."[21] The geographer H. J. MacKinder captured the emergence of this suburban, commuting nature of urban life when he wrote in 1902:

> In a manner all South-Eastern England is a single urban community; for steam and electricity are changing our geographical conceptions. . . . The metropolis in its largest meaning includes all the counties for whose inhabitants London is "Town," whose men do habitual business there, whose women buy and spend there, whose morning paper is printed there, whose standard of thought is determined there.[22]

By the first years of the new century, the expansion of cheap and fast modes of transportation meant that the West End had simply become "Town" for southern England. This trend had been long in the making. Indeed, mid-nineteenth-century observors similarly reported the presence of suburbanites and other visitors traveling to the city center. The difference now was the ease with which this occurred.

In May 1907 the *Evening News* printed a series of articles and letters from suburban women on the relative merits of shopping in their neighborhoods or in the West End. Women from Clapham Common, Wimbledon, and other areas of suburban London acknowledged that their local shops were "up-to-date" and fine for "a hurried dress or hat alteration," but most agreed that going to the West End was special. Mrs. Whilton from Wimbledon was particularly adamant. She wrote that since "we have the cheap District Railway to Victoria . . . in a few minutes time one is in the thick of the sales. It is lovely. I never do my shopping in our suburb if I can help it."[23] Another correspondent observed home that although she did not live there, the West End was familiar territory. "We prefer," she wrote, "to take an excursion straight to the West End . . . where we know where to go and can get exactly what we want rather than run the risks incurred in trying new and unexplored territory."[24] Such women constituted the "immense" market that so excited Gordon Selfridge.

Of course, by this period the West End was filled with shops and newer forms of mass entertainment. Cinemas, organized spectator sports, and mass circulation newspapers such as the *Daily Mail* vied with music halls and public houses for people's free time and discretionary income.[25] By 1909 London already had ninety cinemas, a number that mushroomed to four hundred by 1912.[26] Arnold Bennett's 1907 novel, *The City of Pleasure: A Fantasia on Modern Themes*, was a prescient tale in which the mass leisure industry had remade urban life as an amusement park. This description of the amusement park, the "City of Pleasure," could also have been a portrait of the Edwardian West End. Its streets were

> lined with multifarious buildings, all painted cream—the theatre, the variety theatre, the concert hall, the circus, the panorama, the lecture hall, the menagerie, the art gallery, the story-teller's hall, the dancing-rooms, restaurants, cafés and bars, and those numerous shops for the sale of useless and expensive souvenirs without which no Briton on holiday is complete. . . . Add to this the combined effect of the music of bands and the sunshine, and do not forget the virgin creaminess of the elaborate architecture, and you will be able to form a notion of the spectacle offered.[27]

The West End was similarly a multifarious nexus of commercialized pleasures. Its streets literally bore the mark of the new advertising age. Posters, electric signs, and store windows had transfigured the cityscape into a riot of swirling commodities. For example, in a 1912 photograph of the corner of Oxford Street and Tottenham Court Road, Dewar's Whiskey, Schweppe's Soda Water, Bovril, Crosse and Blackwell, Pears' Soap, Oakey's Knife Polish, Blogg's Brewery, the Excelsior Theatre, the London Fur Co., J. P. Restaurant's Tea Rooms, and the London Underground filled the visual field of the pedestrian, motorist, and commuter (fig. 10). Victorian sketches had imaginatively constructed the consumer as urban traveler. In Edwardian London, posters, electric signs, and public transport turned the urban subject into a reader and consumer. Thomas Burke, for example, recalled that "it was a habit of mine, as soon as I could read, to spell out all the advertisements when riding in trains and buses and trams. . . . Almost the first entrants in the troupe of memories are—Nixey's Black Lead; Reckitt's Blue; Hinde's Curlers; Sapolio; Epps' Cocoa; Brook's Soap and Monkey Brand; Frame Food; and Whelpton's Purifying Pills."[28]

This "city of pleasure" was increasingly associated with a mass crowd and heterosocial amusement. Several memoirs recalled that working- and lower-middle-class consumers enjoyed a day or night "in Town." In 1908, E. B. Chancellor somewhat romantically mused that Piccadilly Circus, the center of the West End's entertainment district, was the place where "east and west meet . . . on common ground."[29] Three years earlier, an article in the *Queen*, "The Changing West End," had characterized Piccadilly in similar terms. Though many still regarded the street as a male preserve, this journalist claimed that "Picadilly is, indeed a wonderful conglomeration of great mansions, clubs, hotels, and shops where the great, the learned, the rich, and the business man and woman are to be found side by side as it were."[30]

Although far from a democratic public sphere in which all could meet on equal terms, the Edwardian West End entertained a diverse crowd. At the same time,

Figure 10. Street advertising, corner of Tottenham Court Road and Oxford Street, June 1912 (courtesy of Hulton Getty Picture Library).

its growing service-based economy also offered men and women employment. On Sunday afternoons before the war, Ursula Bloom began working at one of the new cinemas. In her memoir she recalled going to London alone to select programs for the cinema, after which she would meet her fiancé for tea at the Coventry Street Lyons. They would dance to its "thrilling" bands and kiss in the back of the new taxis.[31] While Ursula eagerly plunged herself into the heterosocial city, other young women experienced the metropolis as primarily a female world. For example, Eva Slawson and Ruth Slate, two working-class friends, came to the West End to pursue feminist politics and patronize commercial amusements. In 1908 and 1909, they spent much of their free time attending feminist and socialist meetings and lectures and partaking of a myriad of other pleasures. One Saturday afternoon in January the two met at Liverpool Station, went to the National Gallery, discussed politics while having tea at Lyons, and then made their way to the Duke of York's Theatre to see Pauline Chase in *Peter Pan*.[32] For Ruth, Eva, and Ursula, the West End symbolized their entry into a world of work, politics, and pleasure.

Despite the ever-present specter of poverty and unemployment, West End consumer culture was growing along the same lines as that developing in metropolitan America. If on a smaller scale, the same nexus of merchants, bankers, journalists, advertisers, and artists transforming American culture was at work in the West End.[33] But English consumer culture emerged in a very different setting. By the time Selfridge arrived in England, Americans were flexing their economic muscles while the English were becoming obsessed with their own failures. Indeed, the new century began with the Prince of Wales exhorting British business to "wake up if she intends to maintain her old preeminence in her colonial trade."[34] Of course, shopkeepers were not in the same position as manufacturers, but similar concerns of failure, backwardness, and national decline also obsessed the retailing community.

During this period, novel business practices were often tainted with the brush of foreignness, associated either with the vulgar mass society of America or the rarified, effeminate, and extravagant culture of France. Certain consumer practices, such as organized sport, could of course promote the idea of a national or "British" identity, but these tendencies worked against a competing perception that commercialism was a foreign import.[35] Whether for good or ill, advertising and display, two hallmarks of consumer culture, seemed vaguely foreign and inevitably brought home England's declining position in the world economy. Though anti-Semitism certainly existed in England, the British shopkeeper most feared American "foreigners" during these years. Such anxieties were not simply the outcome of national hysteria. Gordon Selfridge was, in fact, among a cohort of extremely wealthy and powerful Americans who saw Edwardian London as profitable territory. One of the most notorious was the transport financier Andrew Yerkes, who, like Selfridge, had made his first fortune in Chicago. Yerkes has been credited with having completely remade London's Tube railways during the first years of the new century. Among other things, he raised the capital to electrify the District Line and to initiate three new lines as well. Much of this money also came from America. Indeed, some of the capital for the Charing Cross, Euston, and Hampstead Line was rumored to have come from the department store magnate Marshall Field, but this was later denied.[36]

In recalling the changes he had witnessed in early-twentieth-century London, Thomas Burke labeled "the first quarter of this century . . . London's American Phase." He argued that nearly all aspects of modern London, especially its commercial culture, were literally "American" or had been inspired by "American" models: "the tube railways . . . the bulk of our entertainment . . . our latest hotels . . . our snack-bars and all-night supper stands . . . our electric night-signs . . . our street songs . . . our popular press . . . our newest buildings . . . our one-way streets and automatic traffic controls [and our] giant Stores . . . are American [in] origin."[37] As Burke saw it, American commercialism had, in effect, colonized England and especially its cities. English consumer culture had its own indigenous history, which scholars have now traced back for centuries, yet in the early 1900s, advertising, publicity, and display often seemed more American than English.[38] Despite the work of groups like the Lady Guides and editors of women's magazines, the alliance between consumerism and national identity did not fit in twentieth-century England as it did in the United States. Consumerism was rapidly becoming a way of life, but it appeared to arrive, much like American tourism, as a foreign occupying army. Selfridge tried to separate the perception that consumerism was in itself American, but his success only solidified the belief that mass culture was American culture.

Many Edwardian traders were especially suspicious about serving the masses as a whole instead of selling separately to distinct classes. Of course, some drapers, furniture retailers, and even grocers had built imposing commercial palaces in the main shopping streets of the West End to capture the mass market.[39] Harrod's of Knightsbridge started as a small grocer's in 1849, but after becoming a limited liability company in 1889 it quickly grew into a mammoth store. It prospered under the direction of Richard Burbidge, a former manager of Whiteley's.[40] Yet many stores did not look like those in Chicago, New York, Boston, and Philadelphia. Some grew into huge, luxurious drapers, furnishers, and toy stores without combining diverse lines of trade. When the furniture firm of Waring and Gillow's opened its new Oxford Street store in 1906, trade journals and newspaper reports heralded it as the "largest furnishing emporium in the world."[41] Over a hundred thousand visitors came to view this "Furniture Palace" on its opening day, and even Queen Alexandra was treated to a private shopping trip.[42] Once inside, shoppers could wander through a hundred galleries of furnished rooms and model houses. They could enjoy a cup of tea in the ladies' room, read and write letters in the adjoining reading room, or eat a full meal in the "prettily decorated restaurant."[43] Not surprisingly, perhaps, the enterprising Sam Waring (later Lord Waring) initially joined Selfridge as a business partner, but pulled out of the deal before the department store opened.[44] Waring and Gillow's, like Heal's in Tottenham Court Road, was a huge enterprise, with modern display techniques and store services, but it was not a department store.[45]

Although many Britons considered these stores modern, Selfridge and other Americans thought they were "backward" because they were not department stores in the American or French sense. The prestigious firm of Marshall and Snelgrove's had made its name by trading in silks, furs, carpets, and drapery goods, but it was famous for not moving into furniture, men's clothing, groceries, and the like. The owners' philosophy was that "drapery and dressmaking afforded them all the scope they wanted." Snelgrove apparently defended this position by saying, "We know what we are and we mean to stick to it."[46] In 1890, their store had only twenty-five different departments but was quite profitable and was described as "an ornament to the metropolis . . . the whole forming a splendid example of systematic organization."[47] The Edgeware Road silk mercers and drapers, Messrs. E. & R. Garrould's, sold virtually every sort of household item, but they too did not branch into men's clothing or provisions. Garrould's was popular with the middle and upper-middle classes, even though its forty departments were divided into nine large shops in two different streets.[48] Peter Robinson's, "the birthplace of the blouse," employed almost two thousand workers in over a hundred different departments but was dedicated to selling predominantly "ladies' wear."[49] Liberty's too was considered a very up-to-date business, a "pioneer of commerce," but until the 1920s the store was housed in a series of separate shops along Regent Street.[50] This collection of shops enjoyed the reputation of having revolutionized English furniture and clothing design and of encouraging Britons to cover themselves with "dainty, flowing silks" and decorate with "dreamy, romantic looking furniture."[51] Some shops such as Jay's Mourning Warehouse, Swan and Edgar's, John Barker's, Robinson and Cleaver's, Harvey Nichol's, and others had made Regent Street, Oxford Street, High Street, Kensington, and Knightsbridge elegant and modern shopping centers. These expensive commercial palaces underwent a good deal of expansion at almost the same time that American stores took on their modern visage, but they did not reach the scale or diversity of many of their American or French rivals.

The architecture, nature of display, advertising, and internal organization of English stores often reflected the proprietor's wish to sell to a specific class of shopper. Stores that remained dedicated to an aristocratic and upper-middle-class market, such as those in Bond Street and the Burlington Arcade, typically remained quite small, rarely advertised, and spent little effort on window display.[52] One retail expert, discussing the persistence of rigid social distinctions in England, argued that English houses were smaller than American firms because the practice of selling to "all classes of trade can hardly be imagined over here." "In England," he wrote, "classes are more definitely divided; houses are recognized as doing one kind of business, and every question of policy has to be governed by this fact."[53] London's shopping streets were also thought to represent and reinscribe these same social differences. A 1906 shopping guide explained, for example, that "Regent Street is for wealthy suburbans and Bayswater, Oxford Street is for the world, but Bond Street is for princes and Park Lane."[54] Somewhat ironically, then, the Edwardian West End was understood as a meeting ground of rich and poor, east and west, not because businesses necessarily catered to the masses, but because the neighborhood had many enterprises that served different social groups.

If ideas about class difference shaped the nature of London's stores, they also entered into the relationship between West End traders and their aristocratic and royal landlords. Because of the leasehold system prevalent in this area of the city, wealthy landlords and the English Crown had an unusual degree of control over the nature of trade and building design.[55] Landlords could restrict the types of trade that could be conducted on their property. Traders who leased from the duke of Westminster, for example, had to accept his architects' plans when they built or redesigned their shops. Tensions were particularly high in the last years of the century because many of the ninety-nine-year leases were coming due at a time of a severe collapse in property values.[56]

A glaring example of the tense relations between London's commercial and aristocratic classes came in 1903, when the Portland Estate trustees placed an injunction on John Lewis for attempting to annex adjoining properties to enlarge his Oxford Street store. Lewis fought back in the courtroom but also by publishing a pamphlet, *Our Ground Landlords in the Twentieth Century*, in which he accused the Portland Estate of exercising despotic, feudal powers and inhibiting the progress of business.[57] While John Lewis tussled with Lord Portland, Regent

Street shopkeepers were enmeshed in a battle with their landlord, the Crown. All parties in this dispute agreed that Regent Street's once famous shops had become somewhat dilapidated and were in dire need of redevelopment. Even in the 1880s, the *Architect* described the shops in "the most stately business street in London" as "tottering piles of old materials." One of the shops was described as having a "showy glass front and a showy mahogany counter, perhaps a showy carpet. . . . The ceiling is low, the lighting is bad, and the ventilation best be expressed in plain vulgarity by the single word *sweat*."[58] Something needed to be done, but the Crown and tenants could not agree upon a style of architecture that would reflect their divergent visions of the street.

The Crown's architects wanted Regent Street to display London's status as the "imperial" capital.[59] Regent Street's shopkeepers, instead, yearned for a commercial avenue that would appeal to the diverse public they now served. Regent Street had once sold exclusively to the wealthy and thus had relied less on window display to attract passersby than did Oxford Street or Westbourne Grove. But after the turn of the century, many of the street's shops were patronized by a fairly broad market.[60] Their proprietors believed that the expansion and electrification of the Tube had contributed to this change. In 1907, for example, restaurant, theater, and store owners all reported a surge in business after the recent opening of the Piccadilly Circus Station.[61] Regent Street traders argued that the Crown's plans, designed by Richard Norman Shaw, would not appeal to trade of this nature. Instead of vast expanses of uninterrupted glass, Shaw's design was a street of heavy, monumental stone arches and pillars. The shopkeepers asserted that Shaw's minimal use of plate glass would not allow enough light into their stores nor would it enable them to install dramatic window displays that would attract a large shopping crowd. The complaint of one trader printed in the *Evening News* in 1907 summarized the feelings of the nearly sixty affected shopkeepers. "The last thing which a shop requires is anything like a suggestion of sternness and cold grandeur; a shop should be alluring, attractive, essentially feminine in its characteristics." He concluded that "a show of dainty feminine finery would look hopelessly silly and frivolous in a severe, not to say forbidding, classical frame."[62] Shaw's design ignored what was perceived as the "feminine" and "mass" nature of modern Regent Street. At a meeting of shopkeepers, one trader protested the design because although "there is a high class of shopkeeper who do not require a big window shop . . . that is not the trade which is done in Regent Street. The Regent Street shopkeeper needs a large number of customers, and wants to catch a floating population."[63]

Shaw and his supporters called the shopkeepers' ideas and their trade vulgar. In an article published in the *Nineteenth Century and After*, the famed architect Aston Webb sided with Shaw and hinted that the "appalling mixture of plate glass, looking glass and tawdry wood and brass work . . . results in increased sales for a time, but there can be little doubt but that it leads in the long run to the deterioration of the character of the street and the shops as a first-class business property."[64] An author of a letter in the *Daily Mail* put it bluntly: "I am very sorry to see Regent-Street Philistines protesting against your supporting piers. . . . Can it be true that a person is deterred from buying things he sees in a shop window because he thinks that with a larger space he would find things to his taste. . . . It is a vulgar age."[65] Another complained, "Things are coming to a pretty pass when the architectural efforts of an Imperial city are to be ruled by the blatant, advertising, competitive vulgarities of the unscrupulous linen-draper."[66] The battle lines were drawn between the shopkeeper's "feminine," glass-loving, commercial proposals and the Crown's "masculine," heavy stone, imperial designs. In this conflict, mass commerce and its feminine appeal threatened the British Empire and British masculinity. Some of the same animosities that shaped the struggles over consumer credit and liquor licenses in Victorian Bayswater were thus still in place. Yet those opposed to mass culture now added the popular rhetoric of empire to halt certain types of retail development. The frivolous and feminine world of shopping was accused of damaging London's stature as an imperial capital. The linen drapers eventually had their way, defeating the construction of Shaw's Regent Street. However, the battle delayed Regent Street's rebuilding until after the First World War. While some properties were completed earlier, much of Edwardian Regent Street's glamorous image was buried under construction debris and government documents.[67]

Local conflicts, political rivalries, and the peculiar nature of class, gender, and national ideologies meant that as late as 1909 only a few London stores approximated the size, services, and sensationalism of Marshall Field's in Chicago or the Bon Marché in Paris. Gordon Selfridge delighted in this difference, believing that English retailers' "old-fashioned" approaches meant that London was fresh or open territory. In his estimation, rather than "presenting a unified whole," West End stores were really an "agglomeration of shops" that were "formless and inefficient." Their "subdued and disciplined" interiors and employees discouraged browsing and fantasizing about goods. This was especially true since most English stores still employed shopwalkers, men who strongly encouraged customers to buy something. Selfridge remembered that when he had attempted just to look around a London shop, the shopwalker abruptly told him to " 'op it."[68]

Although Americans were increasingly shopping in London, many shared Selfridge's sense that English shops were cluttered and uncomfortable. In her *Shopping Guide to Paris and London*, Frances Waxman warned American readers not to be disconcerted when entering the choice London shops, where "things are so strewed about and piled up and hung up that it requires a 'seeing eye' to pick out the good from the bad."[69] Evidently, money could not buy better service. On a London visit in 1900, Andrew Carnegie complained:

> Just look at the jumble in the windows . . . so much stuff that you cannot take it all in. And when you go into a shop they treat you most indifferently. You are scowled at if you ask for goods out of the ordinary, and you are made to feel uncomfortable if you do not buy. These shop people drive away more people than they attract. . . . What London wants is a good shaking up.[70]

Selling Selfridge's

Harry Gordon Selfridge would indeed give London a "shaking up." In less than a year, he constructed the largest, most expensive, luxurious, and publicized store in England.[71] The store's architecture, interior decor, organization, and advertising all addressed Andrew Carnegie's criticism of English shops. Selfridge encouraged the public to see his store as beautifully ordered and designed and as attracting rather than repelling customers. Unlike many London traders, Selfridge was determined to sell to the masses.

After winning a struggle with the London County Council and the Marylebone authorities over building size and regulations, Selfridge chose what was then an innovative steel-frame structure to house his monument to mass consumption on the western end of Oxford Street.[72] This neighborhood was quite near Mayfair's stately mansions, but it also was both home and workplace to perhaps several thousand working- and lower-middle-class Londoners. Selfridge did not open a marketplace where none had existed. Rather, he replaced a number of small traders with a single giant shop. On a much larger scale and a faster pace than Whiteley had done, Selfridge destroyed a community of retailers who had occupied or were near the stretch of Oxford Street between Orchard and Duke Streets. Selfridge razed dozens of shops, including drapers, milliners, dressmakers, tailors, antique dealers, hairdressers, fishmongers, upholsterers, tobacconists, stationers, a public house, stables, and warehouses. He also demolished tenements, a school, a home for working girls, and property that had been in the hands of the Dorothy Restaurant, that all-female eaterie which had been started by a Girton graduate in 1888.

In record time, Selfridge replaced this older neighborhood with what the *Daily Chronicle* called his "Shopping Palace."[73] The new emporium overshadowed its neighbors with its eight floors, six acres of floor space, nine passenger lifts, and a hundred departments.[74] Much of the store was also devoted to so-called amenities, including many "resting places," dining and club rooms, reading and writing rooms. At eighty feet high, with huge stone columns and twenty-one of the largest plate-glass windows in the world, Selfridge's struck even the most critical Londoner as an imposing visual spectacle (fig. 11).

The interior, like the exterior, was considered by many to be an architectural masterpiece. The selling space had wide aisles, electric lighting, crystal chandeliers, and a striking color scheme: all-white walls contrasted with thick green carpets. Although not everyone agreed with the reporter who described the interior as presenting a "scene of unexampled perfection," architectural circles generally bestowed high praise on this ambitious new venture.[75] While doing so, they salvaged English reputations by portraying its design as a merger of old and new. As one reporter explained it, "The construction of the building is purely American, although the outer architecture is elegantly English." It thus blended "the best construction of enlightened modernity and the finest architecture of history."[76]

Figure 11. Selfridge's department store just after it opened. Note the curtains drawn over the windows. *Builder*, April 1909 (by permission of the British Library, shelf mark LD 35).

Selfridge hoped that the mere sight of his building would strike awe in the hearts of Londoners. But he also taught Londoners to look at his store by turning its opening into a special event and encouraging consumers to think of the store as a theater. His show windows were the centerpiece of this shopping drama, and their unveiling served as its opening act. Before the building was complete, Selfridge covered his windows with large silk curtains, the type typically found in the theater. The analogy between the stage and store that the curtains suggested was not lost on Selfridge's audience. "Most impressive of all," one reporter had felt, "were the lights and shadows behind the drawn curtains of the great range of windows suggesting that a wonderful play was being arranged."[77]

At exactly nine o'clock on opening day, March 15, 1909, buglers began playing while employees drew back the curtains and revealed a sight so entertaining that one reporter imagined the window-gazing crowd as spectators of "a tableau in some drama of fashion." Instead of each window being piled high with goods, mannequins held lifelike poses in front of painted backgrounds. One reporter described them as "depicting a scene such as Watteau would have loved, and where ladies of the old French court would have wandered."[78] Nearly all reports of the opening emphasized the "new sensation" created by such "lofty" windows with their "delicately painted" backgrounds.[79] Not every expert agreed that Selfridge's window dressing was more effective than older methods were, however. The *Drapery Times*, for example, commented that "the windows, which, in point of size are perhaps the finest in Oxford Street, are, to my mind, spoilt rather than otherwise, by the display of few goods, valuable space being unnecessarily taken up with painted backgrounds and the like."[80] Whether they liked the windows or not, these journalists still credited the American store with the production of a new visual landscape. Both inside and outside the windows, theatrical techniques helped Selfridge invest ordinary goods with cultural and social meanings, meanings filtered through and interpreted by a sympathetic media.[81]

While reporting on Selfridge's opening, the press broadcast the windows' message to a incalculable number of potential shoppers. Readers unable or unwilling to venture to the West End vicariously looked at his windows and wandered in his shop when they read about this spectacle in dozens of journals, magazines, and newspapers. Selfridge's opening significantly tightened the already close relationship between mass retailing and mass journalism. Gordon Selfridge produced Edwardian commercial culture in partnership with the press. Even while criticizing the new "monster shop," journalists repetitively figured consumption as a female, public, and sensual entertainment. Thus, in 1909 countless English writers joined a maverick American entrepreneur to create an international culture of pleasure on the western border of the West End.

The friendship Gordon Selfridge forged with the press was intimately connected to the growing presence of pictorial advertising in this medium. Since at least the 1880s, commercial artists had drawn full- and half-page black-and-white and sometimes color illustrations to sell soap, cocoa, patent medicine, corsets, and numerous other commodities in the periodical press.[82] In contrast to the "artistic" nature of Pears' soap ads, however, most retailers had advertised sparingly with simple columns of text announcing a special sale or promotion. They tended to avoid new printing technologies that produced better and cheaper illustrations. Many ignored the press altogether, relying instead on short circulars or fifteen-hundred-page catalogs.[83] Some catalogs were quite attractively designed so that, according to one business expert, "numerous women look upon the catalogues from Harrod's, Wooland's, Dickins and Jones, etc., as valuable presents, and would not part with them under any consideration."[84] These cherished possessions were, as one scholar has recently explained, disseminators of modernity, in that they constructed consumers as spectators.[85] They were, however, expensive to produce and often did not keep up with the swift pace of fashion's changes. Edwardian advertising managers of the newer and cheaper papers began to court the big shop's custom, attempting to dismantle what had long been a prejudice against newspaper advertising.[86] Change was coming, but an advertising expert despairingly complained in 1904 that no department store in London "is enterprising enough to emulate Mr. John Wanamaker, who published day by day usually a whole page (which he calls his editorial talk) devoted to chronicling the news of the store." This expert was convinced that "the first big house which did adopt this principle would probably be crowded day by day and the others would be compelled to follow."[87]

Gordon Selfridge would bring these American-style publicity techniques to London. "I want to be able to walk through my advertisements to an audience of five millions," Selfridge confidently declared,[88] for he saw newspaper advertising and publicity as the key to the mass market.[89] Between March 15 and March 22, Gordon Selfridge, therefore, hit London with a media blitz the likes of which it had never seen. Thirty-two richly illustrated advertisements drawn by some of the most well known British graphic artists appeared in ninety-seven pages of the daily and weekly press.[90] Although Selfridge wrote most of the copy, he gave free reign to the commercial artists to illustrate the ideas he wished to convey. Many of these same artists were also currently selling the city for London Underground's poster campaign, launched in 1908.[91] Selfridge adopted what were then considered graphically sophisticated advertisements on an especially grand scale. Even the relatively subdued *Times* called the campaign "an epoch in the history of English retail advertising."[92] The Selfridge cartoons, wrote the *Newsbasket*, were "the most complete attempt to combine art with advertising that has been made in this country."[93] The cartoons were considered so successful that, according to *Advertising World*, they were "appropriated" by the Indian Tea Company and New York's Gimbel's department store later that same year.[94]

Selfridge certainly believed that advertising paid, for his opening campaign alone cost him thirty-six thousand pounds.[95] In justifying this investment, Selfridge explained in the British journal *Modern Business* that "honest advertisement" was of tremendous commercial value.[96] Selfridge, like many American admen of his generation, had what Lears described as a "progressive faith in the beneficent powers of 'publicity.' "[97] He spent so much money on advertising not only to appeal directly to shoppers, but also to win the support of the press. As we saw in the last chapter, magazines and newspapers were becoming dependent on advertising revenue during these years. Editors thus found it difficult to criticize the very institutions that supported them. Selfridge left nothing to chance, however. He sought journalists' admiration through old-fashioned personal influence. Selfridge forged friendships with the leading media moguls of the day, including Arnold Bennett, Lord Northcliffe, and Ralph D. Blumenfeld, the American-born editor of the conservative *Daily Express*.[98] Selfridge likewise appealed to rank-and-file journalists, honoring them with a pre-opening dinner, personally escorting them through the new emporium, and always allowing them free use of telephones and other store services. He maintained his relationship with the press by hiring a journalist as a full-time publicist and by constantly entertaining editors. Although the press had already actively promoted shopping, Selfridge made sure that his store received the loudest praise. Department stores and the press, therefore, formed a tight alliance as they sought to create a class of consumers with a new taste for consuming.

The main themes of the opening week ad campaign resurfaced in unpaid publicity, or "news articles" about the store in countless English and foreign newspapers, journals, fashion magazines, religious newspapers, and trade papers. The publicity that the store received was truly phenomenal. Articles about Selfridge's appeared in North America and Europe and throughout the Empire.[99] After the opening, this publicity died down somewhat as Selfridge advertised in a more conventional manner in the leading national daily newspapers. These ads focused more on selling commodities than on the department store or the pleasures of shopping, but because their content changed constantly, these ads provoked a sense of urgency.[100] As goods did not remain stable in the advertisements, readers might worry that they would also quickly disappear from the store's shelves. This encouraged people all over Britain to read the daily papers in order to follow the specials in Oxford Street. To be a good shopper came to mean someone who read the papers, learned what bargains were available, and shopped often.

Selfridge conflated the advertising and editorial sections of newspapers most directly with the "daily column" that he began publishing in 1912 under the pen name "Callisthenes."[101] Selfridge chose this name because Callisthenes was a nephew of Aristotle who had traveled with and documented Alexander the Great's exploits. According to Selfridge, Callisthenes was history's first press agent.[102] Nearly ten thousand of these articles ran in the daily papers from 1912 until 1939.[103] Callisthenes glorified Selfridge's exploits largely by discussing such topics as the "principles" of modern day shopkeeping, the importance of consumption in the evolution of commerce, or the pleasures of a shopping expedition or a department store luncheon party. Although these articles looked quite unlike other advertisements, they still told readers how to think about shopping.

Of course, critics recognized that by advertising so extensively Selfridge had bought the allegiance of the press. One journalist, for example, complained that "simultaneously with the appearance of huge and profitable advertisements in their columns the newspapers burst forth into rapturous laudations of Mr. Selfridge. Few of them, kind friends, have ever broken into laudations over you or me. But, then, we don't advertise."[104] The *Shoe and Leather Record* similarly complained that Selfridge "bought his crowd" through "buying" the newspaper press with his advertisements.[105] "The help of the Press has been bought at the cost of many thousands," reported the *Anglo-Continental*.[106] These critics correctly perceived that Selfridge's advertising was reinforced by the "rapturous laudations" in the press. Even while protesting, however, they implied that Selfridge's tactics worked, that one could buy the press.

Selfridge's shop and his advertisements were part of a larger cultural transformation in which consumers were addressed primarily as spectators. As we have seen, magazine readers already associated the process of reading with shopping and looking. By the turn of century, however, professional advertisers had begun to theorize about this shopping spectator. As Stuart Culver, Jackson Lears, William Leach, and others have argued, by the 1890s professional advertisers placed their faith in the persuasive force of "eye appeal."[107] English advertisers and retailers, particularly those interested in attracting female consumers, also believed in the psychological force of images. An article in the *Retail Trader* in 1910, for example, compared the window dresser to a stage manager: "Just as the stage manager of a new play rehearses and tries and retries and fusses until he has exactly the right lights and shades and shadows and appeals to his audience, so the merchant goes to work, analyzing his line and his audience, until he hits on the right scheme that brings the public flocking to his doors."[108] Trade journals emphasized women's supposed aesthetic sense, love of music,[109] enjoyment of "attractive" illustrations,[110] "artistic" packaging, and "dainty surroundings."[111] One "specialist" summarized: "We are beginning to see that people are influenced more through the eye than any other organ of the body."[112] While reporting on Selfridge's opening-week window displays, the *Daily Chronicle* put it simply: "The Modern Shop is run on the principle that the public buys not what it wants but what it sees."[113] Although Gordon Selfridge stimulated consumers' visual pleasures, he also asked them to associate shopping with an almost inconceivable range of other sensual and social pleasures.

"A Time of Profit, Recreation, and Enjoyment"

The most striking aspect of Selfridge's advertising, especially the opening week cartoons, was that it fit so perfectly within already accepted understandings of gender, shopping, and the Edwardian West End.[114] In reading Selfridge's advertisements and the publicity that the store generated, one can almost hear the voices of William Whiteley, Frances Power Cobbe, Edith Davis, and the countless other men and women who had characterized all or part of the West End as a female territory. When journalists wrote about the store's opening and its advertisements, they incorporated Selfridge's idiom because in some sense they already spoke the same language. In many respects, Gordon Selfridge had himself learned to talk about shopping and shoppers from reading the papers. He often adopted the excessive verbiage of the advertorial, as well as the tropes of the urban sketch, the guidebook, and the feminist tract. Thus, Selfridge departed from his English competitors not in specific arguments, but in his ability to weave together what were by now orthodox beliefs and make them his own. Advertising and newspaper publicity paralleled each other in such a way that whatever Selfridge said appeared as the truth.

At their most basic level, the opening week ads worked upon an association between femininity, visual pleasure, and abundance.[115] The feeling of abundance emanated not from the campaign's subject matter, but its volume, repetition, and cost. For months newspaper reports had told the British public that Selfridge had spent an enormous sum on his building and his advertising. The thirty-two initial cartoons that appeared in nearly all the daily and evening papers during the middle week of March in 1909 gave the impression that Selfridge's message was simply everywhere and addressed to everyone. Though Selfridge often advertised in the ladies' papers, this campaign targeted all types of readers. It did not include *The Times*; however, though Lord Northcliffe admired Selfridge, he refused to participate in this advertising extravaganza.[116]

The visual pleasures of shopping were derived from the ads' form as much as their content. They were considered, as already mentioned, works of art, something to look at as much as read. At the same time, since many of the illustrations incorporated images of the store, the idea of looking at the ad and looking at the

Figure 12. Selfridge's advertisement drawn by F. V. Poole, "Lady London," March 1909 (courtesy of Selfridges' Department Store Archive).

store became conflated. These two forms of pleasurable looking gave way to a third in those cartoons which prominently displayed the shopper or shopping crowd. In many but not all of the ads the newspaper reader gazed upon a female body. Selfridge's ads thus asked both men and women to look at a "beautiful" store, a lovely woman, and a compelling ad. An example of this dynamic appeared in "Lady London," one of the opening week ads illustrated by F. V. Poole (fig. 12). Poole's design transformed the already tight relationship between women, the department store, and the city into an enticing image. He represented "London receiving her Newest Institution" by drawing London as a statuesque goddess protectively holding the new department store.[117] As Rachel Bowlby has pointed out, this image implied that the store's success was literally in women's hands.[118] Yet here London is no ordinary British matron, but rather a combination of Nike and her secularized version, Fame. Crowned with a garland of buildings and wearing wings of flying drapery, this allegorical female frequently symbolized, according to Marina Warner, the desire for success.[119] Lady London personified the metropolis as a female shopper and endowed her with tremendous power.

Advertisements such as Lady London cannot be said to mean one thing to everyone at any one moment. Yet by 1909 the newspaper reading public would have been so familiar with the idea of shopping as a female pursuit and with the department store as the shopper's favorite stomping ground, that few could have avoided reading Poole's ad in this way. If they had any doubts about the ad's meaning, though, they needed only to turn to the editorial pages; nearly all of the papers in which Selfridge advertised, and a good many in which he did not, felt compelled to comment upon and rework the themes developed in the opening campaign.

Selfridge asked women to travel to the city, become part of the urban crowd, and to experience the store as a public place. Indeed, the department store became newsworthy not because of the commodities it sold, but because of its definition as a social and cultural institution for women. Advertising and newspaper publicity promoted Selfridge's as a "sight" and shopping as female entertainment. Within days, Selfridge's had become, trumpeted the *Daily Telegraph*, "one of the sights of London."[120] A reporter for the *Church Daily Newspaper* tersely captured Selfridge's agenda by proclaiming that, at Selfridge's, "Shopping" had become "An Amusement."[121] Whether imagined as an absolute need, a luxurious treat, a housewife's duty, a social event, or a feminist demand, shopping was now always a pleasure.

In writing about the new emporium, the *European Mail* exclaimed that Selfridge's was quite simply "Modernity's Creation."[122] This headline picked up upon one of Selfridge's main strategies: to define consumer pleasure as in itself a "modern" phenomenon. He claimed that his store offered amusements that had supposedly not existed in the past. In Selfridge's vision of history, Victorian shopping had once been work because shops had been dark, their windows had been cluttered and ugly, and shop assistants had been rude. In contrast, Selfridge's had launched a "new era" in which shopping became an amusement. The "repressive" spirit of Victorian shopkeeping had not died, however. Selfridge's ads implied that most West End shops still lived in this unpleasant and uncomfortable past.

Selfridge's early advertising, therefore, tended to undermine the claims of preexisting urban commercial culture in order to heighten the excitement for and enjoyment of his new enterprise. The earliest advertisements often asserted that Selfridge's had transformed shopping from labor into leisure. A typical advertisement loudly proclaimed that the emporium influenced the "shopping habit of the public." "Previous to its opening . . . shopping was merely part of the day's WORK. . . . To-day, shopping—at Selfridge's . . . is an important part of the day's PLEASURE, a time of PROFIT, RECREATION, and ENJOYMENT, that no Lady who has once experienced it will willingly forgo."[123] Another emphasized that "not until Selfridge's opened had English ladies understood the full meaning of 'shopping made easy.' Never had it been quite such a delightful pastime."[124]

Most of Selfridge's ads, especially the opening cartoons, set out to teach readers how to enjoy this "delightful pastime." They did not all do so, however. At least four of the initial advertisements, for example, pictured idealized images of male construction workers, with each declaring that the store was "a monument to British labor" and a sign of the "strong endurance . . . indomitable grit and pluck" of the "British Workman."[125] Others claimed that Selfridge's demonstrated "honest" business practices such as "Integrity, Sincerity, Courtesy and Value."[126] Children were also asked to visit "Babyland" or to eat something "really nice" in the Luncheon Hall.[127] Perhaps some of the most curious advertisements implied that Selfridge's brought the "world" to London. Using the graphic styles associated with Germany, France, and Ireland, a series of ads told foreign shoppers they would find a bit of their homeland in Oxford Street. Each of these drew upon different artistic traditions and no doubt created diverse responses in their readers. However, their collective effect suggested that the store offered something for everyone, and that, although it was brand new and had no established traditions, Selfridge's was a trustworthy enterprise.

The most common theme, however, was the transformation of shopping into leisure. Several ads observed that shopping at Selfridge's offered women access to a publicly oriented social life. These pictured shopping as a female pleasure but one associated with a newly emerging consumer-based heterosocial urban culture. Its romantic possibilities, for example, were subtly encoded in the imagery of the opening day advertisement, "Herald Announcing the Opening," drawn by Bernard Partridge. In this cartoon the department store/Gordon Selfridge is figured not as a modern institution but as a medieval prince mounted atop a faithful steed (fig. 13). The powerful muscles and overwhelming size of the animal underscored the handsome herald's appeal. Not unlike Selfridge himself, the messenger rides into the countryside to summon ladies and their spending power to the urban center. The economic and international aspects of the buyer-seller relationship were encoded in the store's symbol, a capital *S* that appeared as a combination of a pound and dollar sign, emblazoned on the breastplate of the herald's armor. Yet this illustration also obscures the "foreign" background of the owner and his business methods by linking the venture to a representation of ancient English "tradition" and currently popular images of empire.[128] Novelty and tradition, sensuality and consumption, America and England were thus bound together in a pastiche of medieval and Edwardian romantic imagery.[129]

A second cartoon, "Leisurely Shopping," emphasized the romantic pleasures of shopping by representing a fashionably dressed couple enjoying tea together (fig. 14). The attractive couple is less interested in each other, however, than in the viewer, who as the object of their gaze is also invited to enjoy looking at the couple. Man or woman, the reader becomes both object and subject of a desiring gaze. The pleasures of shopping are symbolized by the sexual exchange of the couple and in the voyeuristic pleasures of the reader. In contrast to this somewhat provocative drawing, the written text just hints at this sexual interplay. "Shopping at Selfridge's," it claims, is "A Pleasure—A Pastime—A Recreation . . . something more than merely shopping."[130] The advertisement constructed heterosexual and consumer desire in relation to each other and linked both to a public culture of display.[131]

T. Friedelson also united consumption with heterosocial culture and modern upper-class Society by promoting the visual and social pleasures of window shopping after hours. In "Selfridge's by Night," Friedelson illustrated a fashionable crowd streaming out of motorcars and carriages to gaze at the store's brightly lit

Figure 13. "Herald Announcing the Opening," March 1909. Advertisement drawn by Bernard Partridge (courtesy of Selfridges' Department Store Archive).

windows (fig. 15). Together the image and text implied that window shopping was an exciting but respectable evening entertainment. "By Night as well as Day, Selfridge's will be a centre of attraction," the copy boasted. The "brilliantly lit" and "frequently re-dressed" windows promised "to give pleasure to the artistic sense of every passer-by, and to make the 'Window Shows at Selfridge's in Oxford Street' worth a considerable detour to see."[132] This picture of evening street life encouraged shopping by suppressing the better-known image of the West End after dark.

The notion of the public realm as a romantic space was in part a calculated attack on the reigning portrayal of the urban center as host to prostitution, gambling, and other illicit activities. Like the managers of West End restaurants, hotels, and theaters, Selfridge rebuilt the city's image as a modern, heterosocial, commercial pleasure center. These were, however, "respectable" or "licit" pleasures. Peter Bailey has observed that during this period capitalist managers promoted a

Figure 14. "Leisurely Shopping," March 1909. Advertisement drawn by Stanley Davis (courtesy of Selfridges' Department Store Archive).

Figure 15. "Selfridge's By Night," March 1909. Advertisement drawn by T. Friedleson (courtesy of Selfridges' Department Store Archive).

new form of open, licit sexuality.[133] A distinct form of modernity was constructed then through the promotion of a capitalist-inspired heterosexual culture.

Both store advertisements and newspaper publicity situated the department store within the commercial spaces of the metropolis. For example, in 1912 a Callisthenes column explained that "abroad, it is the cafés, which are the familiar, lovable places where the populace resort to . . . to meet their friends, to watch the world and his wife, to take a cup of coffee, or drink a glass of lager or absinthe." However, in London "it is the Big Stores which are beginning to play the part of the charming foreign café; and . . . it was Selfridge's who deliberately began to create the necessary atmosphere."[134] Department stores, these ads implied, offered middle-class women a simulacrum of social spaces they had rarely entered and that had been until recently tinged with associations of the sexual marketplace.

Gordon Selfridge went further, however, and encouraged bourgeois women to experience city life by themselves, to take up the position of that modern urban character the *flâneur*, or, in this case, the *flâneuse*. Advertising drew upon the portrait of female urban explorer that had been developed in novels, magazines, and newspapers since at least the mid-nineteenth century, but then argued that the *flâneuse* should always include the department store in her ramble. "What a wonderful street is Oxford-street," claimed one ad, for "it compels the biggest crowds of any street in London." "When people come here, they feel they are in the centre of things. . . . Oxford Street is the most important highway of commerce in the world."[135] Advertising itself was characterized as the modern manifestation of *flânerie* in "An Ode to London in the Spring, The Gentle Art of Advertisement." This "ode" privileged the pleasures of an urban walk over a country stroll:

> Although the country lanes are sweet
> And though the blossom bloss,
> Yet what are these to Regent Street
> Or even Charing Cross?
> So catch a train, and thank your stars
> That there are trains to catch
> And make your way this very day
> To London, with dispatch . . . [136]

Selfridge's advertising adopted the idea of the *flâneuse* developed elsewhere, but unlike her other manifestations, she typically meandered through the different departments at Selfridge's and gained her distanced bird's-eye view of London and its swarming tide from the store's roof garden.

She was also asked to come home. In the department store women could enjoy the pleasure of men's company, could experience the pleasures of *flânerie*, but could also experience social and yet domestic pleasures of the aristocracy and wealthy bourgeoisie. These ads represented the department store as both a public and private place. For example, in Lewis Baumer's opening-week advertisement, "At Home," middle-class shoppers were invited to a gathering of fur-wrapped and elegantly coiffed Society ladies. The picture and caption played on the two meanings of being at home. The illustration represented the formal ritualized sense of the term as a social event, while the text reminded readers of the comfortable domestic connotation of feeling "at home."[137] Other ads similarly portrayed Selfridge's as a formal "event" in the Season's calendar. "Shopping," at Selfridge's, one ad explained, "has all the appearance of a Society gathering. . . . It holds a recognised position on the programme of events, and is responsible sartorially for much of the success of each function that takes place."[138] These sorts of advertisements drew readers into the "private" sphere of West End elite culture. They implied one could be a part of Society if one consumed the right goods at the right shop.[139]

Gordon Selfridge and his commercial artists designed and publicized the department store, then, as a blend of elite and mass culture, mirroring the world of Ascot and the amusement park.[140] Ads and articles described the store as a carnival, a fair, a public festival, a tourist sight, a women's club, and a pantomime. Several pieces compared Selfridge's to the Crystal Palace or the Franco-British Exhibition. The *Daily News* even touted the department store as a "new White City . . . especially for women."[141] This carnivalesque atmosphere heightened in July, when Selfridge displayed the Bleriot airplane, the first to fly between France and England, on the roof of his store. Despite his competitors' accusation that he was engaging in a cheap American publicity stunt, huge crowds rushed to his rooftop.[142] The *Daily Telegraph* reported that "the public interest in the monoplane yesterday was immense. Throughout the entire day, without cessation or diminution, a constant stream of visitors passed into Selfridge's and circled round the historic implement."[143] The stunt proved so successful that Selfridge eventually opened a rifle range, putting ground, and skating rink on the top of the store.

Shopping was exciting and thrilling because it was "modern," but also because it could carry shoppers back in time. Selfridge even claimed that his emporium recaptured the sociability of the early-modern marketplace with its mixed-class and mixed-sex culture. In 1913, for example, Selfridge discussed his store as a modern reincarnation of "the great Fairs" that flourished before "small shops began to do business behind thick walls and closed doors." With his own romantic vision of the history of commerce, he continued:

> We have lately emerged from a period when merchandising and merrymaking were kept strictly separate. "Business was Business." . . . But to-day . . . stores—the modern form of market—are gaining something of the atmosphere of the old-time fair at its best; that is, before it became boisterous and degenerate. The sociability of Selfridge's is the sociability of the fair. It draws its visitors from far and near . . . to sell to them or merely to amuse and interest them.[144]

Selfridge posited that mass retailing reunited elite and popular culture, which he argued had been separated during the Victorian era. This rift had limited the pleasures of shopping and urban culture. This argument might be said to have been part of the larger denigration of all things Victorian that so marked early-twentieth-century culture. Albeit for very different purposes, Gordon Selfridge and the artists and writers of Bloomsbury shared an interest in defining the Victorians as repressed and themselves as liberated.

In particular, Selfridge claimed that he not only satisfied women, he emancipated them. Several ads closely replicated the arguments of feminists and clubwomen except that Selfridge painted his shop as the ideal female "rendezvous" or public meeting place. In a Callisthenes column, "Where Shall We Meet," for example, the store was marketed as a haven for shoppers stranded in an unfriendly and supposedly inhospitable city. Before Selfridge's, the ad claimed, women had to resort to "a cold and draughty waiting-room at a railway station" or perhaps "a bleak, dusty, congested traffic-centre, such as Oxford Street." This supposed lack of an "ideal rendezvous in London" was "called another of woman's wrongs." While "the City man had a number of favoured resorts . . . the poor ladies 'out shopping' have been at a single disadvantage."[145] By building a "private" place in public, Selfridge later told one of his executives, "I helped to emancipate women. . . . I came along just at the time when they wanted to step out on their own."[146]

Gordon Selfridge clearly knew that his store was not the only place for women to meet, eat, or rest while in town. Before he opened Selfridge's he had studied London's other stores and women's clubs to gain a sense of what types of venues were popular with London's women. Yet he cultivated a feminist image and was an outspoken supporter of women's suffrage and female business capabilities. Whether or not he genuinely saw himself as aiding women's emancipation, such claims were a successful advertising strategy. This approach appealed to "progressive women" and gave the department store a modern and "progressive" appearance. This feminist image essentially inverted the relationship between women's growing freedoms and the department stores. Though stores had in fact benefited from women's increasingly public lifestyles, such ads made it appear as though the stores had created a hospitable public space for women and that this was equivalent to their "emancipation."

Many ads characterized the department store as bringing greater equality between the sexes, classes, and nations. When Selfridge advertised his restaurants and other "resting places," he maintained, for example, that such amenities served both individual and social needs. He marketed the main restaurant, which could seat up to three thousand patrons a day, as the largest and best in London.[147] It was said to have "excellent" food at "popular prices."[148] Few luncheon and tearooms in London were thought to have finer decor.[149] After lunch, patrons were encouraged to rest in the library, reading, and writing rooms. French, German, American, and Colonial reception rooms also welcomed foreigners and allowed English shoppers to travel to foreign lands. The German shopper, for example, could relax in a dark oak reception room decorated with old tapestries and designed to be a replica of a "sitting room in the Fatherland."[150] A fatigued or ill shopper had the choice of a first aid room, which "looked very dainty and inviting,"[151] or she could take a "rest cure" in the Silence Room. Here, talking was forbidden so "customers may retire from the whirl of bargains and build up energy."[152] Double windows excluded "street noises," while soft lights and chairs with deep cushions enabled shoppers "to find peace and recuperation." While the shopper rested, a maid and "skilled needlewoman" were always available "in case of any little accident to a button or hook-and-eye which might have occurred during the rough and tumble of a day's shopping."[153]

Shopping was thus likened to a "rest cure" that reduced rather than increased anxiety. Underlying this nurturing image, however, lay the more traditional view of the city as dangerous and dirty and the female body as weak and in need of comfort and protection. Although Selfridge encouraged women to enter the city, like a good Victorian patriarch, he also protected them once they were there.

Selfridge promised these women more than comfort, however. He offered them a space for legitimate indulgence. Modern shopping was more than just buying, but it was also more than "just looking."[154] Shopping was a visual culture of, as William Leach has put it, "color, glass and light," but it also was a bodily culture stimulating all the senses.[155] Its decor and displays allowed one to feast one's eye and enjoy the feel of fine fabric. Its restaurants and services invited shoppers to "treat" themselves to "delicious" luxuries. Even a visit to the bargain basement could become a sensual wonderland for the frugal shopper: "What a shining feast for the eyes are the ribbon tables; what filmy piles of blouses are here. . . . What a forest of silken and velvet flowers; what delicious scents are wafted to us from that mound of tinted soaps."[156] In this passage, materials provided "feasts" for the eyes, while colors and scents were "delicious." Oral, tactile, and visual pleasures defined and amplified one another in kinesthetic array. All appetites were united in a single desiring body.

Many early ads focused on the orally gratifying aspects of shopping. Shoppers were enticed with bonbons and sweetmeats packaged in replicas of famous Italian monuments, buildings, and statues in three different types of marble.[157] Sweets became "wonderfully nourishing," a "benefit," even a "necessity," which made "an appetising and delicious appeal to every visitor in the Store."[158] The American-style soda fountain, a unique temptation, stood at the center of the store's oral appeal. Luxurious ingestion almost became the heart of the consumer experience. A typical ad showed how the soda fountain transformed women who "hated shopping" into avid practioners of the art. Two "large iced strawberries" could thoroughly reform a woman who had found shopping "frightfully boring" and another who thought it "a most decadent development" and a "hotbed of frivolous, senseless adornment."[159]

As if to contain the radical possibility of asking women to indulge in such public, bodily pleasures, Selfridge's also was frequently imagined as a huge glorified bourgeois household, sustaining family life in the heart of the city. After defining "afternoon tea" as "the chief ritual to the household gods," an "unrivalled and unassailable" custom that had "long since stood the test of time . . . one of the mainstays of family life," an advertisement reminded shoppers that "even when away from home, the solace of afternoon tea cannot be dispensed with."[160] This ad both created and used preexisting domestic associations of afternoon tea with family, stability, and tradition in order to connect a new American-owned store with notions of bourgeois Englishness, to make local customers feel at home and visiting tourists feel English. Sensual pleasures were thus given moral validity when placed within the language of domesticity and Englishness.

Selfridge's thereby became a home away from home, offering its customers space for what had been considered private forms of socializing. One journalist reported that women were even inviting their friends to formal shopping parties. This reporter claimed that these "parties are a new thing, which have sprung into existence to meet a new need. . . . The parties are small, select, numerous, and earnest."[161] They included buying, but emphasized dining and browsing with friends. Selfridge marketed public dining, a common activity for nearly forty years, as new, modern, and fun, as an updated image of Victorian women's culture. Here, female friendship, like the family, became a vehicle for legitimizing consumption.

Selfridge and his supporters walked a tightrope between praising and denigrating the home and often did both at once. Indeed, Gordon Selfridge believed that women were responsive to the "sensuous appeal of beauty" of his store because they had "little opportunity of escaping the deadening routine of homelife."[162] His advertising reflected this notion and figured the private home as lonely and isolating. "Women needed Selfridge's," according to one ad, "to break the monotony that had invaded and made dull a daily round." Selfridge's provided "the variety which is the spice of life."[163] "I was lonely," complained one housewife, "so I went to Selfridge's . . . one of the biggest and brightest places I could think of. I wanted crowds . . . a happy place . . . 'home' in the open . . . caught up in a whirl of these jolly human, little businesses; made part of the crowd; all sense of isolation swept away."[164] Another ad similarly presented the bourgeois home, in contrast to the department store, as lonely, isolating, and especially dull. "I have a friend, and I want to meet her. Where shall the meeting-place be?" asked one character in this ad. "At my home? I don't think so: women spend so much time among their own all too familiar chintzes," she complained. This consumer "wanted a place with music, where there were plenty of things to see, and a companionable sense of crowds."[165] If Selfridge's offered lonely housewives companionship, the department store also provided them with privacy and solitude, as several journalists pointed out. It was the absence of the shopwalker that was the key to the "new sensation" of shopping at Selfridge's. "Safe from the tyranny of the shopwalker," the editor concluded, "shopping becomes what shopping should be—a matter for individual speculation, for individual choice, and for individual satisfaction."[166]

Selfridge's opening campaign, daily advertisements, Callisthenes' column, and the free publicity in countless newspaper articles formed a chorus that loudly sang the pleasures of shopping. Everything about Selfridge's was characterized as a pleasure. The services and entertainments the store offered, the spectacle it physically presented to passersby and shoppers, and the treatment customers received from employees all made Selfridge's department store a unique female pleasure center. Selfridge's ads and publicity basically implied that all the pleasures of the city could be found in this new store. Under one roof, one could find restaurants, tea shops, women's clubs, and entertainments. "Selfridge's is a city epitomised—a compact concentration of the most attractive shops, of all the comforts and conveniences of modern life open to everyone," opined a *Daily News* reporter.

It is perhaps all too easy to fit the story of Selfridge's into a well-worn narrative about gender relations in which a dashing stranger swept British maidens off their feet. However, this story is not as simple as it appears. Women helped create, finance, and promote the business, and Selfridge's also tried to appeal to, or one might say constitute, the male consumer. Thus the store both articulated and yet undercut any simplistic dichotomy between male producer and female consumer.

Female employees, journalists, and copywriters contributed to the making of Selfridge's, while women apparently were increasingly investing in these large shops. In April of 1909 the *Financial News* ascertained that between 12 and 15 percent of all the shareholders in the leading drapery and furnishing establishments in London were women. It thus concluded that "the lady investor wields a huge and constantly—increasing power in the financial affairs of the world," since she could influence store policy as shareholder and as shopper.[167] A phenomenal 49 percent of Selfridge's private investors were women, a fact the *Drapery Times* attributed to the store's unprecedented advertising campaign.[168] More surprisingly, although many were listed only as married women, spinsters, and widows, many of the small investors were domestic servants, nurses, governesses, and schoolteachers. While more research needs to be done on the role of these female capitalists, it is obvious that, as with the Victorian family firm, women were the "hidden" investors in public companies in the early-twentieth century. Indeed, they were not so hidden that financial experts failed to recognize their economic significance.[169] Ironically, in addition to drawing bourgeois ladies to his store, Selfridge's advertising may have also attracted working- and lower-middle-class women to invest in his concern. Presumably, they too would profit from its success.

The growth of such businesses relied then on women as workers, investors, and shoppers. Women also played an informal role in the promotion of these ventures. Word of mouth was extremely important in establishing or ruining a store's reputation, and in this sense women could wield considerable influence on a business's success. For example, in 1910 a Mrs. Stafford of Museum Cottage, Oxford, received a postcard from "Nannie." On the back of a picture of a London hotel read this short note: "Shall leave London tomorrow at 1.45, arrive at Oxford at 3. Am just off to Selfridges to tea with Annie Coleman. Had a P.C. [postcard] from Aunty. Much Love, Nannie."[170] By 1910 the store was already a household word for a network of women. Nannie's postcard advertised an entire matrix of urban commercial activities including the system of public transport, a hotel, and a department store. Postcards, letters, and gossip thus also contributed to the imaginary creation of the West End. When "Sallie" sent her sister in Shropshire a postcard in 1911, she told of visiting the zoo and witnessing a motor accident, but she also exclaimed, "I have been to see the shops, they are lovely."[171] Nannie and Sallie both experienced and promoted, if they did not financially profit from, West End commercial culture.

"Man's Best Buying Center"

But was that West End as dominated by women as Selfridge's ads and newspaper reporters had implied? The media surely presented the city as given over to women. A recurrent image of the sales season was of London's West End occupied by an army of female shoppers. Under the headline "Stores' Carnival, London's Great Shopping Week" the *Daily Mail* told its readers: "The women of London are preparing for a week of pure joy. . . . All the tubes and motor-omnibuses and horse vehicles of London will take ladies by the thousand to see the fascinating displays of these establishments."[172] Another reporter wrote that "the West End was given over to women" and that their laughter and the "rustle of silken skirts" enlivened the sound of buses crawling through the slush of the streets.[173] Military language often peppered these reports, emphasizing a sense of invasion of the city by an "army in furs and feathers."[174] This image of the shopping hordes was indeed a ubiquitous means of describing shoppers, particularly during sale season.[175]

However, a photograph of Selfridge's on opening day reveals quite a different image of this crowd (fig. 16). If one looks closely at this picture, few silken skirts, furs, and feathers may be seen. Instead, darkly suited men crowded the sidewalk outside of the store. London's men may have come simply to see what the fuss was about. They may also have come because Selfridge's was one of the first department stores to directly target the male consumer. From the start, Selfridge's had also pushed itself as "The Man's Best Buying Centre." Instead of describing the lingering pleasures of shopping, however, Selfridge's appealed to male customers by emphasizing the convenience with which "you may clothe yourself from head to foot in an entire outfit of fashionable ready-made clothing in a twinkling of an eye, whatever your size and shape."[176] Men were not really expected to browse, but to buy something easily and quickly, in a "twinkle of an eye," and then leave as soon as possible.

J. F. W. Woolrich's ad "The Man's Best Buying Centre" played with this difference between male buying and female shopping. In this advertisement men like women meet their friends at Selfridge's, but they do so outside the store. They do not drink tea, flirt with women, or otherwise enjoy themselves. The text focuses on men's dislikes rather than their pleasures. Men supposedly liked Selfridge's because it diminished rather than extended their shopping: "With intimate knowledge of Men's Dislikes as well as of their predilections in Shopping we have planned the Departments that are devoted to their service with an eye to avoid the one and minister to the other. Gentlemen whose desire in entering a shop is to make a purchase quickly and depart as soon as possible will find Selfridge's exactly to their mind." In another ad a wife asks her husband if he will come Christmas shopping with her. He replies as any average, virile middle-class male would: "Shopping! Rather not. Now look here, dear, you know how I hate and loathe the beastly shops. . . . No, I simply won't go; well, if I do, I want you to clearly understand that I won't go inside and I won't carry parcels. I simply—

Figure 16. Photograph of Selfridge's Opening Day, March 15, 1909 (courtesy of Hulton Getty Picture Library).

Selfridge's! Oh! Well, that's another thing."[177] Selfridge's eventually devoted a great deal of advertising designed to lure the male consumer into the female arena of the department store. Because of shopping's association with femininity, however, the male shopper had to have his masculinity reinforced. Selfridge's sustained a distinction between male and female spaces, activities, and consumer habits, but used this difference to sell more goods.[178] Indeed, this campaign carefully found a way to target men while at the same time bolstering the image of consumption as feminine. Even though men shopped, the image of the shopper and shopping crowd was still resolutely gendered as feminine.[179] Although Selfridge could claim to be "Man's Best Buying Center," in 1909 journalists were not able to see shoppers as masculine.

"British Shes Should Shop at British Stores"

Journalists' stories about shopping were thus hardly factual statements or straightforward reports. They were essentially advertising that promoted a desired or ideal vision of the shopping public. Not all reporters regurgitated Selfridge's message, however. As we have already seen, some were quite nervous about the impact this American upstart was having on London's business community. This anxiety was best expressed by the journalist who cleverly wrote "British Shes Should Shop at British Stores."[180] Quite a few journalists reacted to Selfridge with disdain and predicted that his methods would not take hold on English soil. The *Drapery Times* admitted that the store's opening and spectacular publicity had created a crowd but questioned "the possible weakness of inviting people to walk round without being asked to purchase." This writer worried that the masses would interfere with "those people who go to make purchases," since they would be barred from receiving "the attention which they want." Did a mass audience equal mass consumption? Perhaps not, but the author admitted that as much as he disliked Selfridge's methods, "an alternative form of attracting potential customers is difficult to alight upon."[181]

Others defended British pride by maintaining that the crowd Selfridge's had created simply proved that the whole of the West End, not just Selfridge's, was one of the best shopping centers in the world.[182] One reporter, for example, focused on Oxford Street:

> It is extremely doubtful that there is another street in the world which contains so many huge shops, or, rather stores—for they can provide you with anything from a pin to a steam-engine—as Oxford Street, London. America may be able to boast of the great Philadelphia store of Wanamaker . . . of Siegel Cooper and Co. the great store of New York . . . but it cannot point to a spot like the Oxford Street quarter mile, where so many huge business worth millions are concentrated.[183]

Oxford Street, from Marble Arch in the west to High Holborn in the east, had become "one continuous drapers shop."[184] The *Draper* explained that most Oxford Street shops were "drapers pure and simple . . . not stores on the Harrodian principle. They are all fashion marts, and as such are enshrined in the hearts of every woman."[185] If British stores were not as spectacular as those in Philadelphia, New York, and Chicago, British shopping streets could be said to dwarf those in foreign cities. The *Advertiser's Weekly* asserted that Oxford Street was "one vast store," not because of its numerous large shops but because of advertising, and Selfridge was so important because he encouraged its use. Now "every day some new reason is given to large numbers of readers why this thoroughfare demands an urgent visit." The result of this competitive advertising was "to emphasise the fascinations of Oxford Street, and more and more to establish in the readers' mind the prestige of the thoroughfare as a place of great shops."[186] In this context, large and diverse shopping crowds proved that the West End was a preeminent shopping center and England was a prosperous place. One journalist concluded that the "young and well-dressed" crowd shopping in the West End were "living evidences of the good fact that in this big city of ours the middle-class is substantial and prosperous, with a good margin for the little luxuries of life."[187]

Despite the obvious resentment that many retailers had for the American entrepreneur, most felt obliged to adopt his successful strategies. As trade competition grew fierce in Edwardian London, virtually all retailers professed that their enterprises were pleasure centers. Established shops increased their advertising budgets,[188] spruced up their windows, rebuilt and redesigned their interiors.[189] Harrod's jubilee celebration even rivaled Selfridge's spectacle. The Knightsbridge store desperately searched for a reason to celebrate shopping and found an anniversary that precisely coincided with Selfridge's opening. It ardently advertised and celebrated the event with special decorations and unusual entertainments. The furniture department became a concert hall decorated with purple-and-white muslin and garlands of crimson rambler roses. Shoppers enjoyed the music of the London Symphony Orchestra, a famous Spanish opera singer, and other well-known performers.[190] According to a sympathetic reporter, at Harrod's "shopping was a pleasure and nervous headaches or aching feet were conspicuously absent."[191] Harrod's also spent a great deal of money publishing a souvenir, *The House That Every Woman Knows*, in which the store portrayed itself as a Society rendezvous. In a not-too-subtle gibe at Selfridge's American background, the booklet clearly stated that Harrod's was "an English Institution which commands the admiration of the world."[192] Two years later, one of Harrod's catalogs, "Brochure of Progress," observed that the Edwardian store was "one of the brightest and most attractive centres in London."[193]

Not to be outdone, Whiteley's built an entirely new store in Queen's Road and celebrated its opening in 1911 in much the same way that Selfridge's had done two years earlier. One of Whiteley's ads welcomed "all customers and friends, all visitors and sightseers" to visit "their Great New store."[194] Newspapers such as the *Daily Express* reported on the festivities in much the same way as they had on Selfridge's opening. Apparently the paper's editor did not think it strange to describe the militant suffragettes' window-smashing campaign on the front page and then write this headline for the article on Whiteley's, "The Great Siege of London: Lord Mayor a Prisoner of 100,000 women—Enchanted Castle of Commerce." The article then explained that the Lord Mayor had participated in the store's opening festivities, but he soon became trapped by the "battalions" of women who "poured into Queen's-road."[195]

As we have already seen, drapers were not the only traders who were characterizing their venues as popular pleasure centers during this period. In 1909, Lyons built its five-story Corner House in Piccadilly. In addition to several dining rooms, the Corner House had a soda fountain, café, bars, hairdresser, shoe-shine parlor, and theater-booking agent.[196] When another Lyons Corner House opened opposite Bond Street Tube station in Oxford Street in 1916, the event was also celebrated with special concerts featuring a "Ladies Orchestra." Lyons advertised itself as a popular café bringing entertainment to the masses.[197]

Trade competition in the West End had not led to a price war but to a battle over shoppers' pleasures. Not all London stores claimed that they offered new features for lady shoppers, however. In fact, stores such as Liberty's, Heal's, and the shops in Bond Street and the Burlington Arcade used architecture and promotional material to cultivate an old-fashioned image. They implied that it was their small-scale and traditional service that made their shops pleasurable.[198] Heal's, for example, told customers in 1909 that "you will find Heal's shop to be not a modern store with wholesale and impersonal methods, but a shop of the old school with a rare and established standard of taste, and . . . with a trading code dating from a less aggressive and commercial age."[199] Heal's was by no means the only London store to use their age rather than their modernity to appeal to shoppers. In the 1920s, Liberty's even went so far as to rebuild their modern store encased in a Tudor facade.[200]

With so many shops, eateries, and women's clubs all highlighting their own elegance and comfort, the whole of the Edwardian West End became a female playground. Praising this development, the *British Congregationalist* wrote simply that "shopping becomes amusing and fascinating when it involves a visit to the West End."[201] Together with an enthusiastic press, Selfridge's and other English retailers collectively represented the West End as an environment of pleasurable consumption. Despite his monumental efforts, Gordon Selfridge was never the sole source of pleasurable consumption. Even quite supportive reporters described the store as only one of the many West End shops serving women goods and pleasures:

> London's greatest shopping week began yesterday. . . . Selfridge's had flung open its doors. Harrod's was celebrating its sixtieth year of success, and every West End firm vied with one another to dazzle and entertain its customers. Oxford-street, Regent-street, and Brompton-road were crowded with eager shoppers. Never before has it been possible for the twentieth-century woman to indulge in such an orgy of shopping.[202]

In the Edwardian newspaper the female shopping crowd conjured up images of modernity, the mass market, and mass culture. As England's relative economic strength waned, as the roles and ideals of the sexes and the classes shifted, and as the feminist movement presented a far more frightening image of public femininity, the department store and its public women were perceived quite differently in the 1900s than they had been thirty years earlier. Though some clearly worried that shopping crowds symbolized British decline in the face of Americanization, others believed that so many "British Shes" proved that British business could still compete with its American rivals.

Of course, many resented the mass culture that Selfridge had brought to Oxford Street. Writing in 1926, E. B. Chancellor complained of Oxford Street's "garish shops" and its "flashy and tawdry" nature.[203] In her essay "Oxford Street Tide," Virginia Woolf also disparaged the street's artificiality and its "garishness and gaudiness." She called it a "forcing house of sensation" in which "the mind becomes a glutinous slab that takes impressions and Oxford Street rolls off upon it a perpetual ribbon of sights, sounds and movement." Here is the classic modernist critique of mass culture. Woolf was so sure that the swirling superficial sensations of this culture weakened one's mental faculties that she abruptly ended her essay with the admission that "it is vain to try to come to a conclusion in Oxford Street."[204]

For better or worse, twentieth-century Oxford Street had come to epitomize the mass-produced, impersonal world of the large corporation and the fast-paced, chaotic world of commodity culture. Though many decried such developments, this view of Oxford Street, its department stores, and its shoppers was a deliberate creation of countless retailers, advertisers, and journalists.

There is no question, however, that Gordon Selfridge had a tremendous impact on London's commercial culture. "It would be difficult," a Bond Street dressmaker remarked, "to indicate any individual who has done personal work of greater consequence than Mr. Selfridge. He has taught the possibilities of the departmental store. He has introduced a new architecture into commerce."[205] He was not, however, singularly responsible for what this businessman and the *Daily Express* called "a new era of shopping." That era had been created some time before Selfridge crossed the Atlantic and it continued to appear as "new" long after his store had become a fixture in the West End landscape.

Scholars have frequently observed that the department stores were "proponents" of "modern consumer culture."[206] These businesses taught people how to consume, but more importantly how to think about consumption, to associate it with personal satisfaction and individual pleasures. In particular, the department store urged women to see buying as a form of leisure. Whether or not we interpret these pleasures as false or illusory, there is no question that department stores promoted and defined female pleasures in order to sell their goods. What I have argued here, however, is that the notion of department store singularity, female agency and pleasure should not be taken as given, but as a narrative that structured transformations in the media, urbanization, and gender identities. It also rested on conflicting notions of class and Englishness. The meanings that the department store conveyed about commodities and the act of consumption thus did not emanate directly from its showcases and its plate-glass windows.

Finally, a word must be said about the role of the historian in this chapter. Gordon Selfridge stood out from other retailers in part because of his faith in advertising and publicity. He also set himself apart by consciously fashioning himself and the department store as active historical agents. In a variety of places, Selfridge argued that the department store was the most modern form of all commercial activity.[207] Above all else, Gordon Selfridge secured his place in history by insuring that his store would have an extremely comprehensive archive. Far more extensive than those in other London stores, Selfridge's archive includes virtually every advertisement and article that was written about the store in its early years. Because there are few personal or financial papers included, this archive imparts the store's public image. It reveals the history that Gordon Selfridge wanted historians to tell. He wanted scholars to view him as an innovator who knew how to please women better than anyone else. I have attempted to explain rather than accept this narrative. My primary goal has been to explore how Selfridge, and by implication the department store, became identified with the launch of a new epoch. Although he clearly reworked preexisting meanings and structures, I have consciously not placed this chapter at the end of the book since he did not have the final word about the department store or female pleasure. Selfridge wanted to be remembered as one of the most important actors in London's commercial history. This story worked because many people, including scholars, participated in its telling.

• CHAPTER SIX •

Acts of Consumption: Musical Comedy and the Desire of Exchange

HATS

Some people say success is won by dresses,
Fancy that!
But what are dresses without a Hat?

If you would set men talking when you're walking out to shop,
You'll be all right if you're all right on top!

That's the last Parisian hat,
so buy it,
and try it!
Keep your head up steady and straight,
though you're fainting under the weight!
We'll declare that you are sweet
Men will wait outside on the street
If you have that hat![1]

THIS HIT SONG from George Edwardes's production *Our Miss Gibbs* charmed audiences at the Gaiety Theater throughout 1909. Just as Selfridge's symbolized mass consumption that year, Edwardians identified the Gaiety with musical comedy, a new form of mass entertainment that had flourished since the early 1890s.[2] These two institutions shared more than mere name recognition, however, for the form, content, and staging of musical comedy intersected with the growth of mass distribution. Musical comedy reinforced but did not replicate the view of consumption and gender promoted by large-scale retailers. Without propagating identical consumer cultures, the stage and store collectively constructed a large heterosocial consuming crowd in the *fin de siècle* West End.

As Joel Kaplan and Sheila Stowell have recently shown, the prewar theater and fashion industry were involved in a mutually satisfying relationship.[3] Late-Victorian and Edwardian business had a deep and abiding faith that "theatrical" environments put shoppers in a mood to consume. This belief, built upon a particular vision of the consumer, sanctioned the virtual convergence of theater and department store. As we have seen, Selfridge's show windows were decorated with the curtains, painted backgrounds, lighting, and arrangements of a stage set. Fashion shows, concerts, and other entertainments held within the store also turned shopping into a spectacular show. Selfridge and other moguls of the mass market as well as elite fashion designers also sold consumerism on the West End stage. Gordon Selfridge and Richard Burbidge of Harrod's, for example, financed plays that championed their shops and their understanding of shopping. *Our Miss Gibbs* was in fact Burbidge's response to Selfridge's domination of the Edwardian press. Burbidge turned to the theater and musical comedy to sell his vision of Harrod's and consumer culture.

Yet while retailers were borrowing theatrical techniques and using the stage to sell their wares, the West End theater also found its audience in the world of the shops.[4] In 1894, H. J. W. Dam, the author of the immensely popular musical comedy, *The Shop Girl*, told an interviewer, "As many thousands of people do business at the large shops and stores in London, . . . [I realized] the stores formed an excellent sphere to make the basis of a musical piece."[5] Dam was among a number of "modern" authors who saw the stores as an appropriate setting for musical comedy. He recreated the department store onstage to convert West End shoppers into theater audiences. Dam and his theatrical colleagues imagined audiences as shoppers who were as happy to consume goods and images in the darkened halls of the theater as they were in the brightly lit department stores that were but a few blocks away.

Stage and store created similar material environments but emphasized somewhat different pleasures. Selfridge had hinted at the heterosexual pleasures one might find at his store, but generally he advertised the department store as a world of women. The impresarios of the musical comedy such as George Edwardes promised both men and women a luxurious visual, sensual, and erotic shopping experience. In "Hats," for example, a French milliner working in "Garrod's" department store sings the praises of shopping and flirting. The song makes fun of the excesses of an age devoted to large hats and conspicuous consumption, but it also declared that buying the latest Parisian creation would guarantee women success with men. In dozens of similar productions the boundaries between sexual and economic exchange all but disappeared. Buying and selling became a game of courtship, marriage, and heterosexual pleasure. The cast of characters were none other than the debtors, disorderly shoppers, aggressive entrepreneurs, male pests, annoying shopwalkers, and glamorous shop girls that we met elsewhere in the West End. Yet in musical comedy, their economic and social struggles turned into an erotic drama.

In slightly different ways, historians Peter Bailey and Tracy Davis have both argued that musical comedies managed sexuality in a way that supported the interests of corporate capitalism and patriarchal gender relations.[6] This genre certainly reworked the long-established erotic tradition of men looking at women and women making a spectacle of themselves. Actresses' bodies were commodified and consumed by male audiences. However, musical comedy was also a mass cultural form invented to attract men and women from the upper classes to the upper levels of the working classes. Its construction and narrative structure commodified female bodies while also constituting a female spectator and attempting to displace the misgivings attendant with both developments. As the unstable and fluid quality of class and gender identity moved the narrative and inspired the humor in musical comedy, anxieties associated with mass consumer culture were commodified and, in a sense, enjoyed.

Set within a profoundly materialistic world, musical comedy commented upon the production of desire and new types of sociability in sites of mass consumption. It brought desire under control, however, as women's lust for goods and men's lust for women inevitably led to innocent flirtation, a happy marriage, and social stability. Department store musical comedies thus housed socially acceptable yet erotic narratives about the mingling of classes, sexes, and money. By packaging anxieties about consumer culture as entertainment, the theater came to define new "modern" sexual and class identities. It also provided a venue for both producers and consumers to explore the profits, pleasures, and problems of consumer society.

In the twentieth century, the West End and Broadway remain the two most famous theater districts in the world.[7] Although facing financial crises throughout its recent history, the "West End" is still shorthand for quality theater and extravagant productions. This is a complex history that is far too large to explore fully here. Rather, this chapter focuses on the genre of musical comedy in order to look at the intersections between theater and other sites of consumption. On one level, it illuminates the mechanisms that created what Adorno and Horkheimer identified as the "culture industry"—that is, the technical and economic merger of advertising and culture. As they and others have argued, mass cultural forms like musical comedy expressed an ethic of amusement that revealed "the influence of business."[8] This culture industry did not completely dominate society and politics, but as I will show here, it did profoundly reshape metropolitan class and gender relations.

"Going Up West"

Before looking at department store musical comedies or the promotional relationship between the stores and the stage, we must situate the theater within the nexus of commercial and illegal pleasures that defined the turn-of-the-century West End. By this period men and women, the working class and the wealthy, local residents and foreign tourists thought of the West End as a special arena. It was the place for a day in the city, a big night out, or a week of shopping and sightseeing. The theater's growth paralleled the expansion of retailing and catering and shared economic and discursive characteristics with these other modes of consumption.

The theater industry expanded throughout Britain in the latter part of the nineteenth century. However, the dramatic West End—theaters in the area bounded by the Strand, Kingsway, Oxford Street, and New Bond Street—acquired a special aura as the center of fashionable and refined entertainment. Not all West End theaters were actually located within these boundaries nor were all those situated within it considered West End. Nevertheless, the managers of what became West End theaters manipulated pricing, show times, ticket sale locations, and choice of theatrical fare to target wealthy audiences. They also added restaurants and introduced the matinee to prompt the middle classes to see theatergoing as a respectable and fashionable social ritual.[9]

Critics as well as theatrical impresarios created the West End's aura by repeatedly drawing distinctions between art and vulgar entertainment. For example, in discussing the highly centralized nature of England's drama, the critic William Archer wrote in 1894 that "the whole of literary life of the stage . . . is centred in some dozen or fifteen theatres in the West End of London. . . . A great many plays are produced at East End, suburban, and provincial theatres; but they are absolutely ephemeral and 'negligible' the 'penny dreadfuls' of the drama."[10] Like many of his contemporaries, Archer viewed London's dramatic world as a stark contrast between high art and low entertainment, between East and West, center and periphery. Yet this was never a hard-and-fast division. Wealthy men joined the working-class audiences at the music halls such as the Alhambra Palace and the Empire in Leicester Square; until the end of the nineteenth century, the working classes filled the pit or the gallery in West End theaters such as the Adelphi, the Princess, Drury Lane, and the Gaiety.[11]

In the 1870s, John Hollingshead, then manager of the Gaiety Theater, believed that by introducing the matinee he would draw in wealthy women and tourists.[12] He later claimed that the matinee became an immediate success and even an "expected function."[13] After its advent, middle-class women frequently rounded off a day of shopping and sightseeing with an afternoon in the theater.[14] Yet the practice of combining shopping and theatergoing had begun much earlier, if on a smaller scale.

While studying her family's diaries, Ursula Bloom discovered that her great-aunt savored a night at the theater when she visited mid-Victorian London. At the age of twenty-four, this aunt traveled alone to the city to see several productions at Drury Lane and the Royal Opera. On one such visit, she brought Bloom's mother with her, and the two women enjoyed a hectic November week of shopping, playgoing, and sightseeing.[15] Female Londoners went to the theater with even greater regularity than provincial dwellers. Jeanette Marshall, a middle-class girl growing up in London in the early seventies, went to the opera dozens of times each season. As she grew older, Marshall relished many other forms of dramatic entertainment.[16] Even relatively impoverished middle-class families saw the theater as a special but not exceptional occasion. Molly Hughes fondly remembered her first visit to a "real play" during her Christmas holiday of 1882. After consulting her mother, Molly's brothers took her to see a farce at the Criterion. Years later when the play itself was forgotten she remembered the experience of a night out, including "such a meal as I had never dreamt of."[17] Although Molly enjoyed an adult entertainment, many middle-class children were introduced to the theater and music hall stars during the Christmas season, when special children's plays and pantomimes were produced.[18] By the second half of the century, then, West End audiences were increasingly but not exclusively upper-class patrons and middle-class suburban, provincial, and foreign tourists.[19] As early as 1871, the *Atheneum*'s drama critic believed that English "country people . . . incited by the advertisements and criticism they have seen in the London papers," were the foremost sponsors of West End theater.[20]

Until the late 1880s, however, families such as Molly's viewed a night out in the West End as a special event because it was still a rather expensive, inconvenient, and at times downright unpleasant experience. Most playhouses were situated in and around the Strand and were served by only the Charing Cross Underground Station. T. C. Newman recalled that a trip to the West End from a middle-class western suburb could be a cumbersome undertaking. A family "living in Kensington," he remembered, would first eat their evening meal "soberly at home." "After dinner," the tedious trip began with "a walk to the nearest station if it were not too far, or . . . by 'growler' or hansom cab. Then there would be the slow journey in the smokey, sulphurous atmosphere of the Inner Circle Railway to Charing Cross and then the walk up Villiers Street to the Strand, and so on foot to the theatre."[21] Dramatic pleasure was hampered, then, by slow and difficult transportation. Newman failed to mention, however, other obstacles to middle-class comfort.

As Tracy Davis has shown, the theater district was firmly nestled within a neighborhood that offered a wide selection of sexual and other sorts of illegal commercial pleasures. The Strand and surrounding streets were filled with gaming houses, brothels, and pornography shops. Similar amusements were on sale within the theater. The Empire promenade, for example, was a famous site of prostitution and its gallery a notorious rendezvous for homosexual men.[22] In 1894, Mrs. Ormiston Chant launched a famous attack upon what she viewed as the toleration of vice at the Empire, but in 1902 the Empire's promenade was still described as "a strange spectacle—this exchange, this traffic, this Fair Flesh."[23]

Nevertheless, by the late eighties and nineties the physical contours of the theatrical West End had changed dramatically. The construction of Northumberland Avenue, Charing Cross Road, and Shaftesbury Avenue facilitated the flow of middle-class suburbia to dozens of new theaters and music halls.[24] In 1889 the *Building News* observed that because of these new streets a visitor no longer had to travel "the tortuous" and "unsavory" route through Seven Dials.[25] The journal delighted in the way that urban renewal had cut through notorious slums and separated the fashionable, entertaining West End from nearby danger zones, though this "renewal" had not swept away all of the locale's unsavory elements. The erotic spectacle at the Empire and elsewhere remained even as the fin de siècle theater district was enlarged and made increasingly accessible for a mixed-sex, middle-class audience.[26]

At the same time that the physical landscape of the eastern half of the West End was being remade, vast sums were being spent on the construction and remodeling of luxurious theaters. Among other theaters, the Shaftesbury, the Garrick, the Apollo, the Globe, the Queen's, the Aldwych, the Strand, Prince's, Her Majesty's, Daly's, and Wyndham's were all built during the turn of the century. These new dramatic palaces further cemented the image of the West End as

England's paramount entertainment center.[27] The same corporate structures that aided the growth of department stores in these years also financed theatrical construction. A large and mobile middle- and lower-middle-class market, excited by newspaper advertising and reviews, kept the theaters profitable.[28]

During Edward VII's reign it had become, according to Ursula Bloom, "a social gaffe if one could not discuss the latest plays with a personal knowledge of their attributes, and on a Saturday night every little family in suburbia had an early meal and took the 'bus into the West End to attend some entertainment or other."[29] Foreigners, especially Americans, spent as much time and money in the West End theater as they did in its shops.[30] Revolted by this modern mass audience, Henry James characterized it as "the *omnium gatherum* of the population of a big commercial city . . . flocking out of hideous hotels and restaurants, gorged with food, stultified with buying and selling and with all the sordid speculations of the day."[31] Mario Borsa, the author of *The English Stage of To-Day*, was much kinder. Along with "elegantly attired ladies" and "well-groomed male escorts," he saw "shopmen, clerks, and spinsters in pinz-nez, but more numerous still are the shop girls, milliners, dressmakers, typists, stenographers, cashiers of large and small houses of business, telegraph and telephone girls, and thousands of other girls whose place in the social scale is as hard to guess as it is to define."[32]

As Henry James had so critically pointed out, the modern mass audience did not treat theatergoing as an isolated event. James may have wanted to elevate or isolate the theater from what he viewed as the crass and vulgar elements of modern life, yet physically and financially the theater district was an integral part of a larger neighborhood of both legal and illegal amusements. Its proximity to London's most fashionable shopping streets meant that audiences associated the theater with shopping or working in large department stores. Stores, hotels, restaurants, and theaters sometimes even shared the same buildings, owners, and patrons.[33] The Criterion, for example, was a large entertainment complex that included a variety of dining rooms and rest rooms catering to different tastes and incomes. Guidebooks, women's magazines, and department store and restaurant advertising encouraged consumers to think of the West End as a site where one could indulge in diverse forms of consumption. The fact that theater-booking desks were regular features of department stores and restaurants also underscored the interconnections between different consuming amusements.[34]

In the West End, shopping, dining, sightseeing, and playgoing were engaged in and thought about together. As Michael Bonavia later recalled, "Going Up West never had any connection with geography; it meant shopping in Oxford Street or visiting a theatre."[35] Shopping and theatergoing were thus integrated forms of consumption in the late-nineteenth and early-twentieth centuries. Each, of course, could be enjoyed separately. One might shop or go to a play in many London neighborhoods or in any major town in England. But in the West End, buying images and buying goods were overlapping experiences that intensified and amplified one another. The late-Victorian West End thus had become a site in which a diverse audience both "provisioned and envisioned" itself.[36]

Selling to the Modern Audience

The department store and the theater were not just neighbors. They were partners dedicated to igniting insatiable consumer appetites. Their relationship blossomed during the fin de siècle as they recognized a common goal, the creation of the "*omnium gatherum* of the population of a big commercial city," or put simply, the mass market. This mass entity included elegantly attired ladies, well-groomed male escorts, shopmen, clerks, and spinsters, shop girls, milliners, dressmakers, typists, stenographers, and cashiers. Although clearly a congregation of buyers and sellers, this audience in the theater became a collective of consumers. The mutual aspiration to sell amusement to this modern audience contributed to a literal and figurative merger of stage and store.[37]

With the opulent atmosphere of the department store, restaurant, and hotel, the late-Victorian theater translated consumption into visual pleasure and spectacle. As we have seen, the Victorian public acquired a taste for spectacle while reading magazines, walking along the streets, shopping, traveling, and visiting museums, exhibitions, and other entertainments. The theater was a part of this spectacular culture, but it had not always been so. According to one historian, early-nineteenth-century "aural" theater only slowly gave way to highly pictorial productions that conveyed meaning as much through the look of the set and costumes as through dialogue and plot.[38] By 1870, this transformation had been all but accomplished, for as the critic Percy Fitzgerald wrote, "We go not so much to hear as to look." Fitzgerald compared the theater to a "gigantic peep-show [in which] we pay the showman and put our eyes to the glass and stare." When he looked at this peep show, Fitzgerald saw the commodity-filled world of the shop, the store catalog, and the bourgeois interior. He wryly pointed out that because the "most complicated and familiar objects . . . [are] dragged upon the stage . . . when we take our dramatic pleasure we have the satisfaction of not being separated from the objects of our daily life." "Within the walls of the theatre," he remarked, "we meet again the engine and train that sets us down almost at the door; the interior of hotels, counting-houses, shops and factories."[39] To the great dismay of this critic, late-Victorian theater mimetically produced the spaces and commodities of an ideal bourgeois material world.[40]

In mainstream theater—especially comedy—trains, shops, hotels, and other sites of consumption became the locus of the bourgeois imagination. This vision helped Britons accommodate themselves to the intensely urban world they had built. As we will see, it contributed to the commercialization of the city and urban culture. If the New Drama of Ibsen and others depicted modern life as one of fraught social relations, the commercial theater interpreted it as a richly material world of exteriors, interiors, furnishings, and costumes.

This dramatic city bore a striking likeness to the urban sketches published in the popular and women's press. A high level of inbreeding and cross-fertilization in the literary world may partly account for this similarity. Authors like H. J. W. Dam and George Sims, for example, were adept dramatists and journalists. Sims is often remembered for his 1883 exposé on London's slums, *How the Poor Live*, but he was better known as the author of popular melodrama.[41] Owen Hall, the author of several hit musical comedies, was actually a solicitor by the name of James Davis. His sister Eliza was a popular journalist, well known for her contributions to the *Queen*, *Truth*, and other late-Victorian papers.[42]

These writers nearly all believed that spectacle carried a special message to a female public, or at least a feminized public, of mass consumers. By this period, women's visual pleasure was thought to be derived from their consumer desires. Such desires were in turn triggered by a visually rich landscape viewed in a particularly sensuous physical setting. It is this conception of consumer psychology, as much as pure economic interest or personal relationships, which created the partnership between journalism, the fashion industry, and the theater.[43]

Critics, playwrights, and retailers assumed that women's acute visual sense and passion for finery led to their enjoyment of the material aspects of performances. By the 1880s, trade journals commented on stage fashions because editors believed that women attended the theater to learn about the latest designs. The *Warehousemen and Drapers' Trade Journal*, for example, told its readers that it described actresses' dresses because "it frequently happens that a fashion makes its first appearance on the stage, and afterwards is adopted by the feminine public at large." Since actresses now "dress in every way in accordance with the rank and position in the world of personages they represent," the journal commented, "the borrowing of styles and fashions from actors and actresses ceases to be reprehensible." It was no longer "uncommon," the author suggested, "for the audience to applaud a successful toilette as they would a graceful pirouette or bit of eloquent by-play."[44] The irony, of course, is that such articles encouraged drapers, milliners, and other retailers to attend the theater and recreate stage fashions.

The understanding of the theater as store window developed as the stage and actresses gained social recognition and respectability. As this occurred, drapers such as Liberty's and Debenham and Freebody's, "dressmakers of the highest repute," and furnishers such as Gillow's agreed to present their newest wares on the West End stage.[45] These businesses also unintentionally altered attitudes toward actresses and the theater. Though many still regarded actresses as immoral public women, a few had attained the sobriquet of "beauty" or star. Actresses and Society "beauties" were coming to represent a new kind of femininity that was closely tied to the mass production of images. Their portraits were widely circulated and displayed, for example, in shop windows as *cartes de visite*. As one unhappy observer noted, "Pretty, popular and virtuous ladies in society" were being "paraded in the shop windows in the company of burlesque actresses." Some, like this critic, were shocked by this public display, but by the late 1870s these portraits encouraged the movement of actresses into the respectable and fashionable world.[46] These portraits reappeared, however, as advertisements selling products and presenting the idea that a beautiful image could be purchased.[47] The late-Victorian actress was thus strongly identified with fashion and consumption.

Drama reviews in women's magazines, theatrical journals, and the daily papers deepened the association between consumption and the stage and encouraged readers to adopt the look and style of the actress. By focusing attention on costumes and sets, rather than on acting, writing, or directing, the press asked audiences to see theatergoing as a prelude to shopping and to link shopping with a radical re-fashioning of the self.[48] Reviewers simply assumed that audiences naturally viewed plays from their vantage point as shoppers. The editor of a new weekly amusement guide, for example, nonchalantly remarked in 1896 that "the stage is the leader of fashion in dress among both ladies and gentlemen. Illustrated notes will be written by experts upon the dresses in popular plays."[49] The *Lady*'s critic patriotically wrote that instead of looking to France for the latest fashions, English ladies could find them at home. If they patronized those theaters "devoted to comedies and vaudeville," readers would surely find "something novel in the way of dainty gowns, this critic promised."[50]

At times reviews became almost pure advertisement. One critic found the 1910 comedy *Priscilla Runs Away* "a very amusing play," but especially commented that "to the feminine playgoer it affords a very valuable opportunity of studying the latest fads and fancies of La Mode."[51] The "Paquin gown" worn in the first act by Miss Nedson Terry and the numerous others designed by Messrs. Debenham and Freebody became the focus of this review. In "Dresses as the Lyceum Pantomime," the reviewer found Cinderella looking

> sweet in her russet woodland attire, artistic in her rags, superb in her Princess dress (which is composed of the richest satin, covered with a fine, filmy lace, which clings gracefully round her dainty figure, caught here and there with diamond buckles, whilst a girdle of the same precious stones glitters at her waist. And her train is a marvel in itself, for each yard has taken a fortnight to manufacture, and no rainbow hue is missing from its folds, and over all is worked upon the satin an exquisite pattern of old lace). As a dress it is unique, and veritably a part of Fairyland.[52]

The string of adjectives—*glittering*, *filmy*, *exquisite*, *graceful*—the paragraph-length sentences, and the references to "fairyland" replicated the abundant style of commodity culture on sale elsewhere.[53] This was the prose of the fashion world, the advertisement, and the shop window.

Such reviews were frequently accompanied by photographs or illustrations of sets and costumes. Together text and image taught readers what to look for when they went to a play, reminded them of what they had seen if they had already gone, and allowed those who would never attend vicarious access to this fashionable event. Articles and advertisements in theatrical journals and programs directed readers to the vendors who would make them look and live like stars. B. J. Simmons and Co., for example, advertised that their firm had designed the "costumes for the Blue Moon Scene, the Irish Girls, and the Moonbeam dance in 'Our Miss Gibbs.' " A West End shoe store likewise told the readers of the fan magazine the *Play Pictorial* that Miss Gertie Miller, the female lead in *Our Miss Gibbs* says, "Your shoes always give me satisfaction."[54]

Not all reviewers endorsed what they perceived as a mutation of drama into advertisement, but they reluctantly contributed to the process. An 1881 *Era* piece disparaged *Youth* as "an excellent example of the overblown Drury Lane spectacle style," but then told readers, in detail, that this "overblown" style was provided by Messrs. Gillows: "The splendid rooms of the hero," for example were as "luxurious as an Eastern seraglio," had "rich curtains and hangings, an exquisite conservatory with a fountain sending up a jet of real water, lovely flowers, gorgeous paintings, costly and luxurious carpets upon which the footstep falls unheard."[55] Critics thus ambivalently sold plays and the larger culture of consumption. Most, however, seemed to have few doubts about the commercialization of the theater. In 1909, an editorialist for the *Lady's Realm* assured readers that the stage would long remain "the glass of fashion" and that even men sought sartorial guidance while enjoying a night out at the theater.[56]

Although theatrical reviews encouraged female playgoers to concentrate on the fashions paraded onstage, this was by no means the only dynamic between audience and performer. The popular male impersonator Vesta Tilley was one of the leaders of male fashions during this period.[57] Men thus looked at other men, or women dressed as men, to become acquainted with the latest fashions. Although many of the plays' narratives revolved around heterosexual courtship, alternative forms of desire also circulated in the theater. Tracy Davis has documented how the erotic environment outside and inside the auditorium encouraged male audiences to see actresses, like prostitutes, as purchasable erotic entertainment. Particular types of cloth and decoration, "revealing" designs, gestures, and figural composition were already encoded with sexual meaning and enhanced the "sense that the actress was inseparable from the whore and synonymous with sex."[58] Such associations may have worked both against and with the homosexual/homosocial subtext of an amusement that regularly relied on cross-dressing, often housed homosexual activities, and which by the time of the Wilde trials was publicly invested with homosexual meanings.

Consumers no doubt came away with many readings of the plays and of the profuse, commodity-thick prose that surrounded the opening of each new play. These texts could inspire consumption or perpetuate the tradition of home dressmaking—albeit a practice that also involved quite a bit of shopping. While some readers yearned for the goods they read about, others remained happy not to "buy" the styles paraded onstage. Fashion journalism and the commercial theater it endorsed radically collapsed the distinction between actress and audience, the prostitute and the respectable lady, the play and "real life." This was Eliza Linton's greatest fear. Instead of bemoaning the nexus of consumption, public display, and femininity, commercial theater thrived upon this relationship and the idea that gender difference was produced in and through the dynamic of looking and being looked at.

The career of the couturiere Lady Duff-Gordon, known as "Lucile," embodied the complex relationship between the stage, fashion industry, and female audience. Lucile had made clothes since she was a young girl, but she attempted to earn money from her talent only after her husband left her for a chorus girl.[59] If the stage had lured away her husband, Lucile found it could also give her financial independence and even artistic inspiration. Lucile later claimed that her first professional dress had been "inspired by a tea gown she had seen Letty Lind wear on stage."[60] She also believed that she became "established" only after designing the costumes for the leading actresses in Charles Wyndham's production of *The Liars*.[61] After this success, Lucile eventually became one of the most sought-after English designers, with shops in Paris and New York and gowns draping the leading ladies of the London and Broadway stages.[62]

Like many of her fellow retailers, Lucile believed that theatrical environments triggered a psychological urge to purchase goods. "All women," she argued, "make pictures for themselves. They go to the theatre and see themselves as the heroine of the play, they watch Marlene Dietrich or Greta Garbo acting for them in the cinema, but it is themselves they are watching really."[63] Lucile felt that a woman's identification between the audience/shopper and model/actress was an essential facet of her buying clothes. Women would buy clothes, she maintained, once they abandoned a sense of difference between their real and ideal self.

Music, lighting, and a luxurious, comfortable environment allowed women to dispense with their "real" self and see themselves as the actress or model parading before them. Lucile facilitated the process in her shop through the development of what she termed "the mannequin parade." Claiming to be the originator of the fashion show, Lucile made shopping "as entertaining to watch as a play." She later described herself as a director, preparing "the *mise-en-scène* for this first dress parade . . . [with] soft, rich carpet laid down in the big showroom, and beautiful, grey brocade curtains . . . hung across the windows. At one end of the room I had a stage, a miniature affair, all hung with mist olive chiffon curtains, as the background, which created the atmosphere I wanted."[64] This dramatic environment stimulated the identification between shopper and model. "It is impossible," Lucile professed, "to over-estimate the effect of environment on a woman, for women are infinitely more adaptable than men, they become part of their surroundings." Whether in the shop or the theater, "when the lights are lowered to a rosy glow, and soft music is played and the mannequins parade, there is not a woman in the audience, though she may be fat and middle-aged, who is not seeing herself look as those slim, beautiful girls look in the clothes they are offering her. And that is the inevitable prelude to buying clothes."[65]

After Lucile opened her Paris shop, the *Daily Graphic* noted that her great talent lay in the display, or "stage-setting," of her dresses. She did not just "set a number of 'mannequins' parading up and down, each wearing a different costume, and all having the same background," but set off those fashions with "music, appropriate backgrounds, effective lighting, [and] gestures to suit the purpose." This journalist agreed these effects "put her clients in the atmosphere for properly appreciating her creations."[66]

Despite her fame, Lucile's understanding of consumer psychology was similar to that of other retail experts. In 1910 the *Retail Trader* advised shopkeepers that if they wanted their windows to appeal to female passersby, they needed to drape "articles of personal attire" over lifelike mannequins because "these figures in the shop windows represent their [women's] ideals of themselves—show themselves up as they would like to appear."[67] As discussed in the previous chapter, another expert in the *Retail Trader* compared the window dresser to a stage manager, since each works with "lights and shades and shadows and appeals to his audience."[68] Edwardian retailers who sold "fashionable" commodities imagined their audience in almost identical terms as the theatrical world. Both shoppers and audiences were thought to have a heightened "taste for spectacle" and a particularly alert visual sense. As Stuart Culver has argued for the American context, the turn-of-the-century window dresser attempted to "transform the 'passive throng' on the city streets into an audience of absorbed spectators."[69]

Of course, some fashion experts warned that to be well dressed, women needed to gain an accurate, not ideal, self-image. *The Gentlewoman's Book of Dress*, for example, advised a woman to first learn "her own deficiencies" as well as "her good points."[70] Jean Worth, the son of the famed Charles Worth, also encouraged women to "draw a mental picture" of themselves before choosing material for a gown.[71] These experts encouraged faithful rather than fanciful self-portraits. Women must, these authors argued, both learn how to look at themselves as others saw them and as they would like to be seen. Whether retailers thought women should carefully examine their real image or whether they should imagine themselves as fashion models or actresses, all of these fashion experts felt that a central aspect of shopping for clothes involved women looking at themselves. In this sense, the female gaze was directed at the female body, whether one's own or that of an ideal self.

This vision of the shopper as spectator particularly applied to dress goods, however. When advertising "necessities" such as bread the *Progressive Confectioner* told bakers that "you must use good sound logical reasoning with her. . . . Take her into your confidence and tell her all about your bakery . . . how your bread is made . . . how the high standard of quality is kept up. . . . She must be convinced by sane and sensible arguments, she has reasoning powers of her own."[72] This article characterized consumers as rational beings persuaded through logical argument—a view quite unlike that held by the fashion trades.

The point here is twofold. By the Edwardian period, advertisements constructed diverse identities and attitudes toward goods, but ads were also a ubiquitous, chameleonlike cultural form. The advertisement had found its way into a range of cultural practices and locales such as the theater. Even private theatricals bore the imprint of the brand name. In 1900 the *Queen* announced that "advertising parties" had become all the rage. Guests evidently arrived at private homes dressed as a character in a popular advertisement, such as that for Hovis Bread or Carter's Liver Pills. The hostess then awarded a prize to the guest who achieved the "best representation" and the person who correctly guessed the most advertisements.[73] By the 1920s audiences were well aware that plays were both art and advertisement. This recognition inspired the humor in a short skit produced in 1927, aptly titled *The Show Window.* Before the play started the audience was informed that because the financial credits had accidentally been forgotten from the program, the producers had found "another way of giving credit." The skit involved a "smartly dressed lady," "a man," and "a maid" complimenting each other on their stylish clothing or their fair complexion. The receiver of the compliment then turned to the audience and mentioned the brand name—Palmolive, Yardley's, Peter Robinson's, and so on—responsible for his or her good looks.[74]

Advertising had thus moved far beyond the shop sign, trade card, poster, and illustrated paper. It had become a central, indeed pervasive, part of diverse mass cultural forms. Therein lay its force. English society, particularly its wealthier members, had long distrusted blatant puffery. Some entrepreneurs such as Gordon Selfridge had countered such suspicions by seeking free publicity. He also sought other realms for self-promotion, such as the theater. The sociologist Colin Campbell has cautioned that "advertisements (and other product-promoting material) only constitute one part of the total set of cultural influences at work upon consumers."[75] This reminder, however, fails to acknowledge that to a certain extent the advertisement was inserted in less than obvious ways into many cultural realms.

Cinema provides the most well known and thoroughly studied example of the relationship between advertising and the media.[76] The promotional possibilities of the cinema were recognized almost in its earliest incarnations, especially in the United States. But even in England this was true. As early as 1898 an enterprising Manchester draper mounted a cinematograph above his door to advertise the opening of his newest branch. The *Drapers' Record* believed this to be the first time the cinema had advertised a business.[77] It would certainly not be the last. In America, short dramas, comedies, and fashion shows filmed in the first decades of the twentieth century "functioned as living display windows . . . windows that were occupied by marvelous mannequins swathed in a fetish-inducing ambiance of music and emotion."[78] Product "tie-ups" promoted goods on screen, and retailers like Macy's department store sold their own lines of cinema fashions. In order to display as many products as possible, Hollywood movies were often set in fashion salons, department stores, beauty parlors, and middle and upper-class homes. According to Charlotte Herzog, these films literally borrowed the fashion show's ability to "suggestively promote" the sale of clothes.[79] Of course, as Jane Gaines has argued, one can imagine motion picture spectators as "casual shoppers," browsing, but not buying.[80] In her seminal essay "The Film Viewer as Consumer," Jeanne Allen described at least three points of convergence between film viewing and consumerism: film viewing meant "participation in a consumer environment"; it "fostered a liaison" with other "consumer behavior[s]" such as shopping; and "The commercial relations between the film industry and other business existed to produce commercial films or exhibit commercial products in theatrical films."[81] As we have seen, and as Allen herself recognized, all three of these elements were present in the West End theater.

The fin de siècle theater provided direct participation in a consumer environment, was physically situated within a larger shopping district, and had direct commercial relations with other businesses, particularly the fashion industry. Film "inherited" the relationship between consumption and theater, but presented it to an even broader audience. Given the direct influence of theater on early cinema, and jockeying between cinema and theater for audiences, the similarity between the two forms should not be surprising.[82] As the twentieth century wore on this resemblance became less pronounced. West End theater maintained and indeed strengthened an elitist image, while American cinema became the quintessential mass entertainment.[83] The expense involved in staging elaborate productions (which had been designed to appeal to mass female tastes) led to soaring prices and the eventual disappearance of poorer audiences. Cinema, in contrast, distributed opulent material worlds at cut-rate prices.[84]

Both cinema and theater, however, constituted gender difference as a relationship between a male spectator and a desirable female image. The feminine spectacle has a specific history that Abigail Solomon-Godeau has shown was central to the culture of modernity emerging after the French Revolution.[85] If the female body became spectacle in fiction, painting, advertising, pornography, photography, and, as we have seen, journalism and the theater, narrative cinema, Theresa de Lauretis has explained, offered the "most complex expression and widest circulation" of the representation of woman as spectacle.[86] Laura Mulvey similarly argued that in film the "pleasure in looking has been split between active/male and passive/female," in which the woman "displayed as sexual object . . . holds the look, plays to and signifies male desire."[87]

Other scholars have explored how female audiences might have viewed glamorous but commodified feminine images. Herzog, for example, has suggested that women adopt a male perspective to essentially "learn how to transform themselves into a 'look' by comparison with another woman who is looked at."[88] In this formulation the consumer is thought to be identifying with the woman onstage and adopting a male perspective—that is, imagining how she would look to a male spectator. This temporary adoption of the male perspective may not be transgressive, however, since it reinforces the masculine identification with the look.[89] For Mary Ann Doane the female spectator "is invited to witness her own commodification . . . to buy an image of herself insofar as the female star is proposed as the ideal of feminine beauty."[90] In this scenario the female viewer is but a shopper purchasing her own commodification. If one accepts this perspective, there are female audiences, but no female spectators, since that position is always masculine. Miriam Hansen has emphasized this point by arguing that while the movie industry increasingly catered to female audiences, it structured the spectator as masculine. "The theoretical spectator and actual movie-goer," she tells us, "are not one and the same."[91]

While many of these theories of spectatorship have been extremely useful in opening up a way of understanding the perpetuation and creation of gender difference in the twentieth century, they have also been faulted for using psychoanalytic frameworks that present a timeless view of the spectator and spectacle. As we have seen, however, this contemporary scholarship reflects the popular understandings of gender, audiences, and consumption at the time that film was evolving. It was not inevitable that the female film viewer or theatergoer should purchase her own commodification, but this was the primary way that female audiences were conceived during the fin de siècle. Yet, in contrast to those theorists who argue that the spectator was always conceived as masculine, I want to suggest that theatrical managers, writers, and retailers also constructed a female spectator.

Fin de siècle culture producers assumed that both male and female viewers enjoyed looking at an attractive young actress. This figure was so common on the turn-of-the-century stage because theater owners wanted to appeal to a mixed-sex, mass audience. Entrepreneurs attracted heterosocial audiences by constructing narratives that emphasized heterosexual pleasure and gender difference. They envisioned audiences as looking at and desiring different aspects of the same production. They believed that male audiences desired youthful female bodies and female audiences coveted the clothing covering those bodies. The narrative structure of nearly all musical comedy turned these separate passions into a successful heterosexual relationship. Playwrights, fashion designers, theater owners, and critics created performances that conformed to this understanding of sexual difference, consumption, and a gendered public. John Hollingshead, the Gaiety's first manager, wrote that the "English stage . . . governed by the laws of commerce, must stand behind its counter to serve its customers."[92] After Hollingshead left the Gaiety, George Edwardes made the shop girl the heroine of musical comedy because he felt she served the audience what it wanted.

"The Romance of a Shop Girl"

Associated with George Edwardes and the theaters he managed, Daly's and the Gaiety, musical comedies were wildly popular with a heterosocial, middle- and lower-middle-class audience.[93] Paralleling the growth of West End commercial culture, musical comedy addressed the tensions and pleasures of that culture. This genre staged consumption in a comedic and playful light, a surefire source of humor, romance, and spectacle. It situated consumption firmly in the realm of leisure and courtship, not in that of economics and work. Consumption rather than production was presented as the source of social and sexual identities, as virtually every play staged a feminine and consumer-based version of the self-made man.

In the remainder of this chapter, I will discuss several plays that reveal aspects of the relationship between musical comedy and urban consumer culture. Then I will turn to a more focused reading of two extremely popular department store musical comedies, *The Shop Girl* (1894) and *Our Miss Gibbs* (1909). Not only were these two among the most successful of the genre, their comparison helps illuminate how gender ideals, commercial culture, and musical comedy shifted and intersected during the fin de siècle.

Between the 1890s and 1920s, the English theater became a promotional arena that also questioned the nature of consumption, commodification, and consumer desire. As Thomas Richards made clear in his study of commodity culture, the spectacle did not fully replace all social life, nor did it supplant all cultural arenas.[94] Even at its most commercial moments, the stage was also a forum that posed questions about the nature and impact of consumer culture. As Jean-

Christophe Agnew has written of Elizabethan and Jacobean drama, fin de siècle theater "thematized representation and misrepresentation as the pivotal problems of drama . . . [and] invoked the same problematic of exchange—the same questions of authenticity, accountability, and intentionality" that were present in the marketplace.[95]

In turn-of-the-century Britain, the growth of the mass market, rapid industrialization, and urbanization resulted in an almost obsessive concern with the nature of representation, accountability, and authenticity. The use and misuse of consumer credit, for example, had turned upon these very themes. Harrowing tales of recalcitrant debtors and fraudulent consumers in trade journals conveyed the idea that one simply could not detect the real from the fake customer. In these stories and onstage, shoppers played the trickster masquerading as an authentic buyer out to ruin a gullible trader. The relationship between facade and interior thus plagued buyers and sellers and became a dominant theme in the stories they told.

As certain areas of the city became spaces of mass pleasure, the physical separation and distinct rhythms of male and female middle-class life seemed less pronounced. The city street also cut across and through Victorian class and gender ideology. While streets could physically separate working- and middle-class areas, they could also be arenas that brought the classes together in ways which were uncomfortable and erotic. In the new public arenas of the late-Victorian city, gender relations and sexual desire had already become a complex game of exhibitionism and voyeurism, masquerade and detection. And nowhere was this "new historic regime of seeing and 'not-seeing,' of representable and unrepresentable" more apparent than in the theater.[96]

The stage did not simply address or exploit the anxieties and pleasures stimulated by capitalist transformation and urbanization, but as Agnew has explained, it constituted new ways of thinking about identity and market relations.[97] The Edwardian theater in particular positioned the slippery relationship between "real" and "false" selves as the primary dilemma in mass society. Musical comedy, the most popular genre of the era, cast this dilemma as both a comedic and a romantic problem. Its comedy exposed the aggression inherent in market relations, while its romance attempted to turn hostility and conflict into heterosexual desire.

Like the tea shop, the large-scale restaurant, and the department store, the musical comedy was introduced to appeal to a broad audience, while making a particular bid for middle-class women.[98] From the late sixties until 1886, the Gaiety had largely offered burlesque and was quite popular with "the young men of the town."[99] In the words of its first manager, the Gaiety was no "platform for the display of grandmothers and maiden aunts." It exhibited "physical beauty."[100] This philosophy meant that scantily clad young women, known as Gaiety Girls, and eccentrically dressed men became the stock-in-trade at the Gaiety of the 1870s and 1880s.[101] In 1886, George Edwardes took over the somewhat ailing theater. To bring back its former popularity, he renovated the playhouse and the productions and transformed it into what one woman's magazine called a "ladies theatre." Edwardes redecorated the auditorium in "Moorish style" and "scientifically arranged and vastly improved" the ventilation. But most importantly, this reporter observed, was that Edwardes "boldly abandoned burlesque, and [made] a brave bid for victory with genuine English comic opera."[102] It wasn't until the full development of the musical comedy in the midnineties, however, that burlesque leg shows completely disappeared. In the early nineties, the middle-class Londoner Jeanette Marshall complained that she never liked the Gaiety as much as her husband, had; he particularly enjoyed the company of Gaiety Girls. She wrote in her diary that "the tights are certainly most unbecoming to women with fat legs. . . . I cannot see why the becomingness of skirts is not recognized."[103] Edwardes responded to these sorts of complaints, believing that to keep male patrons and win over female customers he needed to emphasize "the becomingness of skirts."

Although a new theatrical form in the 1890s, the musical comedy was a hybrid that blended elements of British and French farce, burlesque, and the comic operas of Gilbert and Sullivan. Both farce and its sibling, musical comedy, relied upon a great deal of physical humor, verbal play, and disguise. Serious emotions and ideas were frequently undercut by visual and verbal gags, often added during the performance by the actor or actress, that can only be guessed at from remaining scripts. Farcical comedy especially exploited verbal misunderstandings that were amplified or created by social differences. The cast therefore usually included a range of different elites peppered with a few intelligent working-class characters.[104]

Musical comedy kept many of the elements of farce, but gave a more central role to members of the serving classes, particularly the favored heroine of the day, the shop girl. This intelligent working girl used her knowledge of consumption and human nature to resolve the dilemmas that she and others faced. The nature of identity was always ambiguous, however, since the actors frequently impersonated members of the "opposite" class. This inversion might be seen as a challenge to the social system. Yet any radical reading was undermined by the audience's complete awareness of the masquerade. While the characters were fooled by disguise, the audience always knew who was who. Indeed, the denouement almost always diminished the radical potential of social inversion by revealing that the shop girl, who had such stellar success and authority throughout the play, was not actually born into the lower orders. At the play's conclusion, the working girl was restored to her rightful place among her class. This genre therefore drew upon elements of European popular culture—namely, the social inversion of the carnival—but exposed its fictions as fictional.

Musical comedy also maintained certain aspects of the burlesque tradition, but it banished the leg shows and other overt appeals to male voyeurism.[105] In 1909 Max Beerbohm wrote of the new genre: "All the classes mingle on the easiest terms. Everyone wants everyone else to have a good time and tries to make everything easy and simple all round. This good time, as I need hardly say, is of a wholly sexual order. And yet everyone from the highest to the lowest is thoroughly good . . . an innocent libertinism."[106] The idea of "innocent libertinism" was an ever-present feature of Edwardian mass culture. This description of musical comedy echoed Joseph Lyons's promotion of restaurant dining as a "free trade in pleasure" and Gordon Selfridge's advertising of the department store as an exciting but safe aspect of modern urban life.

Musical comedy's thematic treatment of class, gender, sexuality, and consumption, as well as its staging and promotion simultaneously critiqued and facilitated the development of urban commercial culture and mass society. The backdrop for its "innocent libertinism" was nearly always a site of exchange: a shopping street, a tea shop, a dressmaker's, an exhibition, a restaurant, the theater itself, or, most popular of all, a department store. These locations offered wonderful promotional possibilities for real-life retailers, seemed very "up-to-date," and allowed for the mixture of strangers that was central to the play's romance and comedy. Many productions moved easily between different sites of consumption. The most extreme example of this was George Grossmith's farce *Come Inside* (1909). While its script no longer exists, a *Pall Mall Gazette* review gives a flavor of the intertextual quality of Edwardian mass culture. In the first scene a male "matinee idol" becomes "the prize" for a female "beauty who wins the most votes in a 'Daily Blither' competition." The Blither's beauty contest is staged as a "glorious assembly of ladies in Pelfridge's beauty parlour." This scene thus self-consciously caricatures Selfridge's, beauty contests, mass-circulation newspapers like the *Daily Mail*, and the emergence of the modern fan club. This phenomenon had appeared only the year before.

According to Kaplan and Stowell, in 1908 the admirers of the matinee idol Lewis Waller had formed a club of KOW Girls, otherwise known as the "Keen Order of Wallerites." In addition to faithfully buying tickets to all of Waller's shows, KOW girls eagerly consumed an array of promotional products, including a Waller "personality puppet."[107] The KOW Girls and their parody in *Come Inside* lampooned and celebrated an emerging star system that made both young men and women into sex objects. Members of the fan club evidently enjoyed playing with the relationship between performance and real life and looking at handsome young men such as Waller.

The second act of *Come Inside* shifted almost seamlessly from Pelfridge's department store to the "Back of a Weekly paper." In this scene, a Mr. Lulli Vallie falls in love with the "girls" he has seen in advertising posters. The central scene of this act is basically a fashion show displaying women's bodies and beautiful clothes. Throughout the play, characters replicate the frenetic experience of the Edwardian shopper as they literally move between the theater, department store, mass circulating newspaper, and advertising poster. This movement also enacted the psychic play between image and reality that set designers, window dressers, and retailers so hoped to inspire; but it is humorously a man, Mr. Lulli Valli, who becomes enraptured with advertised images of women. The play evidently was an "immediate success" because, according to one reviewer, of its "lavish and complete" mise-en-scène and "magnificent costumes."[108] The critic assured readers that the treatment of the "great West-end house of business [Selfridge's] which is so freely satirized in this piece" was of "the utmost good-nature all the time."[109]

Comedies such as this one played with the similarity between shopping and playgoing to encourage female shoppers literally to "come inside" the playhouse. In 1913, for example, Mark and Sydney Blow advertised the Queen's Theater in Shaftesbury Avenue as a shopper's rendezvous, where the public could "meet one's friends, write letters, read all the papers and magazines, use the telephones, send messages by hand, take tea, and generally make themselves at home, as at Selfridge's." Mark Blow told a journalist that he hoped the Queen's would become an "anchor in the intervals between shopping and lunch and more shopping and dinner." They opened the new theater with *This Way, Madame*, a play about a fashionable dressmaker's. Mark Blow explained that when ladies "read the title of 'This Way, Madame' in the theatrical advertisements of the newspapers . . . they will accept its invitation by day as well as by night."[110]

This Way, Madame touted the Queen's Theater as a female public space while also advertising haute couture designs and expensive furnishings. The central scene in the play's second act was comprised of "beautiful mannequins" dressed in "beautiful evening gowns" parading before "a tall, beautiful" customer, the Baroness des Herbettes in a fashionable Rue de la Paix dressmaker's. According to the precise stage directions, the beauties were displayed in a "sumptuous" room decorated with "white and pink marble panels," heavy mahogany doors, a ceiling "painted in a very French style, the subject being cupid hunting cherubs and angels." There were also "several ottomans, draped white and pink against the walls . . . marble tables . . . double doors covered with materials, flowers in profusion . . . *everything to suggest luxury*."[111] Such a combination of lavish costumes and set design, a display of "beauties," and the theater's new amenities pleased both female and male audiences, if not necessarily in quite the same way. For over twenty years, the musical comedy had rarely varied from the basic formula of fashion parade and opulent furnishings.

In the early, extremely successful musical comedy *The Shop Girl* (1894–96), the lyrics, plot, and mise-en-scène linked consumption, performance, and romance. Its author, H. J. W. Dam, set the first act in the Royal Stores, a department store he claimed to have modeled after Whiteley's and the Army and Navy Stores. Dam picked this locale because he felt audiences liked watching their everyday experiences onstage. In an interview published in *Sketch* magazine, Dam opined: "The taste of the public is becoming more local and real. The whole tendency of the serious drama is toward realization in the life of today. My idea was that this is equally true of the comedy stage." However, in a derogatory fashion reminiscent of Henry James, Dam offered that "people will readily pay to see on the stage what they can see in the streets for nothing." Dam emphasized that his choice had been determined by public taste rather than his particular interests. However, this was no doubt the world he inhabited. As an American journalist, he had worked for some time on the London edition of the *New York Herald* and was known "as a writer on up-to-date scientific subjects."[112] "Scientific" evidently meant anything that reflected contemporary society.

Musical comedies were never the product of one author, however. Each was shaped by songwriters, composers, set designers, performers, producers, and theater managers. So while Dam emphasized the "realistic," modern image of the department store when describing his choice of setting, Ivan Caryll, Adrian Ross, and Lionel Monckton's music almost mocked Dam's vision of modernity. In *The Shop Girl*'s first act, for example, a chorus of shoppers and shop workers sing the praises of the department store:

> The noble institution of financial evolution
> Is the glory of English trade.
> It's the wonder of the nation as a mighty aggregation
> of all objects grown or made.

The shop assistants then lampoon this "glory of English trade" when they croon that "the loyal, royal stores" is "a daily dress rehearsal" that sells: "Dress goods / tinned food / Bric a Brac and Parrots / Pipe racks, red wax, fishing goods galore."[113] The song faintly recalls the pathetic effigy of William Whiteley that Bayswater's butchers dragged through Westbourne Grove twenty years before. Like the effigy, it too parodied the particular combination of commodities sold by Universal Providers. By the 1890s, however, the department store was a readily accepted institution. Far from condemning the department store, the lyrics playfully satirized this symbol of English economic prowess, claiming it as a site of performance and leisure.

As much as Dam sought to bring realism to the comedy stage, the play's narrative ultimately reinforced the fantastic portrait of the department store. The action takes place in two acts and two commercial settings, a department store and charity bazaar. These locales allowed for the mixture of classes and sexes that provided the essence of musical comedy. In both places economic and sexual pleasure are interchangeable. The play's humor is predicated on the similarity between the erotics of consumer culture and the economics of sexual attraction. Like many such comedies, the plot circles around the question of true identity and true love in a mass consumer society. It is set in motion when a solicitor enters the Royal Stores not to buy goods but to find a foundling shop girl who has unknowingly inherited a great fortune. After countless twists and turns, singing and dancing, sexual innuendo, and various cases of mistaken identity, the missing shop girl is discovered and thus comes into her fortune. She then marries the penniless but good son of the solicitor. The play thus is brought to its happy ending.

This romantic narrative presented the department store as a luxurious site of all-consuming pleasures, but also as a site of cross-class heterosexual interaction. In these stores, shop girls encounter aristocrats, male assistants flirt with wealthy female shoppers, and customers ogle each other.[114] Buying and selling are equivalent and interdependent activities. Selling in this marketplace always buys the working-class girl a wealthy spouse. On another level, the dynamic in the theater itself replicated this romantic narrative. Male audiences found themselves invited into the supposedly female space of the stores. Rather than being emasculated by the experience, they are asked to consume a spectacle of feminine bodies, to be attracted to a commercialized female ideal. Many men, like Mr. Lulli Valli in

Come Inside, actually fell in love with these female images and adopted the role of Stage Door Johnnie.

The extremely popular "girl" comedies such as *The Shop Girl* made sexually alluring heroines of female service workers, valorized male voyeuristic pleasure, and, according to Peter Bailey, provided a reassuring response to "contemporary challenges to male domination and sexual identity."[115] In contrast to the image of sexual anarchy represented by Oscar Wilde's conviction in 1895 and the plays of Ibsen and other serious authors of the day, musical comedy offered narratives of heterosexual romance.

In the West End musical comedy, the working-class "girl" uses commodities to create a glamorous persona and capture male attention. Instead of being portrayed as a hapless victim, she becomes an actress whose femininity acknowledges, glorifies, and masters performance. The props for this performance are the clothing, makeup, and style of commodity culture. Far from being abused by capitalism, this shop girl manipulates capitalists through her mastery of performance and disguise. The theme of working girl winning a husband via her fashionable style was repetitiously played out in virtually all of the comedies of the era. In Dam's production, the shop girl heroine, played by Ada Reeve, sings:

> When I came to the shop some years ago
> I was terribly shy and simple;
> with my skirt too high and my hat too low
> and an unbecoming dimple.
> But soon I learnt with a customer's aid
> how men make up to a sweet little maid;
> and another lesson I've learnt since then
> How a dear little maid "makes up" for men.
> A touch of rouge that is just a touch
> and black in the eye, but not too much;
> and a look that makes the Johnnies stop
> I learnt that all in the shop, shop, shop!

Once she learned to "make up for men," this shop girl chirped, "I think the proper thing to do / Is to watch for a wealthy Johnny! . . . I won't take no less than a noble peer / with twenty-thousand a year" (fig. 17). Throughout the play, the shop girl is the most skilled consumer and consequently wins the most male attention. While these women sing that they want to marry for money, their songs neither support nor condemn the economics of modern marriage or the romance of consumption. After demonstrating the economic calculus behind most gender relations, the play's conclusion denies this point. The millionaire shop girl eventually marries for love. The play thus pokes fun at the materialistic, commercial age of which it was also a part.

The actual grievances shop workers experienced were either ignored or presented as temporary because the shop girl never remains a worker in these stories. At some point in the play she usually changes places with an upper-class shopper.

Figure 17. Ada Reeve as the "Shop-Girl." *Sketch*, December 1894 (by permission of the British Library, shelf mark LD 52).

In *The Shop Girl*'s second act this social fluidity becomes a primary source of humor and of romantic and visual pleasure. In one song an "actress" sings that she will marry well, and thus "a duchess will develop from a dancer." Following this song, the shoppers and actresses exchange roles. The store's customers and a troupe of actresses tend the booths at the charity bazaar while the Royal Stores' employees perform *Hamlet*. These reversals demanded dozens of new dresses and several spectacular sets. Presumably to keep male audiences happy, the Shakespearean scene also stripped the Gaiety Girls of their dresses. By exposing actresses' legs this musical comedy reverted to the burlesque traditions of the old Gaiety.

This social inversion also laid to rest a labor dispute that had been raised briefly in the first act. Early in the play the Royal Stores' workers had resolved to strike if the store's owner, Mr. Hooley, refused to pay them overtime for selling in his many charity bazaars. The conflict disappears from the plot, but in effect it is solved by the transformation of shop assistants into actresses and then heiresses.[116]

This presentation of class struggle and its resolution worked both as a muted form of social commentary and a device to create a "contemporary" and "realistic" feel.

The fin de siècle was marked by its social conflicts and by its obsession with the fantastic possibilities of cross-class romantic alliances. Although attachments between lower-class women and upper-class men had long found a place in English literature, in the early-twentieth century "real life" romances became popular media events as a bevy of show girls and fashion models married into money and nobility.[117] One of Lucile's models wed a Wall Street financier and another married into "one of the oldest families in Scotland" and was presented at Court.[118] A number of Gaiety Girls also became peeresses. Gertie Miller, the shop girl heroine in *Our Miss Gibbs*, eventually became the countess of Dudley after the death of Lionel Monckton, her first husband. Monckton had been part of a team that had worked on the music of both *The Shop Girl* and *Our Miss Gibbs*. Denise Orme, one of the aristocratic shoppers in *Our Miss Gibbs*, eventually became Baroness Churston. Although these marriages were not a common occurrence, the popular press saw to it that they were common knowledge. Life imitated art as "girls" played workers in order to become "ladies."

One of the most notorious alliances between a wealthy man and a chorus girl, however, was that between Gordon Selfridge and the music hall star Gaby Deslys. This French blonde originally appeared in London on the Gaiety's stage, but eventually became well known for her performances at the Alhambra, her daring publicity photos, and her famous lovers. The aging entrepreneur lavished his considerable fortune on Gaby's upkeep. In a glaring example of conspicuous consumption, Selfridge took Gaby "shopping" every Sunday afternoon, walking her through his store and giving her anything she wanted. Such extravagance eventually led the millionaire American into an impoverished old age. Other West End traders, however, profited from Selfridge's notorious affair. Gaby Deslys's biographer noted that "Gaby's" tea shops and hat shops popped up all over the West End, one even surviving until the 1950s.[119]

Partly due to their outrageous romances, fin de siècle store owners had become quasi celebrities. In a more dramatic conclusion than even Emile Zola could have dreamed up for his department store owner, Octave Mouret, William Whiteley's lifetime of philandering led to his much publicized murder. In 1907 the Universal Provider was shot to death in his store by a man claiming to be his illegitimate son. This event and Selfridge's affair only added to the exciting image of the Edwardian department store.[120] As a young man Whiteley had strenuously defended the morality of the department store, casting himself as the model of patriarchal respectability. His death undid some of this hard work, but by this period middle-class shoppers hardly would have stayed away from this famous shop simply because of the improprieties of the founder. The shop's association with its famous owner was further weakened, however, as the old Whiteley's was entirely replaced in 1911 by a huge modern edifice. After the First World War, retail mergers would further separate the personality of founders or managers from a store's reputation. Indeed, Whiteley's became one of many ailing businesses that Selfridge's acquired in the 1920s.

The strongest tie between retailers and actresses during this period was an economic not romantic one, however. Actresses lent their names to countless advertisements and numerous charities. In 1911, Harrod's boasted that "well-known actresses" were selling British perfume in honor of the "All-British Shopping Week."[121] Selfridge's, in turn, allowed peeresses "experienced in bazaars" the sensation of selling in a "real shop"—all for the good of charity, of course.[122] A particularly strange conflation of the actress and shop assistant came in 1911 when Selfridge's employees appeared at the Court Theater in *The Suffrage Girl.* Kaplan and Stowell describe the piece, written by Percy Nash, a Selfridge executive, as "a bizarre attempt to accommodate women's suffrage to the conventions of the shop-girl musical."[123] If bizarre, *The Suffrage Girl* acted out the complex intersection between consumption and the theater, notions of modern femininity, and the mass market.

Audiences may have flocked to plays like *The Shop Girl* night after night because they touched on contemporary events and because they offered a display of beautiful women and handsome furnishings and fancy dresses. The service workers in the audiences may have also appreciated seeing themselves at the center of the narrative rather than as mere cogs in the wheels of modern commerce. Whatever its particular appeal, the incredible popularity of musical comedy and *The Shop Girl* in particular suggests that its formula gratified a very broadly defined audience.[124]

The shop girl heroine captured the hearts of this diverse audience while also lending a modern aura to a theatrical genre that was not wholly original. As one of several symbols of the 1890s New Woman, the glamorous shop girl was a crucial aspect of the musical comedy's presentation of contemporary life. Although women probably did not surpass male workers in the service economy as a whole until World War I, they already dominated certain trades and a few highly visible departments.[125] An employee hired by Harrod's in 1888 believed that she was among the first wave of female assistants engaged to replace male clerks. Miss Fowle remembered her arrival in somewhat sexual and definitely theatrical terms, recalling that on her first day, "several of the junior members of the staff peer[ed] round showcases to see the 'beauty chorus' arrive."[126] Female department store assistants were nearly all young, and their liminal position between the upper levels of the working class and the lower reaches of the middle class made the shop girl the ideal focus of both concern and delight and sometimes both at once.[127] Their highly public lifestyle as workers, residents, and consumers in the West End also added to the shop girl's theatrical popularity.

In literature, social investigations, and the theater, the shop girl had become an emblem of modernity by the 1890s. Like the prostitute in the 1880s, the shop girl appeared to be a public figure produced by the twin engines of urbanization and industrialization. Feminists and socialists intensively studied labor conditions in the department stores and related institutions, but when these reformers reported their findings, they did not see the shop girl as a consuming beauty. Rather, they saw a sick, lonely, overworked victim of long hours, low wages, poor working and living conditions, treacherous male employers, and fickle female shoppers.

Dozens of tracts, plays, novels, and newspaper exposés invoked a melodramatic mode to cast the female shop assistant as victim of upper-class greed and vanity. In *Shop Slavery and Emancipation*, the Fabian William Paine wrote of the large drapers: "In its front doors are flung wide open to vanity, from its back doors goes forth oppression."[128] Both store owners and their feckless customers supposedly abused service workers. The authors of *The Working Life of Shop Assistants* complained that a woman who regards shopping "not as a matter of business, but as a sort of recreation or pastime" selfishly ignores "the comfort and convenience of shopworkers."[129] In this view, shoppers' pleasure increased workers' labor. Socialists and feminist playwrights such as H. G. Wells, G. B. Shaw, Cicely Hamilton, and Harley Granville-Barker portrayed the shop girl as the victim of advanced capitalism in a number of productions including Granville-Barker's *The Madras House* and Hamilton's *Diana of Dobson's*.[130]

In Gissing's 1893 novel, *The Odd Women*, the shop girl Monica represents a new type of woman who enjoys wandering London's streets on her own and marries a man she meets on one of these adventures. Betraying Gissing's uncertainty about the New Woman, the novel follows Monica through her unhappy marriage, near adultery, and eventual death. One of her coworkers meets a worse fate and falls from shop girl to prostitute.[131] Gissing's shop girls are exploited by their work and by a patriarchal society in which women have few options. The class and gender relations in Gissing's novel and in the reforming exposés and plays were much closer to those enacted in contemporary melodrama than in those portrayed in musical comedy, however.

Melodramas set in department stores typically have the male customer or the store owner sexually harass the shop girl. For example, in *The Shop Girl and Her Master*, the "wicked son" of the emporium's owner vows to make one of the shop girls his mistress. In the opening scene, an experienced employee warns the impressionable new assistant not to "go about" with the owner's son. She is not so much concerned with the girl's safety but with the reputation of shop girls: "It is that that gives we shop girls a bad name and makes people think we are all for sale the same as the goods that hang around the shop." The ingenue responds simply: "And so we are for sale. Women are all for sale, we all have our price whether we are shop girls or Duchesses."[132] William Melville's 1910 melodrama, *Shop-Soiled Girl*, similarly follows the story of two shop girls, one who is seduced and abandoned by a "gentleman" and another who virtuously resists the attention of both the shopwalker and the male customers. Eventually the latter is rewarded by a marriage to a prosperous young man. Such a stark dichotomy between virtue and vice, common in melodrama, is absent from musical comedy. While both forms were often set in department stores, the relations between the sexes in melodrama are far from those in musical comedy.

While these melodramas clearly commented on the commodification of women and sexuality, they were wedded to Victorian constructions of class and gender, which were less popular with West End audiences during this period. Peter Brooks's description of the melodramatic mode as defined by intense "emotionalism; moral polarization and schematization; extreme states of being, situations, actions; overt villainy, persecution of the good and final reward of virtue" was less apparent in musical comedy.[133]

Instead of constructing a world divided into virtuous and fallen women, musical comedies put "girls" in charge of their own commodification. They reworked the well-trodden image of the sexually knowledgeable shop girl into a new feminine ideal that stressed youth, style, and performance. Consumption was pleasurable in itself and because it attracted male attention and marriage. The girl's marriage to an upper-class man resolved the class and gender tensions that plagued the urban center. If shoppers and shop girls had both complained about the leering male pest, in the farce *Just in Time* the shop girl heroine sings, "I love to see / men look at me."[134] This delight in self-display and the open acknowledgment of the sexual dynamics in public places may have been read by some women as giving voice to their sexual independence or autonomy. However, in musical comedy such flirtation was a prelude to marriage and an end to the shop girl's working days. Marital unions rather than labor unions thus solved the plight of the shop girl. It is no wonder that in speaking about musical comedy in 1909, Max Beerbohm concluded, "All the Tory in me rejoices."[135] Yet if Beerbohm was satisfied that this genre displayed an "innocent libertinism," a closer examination of the character of the shopper reveals the aggressive side of its humor. The romance of the shop girl and aristocrat barely contained the hostilities that marred the relationship between buyers and sellers and men and women in London's West End.

The Shopper's Character

If romance brought men and women from different classes together, musical comedy's humor separated them. The use of puns, impersonation, coincidence, mistaken identities, and physical gags emphasized class and gender difference and exposed the tensions between social groups. A good many of the jokes humiliated particular characters, especially female shoppers. The comedic elements and the romantic plots therefore treated consumption quite differently. While the romantic plot rewarded the shop girl for consuming goods, its comedy made the female shopper the butt of jokes.

In contrast to the young and alluring shop girl, the female shopper was typically depicted as elderly, ugly, and foolish. Male attention swirled around the shop girl and avoided the shopper. Audience attention likewise was directed to the shop girl and visited the shopper only for a few comic moments. The shopper was frequently a minor character who would not consume, would not pay for what she bought, or would purchase too much. Both disorderly and peripheral, she became the object of contempt and derision, as the name of one of the Royal Stores' customers, "Lady Dodo," suggests. Lady Dodo's consumption is neither attractive nor meaningful. It is wasteful, disruptive, and economically harmful.

In a sense, the shop girl and shopper serve as foils representing two faces of the female consumer.

In *The Girl from Kay's* (1902), a satire of Jay's, the fashionable Regent Street mourning warehouse-turned-emporium, a shop assistant laments:

> If you'd like to know the ways of customers at Kay's,
> we observe a most remarkable variety.
> There's a lady coming there with Victoria and Pair,
> She's a duchess in the very best Society!
> And she makes us kill ourselves,
> getting velvets from the shelves.
> Till the pile of goods is big enough to bury her,
> Then she says "that's very nice,
> twenty guineas is the price,
> Give me half a yard of ribbon for my terrier."

In most musical comedies wealthy women go shopping but they do not buy anything. The third verse, for example, mocks a

> lady from the West, who is anxious to be dressed
> in the very latest fashion and material . . .
> so she tries on this and that, here a coat and there a hat and
> selects the newest models, say a score or two,
> then she says,
> "I rather guess that's a dreadful cunning dress,
> But I'll go around to see another store or two!"[136]

In the music hall skit *The Toy Shop* (1915) a male assistant almost attacks a female customer who looks but buys nothing. The shop assistant plots against her, telling the audience, "I hate customers and as for women if I get a woman in here I'll strangle her, they come inside and look at everything in the shop, run me up and down to fetch everything and buy nothing, the governor gets the hump, and I get the sack, and everything goes wrong. . . . If I get a woman in here I'll cut her leg off."[137] In skits performed primarily before working- and lower-middle-class audiences buying and selling often became overt expressions of class and gender antagonism.

Such tensions were muted but still present in West End productions. Gordon Selfridge lampooned himself and his customers when he supported the one-act farce *Selfrich's Annual Sale* (1910). The skit presents the Oxford Street emporium as a single department selling everything: "hats, cheese, gowns, toys, ribbons and live animals." The walls exhibit notices that satirize Selfridge's advertising and store services. One reads, "Our prices are made to suit our customers—they are the lowest of the low." Before a sale begins Selfrich tells his two assistants, Miss Marshall and Miss Snelgrove (a play on one of his chief rivals, Marshall and Snelgrove's), "Never before have the public had the opportunity of buying last season's things at such vastly increased prices."[138]

Once the doors open, however, the customers seek their revenge. One "old lady" tries to match ribbon without the original pieces so she asks Selfrich to come to her suburban home. When he refuses, she shouts, "You're the most impertinent and disobliging young man I've ever come across. I shall certainly report you." An array of annoying and troublesome customers follows this performance, with each trying Mr. Selfrich's patience. Each customer's outlandish request intentionally satirizes but also advertizes Selfridge's services, including his return policy and his payment plans and the idea of the store as a shopper's rendezvous. One woman wants to buy a bottle of ammonia on installment and a "German with problem feet" removes his boots to show Selfrich that the socks he bought at the store two years before now have holes. He, of course, wants to return the socks. When asked if they "want to buy anything?" the customers shout in unison, "Buy anything! Why should we?" Finally, a different type of customer comes into the shop. She tells Mr. Selfrich, "Say here, I want a shirtwaist—white cashmere—two dollars, my name is Sadie N. Vandergilt—Hotel Cecil—here's the bill, thank you. I won't detain you." Selfrich asks this wonder customer, "You are an American?" She responds quickly, "Sure, I am! And I know what I want!" "Thank God!" the American entrepreneur answers.

Except for Sadie Vandergilt, Selfrich's customers look like buffoons who have read advertisements at face value, using the store as a "rendezvous" without buying any of its goods. The only "rational" customer is the one who actually makes a purchase, and she of course is an American. While *Selfrich's Annual Sale* expressed popular anxieties about advertising and mass consumer culture, it also made fun of English fears of economic decline and Americanization. No doubt the real-life Gordon Selfridge enjoyed being lampooned in this way because he believed that all publicity is good publicity. Nevertheless, *Selfrich's Annual Sale* revealed a deep fear that English consumers were not buying enough. The unruly customer was both a "real" thorn in the side of shop workers and a symbol of more general worries plaguing Victorian and Edwardian business. The key problem in this capitalist economy was how to expand one's market, to stimulate desires and channel them into sales. Advertisers, entrepreneurs, and economists assumed that financial success lay in arousing but also controlling female desire.

While laughing at the shopper, the shop workers in the audience could also find an acceptable way to avenge themselves. The troublesome shopper was certainly a stock character in trade journals of the era. The drapers' press constantly complained about shop rovers, shop prowlers, or the more frequently named "tabby." Like the kleptomaniac, the tabs or tabby was a customer who consumed time and space not goods. "Shopping A La Fin Du Siecle [*sic*], or How Irene Worried the Drapers," a poem published in the *Drapers' Record*, closely resembles the assistant's song in *The Girl From Kay's*:

> Irene Smith, a maid of bluest blood—
> Her gens ennobled 'ere the
> mighty flood
> . . . .

claimed blood with keen old "Wealth of Nations"
Smith,
. . . . . .
Her stately beauty shall your soul amaze!
She is a fashion plate of loveliness
. . . .
Soon noble shop-fronts claim her willing eye,
With softest vestures, soothing as a sight,
Yet on, still on, her pretty feet must move—
But note, dear reader, how my measure drops—
She's come to Regent Street "To see the Shops."[139]

The poem follows Irene through the Haymarket, Regent Street, and Oxford Street, as she enters store after store without buying anything. The "pretty maid" who went shopping but did not buy anything was a frequent subject of satire in trade journals by the end of the century, as she was literally more common on the streets.[140]

More often than not, the "tab" was an ugly creature, an old, almost witchlike character who brought havoc to the draper's counter. The rover's "chief delight would seem to exist in ransacking an entire stock without making a single purchase," while *prowler* was simply another word for kleptomaniac or thief, who went about "not to inspect but to 'lift' these productions."[141] This woman was usually characterized as an old and ugly pest who often brought her lap dog to the store with her (figs. 18 and 19).[142]

In Edwardian England, the troublesome customer was laughed at and scientifically studied. By this period, trade journals and guides divided the shopper into various types, such as the Easygoing Customer, the Particular Customer and the Suspicious Customer.[143] Shopkeepers were told that if they practiced the "art of salesmanship" or consumer psychology, they could turn these shoppers into purchasers. Throughout the 1920s and 1930s, shop assistants were taught the intricacies of the art of selling when they attended one of many schools for shop assistants sponsored by the Draper's Chamber of Commerce or by large companies such as the Gramophone Company Limited.[144] Staff training, like categorizing and satirizing customers, attempted to control unruly public women. Retailers were involved in a complicated task; they wanted to encourage desire but ensure that it led to a purchase. In musical comedy, the shop girl's desires were satisfied through marriage. The unruly customer was censored for not bringing her desires to a productive and socially acceptable conclusion.

Theater of Desire

The beautiful shop girl, the troublesome shopper, and the sumptuous emporium each played an important part in the most popular musical comedy of the era, *Our Miss Gibbs* (1909). Harrod's backed this comedy set in "Garrod's" as a kind

Figure 18. "The Lady Who Bargains, But Never Buys," *Woman's World*, 1889 (by permission of the British Library, shelf mark pp. 6004ob).

of preemptive strike before Selfridge's launched its grand opening.[145] The play was set within a "Shopping Compendium 'de luxe.' " The stage directions urged the set designer to emphasize "the sumptuousness of the architecture, decorations and general arrangements, [more] than any actual display of goods. The main feature of the scene is the luxury which makes shopping a matter of enjoyment and not a fag." The waiting rooms, dining rooms, club facilities and other services that department stores offered were therefore also available at Garrod's. However, the mise-en-scène was not supposed to be a "photographic reproduction of any part of the stores, but a 'composite' conveying to the audience the idea of its being 'Harrod's' by certain recognizable points" (fig. 20).[146]

In effect *Our Miss Gibbs* dramatized "the new era of shopping." Although first performed before Selfridge's opened, the stage directions read like the new store's advertising:

> The "Ladies Club" is one of the instances of the many innovations, and a vista of the club rooms is seen. A lady gets tired? She can take a reviving massage. Hungry? She can have an exquisite little dejeuner. She fears burglars as she is going abroad? She can place all her jewels in a safe deposit. She has spent all her

Figure 19. "A Tab," *Drapers' Record*, March 1897 (by permission of the British Library, shelf mark LD 167).

Figure 20. Opening Chorus, *Our Miss Gibbs. Play Pictorial*, May 1909 (by permission of the British Library, shelf mark pp. 5224db).

money and wants to cash a cheque? Well, there is the bank in the Royal Exchange. She wishes to secure seats at the theatre and communicate with friends? There is the box office and post office. She is going abroad. There is the travel bureau to take all of the trouble out of her hands.

In the opening scene the audience watches a "crowd of well-dressed women" engaged in the "refined enjoyment" of shopping. Ladies tick off shopping lists written in golden notebooks, lunch on "some of Fipp's dainty souffle ices," glow "from an invigorating massage," and gossip in "the ladies' club." This world of women is quickly invaded, however, by a group of "fashionable Men about town," who are directed to sing "something to the effect that instead of, as in the old days, shopping being a bore, it is now a joy, everything, even the opportunity for flirting being provided for." Here, the pleasure of shopping is clearly understood to be sexual. As in most of the musical comedies of this sort, little buying and selling of commodities takes place. Rather, the stores become a venue for customers to meet the opposite sex. The young Men about Town visit the store everyday in order to court Mary, the shop girl heroine. Although only a "simple Yorkshire lass," Mary Gibbs has won the hearts of her male and female customers alike, including Lord Eynsford, although he is already engaged to a woman of his own class, Lady Betty.

Mary Gibbs is not the innocent victim of Victorian melodrama or even the relatively innocent heroine of *The Shop Girl*. Throughout the play, she manipulates both her employer and customers in order to move up the social ladder. At first glance, she appears to be something of a New Woman, singing that she wants "to lead a single life." On closer inspection, this stance allows her to play various admirers off each other. She apparently cares for Eynsford, who has disguised his true identity and claimed to be a bank clerk; but when he asks if she would love him more if he were wealthy, Mary responds that although she would not love him more, "it must be nice to have everything you want and a little bit over." Mary then defends this mercenary thought with the comment: "I'm just a woman, that's all." Whether said ironically or not, Mary plays for her own gain with the age-old image of female acquisitiveness.

Miss Gibbs also uses her customers' weakness for goods and the store's desire to promote its image to acquire her own fripperies. When Mrs. Farquhar, an "impecunious woman of fashion," finds her store credit has dried up, she turns to Mary for help. In Mrs. Farquhar we meet the shopper as trickster who even sings about her talents: "Though I've very little money in the bank / yet I mix with nobility and rank / and I've never yet / ever paid a debt. . . . A little bit of sense and confidence . . . a little bit of skill to dodge a bill / There you have got, the way to be rich when your not." Yet this debtor's luck has all but run out. With no credit, no money, and in need of a new Ascot gown she turns to Miss Gibbs for help, explaining that "a woman who can't get her Ascot gowns paragraphed is as much out of it as a Labour Member at a Royal Garden Party." Mary helps out by telling the manager, Mr. Toplady, that Mrs. Farquhar has asked her to join her at Ascot, "and introduce me to the fine folks . . . and now she says she can't go because you won't let her have a new frock." She asks Toplady for a gown for Farquhar and several for herself since she will represent "the Girl from Garrod's," whose fashionable image will be good for business (fig. 21). Toplady reluctantly agrees and throws in several hats as well. Both the customer and shop girl are thus represented as voracious consumers who exploit without challenging society's conventions.

Commodities, particularly clothing, provided the basic tools for playing with one's identity. In this marketplace, everyone masquerades as something he or she is not. The milliner Mme Jeanne pretends to be "a step-daughter of the maid of Orleans, from the Rue de la Paix." Although she is "very French in appearance," she turns out to be an ordinary girl from Scotland. Mme Jeanne confides to a Lady Betty, "Aum Scotch when it's a matter of sentiment—and aum French when its a matter of business." In musical comedy, nationality and class are as easy to change as one's hat. A master of disguise, Jeanne is also a master of attraction. It is she who sings the ode to consumer culture that opened this chapter. "Hats" satirized but inscribed the role of commodities in the attraction of the opposite sex. In this song, consumption was equated with making a spectacle of oneself, trying to attract male attention, particularly their admiring gazes. As Jeanne sings, "If you would set men talking when you're walking out to shop / You'll be all right if you're all right on top!" Indeed, the hats in this performance were in themselves spectacles. They cost sixty guineas each, were designed by the

Figure 21. Gertie Miller as Mary Gibbs. *Play Pictorial*, May 1909 (by permission of the British Library, shelf mark pp. 5224db).

famous hat shop Maison Lewis, and were brought from the shop by "experts" for each day's performance.[147]

In comedies such as *Our Miss Gibbs* women's use of commodities to purchase male attention was favorably compared to aristocratic marriages that were arranged for social and economic reasons. In fact, Lord Eynsford and Lady Betty's relationship appears vulgar when set next to the truer emotions expressed between Eynsford and Mary Gibbs. Thus the "dream worlds of mass consumption" are represented as allowing for a freer mingling between the classes and sexes and as providing fertile ground for the growth of "genuine" feelings. Once Mary learns Eynsford's true identity, however, she initially refuses to marry him, asserting that "a wife should never be below a husband in station." Class difference becomes superficial, though, when it is revealed that Eynsford's wealth comes from the soap industry, that the family title was itself purchased, and that Eynsford's own mother was in fact a working girl. Mary eventually gives in to her feelings for Eynsford and agrees to become his wife. The narrative implies that social status is founded on wealth and consumption rather than on blood. The classes mingle in these urban amusements, but class differences are never erased. The department store and the theater become the venue for staging a modern class and gender order in which social identities are maintained and produced by consumption.

"Wanting things" had long been seen as a natural feminine trait. Onstage this desire is most directly understood as sexual, as women's consumer desire becomes an acknowledged aspect of their appeal to men. The "ugly" women in these comedies are those who shop but do not buy into this scenario. The shopper who is out for her own pleasure, who is looking but not buying, is ridiculed and contrasted with the heroine, the glamorous, consuming shop girl. Miss Gibbs, who "wants things" and uses them to capture male attention, has thus become a cultural heroine. From the treatment of the shop girl in 1894 to that of the independent Miss Gibbs in 1909 a noticeable shift had occurred. Both are spunky and glamorous, but the open acceptance of the use of goods in the creation of sexual desire is brought to the foreground in the latter production. Working is presented as a means to move to the other side of the counter, to marry well, acquire money, and lavishly spend it. The pleasures of shopping come not from socializing with other women, from one's presence in public, or from the commodities per se, but from the social advancement and sexual pleasure that a correctly purchased image will bring. Buying and selling are essentially interchangeable activities, both being acts in a play about heterosexual romance. In these theatrical department stores, men are invited to look at women, who are in turn invited to actively pursue men by turning themselves into fashionable images. The theater had turned buying and selling into a romantic comedy.

The fin de siècle theater promoted mass consumption and carved out an ambiguous role for women as both spectators and spectacles. This duality marked the "modern" feminine ideal and reworked the "fallen" image of the public woman into the sexy, youthful modern girl. Publicness or publicity became championed as the state in which women acquired an alluring femininity. By the first decades of the new century, the scandalized "Girl of the Period" of the 1860s had become the adorable and worshiped Gaiety Girl of musical comedy, an ideal of twentieth-century femininity. Publicity surpassed domesticity as the ideal realm of gender and even of class formation.

Social inversion, the use of masquerade, and the marketplace setting tied musical comedy to medieval and early-modern popular culture. As Bakhtin and others have pointed out, the marketplace had traditionally housed both theatrical spectacle and comedy.[148] The carnivalesque department store of musical comedy might have had a tint of the unofficial for some viewers, but generally it played with the traditions of European popular culture to sell commodities. Peter Stallybrass and Allon White have argued that during the nineteenth century, "the bourgeoisie labored to produce the economic as a separate domain, partitioned off from the festive calendar, so they labored *conceptually* to re-form the fair as *either* a rational, commercial, trading event or a popular pleasure ground."[149]

This history of the Victorian and Edwardian West End reveals a bourgeoisie divided between those who worked to separate the market and the theater and those who believed that financial success came from a marketplace that sold pleasure in a theatrical setting. There were many who for various reasons condemned popular theater and mass culture. However, a significant proportion of the business community and their customers cultivated its growth and resolutely believed that institutions such as musical comedy and the department store added a healthy playfulness to urban life. While William Whiteley assured critics that he was not inviting prostitutes into his store, he did not eschew all bodily or sensual pleasures or theatrical elements. Whiteley's critics also turned to the theatrical and comic, if aggressive, idiom of the charivari to censor what appeared to be new and threatening about this draper vending meat, hot lunches, and wine. Those who vented their frustrations in the local paper and trade journals used grotesque exaggeration and satire as the appropriate language of censorship. The excesses of mass consumption were simply ripe for comic rebuke. Onstage, these fears about the body, the market, and excess were reworked into a heterosexual culture of amusement.

One should not see this development as implying that advertising and spectacle had come to dominate urban life. Even in the intensely commercialized environment of the West End, satire served as both promotion and critique. Criticism and promotion were by no means oppositional categories. They were in a dialogue with one another and intersected and reworked each other's themes. This point will be further explored in the epilogue, but by way of conclusion, this chapter will turn to one more story of the Edwardian shop girl in London's West End.

In her 1908 short story, "The Tiredness of Rosabel," Katherine Mansfield follows an exhausted, starving Rosabel home from her work at a West End department store to her dreary lonely flat in Westbourne Grove. Rosabel is alienated and disgusted by the commercial landscape. While riding home, she is "sickened by the smell of warm humanity . . . oozing out of everybody on the 'bus," and bored by the advertisements that seem to define the modern city. "How many times had she read these advertisements—Sapolio Saves Time, Saves Labour'—'Heinz's Tomato Sauce'—and the inane and annoying dialogue between doctor and judge concerning the superlative merits of 'Lamplough's Pyretic Saline.' "[150] Mansfield thus presents the modern commercial metropolis as intensely lonely and physically painful.

Rosabel finds little relief at home, however. As soon as she is in her small room she recalls the spoiled behavior of a female customer. She also remembers flirting with this woman's fiancé as a kind of revenge but also to satisfy her own desires. This memory leads Rosabel into a fantasy. "Suppose," she muses, she and her customer had "changed places." She would have bought hats, ridden in carriages, dined at the Carlton, gone to balls, and enjoyed the caresses of her lover. While her dream reworked the basic romantic theme of musical comedy, its conclusion exposed the unreality of this fantasy. Rosabel awakes from her dream "shivering"

• EPILOGUE •

The Politics of Plate Glass

On a rainy Friday evening, the first day of March 1912, the sound of shattering glass echoed throughout London's West End:

> Shortly before six o'clock a band of women carried out such a window-breaking campaign in the principal streets of the West-End as London has never known. . . . Nothing was heard in the Strand, Cockspur Street, Downing Street, Whitehall, Piccadilly, Bond Street or Oxford Street but the fall of shattered glass and the angry exclamations of the shopkeepers.[1]

In less than an hour, members and supporters of the militant suffrage organization, the Women's Social and Political Union, struck nearly four hundred shop windows and did approximately five thousand pounds' worth of damage. That night and in the days to follow, middle-class women traveled to the West End to protest their exclusion from national politics. While the Suffragettes had also raided government offices and politicians' homes, during this week they visited the best shops in London. From Regent Street to Westbourne Grove, virtually no major department store or fashionable shop was spared in this assault.

As the WSPU leaders had hoped, the protest garnered a great deal of attention in the daily press. By and large, journalists were struck by the event's spectacular nature and its apparent irony. Most could not help but structure their report around the ironic image of the shopper-turned-terrorist. In writing about the episode, a *Daily Telegraph* journalist, for example, commented, "Suddenly women who had a moment before appeared to be on peaceful shopping expeditions produced from bags or muffs, hammers, stones and sticks, and began an attack upon the nearest windows."[2] When the *Daily Mail* described the protest, the paper emphasized how the "brilliantly lighted streets" of the "shopping quarter of London had plunged into a sudden twilight."[3] The *Evening Standard* reported that the West End's "leading streets" looking "almost as if the town were in a state of siege."[4] According to another journalist, the Suffragettes' visit transformed "the whole of the West End of London" into "a city of broken glass."[5]

Like these reporters, shopkeepers were beguiled but also enraged that shoppers would turn against them with such a fury. Mr. Lasenby Liberty, for example, wrote in a letter to the *Standard* that "as a vicarious victim of the recent raid," he wanted Mrs. Pankhurst herself "to state the mental process by which they deem the breaking of the very shrines at which they worship will advance their cause."[6] Traders like Liberty were confused by shoppers' violence and the seemingly indiscriminate nature of their attack, since the rebels showed both supporters and opponents of women's suffrage equal treatment. West End drapers were particularly frantic, however. Although a reporter for the *Draper and Drapery Times*

Figure 22. Swan and Edgar's damaged window being repaired after the Suffragettes' protest in 1912. Compare this view with that of the cover illustration. They reveal two quite different images of this shop in 1912.
Emmeline Pankhurst, *My Own Story* (London: Eveleigh Nash, 1914).

admitted that restaurants, jewelers, confectioners, and other businesses were assaulted, the big drapery houses, such as Swan and Edgar's, Marshall and Snelgrove's, D. H. Evans, Jay's, Liberty's, and Robinson and Cleaver's, "by reason of their juxtaposition, suffered special attack" (fig. 22).[7] These retailers were concerned that not only had the event cost them their windows and forced them to close their shops several hours early, but that it would have a lasting impact on the image of the district as a whole. As one shopkeeper explained, "The damage to their business was great because respectable women no longer dared approach their windows lest they should be suspected of a felonious act."[8] The shopkeepers thus feared that "respectable women" would avoid shopping lest they be marked as a Suffragette, arrested, and possibly imprisoned.

Although both wealthy and working women were among the window smashers, journalists initially saw the demonstration as a conflict between fashionable shoppers and shopkeepers. The protest's drama came from the sight of broken glass, from the sense of a glittering arena being plunged into darkness, and from the idea of shoppers turning against, as Liberty put it, "the shrines at which they worship." Perhaps most upsetting to the traders and the police was their inability to discern shopper from Suffragette. Moreover, when Suffragettes told the story, they admitted that they began the protest by pretending to be on shopping expeditions. Mary Richardson, one of those who had attacked Liberty's windows, recalled that until the appointed time, she and her fellow protesters "walked up and down [Regent Street] and tried to give the impression that we were interested in the goods displayed." After the deed was done, Richardson was nearly arrested but for her excuse that she was "only admiring the carpets."[9] Although two "ladies" who had evidently witnessed the felonious act attempted to convince a constable that Richardson was guilty, she and many others escaped capture by posing as shoppers.

When the Suffragettes later explained their actions, they reinforced the point that there was no essential difference between themselves and "legitimate" shoppers. WSPU leaders answered Liberty and his fellow traders by stating that they had not meant this as a direct attack on shopkeepers. Rather, they were reminding West End retailers that since they depended upon wealthy women's support and patronage, they must use their voting rights to support the rights of women. In a letter addressed to the retailers, the WSPU explained that "the Suffragettes bear no grudge against you personally. . . . On the contrary, the women are good friends to you, and without them and their support what would become of that flourishing business of yours?"[10] In one sense, then, the window-smashing campaign was a form of blackmail. Although feminists probably could not have organized a full-scale boycott against shopkeepers who would not support their cause, they broke retailers' windows to encourage them to become their advocates and vote against the Liberal government.

The demonstration as well as the media's and the militants' explanations of it depended upon the idea that the Suffragettes were West End shoppers. The Suffragettes recognized themselves as consumers and partly accepted retailers' claims that shopping was a female "right" or form of "emancipation." While men had occasionally smashed shopkeeper's windows, the feminists' protest had special significance. For years men like Lasenby Liberty, William Whiteley, and Gordon Selfridge had professed to be on women's side, claiming their goal was to please them in any way possible. In March of 1912, the Suffragettes told shopkeepers that women were not altogether happy.

Aside from the obvious fact that the window smashers did not actually speak for all women and that not all West End traders were politically enfranchised men, the protest was an effective reworking of entrepreneurial discourse. The militants argued that political rights, not department stores, brought about female emancipation and independence. Nevertheless, they acknowledged that a large segment of the English economy depended on women's happiness and compliance. But like the women who had founded or joined women's clubs, they wanted to use this apparent power to gain admission to other aspects of the public sphere. In 1912 some women made a spectacle of themselves to make it clear that women must have access to the halls of Parliament as well as the "halls of temptation."

Although this episode most directly raises questions about the relationship between consumption and politics, it also touches on many of the themes that have been explored in this book. The Suffragettes' protest and the reaction to it rested on the fact that in the late-Victorian and Edwardian metropolis, identities were inherently fluid, ambiguous, and overlapping. As we have seen, shoppers were often characterized as disorderly figures, as prostitutes, drunkards, debtors and other viragoes. The proximity of feminist, commercial, and illicit spaces in London's West End meant that there had long been a confusion about how to identify shoppers, prostitutes, and feminist activists. Though many observers worried about how to separate one type of public woman from another, this proved to be an impossible task. Instead of lamenting this problem, however, the Suffragettes delighted in and used the ambiguities of metropolitan life.

The window-smashing campaign may also be read as a moment in which different meanings of the city and its subjects interacted with each other. This study has explored how the city of pleasurable consumption developed in relation to other facets of the West End, including its place as the home of Society, as a market of illicit pleasures, and as a tourist sight. Throughout this book, I have argued that the metropolis was not experienced as a series of unconnected layers or isolated institutions. Department stores, women's clubs, and the theater, for example, took on their individual significance in relation to the others and to other sites in the city. The militants' protest highlights how the political West End also abutted the commercial realm.

The Suffragettes' protest dramatically illustrates the city's instability. Regent Street, Oxford Street, Westbourne Grove, and the like were primarily understood as sites of consumption, yet this was never their only function or meaning. Retailers certainly wanted to control the image and uses of their neighborhood, but they could never fully achieve this goal. Aristocrats, jurists, and various government bodies often obstructed shopkeepers' efforts to define their neighborhood. At the same time, feminists such as Frances Power Cobbe appeared to be allied with retailers because she too believed that women's presence in the West End was a sign of improvement and progress. Yet other feminists would also set up alternative definitions of the West End and bourgeois femininity.

Though the Suffragettes rejected many of the strategies and beliefs of earlier feminists like Cobbe, they were similarly expanding dominant definitions of women's needs, desires, and place in the city. In some respects, however, the Suffragettes turned from liberal ideals about economic and political rights toward more radical arguments. When they raided the West End, they were not only reconstructing the neighborhood's status as a female pleasure center, but were also engaging in a well-established tradition of radical protest.

Precisely because the West End represented such a concentration of power, prestige, and wealth it had tremendous symbolic importance as a site of political demonstrations and struggle. At various moments—including the Chartist demonstrations in the 1840s, the unemployed riots in the 1880s, and the IRA bombings and Poll Tax riots of more recent times—the West End has been the locus of radical protests and a good deal of window breaking.[11] The point, then, is not that political public spaces became commercial or vice versa. Rather, these two meanings were both present and necessary to each other.

Though this book has only peripherally looked at the history of public protest in London's West End, the intersections between the shopper's London and the Suffragette's city illuminate how the commercial and political realms overlapped during this period. Historians have argued, for example, that the development of feminism into a mass movement partly depended upon the types of transformations in the media and public spaces that this book has laid out. The most basic aspect of this argument is that, as Lisa Tickner has observed, department stores, tea shops and other resting places "open[ed] up to middle-class women the hitherto masculine domain of modern, public, urban life."[12] Suffragists held meetings in well-known restaurants, tea shops, women's clubs, and department stores, and by the Edwardian period both they and conservative women viewed this realm as their territory. For several decades, women's magazines, feminist journals, the Lady Guides, and entrepreneurs had made wealthy women familiar with the West End. This familiarity was put to work in the window smashing campaign. Before the demonstration started, for example, many of the window-smashers met at the Gardenia Restaurant in Catherine Street. Later, after some of the rebels' cases were dismissed in court, they went together to discuss what had happened in a nearby Lyons' café.[13] The Suffragettes fully exploited their urban knowledge to engage in and help organize their protest.

The WSPU and other suffrage organizations like the Artists' Franchise League and Women's Freedom League also used newspapers, advertising, fashion, and the theater to construct a new type of spectacular mass politics and to market their cause. Tickner and other scholars who have explored the style of feminist politics in this era have shown how suffragists employed images of modern, active womanhood legitimated by "the new commerce."[14] For example, when the WSPU chose colors as the symbols for their movement, they essentially branded their cause and sought to capture that "appeal to the eye" that Edwardian window dressers, set designers, and advertisers believed was so essential to successful selling. In fact, the rationale behind choosing to identify their movement with purple, white, and green could have been written by an advertising expert. The colors, this editorialist explains, "make that appeal to the eye which is so irresistible. The result of one of our processions is that this movement becomes identified in the mind of the onlooker with colour, gay sound, movement and beauty."[15]

Critics of the WSPU turned the movement's commercialism against it, however. For example, Francis Latham, an antisuffragist, wrote after a suffrage demonstration: "But for the opportunity to display themselves to the admiring gaze of men, in pretty costumes, big hats, carrying flowers . . . very few damsels would have appeared on the scene. The summer procession was merely an attractive show, without the slightest political significance."[16] Sounding like a latter-day Eliza Linton, Latham condemned women's politics as a form of frivolous and inappropriate self-display and nothing more. The antisuffrage feminist Janet Courtney was much kinder though she too described the Pankhursts as "publicists of the first order. . . . Christabel . . . embodied the very spirit of successful advertisement. What a saleswoman she might have been."[17]

And yet as the feminist movement adopted the tools of mass commerce, it also promoted commercial culture. WSPU leaders even debated about the nature of advertising with experts in trade journals such as *Modern Business*.[18] *Votes for Women* included guides to London's shops and advertising alongside discussions of militant strategy. Its regular column "The World We Live In" offered fashion advice and hints on how to shop "at the Sales."[19] Feminists engaged in quite a bit of their own selling as well. When the London Society for Women's Suffrage took over a shop at 100 Westbourne Grove, the *Bayswater Chronicle* favorably reported that the windows of this "center of attraction . . . made a marvelous display of cartoons and posters."[20] By the Edwardian period, the Suffragists had joined Whiteley's in Westbourne Grove and contributed to the street's reputation as an attraction. Of course, while feminists adopted commercial techniques, capitalist entrepreneurs also happily exploited the language and sensation created by feminists.[21] Department stores sold suffrage paraphernalia and fashions and advertised in the feminist papers. Selfridge even flew a Suffragette flag over his store in 1909.[22]

The window-smashing episode momentarily soured the relationship between West End merchants and feminists, but according to Christabel Pankhurst, "The shops calmed down wonderfully in the end, and even continued to advertise in our papers. Indeed, Mrs. Marshall, who was our honorary canvasser for advertisements, would have it that those whose windows were not broken were a little piqued at being so neglected."[23] If Christabel's assessment has any truth in it at all, then we return to the situation William Whiteley found himself in on Guy Fawkes Day in 1876. The Universal Provider and Edwardian merchants were often the target of a great deal of discontent, but they were not ultimately harmed and may even have been helped by the publicity that typically surrounded public protests. Any retailer who had worried that respectable ladies would stop shopping in the West End because of the Suffragettes' actions would soon find those fears had been unwarranted.

In Edwardian London, women's emancipation and consumer pleasures had merged to a certain degree. This was not simply an appropriation by marketing strategists of liberal feminist arguments about personal autonomy and rights. Rather, an idea of female independence within the public realm had been common to both entrepreneurial and feminist thought since at least the mid-nineteenth century. These two strands of bourgeois culture had similarly promoted a view of the Victorian woman that departed from that advanced by religious and secular moralists. Feminists and entrepreneurs had argued, and sometimes quite stridently, that public women were not necessarily immoral or fallen. They had created similar female public spaces and had used the media to promote those spaces. Of course, their conceptions of women's role within the public were often, but not always, quite different and at times antagonistic. And neither feminist nor entrepreneurial discourse wholly overturned traditional notions of femininity. Indeed, twentieth-century marketers increasingly promoted the ideal of a modernized housewife who cheerfully consumed goods to improve the domestic haven. In the first decades of the twentieth century, however, feminists and entrepreneurs used novel forms of publicity, advertising, and spectacle to appeal to the masses. Before the First World War, militant feminists and large-scale businesses relied upon the same techniques to create a female crowd. However, if the feminist crowd became truly threatening, the shopping mob came to be viewed as a welcome sight in an unstable economy.

When the militants attacked West End commerce they were not protesting consumer culture, the commodification of women, or women's pleasures. Like the founders of women's clubs, they used public identities and public spaces sanctified by the new commerce to reshape national politics and the public sphere. The Suffragettes' 1912 expedition to the West End illuminates, however, that at particular historical moments consumer practices may become political. Although their histories have been popularly conceived of as occupying separate social realms, shopping and politics have been deeply intertwined. Studies of state formation and nationalism and of the labor and youth movements have also pointed to the convergence of consumerism and politics.[24] This research points out that the spaces and practices of consumption may at once have social, cultural, economic, and political significance. Consumption may be both liberating and exploitive, depending upon specific historical circumstances. The meaning of consumption and the identity of consumers, nevertheless, have rarely been entirely fixed by corporate capitalism.

Shopping became one of the primary fault lines in Victorian and Edwardian culture because it challenged received notions of stable class and gender identities and clearly demarcated physical spaces. When individuals debated the West End's pleasures, they confronted concerns about industrialization, urbanization, and modernity. They discussed the relationship between what were perceived as transformations in the public sphere and private changes in family life, sexuality, relations between men and women, and relations between women and commodities. Indeed, as the chapter on Selfridge especially highlighted, they also defined the relationship between England and other nations.

Before the First World War altered the meaning of women's identities and place in public life, shopping was one of the broadest avenues that bourgeois women traveled into the city. Certainly, the First World War did not completely shift the nature of London's West End and the ideal of the female shopper. However, the economic dislocations and shifting class and gender relations that the War had hastened introduced a new era of shopping in London's West End. Retail mergers and corporate restructuring in the 1920s, urban redevelopment and the ever-expanding nature of suburban London, and new media such as the cinema and new modes of transportation such as the automobile altered commercial culture considerably in early-twentieth-century Britain.[25]

In London's West End between the 1860s and 1914, bourgeois women's role in the city was most clearly that of shopper and pleasure seeker. This was never her only place in the metropolis, nor was shopping merely a frivolous pastime or an inconsequential aspect of London's history. For women with few public activities and limited employment and educational options, shopping allowed them to occupy and construct urban space. It also permitted them to define or reject individual and familial identities. When Victorian and Edwardian women shopped, they were central actors in the English economy; they altered the city and ideals of bourgeois femininity; they inhabited and built the public spaces of the modern metropolis. The public was therefore never a unitary or autonomous masculine territory. As producers and consumers, workers and shoppers, writers and readers, middle-class women wandered into the Victorian and Edwardian West End. As Brontë's Lucy Snowe had mused, being alone in London was an "adventure" that could be experienced as both an "irrational" and a "real pleasure."

· NOTES ·

Introduction
"To Walk Alone in London"

1. Charlotte Brontë, *Villette* (1853; reprint, London: Penguin, 1979), 109.

2. Rose Barton, *Familiar London* (London: Adam and Charles Black, 1904), 3, 8–11.

3. Two recent studies on gender and late-Victorian London that I have found especially useful have been Judith R. Walkowitz, *City of Dreadful Delight: Narratives of Sexual Danger in Late-Victorian London* (Chicago: University of Chicago Press, 1992); and Deborah Epstein Nord, *Walking the Victorian Streets: Women, Representation, and the City* (Ithaca: Cornell University Press, 1995). For related studies, also see Judith R. Walkowitz, *Prostitution and Victorian Society: Women, Class and the State* (Cambridge: Cambridge University Press, 1980); Elizabeth Wilson, *The Sphinx in the City: Urban Life, the Control of Disorder, and Women* (Berkeley: University of California Press, 1991); Lynda Nead, *Myths of Sexuality: Representations of Women in Victorian Britain* (Oxford: Basil Blackwell, 1988); Christine Stansell, *City of Women: Sex and Class in New York, 1789–1860* (Urbana: University of Illinois Press, 1987); Kathy Peiss, *Cheap Amusements: Working Women and Leisure in Turn-of-the-Century New York* (Philadelphia: Temple University Press, 1986); Mary P. Ryan, *Women in Public: Between Banners and Ballots, 1825–1880* (Baltimore: Johns Hopkins University Press, 1990).

4. Though many historians have studied aspects of the West End, there has been no full-length history of this neighborhood. For an overview of its history see D. F. Stevens, "The Central Area," in *Greater London*, ed. J. T. Coppock and Hugh C. Prince (London: Faber and Faber, 1964), 167–201. Also see Patricia Garside, "West End, East End: London, 1890–1914," in *Metropolis, 1890–1920*, ed. Anthony Sutcliffe (Chicago: University of Chicago Press, 1984), 221–58. Walkowitz discusses the West End as a commercial site in the 1880s in *City of Dreadful Delight*, 24–25 and 46–49. Also see Gavin Weightman and Steve Humphries, *The Making of Modern London, 1815–1914* (London: Sidgwick and Jackson, 1983), 40–69; Hermione Hobhouse, *A History of Regent Street* (London: Macdonald and Jane's in association with Queen Anne Press, 1975); Lynn Walker, "Vistas of Pleasure: Women Consumers and Urban Space in the West End of London, 1850–1900," in *Women in the Victorian Art World*, ed. Clarissa Campbell Orr (Manchester: Manchester University Press, 1995), 70–85; Alistair Service, *London, 1900* (London: Granada, 1979), 119–45; Donald J. Olsen, *The City as a Work of Art: London, Paris, Vienna* (New Haven: Yale University Press, 1986), 189–209. Other related studies include James Winter, *London's Teeming Streets, 1830–1914* (London: Routledge, 1993); H. J. Dyos and Michael Wolff, eds., *The Victorian City: Images and Reality*, 2 vols. (London: Routledge and Kegan Paul, 1973); Donald J. Olsen, *The Growth of Victorian London* (London: B. T. Batsford, 1976); F. H. W. Sheppard, *London, 1808–1870: The Infernal Wen* (Berkeley: University of California Press, 1971); Steen Eiler Rasmussen, *London: The Unique City*, rev. ed. (Cambridge: MIT Press, 1982), 271–91; Robert Gray, *A History of London* (London: Hutchinson, 1978); Christopher Hibbert, *London: The Biography of a City* (London: Longmans, 1969); and Roy Porter, *London: A Social History* (Cambridge: Harvard University Press, 1995).

5. Jean-Christophe Agnew, "Times Square: Secularization and Sacralization," in *Inventing Times Square: Commerce and Culture and the Crossroads of the World*, ed. William R. Taylor (New York: Russell Sage Foundation, 1991), 2. I have been informed by work on commercial culture and the American city. See, for example, William Leach, *Land of Desire: Merchants, Power, and the Rise of a New American Culture* (New York: Pantheon, 1993); Lewis A. Erenberg, *Steppin' Out: New York Nightlife and the Transformation of American Culture, 1890–1930* (Westport, Conn.: Greenwood, 1981); Stuart M. Blumin, *The Emergence of the Middle Class: Social Experience in the American City, 1760–1900* (Cambridge: Cambridge University Press, 1989); and Gunther Barth, *City People: The Rise of Modern City Culture in Nineteenth-Century America* (Oxford: Oxford University Press, 1980).

6. "London as a City of Pleasure," *Saturday Review*, July 27, 1872, 110.

7. *Evening News*, May 9, 1907, 1.

8. *Evening News*, May 13, 1907, 3.

9. *Modern Business* 2, no. 5 (December 1908): 573.

10. Elizabeth Kowaleski-Wallace argues in *Consuming Subjects: Women, Shopping, and Business in the Eighteenth Century* (New York: Columbia University Press, 1997) that the eighteenth-century shopper was also a feminine subject. However, Jennifer Jones suggests that the shopper was frequently gendered as masculine during this period in France. Jennifer Jones, "*Coquettes* and *Grisettes*: Women Buying and Selling in Ancien Régime Paris," in *The Sex of Things: Gender and Consumption in Historical Perspective*, ed. Victoria de Grazia with Ellen Furlough (Berkeley: University of California Press, 1996), 25–53. In the late-twentieth century the close identification between women and consumption is no longer as fixed as it was in the nineteenth. On this change, see Frank Mort, *Cultures of Consumption: Masculinities and Social Space in Late-Twentieth-Century Britain* (London: Routledge, 1996).

11. Michel Foucault, *The History of Sexuality*, vol. 1, *An Introduction*, trans. Robert Hurley (New York: Vintage Books, 1980), 45. Though there are many studies of Victorian sexuality, there are few explorations of the broader history of pleasure during this period. Particularly helpful works, however, are Peter Bailey, "Parasexuality and Glamour: The Victorian Barmaid as Cultural Prototype," *Gender and History* 2, no. 2 (Summer 1990): 148–72; Frederic Jameson, "Pleasure: A Political Issue," in *Formations of Pleasure*, ed. Frederic Jameson (London: Routledge and Kegan Paul, 1983), 1–14; Lawrence Birken, *Consuming Desire: Sexual Science and the Emergence of a Culture of Abundance, 1871–1914* (Ithaca: Cornell University Press, 1988). Other works on gender, desire, and Victorian culture include Mary Poovey, *Uneven Developments: The Ideological Work of Gender in Mid-Victorian England* (Chicago: University of Chicago Press, 1988); Catherine Gallagher and Thomas Laqueur, ed. *The Making of the Modern Body: Sexuality and Society in the Nineteenth Century* (Berkeley: University of California Press, 1987); Elaine Showalter, *Sexual Anarchy: Gender and Culture at the Fin-de-Siècle* (London: Penguin, 1990).

12. Meaghan Morris, "Things to Do with Shopping Centres," in *Grafts: Feminist Cultural Criticism*, ed. Susan Sheridan (London: Verso, 1988), 221.

13. For the history of Victorian fashion, see Elizabeth Wilson, *Adorned in Dreams: Fashion and Modernity* (London: Virago, 1985), 134–54; Christopher Breward, *The Culture of Fashion: A New History of Fashionable Dress* (Manchester: Manchester University Press, 1995); Valerie Steele, *Fashion and Eroticism: Ideals of Feminine Beauty from the Victorian Era to the Jazz Age* (New York: Oxford University Press, 1985); Alison Gernsheim, *Victorian and Edwardian Fashion* (New York: Dover, 1963). On French fashions, see Philippe Perrot, *Fashioning the Bourgeoisie: A History of Clothing in the Nineteenth Century*, trans. Richard Bienvenu (Princeton: Princeton University Press, 1994). On material culture, see Asa Briggs, *Victorian Things* (Chicago: University of Chicago Press, 1988); and Adrian Forty, *Objects of Desire* (New York: Pantheon, 1986).

14. For a discussion of shopping as leisure, see Rachel Bowlby, *Just Looking: Consumer Culture in Dreiser, Gissing, and Zola* (London: Methuen, 1985); and Anne Friedberg, *Window Shopping: Cinema and the Postmodern* (Berkeley: University of California Press, 1993). For anecdotal histories of shopping, see Alison Adburgham, *Shops and Shopping, 1800–1914: Where and in What Manner the Well-Dressed Englishwoman Bought Her Clothes*, 2d ed. (London: Barrie and Jenkins, 1989); and her *Shopping in Style: London from the Restoration to Edwardian Elegance* (London: Thames and Hudson, 1979); Dorothy Davis, *Fairs, Shops; and Supermarkets: A History of English Shopping* (Toronto: University of Toronto Press, 1966); Molly Harrison, *People and Shopping: A Social Background* (London: Ernest Benn, 1975); and John Benson, *The Rise of Consumer Society in Britain, 1880–1980* (London: Longman, 1994), 59–81.

15. Kowaleski-Wallace, *Consuming Subjects*, 75. For similar arguments, see Claire Walsh, "The Newness of the Department Store: A View from the Eighteenth Century," in *Cathedrals of Consumption: The European Department Store, 1850–1939*, ed. Geoffrey Crossick and Serge Jaumain (Aldershot: Ashgate, 1999); and G. J. Barker-Benfield, *The Culture of Sensibility: Sex and Society in Eighteenth-Century Britain* (Chicago: University of Chicago Press, 1992), 189–90.

16. Though the nineteenth-century middle classes did not live in neatly divided spheres, this ideal was central to the construction of their class identity. Leonore Davidoff and Catherine Hall, *Family Fortunes: Men and Women of the English Middle Class, 1780–1850* (Chicago: University of Chicago Press, 1987). Davidoff has recently discussed the value of this concept in "Regarding Some 'Old Husbands' Tales: Public and Private in Feminist History," in *Worlds Between: Historical Perspectives on Gender and Class* (New York:

Routledge, 1995), 227–76. For a critique of the separate spheres metaphor in women's history, see Amanda Vickery, "Golden Age to Separate Spheres? A Review of the Categories and Chronology of English Women's History," *Historical Journal* 36, no. 2 (June 1993): 383–414; and Linda Kerber, "Separate Spheres, Female Worlds, Woman's Place: The Rhetoric of Women's History," *Journal of American History* 75, no. 1 (June 1988): 9–39.

17. Henri Lefebvre, *The Production of Space*, trans. Donald Nicholson-Smith (Oxford: Basil Blackwell, 1984), 73. Gottdiener summarizes Lefebvre's view of space as "simultaneously a means of production . . . part of the social relations of production . . . an object of consumption, a political instrument, and an element in the class struggle." Mark Gottdiener, *The Social Production of Urban Space* (Austin: University of Texas Press, 1985), 123.

18. Michel de Certeau, *The Practice of Everyday Life*, trans. Steven F. Rendall (Berkeley: University of California Press, 1988), 117. For related arguments about the interdependent construction of places, consumption, and identities, see Robert D. Sack, "The Consumer's World: Place as Context," *Annals of the Association of American Geographers* 78, no. 4 (December 1988): 642–64; and P. D. Glennie and N. J. Thrift, "Modernity, Urbanism, and Modern Consumption," *Environment and Planning D: Society and Space* 10, no. 4 (August 1992): 423–43.

19. Walkowitz shows that feminists reworked preexisting cultural constructs but they were not free to invent entirely new meanings. Walkowitz, *City of Dreadful Delight*, 9.

20. Most studies of late-Victorian middle-class women have characterized this period as one of limited but growing educational, work, and political options. See, for example, the sections on the middle classes in Jane Lewis, *Women in England, 1870–1950: Sexual Divisions and Social Change* (Sussex: Wheatsheaf Books; Bloomington: Indiana University Press, 1984); and Jane Lewis, ed., *Labour and Love: Women's Experience of Home and Family, 1850–1940* (Oxford: Basil Blackwell, 1986); Martha Vicinus, ed., *A Widening Sphere: Changing Roles of Women* (Bloomington: Indiana University Press, 1977); Pat Thane, "Late-Victorian Women," in *Late-Victorian Britain*, ed. T. Gourvish and A. O'Day (London: Macmillan, 1987); David Rubinstein, *Before the Suffragettes: Women's Emancipation in the 1890s* (New York: St. Martin's Press, 1986); Martha Vicinus, *Independent Women: Work and Community for Single Women, 1850–1920* (Chicago: University of Chicago Press, 1985); Ellen Ross, *Love and Toil: Motherhood in Outcast London, 1870–1918* (Oxford: Oxford University Press, 1993); Dina M. Copelman, *London's Women Teachers: Gender, Class, and Feminism, 1870–1930* (New York: Routledge, 1996); Tracy C. Davis, *Actresses as Working Women: Their Social Identity in Victorian Culture* (New York: Routledge, 1991); Lisa Tickner, *The Spectacle of Women: Imagery of the Suffrage Campaign, 1907–1914* (Chicago: University of Chicago Press, 1988); Lee Holcombe, *Victorian Ladies at Work: Middle-Class Working Women in England and Wales, 1850–1914* (Hamden, Conn.: Archon Books, 1973); Patricia Hollis, *Ladies Elect: Women in English Local Government, 1865–1914* (New York: Clarendon Press, 1987); F. K. Prochaska, *Women and Philanthropy in Nineteenth-Century England* (Oxford: Clarendon Press, 1980); Patricia Jalland, *Women, Marriage, and Politics, 1860–1914* (Oxford: Clarendon Press, 1986).

21. Nord, *Walking the Victorian Streets.*

22. Indeed, I first discovered Lucy Snowe in Wilson's discussion of her evocative urban ramble. Wilson, *The Sphinx in the City*, 30–31.

23. Raymond Williams, *The Country and the City* (New York: Oxford University Press, 1973), 233; Janet Wolff, "The Culture of Separate Spheres: The Role of Culture in Nineteenth-Century Public and Private Life," in *The Culture of Capital: Art, Power, and the Nineteenth Century Middle Class*, ed. John Seed and Janet Wolff (Manchester: Manchester University Press; New York: St. Martin's Press, 1988), 126–28; Janet Wolff, "The Invisible Flâneuse: Women and the Literature of Modernity," *Theory, Culture, and Society* 2, no. 3 (1985): 37–46; Griselda Pollock, *Vision and Difference: Femininity, Feminism, and Histories of Art* (London: Routledge, 1988), 50–90.

24. This is a central argument in Nord, *Walking the Victorian Streets*; and Walkowitz, *City of Dreadful Delight*, chap. 1.

25. Walkowitz, *City of Dreadful Delight*; Winter, *London's Teeming Streets*; Nord, *Walking the Victorian Streets*; Ross, *Love and Toil*; Gareth Stedman Jones, *Outcast London: A Study of the Relationship between the Classes in Victorian Society*, rev. ed. (New York: Pantheon, 1984); David Feldman and Gareth Stedman Jones, eds., *Metropolis London: Histories and Representations since 1800* (London: Routledge, 1989); Nigel Thrift and Peter Williams, eds., *Class and Space: The Making of Urban Society* (London: Routledge and Kegan Paul, 1987). These histories illuminate David Harvey's argument that the "command over space" is a central means of achieving power and dominance within the world of commodity ex-

change. David Harvey, *Consciousness and the Urban Experience: Studies in the History and Theory of Capitalist Urbanization* (Baltimore: Johns Hopkins University Press, 1985), 22.

26. Walkowitz, *City of Dreadful Delight*, 20; Griselda Pollock, "Vicarious Excitements: *London: A Pilgrimage*, by Gustave Doré and Blanchard Jerrold, 1872," *New Formations* 2 (Spring 1988): 25–50; Asa Briggs, *Victorian Cities* (1963; reprint, Berkeley: University of California Press, 1993), 314–19; Showalter, *Sexual Anarchy*, 5–6.

27. Brontë, *Villette*, 109.

28. See, for example, L. D. Schwarz, *London in the Age of Industrialisation: Entrepreneurs, Labour Force, and Living Conditions, 1700–1850* (Cambridge: Cambridge University Press, 1992); Peter Earle, *The Making of the English Middle Classes: Business, Society, and Family Life in London, 1660–1730* (Berkeley: University of California Press, 1989); F. J. Fisher, "The Development of London as a Centre of Conspicuous Consumption in the Sixteenth and Seventeenth Centuries," in *Essays in Economic History*, vol. 2, ed. E. M. Carus-Wilson (London: Edward Arnold, 1962), 197–207. On consumerism and early-modern urban culture, see Peter Borsay, *The English Urban Renaissance: Culture and Society in the Provincial Town, 1660–1770* (Oxford: Clarendon Press; New York: Oxford University Press, 1989).

29. William Harvey, *London Scenes and London People* (London: W. H. Collingridge, 1863), 89. For a history of the City in the nineteenth century, see David Kynaston, *The City of London*, vol. 1. *A World of Its Own, 1815–1890* (London: Chatto and Windus, 1994).

30. On the role of monarchy and divisions of the city, see R. Malcolm Smuts, "The Court and Its Neighborhood: Royal Policy and Urban Growth in the Early Stuart West End," *Journal of British Studies* 30, no. 2 (April 1991): 117–49; Lawrence Stone, "The Residential Development of the West End of London in the Seventeenth Century," in *After the Reformation: Essays in Honor of J. H. Hexter*, ed. Barbara Malament (Philadelphia: University of Pennsylvania Press, 1980), 167–212; L. D. Schwarz, "Social Class and Social Geography: The Middle Classes in London at the End of the Eighteenth Century," *Social History* 7, no. 2 (May 1982): 167–85; and E. J. Power, "The East and West in Early Modern London," in *Wealth and Power in Tudor England: Essays Presented to S. T. Bindoff*, ed. E. W. Ives, R. J. Knecht, and J. J. Scarisbrick (London: University of London Press, 1978).

31. John Summerson, *Georgian London*, 3d ed. (Cambridge: MIT Press, 1978); Donald J. Olsen, *Town Planning in London: The Eighteenth and Nineteenth Centuries*, 2d ed. (New Haven: Yale University Press, 1982); Hermione Hobhouse, *Thomas Cubbitt: Master Builder* (New York: Universe Books, 1971); George Rudé, *Hanoverian London, 1714–1808* (Berkeley: University of California Press, 1971).

32. Frances Wey, *A Frenchman Sees the English in the 'Fifties*, trans. Valerie Pirie (1856; reprint, London: Sidgewick and Jackson, 1935), 72–73.

33. Percy White defined the West End in this way in his novel *The West End* (London: Sands, 1900). On the history of "Society," see Leonore Davidoff, *The Best Circles: Women and Society in Victorian England* (Totowa, N.J.: Rowman and Littlefield, 1973).

34. W. D. Rubinstein, *Elites and the Wealthy in Modern British History: Essays in Social and Economic History* (Sussex: Harvester Press; New York: St. Martin's Press, 1987), 36.

35. P. J. Atkins has looked at this aspect of the West End's history in "The Spatial Configuration of Class Solidarity in London's West End, 1792–1939," *Urban History Yearbook* 17 (1990): 36–65; and in "How the West End Was Won: The Struggle to Remove Street Barriers in Victorian London," *Journal of Historical Geography* 19, no. 3 (1993): 265–77. For an exploration of the struggle between the aristocracy and the middle classes in provincial cities, see David Cannadine, *Lords and Landlords: The Aristocracy and the Towns, 1774–1967* (Leicester: Leicester University Press, 1980).

36. Jerrold E. Seigel, *Bohemian Paris: Culture, Politics, and the Boundaries of Bourgeois Life, 1830–1930* (New York: Viking, 1986), 3.

37. *Illustrated London News*, April 21, 1866, 393.

38. *The Shops and Companies of London and the Trades and Manufactories of Great Britain* 1 (1865): 33.

39. Porter, *London*, 109.

40. Boswell's *Life of Johnson*, quoted in Jonathan Raban, *Soft City* (London: Collins Harvill, 1988), 92–93.

41. Adburgham, *Shops and Shopping*, 7. Indeed, the social hierarchy was enacted every time a customer forced a trader out of his or her shop into the street. One wealthy woman recalled "driving into Ashford in the dog cart and we stopped outside the fishmonger. He would come out in his striped apron and ask what we wanted. We'd just sit there and he'd go and get it and put it in the cart and we'd go again. That happened at most shops. Practically no one went into a shop at all. My mother

never set foot in a butcher's shop in her life." Quoted in Michael J. Winstanley, *The Shopkeeper's World, 1830–1914* (Manchester: Manchester University Press, 1983), 53.

42. See, for example, Adburgham, *Shops and Shopping*, 231; William Lancaster, *The Department Store: A Social History* (London: Leicester University Press, 1995), 171–92; Leach, *Land of Desire*; William R. Leach, "Transformations in a Culture of Consumption: Women and Department Stores, 1890–1925," *Journal of American History* 71, no. 2 (September 1984): 319–42; Wilson, *Adorned in Dreams*, 150; Mica Nava, "Modernity's Disavowal: Women, the City, and the Department Store," in *Modern Times: Reflections on a Century of Modernity*, ed. Mica Nava and Alan O'Shea (London: Routledge, 1996), 38–76. Among the many cultural histories of the department store see David Chaney, "The Department Store as a Cultural Form," *Theory, Culture, and Society* 1, no. 3 (1983): 22–31; Rudi Laermans, "Learning to Consume: Early Department Stores and the Shaping of Modern Consumer Culture, 1860–1914," *Theory, Culture, and Society* 10, no. 4 (November 1993): 79–102. On French stores see Michael Miller, *The Bon Marché: Bourgeois Culture and the Department Store* (Princeton: Princeton University Press, 1981); Rosalind Williams, *Dream Worlds: Mass Consumption in Late-Nineteenth-Century France* (Berkeley: University of California Press, 1982); Theresa McBride, "A Woman's World: Department Stores and the Evolution of Women's Employment, 1870–1920," *French Historical Studies* 10, no. 4 (Fall 1978): 664–83; and Lisa Tiersten, "Marianne in the Department Store: Gender and the Politics of Consumption in Turn-of-the-Century Paris," in *Cathedrals of Consumption: The European Department Store, 1850–1939*, ed. Geoffrey Crossick and Serge Jaumain (Aldershot: Ashgate, 1999). For a gendered analysis of Australian stores, see Gail Reekie, *Temptations: Sex, Selling, and the Department Store* (St. Leonards, Australia: Allen and Unwin, 1993). For the Russian context, see Christine Ruane, "Clothes Shopping in Imperial Russia: The Development of a Consumer Culture," *Journal of Social History* 28, no. 4 (Summer 1995): 765–82. On American stores, see Susan Porter Benson, *Counter Cultures: Saleswomen, Managers, and Customers in American Department Stores, 1890–1940* (Urbana: University of Illinois Press, 1988); Elaine S. Abelson, *When Ladies Go a-Thieving: Middle-Class Shoplifters in the Victorian Department Store* (Oxford: Oxford University Press, 1989).

43. Bowlby, *Just Looking*, 1; Thomas Richards, *The Commodity Culture of Victorian England: Advertising and Spectacle, 1851–1914* (Stanford, Calif.: Stanford University Press, 1990); Guy Debord, *Society of the Spectacle*, rev. ed. (Detroit: Black and Red, 1983). For similar arguments, see Friedberg, *Window Shopping*; and the collection of essays in Leo Charney and Vanessa R. Schwartz, *Cinema and the Invention of Modern Life* (Berkeley: University of California Press, 1995). Historian Lori Anne Loeb has studied the construction of gender identities and Victorian advertising, though she generally eschews the theoretical frameworks suggested by Debord and others. Lori Anne Loeb, *Consuming Angels: Advertising and Victorian Women* (New York: Oxford University Press, 1994).

44. Neil McKendrick, John Brewer, and J. H. Plumb, eds., *The Birth of a Consumer Society: The Commercialization of Eighteenth-Century England* (Bloomington: Indiana University Press, 1982). Also see Neil McKendrick, "Home Demand and Economic Growth: A New View of the Role of Women and Children in the Industrial Revolution," in *Historical Perspectives: Studies in English Thought and Society*, ed. Neil McKendrick (London: Europa Press, 1974), 152–210; Lorna Weatherill, *Consumer Behaviour and Material Culture in Britain, 1660–1760* (London: Routledge, 1988); Beverly Lemire, *Fashion's Favorite: The Cotton Trade and the Consumer in Britain, 1660–1800* (Oxford: Oxford University Press, 1992). *The Birth of a Consumer Society* was not singularly responsible for launching the study of consumption, however. Harold Perkin suggested its importance to industrialization in *The Origins of Modern English Society, 1780–1880* (London: Routledge and Kegan Paul, 1969), 91–95. Joan Thirsk, *Economic Policy and Projects: The Development of Consumer Society in Early Modern England* (Oxford: Clarendon Press, 1978); and Chandra Mukerji, *From Graven Images: Patterns of Modern Materialism* (New York: Columbia University Press, 1983), also contributed to this interest. For a useful discussion of the literature of consumption and production and the historiography of the Industrial Revolution, see Ben Fine and Ellen Leopold, "Consumerism and the Industrial Revolution," *Social History* 15, no. 2 (May 1990): 151–79. For criticisms of much of this work, see Colin Campbell, *The Romantic Ethic and the Spirit of Modern Consumerism* (Oxford: Basil Blackwell, 1987).

45. The project resulted in three volumes of collected essays: John Brewer and Roy Porter, eds. *Consumption and the World of Goods* (Lon-

don: Routlege, 1993); Ann Bermingham and John Brewer eds., *The Consumption of Culture, 1600–1800: Image, Object, Text* (London: Routledge, 1995); John Brewer and Susan Staves, eds., *Early Modern Conceptions of Property* (London: Routledge, 1995). John Brewer has also recently published his own study, *The Pleasures of the Imagination: English Culture in the Eighteenth Century* (London: HarperCollins, 1997).

46. For an overview of this debate and its problems, see Gareth Shaw, "The Evolution and Impact of Large-Scale Retailing in Britain," in *The Evolution of Retail Systems, ca. 1800–1914*, ed. John Benson and Gareth Shaw (Leicester: Leicester University Press, 1992), 135–65. See also Gareth Shaw, "The European Scene: Britain and Germany," in Benson and Shaw, *Evolution of Retail Systems*, 17–34. Some classic works on retailing are James B. Jefferys, *Retail Trading in Britain, 1850–1950* (Cambridge: Cambridge University Press, 1954); David Alexander, *Retailing in England during the Industrial Revolution* (London: University of London, Athlone Press, 1970); and Peter Mathias, *Retailing Revolution: A History of Multiple Retailing in the Food Trades Based upon the Allied Suppliers Group of Companies* (London: Longmans, 1967). Also see the more recent Lorna Mui and Hoh-Cheung Mui, *Shops and Shopkeeping in Eighteenth-Century England* (Kingston: McGill-Queen's University Press and Routledge, 1989).

47. On the persistence of older retail practices, see Martin Phillips, "The Evolution of Markets and Shops in Britain," in Benson and Shaw, *The Evolution of Retail Systems*, 53–75. On the shift from the verbal to the visual, see Davis, *Fairs, Shops, and Supermarkets*, 258.

48. Davidoff and Hall, *Family Fortunes*, 29–30.

49. Thorstein Veblen made a similar argument in *The Theory of the Leisure Class* (1899; reprint, London: Penguin, 1984). However, I emphasize a very different aspect of the relationship between consumption, public space, and social identities.

50. For an overview of scholars' use of consumer culture in European history, see Lisa Tiersten, "Redefining Consumer Culture: Recent Literature on Consumption and the Bourgeoisie in Western Europe," *Radical History Review* 57 (Fall 1993): 116–59. Among the many general works on consumer culture, see Grant McCracken, *Culture and Consumption: New Approaches to the Symbolic Character of Consumer Goods and Activities* (Bloomington: Indiana University Press, 1988); Mike Featherstone, *Consumer Culture and Postmodernism* (London: Sage, 1991); Frederic Jameson, "Postmodernism and Consumer Society," in *Postmodern Culture*, ed. H. Foster (London: Pluto Press, 1985); Ben Fine and Ellen Leopold, *The World of Consumption* (London: Routledge, 1993); Martyn J. Lee, *Consumer Culture Reborn: The Cultural Politics of Consumption* (London: Routledge, 1992); Don Slater, *Consumer Culture and Modernity* (Cambridge: Polity, 1997); Daniel Miller, *Material Culture and Mass Consumption* (Oxford: Basil Blackwell, 1987); and his recent *Acknowledging Consumption: A Review of New Studies* (London: Routledge, 1995). Also see Douglas Kellner, "Critical Theory, Commodities, and the Consumer Society." *Theory, Culture, and Society* 1, no. 3 (1983): 66–83. Most of the recent historical studies of British consumerism have focused on the twentieth century; see Benson, *Rise of Consumer Society*; Mort, *Cultures of Consumption*; and Gary Cross, *Time and Money: The Making of Consumer Culture* (London: Routledge, 1993).

51. Jean Baudrillard, *Selected Writings*, ed. Mark Poster (Stanford, Calif.: Stanford University Press, 1988), 21–22.

52. Mort, *Cultures of Consumption*, 7.

53. Jürgen Habermas, *The Structural Transformation of the Public Sphere: An Inquiry into a Category of Bourgeois Society*, trans. Thomas Burger (1962; reprint, Cambridge: MIT Press, 1991). While Habermas significantly broke with Theodor Adorno and Max Horkheimer, he basically adopted the view of mass culture presented in *Dialectic of Enlightenment*, trans. John Cumming (1944; reprint, New York: Herder and Herder, 1972). For similar arguments, see Richard Sennett, *The Fall of Public Man: On the Social Psychology of Capitalism* (New York: Vintage, 1978); and Michael Sorkin, ed., *Variations on a Theme Park: The New American City and the End of Public Space* (New York: Hill and Wang, 1992).

54. In *Consuming Angels*, for example, Loeb suggests that the prevalence of sensual, even erotic, advertised images of women implied that the middle class embraced materialistic hedonism. One cannot, however, assume that these images reveal much about the psychology of the consumer. Benson discusses the question of female emancipation and consumption in *Rise of Consumer Society*, 180–203. For an analysis of the way in which theorists have failed to examine the advertising industry's self-image, see Jackson Lears, *Fables of Abundance: A Cultural History of Advertising in America* (New York: Basic Books, 1994), 19.

55. de Grazia, *The Sex of Things*, 7.

56. Joan Wallach Scott, *Gender and the Politics of History* (New York: Columbia University Press, 1988), 46.

Chapter One
"The Halls of Temptation"

1. "Guy Fawkes Day in Westbourne Grove," *Bayswater Chronicle*, November 11, 1876. This newspaper changed names from the *Bayswater Chronicle and West London Journal* to the *Paddington, Kensington, and Bayswater Chronicle* in 1875, but it was generally known as the *Bayswater Chronicle* (hereafter *BC*). For Whiteley's history see Richard S. Lambert, *The Universal Provider: A Study of William Whiteley and the Rise of the London Department Store* (London: George G. Harrap, 1938); Adburgham, *Shops and Shopping*, 150–57; Lancaster, *The Department Store*, 20–24 and 130–36.

2. E. P. Thompson, "Rough Music," in *Customs in Common: Studies in Traditional Popular Culture* (New York: New Press, 1991), 519; D. E. Underdown, "The Taming of the Scold: The Enforcement of Patriarchal Authority in Early Modern England," in *Order and Disorder in Early Modern England*, ed. Anthony Fletcher and John Stevenson (Cambridge: Cambridge University Press, 1985), 116–36; Natalie Zemon Davis, *Society and Culture in Early Modern France* (Stanford, Calif.: Stanford University Press, 1975), chaps. 4 and 5. On charivari and Victorian marriage, see John R. Gillis, *For Better or Worse: British Marriages, 1600 to the Present* (New York: Oxford University Press, 1985), 130–34; and A. James Hammerton, *Cruelty and Companionship: Conflict in Nineteenth-Century Married Life* (New York: Routledge, 1992), 15–33.

3. Thompson, "Rough Music," 481.

4. Robert D. Storch, " 'Please to Remember the Fifth of November': Conflict, Solidarity, and Public Order in Southern England, 1815–1900," in *Popular Culture and Custom in Nineteenth-Century England*, ed. Robert D. Storch (London: Croom Helm, 1982), 74.

5. Butchers often brought out their marrow bones and cleavers when mocking a local priest or other public figure. T. F. Thiselton-Dyer, *British Popular Customs, Present and Past* (London: George Bell, 1876), 411.

6. For the history of some of these changes, see Gareth Shaw, "The Evolution and Impact of Large-Scale Retailing in Britain," and "The European Scene: Britain and Germany," in *The Evolution of Retail Systems*, 135–65, 17–34. Also see Gareth Shaw and M. T. Wild, "Retail Patterns in the Victorian City," *Transactions of the Institute of British Geographers* 4 (1979): 278–91; Lancaster, *The Department Store*; Jefferys, *Retail Trading in Britain*; John William Ferry, *A History of the Department Store* (New York: Macmillan, 1960); Hrandt Pasdermadjian, *The Department Store: Its Origins, Evolution, and Economics* (London: Newman Books, 1954). Among the many business histories, Michael Moss and Alison Turton, *A Legend of Retailing: The House of Fraser* (London: Weidenfeld and Nicholson, 1989) provides the clearest overview. Also see Hamish Fraser, *The Coming of the Mass Market, 1850–1914* (Hamden, Conn.: Archon, 1981). Despite their differences, all of these scholars argue that the period of the department store's greatest growth and transformation came between 1880 and 1914.

7. "Wholesale Butchery in Bayswater," *BC*, November 11, 1876.

8. For a discussion of the legacy of corporate structures and the European petit bourgeoisie, see Geoffrey Crossick and Heinz-Gerhard Haupt, *The Petite Bourgeoisie in Europe, 1780–1914: Enterprise, Family, and Independence* (London: Routledge, 1995), 16–37. On the problems small shopkeepers faced during this era, see ibid., 64–70, and Winstanley, *The Shopkeeper's World*. The food trades were especially vulnerable. Christopher Hosgood, "The 'Pigmies of Commerce' and the Working-Class Community: Small Shopkeepers in England, 1870–1914," *Journal of Social History* 22, no. 3 (Spring 1989): 439–60.

9. There is a huge literature on the cultural, social, technological, and structural causes of English economic failures in the late-nineteenth century. See, for example, Martin J. Wiener, *English Culture and the Decline of the Industrial Spirit, 1850–1980* (Cambridge: Cambridge University Press, 1981). Among Wiener's many critics, see W. D. Rubinstein, *Capitalism, Culture, and Decline in Britain, 1750–1990* (London: Routledge, 1993). Economic historians have argued recently that only selected industries failed and that failure was more relative than absolute. See, for example, Sidney Pollard, *Britain's Prime and Britain's Decline: The British Economy, 1870–1914* (London: Edward Arnold, 1989); Bernard Elbaum and William Lazonick, eds., *The Decline of the British Economy: An Institutional Approach* (Oxford: Clarendon Press, 1986). For a useful overview of these debates, see James Raven, "Viewpoint: British History and Enterprise Culture," *Past and Present* 123 (May 1989): 178–204.

10. Mary Poovey, *Making a Social Body: British Cultural Formation, 1830–1864* (Chicago: University of Chicago Press, 1995), 4. Asa Briggs argued that during the 1890s the term "the masses" shifted from meaning a threatening crowd to a consuming public. Asa

Briggs, *Victorian Cities*, 49; and "The Human Aggregate," in *The Victorian City: Images and Realities*, (London: Routledge and Kegan Paul, 1973), 1:83–104. Both marketing and sociological investigation developed in part to be able to quantify, see, and control the masses. Indeed, marketing grew out of the turn-of-the-century poverty studies. See T. A. B. Corley's work on Seebohm Rowntree's social investigations and the marketing of his family's cocoa in "Consumer Marketing in Britain, 1914–1960," *Business History* 29 (October 1987): 69; Francis Goodall, "Marketing Consumer Products before 1914: Rowntrees and Elect Cocoa," in *Markets and Bagmen: Studies in the History of Marketing and British Industrial Performance, 1830–1939*, ed. R. P. T. Davenport-Hines (Aldershot: Gower, 1986), 16–56; and Robert Fitzgerald, *Rowntree and the Marketing Revolution, 1862–1962* (Cambridge: Cambridge University Press, 1995).

11. William Taylor, "The Evolution of Public Space in New York City: The Commercial Showcase of America," in *Consuming Visions: Accumulation and Display of Goods in America, 1880–1920*, ed. Simon J. Bronner (New York: W. W. Norton, 1989), 291, 300.

12. Wolfgang Schivelbusch, *The Railway Journey: The Industrialization of Time and Space in the Nineteenth Century* (Berkeley: University of California Press, 1986), 54.

13. Geoff Eley has argued that since the inception of the public sphere in the eighteenth century, there have been many "competing publics." "Nations, Publics, and Political Cultures: Placing Habermas in the Nineteenth Century," in *Habermas and the Public Sphere*, ed. Craig Calhoun (Cambridge: MIT Press, 1992), 306. Also see chapter 3 below.

14. Sociologists and anthropologists have spent a good deal of effort delineating the relationship between consumer practices and social identities. See, for example, Veblen, *The Theory of the Leisure Class*; Pierre Bourdieu, *Outline of a Theory of Practice*, trans. Richard Nice (Cambridge: Cambridge University Press, 1977); and *Distinction: A Social Critique of the Judgement of Taste*, trans. Richard Nice (Cambridge: Harvard University Press, 1984); Mary Douglas and Baron Isherwood, *The World of Goods* (New York: Basic Books, 1979); Arjun Appadurai, ed., *The Social Life of Things: Commodities in Cultural Perspective* (Cambridge: Cambridge University Press, 1986); Miller, *Material Culture and Mass Consumption*.

15. For maps of the fashionable the West End shopping district, see P. G. Hall, *The Industries of London since 1861* (London: Hutchinson, 1962), 46; and Ferry, *A History of the Department Store*, 193.

16. Michel Foucault, "Of Other Spaces," trans. Jay Miscowiec, *Diacritics* 16, no. 1 (Spring 1986): 23. G. K. Chesterton captured this point beautifully in his satire of Whiteley and Paddington's contentious political culture, *The Napoleon of Notting Hill* (London: John Lane, 1904).

17. G. A. Sala, "Young London: Westbourne-Grove and Thereabouts," *Daily Telegraph*, June 2, 1879, 5. Sala's two most famous London rambles, *Twice Round the Clock, or The Hours of the Day and Night in London* (1859; reprint, New York: Humanities Press; Leicester: Leicester University Press, 1971) and *London Up to Date* (London: Adam and Charles Black, 1894). George Augustus Sala (1828–95) was described in 1885 as "the most popular journalist in London . . . an author, engraver, lecturer, critic, caricaturist, and pantomime writer . . . correspondent to the *Daily Telegraph* . . . the most witty and amusing writer in the world." [Count Paul Vasili], *The World of London* (London: Sampson Low, Marston, Searle, Rivington, 1885), 207.

18. Sala, "Young London," *Daily Telegraph*, June 5, 1879, 5.

19. Sala, "Young London," June 2, 1879, 5. Also see Walkowitz's analysis of his representation of gender and shopping in "Going Public: Shopping, Street Harassment, and Streetwalking in Late Victorian London," *Representations*, no. 62 (Spring 1998): 1–30. Thanks to Judy Walkowitz for allowing me to read a draft version of this essay before it appeared. For another reading of orientalist images of consumerism, see Peter Wollen, "Fashion/Orientalism/The Body," *New Formations* 1 (Spring 1987): 5–33.

20. "A Strange Critic in Asia Minor," *BC*, June 14, 1879.

21. The argument that public transport allowed for the creation of separate, socially homogenous neighborhoods has been most forcefully put forth by Olsen, *Growth of Victorian London*. Stuart Blumin similarly pointed out that in America "the city was sorting its classes of people into increasingly distinct institutions and spaces." *Emergence of the Middle Class*, 146.

22. H. J. Dyos, *Victorian Suburb: A Study of the Growth of Camberwell*, 2d ed. (Leicester: Leicester University Press, 1977); and Alan A. Jackson, *Semi-Detached London: Suburban Development, Life, and Transport, 1900–1939* (London: Allen and Unwin, 1973); H. J. Dyos and D. A. Reeder, "Slums and Suburbs," in *The Victorian City* 1:359–86; Hugh C. Prince, "North-West London, 1814–1863,"

and "North-West London, 1864–1914," in *Greater London*, ed. J. T. Coppock and Hugh C. Prince (London: Faber and Faber, 1964), 80–141; F. M. L. Thompson, *Hampstead: Building a Borough, 1650–1964* (London: Routledge and Kegan Paul, 1974); F. M. L. Thompson, ed., *The Rise of Suburbia* (Leicester: Leicester University Press, 1982); Michael Jahn, "Suburban Development in Outer West London," in Thompson, *Rise of Suburbia*, 94–156; and D. A. Reeder, "A Theatre of Suburbs: Some Patterns of Development in West London, 1801–1911," in *The Study of Urban History*, ed. H. J. Dyos (New York: St. Martin's Press, 1968), 253–71.

23. Michael Miller explored the relationship between the department stores and the boulevards in *The Bon Marché*, 19–20, 35. Philip G. Nord argued that the connection between department stores and the new Paris was a key aspect of shopkeeper politics. *Paris Shopkeepers and the Politics of Resentment* (Princeton: Princeton University Press, 1986).

24. Mona Domosh argues that the particular character and structure of the city's elite classes shaped commercial development. Mona Domosh, "Shaping the Commercial City: Retail Districts in Nineteenth-Century New York and Boston," *Annals of the Association of American Geographers* 80, no. 2 (June 1990): 268–84.

25. Gareth Shaw discusses store location in Victorian London in "The Role of Retailing in the Urban Economy," in *The Structure of Nineteenth Century Cities*, ed. James Johnson and Colin G. Pooley (London: Croom Helm and New York: St. Martin's Press, 1982), 171–94. Also see Jeanne Catherine Lawrence, "Geographical Space, Social Space, and the Realm of the Department Store," *Urban History* 19, no. 1 (April 1992): 64–84. Some historians have argued that the first department stores appeared in the north of England in the early-nineteenth century. Lancaster, *The Department Store*, chap. 1; Adburgham, *Shops and Shopping*, 18–19; and Asa Briggs, *Friends of the People: The Centenary History of Lewis's* (London: B. T. Batsford, 1956). For a store outside of London, J. H. Porter, "The Development of a Provincial Department Store, 1870–1939" *Business History* 18 no. 1 (January 1971): 64–71.

26. For portraits of these residential neighborhoods, see Walter Besant, ed. *The Fascination of London: Mayfair, Belgravia, and Bayswater* (London: Adam and Charles Black, 1903); George Clinch, *Mayfair and Belgravia: Being an Historical Account of the Parish of St. George, Hanover Square* (London: Truslove and Shirley, 1892); E. Beresford Chancellor, *Wanderings in Marylebone: A Gossip about the Squares and the Streets and their Past Residents* (London: Dulan, 1926); *Wanderings in Piccadilly, Mayfair, and Pall Mall* (London: Alston Rivers, 1908); *Knightsbridge and Belgravia: Their History, Topography, and Famous Inhabitants* (London: Sir Isaac Pitman, 1909); *The West End of Yesterday and To-day: Being Studies in London's History and Topography during the Past Century* (London: Architectural Press, 1926); Arthur W. Dasent, *The History of St. James's Square and the Foundation of the West End* (London: Macmillan, 1895); *Picadilly in Three Centuries* (London: Macmillan, 1920); and P. H. Ditchfield, *London's West End* (London: Jonathan Cape, 1925). For a more recent overview, see Carol Kennedy, *Mayfair: A Social History* (London: Hutchinson, 1986); and Reginald Colby, *Mayfair: A Town within London* (London: County Life, 1966); Gordon Mackenzie, *Marylebone: Great City North of Oxford Street* (London: St. Martin's and Macmillan, 1972).

27. In the 1870s, William Ablett, an "old draper," described W. Tarn and Co. of Newington; Aldeson and Harvey of Lambeth; Harvey Nichols and Co. of Knightsbridge; Shoolbred of Tottenham Court Road; Whiteley of Westbourne Grove; Rotherham of Shoreditch; Spencer, Turner, and Co. of Lisson Grove as "mammoth, but honest firms," places were customers felt they received "the best market value for their money." William Ablett, *Reminiscences of an Old Draper* (London: Sampson Low, Marston, Searle, and Rivington, 1876), 43.

28. Sir Walter Besant, *London in the Nineteenth Century* (London: Adam and Charles Black, 1909), 29–30.

29. Katherine Chorley, *Manchester Made Them* (Faber and Faber, 1950), 149, cited in Carol Dyhouse, "Mothers and Daughters in the Middle-Class Home, ca. 1870–1914," in *Labour and Love: Women's Experience of Home and Family, 1850–1940*, ed. Jane Lewis (Oxford: Basil Blackwell, 1986), 31.

30. L. McDowell has argued that the "division of urban space reflects and influences the sexual division of labour, women's role in the family, and the separation of home and work life." "Towards an Understanding of the Gender Division of Urban Space," *Environment and Planning D: Society and Space* 1, no. 1 (March 1983): 62. However, large metropolitan areas also defy neat divisions between male and female, domestic and productive, rich and poor. When contemporaries drew such sharp distinctions, they were not merely describing reality, but were attempting to create that reality. On gender and the confusion of the big

city, see Ryan, *Women in Public*, 60–61; and Walkowitz, *City of Dreadful Delight*. For a general discussion of gender relations and spatial settings see the introduction to *Women in Cities: Gender and the Urban Environment*, ed. Jo Little, Linda Peake, and Pat Richardson (New York: New York University Press, 1988). On gender, consumption, and suburbia, see Roger Miller, "Selling Mrs. Consumer: Advertising and the Creation of Suburban Socio-Spatial Relations, 1910–1930," *Antipode* 23, no. 3 (1991): 263–301.

31. Wilson, *The Sphinx in the City*, 45.

32. This separation was a very slow and uneven process. See Davidoff and Hall, *Family Fortunes*, 364–69. Winter argued that while working women and girls were increasingly involved in urban life, "a move to a leafy middle-class suburb meant that wives and daughters would enter the streets of the central city only occasionally to shop or to attend concerts, to go to the theater, or to participate, with some male escort, in special events." *London's Teeming Streets*, 177. Many studies have replicated without interrogating the Victorian ideal of separate male and female spheres by studying only middle-class women's role within the home. See, for example, Patricia Branca, *Silent Sisterhood: Middle-Class Women in the Victorian Home* (London: Croom Helm, 1975).

33. Sala, *Twice around the Clock*, 161–63.

34. Mayhew, *The Shops and Companies of London*, 86.

35. *Warehousemen and Draper's Trade Journal* (hereafter *WDTJ*), July 12, 1873, 374.

36. Mary Poovey noted that the "domestic ideal of female nature . . . was both inherently contradictory and unevenly deployed, [and] it was open to a variety of readings that could be mobilized in contradictory practices." Poovey, *Uneven Developments*, 15. Elizabeth Langland has recently made a similar argument in *Nobody's Angels: Middle-Class Women and Domestic Ideology in Victorian Culture* (Ithaca: Cornell University Press, 1995).

37. See, for example, Frank Bullen's recollections of working as a delivery boy and shop assistant in Westbourne Grove in the 1870s in *Confessions of a Tradesman* (London: Hodder and Stoughton, 1908), 22–28. Sir William Bell, M.P., described the Westbourne Grove of his boyhood as a kind of sexual playground. As an adolescent Bell went to Whiteley's every day to flirt with a young shop assistant in the chemistry department. Sir William Bell, "Some Recollections of Bayswater Fifty Years Ago," *BC*, July 21, 1923. In his student days, H. G. Wells walked through the Grove every day on his way to university. H. G. Wells, *Experiment in Autobiography* (New York: Macmillan, 1934).

38. F. M. L. Thompson, *Rise of Suburbia*, 20.

39. Similar conflicts existed in suburbs across in Britain. See David Cannadine, "Victorian Cities: How Different?" in *The Victorian City: A Reader in British Urban History, 1820–1914*, ed. R. J. Morris and Richard Rodger (London: Longman, 1993), 126–27.

40. Sala, "Young London," *Daily Telegraph*, June 2, 1879, 5.

41. One journalist described Bayswater as extending from "Westbourne Terrace to Notting-hill, and from Hyde Park and Kensington Gardens to the Harrow-road, covering nearly a mile square." *Paddington Times*, May 6, 1876. Baker noted, "Bayswater has come to be the name for the whole of the former Paddington metropolitan borough south of the railway." During the mid- and late-Victorian years it was the term used for "the south-western part of Paddington, from the Kensington boundary eastward to Lancaster Gate Terrace and Eastbourne Terrace and from Bayswater Road northward to Bishop's Bridge Road and Westbourne Grove," T. F. T. Baker, *A History of the County of Middlesex*, vol. 9, *Hampstead and Paddington* (Oxford: Oxford University Press, 1989), 204. As with the West End as a whole, however, these boundaries were never as fixed as maps suggest.

42. Baker, *County of Middlesex*, 185.

43. See, for example, Dyos's analysis of Camberwell's population in *Victorian Suburb*, 53–56; and Jahn's "Suburban Development."

44. Sheppard, *London, 1808–1870*, xvii, 84.

45. Baker, *County of Middlesex*, 177–81. For a comprehensive study of transport in the Victorian era, see the first volume of T. C. Barker and Michael Robbins, *A History of London Transport: Passenger Travel and the Development of the Metropolis* (London: George Allen and Unwin, 1974). Despite the development of mass transit, Whiteley and one of his neighbors ran their own omnibus service from the Grove to St. John's Wood, Maida Vale, and Camden Town. Michael Bonavia, *London before I Forget* (Upton-upon-Severn, Worcs.: Self-Publishing Association, 1990), 131.

46. On Bayswater's demography, see Baker, *County of Middlesex*, 204–12; Reeder, "A Theatre of Suburbs." During the late 1830s and 1840s, working people occupied small houses along Bishop's Road and Westbourne Grove. Lambert, *Universal Provider*, 59. Bayswater Road in the 1840s was known for its "plebeian tea-gardens." "Bayswater Fresco," *Punch* 5 (1843): 137.

47. Atkins, "The Spatial Configuration of Class Solidarity," 53–55. Bayswater also had a relatively wealthy Jewish population. Gerry Black, *Living Up West: Jewish Life in London's West End* (London: London Museum of Jewish Life, 1994), 10.

48. Thomas Charles Newman, *Many Parts* (London: Hutchinson, 1935), 106.

49. Emily Constance Cook, *Highways and Byways in London* (London: Macmillan, 1903), 295. In 1879 a journalist noted that "Asia Minor . . . is the favourite home of merchant princes, of travellers, painters, men of science, literature, of orientalists, of the elite of home and foreign society . . . and women who are their mothers, wives and sisters." *BC*, June 14, 1879.

50. Alfred Cox, *The Landlord's and Tenant's Guide* (1853), quoted in Olsen, *The Growth of Victorian London*, 164.

51. Peter Cunningham, *London in 1857*, 4th ed. (London: John Murray, 1857), xiii.

52. *Paddington Times*, May 6, 1876.

53. In the 1880s "scores" of City merchants and bankers commuted from Bayswater to the City on the 'bus. Newman, *Many Parts*, 45.

54. By the 1920s and 1930s Westbourne Grove was filled with decidedly "down-market" establishments. See Bonavia's description in *London before I Forget*, 131–32. A 1924 book on London's shops advised that Bayswater should be visited because of Whiteley's, but it did not recommend any other shops in the area. Elizabeth Montizambert, *London Discoveries in Shops and Restaurants* (London: Women Publishers, 1924), 5. In a guide published in 1934, the author called Whiteley's "a shopping centre in itself," but it is not "in one of London's shopping centres." Thelma Benjamin, *London Shops and Shopping* (London: Herbert Joseph, 1934), 158. Brompton Road, the main commercial street in Kensington and the site of Harrod's department store, underwent the same sort of change a decade or so later. See Harold Clunn, *The Face of London: The Record of a Century's Changes and Development* (London: Simpkin and Marshall, 1932), 333. Harrod's began expanding from a small grocery shop in the late sixties, but it did not become a full department store until after 1889, when Charles Digby Harrod retired and the store was floated as a limited liability company. At that point, Richard Burbidge, a former manager at Whiteley's, was appointed general manager. Tim Dale, *Harrod's: The Store and the Legend* (London: Pan Books, 1981).

55. "Westbourne Grove," *London Post Office Directory* (London: Frederick Kelly, 1860).

56. *Builder* 21 (1863), 766–67, quoted in Olsen, *The Growth of Victorian London*, 168.

57. *Building News* 6 (1860), 593, quoted in Olsen, *Growth of Victorian London*.

58. Lambert, *Universal Provider*, 60–61.

59. Quoted ibid., 58–59.

60. Ablett, *Reminiscences of an Old Draper*, 193.

61. "Modern Paris," *Building News*, February 1, 1861, 80.

62. By the early 1870s, trade journals recognized that the larger drapers such as Whiteley's did an "immense suburban and provincial trade." *WDTJ*, December 14, 1872, 447.

63. Sala, "Young London," *Daily Telegraph*, June 2, 1879, 5.

64. "Westbourne Grove," in *London Post Office Directory* (London: Frederick Kelly, 1870). In its heyday in the 1870s and 1880s, the Grove included many other fashionable shops, such Arthur's Stores, Owen's, and the haute couture fur salon originally known as the Arctic Fur Store, later known as Bradley's. Bonavia, *London before I Forget*, 131.

65. Sala, "Young London," *Daily Telegraph*, June 2, 1879, 5.

66. Lambert, *Universal Provider*, 60–61; Adburgham, *Shops and Shopping*, 149–59.

67. Sala, "Young London," *Daily Telegraph*, June 2, 1879, 5.

68. *Modern London, the World's Metropolis: An Epitome of Results* (London: Historical Publishing, 1890), 194.

69. The union of commerce and royal spectacle was developed to a much greater extent in the 1887 and 1897 jubilee celebrations, however. See Thomas Richards, "The Image of Victoria in the Year of Jubilee," *Victorian Studies* 31, no. 1 (Autumn 1987): 7–32; and Victoria Smith, "Constructing Victoria: The Representation of Queen Victoria in England, India, and Canada, 1897–1914" (Ph.D. diss., Rutgers University, 1998), chap. 1. As we will see in chapter 3, Princess Alexandra's procession altered women's relationship to London by encouraging the prestigious men's clubs to open their doors to women. Many middle-class women also ventured to London to view the procession. Two sisters from Kent, for example, Emily and Ellen Hall, remembered wandering all over the city and being crushed by the crowds. Emily even left her crinoline at home to ease her walk through the crowds in Oxford and Regent Streets. A. R. Mills, ed., *Two Victorian Ladies: More Pages from the Journals of Emily and Ellen Hall* (Letchworth, Herfordshire: Garden City Press, 1969), 88.

70. This view of the store's origins appears in Lambert, *The Universal Provider*, 18–21;

Adburgham, *Shops and Shopping*, 150; and most recently in Lancaster, *The Department Store*, 20. It was also part of store mythology and was described in two internal histories, "Whiteley's, 1863–1963" (London: Whiteley's, 1963) and "A Short History of Whiteley's" (publishing details unknown). Whiteley's archive, Westminster City Archives, London. Other retailers also remembered being inspired by visits to exhibitions. Paul Poiret, for example, recalled being taken to the 1889 Exhibition and wondered: "I have often asked myself whether my taste for colour was not born on that night, amidst the phantasmagoria of pinks, greens, and velvets." Paul Poiret, *My First Fifty Years*, trans. Stephen Haden Guest (London: Victor Gollancz, 1931), 18.

71. See, for example, Asa Briggs's discussion of William Whiteley and the Crystal Palace in *Victorian People: A Reassessment of Persons and Themes, 1851–1867*, rev. ed (Chicago: University of Chicago Press, 1975), 40.

72. Richards, *The Commodity Culture of Victorian England*, 21.

73. Walter Benjamin, "Paris, Capital of the Nineteenth Century," in *Reflections: Essays, Aphorisms, Autobiographical Writings*, ed. Peter Demetz, trans. Edmund Jephcott (New York: Harcourt, Brace, Jovanovich, 1978), 152–53.

74. Karl Marx, *Capital: A Critique of Political Economy* (1867; reprint, New York: Modern Library, 1936), 81.

75. Bowlby, *Just Looking*, 8. On display and the Great Exhibition, see Briggs, *Victorian Things*, 52–102; Forty, *Objects of Desire*; Paul Greenhalgh, *Ephemeral Vistas: The Expositions Universelles, Great Exhibitions, and World's Fairs, 1851–1939* (Manchester: Manchester University Press, 1988). For the prehistory of the Crystal Palace, see Toshio Kusamitsu, "Great Exhibitions before 1851," *History Workshop* 9 (Spring 1980): 70–89. There has been a good deal of research on exhibitions, French design, and commercial history; see Williams, *Dream Worlds*, 64–66; Whitney Walton, *France at the Crystal Palace: Bourgeois Taste and Artisan Manufacture in the Nineteenth Century* (Berkeley: University of California Press, 1992); Deborah Silverman, *Art Nouveau in Fin-de-Siècle France: Politics, Psychology, and Style* (Berkeley: University of California Press, 1989); Leora Auslander, *Taste and Power: Furnishing Modern France* (Berkeley: University of California, 1996), 203–10.

76. *Queen*, March 3, 1866, 159.

77. See McKendrick, *The Birth of a Consumer Society*, especially chaps. 3 and 4.

78. On early and mid-Victorian amusements, see Richard D. Altick, *The Shows of London* (Cambridge: Harvard University Press, Belknap Press, 1978).

79. The introduction of gaslight and the development of plate glass reinforced the understanding of the shop window as a stage or exhibition. Wolfgang Schivelbusch, *Disenchanted Night: The Industrialization of Light in the Nineteenth Century*, trans. Angela Davies (Berkeley: University of California Press, 1988). See Ablett's discussion of the introduction of expensive shop fittings between the 1820s and 1860s, in *Reminiscences of an Old Draper*, 90; "The London Shop Fronts," *Chamber's Journal* (October 1864): 670–72; and Major Chambre, *Recollections of West-End Life with Sketches of Society in Paris, India, etc.* (London: Hurst and Blackett, 1858), 245–46. Plate glass was first used in very elite houses, notably Swan and Edgar's in Regent Street and Harvey's of Ludgate Hill. *WDTJ*, June 10, 1882, 397.

80. Tony Bennett, "The Exhibitionary Complex," *New Formations* 4 (Spring 1988): 85.

81. Friedberg, *Window Shopping*, 15. This had repercussions for the constitution of racial as well as class and gender identities. Timothy Mitchell, *Colonising Egypt* (Berkeley: University of California Press, 1991), 1–33.

82. Scholars have failed to arrive at an adequate definition of the department store. Jefferys defined a department store as "a large retail store with four or more separate departments under one roof, each selling different classes of goods of which one is women's and children's wear." Jefferys, *Retail Trading in Britain*, 326. This definition fits stores dating back much earlier than 1850 and excludes some that expanded by acquiring small shops in the same street.

83. Although Lewis's served a very different clientele than Whiteley's, the Liverpool store faced the same sorts of attacks from local traders as Whiteley encountered. Briggs, *Friends of the People*, 39–43. For shopkeepers' reactions to the department store, see Crossick and Gerhard-Haupt, *The Petite Bourgeoisie in Europe*, 49–52 and 158–59; Christopher Hosgood, " 'A Brave and Daring Folk': Shopkeepers and Associational Life in Victorian and Edwardian England," *Journal of Social History* 26, no. 2 (Winter 1992): 285–308. On shopkeepers' politics, see Winstanley, *The Shopkeeper's World*; Geoffrey Crossick, "Shopkeepers and the State in Britain, 1870–1914," in *Shopkeepers and Master Artisans in Nineteenth-Century Europe*, ed. Geoffrey Crossick and Heinz-Gerhard Haupt (London: Methuen, 1984), 239–69; and Geoffrey Crossick, "The Emergence of the Lower Middle-Class

in Britain: A Discussion," in *The Lower Middle Class in Britain, 1870–1914*, ed. Geoffrey Crossick (New York: St. Martin's Press, 1977), 11–60; Thea Vigne and Allen Hawkins, "The Small Shopkeeper in Industrial and Market Towns," in Crossick, *Lower Middle Class in Britain*, 184–209. For an excellent assessment of the French situation, see Nord, *Paris Shopkeepers*. Nord argues that shopkeepers' resentment focused on the department stores because they symbolized broader shifts in the urban and commercial economy.

84. In 1867 Whiteley's included the following departments: Silks, Dresses, Linens, Drapery, Mantles, Millinery, Ladies' Outfitting, Haberdashery, Trimming, Gloves, Hosiery, Ribbons, Fancy Goods, Jewellery, Lace, Umbrellas, Furs, and Artificial Flowers. Gross profits were estimated to be around £4,500 for that year. Soon thereafter Whiteley added a dressmaking service, men's outfitting, and a furnishing drapery. Lambert, *The Universal Provider*, 67–72. Traders believed that competition was intensifying in these years, but if anything grocers faced greater competition than drapers did. In 1872 the *WDTJ* reported that there were 1,200 drapers and 2,500 retail grocers in London. This may explain why Whiteley inspired the greatest hostility when he moved into the food trades. "Malthusian Trading—The Surplus Shopkeeper," *WDTJ*, December 14, 1872, 447–48.

85. Henry Walker, "Whiteley's Liquor License," *Bayswater Chronicle*, March 23, 1872. Walker, the brother of Thomas Walker, who was the editor of the *Daily News*, edited the *BC* from 1872 until 1899. His obituary described him as "a pioneer of liberal thought in the realm of science . . . devoted to promotion of Scientific Knowledge, the Early Closing Association and the Saturday half-holiday movement. . . . He rejoiced in the progress of the education of women, and their entrance into higher scholarship and science. . . . [He was] a staunch Gladstonian in politics . . . [and had] sympathies with collectivist ideas." *BC*, February 17, 1900. However, many liberals disliked the magistrates' role in regulating the alcohol trade. For example, the radical liberal George Broderick called the magistrates' power to renew and grant new licenses a "despotic" example of "unlimited magisterial power." "Local Government in England," in *Local Government and Taxation*, ed. J. W. Probyn (London: Cassell, Petter, and Gilpin, 1875), 36.

86. This question was a prominent theme in nearly all texts that depicted shopping in this period. See *Drapier and Clothier* 1 (July 1859); Mayhew, *Shops and Companies of London*, 5, 86; "Shopping without Money," *Leisure Hour* (1865): 110–12; "Going a Shopping," *Leisure Hour* (1866): 198–200; "The Philosophy of Shopping," *Saturday Review*, October 16, 1875, 488–89; "Ladies Shopping," *WDTJ*, July 12, 1873, 374.

87. *BC*, March 23, 1872. This strategy for limiting trade was an old one. In 1816 West End shopkeepers complained to Parliament that among "the numerous evils" associated with bazaars was the way they increased "places of public promenade [and] intrigue." Like those who opposed the department stores, however, these traders helped construct the perception that all women in public were prostitutes. Gary R. Dyer, " 'The Vanity Fair' of Nineteenth-Century England: Commerce, Women, and the East in the Ladies Bazaar," *Nineteenth-Century Literature* 46, no. 2 (September 1991): 205.

88. Robert Thorne, "Places of Refreshment in the Nineteenth-Century City", in *Buildings and Society: Essays on the Social Development of the Built Environment*, ed. Anthony D. King (London: Routledge and Kegan Paul, 1980), 235. Descriptions of West End nightlife nearly always characterize the women who drink, dance, and dine in public as prostitutes. See, for example, J. Ewing Ritchie, *The Night Side of London* (London: William Tweedle, 1857); Stephen Fiske, *English Photographs* (London: Tinsley Brothers, 1869); Donald Shaw, *London in the Sixties* (London: Everett and Co., 1908); Ivan Bloch, *Sexual Life in England Past and Present*, trans. William Forstern (London: Francis Aldor, 1938); and Henry Mayhew, *London's Underworld*, ed. Peter Quennell (1862; reprint, London: Bracken Books, 1983), 121–27.

89. Davis, *Actresses as Working Women*, 139–45; Walkowitz, *City of Dreadful Delight*, 50–52. In his detailed description of West End prostitution Henry Mayhew portrayed its streets and shops as both commercial and sexual marketplaces. He also identified milliners, dressmakers, servants, those who served at bazaars, and "frequenters of fairs" as especially prone to entering the illicit trade. Mayhew, *London's Underworld*, 38.

90. *Paddington Times*, March 30, 1872.

91. Brian Harrison, *Drink and the Victorians: The Temperance Question in England, 1815–1872* (Pittsburgh: University of Pittsburgh Press, 1971), 303.

92. Walter Benjamin, "Central Park," trans. Lloyd Spencer, *New German Critique* 34 (Winter 1985): 40. Also see Susan Buck-Morss's analysis of Benjamin's treatment of the prostitute as commodity, "The Flâneur, the Sandwichman, and the Whore: The Politics of

Loitering," *New German Critique* 39 (Fall 1986): 99–140; and her longer study, *The Dialectics of Seeing: Walter Benjamin and the Arcades Project* (Cambridge: MIT Press, 1989).

93. Amanda Anderson, *Tainted Souls and Painted Faces: The Rhetoric of Fallenness in Victorian Culture* (Ithaca: Cornell University Press, 1993), 2. Also see, Walkowitz, *Prostitution and Victorian Society* and *City of Dreadful Delight*; Nead, *Myths of Sexuality*, 110–35; Wilson, *The Sphinx in the City*, 55–57; Kathy Peiss, "Making Up, Making Over: Cosmetics, Consumer Culture, and Women's Identity," in de Grazia and Furlough, *The Sex of Things*, 315; Christine Buci-Glucksmann, "Catastrophic Utopia: The Feminine as Allegory of the Modern," *Representations* 14 (Spring 1986): 220–29; Laurie Teal, "The Hollow Women: Modernism, the Prostitute, and Commodity Aesthetics," *Differences: A Journal of Feminist Cultural Studies* 7, no. 3 (Fall 1995): 80–108; Mariana Valverde, "The Love of Finery: Fashion and the Fallen Woman in Nineteenth-Century Social Discourse," *Victorian Studies* 32, no. 2 (Winter 1989): 169–88; Daniel A. Cohen, "The Murder of Maria Bickford: Fashion, Passion, and the Birth of a Consumer Culture," *American Studies* 31, no. 2 (Fall 1990): 5–30. Also see the editorial on crime and the love of "dress" among male and female shop assistants, *BC*'s February 10, 1872; and Arthur Sherwell, *Life in West London: A Study and a Contrast* (London: Methuen, 1897), 145–48.

94. "The Girl of the Period," *Saturday Review*, March 14, 1868, 339–40. On the reaction to Linton's *Saturday Review* essays, see Nancy Fix Anderson, *Woman against Women in Victorian England: A Life of Eliza Lynn Linton* (Bloomington: Indiana University Press, 1987), 117–36. Also see Herbert Van Thal, *Eliza Lynn Linton, the Girl of the Period: A Biography* (London: George Allen and Unwin, 1979).

95. *Saturday Review*, October 16, 1875, 488.

96. "London Girls of the Period: The West End Girl," *Girl of the Period Miscellany* 1, no. 3 (May 1869): 92.

97. *BC*, March 23, 1872. Spencer, Turner and Boldero in Lisson Grove was even larger, however, with its approximately one thousand employees. *WDTJ*, December 21, 1872, 643.

98. *BC*, March 23, 1872. Whiteley made a similar argument about customers' "convenience" in "How to Succeed as a Shopkeeper: A Practical Article by William Whiteley," *London Magazine*, newspaper clipping, Whiteley's Archive, Westminster City Archives.

99. *BC*, March 23, 1872.

100. Biagini argued that one of the factors that led to the defeat of the Liberal government in 1874 was an "unholy alliance between publicans and priests." Eugenio Biagini, *Liberty, Retrenchment, and Reform: Popular Liberalism in the Age of Gladstone, 1860–1880* (Cambridge: Cambridge University Press, 1992), 119. Initially the drink trade was divided on the issue of licensing reform, but over time they developed a strong alliance with the Conservative Party. Harrison, *Drink and the Victorians*, 280–82.

101. *Paddington Times*, March 9, 1872. Of course, while the publicans criticized certain forms of mass culture, their trade was also commercializing during these years. Mark Girouard, *Victorian Pubs* (New Haven: Yale University Press, 1984); Brian Harrison, "Pubs," in *The Victorian City: Images and Reality* (London: Routledge and Kegan Paul, 1973), 1:161–90; Peter Bailey, ed., *Music Hall: The Business of Pleasure* (Milton Keynes and Philadelphia: Open University Press, 1986); Dagmar Kift, *The Victorian Music Hall: Culture, Class, and Conflict*, trans. Roy Kift (Cambridge: Cambridge University Press, 1996).

102. Middlesex County Sessions Records, County Licensing Committee, (hereafter MCSR, CLC) Hanover Square Division (St. Georges), Greater London Record Office (hereafter GLRO), MA/C/L 1878/70. For a history of the Gallery, see Susan P. Casteras and Colleen Denny, eds. *The Grosvenor Gallery: A Palace of Art in Victorian England* (New Haven: Yale University Press, 1996). When Robinson and Cleaver's, a large Regent Street draper's, applied to the crown commissioners to open a restaurant, their letter similarly explained that this venue would be highly "respectable" and would never become a "nuisance." Horner to Crown Lessees of 156 and 158 Regent Street, April 3, 1907, Public Record Office (hereafter PRO), CRES 35/2376.

103. MCSR, CLC, Hanover Square Division (St. Georges), GLRO, MA/C/L/1878/71.

104. MCSR, CLC, Paddington Division, GLRO, MA/C/L/1880/35.

105. MCSR, CLC, Paddington Division, GLRO, MA/L/1880/50.

106. MCSR, CLC, St. James Division, GLRO, MA/C/L/1878/74.

107. MCSR, CLC, Strand Division, GLRO, MA/C/L/1878/94. On the Adelaide Gallery, see Altick, *The Shows of London*, 377–89.

108. MCSR, CLC, Strand Division, GLRO, MA/C/L/1878/110.

109. On the history of these images of consumption, see, for example, Joyce Appleby,

"Consumption in Early Modern Social Thought," in Brewer and Porter, *Consumption and the World of Goods*, 162–73; and John Sekora, *Luxury: The Concept in Western Thought, Eden to Smollet* (Baltimore: Johns Hopkins University Press, 1977).

110. For an analysis of how Smith and early political economists imagined consumption as a positive social force, see McKendrick, "The Consumer Revolution of Eighteenth-Century," in McKendrick, Brewer, and Plumb, *The Birth of a Consumer Society*, 15–19. Appleby, "Consumption in Early Modern Social Thought," 167–71. Also see Albert O. Hirschman's analysis of Mandeville and Smith in *The Passions and the Interests: Political Arguments for Capitalism before Its Triumph* (Princeton: Princeton University Press, 1977); and Istvan Hont and Michael Ignatieff, *Wealth and Virtue: The Shaping of Political Economy in the Scottish Enlightenment* (Cambridge: Cambridge University Press, 1983).

111. *WDTJ*, April 15, 1872, 4. For a slightly different formulation of these oppositional portraits of the consumer, see Rachel Bowlby, *Shopping with Freud* (London: Routledge, 1993), 3.

112. *WDTJ*, April 15, 1872, 17. Decades later retailers were still uncertain about the value of adding restaurants and other amenities. One wrote, for example, "Many of the larger houses have during recent years added restaurants to their attractions. . . . These new notions are good if they attract the right people, but unless care be exercised the restaurant can easily be the means of losing more than is garnered." Samson Clark, *Short Talks with Drapers* (London: Trade Press Association, 1916), 141.

113. *WDTJ*, April 15, 1872, 17.

114. "Lunch with the Linendrapers," *Graphic*, August 3, 1872, 98. For a similar appraisal, see *Grocery News and Oil Journal*, March 22, 1872, 121.

115. *Graphic*, August 3, 1872, 98.

116. Throughout Britain, stationers, ironmongers, and others resented being undersold by the ever-expanding "modern draper." "The Modern Draper—Ironmongery," *Drapers' Record*, December 9, 1893, 1369. For another view, see "How a Draper Developed into a Furnisher, by One Who Has Tried It," *Drapers' Record*, November 2, 1895, 260.

117. For specific details of the many conflicts between Whiteley and these bodies see Lambert, *Universal Provider*, especially 80–115; and the Paddington Vestry Minutes, especially vol. E, F, and G, which cover 1874–82. On shopkeepers and local government, see E. P. Hennock, "The Social Composition of Borough Councils in Two Large Cities," in *The Study of Urban History*, ed. H. J. Dyos (New York: St. Martin's Press, 1968), 318–35. For a history of London's government during these years, see David Owen, *The Government of Victorian London, 1855–1889: The Metropolitan Board of Works, the Vestries, and the City Corporation*, ed. Roy MacLeod (Cambridge: Harvard University Press, Belknap Press, 1982); John Davis, *Reforming London: The London Government Problem, 1855–1900* (Oxford: Clarendon Press, 1988); Ken Young and Patricia L. Garside, *Metropolitan London: Politics and Urban Change, 1837–1981* (London: Edward Arnold, 1982). For an earlier period, see F. H. W. Sheppard, *Local Government in St. Marylebone, 1688–1835* (London: University of London, Athlone Press, 1958).

118. *BC*, April 10, 1875.

119. Lambert, *The Universal Provider*, 79–83.

120. *BC*, December 9, 1876.

121. *BC*, April 26, 1879.

122. *BC*, December 15, 1877.

123. "Whiteley's Grand Provision Emporium," *Paddington Times*, November 4, 1876.

124. Emile Zola, *The Ladies' Paradise* (1883; reprint, Berkeley: University of California Press, 1992).

125. The *Paddington Times* described Whiteley's as "a thing of beauty and a realm of thought" in an article, "Whiteley's Christmas Bazaar," published on December 2, 1876.

126. "Why is Whiteley's So Often Burned Down?" *Pall Mall Gazette*, August 10, 1887, 3.

127. *BC*, March 10, 1877. A similar point was made in the first issue of what would become the most popular drapers' journal, the *Drapers' Record*. In "Sites for Shops," the author recommended opening up near one of the "colossal establishments" because there "it is a tendency of the times for ladies to go to a certain central spot to make their purchases." When they did not find what they needed in the large shops, shoppers would venture into a neighboring small shop. *Drapers' Record*, August 6, 1887, 6.

128. *BC*, March 26, 1881.

129. Newman, *Many Parts*, 103.

130. A. M. W. Stirling, ed., *Victorian Sidelights: From the Papers of the Late Mrs. Adams-Acton* (London: Ernest Benn, 1954), 247.

131. See, for example, *BC*, June 22, 1878; February 22, 1879; April 26, 1879; May 3, 1879; June 14, 1879; June 21, 1879; July 5, 1879; and July 19, 1879. Also see "In Westbourne Grove," by Claribel, which started in April of 1887.

132. *BC*, May 3, 1879.

133. *BC*, November 1, 1879.

134. *BC*, October 30, 1880.

135. *BC*, October 28, 1882.

136. *BC*, January 7, 1882. See a similar description of Saturday shopping, in *BC*, February 16, 1884. Whiteley tried to commission William Powell Frith to paint a picture of Westbourne Grove that would capture this public of nobility, gentry, street beggars, and toy sellers, "all the variety and characters that Westbourne Grove always presents." Although he later regretted it, Frith refused this commission. W. P. Frith, *My Autobiography and Reminiscences*, 7th ed. (London: Richard Bentley, 1889), 288.

137. In one brief moment of wishful thinking, the *Drapers' Record* published a piece in 1888 on the "decline of Whiteley's system." The author did not believe that the small shop would be revived, but felt that "everything is done on such a colossal scale that it is impossible . . . to go in for the sale of every article of modern requirements." *Drapers' Record*, February 11, 1888, 32. A few months later, the author of "The Fate of the Small Tradesman" noted that the problem with the small shops was not that they were small per se, but that many traders were "old-fashioned." This expert believed that small and large could survive together if small shops were run on the same efficient modern lines as large ones. *Drapers' Record*, April 28, 1888, 305.

138. Whiteley abandoned his greengrocery business later in 1877. The same year his annual net profit fell to £60,000 from the £66,000 reached in 1876, and continued to fall to £50,000 in 1880. Lambert, *The Universal Provider*, 94. Some of these problems were related to a series of suspicious fires in the 1880s. It was after one such conflagration in 1887 that the *Pall Mall Gazette* (hereafter *PMG*) denounced the Universal Provider. *PMG*, August 8 and 10, 1887, and the *Drapers' Record*, August 13, 1887, 21. The author of "Round Town," a column in the *Drapers' Record*, wondered whether the recent success of High Street, Kensington, was hurting Westbourne Grove's "high position in the estimation of the shopping public." *Drapers' Record*, August 15, 1894, 741.

139. On middle-class co-operatives, see J. Hood and B. S. Yamey, "Middle-Class Co-operative Retailing Societies in London, 1864–1900," in *Economics of Retailing*, ed. K. A. Tucker and B. S. Yamey (London: Penguin, 1973), 131–45; Jefferys, *Retail Trading in Britain*, 16–17; E. D. Wainwright, *Army and Navy Stores Limited Centenary Year* (London: The Stores, 1971); *Yesterday's Shopping: The Army and Navy Stores Catalogue, 1907*, facsimile (Devon: David and Charles Reprints, 1969). For a recent study of all types of cooperatives, see Martin Purvis, "Co-operative Retailing in Britain," in Benson and Shaw, *The Evolution of Retail Systems*, 107–34; and Peter Gurney, *Co-Operative Culture and the Politics of Consumption in England, 1870–1930* (Manchester: Manchester University Press, 1996). For the competition between the co-operatives and the stores, see Mrs. Wigley, "Domestic Puzzles: Where shall I Buy—Shops or Stores?" *Leisure Hour*, 28 (1879): 331–33. On small shopkeepers' anger toward the co-operatives, see *The Times*, February 1–6, 1872; *Saturday Review*, August 1, 1874; November 25, 1876; January 25, 1879; April 10, 1880. See also, Maurice C. Moore, *Fighting the Enemies of the Shopkeeper* (London: Drapers' Record, 1915). Crossick and Haupt explore this anxiety in *The Petite Bourgeoisie in Europe*, 159–60.

140. Extract from the *Daily Graphic* (New York), May 12, 1876, quoted in *William Whiteley's Diary: Almanac and Handbook of Useful Information for 1877* (William Whiteley's, 1877). The diary was published annually from 1877 to 1915. Also see the publicity in the *Drapers' Record*, November 17, 1888, 575; and *WDTJ*, Dec 16, 1882, 874.

141. E. J. Hobsbawm, *Industry and Empire: From 1750 to the Present Day* (Harmondsworth: Penguin, 1987); Fraser, *Coming of the Mass Market*; Richards, *Commodity Culture of Victorian England*; E. S. Turner, *The Shocking History of Advertising!* (New York: E. P. Dutton, 1953); Blanche B. Elliott, *A History of English Advertising* (London: B. T. Batsford, 1962); T. R. Nevett, *Advertising in Britain: A History* (London: Heinemann, on behalf of the History of Advertising Trust, 1982); Diana Hindley and Geoffrey Hindley, *Advertising in Victorian England, 1837–1901* (London: Wayland Publishers, 1972). For an example of the "science" of advertising, see Thomas Smith, *Successful Advertising: Its Secrets Explained*, 7th annual ed. (London: Mutual Advertising Agency, 1885).

142. It was common practice for servants to take their employers' children shopping with them. Ellen Jane Panton remembered loathing her daily walks in Westbourne Grove with her governess. *Leaves from a Life* (London: Eveleigh Nash, 1908), 45.

143. *BC*, April 2, 1881. Also see March 7, 1891.

144. *BC*, July 11, 1885.

145. *BC*, October 19, 1879.

146. David Scobey, "Anatomy of the Promenade: The Politics of Bourgeois Sociability in Nineteenth-Century New York," *Social History* 17, no. 2 (May 1992): 203–27. Of course, there are many uses of the very same street. For ex-

ample, the charivari that erupted in Westbourne Grove demonstrated the way in which the street was seen as a site of lower-middle-class protest and corporate identities. For some compelling studies of street politics in the nineteenth century, see Susan G. Davis, *Parades and Power: Street Theatre in Nineteenth-Century Philadelphia* (Philadelphia: Temple University Press, 1986); Ryan, *Women in Public*, chap. 1; and P. G. Goheen, "The Ritual of the Streets in Mid-Nineteenth-Century Toronto," *Environment and Planning D: Society and Space* 11, no. 2 (April 1993): 127–45. Atkins, like Scobey, sees certain social spaces as "authored, produced, controlled, manipulated and consumed by the élite for their own reproduction as a class." Atkins, "How the West End was Won," 274–75. However, gender, trade, and political allegiances were among those factors which worked against a shared elite vision or dominance of the street.

147. Peiss, *Cheap Amusements*, 57. See also Stansell, *City of Women*; and François Barret-Ducrocq, *Love in the Time of Victoria: Sexuality, Class, and Gender in Nineteenth-Century London*, trans. John Howe (London: Verso, 1991), 9.

148. *BC*, May 18, 1878.

149. *BC*, January 12, 1878; August 31, 1878; April 24, 1880; April 6, 1889; December 24, 1887; September 24, 1892.

150. *BC*, October 18, 1879.

151. Samuel L. Clemens, *A Tramp Abroad*, ed. Charles Neider (New York: Harper and Row, 1977), 290.

152. See Walkowitz, *City of Dreadful Delight*, 50–52, and "Going Public"; Winter, *London's Teeming Streets*, 176–86.

153. Osbert Lancaster, *All Done from Memory* (London: John Murray, 1953), 38.

154. Panton, *Leaves from a Life*, 41. On Panton's career as a "taste professional" and part of the movement that brought aesthetic sensibilities to middle-class home decor see Nicholas Cooper, *The Opulent Eye: Late Victorian and Edwardian Taste in Interior Design* (London: Architectural Press, 1976), 9. Despite her "rage" at the big stores, in her later works on home decoration she often recommended these shops as places where the latest fashions in fabric and furnishings could be purchased at moderate prices suitable to middle-class incomes. Ellen Jane Panton, *Homes of Taste: Economical Hints* (London: Sampson Low, Marston, Searle, 1890) and *Leaves from a Housekeeper's Book* (London: Eveleigh Nash, 1914).

155. *BC*, June 12, 1880. A letter in response to this issue suggested that true "ladies" do not speak of themselves as such and therefore the author may have been a shop assistant or servant. *BC*, June 26, 1880.

156. *BC*, June 29, 1880. Also see *BC*, June 26, 1880.

Chapter Two
The Trials of Consumption

1. This quote appears both in "A Husband and His Wife's Dresses," *The Times*, August 6, 1892, 6; and in *WDTJ*, August 13, 1892, 747.

2. In 1881, for example, there were over a million proceedings heard in the county courts. The majority of these involved drapers seeking unrecovered debts. *WDTJ*, June 17, 1882, 414. For a quantitative analysis of debt and the county court system, see Paul Johnson, "Small Debts and Economic Distress in England and Wales, 1857–1913," *Economic History Review* 46, no. 1 (February 1993): 65–87. For an earlier period, see Margot Finn, "Debt and Credit in Bath's Court of Requests, 1829–1839," *Urban History* 21, pt. 2 (October 1994): 211–36. Though most of London's county court records no longer exist, many of the decisions and testimonies were printed in trade journals and newspapers. While incomplete and sometimes inaccurate, these reports usefully show us how retailers understood the law and its impact.

3. These categories were never static, but in the second half of the nineteenth century, the "family" was undergoing a major cultural, social, and economic reevaluation, as a result of changes in divorce and married women's property reform. See Mary Poovey's discussion of this in *Uneven Developments*, 51–88. Although "agency" has taken on a very general meaning in feminist scholarship, in nineteenth-century legal discourse it specifically implied a woman's ability to act as a financial agent for her husband, father, brother, or employer.

4. Davidoff and Hall, *Family Fortunes*.

5. For an analysis of the social meaning of credit, see Craig Muldrew, "Interpreting the Market: The Ethics of Credit and Community Relations in Early Modern England," *Social History* 18, no. 2 (May 1993): 163–83. Scott Sandage has argued, however, that the moral assessment involved in face-to-face lending actually remained as credit became "rationalized." Scott Sandage, " 'Small Man, Small Means, Doing Small Business': Credit Re-

porting and the Commodification of Character, 1840–1880" (paper presented at the Warren Susman Memorial Graduate History Conference, Rutgers University, New Brunswick, N.J., April 1993). I have borrowed the term "cultural transaction" from Sandage's excellent study.

6. Rosalind Williams made this point when she discussed the introduction of the installment plan in France during the 1870s. Williams, *Dream Worlds*, 92–94. However, in some industries standardized credit was introduced not as a marketing tool but as a way to solve problems in financing production. For the use of credit in the U.S. auto industry, see Martha L. Olney, *Buy Now, Pay Later: Advertising, Credit, and Consumer Durables in the 1920s* (Chapel Hill: The University of North Carolina Press, 1991).

7. Melanie Tebbutt, *Making Ends Meet: Pawnbroking and Working Class Credit* (New York: St. Martin's Press; Leicester: Leicester University Press, 1983); Paul Johnson, "Credit and Thrift and the British Working Class, 1870–1914," in *The Working Class in Modern British History: Essays in Honour of Henry Pelling*, ed. Jay Winter (Cambridge: Cambridge University Press, 1983), 147–70; Paul Johnson, *Saving and Spending: The Working Class Economy in Britain, 1870–1939* (Oxford: Oxford University Press, 1985), 144–92; Stedman-Jones, *Outcast London*, 87–88; Ross, *Love and Toil*, 81–84. Also see the analysis of working-class consumption and credit in Judith G. Coffin, *The Politics of Women's Work: The Paris Garment Trades, 1750–1915* (Princeton: Princeton University Press, 1996), 81–88.

8. There have, however, been excellent studies of credit, debt, and the family economy among England's elite classes prior to the nineteenth century. John Habakkuk, *Marriage, Debt, and the Estates System: English Landownership, 1650–1950* (Oxford: Clarendon Press, 1994), especially chap. 4. Habakkuk does not spend much time on the late-nineteenth and twentieth centuries. Also see Margaret R. Hunt, *The Middling Sort: Commerce, Gender, and the Family in England, 1680–1780* (Berkeley: University of California Press, 1996), 22–46 and 125–29; and William Chester Jordan, *Women and Credit in Pre-industrial and Developing Societies* (Philadelphia: University of Pennsylvania Press, 1993).

9. The use of credit in retailing stemmed from the shortage of coin in the eighteenth century. See Davis, *Fairs, Shops, and Supermarkets*, 185; John Brewer, "Commercialization and Politics," in McKendrick, Brewer, and Plumb, *Birth of a Consumer Society*, 208–9. For a broader account of the role of credit and the eighteenth-century economy, see B. L. Anderson, "Money and the Structure of Credit in the Eighteenth Century," *Business History* 12, no. 2 (July 1970): 85–101. On credit and business failure, see Julian Hoppit, *Risk and Failure in English Business, 1700–1800* (Cambridge: Cambridge University Press, 1987), 140–60. For the role of credit and the rural economy, see B. A. Holderness, "Credit in English Rural Society before the Nineteenth Century, with Special Reference to the Period 1650–1720," *Agricultural History Review* 24, pt. 2 (1976): 97–109.

10. See the discussion of the shifting nature of Victorian business and credit fraud in George Robb, *White-Collar Crime in Modern England: Financial Fraud and Business Morality, 1845–1929* (Cambridge: Cambridge University Press, 1992), 66–79.

11. Gareth Shaw has argued that the increased use of cash in the drapery trades "improved" these shops' "performance" and aided their expansion into department stores. Shaw, "The Evolution and Impact of Large-Scale Retailing in Britain," in Benson and Shaw, *The Evolution of Retail Systems*, 137. See also Mathias, *Retailing Revolution*, 47. Department stores eventually reestablished limited forms of credit, but accounts were given only to select customers. Adburgham, *Shops and Shopping*, 234; and Benson, *Counter Cultures*, 90.

12. P. S. Atiyah, *The Rise and Fall of the Freedom of Contract* (Oxford: Clarendon Press, 1979), 182–83.

13. Even wives who had separate property had only very limited power to make a contract with reference to it. C. A. Morrison, "Contract," in *A Century of Family Law, 1857–1957*, ed. R. H. Graveson and F. R. Crane (London: Sweet and Maxwell, 1957), 121–22. More recent research, however, indicates that early modern wives may have had more control over their separate property than had been thought. See, for example, Hunt, *The Middling Sort*, 158–61. Susan Staves has suggested that it may have been more difficult for women to alienate their separate property by the early-nineteenth century than it had been earlier. Susan Staves, *Married Women's Separate Property in England, 1660–1833* (Cambridge: Harvard University Press, 1990), 152–53. For an overview, see Amy Louise Erickson, *Women and Property in Early Modern England* (London: Routledge, 1993).

14. Finn has pointed to the same discrepancy between married women's official legal nonexistence and their actions as economic agents in the marketplace and the courtroom.

Margot Finn, "Women, Consumption, and Coverture in England, ca. 1760–1860," *Historical Journal* 39, no. 3 (September 1996): 709.

15. Much of this ridicule came from humor magazines such as *Punch*. See, for example, the series "The Physiology of the London Idler," which appeared in the third volume of *Punch* in 1842. For a biting portrait of the male shopper, see "The Husband Out Shopping with His Wife," in Mayhew, *The Shops and Companies of London* 1:86. For further discussion of images of the male shopper, see chap. 4 below. For an earlier period, see David Kuchta, "The Making of the Self-Made Man: Class, Clothing, and English Masculinity," in de Grazia and Furlough, *The Sex of Things*, 54–78. For a discussion of masculine consumer practices in nineteenth-century France, see Leora Auslander, "The Gendering of Consumer Practices in Nineteenth-Century France," in de Grazia and Furlough, *The Sex of Things*, 85–99.

16. On these traveling drapers, see Gerry R. Rubin, "From Packmen, Tallymen, and 'Perambulating Scotchmen' to Credit Drapers' Associations, ca. 1840–1914," *Business History* 28, no. 2 (April 1986): 206–25.

17. "Ladies Shopping," *WDTJ*, July 12, 1873, 374. Mayhew, *Shops and Companies of London* 1:86; Sala, *Twice around the Clock*, 161–63.

18. T. J. Jackson Lears argues that in American culture the itinerant peddler personified the emerging market and was frequently portrayed as seducing wives with his salesmanship. T. J. Jackson Lears, "Beyond Veblen: Rethinking Consumer Culture in America," in *Consuming Visions: Accumulation and Display of Goods in America, 1880–1920*, ed. Simon J. Bronner (New York: W. W. Norton, 1989), 78–80.

19. *Drapier and Clothier* 1 (May 1859), 11. Despite all the legal changes that will be described in this chapter, this same scenario still haunted judges in Edwardian England. A magistrate for the city of Leeds wrote in 1906:

> Under an expanding system of credit, articles of adornment are palmed off upon the wife by unscrupulous traders, and purchased by her without the husband's knowledge—or, perchance, wages handed over for rent and necessaries are wasted by her in gaming or drinking, or misapplied to the cash purchase of trinkets, leaving the butcher and baker to sue for their bills. Soon afterwards comes the County Court summons, served on the wife who destroys it or conceals it from her husband. The plaintiff gets judgment after giving little or no proof of the wife's agency, or, perhaps, she appears and admits the debt. Next comes the judgment order under which a few installments may possibly be paid—then, when default occurs, there arrives the judgment summons, followed by commitment and arrest.

Charles M. Atkinson, "Imprisonment for Debt," *Law Magazine and Review* 31 (1906), 140–41, quoted in V. Markham Lester, *Victorian Insolvency: Bankruptcy, Imprisonment for Debt, and Company Winding-Up in Nineteenth-Century England* (Oxford: Clarendon Press, 1995), 118–19.

20. "Puffing Impostors—A Few Words to All Ladies Making Purchases," *Drapier and Clothier* 1, no. 3 (July 1859): 86–87.

21. For examples of household manuals that represented debt in this way, see J. H. Walsh, *A Manual of Domestic Economy: Suited to Families Spending from £100 to £1,000 a Year*, 2d ed. (London: Routledge, 1857); Mrs. Warren, *How I Managed My House on Two Hundred Pounds a Year*, 4th American ed. (Boston: Loring, 1866); Florence Stacpoole, *Handbook of Housekeeping for Small Incomes* (London: Walter Scott, 1897); *Cassell's Household Guide: Being a Complete Encyclopedia of Domestic and Social Economy*, 3 vols. (London: Cassell, Petter, and Galpin, 1869–71); Mrs. C. E. Humphrey, *The Book of the Home: A Comprehensive Guide on All Matters Pertaining to the Household* (London: Gresham, 1910). The popular press also hinted that a woman's debts would bring about her moral ruin. See, for example, Coralie Stanton and Heath Hoskin, "Everyone Must Pay," *Ladies Home Paper: A Weekly Journal for Gentlewomen*, February 13, 1909, 8; Violet Lady Greville, "A Lady Dressmaker," *Queen*, October 4, 1913, 614. On the centrality of debt in the narrative structure of Dickens's fiction, C. R. B. Dunlop, "Debtors and Creditors in Dickens' Fiction," *Dickens Studies Annual: Essays on Victorian Fiction* 19 (1990): 25–47.

22. For an analysis of the invention of the female kleptomaniac and her social and cultural meanings, see Abelson, *When Ladies Go a-Thieving*; Patricia O'Brien, "The Kleptomania Diagnosis: Bourgeois Women and Theft in Late-Nineteenth-Century France," *Journal of Social History* 17 (Fall 1983): 65–77.

23. See, for example, the fate of one husband described by Henry Mayhew, *London Labour and the London Poor* (1851; reprint, London: Frank Cass and Co., 1967), 1:333.

24. Samuel Smiles, *Thrift* (London: J. Murray, 1875), 261.

25. This fear was related to increasing material expectations, perhaps more than to inflationary pressures. See, for example, W. R. Greg, "Life at High Pressure," *Contemporary Review* 25 (March 1875): 623–38, esp. 632–34; "The Cost of Living," *Cornhill Magazine* 31 (January–June 1875): 412–21. For an examination of the large body of "cost of living" literature, see J. A. Banks, *Prosperity and Parenthood: A Study of Family Planning among the Victorian Middle Classes* (London: Routledge and Kegan Paul, 1954), 58.

26. Smiles, *Thrift*, 252–53.

27. Jean-Christophe Agnew's, *Worlds Apart: The Market and the Theater in Anglo-American Thought, 1550–1750* (Cambridge: Cambridge University Press, 1986) is among the most compelling analyses of identity and market changes. For comparative anxieties in nineteenth-century America, see Karen Halttunen, *Confidence Men and Painted Women: A Study of Middle-Class Culture in America, 1830–1870* (New Haven: Yale University Press, 1982). Also see Warren Susman's classic article, "Personality and the Making of Twentieth-Century Culture," in *Culture as History: The Transformation of American Society in the Twentieth Century* (New York: Pantheon Books, 1984).

28. Smiles, *Thrift*, 259–61.

29. Although imprisonment was abolished with the 1869 Debtors Act, small debtors could be and were jailed until 1970. Nearly 10,000 were imprisoned each year just before the First World War, and the number was still averaging at 7,000 persons annually, or 14 percent of the prison population, between 1961 and 1964. See O. R. McGregor, *Social History and Law Reform* (London: Stevens and Sons, 1981), 36–38. See also G. R. Rubin, "Law, Poverty, and Imprisonment for Debt," in *Law, Economy, and Society, 1750–1914: Essays in the History of English Law*, ed. G. R. Rubin and David Sugarman (Abingdon: Professional Books, 1984), 241–99; and Lester, *Victorian Insolvency*, 88–122. Legal manuals advised solicitors and creditors well into the twentieth century on how and when to imprison reluctant debtors. See, for example, Herbert Broom, *The Practice of County Courts* (London: W. Maxwell, 1852); John Cook, *A Guide to the Recovery of Debts in the County Courts* (London: T. Pettitt, 1878); John Mayhew, *Tradesman's Guide to the Practice of the County Courts*, 3d ed. (London: Simpkin, Marshall, 1880); *County Court Practice Made Easy, or Debt Collection Simplified*, 5th ed., rev. (London: Effingham Wilson, 1922), 65–67, 115.

30. Smiles, *Thrift*, 274.

31. See n. 7 and Banks, *Prosperity and Parenthood*, 54.

32. Alexander, *Retailing in England*, 176.

33. Benson, for example, related the growth of consumer society in Britain after 1880 by attempting to document changes in income levels. Benson, *Rise of Consumer Society*, 11–29.

34. Quoted in Alexander, *Retailing in England*, 176. Dorothy Constance Peel presented a similar image of the difficulties of collecting payment from the aristocracy in *Life's Enchanted Cup: An Autobiography, 1872–1933* (London: John Lane and the Bodley Head, 1933), 129–34.

35. Lady Jeune, "The Ethics of Shopping," *Fortnightly Review* 57 (January 1895): 123.

36. Lady Lucy Christiana Sutherland Duff-Gordon, *Discretions and Indiscretions* (London: Jarrolds, 1932), 54. "Machinka," another upper-class dressmaker, had similar problems. Beryl Lee Booker, *Yesterday's Child, 1890–1909* (London: John Long, 1937), 70. These difficulties also plagued shopkeepers who served lower-class customers. John Birch Thomas, *Shop Boy: An Autobiography* (London: Routledge and Kegan Paul, 1983), 7–8.

37. Andrews and Co., 71 Tottenham Court Road, to H. Flower Esq., November 21, 1883, trade card/bill head collection in the Print Room, Guildhall Library. Though it was common practice for shops to charge interest on outstanding accounts, customers seem to have been quite put off by this practice. For example, Marion Sanbourne, the wife of Linley Sanbourne, recalled that although she "Paid bill at Millers only owing since 23rd of last month & they charged 1/- extra on small account of 3/6d never felt more angry—meanness of supposed west-end shops—pity they do not follow example set by Barkers." Shirley Nicholson, *A Victorian Household: Based on the Diaries of Marion Sanbourne* (London: Barrie and Jenkins, 1988), 69.

38. A. Barrett and Sons to J. Flower, Esq., April 29, 1908, trade card/bill head collection, Guildhall Library, London.

39. Ablett, *Reminiscences of an Old Draper*, 22. On book debt and business failure see Alexander, *Retailing in England*, 175–85.

40. Brian Abel-Smith and Robert Stevens, *Lawyers and the Courts: A Sociological Study of the English Legal System, 1750–1965* (London: Heinemann, 1967), 32–36. On traders' reluctance to turn to legal remedies, see Tebbutt, *Making Ends Meet*, 121. On the power of the summons to settle the debt, see *The County Courts* (London, 1852).

41. *Our County Courts: The Practice Contrasted with that of the Superior Courts; with suggestions for the Improvement of Both*, 1857,

quoted in W. L. Burn, *The Age of Equipoise: A Study of the Mid-Victorian Generation* (London: George Allen and Unwin, 1964), 138.

42. Though the courts were partly the work of legal reformers such as Lord Brougham, this critic wrote that "Whig Law legislators" treated these courts with "suppressed contempt." *County Courts Chronicle*, September 1, 1865, 191.

43. The social implications of both the civil law and the operation of the small courts are just beginning to receive scholarly attention. For a discussion of this literature, see Sugarman and Rubin's introduction to *Law, Economy, and Society*, esp. 43–47. For a more detailed social history of the county courts and debt enforcement, see Rubin's "The County Courts and the Tally Trade, 1846–1914" and "Law, Poverty, and Imprisonment for Debt, 1869–1914" in Rubin and Sugarmen, *Law, Economy, and Society*; and Paul Johnson, "Class Law in Victorian England," *Past and Present* 141 (November 1993): 147–69.

44. On the anti-trade attitude of the county court judges see Rubin, "The County Courts and the Tally Trade," 321–48. Paul H. Haagen found that similar attitudes among eighteenth-century legislators explained their reluctance to reform debt law. "Eighteenth-Century English Society and the Debt Law," in *Social Control and the State: Historical and Comparative Essays*, ed. Stanley Cohen and Andrew Scull (Oxford: Basil Blackwell, 1983), 222–47. His argument that debt law was central to the systems of deference in this period is an intriguing one that might be explored in relationship to the nineteenth-century reforms.

45. In 1851 Rees claimed that he had forbidden his wife to pledge his credit beyond her fifty pound annual allowance. She evidently did so when she bought clothing for herself and her daughters from Jolly and Sons. The jury for the lower court found that the goods were necessaries and that Mrs. Rees's allowance should have covered the amount, but that Mr. Rees had not paid it on a regular basis. Thus, he was required to pay Jolly and Sons this amount even though he had privately forbidden his wife to make these purchaces. When the case moved to the Court of Common Pleas, however, this decision was overturned. Mr. Rees's private injunction against his wife was enough to absolve him from paying for her purchases. For contemporary discussion of the case and a reprint of the court's decision, see *County Courts Chronicle*, June 1, 1864, 98–99. Also see Atiyah, *The Rise and Fall of the Freedom of Contract*, 485–86.

46. *The Times*, February 2, 1864, 9.

47. On the legal treatment of wives' debts, see Morrison, "Contract," 116–21. For a history of married women's property law, see Lee Holcombe, *Wives and Property: Reform of the Married Women's Property Law in Nineteenth-Century England* (Toronto: University of Toronto Press, 1983); Mary Lyndon Shanley, *Feminism, Marriage, and the Law in Victorian England* (Princeton: Princeton University Press, 1989); Caroline Norton, *Caroline Norton's Defense: English Laws for Women in the Nineteenth Century* (1854; reprint, Chicago: Academy, 1982); Poovey, *Uneven Developments*, 51–88; and R. J. Morris, "Men, Women, and Property: The Reform of the Married Women's Property Act, 1870," in *Landowners, Capitalists, and Entrepreneurs: Essays for Sir John Habakkuk*, ed. F. M. L. Thompson (Oxford: Clarendon Press, 1994). Norma Basch, *In the Eyes of the Law: Women, Marriage, and Property in Nineteenth-Century New York* (Ithaca: Cornell University Press, 1982); and Carole Shammas, "Re-assessing the Married Women's Property Acts," *Journal of Women's History* 6, no. 1 (Spring 1994): 9–30, illuminate comparable developments in the United States.

48. On the Lords' alterations of the original bill, see Shanley, *Feminism, Marriage, and the Law*, 49–78. Only earnings, investments, and property owed to the wife as the beneficiary of someone who died intestate and legacies of less than two hundred pounds became a married women's separate property. Proponents complained that a woman's money earned before marriage or before the act passed would not become her separate property, nor would money deposited in savings banks or similar institutions, unless she had made a special application for her account to be so registered (70–75).

49. Erickson, *Women and Property in Early Modern England*, 107.

50. Shanley, *Feminism, Marriage, and the Law*, 70–71.

51. Courtney Stanhope Kenny, *The History of the Law of England as to the Effects of Marriage on Property and on the Wife's Legal Capacity* (London: Reeves and Turner, 1879), 17.

52. Shanley, *Feminism, Marriage, and the Law*, 105–7.

53. Robert Malcolm Kerr, *The Commentaries on the Laws of England of Sir William Blackstone, Adapted to the Present State of the Law*, 4th ed. (London: John Murray, 1876), 1:418.

54. The *Cornhill Magazine* published a short essay on trade journals in which the author wrote: "The Trade Journal is the modern expression of the old trade guild, watchful to educate, to advise, to help, to protect." "Trade

Journals," *Cornhill Magazine* 54 (1886): 537. On the history of the trade press, see Christopher Hosgood, "The Shopkeeper's 'Friend': The Retail Trade Press in Late-Victorian and Edwardian Britain," *Victorian Periodicals Review* 25, no. 4 (Winter 1992): 164–72.

55. "Husbands and Other Debtors," *WDTJ*, April 4, 1874, 151. It was estimated that nine out of ten cases involving a dispute over a husband's liability for a wife's purchasing involved drapery goods. *Drapers' Record*, October 5, 1889, 424.

56. See, for example, "*Kenny v. Caldwell Huddersfield County Court*," *WDTJ*, May 1, 872, 46; "*Allen v. Field, Dublin Court of Exchequer*," *WDTJ*, December 21, 1872, 474.

57. *WDTJ*, March 21, 1874, 127.

58. "Husbands, Wives, and County Courts," *WDTJ*, March 21, 1874, 127.

59. Horace Wyndham, *Feminine Frailty* (London: Ernest Benn, 1929), 36–45. Laura Bell (Mrs. Thistlethwayte) began her career as a draper's assistant. She then became a prostitute, the wife of an aristocrat, and finally a famous lay preacher. Her life was described in several Victorian memoirs such as the anonymously written *Fifty Years of London Society, 1870–1920* (New York: Brentano's, 1920).

60. Wyndham, *Feminine Frailty*, 44–47.

61. "*Debenham and Freebody v. Mellor*," *WDTJ*, March 27, 1880, 199. There is some confusion over the defendant's name, reported originally as Mellor; once it reached the House of Lords, it was spelled Mellon. I have used the latter spelling, as it is that used in present legal texts.

62. Baudrillard, *Selected Writings*, 37–45; William Leiss, *The Limits to Satisfaction: An Essay on the Problem of Needs and Commodities* (Toronto: University of Toronto Press, 1976).

63. "*Debenham and Freebody v. Mellor*," *WDTJ*, March 27, 1880, 199; *The Times*, March 25, 1880, 3. Bramwell (1808–92) was the son of a banker and quite involved in reforming commercial law. W. R. Cornish and G. de N. Clark, *Law and Society in England, 1750–1950* (London: Sweet and Maxwell, 1989), 637.

64. "A Husband's Liability," *WDTJ*, April 3, 1880, 213.

65. "A County Court Justice, *Debenham v. Mellor*," *WDTJ*, April 3, 1880, 216.

66. "Liability of Married Women," *Drapers' Journal*, June 10, 1880, 3.

67. Quoted in *Drapers' Journal*, June 10, 1880, 4. A few years later, tradesmen worried that this fear was lessening and that husbands were beginning to prefer "a few minutes in the witness-box" rather than a payment of "fifty or a hundred pounds." *Drapers' Record*, October 28, 1893, 1027.

68. "*Debenham and Freebody v. Mellon*," *The Times*, November 25, 1880, 4.

69. "*Debenham and Another v. Mellon*," *The Times*, November 29, 1880, 4.

70. *The Times*, November 29, 1880, 9.

71. *The Times*, November 30, 1880, 5.

72. Hansard Parliamentary Debates, 3d ser., vol. 252 (1880): 1536.

73. "The Married Women's Property Bill," *WDTJ*, June 19, 1880, 386–87.

74. Hansard Parliamentary Debates, 3d ser., vol. 252 (1880): 1543.

75. *Women's Suffrage Journal* 13 (September 1882): 131, quoted in Shanley, *Feminism, Marriage, and the Law*, 124.

76. *WDTJ*, September 9, 1882, 633.

77. Shanley, *Feminism, Marriage, and the Law*, 126–30.

78. *WDTJ*, April 22, 1882, 280.

79. "Creditors and Marriage Settlements," *WDTJ*, December 1, 1883, 814.

80. *WDTJ*, August 14, 1883, 530.

81. "Married Women's Contracts," *Drapers' Record*, May 17, 1890, 653.

82. *Drapers' Record*, March 22, 1890, 424; May 17, 1890, 653.

83. *Drapers' Record*, November 1, 1890, 643.

84. "Important Decision under the Married Women's Property Act," *Drapers' Record*, May 11, 1889, 562. In 1854 Caroline Norton described the same situation. She pointed out that the laws allowed her husband to "defraud" her creditors, and as a married woman she had only to plead coverture: "Because I am Mr. Norton's wife I can cheat others, the tradesmen who have supplied me would (by the law of England) utterly lose their money." Norton, *Caroline Norton's Defense*, 96.

85. "Married Women's Rights," *Drapers' Record*, August 2, 1890, 139; "Married Women's Liability," *Drapers' Record*, May 24, 1890, 694; May 2, 1891, 785.

86. "Husband and Wife," *Drapers' Record*, November 21, 1891, 993.

87. "Married Women's Debts," *Drapers' Record*, April 13, 1895, 75.

88. *Drapers' Record*, May 2, 1891, 792. This writer did not feel that English law was promoting commercial expansion. It may be that consumer credit was treated quite differently in this respect than were other forms of commercial credit and contracts. On the relationship between the law and such commercial transactions, see R. B. Ferguson, "The Adjudication of Commercial Disputes and the Legal System in Modern England," *British Journal of Law and Society* 7, no. 2 (Winter 1980): 141–57 and his "Commercial Expectations and the Guarantee of the Law: Sales Transactions in Mid-

Nineteenth-Century England," in Rubin and Sugarmen, *Law, Economy, and Society*, 192–214.

89. Morrison, "Contract," 121–26.

90. "County Courts," *London Society* 6 (January 1867): 455.

91. In practice, most working-class husbands relinquished control of family monies to their wives. Farther up the social scale, wives traditionally had less direct control over domestic expenditure. Viviana A. Zelizer, "The Social Meaning of Money: 'Special Monies,'" *Journal of American Sociology* 95, no. 2 (September 1989): 357. On financial tensions within the family, see Ellen Ross, "'Fierce Questions and Taunts': Married Life in Working-Class London, 1870–1914," *Feminist Studies* 8, no. 3 (Fall 1982): 575–602; Pat Ayers and Jan Lambertz, "Marriage Relations, Money, and Domestic Violence in Working-Class Liverpool, 1919–1939" in *Labour and Love: Women's Experience of Home and Family, 1850–1940*, ed. Jane Lewis (Oxford: Basil Blackwell, 1986), 195–219; Tebbutt, *Making Ends Meet*, 37–38; A. James Hammerton, "Victorian Marriage and the Law of Matrimonial Cruelty," *Victorian Studies* 33, no. 2 (Winter 1990): 278; and Hammerton, *Cruelty and Companionship*, 113–14.

92. See, for example, the way that Jane and Thomas Carlyle fought over money. After one such "money row," Jane wheedled more money out of her husband by drawing up a parliamentary style budget that outlined her expenditures. See Joan Perkin's discussion of this incident in *Women and Marriage in Nineteenth-Century England* (London: Routledge, 1989), 245.

93. Maria Lydia Blane Wood to her mother, June 4, 1860, reprinted in Jane Van Sittart, ed., *From Minnie, with Love: The Letters of a Victorian Lady, 1849–1861* (London: Peter Davies, 1974), 177–78.

94. Blane to her mother, October 10, 1860, *From Minnie, with Love*, 181.

95. On the specific mechanisms of the county courts, see Johnson, "Small Debts and Economic Distress," 66–69.

96. For example, in *Thomas Wallis v. Grossmith* the judge found Mrs. Grossmith's purchases showed no "extravagance," so Mr. Grossmith was found liable. *Drapers' Record*, October 5, 1889, 428.

97. "Law for Ladies," *Lady*, March 12, 1885, 138.

98. *The Times*, June 5, 1880, 6; *Drapers' Journal*, June 10, 1880, 3.

99. After the decision of Debenham and Mellon in the Court of Appeal, there was a great deal of discussion in the trade press as to whether any clothing could be considered necessary. See, for example, *WDTJ*, April 3, 1880, 212.

100. Their case was heard in this court rather than in the county court because of the size of the debt. There was some inconsistency as to the limits heard in the county courts during this period, but the generally accepted limit was fifty pounds.

101. *Floyd v. Hallmann and Wife, The Times*, March 20, 1896, 14; *WDTJ*, March 28, 1896, 363.

102. *The Times*, March 20, 1896, 14.

103. Moving in society had profound social, political, and economic importance, and required a great deal of conspicuous consumption. Davidoff, *Best Circles*, 68.

104. *The Times*, March 20, 1896, 14.

105. Ibid.

106. Ibid.

107. "*Burberry's v. Mayer and Another*, High Court of Justice, King's Bench Division," *The Times*, January 20, 1909, 3. Occasionally tradesmen found themselves at a loss when a couple had separated and the wife gave the husband an allowance. A West End jeweler's sued a husband for a hundred pounds for a pearl necklace they had sold to his wife. During the trial it became clear that the wife, the daughter of Peter Robinson, the successful West End draper, had all the money in the family. They had sued the wrong party, but the judge made them abide by that choice. "*Halford and Sons v. Price and Another*, High Court of Justice, King's Bench Division," *The Times*, April 19, 1910, 3.

108. "A Wife's Liability," *Drapers' Record*, August 1, 1891, 217.

109. "A Husband's Responsibility," *Retail Trader*, January 1913, 16.

110. Veblen had argued that a wife's "conspicuous consumption" helped "establish the good name of the household and its master." Veblen, *Theory of the Leisure Class*, 81.

111. "Whiteley's General Catalogue for 1885," xxxiii. Whiteley's Store Archive, Westminster City Archives, London. In 1892 Dickins and Jones explained in their catalogue: "Madame, We beg to inform you that our Half-Yearly Sale, at Reduced Prices for Ready Money, will commence on Monday Next, February 8th. . . . The entire stock will undergo a considerable reduction in price, and many lots of fashionable goods, purchased at a large discount for cash, will be included in the Sale, at about half their value." Dickins and Jones, "Annual Sale Catalogue," February 1892, HF/9/1, House of Fraser Archives, Business Records Center, University of Glasgow.

112. See n. 11 and Adburgham, *Shops and Shopping*, 143, 170.

113. Fred W. Burgess, *The Practical Retail Draper: A Complete Guide for the Drapery and Allied Trade*, 5 vols. (London: Virtue and Co., 1912), 1:213.

114. Alexander, *Retailing in England*, 183; Miller, *The Bon Marché*, 54–55.

115. See, for example, *WDTJ*, April 3, 1880, 213 and November 5, 1892; and "Married Women's Debts," *Drapers' Record*, April 13, 1895, 75. Stores also turned to debt collection agencies. For example, in 1920 the Tottenham Court furniture giant, Heal's, tried to deduct 2 percent from the commissions of assistants who had authorized large sales that subsequently became bad debts. The workers protested and were able to convince the management to deduct only 1 percent from their commission. Heal's Board of Directors, minute books, March 26, 1920, and March 9, 1920. SU78 Heal and Son Archive, Archive of Art and Design, Victoria and Albert Museum.

116. "A Husband's Liability," *WDTJ*, December 4, 1880, 772.

117. "Women and Tradesmen: Various Methods to Cheat Shopkeepers," *Retail Trader* (October 1912): 456.

118. "Hard Cases—Credit," *Retail Trader* 4, no. 48 (November–December 1912): 459.

119. "Husband's Liability," *Drapers' Record*, April 4, 1896, 14.

120. *Drapers' Record*, April 13, 1895, 75.

121. *BC*, November 18, 1876.

122. Ibid.

123. "Local Industries: Cash v. Credit," *Chelsea Herald*, August 30, 1884, 4. In the 1890s, however, the newly married Molly Hughes had found that Whiteley's prices were much higher than those of the local shops in her neighborhood. M. V. Hughes, *A London Home in the 1890s* (1946; reprint, Oxford: Oxford University Press, 1978), 147.

124. Some women felt that being married afforded them greater liberties when out shopping. For example, on the day she married, Beryl Lee Booker found a new pleasure in shopping. After a visit to Marshall and Snelgrove's, she drove to Hatchard's "and bought a hitherto forbidden novel, and then I walked up and down the Burlington Arcade. I was a married woman." Booker, *Yesterday's Child*, 256.

Chapter Three
"Resting Places for Women Wayfarers"

1. *Pall Mall Gazette*, March 4, 1912, 12. Although there was a working-class women's club movement in Britain, this chapter focuses on middle- and upper-class women's clubs. For an account of working women's clubs, see Maude Stanley, *Clubs for Working Girls* (London: Macmillan, 1890).

2. A fairly complete record of women's clubs may be found in the *Englishwoman's Year-Book*, edited by Louisa Hubbard from 1875 to 1916. The 1904 edition lists thirty-six London and twelve provincial clubs in Bath, Clifton, Brighton, Leeds, Liverpool, Manchester, Dublin, Edinburgh, Glasgow, and Inverness.

3. For a discussion of clubs and feminism, see Philippa Levine, *Feminist Lives in Victorian England: Private Roles and Public Commitment* (Oxford: Basil Blackwell, 1990), 66–67; Polly Beals, "Fabian Feminism: Gender, Politics, and Culture in London, 1880–1930" (Ph.d. diss., Rutgers University, 1989), 77–80; and Vicinus, *Independent Women*, 295–99. For clubs and female leisure, see Rubinstein, *Before the Suffragettes*, 222–26.

4. We still need a full-length study of the intersections between feminism and consumerism. For the relationship between the suffrage movement and commercial culture, see Tickner, *Spectacle of Women*; Joel H. Kaplan and Sheila Stowell, *Theatre and Fashion: Oscar Wilde to the Suffragettes* (Cambridge: Cambridge University Press, 1994), 152–84; and the epilogue to this book. Of course, twentieth-century feminist scholars have been among the greatest critics of consumerism. For this point see de Grazia and Furlough, *The Sex of Things*, 275–76. But as Rachel Bowlby has recently suggested, feminism has at times adopted the language of the market. "Soft Sell: Marketing Rhetoric in Feminist Criticism," in de Grazia and Furlough, *The Sex of Things*, 381–88.

5. I use the term *feminist* because it came into popular use in Britain in the 1890s coincident with the period of the greatest expansion of women's clubs, and where it no doubt was used. Much ink has been spilled over whether the term *feminist* should be applied prior to its first inception. Nancy Cott has argued that doing so has led to a misreading of the varied and diverse nature of the nineteenth-century woman's movement. *The Grounding of Modern Feminism* (New Haven: Yale University Press, 1987), 3–4. For a different opinion, see Karen Offen, "Defining Feminism: A Comparative Historical Approach," *Signs* 14, no. 1 (Autumn 1988): 119–57.

6. For general studies, see Philippa Levine, *Victorian Feminism, 1850–1900* (London: Hutchinson, 1987); Olive Banks, *Faces of Feminism: A Study of Feminism as a Social Movement* (New York: St. Martin's Press, 1981); David Morgan, *Suffragists and Liberals: The Politics of Women's Suffrage in Britain* (Oxford: Basil Blackwell, 1975); Jane Rendall, ed., *Equal or Different: Women's Politics, 1800–1914* (Oxford: Basil Blackwell, 1987).

7. For a map with the locations of some of these institutions, see Lynn Walker. "Vistas of Pleasure," in Orr, *Women in the Victorian Art World*, 70–83. Walker's map does not include many of the clubs, however.

8. Glasgow was famous for its tearooms, especially Miss Cranston's "artistic" tearoom. Perilla Kinchin, *Tea and Taste: The Glasgow Tea Rooms, 1875–1975* (Wendlebury: White Cockade, 1991). For an excellent examination of how American clubs reshaped women's relationship to the city, see Sarah Deutsch, "Reconceiving the City: Women, Space, and Power in Boston, 1870–1910," *Gender and History* 6, no. 2 (August 1994): 202–23. Although the club movement was much more developed in the United States than in England, there are striking parallels between Boston and London. Among the many studies of the American movement, see Karen J. Blair, *The Clubwoman as Feminist: True Womanhood Redefined, 1868–1914* (New York: Holmes and Meier, 1980); Theodora Penny Martin, *The Sound of Our Own Voices: Women's Study Clubs, 1860–1910* (Boston: Beacon Press, 1987); and Anne Firor Scott, *Natural Allies: Women's Associations in American History* (Urbana: University of Illinois Press, 1991).

9. For a typical example of this lament during the early 1870s, see "London as It Is and as It Might Be," *Builder*, January 27, 1872, 61–63. Arthur Cawston began his study of urban redevelopment by noting, "London is often described as ugly, but it is not past redemption." Arthur Cawston, *A Comprehensive Scheme for Street Improvements* (London: Edward Stanford, 1893).

10. Winter, *London's Teeming Streets*; Susan D. Pennybacker, *A Vision for London, 1889–1914: Labour, Everyday Life, and the LCC Experiment* (New York: Routledge, 1995), 158–240.

11. This feminist critique was closely tied to the political battles over the regulation of prostitution. Those who were active in the campaign to repeal the Contagious Diseases Acts between the 1860s and 1880s believed that the acts had institutionalized male authority over women and had increased rather than decreased female vulnerability in public. For a careful examination of the politics of prostitution, see Walkowitz, *Prostitution and Victorian Society.* Also see Susan Kent, *Sex and Suffrage in Britain, 1860–1914* (Princeton: Princeton University Press, 1987), 60–79. For related discussions of feminist attitudes toward urban life, see Vicinus, *Independent Women*, especially chaps. 6 and 7; Nord, *Walking the Victorian Streets*, 181–236; Ross, *Love and Toil*; and Walkowitz, *City of Dreadful Delight.* Although her book is technically about how feminists perceived domestic space, chapter 3 of Carol Dyhouse's *Feminism and the Family in England, 1880–1939* (Oxford: Basil Blackwell, 1989) explores how feminists imagined the relationship between public and private. For feminist approaches to public and private space, see Dolores Hayden, *The Grand Domestic Revolution: A History of Feminist Designs for American Homes, Neighborhoods, and Cities* (Cambridge: MIT Press, 1985).

12. Helen Meller has argued, however, that late-nineteenth- and early-twentieth-century planners did not consider women's relationship to the city and essentially reinscribed separate-spheres ideology onto their view of the metropolis. "Planning Theory and Women's Role in the City," *Urban History Yearbook* 17 (1990): 85–98.

13. There has been relatively little work on the catering and hotel industries. Robert Thorne's essay "Places of Refreshment in the Nineteenth-Century City"; Joanne Finklestein's, *Dining Out: A Sociology of Modern Manners* (Oxford: Polity Press in association with Basil Blackwell, 1989), 40; and Jack Simmons, "Railways, Hotels, and Tourism in Great Britain, 1839–1914," *Journal of Contemporary History* 19, no. 2 (April 1984): 201–22 are the most compelling studies. Also see D. J. Richardson, "J. Lyons and Co., Ltd.: Caterers and Food Manufacturers, 1894–1939," in *The Making of the Modern British Diet*, ed. Derek Oddy and Derek Miller (London: Croom Helm, 1976): 161–72; Jackson Stanley, *The Savoy: A Century of Taste*, 3d ed., rev. (London: Frederick Muller, 1989), 23–24; David Bush and Derek Taylor, *The Golden Age of British Hotels* (London: Northwood, 1974). For a fascinating contemporary portrait of the "modern" hotel, see Arnold Bennett's novel *The Grand Babylon Hotel: A Fantasia on Modern Times* (1902; reprint, Harmondsworth: Penguin, 1985). Most recent studies of public amusements in the United States have focused on urban attractions that became popular in the late 1880s and 1890s. Erenberg, *Steppin' Out*; David Nasaw, *Going Out: The Rise and Fall of Public Amusements* (New York: Basic Books, 1993); John F. Kasson, *Amusing the*

Million: Coney Island at the Turn of the Century (New York: Hill and Wang, 1978); Peiss, *Cheap Amusements*; and the excellent collection of essays in Taylor, *Inventing Times Square*.

14. Gustave Doré and Blanchard Jerrold, *London, a Pilgrimage* (1872; reprint, New York: Dover, 1970), 170–71. Although Jerrold and Doré acknowledged the growth of commercialized leisure during this era, they focused on the public house and the music hall and neglected the shopping culture that was also visibly transforming the metropolis. In her excellent analysis of Doré and Jerrold's text, Griselda Pollock noted this absence and discussed the ways in which the texts suppressed aspects of bourgeois modernity that were reshaping the West End. See Pollock, "Vicarious Excitements," 37–38.

15. "London as a City of Pleasure," *Saturday Review*, July 27, 1872, 110. Twenty years before, another journalist similarly argued that the growth of public transportation contribution to "the increased and daily increasing facilities for social enjoyment." *The Art of Dining, or Gastronomy for Gastronomers* (London: John Murray, 1852), 122. In the midst of a lengthy discussion of London's brothels and other illicit entertainments, an American journalist wrote, "No other city, including Paris, spends more money . . . to support music and drama." Daniel Joseph Kerwan, *Palace and Hovel, or Phases of London Life* (1870; reprint, London: Abellard-Schuman, 1963), 154. In the 1880s, a French businessman even commented that he now felt at home in Regent Street because "nowadays, in every part of London café restaurants in the French style are to be found." *WDTJ*, January 30, 1886, 86. For other accounts of London's dining culture, see "Hotels and Restaurants," *Building News* 36 (February 1879): 157–58; Nathaniel Newnham-Davis, *Dinners and Diners: Where and How to Dine in London* (London: Grant Richards, 1899); and his *The Gourmet's Guide to London* (London: Grant Richards, 1914).

16. Peter Bailey, *Leisure and Class in Victorian England: Rational Recreation and the Contest for Control, 1830–1885* (London: Routledge and Kegan Paul; Toronto: University of Toronto Press, 1978), esp. 56–59; Bailey, "Parasexuality and Glamour"; Hugh Cunningham, *Leisure in the Industrial Revolution, ca. 1780–1880* (New York: St. Martin's Press, 1980), 151–78; John Clarke and Chas Critcher, *The Devil Makes Work: Leisure in Capitalist Britain* (Urbana: University of Illinois Press, 1985), 60–71; Eileen Yeo and Stephen Yeo, eds., *Popular Culture and Class Conflict, 1590–1914: Explorations in the History of Labour and Leisure* (Sussex: Harvester Press; Atlantic Highlands, N.J.: Humanities Press, 1981); John K. Walton and James Walvin, eds., *Leisure in Britain, 1780–1939* (Manchester: Manchester University Press, 1983); Stella Margetson, *Leisure and Pleasure in the Nineteenth Century* (New York: Coward-McCann, 1969). Helen Meller has argued that the transformation in attitudes toward leisure in Bristol during the late sixties and early seventies was in part due to what she saw as the emergence of a "Liberal cultural ideal." This ideal drew upon Matthew Arnold's "vision of 'culture' as a socially cohesive force" that could bring both personal fulfillment and break down social barriers. *Leisure and the Changing City, 1870–1914* (London: Routledge and Kegan Paul, 1976), 50–51. Much of the social history of leisure has focused on how the construction and control of leisure has been a site of class tensions, confrontation, and construction. See, for example, A. P. Donajgrodzki, ed., *Social Control in Nineteenth-Century Britain* (London: Croom Helm, 1977).

17. Walkowitz has explored how feminism partly grew from a critique of male sexual pleasures in the city in *Prostitution and Victorian Society* and *City of Dreadful Delight*. Kathy Peiss looked at how the regulation of working women's leisure in New York also involved the promotion of "respectable" amusements. Peiss, *Cheap Amusements*, 163–84. The Left critique of leisure has continued to separate pleasure into appropriate and inappropriate forms. See Fredric Jameson's discussion of this in "Pleasure: A Political Issue."

18. Foucault, *History of Sexuality*. On the production of commercial sexuality, see Bailey, "Parasexuality and Glamour."

19. Harrison has argued that by the 1860s, "the respectable classes" were no longer patronizing pubs as they had previously. Throughout the century, however, the public house remained a transport and recreation center for the lower classes as well as a meeting place for radical and reform organizations. Indeed, pubs were condemned because they were an important aspect of a working-class masculine public sphere. Harrison, "Pubs," 161–90. On the role of pubs as meeting places, also see Girouard, *Victorian Pubs*, 9–10, 46.

20. Some have argued that commercial entertainments like the music hall contributed to the decline of working-class radicalism. See, for example, Gareth Stedman Jones, "Working-Class Culture and Working-Class Politics in London, 1870–1900: Notes on the Remaking of a Working Class," in *Languages of Class: Studies in English Working-Class History, 1832–1982* (Cambridge: Cambridge University Press, 1983), 279–88. Others have suggested

that aspects of mass commercial culture have facilitated the creation of economic and political networks among different classes of men. For the tension between amusement and politics in working-class men's clubs, see John Davis, "Radical Clubs and London Politics, 1870–1900," in Feldman and Jones, *Metropolis London*, 103–28. Also, John Brewer, "Commercialization and Politics," in McKendrick, Brewer, and Plumb, *The Birth of a Consumer Society*, especially 231–62. Drinking establishments were crucial to radical culture but contributed to the masculinization of early-nineteenth-century politics. Dorothy Thompson, "Women and Radical Politics: A Lost Dimension," in *The Rights and Wrongs of Women*, ed. Juliet Mitchell and Ann Oakley (Harmondsworth: Penguin, 1976); Sally Alexander, "Women, Class, and Sexual Difference in the 1830s and the 1840s: Some Reflections on the Writing of a Feminist History," *History Workshop Journal* 17 (1984): 125–49; and Anna Clark, *The Struggle for the Breeches: Gender and the Making of the British Working Class* (Berkeley: University of California Press, 1995).

21. Voluntary associations contributed to the formation of middle-class culture and identities in the first half of the nineteenth century. Davidoff and Hall, *Family Fortunes*, 416–29; R. J. Morris, "Voluntary Societies and British Urban Elites, 1780–1850: An Analysis," *Historical Journal* 26, no. 1 (1983): 95–118; and R. J. Morris, *Class, Sect, and Party: The Making of the British Middle Class, Leeds, 1820–1850* (Manchester: Manchester University Press, 1990), 161–203. Theodore Koditscheck writes that the associational nexus that emerged in the 1830s and 1840s "provided a framework for a systematic bourgeois culture and politics that sought to achieve hegemony over Bradford's restive ruling class." *Class Formation and Urban Industrial Society: Bradford, 1750–1850* (Cambridge: Cambridge University Press, 1990), 251.

22. Cited in Ralph Neville, *London Clubs: Their History and Treasures* (London: Chatto and Windus, 1911), 135. This oft-quoted quip is no doubt referring to the Savages Club, which Sala helped found, but it and the club's name were funny because it inverted the constructions of "white" imperial masculinity that were becoming dominant.

23. Brian Harrison, *Separate Spheres: The Opposition to Women's Suffrage in Britain* (New York: Holmes and Meier, 1978), 98. Clubs, restaurants, and other male gathering places also helped constitute bohemia as a masculine territory. For an anecdotal look at the institutions of bohemia, see Guy Deghy, *Paradise in the Strand: The Story of Romano's* (London: Richards Press, 1958); and George R. Sims, *My Life: Sixty Years' Recollections of Bohemian London* (London: Eveleigh Nash, 1917). Indeed, in describing the history of men's clubs, E. B. Chancellor remarked in an offhand way, "In those days St James's street was practically given over to clubmen; and ladies seldom walked in it unless escorted by a friend or man servant. The argus-eyed, bow-window of Whites was an ordeal not many cared to undergo." Chancellor, *The West End of Yesterday and Today*, 19.

24. Philip J. Ethington, *The Public City: The Political Construction of Urban Life in San Francisco, 1850–1900* (Cambridge: Cambridge University Press, 1994), 208–17, 326–36, 355–69; Ryan, *Women in Public*, 164–71; and Mary Ryan, "Gender and Public Access: Women's Politics in the Nineteenth Century," in *Habermas and the Public Sphere*, ed. Craig Calhoun (Cambridge: MIT Press, 1992), 259–88.

25. Geoff Eley, "Nations, Publics, and Political Cultures," in Calhoun, *Habermas and the Public Sphere*, 289–339. Also see Davidoff's textured rethinking of the meaning of the public in the nineteenth century in "Regarding Some 'Old Husband's Tales.' "

26. Habermas, *Structural Transformation*, 27; and his more recent assessment, "Further Reflections on the Public Sphere," in Calhoun, *Habermas and the Public Sphere*, 421–61.

27. Habermas, *Structural Transformation*, 33. Feminists have argued that while Habermas noted that the public sphere was masculine, he did not see how gender was central to its very construction. Joan B. Landes, *Women and the Public Sphere in the Age of the French Revolution* (Ithaca: Cornell University Press, 1988); Ryan, *Women in Public*, 9–13; Ryan, "Gender and Public Access," 259–88; Nancy Fraser, "Rethinking the Public Sphere: A Contribution to the Critique of Actually Existing Democracy," in Calhoun, *Habermas and the Public Sphere*, 109–42, originally published in *Social Text* 25/26 (1990): 56–80. I agree, however, with recent scholarship that has reconsidered this portrait of female exclusion. See, for example, Mary Thale, "Women in London Debating Societies in 1780," *Gender and History* 7, no. 1 (April 1995): 5–24; and Vickery's assessment of this period, in "Golden Age to Separate Spheres?"

28. Habermas, *Structural Transformation*, 177.

29. Vickery, "Golden Age to Separate Spheres?" 393; and Davidoff, "Regarding Some 'Old Husbands' Tales."

30. Hannah Arendt, *The Human Condition* (Chicago: University of Chicago Press, 1958). Seyla Benhabib has explored the models of

public space in the work of Arendt and Habermas in "Models of Public Space: Hannah Arendt, the Liberal Tradition, and Jürgen Habermas," in Calhoun, *Habermas and the Public Sphere*, 73–98.

31. Richard Sennett has recently written that "the more comfortable the moving body became, the more it also withdrew socially, travelling alone and silent." He felt that "the geography of speed and the search for comfort" led people into an isolated condition. *Flesh and Stone: The Body and the City in Western Civilization* (New York: W. W. Norton, 1994), 338 and 358. For similar arguments, see Sennett's earlier *The Fall of Public Man*; and Schivelbush, *The Railway Journey*, 54. Sennett's view of London's public life moving from a realm of discourse and community to one of silence and anomie because of consumption and its culture of "comfort" fails to characterize women's experience of public life or to account for the vibrant feminist and socialist cultures that emerged in the city.

32. Taylor, "The Evolution of Public Space," 299–302.

33. *Woman's Gazette, or News about Work* 1, no. 1 (October 1875): 1. The journal ran from 1875 to 1879, after which it continued until 1893 as *Work and Leisure: Englishwoman's Advertiser, Reporter, and Gazette*.

34. "Resting-Places for Women Wayfarers," *Woman's Gazette* 3, no. 7 (July 1878): 100–101.

35. For an anecdotal but important study of mealtimes and the organization of daily life, see Arnold Palmer, *Movable Feasts* (London: Oxford University Press, 1952).

36. For example, when thirteen-year-old Georgiana Sitwell visited London in 1837 she traveled with her father in his "chariot," stayed with her aunt, and was "amused" by her cousin. Her memories of London were limited to a daily walk in Hyde Park, a single trip to the Soho Bazaar, and "one or two picture exhibitions." Osbert Sitwell, ed., *Two Generations* (London: Macmillan, 1940), 123.

37. Sitwell, *Two Generations*, 263.

38. Booker, *Yesterday's Child*, 33, 69.

39. Nicholson, *A Victorian Household*, 87.

40. Thorne, "Places of Refreshment in the Nineteenth-Century City," 235. For a grim view of the confectioner, see George Eliot, *Brother Jacob* (1879; reprint, London: Virago, 1984). For a contrast to this gloomy picture, see the description of Stewart's, which had served sweets to Londoners for over two hundred years before it was rebuilt in 1907. Chancellor, *Wanderings in Piccadilly*, 2. Outside of London there were even fewer places for a women to dine in public during the day. On her summer vacation at the seaside in 1884, the middle-class diarist Molly Hughes remembered the difficulty she and her mother had finding a place to eat their midday meal. Following their habit in London, they "made for the commercial centre . . . and certainly found a few shops," but, unlike in London, it was several hours before they could find any respectable eatery. M. V. Hughes, *A London Girl of the 1880s* (Oxford: Oxford University Press, 1979), 72.

41. This was how Gwen Raverat, one of Charles Darwin's granddaughters, described her mother's condition after she returned to Cambridge after a long day of London shopping in the 1890s. *Period Piece: A Cambridge Childhood* (London: Faber and Faber, 1960), 95.

42. Ursula Bloom, *Victorian Vinaigrette* (London: Hutchinson, 1956), 67.

43. John Burnett, ed., *Destiny Obscure: Autobiographies of Childhood, Education, and Family from the 1820s to the 1920s* (London: Routledge, 1994), 119.

44. "Resting-Places," *Woman's Gazette*, 100.

45. There were many images associated with the New Woman of the 1890s. George Gissing's Alice and Virginia Madden are portrayed, for example, as ill, starving, and quietly suffering in *The Odd Women* (1893; reprint, Harmondsworth: Penguin, 1993). Among the several studies of the New Woman, see Ruth Brandon, *The New Women and the Old Men: Love, Sex, and the Woman Question* (New York: W. W. Norton, 1990); Ann L. Ardis, *New Women, New Novels: Feminism and Early Modernism* (New Brunswick, N.J.: Rutgers University Press, 1990); Showalter, *Sexual Anarchy*, 38–58; Nord, *Walking the Victorian Streets*, 181–236; Gail Cunningham, *The New Woman and the Victorian Novel* (London: Macmillan, 1978). For an excellent assessment of how the New Woman was constructed at the intersections between advertising, the periodical press, and high art in the United States, see Ellen Wiley Todd, *The "New Woman" Revised: Painting and Gender Politics on Fourteenth Street* (Berkeley: University of California Press, 1993). For a focus on the periodical press in the United States and England, see Patricia Marks, *Bicycles, Bangs, and Bloomers: The New Woman in the Popular Press* (Lexington: University of Kentucky Press, 1990).

46. *Woman's Gazette* 2, no. 14 (November 1877): 220; and 3, no. 12 (December 1878), 188. The job of recommending and supporting female businesses was increasingly taken up by the mainstream women's press. See, for example, the discussion of "lady" entrepreneurs in "Why Ladies Fail in Business," *Queen*, April

13, 1898, 287; "Ladies in Business: The Conditions of Success—A Collection of Opinions," *Queen*, November 26, 1898, 923; and M. I. Fergusson, "Tea Room and Confectionery Work," *Queen*, May 6, 1905, 558.

47. "Resting Places," *Woman's Gazette*, 101.

48. On the relationship between the *English Woman's Journal* and the LSA, see Jane Rendall, " 'A Moral Engine'? Feminism, Liberalism, and the *English Woman's Journal*," in *Equal or Different*, 128.

49. *Woman's Gazette* 3, no. 11 (November 1879): 172. On this campaign also see Winter, *London's Teeming Streets*, 127; and Walker, "Vistas of Pleasure," 77.

50. Dr. James Stevenson, "Paddington Vestry Report on the Necessity of Latrine Accommodation for Women in the Metropolis" (London: Paddington Vestry Hall, 1879), 4.

51. Ibid., 8–9.

52. Ibid., 10–13.

53. Though Stevenson assumed that stores offered such amenities, very few included ladies' rooms until the late 1880s. When Whiteley's neighbor, William Owen, added a "ladies' lavatory" to his emporium in 1887, the *WDTJ* remarked that this was a "special feature" of the new store. *WDTJ*, October 29, 1887, 924.

54. Stevenson, "Latrine Accommodation," 19–21.

55. "The Twenty-third Annual Report of the Ladies Sanitary Association" (April 1881), 12–14. This company built lavatories for women in Bethnal Green and Ludgate Circus in 1882. "The Twenty-fourth Annual Report of the Ladies Sanitary Association" (April 1882), 16.

56. Walker, "Vistas of Pleasure," 77. Walker's account does not explain why they were installed in Glasgow, Nottingham, and other large towns. Certainly the middle classes were as anxious about bodily functions and women's independence in the provinces as in the capital.

57. See, for example, William Woodward, "The Sanitation and Reconstruction of Central London," in *Essays on the Street Re-Alignment, Reconstruction, and Sanitation of Central London, and the Rehousing of the Poorer Classes* (London: George Bell, 1886), 80; and *Public Conveniences in London: Report by the Medical Officer* (London: LCC, 1928). By the 1920s, central London had nearly thirty female public conveniences, but this medical officer still felt this was quite inadequate, given the numbers of women who visited London each day.

58. See the discussion of Evans and other vestrywomen's careers in Hollis, *Ladies Elect*, 336–54. Hollis argued that by the late 1890s, Progressives, represented by such groups as the London Reform Union, took up the cause of public lavatories for both men and women as part of a drive to improve London's sanitation (341–42).

59. Residents often objected to the vestry's attempts to build urinals and similar conveniences. See, for example, Paddington Vestry Minutes, May 4, 1880, 193; and June 15, 1880, 230; and St. Marylebone Vestry, Public Convenience Subcommittee Minutes, June 30, 1897. The minutes primarily document the decisions taken to maintain preexisting conveniences. One recurrent topic was whether vestrywomen should inspect the conveniences. See, for example, the discussion on March 12, 1896, Westminster City Archives, London.

60. *BC*, June 10, 1899.

61. *BC*, August 8, 1891.

62. Eva Anstruther argued that when women "took to work the need for clubs became apparent." "Ladies' Clubs," *Nineteenth Century* 45 (April 1899): 600.

63. Among the vast literature on middle-class women's employment, see Holcombe, *Victorian Ladies at Work*; Vicinus, *Independent Women*; Hollis, *Ladies Elect*; Rubinstein, *Before the Suffragettes*, 69–93; Copelman, *London's Women Teachers*; Lewis, *Women in England*; Sandra Burman, ed., *Fit Work for Women* (London: Croom Helm, 1979); Ellen Jordan, "The Lady Clerks at the Prudential: The Beginning of Vertical Segregation by Sex in Clerical Work in Nineteenth-Century Britain," *Gender and History* 8, no. 1 (April 1996): 65–81; Meta Zimmeck, "Jobs for Girls: The Expansion of Clerical Work for Women, 1850–1914," in *Unequal Opportunities: Women's Employment in England, 1800–1918*, ed. Angela John (Oxford: Basil Blackwell, 1986), 153–78; and Gregory Anderson, ed., *The White-Blouse Revolution: Female Office Workers since 1870* (Manchester: Manchester University Press, 1988).

64. See, for example, the admiration that the feminist journal the *Englishwoman's Review* bestowed upon "one large drapery establishment in Bayswater" when it opened a reading room for its female employees. The name of the particular store was not mentioned, but it probably was Whiteley's. *Englishwoman's Review* 5 (1871): 186.

65. Frederick Gordon, *Crosby Hall: The Ancient City Palace and Great Banqueting Hall*, 2d ed. (London: Marhent and Lenges, 1868), 13. On women and restaurant dining, see Thorne, "Places of Refreshment in the Nineteenth-Century City," 235. Even some taverns attempted to appeal to women as early as the 1870s. The London Tavern in Fleet Street advertised that it included a "Ladies Dining

Salon" in April of 1870. His Lordship's Larder at no. 111 Cheapside explained in an advertisement that "Ladies—will find a suite of private apartments with female attendants and arranged with the strictest regard to their comfort and suited to the most refined taste." Philip Norman Collection, 23.1 HOB-MCR, Guildhall Libary, London.

66. *Caterer, Hotel Proprietor's, and Refreshment Contractor's Gazette* (hereafter *Caterer*), August 3, 1878, 70.

67. *Caterer*, June 1, 1878, 44. See also "Hotels and Restaurants," *Building News*, February 7, 1879, 157–58.

68. Newnham-Davis, *The Gourmet's Guide to London*, 86. Thomas Verity, "The Modern Restaurant," *Royal Institute of British Architects Transactions* 29 (1878–79): 85–92. By the turn of the century, even the drink trade was beginning to consider how to cater to middle-class women; see "Where Ladies Are Specially Catered For," *Licensing World and Licensed Trade Review*, March 8, 1902, 163.

69. One trade journal even commented that the advantage of large hotels over small ones is that "feminine society" may be found there. *Caterer*, September 7, 1878, 84.

70. Charles Eyre Pascoe, *London of To-Day: An Illustrated Handbook for the Season* (Boston: Roberts Brothers, 1885), 239.

71. In the 1850s and 1860s these clubs were perceived as a "new" feature of urban life. One author wrote in 1852, for example, that "the improvement and multiplication of clubs is the grand feature of metropolitan progress." *The Art of Dining*, 122. For a contemporary discussion of men's clubs, see John Timbs, *Clubs and Clublife in London, with Anecdotes of Its Famous Coffee-Houses, Hostelries, and Taverns, from the Sixteenth Century to the Present Time* (London: Chatto and Windus, 1872; reprint, Detroit: Gale Research, 1967); George James Ivey, *Clubs of the World: A General Guide or Index to the London and County Clubs*, 2d ed. (London: Harrison, 1880); and Neville, *London Clubs*. Also see Anthony Lejeune and Malcolm Lewis, *The Gentlemen's Clubs of London* (London: Dorset Press, 1979). Showalter briefly discusses male clubland and its constructions of masculinity in *Sexual Anarchy*, 11–13.

72. James Henry Leigh Hunt, *A Saunter through the West End* (London: Hurst and Blackett, 1861), 197–98.

73. "The Ladies Reading Room," *Illustrated London News*, January 28, 1861. On the founders of the Langham Place Group, see Sheila R. Herstein, *A Mid-Victorian Feminist: Barbara Leigh Smith Bodichon* (New Haven: Yale University Press, 1985); and Shelia R. Herstein, "The *English Woman's Journal* and the Langham Place Circle: A Feminist Forum and Its Women Editors," in *Innovators and Preachers: The Role of the Editor in Victorian England* (Westport, Conn.: Greenwood, 1985), 61–76; Candida Ann Lacey, *Barbara Leigh Smith Bodichon and the Langham Place Group* (New York: Routledge and Kegan Paul, 1987); Holcombe, *Victorian Ladies at Work*, 5–20; Jane Rendall, "Friendship and Politics: Barbara Leigh Smith Bodichon (1827–1891) and Bessie Rayner Parkes (1829–1925)" in *Sexuality and Subordination: Interdisciplinary Studies of Gender in the Nineteenth Century*, ed. Susan Mendus and Jane Rendall (London: Routledge, 1989), 136–70; and Rendall, " 'A Moral Engine'?"

74. *Englishwoman's Review* 5 (1871): 151–53.

75. *Daily News*, February 2, 1871, 3.

76. Ibid. It is useful to contrast this history with that described in the feminist *Englishwoman's Review* 5 (1871): 183–88.

77. Frances Power Cobbe, "Clubs for Women," *Echo*, March 14, 1871, 2. Cobbe shared certain attitudes about the girls of her day with Eliza Lynn Linton. See, for example, Cobbe's discussion of feminine "vanity and frivolity" in *The Duties of Women: A Course of Lectures* (Boston, George H. Ellis, 1881), 15. For a recent assessment of Cobbe's place in the feminist movement, see Barbara Caine, *Victorian Feminists* (Oxford: Oxford University Press, 1992), 103–49. One may also consult the second volume of Frances Power Cobbe, *The Life of Frances Power Cobbe*, vol. 2 (Boston: Houghton, Mifflin, 1895). Cobbe was a prolific writer, publishing countless books and essays on a variety of topics including antivivisection, domestic violence, and women's suffrage. Cobbe regarded herself as a political conservative, despite her support for women's rights. She was also one of the first professional female journalists in England and by this period was hired to write leading articles in the *Echo*.

78. Cobbe, *Echo*, March 14, 1871, 2.

79. Basel Champneys, ed., *Adelaide Drummond: Retrospect and Memoir* (London: Smith, Elder, 1915), 289.

80. This paper was not a typical ladies' magazine, however. Laurel Brake argues that as editor of the *Woman's World*, Oscar Wilde "cultivated" the new woman and introduced male "homosexual discourse into female space." Laurel Brake, *Subjugated Knowledges: Journalism, Gender, and Literature in the Nineteenth Century* (New York: New York University Press, 1994), 127.

81. Amy Levy, "Women and Club Life," republished in *The Complete Novels and Selected*

Writings of Amy Levy, 1861–1889, ed. Melvyn New (Gainesville: University of Florida Press, 1993): 532–38.

82. Nord does an excellent job exploring Levy's ambiguous position as a writer of the city in *Walking the Victorian Streets*, 197–206. New's introduction is a straightforward biography, yet he too emphasizes Levy's vision of London. New, *Amy Levy*, 35.

83. Levy, "Women and Club Life," 533.

84. For the type of female community Levy would have been referring to, see Nord, *Walking the Victorian Streets*, chap. 6. These writers seemed to desire more solitude and independence than the women who built the separate communities that Vicinus explored in *Independent Women*.

85. Levy, "Women and Club Life," 535.

86. Ibid., 536. It is unclear which clubs Levy joined. According to Melvyn New she was a member of the Men and Women's Club. As Walkowitz pointed out, however, club rules and the personalities of the participants proved quite frustrating for the female members. Walkowitz, *City of Dreadful Delight*, 135–70.

87. Dora Jones, "The Ladies' Clubs of London," *Young Woman* 7 (1899): 411. The club eventually moved to George Street in Hanover Square. It was unfortunate that many of the clubs Levy would have enjoyed were formed after her suicide in 1889.

88. Besant had founded the Authors' Club in 1891. For a discussion of Besant's insult and the establishment of the Writers' Club, see the *Lady*, September 24, 1891, 358; and October 1, 1891, 384. For other accounts of the Writers', see Jones, "The Ladies' Clubs of London," 411; Evelyn Willis, "Ladies' Clubs in London," *Lady's Realm* (1899): 319.

89. Constance Smedley, *Crusaders: The Reminiscences of Constance Smedley* (London: Duckworth, 1929), 54. E. M. Delafield [pseudo.], *Diary of a Provincial Lady* (London: Macmillan, 1930), 56–58, provides a fictional account of this female literary culture. For a contemporary account of some of authors who founded the Writers', see Helen C. Black, *Notable Women Authors of the Day* (1893; reprint, New York: Books for Libraries Press, 1972). Journalists could also join the Society of Women Journalists that was founded by Joseph S. Wood, editor of the *Gentlewoman*. Rubinstein, *Before the Suffragettes*, 85.

90. Of course, political positions were not necessarily changed by such contact. For example, "an old-fashioned woman" was totally unmoved after listening to Mrs. Fawcett speak on the "parliamentary franchise for women" at the Pioneer Club. *Lady*, March 8, 1894, 288.

91. *Englishwoman's Review*, July 16, 1900, 192.

92. Elizabeth Blackwell, "The Somerville Club," *Englishwoman's Review*, August 16, 1880, 337–43.

93. It is not exactly certain if Walker was the club's chairman or if he simply chaired this meeting. See the report of the meeting in *BC*, March 20, 1880.

94. Quoted in Beals, *Fabian Feminism*, 78.

95. *Lady*, January 30, 1890, 128.

96. *Lady*, November 15, 1888, 456.

97. "The Junior Denison Club," *Englishwoman's Review*, April 15, 1886, 187.

98. Hilda Friederichs, "A Peep at the Pioneer Club," *Young Woman* 4 (1895): 302; Dora Jones, "Sketches at the Pioneer Club," *Lady*, April 6, 1895, 585. The club also published a journal, *The Pioneer: A Quarterly Magazine Issued by the Pioneer Club*. The British Library's copy of the journal was unfortunately destroyed and I have not been able to locate another copy.

99. Mary H. Krout, *A Looker On in London* (New York: Dodd, Mead, 1899), 80.

100. On Massingberd's political defeat, see Hollis, *Ladies Elect*, 308–9. As a temperance worker who also worked for women's emancipation, Massingberd confronted the same conservative alliance that had defeated Whiteley's proposal for his liquor license.

101. *Illustrated London News*, February 6, 1897, 194. Massingberd's influence may also be judged by those who attended the memorial service held for her at St. John's Church in Westminster. *Queen*, February 13, 1897, 300.

102. In "Lesbian Perversity and Victorian Marriage: The 1864 Codrington Divorce Trial," *Journal of British Studies* 36, no. 1 (January 1997): 70–98, Martha Vicinus examines the "lesbian" relationship between Emily Faithfull and a married woman, Helen Jane Smith Codrington. For a history of these passionate friendships, see Lilian Faderman, *Surpassing the Love of Men: Romantic Friendship and Love between Women from the Renaissance to the Present* (New York: Morrow, 1981); Caroll Smith-Rosenberg's seminal essay, "The Female World of Love and Ritual: Relations between Women in Nineteenth-Century America," *Signs* 1, no. 1 (Autumn 1975): 1–29; and Rendall, "Friendship and Politics."

103. Leading suffragists such as Mrs. Pethick Lawrence were among its regular speakers. See an announcement of one of her lectures in *Votes for Women* (April 1908): 111. The feminist journal *Shafts* also regularly reported upon the Pioneers' event. Also see "The Pioneer," *Queen*, December 23, 1893, 1081. One of the members of the club's managing committee,

L. T. Meade, was an extremely successful popular author, whom Sally Mitchell has credited as among the authors of a new cultural ideal for young women. Meade's stories constructed a "New Girl," who was more independent and adventurous than her predecessors. Sally Mitchell, *The New Girl: Girls' Culture in England, 1880–1915*, (New York: Columbia University Press, 1995), 1–22.

104. "Ladies' Clubs," *Tinsley's Magazine* 4 (February–July 1869): 368–75.

105. *Saturday Review*, June 20, 1874, 774.

106. Elizabeth Lynn Linton, *The New Woman in Haste and at Leisure* (New York: Merriam, 1895), 52.

107. The periodical press frequently lampooned women's clubs in the 1890s. See, for example, Phil May's "The Smoking Room of a Ladies Club," *Pall Mall Budget*, December 27, 1894, 27. For a discussion of this criticism, see Showalter, *Sexual Anarchy*, 13; and Marks, *Bicycles, Bangs, and Bloomers*, 117–46. Levy's essay was in some respects a direct response to George du Maurier's famous cartoon "Female Clubs v. Matrimony," published ten years earlier. *Punch's Almanack for 1878* 74 (December 14, 1877), n.p. Although women's magazines were generally quite supportive of the club movement, they also enjoyed making fun of these institutions. The *Queen*, for example, published a cartoon in which a husband asks his wife if she is "going out this evening." After she tells him she is going to her "Down-with-Men Club," he threatens to "go home to my father." *Queen*, December 28, 1895, 1010.

108. "The Victoria Club," *Englishwoman's Review*, August 15, 1876, 365.

109. "Women's Clubs in London," *Queen*, November 11, 1893, 801.

110. *Queen*, June 28, 1899, 138.

111. *Queen*, August 18, 1888, 193.

112. Of course, some clubs were still member-owned. Still, they seem to have undergone a similar transition to that of working men's clubs. The growth of pubs and music halls forced working men's clubs to offer "professional" entertainments and ultimately to be run more like businesses. T. G. Ashplant, "London Working Men's Clubs, 1875–1914," in Yeo and Yeo, *Popular Culture and Class Conflict*, 241–70; and Davis, "Radical Clubs and London Politics."

113. B. S. Knollys, "The County Club," *Englishwoman* (May 1895): 203.

114. Willis, "Ladies Clubs in London," 316.

115. "The Empress Club," *The Times*, July 27, 1900, 15; and "Our Ladies' Clubs: The Empress," *Graphic*, April 4, 1908, 477. Another journalist wrote that the new drawing room's "walls, mirror frames, and ceiling are in white, the graceful effects of molding being given by means of patent Daekoria, by which excellent reproductions of this kind of decorative work of all periods may be obtained. The panels of the walls, the hangings, and coverings of the furniture are in crimson Beresford brocade, and the comfortable chairs and lounges, tall, cool palms and tasteful screens make this withdrawing room the ideal of comfort for the rapidly increasing race described by our transatlantic cousins as club women." *Queen*, June 29, 1901, 1064.

116. The Kettledrum was a well-known shoppers' resort, receiving a great deal of attention in the women's press for its "dainty" menu and decor. See *Lady*, December 15, 1892, 768; and *A.B.C. Amusement Guide and Record*, March 7, 1896, 21. Cohen seems to have been the sister of the composer Fred Cohen.

117. *Queen*, November 21, 1896, 954. The Sandringham was thriving two years later, for its proprietors were planning to move it into "lordly premises in Dover-street." *Queen*, January 28, 1899, 138.

118. The London Republican Club, Birbeck Institution, and New Quebec Institute admitted men and women on equal terms. *Women's Suffrage Journal* 4, no. 39 (May 1873), 68. Among other early feminists, Millicent Garrett Fawcett was an active member of the Radical Club, a group founded by her husband in 1865. She was also involved with the Republican Club. One of the Republican Club's stated objectives was to end " 'social and political privileges' on grounds of sex." David Rubinstein, *A Different World for Women: The Life of Millicent Garrett Fawcett* (New York: Wheatsheaf, 1991), 31. A committee of countesses, reverends, and an archdeacon established the mixed-sex Russell Club in Regent Street in 1878. *BC*, April 27, 1878; and May 4, 1878. The editor remarked that the vestrymen should take note that "flaneurs" had immediately started drinking wine in one of the rooms, thus making a joke about their reaction to men and women drinking together at Whiteley's. Many years later, the editor made light of the new mixed-sex Utopian club by arguing that there "is a greater degree of politeness" in such clubs. See *BC*, April 25, 1891. Other mixed-sex clubs included the Cabaret Theatre Club, the New Albany, and the most famous of all, the Bath Club. The Bath was founded in 1894 in Dover Street, primarily for recreational purposes such as swimming and gymnastics. "The Bath Club," *M.P.*, December 17, 1894, vol. 5, S.L. 23, Philip Norman Collection, Guildhall Library, London.

119. For details of this feminine drive into male clubland, see *Lady*, February 27, 1890; May 22, 1890; November 6, 1890; and July 16, 1891. Also see [Vasili], *The World of London*, 268. Female literary luminaries such as Sarah Grand, Mrs. Arthur Stannard, Flora Annie Steel, Marie Corelli, and Flora Hepworth Dixon were honored at a "ladies" dinner at the Vagabond in 1895. On this dinner, see newspaper clipping in vol. 5 of the Philip Norman Collection, S.L. 23, Guildhall Library, London. The source of this clipping is unknown, but the date is June 6, 1895.

120. See for example, "Ladies Clubs," *Nineteenth Century*, 45 (April 1899): 598–611; "Which Club Shall I Join?" *Queen*, December 31, 1898, 1133, and January 28, 1899, 138; Willis, "Ladies' Clubs in London."

121. Jones, "The Ladies' Clubs of London," 409.

122. "The Alexandra," *Queen*, November 25, 1893, 875.

123. Friederichs, "A Peep at the Pioneer Club," 302.

124. Jones, "Sketches at the Pioneer Club," 585.

125. *Lady*, 9 July 1885, 606.

126. "Another Ladies Club," *Queen*, April 18, 1896, 656. During this period, however, the social composition of Victoria's Drawing Rooms had significantly broadened, with the professional classes making up a full quarter of those in attendance. Nancy W. Ellenberger, "The Transformation of London 'Society' at the End of Victoria's Reign: Evidence from the Court Presentation Records," *Albion* 22, no. 4 (Winter 1990): 633–53.

127. "Ladies' Army and Navy Club," *Queen*, April 26, 1902, 716; "The Ladies' Empire Club," *Queen*, May 17, 1902, 839. On the history of the Primrose League and conservative women's political activism, see Beatrix Campbell, *The Iron Ladies: Why Do Women Vote Tory?* (London: Virago, 1987); Linda Walker, "Party Political Women: A Comparative Study of Liberal Women and the Primrose League, 1890–1914," in Rendall, *Equal or Different*, 165–91; Martin Pugh, *The Tories and the People, 1880–1935* (Oxford: Basil Blackwell, 1985).

128. "A New Ladies' Club," *Queen*, July 2, 1910, 12.

129. *Graphic*, March 28, 1908, 445. In addition to holding events at hotels and restaurants, some clubs found permanent homes in these "commercial" institutions. For example, the Ladies' Automobile Club made Claridge's Hotel their headquarters, renting out a variety of sitting and other rooms for their 270 members. See "London's Latest: Hotels Instead of Homes, The Scene of Beautiful Gatherings," *Daily Illustrated Mirror*, June 20, 1904. PCMA/4, Savoy Hotel Archives, Savoy Hotel, London.

130. Margaret Polsen Murray, "Women's Clubs in America," *Nineteenth Century* 47 (May 1899): 847. That same year, Beatrice Barham wrote that American clubs were less concerned with providing an urban rendezvous and were more "serious" in their aim. "Women's Clubs in America," *Englishwoman* 9 (June 1899), 506.

131. Annie Swan Smith, excerpt from *America at Home: Impressions of a Visit in War Time* (London: Oliphants, 1919), republished in *With Women's Eyes: Visitors to the New World, 1775–1918*, comp. and ed. Marion Tinling (Hamden, Conn.: Archon, 1993), 185. A similar argument may be found in Janet E. Courtney, *Recollected in Tranquility* (London: William Heinemann, 1926), 257.

132. Quoted in Dora d'Espaigne, "Lyceum Club: An International Club for Women," *Girl's Own Paper*, 602, ca. 1910, clipping #367.9421, Westminster City Archives, London. For a history of this institution, see Smedley, *Crusaders*; Adelaide Johnson, "The Lyceum Club of London: An Organization of Women Engaged in Literary, Artistic, and Scientific Pursuits," *Critic* 86 (1905): 132–37; See also "What Is the Lyceum Club Doing," *Queen*, October 1, 1904, 539; and *The Lyceum: Monthly Journal of the Lyceum Club*. The club evidently began publishing the journal in 1904, but I have been able to find volumes only from the 1920s. More work could be done on this extraordinary organization. By the 1920s, the club had become an international organization that claimed to have over ten thousand members and thirty clubhouses throughout the world.

133. W. Macqueen-Pope, *Goodbye Piccadilly* (New York: Drake, 1972), 89–91.

134. Vicinus, *Independent Women*, 295–99.

135. "Family Budgets," *Cornhill Magazine* 10 (January–June 1901): 791.

136. See, for example, *Bye-Laws and Regulations* (London: London Lyceum Club, 1934).

137. *Drapers' Record*, January 24, 1894, 195.

138. *Harrod's General Catalogue for 1905* (London: Harrod's, 1905), 13, Harrod's Instore Archive, London. The Edwardian Whiteley's also included several restaurants, luncheon rooms, and "luxurious club rooms." "The New Whiteley's," *Queen*, November 5, 1911, 814; and "The New Whiteley's," *Daily News*, November 23, 1911.

139. Before he opened his store, Selfridge had collected menus, photographs, newspaper

clippings, and other ephemera from famous restaurants and clubs in both Europe and the United States. He replicated many aspects of these urban institutions in his new store. See chapter 5 below.

140. *Evening Standard*, February 16, 1910.

141. *Pall Mall Gazette*, May 17, 1909, 10.

142. One "expert" believed that there were five such tearooms in Bond Street in 1902. This "expert" warned that this was a particularly difficult place to start such a business since the "rents were enormous, sometimes eight hundred a year, sometimes more. . . . The public is so spoilt that it will not have tea except to the accompaniment of flowers and music, dainty gowns and well-dressed hair." "Concerning Tea Rooms," in *Queen*, February 1, 1902, 194.

143. See a description of this venture in the *Lady's Realm* 1 (1897): 215–16 and 331.

144. *Englishwoman's Review*, July 30, 1893, 195.

145. Horace Wyndham, "Ladies' Tea-Shops in London," *Lady's Realm* 7 (1900): 738.

146. *BC*, November 24, 1888. Mrs. Cooper-Oakley opened the Dorothy in Mortimer Street to feed shop assistants and other lower-middle-class workers and students. Its decor was quite sparse in comparison with clubs. See the illustration and article on the restaurant in *Lady*, January 3, 1889, 4–5. It was evidently so successful, however, that within a year a second branch was opened at 446 Oxford Street. The *Lady* commented that "these rooms are the prettiest in London, and best adapted for their purpose. . . . Downstairs there is a very commodious lavatory, fitted with hot and cold water." June 20, 1889, 642. The Dorothy became the butt of satire in a poem, "Diana at Dinner," *Punch, or The London Charivari*, June 28, 1890, 303. For similar enterprises, see "Restaurants for Working Girls," *Queen*, March 26, 1904, 558.

147. "Seventy-Five Years of Catering," (Catering Division J. Lyons and Company, Ltd., n.d.), J. Lyons and Company Limited Archive; Richardson, "J. Lyons and Co." 161–72. Lyons quickly branched out into the restaurant business, owning the luxurious Trocadero as well as the moderately priced Corner Houses. See George Edgar, "Mr Joseph Lyons: A Character Sketch," *Modern Business* 3, no. 3 (April 1909): 207–12.

148. By 1909 there were twenty-four of these "modern" shops. R. Strauss, "Original Retailers: Mr. W. B. Fuller," *Modern Business* 3, no. 5 (June 1909): 450–52.

149. *BC*, February 18, 1899.

150. "Shopping," *Queen*, June 17, 1893, 1015.

151. Richardson, "J. Lyons and Co. Ltd," 166. It is difficult to say how much of the Savoy's innovations were instituted by Richard D'Oyle Carte or his second wife, the college-educated actress Helen Cowper-Black. George Edwardes claimed that "the whole foundation of the Savoy business rested on her." Quoted in Compton Mackenzie, *The Savoy of London* (London: George G. Harrap, 1953), 45. Also see Jackson, *The Savoy*, 21. The most well known of the female hoteliers in this period, however, was Rosa Lewis, the cockney-born "Duchess of Jermyn Street." Daphne Fielding, *The Duchess of Jermyn Street: The Life and Good Times of Rosa Lewis and the Cavendish Hotel* (Harmondsworth: Penguin, 1978).

152. Beatty Kingston, et al. *Homes of the Passing Show* (London: Savoy Press, 1900), 53.

153. Clement Scott, *How They Dined Us in 1860 and How they Dine Us Now* (n.p. 1900), 22.

154. For Edwardian accounts of hotels and the transformation of public life, see, for example, Shaw, *London in the Sixties*; Julius M. Price, *Dame Fashion* (London: Sampson, Low, Marston, 1912), 155; Cook, *Highways and Byways of London*, 32–33. Also see Finklestein, *Dining Out*, 40–50; Thorne, "Places of Refreshment."

155. See, for example, "London Clubs—Their Changing Spirit," *Times*, July 3, 1913; "London Clubs: Their Decline and Its Causes: The Restaurant Habit," *Times*, April 25, 1914.

156. Newnham-Davis, "Is Club-Life Doomed?" *Daily Mail*, December 6, 1906, 5.

157. Champneys, *Drummond*, 289.

158. Evidently the Ladies Army and Navy Club continued to prosper. In 1927 it moved into the mansion formerly belonging to the Earl Spencer. See "Famous Mansion as Women's Club—History and Beauty of Spencer House," dated June 1927, source unknown, Philip Norman Collection, C.57.2, Guildhall Libary, London. For the way clubs were understood during this period, see "A New Club for Busy Women," *Shopping News and Notes* (January 1926): 3–4; "An Ideal Club for Ladies," *Shopping News and Notes* (April 1926): 11, 30–31; "A Distinguished Club in a Historical Setting," *Shopping News and Notes* (May 1926): 17. As late as 1943 an expert on men's clubs wrote about the "infiltration" of clubs by ladies, the new "cock and hen" clubs, and the advent of ladies' clubs as a "modern development." Bernard Darwin, *British Clubs* (London: Collins, 1947), 33. Twentieth-century Londoners were thus quite unaware that dozens of women's clubs had once lined West End streets.

159. Winding-up proceedings for the Ladies Lyceum Club, PRO J13/13795, no. 00275 of 1933. For the fate of other clubs, see winding-up proceedings of the Ladies Clubs Limited, PRO J13/3728, no. 00186 of 1904; and Ladies Carlton Club PRO J13/12390, no. 00309 of 1930. For an example of the expenses that clubs had incurred, see the debt that Heal's was attempting to recover from the Ladies Automobile Club in 1921. Board Meeting Minute Book, October 21, 1921, AAD-1978, SU 78; Heal's Archives, Archive of Art and Design, Victoria and Albert Museum, London.

Chapter Four
Metropolitan Journeys

1. Krout, *A Looker On in London*, 5.

2. A similar relationship existed between men's clubs and the press. Stephen Koss, *The Rise and Fall of the Political Press in Britain: The Nineteenth Century* (Chapel Hill: University of North Carolina Press, 1981), 158–59.

3. Walkowitz, *City of Dreadful Delight*, 41. Raymond Williams explored the diverse narratives of the late-Victorian city in *The Country and the City*, 213–32.

4. Bennet Burleigh quoted in Jones, *Outcast London*, 296.

5. Walkowitz, *City of Dreadful Delight*, 25.

6. Showalter, *Sexual Anarchy*.

7. Andrew Mearns, *The Bitter Cry of Outcast London. An Inquiry into the Condition of the Abject Poor* (London: London Congregational Union, 1883).

8. Margaret Fletcher, *O, Call Back Yesterday* (Oxford: Basil Blackwell, 1939), 73.

9. George Gissing, *In the Year of Jubilee* (1894; reprint, New York: Dover, 1982), 25, 42.

10. Ibid., 61–62.

11. James W. Drawbell, "How the Press Caters for Women's Interests," in *The Press, 1898–1948* (London: Newspaper World, 1948), 118. In her study of how the daily press represented London, Garside briefly notes that in the early part of the twentieth century, "shopping came to dominate the *Illustrated London News*' regular 'Ladies Page.'" Patricia L. Garside, "Representing the Metropolis: The Changing Relationship between London and the Press, 1870–1939," *London Journal* 16, no. 2 (1991): 167. A limited number of women's magazines and books, such as E. E. Perkins, *The Lady's Shopping Manual and Mercury Album* (London: T. Hurst, 1834), offered consumer advice to female readers in the early part of the century.

12. On travel and authenticity, see Erik Cohen, "Authenticity and Commoditization in Tourism," *Annals of Tourism Research* 15 (1988): 371–86. For a structural analysis of tour guides' role in the creation of the "authentic," see Erik Cohen, "The Tourist Guide: The Origins, Structure, and Dynamics of a Role," *Annals of Tourism Research* 12, no. 1 (1985): 5–29; and Elizabeth C. Fine and Jean Haskell Speer, "Tour Guide Performances as Sight Sacralization," *Annals of Tourism Research* 12, no. 1 (1985): 73–95.

13. Gerry Kearns and Chris Philo argue that the "practice of selling places" to businesses, tourists, and residents has an economic logic, but also may operate as a "subtle form of socialization designed to convince local people, many of whom will be disadvantaged and potentially disaffected, that they are important cogs in a successful community." *Selling Places: The City as Cultural Capital, Past and Present* (Oxford: Pergamon, 1993), 3. For the creation of places as tourist sights, see Dean MacCannell, *The Tourist: A New Theory of the Leisure Class* (New York: Schocken Books, 1976); M. Christine Boyer, "Cities for Sale: Merchandising History at South Street Seaport," in Sorkin, *Variations on a Theme Park*, 181–204; Gregory Ashworth and Brian Goodall, eds., *Marketing Tourism Places* (London: Routledge, 1990); Gregory Ashworth and J. E. Tunbridge, *The Tourist-Historic City* (London: Belhaven Press, 1990). In their overview of recent social science literature on consumption and urbanism, Glennie and Thrift argue that "more attention needs to be paid to how centres manage to attract all manner of people to them again and again." "Modernity, Urbanism and Modern Consumption," 439.

14. On tourism and the commodification of vision, see John Urry, *The Tourist Gaze: Leisure and Travel in Contemporary Societies* (London: Sage, 1990); MacCannell, *The Tourist*; James Buzard, *The Beaten Track: European Tourism, Literature, and the Ways to Culture, 1800–1918* (Oxford: Clarendon Press, 1993); and Friedberg, *Window Shopping*. For a review of MacCannell's book and further discussion of the semiotics of tourism, see Georges Van Den Abbeele, "Sightseers: The Tourist as Theorist," *Diacritics* 10, no. 4 (December 1980): 2–14. The history of the tourist gaze has been explored by Judith Adler, "Origins of Sightseeing," *Annals of Tourism Research* 16 (1989): 7–29. Also see Ellen Furlough, "Packaging Plea-

sures: Club Mediterranée and French Consumer Culture, 1950–1968," *French Historical Studies* 18 no. 1 (Spring 1993): 65–81. John Benson sees both tourism and shopping as core facets of the rise of consumer society, but he does not explicitly address their relationship. *The Rise of Consumer Society*, chaps. 3 and 4.

15. Walkowitz, *City of Dreadful Delight*, 18.

16. Several recent studies have argued that women's magazines were agents in the construction of feminine identities, including that of shopper. See, for example, Ros Ballaster, Margaret Beetham, and Sandra Hebron, *Women's Worlds: Ideology, Femininity, and the Woman's Magazine* (London: Macmillan, 1991); Margaret Beetham, *A Magazine of Her Own? Domesticity and Desire in the Woman's Magazine, 1800–1914* (London: Routledge, 1996), 8; Christopher Breward, "Femininity and Consumption: The Problem of the Late-Nineteenth-Century Fashion Journal," *Journal of Design History* 7, no. 2 (1994): 71–89. For a general overview of the women's press, see Cynthia L. White, *Women's Magazines, 1693–1968* (London: Michael Joseph, 1970). For an analysis of contemporary journals, see Janice Winship, *Inside Women's Magazines* (London: Pandora, 1987). For a business history, see Brian Braithwaite, *Women's Magazines: The First 300 Years* (London: Peter Owen, 1995). For the pre-Victorian era, see Alison Adburgham, *Women in Print: Writing Women and Women's Magazines from the Restoration to the Accession of Victoria* (London: George Allen and Unwin, 1972); and Kathryn Shevelow, *Women and Print Culture: The Construction of Femininity in the Early Periodical* (London: Routledge, 1989).

There has been even more work on the relationship between women's magazines and American consumer culture, much of it focusing on the *Ladies' Home Journal.* See Helen Damon-Moore, *Magazines for the Millions: Gender and Commerce in the "Ladies' Home Journal" and the "Saturday Evening Post," 1880–1910* (Albany: State University of New York Press, 1994); and Jennifer Scanlon, *Inarticulate Longings: The "Ladies' Home Journal," Gender, and the Promises of Consumer Culture* (New York: Routledge, 1995). Christopher Wilson has argued that the *Ladies' Home Journal*, like other mass-market magazines, transformed reading into a passive, consumerist activity. He suggests that through innovations in "style, format, and reader participation," journals such as the *Ladies Home Journal* "directly contributed to the rise of consumer culture." Christopher P. Wilson, "The Rhetoric of Consumption: Mass-Market Magazines and the Demise of the Gentle Reader, 1880–1920," in *The Culture of Consumption: Critical Essays in American History, 1880–1980*, ed. Richard Wrightman Fox and T. J. Jackson Lears (New York: Pantheon Books, 1983), 39–64, 42. Also see Ellen Gruber Garvey's recent study, *The Adman in the Parlor: Magazines and the Gendering of Consumer Culture, 1880s to 1910s* (New York: Oxford University Press, 1996).

17. Breward, "Femininity and Consumption," 71, 83.

18. Beetham, Ballaster, and Hebron have argued that "Women's magazines contain, within single issues and between different titles, many competing and contradictory notions of femininity." *Women's Worlds*, 22, also see 12. Beetham has further pointed out how femininities constructed in women's magazines developed in contrast both to shifting notions of masculinity and to gender identities being constructed "outside" of the magazine. Beetham, *A Magazine of Her Own*, 4–5, and pt. 2, "New Woman, New Journalism, the 1880s and 1890s."

19. In her recent study of the various ways in which the "woman reader" was constituted in the nineteenth century, Kate Flint argues that female reading was in a sense always a form of "consumption associated with the possession of leisure time." *The Woman Reader, 1837–1914* (Oxford: Clarendon Press, 1993), 11.

20. One scholar has estimated that there were 48 new middle-class women's magazines started during these years. White, *Women's Magazines*, 58. Beetham found at least 120 female journals founded during this same period. *A Magazine of Her Own?* 122.

21. Joel H. Wiener, "How New Was the New Journalism?" in *Papers for the Millions: The New Journalism in Britain, 1850s to 1914*, ed. Joel H. Wiener (Westport, Conn.: Greenwood Press, 1988), 62; and White, *Women's Magazines*, 63. On the editorial and organizational shifts in the press after the 1850s, see Joel H. Wiener, ed. *Innovators and Preachers: The Role of the Editor in Victorian England* (Westport, Conn.: Greenwood Press, 1985); Laurel Brake, Aled Jones, Lionel Madden, eds. *Investigating Victorian Journalism* (New York: St. Martin's Press, 1990); Alan J. Lee, *The Origins of the Popular Press in England, 1855–1914* (London: Croom Helm, 1976); and Lucy Brown, *Victorian News and Newspapers* (Oxford: Clarendon Press, 1985). The mechanization of newspaper production has been detailed by A. E. Musson, "Newspaper Printing in the Industrial Revolution," *Economic History Review*, 2d ser., 10, no. 3 (1958): 411–26. On the growth of literacy see, Richard D. Altick, *The English Common Reader: A Social History of the*

Mass Reading Public, 1800–1900 (Chicago: University of Chicago Press, 1963); Raymond Williams, *The Long Revolution* (London: Chatto and Windus, 1961). For a study of women, mass periodicals, and the mass public prior to the 1860s, see Sally Mitchell, *The Fallen Angel: Chastity, Class, and Women's Reading, 1835–1880* (Bowling Green, Ohio: Bowling Green University, Poplar Press, 1981), especially chap. 1, "Woman's Place: Penny Weekly Family Magazines of the 1840s and 1850s," 1–21.

22. Two studies of this influential women's magazine are Charlotte C. Watkins, "Editing a 'Class Journal': Four Decades of the *Queen*," in Wiener, *Innovators and Preachers*, 185–200; and Beetham, *A Magazine of Her Own?* 89–111. Though it is extremely difficult to estimate circulation during this period, Watkins believed that the journal's circulation was 23,500 in 1890, falling to 16,000 by 1900. The paper is still published today.

23. White, *Women's Magazines*, 44.

24. Ibid., 42. In comparison, *The Times* had a circulation of 60,000 in 1858. This far surpassed its main rivals, however. T. R. Nevett, "Advertising and Editorial Integrity in the Nineteenth Century," in *The Press in English Society from the Seventeenth to the Nineteenth Centuries*, ed. Michael Harris and Alan Lee (London: Fairleigh Dickinson University Press, 1986), 152.

25. Quoted in Watkins, "Editing a 'Class Journal,'" 186.

26. Beetham argues that it was difficult for the journal's editor to define precisely what constituted women's "news," and that the *Queen* eventually was modeled more upon the *Illustrated London News* than *The Times* or similar paper. Beetham, *A Magazine of Her Own?* 90–96.

27. Charles Cavers, *Hades! The Ladies! Being Extracts from the Diary of a Draper, Charles Cavers, Esq.* (London: Gurney and Jackson, 1933), 18, 32.

28. *Queen*, September 7, 1861, 1.

29. *Queen*, April 12, 1862, 97. White has argued that the *Queen*, like most women's magazines, did not support women's suffrage. *Women's Magazines*, 49–50. However, this was not exactly true. For the *Queen's* relationship to feminist politics, see Theodora Bostick, "The Press and the Launching of the Woman's Suffrage Movement, 1866–1867," *Victorian Periodicals Review* 13, no. 4 (Winter 1980): 125–31.

30. See, for example, the first part of the series "London Interiors: Home of the Spitalfield's Silk-Weaver," *Queen*, September 21, 1861, 36.

31. Watkins, "Editing a 'Class Journal,'" 187.

32. On Greenwood's career, see B. I. Diamond, "A Precursor of the New Journalism: Frederick Greenwood of the *Pall Mall Gazette*," in Wiener, *Papers for the Millions*, 25–45. Greenwood introduced some of the innovations he would bring to the *PMG* in the first issues of the *Queen*. Rosemary T. Van Arsdel has begun to examine the relationship between women's magazines and the new journalism in "Women's Periodicals and the New Journalism: The Personal Interview," in Wiener, *Papers for the Millions*, 243–56. Also see Beetham, *A Magazine of her Own?* chap. 8. Evidently Matthew Arnold coined the term "new journalism" in an article published in the *Nineteenth Century* in 1887. On this point, see Brake, *Subjugated Knowledges*, 83.

33. Watkins, "Editing a 'Class Journal,'" 187–88.

34. Joel Wiener argues that the varying degrees of influence held by proprietors, editors, subeditors, and writers is virtually impossible to determine. Joel H. Wiener, "Sources for the Study of Newspapers," in *Investigating Victorian Journalism*, 155–65.

35. On Yates's career as society gossip, see Joel H. Wiener, "Edmund Yates: The Gossip as Editor," in Brake, Jones, and Madden, *Innovators and Preachers*, 259–74.

36. Peel, *Life's Enchanted Cup*, 64. For the identities of some of the authors and subeditors, see Watkins, "Editing a 'Class Journal.'"

37. Peel, *Life's Enchanted Cup*, 160.

38. "Mrs. M. E. Haweis: A Sketch of Her Life and Work," *Englishwoman*, February 9, 1899, 172–75. Female journalists met with vicious social criticism in the pages of *Punch* and other humor magazines. See Marks, *Bicycles, Bangs, and Bloomers*, 85–87; and John Stokes, *In the Nineties* (Chicago: University of Chicago Press, 1989), 25. Elaine Showalter has argued that by the 1880s many male novelists and writers believed that their profession was being feminized. She notes that during these years approximately 40 percent of the authors being published by the larger houses in England were female and that women writers were also coming to dominate the world of periodical publishing. Showalter, *Sexual Anarchy*, 76–77.

39. Many of these writers considered themselves politically conservative and by no means all female journalists worked for women's magazines. In fact, the first woman writer to draw a fixed salary was Eliza Lynn Linton. Anderson, *Woman against Women*. One of the most influential women journalists in the 1890s was the staunch imperialist Flora Shaw, who dur-

ing this decade was colonial editor for *The Times*. Helen Callaway and Dorothy O. Helly, "Crusader for Empire: Flora Shaw/Lady Lugard," in *Western Women and Imperialism: Complicity and Resistance*, ed. Napur Chaudhuri and Margaret Strobel (Bloomington: Indiana University Press, 1992): 79–87. There is no full-length study of women journalists, however. See Rubinstein, *Before the Suffragettes*, 85–87; and Arnold Bennett, *Journalism for Women: A Practical Guide* (London: John Lane, 1898).

40. *Lady*, February 19, 1885, 1. Like the *Queen*, the journal was a six-penny weekly.

41. *Lady*, October 28, 1886, 351.

42. About the same time Lowe was replaced by a male editor at the *Queen*. The *Lady* sold fewer than 2,500 copies an issue during its first year. Eventually it reached a circulation of just under 18,000 in 1895 and nearly 28,000 by 1905, and is still published today.

43. "Woman's World," *St. James Gazette*, December 20, 1893, 12.

44. Of course, as Marjorie Ferguson has argued in her study of contemporary women's magazines, *Forever Feminine: Women's Magazines and the Cult of Femininity* (London: Heinemann, 1983), when such texts discuss economic or political topics they do so through a feminine lens and thus still underscore a division between male and female.

45. Burton argues that late-Victorian and Edwardian feminists justified their role in the public sphere by identifying "themselves with the national interest and their cause with the future prosperity of the nation state." Antoinette Burton, *Burdens of History: British Feminists, Indian Women, and Imperial Culture, 1865–1915* (Chapel Hill: University of North Carolina Press, 1994), 5.

46. *Lady*, February 19, 1885, 1.

47. *The Gentlewoman: The Illustrated Journal for Gentlewomen*, July 12, 1890, 1.

48. Beetham, *A Magazine of Her Own?* 90.

49. Walter Benjamin, *Charles Baudelaire: A Lyric Poet in the Era of High Capitalism*, trans. Harry Zohn (London: Verso, 1983), 36.

50. Williams, *The Country and the City*, 233. For a related study of American literature, see Dana Brand, *The Spectator and the City in Nineteenth-Century American Literature* (Cambridge: Cambridge University Press, 1991).

51. Anne Friedberg and others have recently discussed tourism and shopping as a kind of *flânerie* in which men and women come to see the world through "a mobilized" and "virtual" gaze. *Window Shopping*, 2. For a related argument, see the introduction and essays in Charney and Schwartz, *Cinema and the Invention of Modern Life*.

52. Pollock, *Vision and Difference*, 67; Wolff, "The Invisible Flâneuse," 37–48. This viewpoint has been most directly pursued in feminist film studies, which will be explored more fully in the final chapter.

53. Buck-Morss, "The Flâneur, the Sandwichman, and the Whore," 105.

54. Bowlby, *Just Looking*, 11.

55. Elizabeth Wilson has criticized Pollock and Wolff for accepting women's absence from the public as fact rather than ideology. Wilson, "The Invisible Flâneur," *New Left Review* 191 (January–February 1992): 104–5. Also see her book *Adorned in Dreams*, 30–31. Mica Nava's "Modernity's Disavowal" is the most recent analysis of this feminist debate.

56. Walkowitz, *City of Dreadful Delight*, 17. See also Priscilla Parkhurst Ferguson, "The Flaneur: Urbanization and Its Discontents," in *Home and Its Dislocations in Nineteenth-Century France*, ed. Suzanne Nash (Albany: State University of New York Press, 1993). On female social reformers and charity workers, see Ross, *Love and Toil*; Walkowitz, *Prostitution and Victorian Society*, esp. 69–147; Vicinus, *Independent Women*, 211–46; Nord, *Walking the Victorian Streets*, 181–236. For twentieth-century women writers, see Susan Merrill Squier, *Virginia Woolf and London: The Sexual Politics of the City* (Chapel Hill: University of North Carolina Press, 1984); Susan Merrill Squier, ed., *Women Writers and the City: Essays in Feminist Literary Criticism* (Knoxville: University of Tennessee Press, 1985); and Christine Wick Sizemore, *A Female Vision of the City: London in the Novels of Five British Women* (Knoxville: University of Tennessee Press, 1989).

57. Nord, *Walking the Victorian Streets*, 4, 117.

58. Friedberg, *Window Shopping*, 36.

59. Brontë, *Villette*, 109.

60. On the panoptic gaze, see Michel Foucault, *Discipline and Punish: The Birth of the Prison*, trans. Alan Sheridan (New York: Pantheon, 1977), 195–228. Although Foucault opposed the spectacle and surveillance, recent scholars have shown how these two modes of looking work together in the modern period. Friedberg, *Window Shopping*; Bennett, "The Exhibitionary Complex"; Jonathan Crary, *Techniques of the Observer: On Vision and Modernity in the Nineteenth Century* (Cambridge: MIT Press, 1990); Schivelbusch, *The Railway Journey*, 61–64, 189–97. Margaret Cohen locates the emergence of "panoramic literature" as a new approach to representing the "everyday" during the July Monarchy. "Panoramic Literature and the Invention of Everyday Genres," in Charney and Schwartz, *Cinema and the Invention of Modern Life*, 228.

Schwartz also argued that panoramas and dioramas flourished in the 1880s and 1890s because they presented "an already familiar version of reality—a reality in which life was captured through motion," "Cinematic Spectatorship before the Apparatus: The Public Taste for Reality in *Fin-de-Siècle* Paris," in Charney and Schwartz, *Cinema and the Invention of Modern Life*, 311.

61. Mayhew, *Shops and Companies*, 86.

62. Lambert, *The Universal Provider*, 62.

63. Lucy's position is much like that of the placeless governess. See, for example, M. Jeanne Peterson, "The Victorian Governess: Status Incongruence in Family and Society," in *Suffer and Be Still: Women in the Victorian Age*, ed. Martha Vicinus (Bloomington: Indiana University Press, 1972) and Poovey, *Uneven Developments*, 126–63.

64. Walter Benjamin, "Paris, Capital of the Nineteenth Century," in *Reflections: Essays, Aphorisms, Autobiographical Writings*, ed. Peter Demetz, trans. Edmund Jephcott (New York: Harcourt Brace Jovanovich, 1978), 156.

65. de Certeau, *The Practice of Everyday Life*, 103.

66. Winter, *London's Teeming Streets*, 10. On the market metaphor, see Max Byrd, *London Transformed: Images of the City in the Eighteenth Century* (New Haven: Yale University Press, 1978), 12; Raban, *Soft City*, 92–93. For related studies of urban representation, see Williams, *The Country and the City*; Andrew Lees, *Cities Perceived: Urban Society in European and American Thought, 1820–1940* (New York: Columbia University Press, 1985); Steven Marcus, "Reading the Illegible," in *The Victorian City*, 1:257–76. According to George Levine, many Victorian artists and authors simply failed to confront the urban experience. "From 'Know-Not-Where' to 'Nowhere': The City in Carlyle, Ruskin, and Morris," in Dyos and Wolff, *The Victorian City* 2:495–516. Also see the related essays in sec. 5 of "Ideas in the Air," in Dyos and Wolff, *The Victorian City* 2:431–84.

67. A typical 1861 essay, for example, extolled the delights of "Refreshment Rooms" in the South Kensington Museum, Mme Tussaud's "exhibition," and the Pantheon and Soho Bazaars. *Queen*, September 21, 1861, 41–42.

68. *Queen*, March 15, 1862, 26.

69. *Queen*, March 29, 1862, 68.

70. *Queen*, March 26, 1864, 239.

71. See, for example, the *Queen*, September 21, 1861, 35–36; October 26, 1861, 145–52.

72. *Queen*, March 3, 1866, 159. In the 1830s, London's streets were illuminated by gaslight, and plate glass began to replace the smaller, older panes in shop windows. Michael R. Booth, *Victorian Spectacular Theatre, 1850–1910* (London: Routledge and Kegan Paul, 1981), 4; Schivelbusch, *Disenchanted Night*.

73. Bennett, "Exhibitionary Complex."

74. Sala, *Twice round the Clock*. Ironically, commercial culture was in part created by writers who were profoundly ambivalent, indeed marginalized, by an expanding mass market in literature. Bowlby, *Just Looking*, 83–117.

75. Mayhew, *The Shops and Companies of London* 1:4. This journal adopted the jingoistic tone of the travel guides to Germany that Mayhew had just completed. Mayhew's biographer labeled this unsuccessful journal "a high-class advertising special." Anne Humpherys, *Henry Mayhew* (Boston: Twayne, 1984), 42.

76. Mayhew, *Shops and Companies*, 5.

77. "Shopping without Money," *Leisure Hour* 14 (London 1865): 110.

78. Raban, *Soft City*, 97. Nord argues that this image of London was common during the early-nineteenth century and owed much to early forms of popular literature. *Walking the Victorian Streets*, 31.

79. "The London Shop-Fronts," *Chamber's Journal of Popular Literature, Science, and Art*, October 15, 1864, 670.

80. "Going a-Shopping," *Leisure Hour* 15 (1866): 198.

81. Victor Fournel, *Ce qu'on voit dans les rues de Paris*, (Paris, 1858), quoted in Walter Benjamin, *Charles Baudelaire*, 69.

82. *Queen*, September 7, 1861, 15.

83. *Queen*, September 21, 1861, 38.

84. This sanitized city that could be pleasurably and safely explored by the bourgeoisie was easily translated into advertising copy that could serve the interests of West End retailers. In the mid-1860s, the Regent Street clothiers H. J. and D. Nicolls published a pamphlet as a "slight memoranda to the guidance of purchasers in this 'the street of streets.' " This advertisement presented Regent Street as an honest, respectable, and safe place. "Where else throughout Europe, could we send a child to purchase with less fear of being impaired upon than in that new fashionable resort." *A Visit to Regent Street* (London: Henry Vizetelly, ca. 1865), 3.

85. Lady Beatrice Violet Greville, *Faiths and Fashions: Short Essays Republished* (London: Longmans, Green, 1880), 248.

86. Greville, *Faiths and Fashions*, 249, 257. For a similarly ambivalent treatment of shopping by a female journalist, see Lady Jeune, "The Ethics of Shopping," *Fortnightly Review*, 57 (January–June 1895), 123–32.

87. Lady Beatrice Violet Greville, *Vignettes of Memory* (London: Hutchinson, 1927), 149.

88. John Berger, *Ways of Seeing* (London: Penguin, 1972), 46.

89. Beetham, *A Magazine of Her Own?* 96.

90. Ibid., 150.

91. Davies observes that a new genre of popular fiction, known as "railway fiction," emerged in the 1840s and by 1851 was already associated with "the unregenerate tastes of the 'unknown public.'" Tony Davies, "Transports of Pleasure: Fiction and Its Audiences in the Later Nineteenth Century," in Jameson, *Formations of Pleasure*, 49.

92. Peel, *Life's Enchanted Cup*, 62, 95.

93. Ibid., 95. Peel, like Greville, remembered that "although I was quietly dressed, and I hope looked what I was, a respectable young woman, there was scarcely a day when I, while waiting for the omnibus, was not accosted" (105–6).

94. *Saturday Review*, August 20, 1881, 231.

95. Ben Singer, "Modernity, Hyperstimulus, and the Rise of Popular Sensationalism," in Charney and Schwartz, *Cinema and the Invention of Modern Life*, 72–99.

96. On the discussion of ladies's carriages, see Stephen Fiske, *English Photographs* (London: Tinsley Brothers, 1869). Schivelbusch argues that after the Briggs murder in a railway compartment in 1864 the English feared that the privacy of the compartment also made them vulnerable. Schivelbusch, *The Railway Journey*, 83–88. See, for example, the *Bayswater Chronicle*'s coverage of the report on ladies' carriages produced by the Board of Trade on July 3 and August 14, 1875. The topic arose again in 1887 when a Miss Scragg was brutally assaulted while traveling from Wellington to Shrewsbury. After this incident the Board of Trade sent a circular to all the railway companies, asking what arrangements they had to insure the safety of single female travelers. See the discussions in *The Times* between August 29 and 30, 1887 and again on September 3, 1887; February 23 and 28, 1888. For similar anxieties in America during this period, see Virginia Scharff, *Taking the Wheel: Women and the Coming of the Motor Age* (Albuquerque: University of New Mexico Press, 1992), 6–7; and Patricia Cline Cohen, "Safety and Danger: Women on American Public Transport," in Helly and Reverby, *Gendered Domains*, 109–23.

97. *Lady*, May 6, 1886, 349; and May 13, 1886, 369.

98. *Lady*, September 8, 1887, 178.

99. *Queen*, August 15, 1896, 294.

100. *Queen*, January 7, 1893, 2.

101. *Queen*, July 29, 1893, 193.

102. *Queen*, July 2, 1900, 2. Compare this to the description of the management of suburban railways in the *Queen*, December 18, 1897, 1150. In 1902, the journal criticized the poor ventilation of London's Central Line as compared to the well-ventilated Parisian Metro. See March 22, 1902, 470. The *Lady's* legal editor frequently informed women of their rights as omnibus passengers. See, for example, *Lady*, December 6, 1888, 550.

103. *Lady*, October 25, 1888, 370.

104. *Lady*, February 5, 1891, 154.

105. *Queen*, March 12, 892, 398.

106. *Queen*, March 29, 1913, 556. The 'bus was often called a "democratic" vehicle. For example, in 1898 the first issue of *The Bus, Tram, and Cab Trades Gazette* claimed that "Everybody rides in omnibuses in these democratic days." October 29, 1894, 14.

107. *Lady*, September 17, 1891, 334.

108. Ibid.

109. *Lady*, August 6, 1891, 172.

110. *Lady*, August 13, 1891, 198.

111. *Queen*, April 12, 1913, 646.

112. New, *The Complete Novels and Writings of Amy Levy*, 386–87.

113. A. France, "The Way for All"; M. Laurence, "Always Warm and Bright," 1912; F. C. Whitney, "For Business or Pleasure," 1913. Publicity Poster Collection, London Transport Museum. More research needs to be done on the image of women and the urban crowd that these posters projected. There is unfortunately not enough space to do so here. Those interested in its history may consult Oliver Green, *Underground Art: London Transport Posters, 1908 to the Present* (London: Studio Vista, 1990); and Christian Barmen, *The Man Who Built London Transport: A Biography of Frank Pick* (London: David and Charles, 1979). For a contemporary discussion of poster art, see W. S. Rogers, *A Book of the Poster: Illustrated with Examples of the Work of the Principal Poster Artists of the World* (London: Greening, 1901); and for the comparison with New York City, see "Subway Advertising," *Outlook* 79 (January 1905): 4–5.

114. There were two posters, "Into the Heart of the Shopping Centres," in 1908 and 1910, artists unknown, and a very similar one by Agnes Richardson, "To the Shopping Centres," 1922. Artist Unknown, "The Only Way to the Theatre," 1912. Publicity Poster Collection, London Transport Museum.

115. Artist Unknown, "Milestones of Progress," 1913. Publicity Poster Collection, London Transport Museum.

116. E. A. Cox, "Look, Shop, Travel, Underground, 1915," Publicity Poster Collection, London Transport Museum.

117. Beetham, *A Magazine of Her Own?* 96.

118. de Certeau, *The Practice of Everyday Life*, 120. For a similar analysis of contemporary shopping, see Mark Gottdiener, "Recapturing the Center: A Semiotic Analysis of Shopping Malls," in *The City and the Sign: An Introduction to Urban Semiotics*, ed. Mark Gottdiener and Alexandros Ph. Lagopoulos (New York: Columbia University Press, 1986), 288–302.

119. On the difference between the way that "tours" and "maps" organize space, see de Certeau, *The Practice of Everyday Life*, 118–22.

120. "Shopping in London," *Lady*, June 28, 1888, 578. On one level, these adventures recast the age-old figures of the country bloke and the urban swell touring around London. Yet these two ladies visited a very different metropolis than that enjoyed by male ramblers in such texts as Pierce Egan's *Life in London*. See Nord's discussion of Egan's text in *Walking the Victorian Streets*, 31–40.

121. *Lady*, June 28, 1888, 578–80.

122. *Lady*, September 3, 1885, 768.

123. *Queen*, April 2, 1892, 520.

124. *Woman's World* (1889): 5.

125. *Lady*, May 31, 1888, 481.

126. *Queen*, April 2, 1892, 520.

127. *The Housewife: A Practical Magazine Concerning Everything in and about the Home* 3 (1888): 41.

128. *Lady*, March 21, 1889, 297. Another essayist similarly asserted that "modern shopping is a liberal education." *Lady*, April 26, 1888, 356.

129. "Shopping Expedition I" appeared in the *Lady*, April 26, 1888, 356. A new expedition appeared about once a month until spring 1889.

130. *Lady*, November 8, 1888, 424.

131. See, for example, *Lady*, May 31, 1888, 481; and *Englishwoman* (October 1895): 160.

132. *Lady*, October 25, 1888, 374.

133. *Englishwoman* 1, no. 1 (March 1895): 69.

134. *Englishwoman* 2, no. 8 (October 1895): 158. See also *Lady*, May 10, 1888, 408.

135. *Lady*, August 16, 1888, 150.

136. *Queen*, January 9, 1897, 62.

137. "Shopping," *Living Age*, December 22, 1906, 758.

138. *Lady*, April 4, 1889, 357. Also *Lady*, April 27, 1893, 514. On the way in which such cultural distinctions constructed social positions, see Bourdieu, *Distinction*.

139. *PMG*, May 26, 1909, 10.

140. *Englishwoman* 1, no. 2 (April 1895): 171.

141. *Lady*, September 6, 1888, 214

142. *Lady*, December 5, 1889, 622.

143. *Queen*, January 5, 1889, 22.

144. Burton, *Burdens of History*. The Lady Guides' political motivations were not those of the women writers analyzed by Nord in *Walking the Victorian Streets*, 181–236.

145. *Progress: The Organ of the Lady Guide Association* (1889–90): 2.

146. *Progress*, 2.

147. Richards, *The Commodity Culture of Victorian England*, 73–118.

148. *Progress*, 2.

149. *Progress*, 35.

150. *Queen*, January 5, 1889, 22.

151. Alden Hatch, *American Express: A Century of Service, 1850–1950* (New York: Doubleday, 1950), 100–101; and Peter Grossman, *American Express: The Unofficial History of the People Who Built the Great Financial Empire* (New York: Crown, 1987), 113. On the American Rendezvous, see Scrapbook, Dr. S. R. Ellison, "A Trip to Europe, April 9th–June 5th, 1898," Ellison Collection, New York Public Library. Whiteley's department store opened a travel agency a few months before the founding of the Lady Guide Association. *Drapers' Record*, November 17, 1889, 575.

152. *Progress*, 3.

153. *Queen*, July 12, 1890, 74.

154. *Particulars, &c. of the Lady Guide Association, Ltd., the London and International Reception, Inquiry, Information, and Supply Bureau*, 71.

155. *Woman's Gazette* 1, no. 5 (February 1876): 76.

156. *Lady*, November 5, 1885, 958.

157. *Lady*, November 12 and 19, 1885. See similar letters in the *Queen*, October 15, 1892, 647; October 6, 1894, 601; September 6, 1896, 461; and October 24, 1896, 792.

158. *Progress*, 4.

159. *Progress*, 5. On the commodification of women's work, see Glenna Matthews, *"Just a Housewife": The Rise and Fall of Domesticity in America* (New York: Oxford University Press, 1987); Ruth Schwartz Cowan, *More Work for Mother: The Ironies of Household Technology from the Open Hearth to the Microwave* (New York: Basic Books, 1983); Hayden, *Grand Domestic Revolution*.

160. *Graphic*, reprinted in *Progress*, 9.

161. *Progress*, 22.

162. "The Lady Guide's Valentine," *Lady*, February 12, 1891, 194.

163. Ibid., 195.

164. Ibid..

165. *Daily Telegraph*, reprinted in *Progress*, 7–8.

166. Recorded by Arthur J. Munby, *Red Note-Books*, 1860–61, quoted in Barret-Ducrocq, *Love in the Time of Victoria*, 52.

167. Walkowitz, *City of Dreadful Delight*, 50–52. Walkowitz developed this theme in her more recent "Going Public."

168. *Spectator*, reprinted in *Progress*, 10.

169. *Daily Telegraph*, reprinted in *Progress*, 7–8.

170. Walkowitz, *The City of Dreadful Delight*. Also see Davis, *Actresses as Working Women*, 139–45.

171. In 1889 the *Lady* even blamed "the American invasion from which Society is suffering" for "the distinct and steady decline in the time-honoured office of a chaperon." *Lady*, February 21, 1889, 185. It was fairly common to worry about the effect of the example of American girls on English youth. See for example, "The Americanising of Our Girls," *Bat*, February 23, 1886, 780.

172. Fletcher, *O, Call Back Yesterday*, 114–15.

173. *Queen*, June 5, 1882, 375. Many thanks to Ana Szolodko for finding this article.

174. *Daily Telegraph* printed in *Progress*, 8.

175. On the connection between tourism, commerce, and urban life, see Neil Harris, "Urban Tourism and the Commercial City," in *Inventing Times Square: Commerce and Culture at the Crossroads of the World*, ed. William Taylor (New York: Russell Sage Foundation, 1991); Simmons, "Railways, Hotels, and Tourism in Great Britain, 1839–1914." For a general social history of travel in Britain, see J. A. R. Pimlott, *The Englishman's Holiday: A Social History* (London: Faber and Faber, 1947); J. K. Walton, *The English Seaside Resort: A Social History, 1750–1914* (Leicester: Leicester University Press, 1983); and Ian Ousby, *The Englishman's England: Travel, Taste, and the Rise of Tourism* (Cambridge: Cambridge University Press, 1990); and the more general John Ash and Louis Turner, *The Golden Hordes: International Tourism and the Pleasure Periphery* (New York: St. Martin's Press, 1976).

176. *WDTJ*, July 19, 1884, 487.

177. "Shopping in London, Paris, and New York," *Drapers' Record*, November 16, 1888, 575; June 1, 1889, 636; August 9, 1890, 169–72.

178. Within a year Lady Guides had accompanied 290 families on sightseeing trips alone. *Lady*, November 6, 1890, 582.

179. "Address delivered upon the opening of the LGA Permanent Offices," printed in *Progress*, 19.

180. *Progress*, 18–19.

181. *Queen*, July 14, 1894, 89.

182. "The Lady Guides," *Queen*, April 5, 1902, 595. The exact date the Association closed its doors is unknown. In 1899 it still was in operation, but they had moved to a single office at 20 Haymarket.

183. Darley Dale, "Occupations for Women—The Lady Guide," *Englishwoman* 9 (April 1899): 317.

184. See, for example, "Shopping by Proxy: An American Idea," *Manchester Guardian*, October 25, 1927, no. #381.2:331.4, Fawcett Library, Newspaper Cuttings Collection.

185. See *West End Advertiser*, (1891); *Shopping: A Journal of Society for Society* (July 1895); *Shopping: A Literary and Artistic Mirror of the World of Women* (August 1902); and *London and Suburban A.B.C. Shopping Guide* (March 1911). A number of journals that began in the 1920s were more successful than earlier attempts. See for example, *Shopping Life: The Only Journal Which Makes a Direct Appeal to the Shopping Public* (November 1921–December 1924); and *Shopping News and Notes* (December 1924–September 1926). There were probably dozens of small guides published in this period, but few have been preserved. See, for example, an advertisement: "What to Buy and Where to Buy It," printed in *The Ladies' Home Paper: A Weekly Journal for Gentlewomen* 11 (April 10, 1909): 8.

186. *Olivia's Shopping and How She Does It: A Prejudiced Guide to the London Shops* (London: Gay and Bird, 1906), 7. There were other quite similar shopping guidebooks such as Frances Sheafer Waxman, *A Shopping Guide to Paris and London* (New York: McBride, Nast, and Co., 1912); and Montizambert, *London Discoveries in Shops and Restaurants*.

187. Early guidebooks and periodicals gave very little attention to London's shops as sights in themselves. See, for example, *Visitor's Guide and Journal of Amusements* (July 1874); W. J. Loftie, *Tourist's Guide through London* (London: Edward Stanford, 1881); *Sights of London Illustrated and Metropolitan Hand-Book for Railways, Tramways, Omnibuses, River Steamboats, and Cabfares* (London: Henry Herber, 1883); and *Tourist's Monthly Holiday Guide to London* (January 1886). In later guides shopping became an important part of a London visit. By the 1902 edition of Baedeker's London guide there is a separate section, "Shops,

Bazaars, and Markets." Karl Baedeker, *London and Its Environs: Handbook for Travellers* 13th ed., rev. (London: Dulau and Co., 1902). For a cultural analysis of Baedeker, see Edward Mendelson, "Baedeker's Universe," *Yale Review* 74, no. 3 (April 1985): 386–403.

188. *A.B.C. Amusement Guide and Record: Being Alphabetical Particulars of All the Theatres, Concerts, Music Halls, Enter tainments with the Times and Prices of Admission*, ed. Frank Chesworth (March 7, 1896–).

189. *Evening News*, May 17, 1907, 3.

190. *Evening News*, May 21, 1907, 2.

191. *PMG*, May 24, 1900, 11.

192. *PMG*, May 10, 1900, 10.

Chapter Five
"A New Era of Shopping"

1. *Daily Express*, March 15, 1909, and the *Standard*, March 16, 1909. Most of the newspapers quoted in this chapter were collected in scrapbooks housed at the Selfridge's Department Store Archive and generally do not have page numbers. The store is now known as Selfridges, but at the time it opened it was Selfridge's.

2. "Never, probably, had the Spring drapery exhibitions been launched with greater competitive enthusiasm," claimed the *Drapers' Record*, April 3, 1909.

3. *Standard*, March 18, 1909.

4. *Daily Express*, March 15, 1909.

5. On the history of Selfridge's, see Gordon Honeycombe, *Selfridges, Seventy-five Years: The Story of the Store, 1909–1984* (London: Park Lane Press, 1984); Reginald Pound, *Selfridge: A Biography* (London: Heinemann, 1960); Alfred H. Williams, *No Name on the Door: A Memoir of Gordon Selfridge* (London: W. H. Allen, 1956); Adburgham, *Shops and Shopping*, 274–77; Ferry, *A History of the Department Store*, 221–31; Lancaster, *The Department Store*, 58–84; and Jeanne Catherine Lawrence, "Steel Frame Architecture versus the London Building Regulations: Selfridges, the Ritz, and American Technology," *Construction History* 6 (1990): 23–46. Also see an earlier version of this chapter in Charney and Schwartz, *Cinema and the Invention of Public Life*; and Nava's, "Modernity's Disavowal." Although I did not see Nava's essay prior to writing this first article, we analyzed one of the same store advertisements.

6. Lears, *Fables of Abundance*, 19.

7. Some scholars have more or less accepted the conclusion that department stores positively rewrote women's social roles and ideas of femininity. Leach, "Transformations in a Culture of Consumption"; Lancaster, *The Department Store*, 171–94; and Benson, *Rise of Consumer Society in Britain*, 180–99.

8. Leach, *Land of Desire*, 69, 86–87, 99; Herman Kogan and Lloyd Wendt, *Give the Lady What She Wants! The Story of Marshall Field and Company* (Chicago: Rand McNally, 1952), 201–15. For broader studies of promotion in America, see Neil Harris, *Cultural Excursions: Marketing Appetites and Cultural Tastes in Modern America* (Chicago: University of Chicago Press, 1990); Susan Strasser, *Satisfaction Guaranteed: The Making of the American Mass Market* (New York: Pantheon, 1989); Bronner, *Consuming Visions*; Stuart Ewen, *Captains of Consciousness: Advertising and the Social Roots of Consumer Culture* (New York: McGraw-Hill, 1976); and Stuart Ewen and Elizabeth Ewen, *Channels of Desire: Mass Images and the Shaping of American Consciousness* (New York: McGraw-Hill, 1976).

9. Robert Hendrickson, *The Grand Emporiums: The Illustrated History of America's Great Department Stores* (New York: Stein and Day, 1979), 86–87.

10. Leach, *Land of Desire*, 27–31.

11. Pound, *Selfridge*, 32.

12. *Brief Guide to London* (London: D. H. Evans and Co., ca. 1890) HF15/1, House of Fraser Archive, Business Records Centre, Glasgow.

13. Pound, *Selfridge*, 28.

14. Moss and Turton, *A Legend of Retailing*, 89–90.

15. George Dangerfield, *The Strange Death of Liberal England, 1910–1914* (1935; reprint, New York: Perigree Books, 1980). For a more recent assessment, see David Powell, *The Edwardian Crisis: Britain 1901–1914* (New York: St. Martin's Press, 1996); and Alan O'Day, ed., *The Edwardian Age: Conflict and Stability, 1900–1914* (Hamden, Conn.: Archon Books, 1979).

16. Recent assessments of wages and prices in the era suggest that the contrast between the late-Victorian and the Edwardian era is not as strong as earlier studies had concluded. Yet the general trends remain in place. Charles Feinstein, "A New Look at the Cost of Living, 1870–1914," in *New Perspectives on the Late Victorian Economy: Essays in Quantitative Economic History, 1860–1914*, ed. James Forman-Peck (Cambridge: Cambridge University Press, 1991), 151–79. Also see T. R. Gourvish,

"The Standard of Living, 1890–1914," in O'Day, *The Edwardian Age*, 13–34; Derek Fraser, "The Edwardian City," in *Edwardian England*, ed. Donald Read (New Brunswick, N.J.: Rutgers University Press, 1982), 56–74.

17. A. J. P. Taylor, "Prologue," in Read, *Edwardian England*, 3. For a broader look at this phenomenon, see Jamie Camplin, *The Rise of the Plutocrats: Wealth and Power in Edwardian England* (London: Constable, 1978). Of course, a great many were buying Lipton's tea and the countless other mass-produced goods lining the shelves of British shops in these years. On working-class expenditure, see Paul Johnson, "Conspicuous Consumption and Working-Class Culture in Late Victorian and Edwardian Britain," *Transactions of the Royal Historical Society* 38 (1988): 27–42; and Johnson, *Saving and Spending*, especially chap. 4 and 7; Ross, *Love and Toil*, 27–55; Fraser, *The Coming of the Mass Market*, 14–26.

18. London County Council Statistics, vol. 35 (1930–31), cited in David R. Green, "The Metropolitan Economy: Continuity and Change, 1800–1939," in *London: A New Metropolitan Geography*, ed. Keith Hoggart and David Green (London: Edward Arnold, 1991), 11.

19. Fraser, "The Edwardian City," 56. Significantly, the electric trams did not take visitors into the interior of the West End. Barker and Robbins, *London Transport* 2:30–34, 100–101.

20. Barker and Robbins, *London Transport*, 44–45.

21. Fred W. Burgess, *The Practical Retail Draper: A Complete Guide for the Drapery and Allied Trade* (London: Virtue and Company, 1912), 1:58.

22. Quoted in P. J. Waller, *Town, City, and Nation: England, 1850–1914* (Oxford: Oxford University Press, 1983), 65–66.

23. *Evening News*, May 10, 1907, 1.

24. *Evening News*, May 7, 1910, 3.

25. The growth of leisure time in the twentieth century has been an important facet of the development of consumer society. See Cross, *Time and Money*; and Benson, *Rise of Consumer Society*, 14.

26. Paul Thompson, *The Edwardians: The Remaking of British Society* (London: Granada, 1977), 197–202; Jonathan Rose, *The Edwardian Temperament, 1895–1919* (Athens: Ohio University Press, 1986), 163–66.

27. Bennett, *The City of Pleasure: A Fantasia on Modern Times* (1907; reprint, New York: Doubleday, 1975), 6–7. Camplin described Bennett's "City of Pleasure" as a metaphor for the extravagant social life enjoyed by elites. *The Rise of the Plutocrats*, 238–51. However, this amusement park mirrors the emergence of London's mass entertainments.

28. Thomas Burke, *London in My Time* (London: Rich and Cowan, 1934), 23–24. Lears demonstrates Americans' ambiguous reaction to this development by quoting one landscape architect who opposed billboards but had to admit that colorful posters, window displays, and electric signs all put the urban passerby "unconsciously in a holiday mood." Lears, *Fables of Abundance*, 294. On the opposition and regulation of these "sky signs," see Turner, *The Shocking History of Advertising!* 161; and Nevett, *Advertising in Britain*, 110–36.

29. Chancellor, *Wanderings in Piccadilly, Mayfair, and Pall Mall*, 76.

30. "The Changing West End," *Queen*, May 13, 1905, 767.

31. Ursula Bloom, *Youth at the Gate* (London: Hutchinson, 1959), 15. Vera Brittain, however, remembered that she and her fiancé, Roland, still had to be chaperoned when they spent a day together amusing themselves in the West End. Vera Brittain, *Testament of Youth* (1933; reprint, Harmondsworth: Penguin, 1989), 114–15. For an analysis of working-class women consumers just after the period being discussed, see Sally Alexander, "Becoming a Woman in London in the 1920s and 1930s," in Feldman and Jones, *Metropolis London*, 245–71. See also the "Reminiscences" of Rachel Brewis in *Costume* 16 (1982): 86–92.

32. Ruth Slawson's diary, January 30, 1909. Tierl Thompson, ed., *Dear Girl: The Diaries and Letters of Two Working Women, 1897–1917* (London: Women's Press, 1987), 138. It is interesting to compare these diaries with that of Lady Cynthia Asquith during this period, for despite their class and other differences, these women spent a great deal of time "consuming" in the West End. Asquith constantly shopped in the West End and was particularly fond of Selfridge's. See, for example, her entries for April 16, 1915; May 7, 1915; October 20, 1915; and December 1, 1915. Lady Cynthia Asquith, *Diaries, 1915–1918* (New York: Alfred A. Knopf, 1969).

33. See, for example, Leach, *Land of Desire*; and the collection of essays, *Inventing Times Square*.

34. Cited in Donald Read, *The Age of Urban Democracy: England, 1868–1914*, rev. ed. (London: Longman, 1994), 385.

35. Benson, *Rise of Consumer Society*, 143–63. Though advertising and other aspects of consumer culture could unify Britons, what I am suggesting here is that during this

period, it also began to be associated as something foreign.

36. On this financier's notorious career, see "Yerkes and American Investment," in Barker and Robbins, *London Transport*, 61–84. For a more general discussion, see S. B. Saul, "The American Impact on British Industry, 1895–1914," *Business History* 3 (December 1960): 19–38.

37. Burke, *London in My Time*, 35.

38. This was a particularly strong theme in business journals at the time. See, for example, *Magazine of Commerce* 4 (February 1904): 120; and the *Drapers' Record*, March 20, 1909. Also see William T. Stead, *The Americanization of the World, or The Trend of the Twentieth Century* (New York: Horace Markley, 1902). Lancaster discusses how English drapers perceived these differences in *The Department Store*, 68–75.

39. Between 1900 and 1914, Macy's, Marshall Field's, Carson, Pirie Scott, Filene's, and many other major shops tore down their old stores and built structures that rose to twenty-five stories in height. Leach, *Land of Desire*, 22. London's stores went through the same process but they never reached the scale of these American buildings. On the development of English department stores after the 1880s, see Ferry, *A History of the Department Store*, 191–272; Pasdermadjian, *The Department Store*, 7 and, more generally, 24–40; Shaw, "The Role of Retailing in the Urban Economy"; Benson and Shaw, *The Evolution of Retail Systems*; Adburgham, *Shops and Shopping*, 271–82; Lancaster, *The Department Store*; Jefferys, *Retail Trading*, 18–20.

40. Dale, *Harrods*, 19–33.

41. *Magazine of Commerce* 9, no. 45 (1906): 46.

42. *Daily Mail*, June 13, 1906, 5.

43. "Souvenir Booklet of the Opening of Waring and Gillows New Building, 162–180 Oxford Street" (June 1906), #420/WAR, Ashbridge Collection, Westminster City Archives, London.

44. For a discussion of their early partnership, see "£1,000,000 Drapery Shop For London," *Drapers' Record*, June 30, 1906, 764–66.

45. "Historical Note on Tottenham Manor and an Old House of Business" (London: Heal and Son's, 1910), #SU4 (1910) Heal's Archives, Archive of Art and Design, Victoria and Albert Museum, London.

46. "Death of Mr. Snelgrove," *Daily Telegraph*, December 4, 1903, 420/MAR, Ashbridge Collection, Westminster City Archives, London.

47. *Modern London, the World's Metropolis: an Epitome of Results* (London: Historical Publishing Company, 1890), 82. For the store's prospectus, see the *Drapers' Record*, February 19, 1898, 457.

48. *Drapers' Record*, November 2, 1889, 548.

49. *Madame*, September 28, 1895, 132.

50. "British Industries: Pioneers of Commerce, Liberty and Co., Ltd," *Citizen*, December 10, 1898, #788/712, Liberty's Archive, City of Westminster Archives, London. See also the *Drapers' Record*, September 17, 1898, 705–7.

51. "The Maker of the 'House Beautiful': The Story of Liberty's," in *Fortunes Made in Business: Life Struggles of Successful People* (1900), 209, 788/9, Liberty's Archive, Westminster City Archives, London.

52. Booker, *Yesterday's Child*, 248; James Bone, *London Echoing* (London: Jonathan Cape, 1948), 132; Cavers, *Hades! the Ladies!* 254.

53. Samson Clark, *Retail Drapery Advertising: A Handbook on Drapery Publicity and Kindred Matters* (London: Simpkin, Marshall, Hamilton, Kent, 1910), 12. This idea persisted into the 1920s. See, for example, P. J. Westwood, "Modern Shop and Store Construction," in *The Modern Shop*, ed. D. MacMillan Muir (London: Blackfriar's Press, 1927), 19.

54. *Olivia's Shopping*, 24.

55. On the politics of property ownership in London, see Olsen, *Town Planning in London*; and Avner Offer, *Property and Politics, 1870–1914: Landownership, Law, Ideology, and Urban Development in England* (Cambridge: Cambridge University Press, 1981), especially 254–313. For the impact of London's building regulations on the structure of large retail showrooms, see Lawrence, "Steel Frame Architecture versus the London Building Regulations."

56. For an example of the tensions between landlords and their shopkeeper tenants, see Frank Banfield, *The Great Landlords of London* (London: Spencer Blackett, 1890). This was originally published as a series of articles in the *Sunday Times* and was intended to call attention to what the author viewed as a monopolistic and feudal system that was a "serious infliction upon the commercial classes" (31).

57. Lewis argued that "landlords are not the absolute owners of the earth on which we live. . . . They hold the land in trust for the community, and their first duty is to afford every facility for the profitable use of the land held by the tenant. Landlords cannot have any equitable right to harass or hinder the industry of tenants, whose labor is the source of the landlord's wealth." John Lewis, *Our Ground Landlords in the Twentieth Century* (1903),

Ashbridge Collection, Westminster City Archives, London.

58. *Architect*, October 22, 1881, 263. Arthur Cates, an architect for the Crown's Land Revenues, blamed the problem on the legal restrictions that entangled property. See his letter to the *Architect*, October 31, 1881, PRO CRES 35/3714. Dickins of Dickins and Jones believed that the Regent Street's shops were in a dire state because "of the mechanisms of obstructions which governmental departments always throw in the way of improvements." Report of a speech he gave on Piccadilly Circus at a meeting between the St. James vestry and the Metropolitan Board of Works. *Metropolitan*, July 16, 1887. PRO CRES 35/2345.

59. For a broader discussion of the building of imperial London, see M. H. Port, *Imperial London: Civil Government Building in London, 1850–1914* (New Haven: Yale University Press, 1995); Arthur H. Beavan, *Imperial London* (London: J. M. Dent, 1901) Also see Harold Clunn, *London Rebuilt, 1897–1927* (London: John Murray, 1927); Service, *London, 1900*; Andrew Saint, *Richard Norman Shaw* (New Haven: Yale University Press, 1976); Hobhouse, *A History of Regent Street*, 112–36.

60. *Daily Telegraph*, April 4, 1907, 8.

61. "Tubes and Trade," *Evening News*, May 7, 1907, 3. For the connection between the Tube and London's major shopping centers, see the *London and Suburban A.B.C. Shopping Guide* (London: Gough Press, 1911).

62. *Evening News*, April 10, 1907, 2.

63. Ibid., 3. The *American Register* commented that Shaw's plans might once again transform Regent Street into a hallmark of fashion because they would "abolish the window display so necessary to a suburban and country custom." May 1, 1909.

64. Aston Webb, "Improved Shop Architecture for London: The New Regent's Quadrant," *Nineteenth Century and After* 60 (July 1906): 165–68. Ironically, Webb would install the first show windows in the Army and Navy Stores in Victoria Street in 1920. Wainwright, *Army and Navy Stores Limited Centenary Year*, 15.

65. "Shop Window Fight—Do We Need Temptations to Buy?" *Daily Mail*, June 12, 1906, 5.

66. Ibid.

67. For the chaos created by rebuilding, see the *Daily Telegraph*, June 1, 1912.

68. Pound, *Selfridge*, 29.

69. Waxman, *A Shopping Guide to Paris and London*, 3. Similar criticisms were leveled at English shops in the 1890s. For example, in 1892 one American woman wrote that "while so remarkable in its general characteristics and in practical resources, the house of Whiteley, neither outside nor inside, by any means compares in attractiveness with our American shops-of-many-wares. The building itself is straggling, homely, and rude in effect . . . narrow, close and stuffy." Mrs. S. A. Brock Putnam, "An American View of London Shops," *WDTJ*, October 1, 1892, 929. There were many, however, who felt that Edwardian shops were improving. See, for example, Cook, *Highways and Byways in London*, 299; *Olivia's Shopping*, 8.

70. Quoted in Richard Kenin, *Return to Albion: Americans in England, 1760–1914* (New York: Holt, Rinehart, and Winston, 1979), 225.

71. The company was initially registered on June 19, 1906, as Selfridge and Waring, Ltd., with a capital of a million pounds divided into 100,000 five-pound reference shares and 500,000 ordinary shares at one pound each. When Waring dropped out of the deal, Selfridge set up Selfridge and Co., Ltd., investing approximately £200,000 more of his own money. On Selfridge's finances, see Pound, *Selfridge*, 33.

72. Lawrence, "Steel Frame Architecture," 23–46. Selfridge and his lawyers spent a great deal of time in Portman's estate offices, but he evidently felt that the estate officers were a bit less obstructionist than others. Pound, *Selfridge*, 35.

73. *Daily Chronicle*, March 15, 1909.

74. Honeycombe, *Selfridges*, 9.

75. *Daily Express*, March 16, 1909. Also see *Builder*, March 20, 1909. This issue published photographs of Selfridge's and the newly rebuilt Debenham and Freebody's. Selfridge's classical design used more glass, and its strong vertical lines emphasized the store's height.

76. *Black and White*, March 20, 1909.

77. *Daily Chronicle*, March 15, 1909.

78. *Daily Chronicle*, March 16, 1909.

79. *Christian World*, March 18, 1909. On the comparison between American and English display techniques, see the *Drapers' Record*, April 3 and 10, 1909. Around 1910 American print ads and show windows began to use more empty space in order to appear less cluttered. Leonard Marcus, *The American Store Window* (London: Architectural Press, 1978), 18–19. Yet American window dressers still had diverse opinions about how best to excite the passersby. Leach, *Land of Desire*, 59–69. Before Selfridge arrived in London, architects and shopkeepers were already rethinking the function of the store window. For an example of

English techniques, see Horace Dan and E. C. Morgan, *English Shop Fronts Old and New* (London: B. T. Batsford, 1907).

80. *Drapery Times*, March 20, 1909.

81. Haug has suggested that this perception of the shop as a stage is still present in the late-twentieth-century understandings of the department store. Wolfgang F. Haug, *Critique of Commodity Aesthetics: Appearance, Sexuality, and Advertising in Capitalist Society*, 8th ed. (Minneapolis: University of Minnesota Press, 1986), 68–69. Of course, goods take on value or meanings in many different ways. Appadurai's introduction to *The Social Life of Things* is a particularly useful overview of many of the key theorists in this field. For critical studies of contemporary advertising, see Sut Jhally, Stephen Kline, and William Leiss, eds., *Social Communication in Advertising: Persons, Products, and Images of Well-Being* (New York and London: Routledge, 1986); Sut Jhally, *The Codes of Advertising: Fetishism and the Political Economy of Meaning in the Consumer Society* (London: Frances Pinter, 1987); Kathy Myers, *Understains: The Sense and Seduction of Advertising* (London: Comedia, 1986); and Judith Williamson, *Decoding Advertisements: Ideology and Meaning in Advertising* (London: Marion Boyars, 1978); and her *Consuming Passions: The Dynamics of Popular Culture* (London: Marion Boyars, 1986).

82. For an analysis of the themes that were most commonly developed in these ads, see Richards, *The Commodity Culture of Victorian England*; and Loeb, *Consuming Angels*. In "Advertising: The Magic System," in *Problems in Materialism and Culture* (London: Verso, 1980), Raymond Williams provides a short history of print advertising and the advertising profession.

83. On retailers' refusal to advertise in newspapers, see Nevett, *Advertising in Britain*, 74. On the store catalog, see Turner, *The Shocking History of Advertising!* 198. Also see Alison Adburgham, *Yesterday's Shopping: The Army and Navy Store's Catalogue, 1907*, facsimile ed. (Devon: David and Charles Reprints, 1969). Many catalogs did not match this example, however. Edward Maxwell wrote in 1904 that most were "marvels of typographical imperfection. . . . They cry Cheap! Cheap! Cheap!" "A Matter-of-Fact Talk on Advertising," *Magazine of Commerce* 4 (February 1904): 120. By 1912 the *Evening Standard* announced that newspaper advertising had replaced the "inanimate" catalogs as the medium of choice for London retailers. January 2, 1912.

84. Berthe Fortesque Harrison, "Advertising from the Woman's Point of View," *Modern Business* 2 (December 1908): 512.

85. On catalogs and American consumer culture, see Alexandra Keller, "Disseminations of Modernity: Representation and Consumer Desire in Early Mail-Order Catalogs," in Charney and Schwartz, *Cinema and the Invention of Modern Life*, 156–82.

86. Turner, *Shocking History of Advertising!* 198. On the alliance between American newspapers and department stores, Michael Schudson, *Advertising, the Uneasy Persuasion: Its Dubious Impact on American Society* (New York: Basic Books, 1984), 4.

87. Maxwell, "Matter-of-Fact Talk on Advertising," 117. On Wanamaker's use of newspaper publicity, see Simon J. Bronner, "Reading Consumer Culture," in *Consuming Visions*, 13–53. In addition to Lears's recent *Fables of Abundance*, another helpful study of American advertising is Roland Marchand, *Advertising the American Dream: Making Way for Modernity, 1920–1940* (Berkeley: University of California Press, 1985).

88. *American Register*, May 1, 1909.

89. Of course, Selfridge did not limit himself to the newspapers. In 1909 London's buses also asked, "Why Not Spend the Day at Selfridge's?" *Rialto*, April 7, 1909.

90. Artists signed their individual drawings, and their names were also republished when the designs were bound into a souvenir booklet. The artists were: Lewis Baumer, R. Anning Bell, Walter Crane, John Campbell, Stanley R. Davis, J. T. Friedelson, E. Grasset, H. A. Hogg, Garth Jones, Will Lendon, Ellis Martin, John Mills, Harold Nelson, Bernard Partridge, Fred Pegram, F. V. Poole, Tony Sarge, E. J. Sullivan, S. E. Scott, Linley Sanbourne, Fred Taylor, Howard Van Dusen, Frank Wiles, J. F. Woolrich. Two women, Miss B. Ascough and Miss S. B. Pearse, drew the two cartoons promoting "Children's Day."

91. Green, *Underground Art*; Barmen, *The Man Who Built London Transport*.

92. *The Times*, March 14, 1909.

93. *Newsbasket*, May 1909. One of the most famous of his opening week cartoons should be well known to scholars of consumer culture, for Rachel Bowlby published it on the cover of her book *Just Looking*.

94. *Advertising World*, November 26, 1910, 551.

95. A typical budget was about £500 a month. Nevett, *Advertising in Britain*, 74.

96. Raymond Blathwayt, "Mr. H. Gordon Selfridge: A Character Sketch," *Modern Business* 2 (August 1908–January 1909): 338, 335–343.

97. Lears, *Fables of Abundance*, 219. Also see Garvey, *The Adman in the Parlor*.

98. Williams, *No Name on the Door*, 28.

99. Some of the many papers in which notices of the new store appeared include: *Barrow News*, *Belfast Evening Telegraph*, *Bolton Evening News*, *Bolton Journal*, *Bristol Times*, *Burton Daily Mail*, *Cork Constitution*, *Cork Examiner*, *Coventry Herald*, *Derby Daily Telegraph*, *Dublin Express*, *Dundee Courier*, *East Anglian Daily Times*, *Leicester Chronicle*, *Manchester Guardian*, *Midland Counties Express*, *Nottingham Echo*, and others. The foreign papers included: *African World*, *Egyptian Morning News*, *Gold Coast Leader*, *Indian Engineering*, *Toronto Evening Telegram*, *Transvaal Critic*, *Brisbane Telegraph*, and numerous German, French, American, and Commonwealth papers. Papers from different Christian faiths such as *Catholic Weekly*, *Christian Commonwealth*, *Christian World*, *Church Daily Newspaper*, and *British Congregationalist* praised the new shop and the pleasures of shopping, as did the *Jewish Chronicle*, *British Journal of Nursing*, *Car*, and *Co-operative News*.

100. George Warrington criticized Selfridge for not continuing the spectacular style of his opening week ads. See "If I Were Selfridge," *Modern Business*, August 4, 1909, 38.

101. Although readers thought Callisthenes was a composite of many English authors, it was a pseudonym for Selfridge and the employees whose copy he revised. Some of these were rebound under the title *Selfridge's of London: A Five-Year Retrospect* (London: Selfridge and Co., 1913).

102. Honeycombe, *Selfridges*, 172.

103. Bonavia, *London before I Forget*, 77.

104. *London Opinion*, March 27, 1909.

105. *Shoe and Leather Record*, March 19, 1909.

106. *Anglo-Continental*, March 20, 1909.

107. Leach, *Land of Desire*, 43; Lears, *Fables of Abundance*; and Stuart Culver, "What Manikins Want: *The Wonderful Wizard of Oz* and *The Art of Decorating Dry Goods Windows*," *Representations* 21 (Winter 1988): 106.

108. "The Show Window," *Retail Trader*, October 25, 1910, 18.

109. Maxwell, "A Matter-of-Fact Talk on Advertising," 118.

110. Harrison, "Advertising from the Woman's Point of View," 511.

111. R. Strauss, "Original Retailers: Mr. W. B. Fuller," *Modern Business* 3 (June 1909): 452.

112. "The Reign of the Artistic," *Success Magazine*, reprinted in *Retail Trader*, May 19, 1910, 16.

113. *Daily Chronicle*, March 16, 1909.

114. Williamson has argued that advertisements are not a " 'single' language"; they "provide a structure which is capable of transforming the language of objects to that of people and vice versa." *Decoding Advertisements*, 12. For an excellent study of how advertising draws upon and reworks "prior meanings," see Timothy Burke, *Lifebuoy Men, Lux Women: Commodification, Consumption, and Cleanliness in Modern Zimbabwe* (Durham, N.C.: Duke University Press 1996), 3.

115. A female image conveying fertility and abundance was a recurrent trope in advertising of the period. Lears, *Fables of Abundance*, especially 101–10.

116. Pound, *Selfridge*, 60.

117. *Evening Standard*, March 16, 1909.

118. Bowlby, *Just Looking*, 20.

119. Marina Warner, *Monuments and Maidens: The Allegory of the Female Form* (New York: Atheneum, 1985), 140. For an analysis of how the classical female worked in other Victorian advertisements, see Loeb, *Consuming Angels*, 34–42.

120. *Daily Telegraph*, March 16, 1909.

121. *Church Daily Newspaper*, March 19, 1909.

122. *European Mail*, March 22, 1909.

123. *Daily Telegraph*, April 11, 1910.

124. *Daily Chronicle*, March 17, 1909.

125. See, for example, the ad entitled "Labor Omnia Vincit," drawn by Harold Nelson.

126. H. A. Hogg's advertisement, "Of Foundation Stones."

127. "Children's Day at Selfridge's," drawn by Bessie Ascough.

128. Mark Girouard, *The Return to Camelot: Chivalry and the English Gentleman* (New Haven: Yale University Press, 1981).

129. This foreshadowed the "capitalist realism" style described by Schudson in *Advertising, the Uneasy Persuasion*, 214–15. Such ads illuminate Haug's argument that "commodities borrow their aesthetic language from human courtship; but then the relationship is reversed and people borrow their aesthetic expression from the world of the commodity." Haug, *Critique of Commodity Aesthetics*, 19.

130. *Daily News*, *Telegraph*, and *Westminster Gazette*, March 19, 1909.

131. Selfridge's advertising illuminates how the consumer was identified as having a "polymorphous potential to desire everything." Birken, *Consuming Desire*, 50.

132. *Daily Chronicle*, March 20, 1909.

133. Bailey, "Parasexuality and Glamour."

134. *Evening Standard*, January 22, 1912.

135. *Evening Standard*, December 11, 1915.

136. *Evening Standard*, May 1912 (specific date not available).

137. *Standard*, March 20, 1909.

138. *Evening Standard* and *Pall Mall Gazette*, May 13, 1912.

139. Various journals debated whether or not Selfridge's fulfilled this goal. The *Lady*, for example, believed that the store made the average woman feel "at home," while *Truth* thought there was a world of difference between the crowd invited to a private social event and that invited to Selfridge's. *Lady*, March 18, 1909; and *Truth*, May 5, 1909.

140. For parallel examples, see Lauren Rabinovitz, "Temptations of Pleasure: Nickelodeons, Amusement Parks, and the Sights of Female Sexuality," *Camera Obscura* 23 (May 1990): 71–89; Tony Bennett, "A Thousand and One Troubles: Blackpool Pleasure Beach," in Jameson, *Formations of Pleasure*, 138–55.

141. *Daily News*, March 22, 1909. See also *Justice*, March 20, 1909.

142. Honeycombe, *Selfridges*, 39.

143. *Daily Telegraph*, July 27, 1909.

144. *Hardware Trade Journal*, March 3, 1913. On the interplay between the market and the theater in the early-modern period, see Agnew, *Worlds Apart*.

145. *Evening Standard*, March 23, 1911.

146. Williams, *No Name on the Door*, 55.

147. *Daily Chronicle*, March 22, 1909.

148. *Church Daily Newspaper*, March 19, 1909.

149. *Morning Leader*, March 17, 1909.

150. *Daily News*, March 22, 1909.

151. *British Journal of Nursing*, March 20, 1909.

152. *Evening Standard*, March 11, 1909.

153. *Daily Mail*, March 12, 1909.

154. On the meaning of this phrase, see Bowlby, *Just Looking*.

155. Leach, *Land of Desire*, 39–70.

156. *Evening Standard*, November 11, 1915.

157. *Morning Post*, October 30, 1915.

158. *PMG*, November 6, 1916.

159. *Evening Standard* and *PMG*, June 20, 1912.

160. *Standard*, April 10, 1911.

161. *Daily Mail*, March 15, 1909.

162. Williams, *No Name on The Door*, 96.

163. *Evening Standard*, April 21, 1911.

164. *Evening Standard*, July 16, 1912.

165. *Evening Standard*, November 23, 1915.

166. *T.P.'s Weekly*, April 2, 1909.

167. *Financial News*, April 10, 1909.

168. " 'Who's Who' at Selfridge's: New facts concerning the holders of the Preference Capital—How the recent promotion has interested an army of small investors—Full list of Shareholders," *Drapery Times*, August 28, 1909, 422–24.

169. On the role of female investment in family firms, see Davidoff, and Hall, *Family Fortunes*, 272–316.

170. Noble Collection, box C23.3, 1910, Guildhall Library. Benson has argued that "women shared both knowledge and the experience of consumption in their kin and friendship networks." Benson, *Counter Cultures*, 5. Businessmen recognized and used this culture in a variety of different ways. See, for example, W. H. Simmonds, *The Practical Grocer: A Manual and Guide for the Grocer and Provision Merchant* (London: Gresham, 1904–5), 4:197.

171. C138 Acc. 5280, Photographic Collection, Westminster City Archives.

172. *Daily Mail*, March 15, 1909.

173. *Daily Express*, March 16, 1909.

174. *Daily Graphic*, March 15, 1909.

175. This image of shopping crowds has become a recurrent trope in the twentieth century. The *PMG*, for example, began its article on the 1920 sales season with the headline: "Hunting in the West End: Women Early on the Warpath." Cited in Maurice Corina, *Fine Silks and Oak Counters: Debenhams, 1778–1978* (London: Hutchinson, 1978), 86.

176. *Daily Express*, March 15, 1909.

177. *Evening Standard* and *Westminster Gazette*, December 1, 1910.

178. In 1914 Selfridge employed the well-known cartoonist Raaz to illustrate Selfridge's as a "Men's Store." Raaz drew more than a dozen different types of men writing letters about their experiences at Selfridges. This was a perhaps an ill-timed campaign, since men would soon be conspicuously absent from London's streets. For analyses of the construction of the male consumer in the late-twentieth century, see Mort, *Cultures of Consumption*; Frank Mort and Peter Thompson, "Retailing, Commercial Culture, and Masculinity in 1950s Britain: The Case of Montague Burton, the 'Tailor of Taste,' " *History Workshop Journal* 38 (Autumn 1994): 106–28; and Frank Mort, "Archaeologies of City Life: Commercial Culture, Masculinity, and Spatial Relations in 1980s London," *Environment and Planning D: Society and Space* 13 (1995): 573–90. Also, see Gail Reekie's analysis of this development in "Changes in the Adamless Eden: The Spatial and Sexual Transformation of a Brisbane Department Store, 1930–1990," in *Lifestyle Shopping: The Subject of Consumption* (London: Routledge, 1992), 170–94; and Sean Nixon, "Have you Got That Look? Masculinities and the Shopping Spectacle," in Reekie, *Lifestyle Shopping*, 149–69.

179. This gendered image of the shopping crowd corresponds to that described by Andreas Huyssen in "Mass Culture as Woman,

Modernism's Other," in *Studies in Entertainment: Critical Approaches to Mass Culture*, ed. Tania Modleski (Bloomington: Indiana University Press, 1986).

180. *Referee*, March 21, 1909. The same attitude surfaced in letters and speeches printed in local newspapers. One letter writer complained that "Borough tradesmen" were being "driven to the wall" by "American Trusts." A local M.P. also used Selfridge as an example of why his constituents should favor tariff reform. *Marylebone Mercury and West London Gazette*, March 20, and April 3, 1909.

181. *Drapery Times*, March 27, 1909.

182. Selfridge boasted that his store accommodated over a million visitors during opening week, but we will never know exactly how many and what types of shoppers came to store. *Daily Chronicle*, March 22, 1909.

183. *Tit Bits*, April 3, 1909. Also see the way in which the Savoy Group promoted London's shops in the booklet *London's Social Calendar* (London: Savoy Hotel, 1914).

184. *Cosmopolitan Financier*, March 20, 1909.

185. *Draper*, April 4, 1909.

186. "Creating the Shopping Centre: The Effect of Advertising on the Popularity of City Thoroughfares," *Advertiser's Weekly*, May 10, 1913.

187. *Daily Express*, May 6, 1909.

188. Messrs. Dickins and Jones Minute Book of Board Meetings, 1909–1914, General Board Meeting Minutes, March 10, 1910, HF/10/1/3, House of Fraser Archives.

189. *The Times*, March 15, 1909, 12.

190. *Daily Express*, March 17, 1909.

191. *Daily Express*, March 16, 1909.

192. *The House That Everywoman Knows* (London: Harrod's, 1909).

193. "Brochure of Progress" (London: Harrod's Stores, 1911), Harrod's in-store Archive.

194. *Daily News*, November 23, 1911, 3.

195. *Daily Express*, November 22, 1911, 5. For a full discussion and illustrations of the new store, see "Current Architecture: Whiteley's New Premises," *Architectural Review* 31 (March 1912): 164–72.

196. John Kings, "The Four Corners of Lyons," *Business Report* (J. Lyons and Co., 1959). J. Lyons and Company, Limited Archives.

197. See, for example, its advertisement in the *Sphere*, September 9, 1916.

198. See, for example, *Old Bond Street as a Centre of Fashion, 1686–1906*, souvenir of the inauguration of the Business of J & G Ross, 32 Old Bond Street, October 18, 1906; *Burlington Arcade: Being a Discourse on Shopping for the Elite* (London: the Favil Press, 1925).

199. John Thorpe, "An Aesthetic Conversion: Being Independent Notes" (London: Heal and Son, 1909). SU 3, 1909, Heal's Archives. Store advertising emphasized the shop's long history. See, for example, "Historical Note on Tottenham Manor and an Old House of Business" (London: Heal and Sons, 1910), SU 4, 1910, Heal's Archives; and "At the Peacock in the Strand" (London: Thresher and Glenny, ca. 1910), 301/363, Thresher and Glenny Archives.

200. Alison Adburgham, *Liberty's: A Biography of a Shop* (London: Allen and Unwin, 1975).

201. *British Congregationalist*, April 16, 1909.

202. *Daily Express*, March 16, 1909.

203. Chancellor, *The West End of Yesterday and To-Day*, 3.

204. Virginia Woolf, "Oxford Street Tide," in *The London Scene: Five Essays by Virginia Woolf* (New York: Random House, 1975), 16–22.

205. Cavers, *Hades! The Ladies!* 212.

206. Laermans, "Learning to Consume," 82. Among the many scholars to have made this point are Bowlby, *Just Looking*; Miller, *The Bon Marché*; Williams, *Dream Worlds*; Chaney, "The Department Store as a Cultural Form"; Abelson, *When Ladies Go a-Thieving*; Benson, *Counter Cultures*; and Leach, *Land of Desire*.

207. H. Gordon Selfridge, *The Romance of Commerce*, 2d ed. (London: John Lane the Bodley Head, 1923).

Chapter Six
Acts of Consumption

1. *Our Miss Gibbs*, produced by George Edwardes, constructed by J. T. Tanner, written by "Cryptos," a team consisting of Adrian Ross, Percy Greenbank, Ivan Caryll, and Lionel Monckton. Add. mss. 1909/3, British Library, Lord Chamberlain's Play's (hereafter LCP). First performed at the Gaiety Theater, January 25, 1909. The Gaiety had several incarnations and two distinct homes. The first Gaiety at 354 Strand was built in 1862, significantly altered in 1886, and finally closed down in 1903. A new Gaiety Theater was opened in Aldwych in 1903. *Our Miss Gibbs* was performed at the new Gaiety, which was managed by George Edwardes at that time. The play manuscripts used in this chapter were

nearly all from the British Library, Lord Chamberlain's Plays Collection. The scripts were often slightly changed after this version was submitted for approval; however, in many cases they are the only surviving copy.

2. There has been very little scholarship on musical comedy, despite its popularity. For a brief overview, see Raymond Mander and Joe Mitchenson, *Musical Comedy: A Story in Pictures* (New York: Taplinger, 1970); and Peter Bailey, " 'Naughty but Nice': Musical Comedy and the Rhetoric of the Girl," in *The Edwardian Theatre: Essays on Performance and the Stage*, ed. Michael R. Booth and Joel H. Kaplan (Cambridge: Cambridge University Press, 1996), 36–60.

3. Kaplan and Stowell, *Theatre and Fashion*. Kaplan and Stowell explore many facets of the relationship between theater and fashion. Their book and Bailey's recent chapter, "Naughty but Nice," touch on some of the same themes of this chapter, but from slightly different perspectives. For Oscar Wilde's negotiation of the relationship between consumerism and theater, see Regina Gagnier, *Idylls of the Marketplace: Oscar Wilde and the Victorian Public* (Stanford, Calif.: Stanford University Press, 1986).

4. Several recent essay collections examine the social, cultural, and economic history of English theater; see Richard Foulkes, ed., *British Theatre in the 1890s: Essays on Drama and the Stage* (Cambridge: Cambridge University Press, 1992); Booth and Kaplan, *The Edwardian Theatre*; and Judith L. Fisher and Stephen Watt, eds., *When they Weren't Doing Shakespeare: Essays on Nineteenth-Century British and American Theatre* (Athens: University of Georgia Press, 1989).

5. H. J. W. Dam, "The Shop Girl at the Gaiety," *Sketch* (November 28, 1894), 216.

6. Bailey, "Parasexuality and Glamour," 166; and Bailey, " 'Naughty but Nice.' " On the erotic nature of Victorian theater more generally see Davis, *Actresses as Working Women*.

7. For an excellent analysis of the emergence of Broadway and New York nightlife, see Lewis Erenberg, "Impresarios of Broadway Nightlife," in Taylor, *Inventing Times Square*, 158–77; and William R. Taylor, "Broadway: The Place That Words Built," in *Inventing Times Square*, 212–31.

8. Adorno and Horkheimer, *Dialectic of Enlightenment*, 144.

9. John Pick, *The West End: Management and Snobbery* (Sussex: John Offard, 1983), chaps. 4–9. Pick argues that West End theater managers made a deliberate decision to exclude working-class audiences from the "artistic" theater and that this ultimately led to the "crisis" of the West End theater in the twentieth century. This process was slow, complex, and never total, however. For contemporary descriptions of West End theater, see Robert Machray, *The Night Side of London* (London: John Macqueen, 1902), 89. Besant, *London in the Nineteenth Century*, 188–91.

10. William Archer, *The Theatrical World of 1894* (London: Walter Scott, 1895), 355.

11. Michael R. Booth, *Theatre in the Victorian Age* (Cambridge: Cambridge University Press, 1991), 7.

12. There are no equivalents to Faye E. Dudden's *Women in The American Theatre: Actresses and Audiences, 1790–1870* (New Haven: Yale University Press, 1994); and Richard Butsch's "Bowery B'hoys and Matinee Ladies: The Re-gendering of Nineteenth-Century American Theatre Audiences," *American Quarterly* 46, no. 3 (September 1994): 374–405 for studies of gender and theater audiences for Britain. In particular, the invention of the matinee and its effect on the class and gender of audiences merits further study.

13. John Hollingshead, *"Good Old Gaiety": An Historiette and Remembrance* (London: Gaiety Theatre Co., 1903), 25.

14. Indeed, some matinee audiences were condemned as frivolous conspicuous consumers sporting oversized, highly ornamented matinee hats. However, at the Court Theatre, home of the New Drama of the 1890s, matinee audiences were filled with New Women. See Dennis Kennedy, "The New Drama and the New Audience," in Booth and Kaplan, *The Edwardian Theatre*, 130–47.

15. Bloom, *Victorian Vinaigrette*, 74–77.

16. Zuzanna Shonfield, *The Precariously Privileged: A Professional Family in Victorian London* (Oxford: Oxford University Press, 1987) 22, 43.

17. Hughes, *A London Girl of the 1880s*, 15–16.

18. J. P. Wearing, "Edwardian London West End Christmas Audiences, 1900–1914," in Fisher and Watt, *When They Weren't Doing Shakespeare*, 230–40.

19. Michael R. Booth, "East End and West End: Class and Audience in Victorian London," *Theatre Research International* 2, no. 2 (February 1977): 99; Dagmar Höher, "The Composition of Music Hall Audiences, 1850–1914," in *Music Hall: The Business of Pleasure*, ed. Peter Bailey (Milton Keynes and Philadelphia: Open University Press, 1986), 74–92; and Dagmar Höher Kift, *The Victorian Music Hall: Culture, Class, and Conflict*, trans. Roy Kift (Cambridge: Cambridge University Press, 1996), 62–74. Class segregation was primarily produced by the differences in seat prices. A

good seat at a West End theater cost between 5s. and 10s. 6d., but the gallery at the Criterion, for example, still cost only 1s. Pick, *The West End*; J. C. Trewin, *The Edwardian Theatre* (Oxford: Basil Blackwell, 1976), 9.

20. Thomas Purnell, *Dramatists of the Present Day* (1871), cited in Booth, *Theatre in the Victorian Age*, 13.

21. Newman, *Many Parts*, 64.

22. Davis, *Actresses as Working Women*, especially chap. 5, "The Geography of Sex in Society and Theatre."

23. Machray, *The Night Side of London*, 84. See also Tracy C. Davis, "Indecency and Vigilance in the Music Halls," in Foulkes, *British Theatre in the 1890s*, 111–31. Also see *Actresses as Working Women*, 154–58; Joseph Donohue, "The Empire Theatre of Varieties Licensing Controversy of 1894: Testimony of Laura Ormiston Chant before the Theatres and Music Halls Licensing Committee," *Nineteenth Century Theatre* 15, no. 1 (Summer 1987): 50–60; and Karl Beckson, *London in the 1890s: A Cultural History* (New York: W. W. Norton, 1992), 110–28.

24. Olsen, *The Growth of Victorian London*, 16.

25. *Building News* 57 (1889), 311, as cited in Olsen, *The Growth of Victorian London*, 304.

26. W. Macqueen-Pope, *Carriages at Eleven: The Story of the Edwardian Theatre* (London: Hutchinson, 1947).

27. For the architectural history of London theaters, see Victor Glasstone, *Victorian and Edwardian Theatres: An Architectural and Social Survey* (Cambridge: Harvard University Press, 1975), esp. 98–114. Other details may be found in Diana Howard, *London Theatres and Music Halls, 1850–1950* (London: Library Association, 1970).

28. Tracy C. Davis, "Edwardian Management and the Structures of Industrial Capitalism," in Booth and Kaplan, *The Edwardian Theatre*, 111–29.

29. Ursula Bloom, *The Elegant Edwardian* (London: Hutchinson, 1958), 108.

30. In a very brief visit to London in 1898, Dr. S. A. Ellison and another couple visited the Lyric Theatre, Her Majesty's Theatre, the Duke of York's Theater, the Tivoli, and the Empire. Dr. S. A. Ellison, "A Trip to Europe, April 9th–June 5th, 1898," Ellison Collection, New York Public Library.

31. Quoted in Gagnier, *Idylls of the Marketplace*, 103.

32. Mario Borsa, *The English Stage of To-Day* (1908), as cited in Booth, *Theatre in the Victorian Age*, 15–16.

33. In November of 1878 the mass caterers Spiers and Pond opened the new Gaiety Restaurant attached to the theater. Hollingshead, *"Good Old Gaiety,"* 41. Late-Victorian entrepreneurs frequently had financial interests in many aspects of the entertainment business. Frederick Gordon, for example, had been a proprietor, director, or member of the board of directors of Bovril, the Gordon Hotels, and the large furnishers Maple's. He directed the transformation of both the Holborn Restaurant and Frascati's into public companies in the 1880s and 1890s. His overseas interests included African mining ventures. For the details, see Gordon's obituary in the *Financial Times*, March 24, 1904, 3.

34. *Daily Mail*, April 14, 1909, 66. See the way that these entertainments are linked in *London's Social Calendar, 1914* (London: Savoy Hotel, 1914), #942.11.31, General Collection, Westminster City Archives. Commenting upon the calendar issued by the Savoy Hotel Company the previous year, the *Queen* noted that the calendar "gives an excellent idea of how the fashionable world of London enjoys itself." June 28, 1913, 1190.

35. Bonavia, *London before I Forget*, 71.

36. I am borrowing this phrase from Agnew, *World Apart*, 33.

37. Stowell and Kaplan have recently shown how the alliance between retailing and the theater inspired audiences and managers to see the latter as a promotional venue. They also argue that the "New Drama" of Ibsen, Shaw, Granville-Barker, and feminist playwrights reacted against the staging of consumption and gender relations within mainstream drama. For the suffrage response, see Kaplan and Stowell, *Theatre and Fashion*, chap. 5. Jan McDonald similarly argues that the New Drama being produced at the Court Theatre challenged the growing commercialism of the West End. *The "New Drama," 1900–1914* (New York: Grove Press, 1986), 5. Also see Simon Trussler, *The Cambridge Illustrated History of British Theatre* (Cambridge: Cambridge University Press, 1994), 260. Of course, this division was not so clear at the time. Actresses in avant-garde productions were often beautifully and fashionably attired and the play's mis-en-scène could be as richly materialistic as that of commercial theater.

38. For an analysis of the pictorial aspects of nineteenth-century drama, see Martin Meisel, *Realizations: Narrative, Pictorial, and Theatrical Arts in Nineteenth-Century England* (Princeton: Princeton University Press, 1983). See also Michael R. Booth, "The Metropolis on Stage," in Dyos and Wolff, *The Victorian City*, 1:211–24.

39. Percy Fitzgerald, *Principles of Comedy and Dramatic Effect* (Tinsley, 1870) cited in Booth, *Victorian Spectacular Theatre*, 15.

40. In discussing Wilde's *The Importance of Being Earnest*, Gagnier points out that the "material images on stage are a direct mimesis of the audience." *Idylls of the Marketplace*, 111.

41. In an interesting episode in the late nineties, Sims urged drapers to keep their windows lit after hours. This campaign served a twofold purpose: it would make the West End both more spectacular and more moral. Sims and his fellow authors were deeply invested in the moralizing potential of the spectacular metropolis. London's drapers responded somewhat negatively, however. "Lights of London," *Drapers' Record*, October 24, 1896, 195, and "More Lights in London," 202.

42. Mander and Mitchenson, *Musical Comedy*, 14.

43. Kaplan and Stowell's *Theatre and Fashion* does an excellent job surveying the nature of this relationship, but does not fully consider how the theater and fashion industry developed a view of the consumer/spectator.

44. *WDTJ*, October 30, 1880, 687.

45. Ibid. Haute couture and mass production and distribution developed together and both were a product of a growing capitalist economy. Steele, *Fashion and Eroticism*, 80.

46. "Beauties in Shop-Windows," *BC*, April 6, 1878. See also "Society Beauties Pictures Sold in Shop-Windows," *BC*, March 30, 1878. For the image of actresses as prostitutes, see Davis, *Actresses as Working Women*, esp. 69–101. Even in Edwardian London, actresses and fashion models were sometimes thought to be women of easy virtue. For a model's reminiscences, see Lou Taylor, "Marguerite Shoobert, London Fashion Model, 1906–1917," *Costume: The Journal of the Costume Society* 17 (1983): 105–10, 109. For the growing respectability of actresses, see Kathy Peiss, "Making Up, Making Over," in de Grazia and Furlough, *The Sex of Things*, 321–22. On the mass circulation of the actress's image see Elizabeth Ann McCauley, *A. A. Disdéri and the Cartes de Visite Portrait Photograph* (New Haven: Yale University Press, 1985); and Avril Lansdell, *Fashion à la Carte, 1860–1900: A Study of Fashion Through Cartes de Visite* (Aylesbury: Shire Publications, 1985).

47. For a discussion of this practice, see "Abuses of Advertisement," *Queen*, February 21, 1903, 310. Even the famous male impersonator Vesta Tilley was used to sell Pond's Vanishing Cream. See the advertisement in the *Daily Graphic*, March 28, 1911, 17. Loeb discusses the actress as "commercial heroine," in *Consuming Angels*, 95–99.

48. Patrice Petro has observed that the image and meaning of women's cinema spectatorship should be read in relationship to the illustrated women's magazines, since together these media constructed the female viewer/reader as consumer. Patrice Petro, *Joyless Streets: Women and Melodramatic Representation in Weimar Germany* (Princeton: Princeton University Press, 1989), 90.

49. *A.B.C. Amusement Guide and Record*, March 7, 1896, 3.

50. *Lady*, February 25, 1890, 225.

51. *Sphere*, July 9, 1910, ii.

52. *Lady*, January 11, 1894, 43.

53. For an extreme example of this tendency see the review of *The Forty Thieves* at Drury Lane in *The Era* in early 1887, reproduced in Booth's *Victorian Spectacular Theatre*, 161–71.

54. Advertising page, *Play Pictorial* 13, no. 80 (May 1909).

55. *Era*, August 13, 1881, as cited in Booth, *Victorian Spectacular Theatre*, 69.

56. "Dress and Democracy in the Drama of To-Day," *Lady's Realm* 26 (May–October 1909): 43–44.

57. Christopher Pulling, *They Were Singing*, quoted in James Laver, *Edwardian Promenade* (London: Edward Hulton, 1958), 92. For the multiple meanings of cross-dressing on the stage, see J. S. Bratton, "Beating the Bounds: Gender Play and Role Reversal in the Edwardian Music Hall," in Booth and Kaplan, *The Edwardian Theatre*, 86–110. For a broader cultural analysis, see Marjorie Garber, *Vested Interests: Cross-Dressing and Cultural Anxiety* (New York: Routledge, 1992). For a discussion of gender as performance, see Judith P. Butler, *Gender Trouble: Feminism and the Subversion of Identity* (New York: Routledge, 1990).

58. Davis, *Actresses as Working Women*, 107.

59. Duff-Gordon, *Discretions and Indiscretions*, 24. Also see Kaplan and Stowell's analysis of Lucile's career in *Theatre and Fashion*, esp. 39–43. For another history of Lucile and her famous sister, Elinor Glyn, see Meredith Etherington-Smith and Jeremy Pilcher, *The 'It' Girls: Lucy, Lady Duff Gordon, the Couturière, and Elinor Glyn, Romantic Novelist* (London: Harcourt Brace Jovanovich, 1986). These designers generally sold to society's elite, actresses, and courtesans, but the respectable and unrespectable clientele never met one another face to face. Steele, *Fashion and Eroticism*, 76.

60. Duff-Gordon, *Discretions*, 41–43. While Lucile later claimed that the stage had inspired her first dress design, Paul Poiret believed that he had acquired "his taste for colour . . . amidst the phantasmagoria of pinks, greens, and velvets" that he witnessed as a child at the

1889 Paris Exhibition. Poiret, *My First Fifty Years*, 18.

61. Duff-Gordon, *Discretions*, 47. In 1909 she claimed to have earned approximately forty thousand pounds.

62. Cecil Beaton, *The Glass of Fashion* (1954; reprint, London: Cassell, 1989), 32.

63. Duff-Gordon, *Discretions*, 76.

64. Ibid., 68. Charlotte Herzog quotes costume historian, Elizabeth Jackimowicz, who wrote that each of the famous designers Chanel, Poiret, and Worth claimed to have originated the first fashion show. Lucile, then, must be added to this list. Charlotte Herzog, " 'Powder Puff' Promotion: The Fashion-Show-in-the-Film," in *Fabrications: Costume and the Female Body*, ed. Jane Gaines and Charlotte Herzog (New York: Routledge, 1990), 134.

65. Duff-Gordon, *Discretions*, 74–76.

66. "Blue Blood and Business—Lady Duff-Gordon's Fashion Salon in Paris," *Daily Graphic*, April 6, 1911, 13.

67. "Good Window Display," *Retail Trader*, September 27, 1910, 24.

68. "The Show Window," *Retail Trader*, October 25, 1910, 18.

69. Culver, "What Manikins Want," 106.

70. Fanny Douglas, *The Gentlewoman's Book of Dress*, Victoria Library for Gentlewomen Series (London: Henry and Co., 1895) 3.

71. Florence Hull Winterburn, *Principles of Correct Dress* (New York: Harper Brothers, 1914), 15.

72. "How to Advertise Bread—The Value of Newspaper Advertising—The Newspaper, the Baker's Shop Window," *Progressive Confectioner* 1, no. 1 (January 1911): 9–10. There were many different ways that the emerging field of consumer psychology conceptualized the consumer. Bowlby began to explore this topic in *Shopping with Freud*, 94–119.

73. *Queen*, April 26, 1900, 681.

74. Anonymous, *The Show Window*, LCP, add. mss. 1927/7. First performed at the Nottingham Hippodrome, February 24, 1927.

75. Campbell, *The Romantic Ethic*, 47.

76. On cinema and its relationship to consumer culture, see Friedberg, *Window Shopping*, and the introduction and essays in Charney and Schwartz, *Cinema and the Invention of Modern Life*; Petro, *Joyless Streets*; Miriam Hansen, *Babel and Babylon: Spectatorship in the American Silent Film* (Cambridge: Harvard University Press, 1991); Gaines and Herzog, *Fabrications*.

77. *Drapers' Record*, March 12, 1898, 629.

78. Charles Eckert, "The Carol Lombard in Macy's Window," *Quarterly Review of Film Studies* 3, no. 1 (Winter 1978): 4.

79. Herzog, "Powder Puff," 137.

80. Jane Gaines, "The Queen Christina Tie-Ups: Convergence of Show Window and Screen," *Quarterly Review of Film and Video Studies* 11 (1988–89): 35.

81. Jeanne Allen, "The Film Viewer as Consumer," *Quarterly Review of Film Studies* 5, no. 4 (Fall 1980): 482. Allen expands this argument in a later article, "*Fig Leaves* in Hollywood: Female Representation and Consumer Culture," in Gaines and Herzog, *Fabrications*, 122–33. In this article she explores how the intersection between film and consumerism played out in the 1926 film *Fig Leaves*.

82. On the relationship between theatrical production and the birth of the cinema, see Nicholas A. Vardac, *Stage to Screen: Theatrical Method from Garrick to Griffith* (1949; reprint, New York: Benjamin Blom, 1968). On the heterogenous nature of early cinema audience in the United States, see Hansen, *Babel and Babylon*, chap. 2.

83. Lary May, *Screening Out the Past: The Birth of Mass Culture and the Motion Picture Industry* (Chicago: University of Chicago Press, 1980).

84. On the soaring costs of theatrical productions, see Pick, *The West End*, especially chaps. 7–9.

85. Abigail Solomon-Godeau, "The Other Side of Venus: The Visual Economy of Feminine Display," in de Grazia and Furlough, *The Sex of Things*, 114.

86. Theresa de Lauretis, *Alice Doesn't: Feminism, Semiotics, Cinema* (Bloomington: Indiana University Press, 1984), 4. See also her *Technologies of Gender: Essays on Theory, Film, and Fiction* (Bloomington: Indiana University Press, 1987).

87. Laura Mulvey, "Visual Pleasure and Narrative Cinema," *Screen* 16, no. 3 (Autumn 1975): 11. For the novel see Bowlby, *Just Looking*; Jeff Nunokawa, "*Tess*, Tourism, and the Spectacle of Women," in *Rewriting the Victorians: Theory, History, and Politics of Gender*, ed. Linda M. Shires (New York: Routledge, 1992), 70–86; and Thomas Richards, *The Commodity Culture of Victorian England*, 206. Tracy Davis and Peter Bailey analyzed the construction of the female body as object of the male gaze in the Victorian theater. They do not, however, show how this construction was related to the emergence of a culture of consumption or theorize about the construction of a female spectators' reaction. Davis, *Actresses as Working Women*, 105–37; Bailey, " 'Naughty but Nice.' " For the American theater, see Robert Allen, *Horrible Prettiness: Burlesque and American Culture* (Chapel

Hill: University of North Carolina Press, 1991).

88. Herzog, "Powder Puff," 158–59.

89. Mary Ann Doane, "Film and the Masquerade: Theorizing the Female Spectator," *Screen* 23, nos. 3–4 (1982): 80.

90. Mary Ann Doane, "The Economy of Desire: The Commodity Form in/of the Cinema," *Quarterly Review of Film and Video Studies* 11 (1988–89):25.

91. Hansen, *Babel and Babylon*, 4.

92. John Hollingshead, "Theatres," in *London in the Nineteenth Century*, ed. Walter Besant (London: Adam and Charles Black, 1909), 205.

93. George Rowell, *The Victorian Theatre, 1792–1914* (Cambridge: Cambridge University Press, 1978), 143–45; Trewin, *The Edwardian Theatre*, 160–62. "The Romance of a Shop Girl" is the title of B. W. Findon's article on *Our Miss Gibbs* in the *Play Pictorial* 13, no. 80 (May 1909): 102–25.

94. Richards, *The Commodity Culture of Victorian England*, 15.

95. Agnew, *Worlds Apart*, 11.

96. Buci-Glucksmann, "Catastrophic Utopia," 221.

97. Halttunen has shown that American theater began to laugh at rather than overtly condemn fashion's excesses as early as the 1840s. Halttunen, *Confidence Men and Painted Women*.

98. Charles Petrie, *The Edwardians* (New York: W. W. Norton, 1965), 39.

99. For the early years of the theater, see John Hollingshead, *Gaiety Chronicles* (London: Archibald Constable, 1898); Hollingshead, "*Good Old Gaiety*." For Edwardes's management see Stanley Naylor, *Gaiety and George Grossmith: Random Reflections on the Serious Business of Enjoyment* (London: Stanley Paul, 1913); and W. Macqueen-Pope, *Gaiety: Theatre of Enchantment* (London: W. H. Allen, 1949).

100. Cited in Derek Parker and Julia Parker, *The Natural History of the Chorus Girl* (London: David and Charles, 1975), 52.

101. In " 'Naughty but Nice,' " Bailey does an excellent job analyzing the many facets of the Gaiety Girl phenomenon, including their status as workers, stage personas, and public images. These different facets coalesced to produce a new product: commodified sexuality. More work needs to be done, however, on the Gaiety Girl as burlesque actress prior to the advent of the musical comedy.

102. *Lady*, October 28, 1886, 344. Mary Ryan briefly examined the transformation of the theater from a site of male homosocial leisure into a heterosocial entertainment. See *Women in Public*, 79–80.

103. Shonfield, *The Precariously Privileged*, 217.

104. This discussion summarizes Jeffrey H. Huberman's analysis in *Late Victorian Farce* (Ann Arbor, Mich.: UMI Research Press, 1986). Also see Jessica Milner Davis, *Farce* (London: Methuen, 1978).

105. English burlesque was tamer than its American counterpart; it was a variety show of broad comedy and strip-tease dancers. However, late-nineteenth-century English burlesque usually featured a chorus of working-class women exposing their legs at some point in the performance. On English burlesque, see V. C. Clinton-Baddeley, *The Burlesque Tradition in the English Theater after 1660* (New York: Benjamin Blom, 1971); John D. Jump, *Burlesque* (London: Methuen, 1971).

106. "At the Gaiety," *Saturday Review*, October 30, 1909, reprinted in Max Beerbohm, *Around Theatres* (New York: Knopf, 1930), 2:722.

107. The KOW Girls also took their name because Waller had played a cowboy in Edwin Royle's, *A White Man* at the Lyric that year. Kaplan and Stowell, *Theatre and Fashion*, 125.

108. *PMG*, April 12, 1909, 12.

109. *M.A.P.*, April 17, 1909, 71.

110. "The Selfridge of Stageland: Queen's Theatre as Public Rendezvous," *Daily Chronicle*, September 17, 1913.

111. *This Way, Madame*, first performed at the Coronet Theatre, September 2, 1913, LCP, add. mss. 1913/30

112. H. J. W. Dam, "The Shop Girl: At the Gaiety," *Sketch*, November 28, 1894, 216. On his career also see *London American*, April 3, 1895, 6.

113. H. J. W. Dam, music by Ivan Caryll with additional numbers by Adrian Ross and Lionel Monckton, *The Shop Girl*, first performed November 22, 1894, Gaiety Theatre. LCP, add. mss., 53562.

114. On a male worker's attempt to raise his station via flirtation, see Robert Buchanan and Charles Marlowe, *The Romance of the Shopwalker*, first performed February 27, 1896 at the Royal Colchester, LCP, add. mss., 53594u.

115. Bailey, "Parasexuality and Glamour," 166–67.

116. Yet this tension between workers and their boss, Septimus Hooley, never entirely disappeared. In fact, when the play was revived in 1920, this scene was extended and Hooley's response was a good deal more vicious than it had been in 1894. In the later version, Hooley answers his employee's complaints by calling them "pilferers of petty cash," "pinchers of pre-

cious patterns," and "lunch-time loungers." Revised version and lyrics by Arthur Wimperis, music by Herman Darewski, *The Shop Girl*, first performed at the Gaiety, March 25, 1920. LCP add. mss. 1920/7.

117. For a discussion of the Gaiety Girls who became peeresses, see Laver, *Edwardian Promenade*, 76–77.

118. Taylor, "Marguerite Shoobert, London Fashion Model," 110.

119. James Gardiner, *Gaby Deslys: A Fatal Attraction* (London: Sidgwick and Jackson, 1986), 106–7, 140.

120. Lancaster, *The Department Store*, 183. Lancaster suggests that Whiteley's behavior perpetuated the store's immoral image.

121. *Daily Graphic*, March 27, 1911, 14.

122. *Standard*, March 19, 1914.

123. Kaplan and Stowell, *Theatre and Fashion*, 183–84.

124. This point has been suggested by Peter Bailey's analysis of mass culture in "Ally Sloper's Half-Holiday: Comic Art in the 1880s," *History Workshop Journal* 16 (Autumn 1983): 4–31.

125. E. B. Ashford, "Women in the Distributive Trades, Displacement Study," *Women's Industrial News* 20, no. 73 (April 1916): 9–14. The *Drapers' Record* commented in 1895 that there was "a growing tendency on the part of drapers to give more and more employment to women in the lighter trades." July 6, 1895, 15.

126. Miss Fowle, March 1921. Miscellaneous unmarked box of short histories at Harrods' In-Store Archive.

127. This mixture of emotions was present in "the morality of shop girls question" which clerics, drapers, and journalists debated around the time of Selfridge's opening. See, for example, "Morality of Shop Girls Question," *Daily News*, February 17, 1909, 9. The best work on the female shopworkers in England remains Holcombe, *Victorian Ladies at Work*, 103–40. Lancaster also discusses their history briefly in *The Department Store*, 137–42 and 177–82. Neither work explores the female work culture discussed so thoroughly by Benson in *Counter Cultures* or how the feminization of the sales staff may have been a cost-cutting measure. For this argument, see McBride, "A Woman's World." For two general works, see Wilfred B. Whitaker, *Victorian and Edwardian Shopworkers: The Struggle to Obtain Better Conditions and a Half Holiday* (Totowa, N.J.: Rowman and Littlefield, 1973); Christina Walkley, *The Ghost in the Looking Glass: The Victorian Seamstress* (London: Peter Owen, 1981).

128. William Paine, *Shop Slavery and Emancipation: A Revolutionary Appeal to the Educated Young Men of the Middle Class* (London: P. S. King, 1912), 82. In the midseventies reform groups such as the Ladies Sanitary Association and local organizations such as the Brighton Association in Favour of Seats behind Counters had attempted to improve working conditions in the department stores and small shops. *Woman's Gazette* (April 1876): 100–101; (May 1876): 124.

129. Sir Joseph Hallsworth and Rhys J. Davies, *The Working Life of Shop Assistants: A Study in the Conditions of Labour in the Distributive Trades* (Manchester: National Labour Press, 1910), 77–78.

130. Harley Granville-Barker, *The Madras House*, ed. Margery Morgan (London: Methuen, 1977); and Cicely Hamilton, *Diana of Dobson's: A Romantic Comedy in Four Acts* (New York: Samuel French, 1925). On the treatment of mass commerce and images of female sexuality in socialist and feminist theater, see Kaplan and Stowell, *Theatre and Fashion*, 108–14, 122–29, and 152–82; Gagnier, *Idylls of the Marketplace*; McDonald, *The "New Drama"*; Sheila Stowell, *A Stage of Their Own: Feminist Playwrights of the Suffrage Era* (Ann Arbor: University of Michigan Press, 1992); Dennis Kennedy, *Granville-Barker and the Dream of Theatre* (Cambridge: Cambridge University Press, 1985); Harry M. Ritchie, "Harley Granville-Barker's *The Madras House* and the Sexual Revolution," *Modern Drama* 15, no. 2 (September 1972): 150–58; and Heidi J. Holder, "'The Drama Discouraged': Judgment and Ambivalence in *The Madras House*," *University of Toronto Quarterly* 58, no. 2 (Winter 1988–89): 275–94.

131. Gissing, *The Odd Women*.

132. Stuart Lonalti, *The Shop Girl and Her Master*, Theatre Royal, Leigh, Lancaster, April 19, 1915, LCP #333A.

133. Peter Brooks, *The Melodramatic Imagination: Balzac, Henry James, Melodrama, and the Mode of Excess* (New York: Columbia University Press, 1985), 11–12.

134. Rich Waldon, *Just in Time*, Royal Princess, Glasgow, July 23, 1915, LCP #3586.

135. Quoted in Bailey, "Parasexuality and Glamour," 166.

136. Owen Hall, *The Girl from Kay's*, Apollo Theatre, November 24, 1902, LCP #1902/33. Ellipsis in original.

137. Anonymous, *The Toy Shop*, first performed July 21, 1915, Palace Doncaster, LCP, 1915/11.

138. Paul A. Rubens, *Selfrich's Annual Sale*, October 24, 1910, Savoy Theatre. LCP, 1910/26. Selfridge also became the source of farce in Fred Maitland, *Number One "Gerrard"—Or*

Selfridge Outdone, April 25, 1912, Empire Liverpool, LCP, 1912/17.

139. *Drapers' Record*, September 13, 1890, 353.

140. *Drapers' Record*, February 20, 1897, 441.

141. *Drapers' Record*, October 3, 1899, 661.

142. *Drapers' Record*, March 20, 1897, 707, and the *Woman's World*, (1889): 5–6, 8.

143. Simmonds, *The Practical Grocer* 1: 188–89.

144. See, for example, "A School for Shop Assistants: Gramophone Company's Novel Training Scheme," *Daily Chronicle*, December 1, 1922; "Drapery Trade Summer School," *The Times*, August 19, 1924; "Draper's Summer School," *The Times*, August 14, 1930. The later was held at Girton College, Cambridge, and was opened with a speech by the Fabian essayist and author of *The Eighteen-Nineties* (1913), Holbrook Jackson. Jackson began by praising Mr. Gordon Selfridge for having "revolutionized the drapery trade in this country."

145. Macqueen-Pope, *Gaiety*, 422.

146. "Cryptos," *Our Miss Gibbs*.

147. Laver, *The Edwardian Promenade*, 76.

148. Mikhail Bakhtin, *Rabelais and His World*, trans. Hélène Iswolsky (Bloomington: Indiana University Press, 1984), 154.

149. Peter Stallybrass and Allon White, *The Politics and Poetics of Transgression* (Ithaca: Cornell University Press, 1986), 30.

150. Katherine Mansfield, "The Tiredness of Rosabel," in *Stories*, selected with an introduction by Elizabeth Bowen (1908; reprint, New York: Vintage Books, 1956), 3–8, 3.

151. Ibid., 8.

Epilogue
The Politics of Plate Glass

1. *Daily Telegraph* quoted in *Votes for Women*, March 8, 1912, 352. For an overview of the campaign and a discussion of its place in the history of the struggle for the vote, see Antonia Raeburn, *The Militant Suffragettes* (London: Michael Joseph, 1973), 166–82; Roger Fulford, *Votes for Women: The Story of a Struggle* (London: Faber and Faber, 1957), 245–54; Andrew Rosen, *Rise Up, Women! The Militant Campaign of the Women's Social and Political Union, 1903–1914* (London: Routledge and Kegan Paul, 1974), 157–60. There had been some window breaking in the West End in November of 1911, but that earlier campaign was primarily directed at government offices. For the most recent assessment of suffragette tactics, see Cheryl R. Jorgensen-Earp, *"The Transfiguring Sword": The Just War of the Women's Social and Political Movement* (Tuscaloosa: University of Alabama Press, 1997).

2. *Daily Telegraph* quoted in *Votes For Women*, March 8, 1912, 352.

3. Cited in Emmeline Pankhurst, *My Own Story* (London: Eveleigh Nash, 1914), 217.

4. *Evening Standard* quoted in *Votes For Women*, March 8, 1912, 354.

5. *Daily Graphic*, March 2, 1912, 6.

6. *Standard*, March 4, 1912, 12.

7. *Draper and Drapery Times*, March 9, 1912, 331–32.

8. *Draper and Drapery Times*, March 16, 1912, 417.

9. Mary R. Richardson, *Laugh a Defiance* (London: George Weidenfeld and Nicholson, 1953), 39–40.

10. "Window Breaking: To One Who has Suffered," WSPU leaflet reprinted in Jane Marcus, ed., *Suffrage and the Pankhursts* (London: Routledge and Kegan Paul, 1987), 183–84. In one instance at least, a window smasher, Lady Rhondda's aunt Janetta, felt so guilty about her act that she went to the very same shop the next day and bought a five-guinea hat to make up for it. See the description of this incident in Janet Courtney, *The Women of My Time* (London: Lovat Dickson, 1934), 165.

11. For a discussion of nineteenth-century London and social protest, see Geoffrey Crossick, "The Organization of Space," in *A New Economic and Social History of Modern Europe*, ed. Heinz-Gerhard Haupt and Albert Carreras (London: Routledge, forthcoming); David Goodway, *London Chartism, 1838–1848* (Cambridge: Cambridge University Press, 1982), 111–14; and Donald Richter, *Riotous Victorians* (Athens: Ohio University Press, 1981).

12. Tickner, *The Spectacle of Women*, 190. Fulford made a very similar argument in *Votes for Women*, 118.

13. Richardson, *Laugh a Defiance*, 43. At the Lyons café, however, a group of men threw cups at Richardson and her militant friends. The café could thus hardly be construed as a safe haven.

14. Tickner, *The Spectacle of Women*, 190; Diane Atkinson, *The Purple, White, and Green: Suffragettes in London, 1906–1914* (London: Museum of London, 1992). See also Vicinus, *Independent Women*, 247–80 and most recently

Kaplan and Stowell, *Theatre and Fashion*, 152–84.

15. *Votes for Women* (1908) cited in Atkinson, *The Purple, White, and Green*, 15.

16. Francis Latham, *Is the British Empire Ripe for Government by Disorderly Women Who Smash Windows and Assault Police?* (London: Simpkin, Marshall, Hamilton, Kent and Co., 1911), 20.

17. Courtney, *Women of My Time*, 174.

18. See the exchange between Mr. Pethick–Lawrence and Keith Thomas, the managing director of the Imperial News Agency, "How Women Might Get the Vote," *Modern Business* 3 (July 1909); 4 (August 1909).

19. *Votes For Women*, January 7, 1910, 285.

20. *BC*, June 13, 1908.

21. For an analysis of this in the United States, see Cott, *Grounding of Modern Feminism*, 145–74; Rayna Rapp and Ellen Ross, "The Twenties Backlash: Compulsory Heterosexuality, the Consumer Family, and the Waning of Feminism," in *Class, Race, and Sex: The Dynamics of Control*, ed. Amy Swerdlow and K. Lessinger (Boston: G. K. Hall, 1982), 93–107.

22. Atkinson, *Purple, White, and Green*, 27.

23. Christabel Pankhurst, *Unshackled: The Story of How We Won the Vote*, ed. Rt. Hon. Lord Pethick-Lawrence (1959; reprint, London: Cresset Women's Voices, 1987), 205.

24. Among the many studies to explore the intersections between politics and consumption, see Auslander, *Taste and Power*; Victoria de Grazia, *How Fascism Ruled Women: Italy, 1922–1945* (Berkeley: University of California Press, 1992); and the introduction and essays in part 3 of de Grazia and Furlough, *The Sex of Things*. Also see Belinda Davis, "Home Fires Burning: Politics, Identity, and Food in World War I Berlin" (Ph.D diss., University of Michigan, 1992); Erica Carter, "Alice in Consumer Wonderland: West German Case Studies in Gender and Consumer Culture," in *Gender and Generation*, ed. Angela McRobbie and Mica Nava (London: Macmillan, 1984); Ellen Furlough, *Consumer Cooperation in France: The Politics of Consumption, 1834–1930* (Ithaca: Cornell University Press, 1991): Gurney, *Cooperative Culture in England*; Dana Frank, *Purchasing Power: Consumer Organizing, Gender, and the Seattle Labor Movement* (Cambridge: Cambridge University Press, 1994); Lizabeth Cohen, *Making a New Deal: Industrial Workers in Chicago, 1919–1939* (Cambridge: Cambridge University Press, 1990), 99–158; Jane Gaines, "Introduction: Fabricating the Female Body," in Gaines and Herzog, *Fabrications*, 5–11; Elizabeth Wilson, "All that Rage," in Gaines and Herzog, *Fabrications*, 28–38; Stuart Hall and Tony Jefferson, *Resistance through Rituals: Youth Subcultures in Post-War Britain* (London: Hutchinson, 1976); Dick Hebdige, *Subculture: The Meaning of Style* (London: Methuen, 1979).

25. This history has yet to be written. However, one may wish to consult Sally Alexander's "Becoming a Woman in London in the 1920s and 1930s," in Feldman and Jones, *Metropolis*, 245–71.

BIBLIOGRAPHY

Archival Sources

City of Westminster Local Archives Centre, London.
- Ashbridge Collection
- Liberty's Archive
- Paddington Vestry Minutes. vols. E–G, 1874–82
- Pamphlet Collection
- Photographic Collection
- Print Collection
- St. Marylebone Public Conveniences Sub-Committee Minutes, 1893–1900
- Thresher and Glenny Archives
- William Whiteley's Archive

Dickins and Jones In-Store Archive. Dickins and Jones Department Store, London.

Ellison Collection. New York Public Library, New York.

Fawcett Library, London.
- Newspaper Cuttings Collection. Box 38.

Greater London Record Office, London.
- Middlesex County Sessions Records. County Licensing Committee
- Hanover Square Division (St. Georges) MA/C/L/1878/68–72
- Paddington Division MA/C/L/1880/31–50
- St. James Division MA/C/L/1880/73–79
- Strand Division MA/C/L/1878/92–113

Guildhall Library, London.
- Noble Collection
- Philip Norman Collection
- Trade Card/Bill Head Collection

Harrod's In-Store Archive. Harrod's Department Store, London.

Heal and Son Archive. Archive of Art and Design, Victoria and Albert Museum, London.

House of Fraser Archive. The Archives and Business Record Centre, Glasgow University, Glasgow.
- Document Class HF6, HF9, HF10, HF11, HF15

Hulton Getty Picture Collection. London.

J. Lyons and Company Limited Archive. Greenford, Middlesex.

Lord Chamberlain's Plays. Department of Manuscripts. British Library, London.

Public Record Office, London.
- Crown Lands England House Department Reports, CRES 19.
- Letters Regarding Crown Leases, CRES 35.
- Home Office, H.O. 45.
- Metropolitan Board of Works, Works 6.
- Metropolitan Police Papers, Mepo. 2, Mepo. 3.
- Winding-Up Proceedings, J13/3727, J13/6238, J13/12390, J13/13795

Publicity Poster Collection. London Transport Museum, London.

Savoy Archives. Savoy Hotel, London.

Selfridges Archive. Selfridges Department Store, London.

Parliamentary Papers

United Kingdom. Hansard Parliamentary Debates, 3d series. Vol. 202 (1870): 395–402, 599–621, 877–94.

———. Hansard Parliamentary Debates, 3d series. Vol. 214 (1873): 327–29, 667–89.

———. Hansard Parliamentary Debates, 3d series. Vol. 218 (1874): 607–14.

———. Hansard Parliamentary Debates, 3d series. Vol. 252 (1880): 1531–45.

———. Hansard Parliamentary Debates, 3d series. Vol. 273 (1882): 1603–11.

Newspapers and Periodicals

A.B.C. Amusement Guide and Record: Being Alphabetical Particulars of All the Theatres, Concerts, Music Halls, Entertainments with the Times and Prices of Admission.

Bayswater Chronicle and West London Journal (BC)

Builder

Building News

Bus, Tram, and Cab Trades Gazette

Caterer, Hotel Proprietor, and Refreshment Contractor's Gazette

County Courts Chronicle

Daily Chronicle

Daily Express

Daily Graphic

Daily Mail

Daily News
Daily Telegraph
Draper
Draper and Drapery Times
Drapers' Journal
Drapers' Record: A Journal Devoted to the Drapery, Outfitting, and Upholstery Trades
Drapery Times
Drapier and Clothier: A Book of General Information for All Traders in and Purchasers of Textile Fabric
Englishwoman: An Illustrated Magazine
Englishwoman's Review of Social and Industrial Questions
Englishwoman's Year-Book
Evening News
Gentlewoman: The Illustrated Weekly Journal for Gentlewomen
Graphic
Grocery News and Oil Journal
Housewife: A Practical Magazine Concerning Everything in and about the Home
Illustrated London News
Ladies' Home Paper: A Weekly Journal for Gentlewomen
Lady: A Journal for Gentlewomen
Lady's Realm
London American: A Chronicle of the American Colony in Europe
London and Suburban A.B.C. Shopping Guide
The Lyceum: Monthly Journal of the Lyceum Club
Madame
Magazine of Commerce
Marylebone Mercury and West London Gazette
Modern Business
Modern Retailing: A Journal for Shopkeepers, Assistants, and Customers
Paddington Times
Pall Mall Gazette (*PMG*)
Play Pictorial
Progress: The Organ of the Lady Guide Association
Punch, or The London Charivari
Queen: The Lady's Newspaper and Court Chronicle
Retail Trader
Saturday Review of Politics, Literature, and Art
Shopkeeper: The Official Organ of the Shopkeeper's and Small Trader's Protection Society
Shopping: A Journal of Society for Society
Shopping: A Literary and Artistic Mirror of the World of Women
Shopping Life: The Only Journal Which Makes a Direct Appeal to the Shopping Public
Shopping News and Notes
Shops and Companies of London and the Trades and Manufactories of Great Britain
Sketch
Sphere
Standard
St. James Gazette
The Times (London)
Tourists' Monthly Holiday Guide to London
Visitors' Guide and Journal of Amusements
Votes For Women
Warehousemen and Drapers' Trade Journal and Review of the Textile and Fabric Manufacturers (*WDTJ*)
West End Advertiser
William Whitely's Diary: Almanac and Handbook of Useful Information for 1877–1915
Woman's Gazette, or News about Work.
Woman's World
Women's Suffrage Journal
Work and Leisure: The Englishwoman's Advertiser, Reporter, and Gazette (formerly *Woman's Gazette*)

Primary Sources

a'Beckett, Arthur William. *London at the End of the Century: A Book of Gossip by Arthur William a'Beckett.* London: Hurst and Blackett, 1900.

Ablett, William. *Reminiscences of an Old Draper.* London: Sampson Low, Marston, Earle, and Rivington, 1876.

Alison Adburgham, ed. *Yesterday's Shopping: The Army and Navy Stores Catalogue, 1907.* Facsimile ed. Devon: David and Charles Reprints, 1969.

"Advertise to the Women Who Buy!" *Advertiser's World* 2, no. 9 (August 1902): 227.

Aleph, William H. *London Scenes and London People.* London: W. H. Collingridge, 1863.

"The Americanising of Our Girls." *Bat*, February 23, 1884, 780.

Amies, Hardy. *Just So Far.* London: Collins, 1953.

Anstruther, Eva. "Ladies' Clubs." *Nineteenth Century* 45 (April 1899): 599–611.

Archer, William. *The Theatrical World of 1894.* London: Walter Scott, 1895.

The Art of Dining, or Gastronomy for Gastronomers. London: John Murray, 1852.

Ashford, E. B. "Women in Distributive Trades, Displacement Study." *Women's Industrial News* 20, no. 73 (April 1916): 9–14.

Asquith, Lady Cynthia. *Diaries, 1915–1918.* Edited by E. M. Horsley. New York: Alfred A. Knopf, 1969.

Baedeker, Karl. *London and the Environs: Handbook for Travellers*. 13th ed., rev. London: Dulau, 1902.

———. *London and the Environs: Handbook for Travellers*. 14th ed., rev. New York: Scribner, 1905.

———. *London and the Environs: Handbook for Travellers*. 16th ed., rev. London: T. Fisher Unwin, 1911.

Banfield, Frank. *The Great Landlords of London*. London: Spencer Blackett, 1890.

Barrington, Cecil V. *The Shop Hours Acts, 1892–1904*. London: Butterworth, 1905.

Barton, Rose. *Familiar London*. London: Adam and Charles Black, 1904.

Bayley, J. Ernest. *Drapery Business Organization Management and Accounts*. London: Sir Isaac Pitman, 1912.

Beaton, Cecil. *The Glass of Fashion*. 1954. Reprint, London: Casell, 1989.

Beavan, Arthur H. *Imperial London*. London: J. M. Dent, 1901.

Beerbohm, Max. *Yet Again*. New York: Alfred Knopf, 1923.

———. *Around Theatres*. Vol. 2. New York: Knopf, 1930.

———. *Last Theatres, 1904–1910*. Introduction by Rupert Hart-Davis. New York: Taplinger, 1970.

Beeton, Isabella. *Beeton's Book of Household Management*. 1861. Reprint, New York: Farrar, Straus, and Giroux, 1969.

Belcher, John. "Whiteley's New Premises." *Architectural Review* 31 (March 1912): 164–72.

Benjamin, Thelma. *London Shops and Shopping*. London: Herbert Joseph, 1934.

Bennett, Arnold. *Journalism for Women: A Practical Guide*. London and New York: John Lane, 1898.

———. *The Grand Babylon Hotel: A Fantasia on Modern Times*. 1902. Reprint, Harmondsworth: Penguin, 1985.

———. *The City of Pleasure: A Fantasia on Modern Times*. 1907. Reprint, New York: Doubleday, 1975.

Bensusan, S. L. "The World's Cafés—By Way of an Introduction." *Idler* 15 (February–July 1899): 125–31.

Benton, Eleanor R. "The Gentle Art of Shopping." *Harper's Weekly*, September 19, 1908.

Besant, Walter. *London in the Nineteenth Century*. London: Adam and Charles Black, 1909.

———., ed. *The Fascination of London: Mayfair, Belgravia, and Bayswater*. London: Adam and Charles Black, 1903.

Billington Grieg, Theresa. *The Consumer in Revolt*. London: Stephen Swift, 1912.

Black, Helen. *Notable Woman Authors of the Day*. 1893. Reprint, New York: Books for Libraries Press, 1972.

Bloch, Ivan. *Sexual Life in England Past and Present*. Translated by William Forstern. London: Francis Aldor, 1938.

Bloom, Ursula. *Victorian Vinaigrette*. London: Hutchinson, 1956.

———. *The Elegant Edwardian*. London: Hutchinson, 1958.

———. *Youth at the Gate*. London: Hutchinson, 1959

Board of Trade. "Handbook on London Trades—Clothing Trades, Part I—Girls." London: Darling and Sons, 1915.

Bonavia, Michael. *London before I Forget*. Upton-upon-Severn, Worcs: Self-Publishing Association. 1990.

Bone, James. *London Echoing*. London: Jonathan Cape, 1948.

Booker, Beryl Lee. *Yesterday's Child, 1890–1909*. London: John Long, 1937.

Booth, Charles. *Life and Labour of the People in London*. 2d Ser. *Industry*. 1902–4. Reprint, New York: Ams Press, 1970.

Brewis, Rachel. "Reminiscences." *Costume* 16 (1982): 86–92.

Brittain, Vera. *Testament of Youth*. 1933. Reprint, Harmondsworth: Penguin, 1989.

Broderick, George C. "Local Government in England." In *Local Government and Taxation*, edited by J. W. Probyn. London: Cassell, Petter, and Galpin, 1875.

Brontë, Charlotte. *Villette*. 1853. Reprint, London: Penguin, 1979.

Broom, Herbert. *The Practice of County Courts*. London: W. Maxwell, 1852.

Buchanen, Robert, and Charles Marlowe. *The Romance of a Shopwalker*. London: Royal Colchester, February 27, 1896.

Bullen, Frank T. *Confessions of a Tradesman*. London: Hodder and Stroughton, 1908.

Burgess, Fred W. *The Practical Retail Draper: A Complete Guide for the Drapery and Allied Trade*. 5 vols. London: Virtue and Co., 1912.

Burke, Thomas. *The London Spy: A Book of Town Travels*. London: Thorton Butterworth, 1925.

———. *London in My Time*. London: Rich and Cowan, 1934.

Burlington Arcade: Being a Discourse on Shopping for the Elite. London: Favil, 1925.

Carey, George Saville. "A Bond-Street Lounger, or A Man with Two Suits at His Back." London: Laurie and Whittle, 1800.

Cassell's Household Guide: Being a Complete Encyclopedia of Domestic and Social Economy. 3 vols. London: Cassell, Petter, and Galpin, 1869–71.

Cavers, Charles. *Hades! The Ladies! Being Extracts from the Diary of a Draper, Charles Cavers, Esq.* London: Gurney and Jackson, 1933.

Cawston, Arthur. *A Comprehensive Scheme for Street Improvements.* London: Edward Stanford, 1893.

Chambre, Major. *Recollections of West-End Life with Sketches of Society in Paris, India, etc.* London: Hurst and Blackett, 1858.

Champneys, Basil, ed. *Adelaide Drummand: Retrospect and Memoir.* London: Smith, Elder, 1915.

Chancellor, E. Beresford. *Wanderings in Piccadilly, Mayfair, and Pall Mall.* London: Alston Rivers, 1908.

———. *Knightsbridge and Belgravia: Their History, Topography, and Famous Inhabitants.* London: Sir Isaac Pitman, 1909.

———. *Wanderings in Marylebone: A Gossip about the Squares and the Streets and Their Past Residents.* London: Dulan, 1926.

———. *The West End of Yesterday and To-day: Being Studies in London's History and Topography during the Past Century.* London: Architectural Press, 1926.

———. *Liberty and Regent Street.* London: Liberty's, 1928.

Chesterton, G. K. *The Napoleon of Notting Hill.* London: John Lane, 1904.

Clark, Samson. *Retail Drapery Advertising: A Handbook on Drapery Publicity and Kindred Matters.* London: Simpkin, Marshall, Hamilton, Kent, 1910.

———. *Short Talks with Drapers.* London: Trade Press Association, 1916.

Clemens, Samuel L. *A Tramp Abroad.* Edited by Charles Neider. New York: Harper and Row, 1977.

Clinch, George. *Mayfair and Belgravia: Being an Historical Account of the Parish of St. George, Hanover Square.* London: Truslove and Shirley, 1892.

Clunn, Harold P. *London Rebuilt, 1897–1927.* London: John Murray, 1927.

———. *The Face of London: The Record of a Century's Changes and Development.* London: Simpkin and Marshall, 1932.

Cobbe, Frances Power. "Clubs for Women." *Echo,* March 14, 1871.

———. *The Duties of Women: A Course of Lectures.* Boston: George H. Ellis, 1881.

———. *The Life of Frances Power Cobbe.* Vol. 2. Boston: Houghton, Mifflin, 1895.

Collins' Guide to London and Neighborhood. Rev. ed. London: William Collins, 1882.

Cook, Emily Constance. *Highways and Byways in London.* London: Macmillan, 1903.

Cook, John. *A Guide to the Recovery of Debts in the County Courts.* London: T. Pettitt, 1878.

"The Cost of High Living." *Cornhill Magazine* 31 (January-June 1875): 412–21.

County Court Practice Made Easy, or Debt Collection Simplified. 5th ed., rev. London: Effingham Wilson, 1922.

"County Courts." *London Society* 6 (January 1867): 455–60.

The County Courts. London, 1852.

Courtney, Janet E. *Recollected in Tranquility.* London: William Heinemann, 1926.

———. *The Women of My Time.* London: Lovat Dickson, 1934.

Cunningham, Peter. *London in 1857.* 4th ed. London: John Murray, 1857.

Dam, H. J. W. *The Shop Girl.* London: Gaiety, November 22, 1894.

———. "The Shop Girl at the Gaiety." *Sketch,* November 28, 1894.

———. *The Shop Girl.* London: Gaiety, March 25, 1920.

Dan, Horace, and Morgan Wilmott. *English Shop Fronts Old and New.* London: B. T. Batsford, 1907.

Dasent, Arthur Irwin. *The History of St. James's Square and the Foundation of the West End.* London: Macmillan, 1895.

———. *Piccadilly in Three Centuries.* London: Macmillan, 1920.

Delafield, E. M. [pseud.]. *Diary of a Provincial Lady.* London: Macmillan, 1930.

Denny, Ernest. *The Gentle Art of Shopping.* London: Samuel French, 1919.

"Diana at Dinner." *Punch, or The London Charivari,* June 28, 1890, 303.

Dickens, Charles. "Debt." *Household Words* 17 (1858): 319–21.

Dickens's Dictionary of London, 1896. 18th ed. London: J. Smith, 1896.

District Railway Guide to London. London: Alfred Boot and Son, 1988.

Ditchfield, P. H. *London's West End.* London: Jonathan Cape, 1925.

Dockrell, E. Morgan. "Women's Clubs." *Humanitarian* 12 (1898): 346–51.

Doré, Gustave, and Blanchard Jerrold. *London, a Pilgrimage.* 1872. Reprint, New York: Dover, 1970.

Douglas, Fanny. *The Gentlewoman's Book of Dress.* Victoria Library for Gentlewomen Series. London: Henry and Co. 1895.

Doyle, Richard, and Percival Leigh. *Manners and Customes of Ye Englyshe.* London: Bradbury and Evans, 1849.

"Dress and Its Cost." London: Ladies' Sanitary Association, ca. 1860.

Duff-Gordon, Lady Lucy Christiana Sutherland. *Discretions and Indiscretions.* London: Jarrolds, 1932.

du Maurier, George. "Female Clubs v. Matrimony." *Punch's Almanack for 1878* 74 (December 14, 1877): n.p.

Edwardes, George. *Our Miss Gibbs.* London: Gaiety, January 25, 1909.

Edwards, Percy J. *History of London Street Improvements, 1855–1897.* London: London County Council, 1898.

Eliot, George. *Brother Jacob.* 1879. Reprint, London: Virago, 1984.

Elliot, J. H. "Imprisonment for Debt." *Westminster Review* 47 (December 1845): 231–41.

"The Etiquette of Modern Society: A Guide to Good Manners in Every Possible Situation." London: Ward, Lock and Co., 1881.

"Family Budgets." *Cornhill Magazine* 10 (January–June 1901): 656–66, 790–800; 11 (June–December 1901): 48–61, 184–91.

Fashionable Rendezvous. London: Harrod's, 1909.

Fearnside, William Gray, and Thomas Harrel, eds. *Holmes's Great Metropolis, or Views of the History of London Being a Grand National Exhibition of the British Capital.* London: Thomas Holmes, 1851.

Fifty Years of London Society, 1870–1920. New York: Brentano's, 1920.

Fiske, Stephen. *English Photographs.* London: Tinsley Brothers, 1869.

Fletcher, Margaret. *O, Call Back Yesterday.* Oxford: Basil Blackwell, 1939.

Friederichs, Hilda. "A Peep at the Pioneer Club." *Young Woman* 4 (1895): 302–6.

Frith, W. P. *My Autobiography and Reminiscences.* 7th ed. London: Richard Bentley, 1889.

Gissing, George. *The Odd Women.* 1893. Reprint, Harmondsworth: Penguin, 1993.

———. *In the Year of Jubilee.* 1894. Reprint, New York: Dover, 1982.

———. *Will Warburton: A Romance of Real Life.* 1905. Reprint, London: Hogarth, 1985.

Gillows and Company. *Gillows: A Record of a Furnishing Firm during Two Centuries.* 2d ed. London: Harrison and Sons, 1901.

"Going a Shopping." *Leisure Hour* 15 (1866): 198–200.

Gordon, Frederick. *Crosby Hall: The Ancient Palace and Great Banqueting Hall.* 2d ed. London: Merchant and Lenges, 1868.

Gosden, Walter, ed. *The Langham Hotel Guide to London: Prepared for the Use of Visitors.* London: Langham Hotel Co., 1898.

Granville-Barker, Harley. *The Madras House.* Edited by Margery Morgan. London: Methuen, 1977.

Greg, W. R. "Life at High Pressure." *Contemporary Review* 25 (March 1875): 623–38.

Greville, Lady Beatrice Violet. *Faiths and Fashions: Short Essays Republished.* London: Longmans, Green, 1880.

———. *Vignettes of Memory.* London: Hutchinson, 1927.

The Grocer's Guide to Window Dressing. London: Grocer, 1911.

Hall, Owen. *The Girl from Kay's.* London: Apollo, November 24, 1902.

Hallsworth, Sir Joseph, and Rhys J. Davies. *The Working Life of Shop Assistants: A Study of the Conditions of Labour in the Distributive Trades.* Manchester: National Labour Press, 1910.

Hamilton, Cicely. *Diana of Dobson's: A Romantic Comedy in Four Acts.* New York: Samuel French, 1925.

———. *Life Errant.* London: J. M. Dent and Sons, 1935.

Harvey, William. *London Scenes and People.* London: W. H. Collingridge, 1863.

Hill, Georgiana. *A History of Dress: From the Saxon Period to the Present.* 2 vols. London: Richard Bentley and Son, 1893.

Hobhouse, Emily. "Women Workers: How They Live, and How They Want to Live." *Nineteenth Century* 47 (January–June 1900): 471–84.

Hoffman, P. C. *They Also Serve: The Story of the Shop Walker.* London: Porcupine Press, 1909.

Hollingshead, John. *Gaiety Chronicles.* London: Archibald Constable, 1898.

———. *"Good Old Gaiety": An Historette and Remembrance.* London: Gaiety Theatre Co., 1903.

"Hotels and Restaurants." *Building News* 36 (February 1879): 157–58.

The House That Everywoman Knows. London: Harrod's, 1909.

Hudson, Derek, ed. *Munby: Man of Two Worlds. The Life and Diaries of Arthur J. Munby, 1828–1910.* London: John Murray, 1972.

Hughes, M. V. *A London Girl of the 1880s.* 1946. Reprint, Oxford: Oxford University Press, 1979.

———. *A London Home in the 1890s.* 1946. Reprint, Oxford: Oxford University Press, 1978.

Humphrey, Mrs. C. E. *The Book of the Home: A Comprehensive Guide on All Matters Pertaining to the Household.* London: Gresham, 1910.

Hunt, James Henry Leigh. *A Saunter through the West End*. London: Hurst and Blackett, 1861.

Ivey, George James. *Clubs of the World: A General Guide or Index to the London and County Clubs*. 2d ed. London: Harrison, 1880.

Jeune, Lady. "The Ethics of Shopping." *Fortnightly Review* 57 (January–June 1895): 123–32.

Johnson, Adelaide. "The Lyceum Club of London: An Organization of Women Engaged in Literary, Artistic, and Scientific Pursuits." *Critic* 86 (1905): 132–37.

Jones, Dora. "The Ladies' Clubs of London." *Young Woman* 7 (1899): 409–13.

Jones, Harry. *East and West London: Being Notes of Common Life and Pastoral Work in Saint James's Westminster and Saint Georges-in-the East*. London: Smith, Elder, 1875.

Josephy, Helen, and Mary Margaret McBride. *London Is a Man's Town (But Women Go There)*. New York: Coward-McCann, 1930.

Kenny, Courtney Stanhope. *The History of the Law of England as to the Effects of Marriage on Property and on the Wife's Legal Capacity*. London: Reeves and Turner, 1879.

Keppel, Sonia. *Edwardian Daughter*. London: Hamish Hamilton, 1958.

Kerr, Robert Malcolm. *The Commentaries on the Laws of England: Of Sir William Blackstone, Adapted to the Present State of the Law*. 4th ed., vol. 1. London: John Murray, 1876.

Kerwan, Daniel Joseph. *Palace and Hovel, or Phases of London Life*. 1870. Reprint, London: Abellard-Schuman, 1963.

Kingston, Beatty, et al. *Homes of the Passing Show*. London: Savoy Press, 1900.

Krout, Mary H. *A Looker On in London*. New York: Dodd, Mead, 1899.

"Ladies' Clubs." *Nineteenth Century* 45 (April 1899): 598–611.

"Ladies' Clubs." *Tinsley's Magazine* 4 (February–July 1869): 368–75.

Ladies Sanitary Association. *Twenty-third Annual Report of the Ladies Sanitary Association*. London: Ladies Sanitary Association: 1881.

———. *Twenty-fourth Annual Report of the Ladies Sanitary Association*. London: Ladies Sanitary Association: 1882.

———. *Report of the Ladies Sanitary Association to the Seventh International Congress of Hygiene and Demography*. London: Jarold and Sons, 1891.

Lancaster, Osbert. *All Done from Memory*. London: John Murray, 1953.

Langford, Howard. *Shopping*. Bedford Palace, September 20, 1921.

Langley, Percival, and Sid Walker. *Shopping*. Palace, East Ham, October 13, 1919.

Latham, Francis. *Is the British Empire Ripe for Government by Disorderly Women Who Smash Windows and Assault Police?* London: Simpkin, Marshall, Hamilton, Kent and Co., 1911.

Levy, Amy. "Women and Club Life." In *The Complete Novels and Selected Writings of Amy Levy, 1861–1889*, edited by Melvyn New. Gainsville: University of Florida Press, 1993.

Libra, J. G. "Shop-Windows." *Building News*, June 24, 1881, 731–34; September 23, 1881, 384–87; October 28, 1881, 552–54; November 4, 1881, 584–85.

Linton, Elizabeth Lynn. *The New Woman in Haste and at Leisure*. New York: Merriam, 1895.

Little, Charles P. *Little's London Pleasure Guide, 1898*. London: Simpkin, Marshall, Hamilton, Kent, 1898.

"Local Industries: Cash v. Credit." *Chelsea Herald*, August 30, 1884.

Loftie, W. J. *Tourists' Guide through London*. London: Edward Stanford, 1881.

———. *The Colour of London: Historic, Personal, and Local*. London: Chatto and Windus, 1914.

Lonalti, Stuart. *The Shop Girl and Her Master*. Leigh, Lancaster: Theatre Royal, April 19, 1915.

London County Council. "Public Conveniences in London." London: London County Council, 1928.

"London Girls of the Period: The West End Girl." *Girl of the Period Miscellany* 1, no. 3 (May 1869): 90–92.

London Lyceum Club, Ltd. *Bye-Laws and Regulations*. London: London Lyceum Club, 1934.

London Post Office Directory. London: Frederick Kelly, 1860, 1870, 1880.

London's Social Calendar. London: 1914.

"The London Shop-Fronts." *Chamber's Journal of Popular Literature, Science, and Art*, October 15, 1864, 670–72.

London, the West End: Nelson's Colour Views. London: T. Nelson, [187?].

Machray, Robert. *The Night Side of London*. London: John Macqueen, 1902.

Maitland, Fred. *Number One "Gerrard"—or Selfridge Outdone*. Empire Liverpool, April 25, 1912.

Mansfield, Katherine. *Stories*. Edited by Elizabeth Bowen. 1908. Reprint. New York: Vintage, 1956.

Marx, Karl. *Capital: A Critique of Political Economy.* 1867. Reprint, New York: Modern Library, 1936.

May, Phil. "The Smoking Room at a Ladies Club." *Pall Mall Budget,* December 27, 1894, 27.

Mayhew, Henry. *London Labour and the London Poor.* Vol. 1. 1851. Reprint, London: Frank Cass, 1967.

———. *London's Underworld.* Vol. 4 of *Londons Labour and the London Poor.* 1862. Reprint, edited by Peter Quennell, London: Bracken Books, 1983.

Mayhew, John. *Tradesman's Guide to the Practice of the County Courts.* 3d ed. London: Simpkin, Marshall, 1880.

Mearns, Andrew. *The Bitter Cry of Outcast London: An Inquiry into the Conditions of the Abject Poor.* London: London Congregational Union, 1883.

Melville, William. *The Shop Soiled Girl.* London: Elephant and Castle, October 3, 1910.

Mills, A. R., ed. *Two Victorian Ladies: More Pages from the Journals of Emily and Ellen Hall.* Letchworth, Herfordshire: Garden City Press, 1969.

Miss Hollamby on Shopping. London, 1906.

Modern Belles: Dedicated to All Beaux. London: J. J. Stockdale, 1818.

Modern London, the World's Metropolis: An Epitome of Results. London: Historical Publishing, 1890.

Montizambert, Elizabeth. *London Discoveries in Shops and Restaurants.* London: Women Publishers, 1924.

Moore, Maurice C. *Fighting the Enemies of the Shopkeeper.* London: Drapers' Record, 1915.

Muir, D. MacMillan. *Regent Street Past and Present.* London: Blackfriars Press, 1925.

———., ed. *The Modern Shop: An Illustrated Description of the Modern Shop.* London and Leicester: Blackfriars Press, 1927.

Murray, Margaret Polson. "Women's Clubs in America." *Nineteenth Century* 47 (May 1989): 847–54.

My Milliner's Bill. London: Court Theater, March 6, 1884.

Naylor, Stanley. *Gaiety and George Grossmith: Random Reflections on the Serious Business of Enjoyment.* London: Stanley Paul, 1913.

Neish, R. "A Woman's Shopping." *Pall Mall Magazine* 24 (May–August 1901): 311–20.

Neville, Ralph Henry. *London Clubs: Their History and Treasures.* London: Chatto and Windus, 1911.

Neville, Ralph Henry, and Charles Edward Jerningham. *Piccadilly to the Mall: Manners, Morals, and Man.* London: Duckworth, 1908.

"New Buildings in the West End." *Building News* 41 (July–December 1881): 349.

"The New Whiteley's." *Daily News,* November 23, 1911.

Newman, Thomas Charles. *Many Parts.* London: Hutchinson, 1935.

Newnham-Davis, Nathaniel. *Dinners and Diners: Where and How to Dine in London.* London: Grant Richards, 1899.

———. *The Gourmet's Guide to London.* London: Grant Richards, 1914.

Nicholson, Shirley. *A Victorian Household: Based on the Diaries of Marion Sanbourne.* London: Barrie and Jenkins, 1988.

Norton, Caroline. *Caroline Norton's Defense: English Laws for Women in the Nineteenth Century.* 1854. Reprint, Chicago: Academy, 1982.

Old Bond Street as a Centre of Fashion, 1686–1906. London: J. and G. Ross, 1906.

Olivia's Shopping and How She Does It: A Prejudiced Guide to the London Shops. London: Gay and Bird, 1906.

Osware, E. R. *Boot's "District" Guide to London.* 8th ed. Issued with the authority of the District Railway Company. London: Sampson Low, Marston, and Co., 1898.

Paine, William. *Shop Slavery and Emancipation: A Revolutionary Appeal to the Educated Young Men of the Middle Class.* London: P. S. King, 1912.

Pankhurst, Christabel. *Unshackled: The Story of How We Won the Vote.* Edited by the Rt. Hon. Lord Pethick-Lawrence. 1957. Reprint, London: Cresset Women's Voices, 1987.

Pankhurst, Emmeline. *My Own Story.* London: Eveleigh Nash, 1914.

Panton, Jane Ellen. *Homes of Taste: Economical Hints.* London: Sampson Low, Marston, Searle, 1890.

———. *Leaves from a Life.* London: Eveleigh Nash, 1908.

———. *More Leaves from a Life.* London: Eveleigh Nash, 1911.

———. *Leaves from a Housekeeper's Book.* London: EveleighNash, 1914.

Particulars, &c. of the Lady Guide Association, Ltd, the London and International Reception, Inquiry, Information, and Supply Bureau. London: Lady Guide Association, 1889.

Pascoe, Charles Eyre. *London of To-Day: An Illustrated Handbook for the Season.* Boston: Roberts Brothers, 1885.

———. *London in Little.* London: Hazell, Watson, Viney, 1891.

Peel, Dorothy Constance. *Life's Enchanted Cup: An Autobiography, 1872–1933*. London: John Lane and the Bodley Head, 1933.

Perkins, E. E. *The Lady's Shopping Manual and Mercury Album*. London: T. Hurst, 1834.

Philip, R. K. *Handy Book of Shopkeeping*. London, 1892.

Philipps, Mrs. Wynford. "Women's Clubs in England." In *Transactions of the International Congress of Women of 1899*. Vol. 7, *Women in Social Life*, edited by the Countess of Aberdeen. London: T. Fisher Unwin, 1900.

Poiret, Paul. *My First Fifty Years*. Translated by Stephan Haden Guest. London: Victor Gollancz, 1931.

Price, Julius M. *Dame Fashion*. London: Sampson, Low, Marston, 1912.

Raverat, Gwen. *Period Piece: A Cambridge Childhood*. London:Faber and Faber, 1960.

Richardson, Mary R. *Laugh a Defiance*. London: George Weidenfeld and Nicholson, 1953.

Ritchie, J. Ewing. *The Night Side of London*. London: WilliamTweedle, 1857.

Rogers, W. S. *A Book of the Poster: Illustrated with Examples of the Work of the Principal Poster Artists of the World*. London: Greening, 1901.

Rubens, Paul A. *Selfrich's Annual Sale*. London: Savoy, October 24, 1910.

Sala, George Augustus. *Twice round the Clock, or The Hours of the Day and Night in London*. 1859. Reprint, New York: Humanities; Leicester: Leicester University Press, 1971.

———. *London Up to Date*. London: Adam and Charles Black, 1894.

Scannell, Dorothy. *Mother Knew Best: An East End Childhood*. London: Macmillan, 1974.

Scott, Clement. *How They Dined Us in 1860 and How They Dine Us Now*. London, 1900.

Selfridge, H. Gordon [Callisthenes]. *Selfridge's of London: A Five Year Retrospect*. London: Selfridge's and Co., 1913.

———. *The Romance of Commerce*. 2d ed. London: John Lane the Bodley Head, 1923.

"Selfridge's Report." *Economist*, June 4, 1910, 1245.

Shaw, Donald. *London in the Sixties*. London: Everett, 1908.

Sherwell, Arthur. *Life in West London: A Study and a Contrast*. London: Methuen, 1897.

Shonfield, Zuzanna. *The Precariously Privileged: A Professional Family in Victorian London*. Oxford: Oxford University Press, 1987.

"Shopping." *Living Age* 33 (December 22, 1906): 758–60.

"Shopping without Money." *Leisure Hour* 14 (1865): 110–12.

The Show Window. Nottingham Hippodrome, February 24, 1927.

Sights of London Illustrated and Metropolitan Hand-Book for Railways, Tramways, Omnibuses, River Steamboats, and Cabfares. London: Henry Herbert, 1883.

Simmonds, W. H. *The Practical Grocer: A Manual and Guide for the Grocer and Provision Merchant*. 4 vols. London: Gresham, 1904–5.

Sims, George R. *My Life: Sixty Years' Recollections of Bohemian London*. London: Eveleigh Nash, 1917.

———, ed. *Edwardian London*. 3 vols. Originally published as *Living London*. London: Cassell and Co., 1902. Reprint, London: Village Press, 1990.

Sitwell, Osbert, ed. *Two Generations*. London: Macmillan, 1940.

Smedley, Constance. *Crusaders: The Reminiscences of Constance Smedley*. London: Duckworth, 1929.

Smiles, Samuel. *Thrift*. London: J. Murray, 1875.

Smith, Annie Swan. "Annie Swan Smith on Women's Clubs." In *With Women's Eyes: Visitors to the New World, 1775–1918*, compiled and edited by Marion Tinling. Hamden, Conn.: Archon, 1993.

Smith, Thomas. *Successful Advertising: Its Secrets Explained*. 7th annual ed. London: Mutual Advertising Agency, 1885.

Social Centres of London: Being a Comprehensive Guide to the Social, Educational, Recreative, and Religious Institutes and Clubs of the Metropolis. London: Polytechnic Reception Bureau, 1892.

Stacpoole, Florence. *Handbook of Housekeeping for Small Incomes*. London: Walter Scott, 1897.

Stacpoole, Margaret de Vere. *London, 1913*. New York: Duffield, 1914.

Stanley, Maude. *Clubs for Working Girls*. London: Macmillan, 1890.

Stead, William T. *The Americanization of the World, or The Trend of the Twentieth Century*. New York: Horace Markley, 1902.

Stevenson, Dr. James. "Paddington Vestry Report on the Necessity of Latrine Accommodation for Women in the Metropolis." London: Paddington Vestry Hall, 1879.

Stirling, A. M. W., ed. *Victorian Sidelights: From the Papers of the Late Mrs. Adams-Acton*. London: Ernest Benn, 1954.

"Subway Advertising." *Outlook* (New York) 79 (January 1905): 4–5.

"Suffragette Parade and Suffrage Breakfast." *Evening Standard and St. James Gazette.* February 20, 1909.

Sutherst, Thomas. *Death and Disease Behind the Counter.* London: Kegan Paul, 1884.

Thiselton-Dyer, T. F. *British Popular Customs: Past and Present.* London: George Bell, 1876.

This Way, Madam. London: Coronet Theater, September 2, 1913.

Thomas, John Birch. *Shop Boy: An Autobiography.* London: Routledge and Kegan Paul, 1983.

Thompson, Tierl, ed. *Dear Girl: The Diaries and Letters of Two Working Women, 1897–1917.* London: Women's Press, 1987.

Timbs, John. *Clubs and Club Life in London, with Anecdotes of Its Famous Coffee-Houses, Hostelries, and Taverns, from the Seventeenth Century to the Present Time.* London: Chatto and Windus, 1872. Reprint, Detroit: Gale Research Co., 1967.

"Tit-Bits" Guide to London. London: George Newnes, 1895.

The Toy Shop. London: Palace Doncaster, July 21, 1915.

"Trade Journals." *Cornhill Magazine* 52 (1886): 512–37.

Van Sittart, Jane, ed. *From Minnie, with Love: The Letters of a Victorian Lady, 1849–1861.* London: Peter Davies, 1974.

[Vasili, Count Paul]. *The World of London.* London: Sampson Low, Marston, Searle, Rivington, 1885.

Veblen, Thorstein. *The Theory of the Leisure Class.* 1899. London: Penguin, 1994.

Verity, Thomas. "The Modern Restaurant." *Royal Institute of British Architects Transactions* 29 (1878–79): 85–92.

A Visit to Regent Street. London: Henry Vizetelly, [1862].

Waldon, Rich. *Just in Time.* Glasgow: Royal Princess, July 23, 1915.

Walford, L. B. *Memories of Victorian London.* London: Edward Arnold, 1912.

Walsh, J. H. *A Manual of Domestic Economy: Suited to Families Spending from £100 to £1,000 a Year.* 2d ed. London: Routledge and Company, 1857.

[Walter]. *My Secret Life.* Reprint. New York: Grove Press, 1966.

Warren, Mrs. *How I Managed My House on Two Hundred Pounds a Year.* 4th American ed. Boston: Loring, 1866.

Waxman, Frances Sheafer. *A Shopping Guide to Paris and London.* New York: McBride, Nast, and Co., 1912.

Webb, Aston. "Improved Shop Architecture for London: The New Regent's Quadrant." *Nineteenth Century and After* 60 (July 1906): 165–68.

Wells, H. G. *Tono-Bungay.* 1908. Reprint, Boston: Houghton Mifflin, 1966.

———. *Kipps.* London: Dalston Theatre, July 25, 1910.

———. *The Wife of Sir Isaac Harman.* 1914. Reprint, London: Hogarth, 1986.

———. *Experiment in Autobiography.* New York: Macmillan, 1934.

Wey, Francis. *A Frenchman Sees the English in the 'Fifties.* Translated by Valerie Pirie. 1856. Reprint, London: Sidgwick and Jackson, 1935.

W. H. E. *"In Difficulties": A Treatise on Trade.* London: West End News, 1878.

"Where Ladies Are Specially Catered For." *Licensing World and Licensed Trade Review,* March 8, 1902, 163.

White, Percy. *The West End.* London: Sands, 1900.

White, William H. "On Middle-Class Houses in Paris and Central London." *Royal Institute of British Architects Transactions* 28 (1877–78): 21–54.

Wigley, Mrs. "Domestic Puzzles: Where Shall I Buy—Shops or Stores?" *Leisure Hour* 28 (1879): 331–34.

Wilkinson, W. E. *The Shops Act, 1912–1934,* London: Solicitors' Law Stationery Society, 1934.

Williams, Montague, Q. C. *Round London: Down East and Up West.* London: Macmillan, 1892.

Winterburn, Florence Hull. *Principles of Correct Dress.* New York: Harper Brothers, 1914.

Woodhead's Directory of Credit Drapers of England and Wales. Manchester: George Woodhead, 1890.

Woodward, William. "The Sanitation and Reconstruction of Central London." In *Essays on the Street Re-Alignment, Reconstruction, and Sanitation of Central London, and the Rehousing of the Poorer Classes.* London: George Bell, 1886.

Woolf, Virginia. *The London Scene: Five Essays by Virginia Woolf.* New York: Random House, 1975.

Wyman's Commercial Encyclopedia of Leading Manufacturers of Great Britain, and Their Productions: Being a Guide to Merchant Buyers All Over the World. 4th ed. London: Wyman and Sons, 1896.

Wyndham, Horace. *Feminine Frailty.* London: Ernest Benn, 1929.

Yearbook of Women's Club Houses. 2d ed. New York: Woman's Journal, 1929.

Zola, Emile. *The Ladies' Paradise.* 1883. Reprint, Berkeley: University of California Press, 1992.

Secondary Sources

Abel-Smith, Brian, and Robert Stevens. *Lawyers and the Courts: A Sociological Study of the English Legal System, 1750–1965*. London: Heinemann, 1967.

Abelson, Elaine S. *When Ladies Go a-Thieving: Middle-Class Shoplifters in the Victorian Department Store*. Oxford and New York: Oxford University Press, 1989.

Abrams, Ann Uhry. "From Simplicity to Sensation: Art in American Advertising, 1904–1929." *Journal of Popular Culture* 10, no. 3 (Winter 1976): 620–28.

Adburgham, Alison. *Women in Print: Writing Women and Women's Magazines from the Restoration to the Accession of Victoria*. London: George Allen and Unwin, 1972.

———. *Liberty's: The Biography of a Shop*. London: Allen and Unwin, 1975.

———. *Shopping in Style: London from the Restoration to Edwardian Elegance*. London: Thames and Hudson, 1979.

———. *Shops and Shopping, 1800–1914: Where and in What Manner the Well-Dressed Englishwoman Bought Her Clothes*. 2d ed. London: Barrie and Jenkins, 1989.

Adler, Judith. "Origins of Sightseeing." *Annals of Tourism Research* 16, no. 1 (1989): 7–29.

Adorno, Theodor W., and Max Horkheimer. *Dialectic of Enlightenment*. Translated by John Cumming. 1944. Reprint, New York: Herder and Herder, 1972.

Agnew, Jean-Christophe. *Worlds Apart: The Market and the Theater in Anglo-American Thought, 1550–1750*. Cambridge: Cambridge University Press, 1986.

———. "Times Square: Secularization and Sacralization." In *Inventing Times Square: Commerce and Culture at the Crossroads of the World*, edited by William R. Taylor. New York: Russell Sage Foundation, 1991.

Alexander, David. *Retailing in England during the Industrial Revolution*. London: University of London, Athlone Press, 1970.

Alexander, Sally. "Women, Class, and Sexual Difference in the 1830s and 1840s: Some Reflections on the Writing of a Feminist History" *History Workshop Journal* 17 (1984): 125–49.

———. "Becoming a Woman in London in the 1920s and 1930s." In *Metropolis London: Histories and Representations since 1800*, edited by David Feldman and Gareth Stedman Jones. London: Routledge, 1989.

Allen, Jeanne. "The Film Viewer as Consumer." *Quarterly Review of Film Studies* 5, no. 4 (Fall 1980): 481–99.

———. "*Fig Leaves* in Hollywood: Female Representation and Consumer Culture." In *Fabrications: Costume and the Female Body*, edited by Jane Gaines and Charlotte Herzog. London: Routledge, 1990.

———. "Palaces of Consumption as Women's Clubs: En-Countering Women's Labor History and Feminist Film Criticism." *Camera Obscura: A Journal of Feminism and Film Theory* 22 (January 1990): 150–58.

Allen, Robert C. *Horrible Prettiness: Burlesque and American Culture*. Chapel Hill: University of North Carolina Press, 1991.

Altick, Richard D. *The English Common Reader: A Social History of the Mass Reading Public, 1800–1900*. Chicago: University of Chicago Press, 1963.

———. *The Shows of London*. Cambridge: Harvard University Press, Belknap Press, 1978.

Anderson, Amanda. *Tainted Souls and Painted Faces: The Rhetoric of Fallenness in Victorian Culture*: Ithaca: Cornell University Press, 1993.

Anderson, B. L. "Money and the Structure of Credit in the Eighteenth Century." *Business History* 12, no. 2 (July 1970): 85–101.

Anderson, Gregory, ed. *The White-Blouse Revolution: Female Office Workers since 1870*. Manchester: Manchester University Press, 1988.

Anderson, Nancy Fix. *Woman against Women in Victorian England: A Life of Eliza Lynn Linton*. Bloomington: Indiana University Press, 1987.

Appadurai, Arjun, ed. *The Social Life of Things: Commodities in Cultural Perspective*. Cambridge: Cambridge University Press, 1986.

Appleby, Joyce. "Consumption in Early Modern Social Thought." In *Consumption and the World of Goods*, edited by John Brewer and Roy Porter. London: Routledge, 1993.

Ardis, Ann L. *New Women, New Novels: Feminism and Early Modernism*. New Brunswick, N.J.: Rutgers University Press, 1990.

Arendt, Hannah. *The Human Condition*. Chicago: University of Chicago Press, 1958.

Ash, John, and Louis Turner. *The Golden Hordes: International Tourism and the Pleasure Periphery*. New York: St. Martin's Press, 1976.

Ashplant, T. G. "London's Working Men's Clubs, 1875–1914." In *Popular Culture and Class Conflict, 1590–1914: Explorations in *the History of Labour and Leisure*, Edited by Eileen Yeo and Stephen Yeo. Sussex: Harvester; Atlantic Highlands, N.J.: Humanities, 1981.

Ashworth, Gregory, and Brian Goodall, eds. *Marketing Tourism Places*. London: Routledge, 1990.

Ashworth, Gregory, and J. E. Tunbridge. *The Tourist-Historic City*. London: Belhaven Press, 1990.

Atiyah, P. S. *The Rise and Fall of the Freedom of Contract*. Oxford: Clarendon Press, 1979.

Atkins, P. J. "The Spatial Configuration of Class Solidarity in London's West End, 1792–1939." *Urban History Yearbook* 17 (1990): 36–65.

———. "How the West End Was Won: The Struggle to Remove Street Barriers in Victorian London." *Journal of Historical Geography* 19, no. 3 (1993): 265–77.

Atkinson, Diane. *The Purple, White, and Green: Suffragettes in London, 1906–1914*. London: Museum of London, 1992.

Auslander, Leora. "The Gendering of Consumer Practices in Nineteenth-Century France." In *The Sex of Things: Gender and Consumption in Historical Perspective*, edited by Victoria de Grazia with Ellen Furlough. Berkeley: University of California Press, 1996.

———. *Taste and Power: Furnishing Modern France*. Berkeley: University of California Press, 1996.

Ayers, Pat, and Jan Lambertz. "Marriage Relations, Money, and Domestic Violence in Working-Class Liverpool, 1919–1939." In *Labour and Love: Women's Experience of Home and Family, 1850–1940*, edited by Jane Lewis. Oxford: Basil Blackwell, 1986.

Bailey, Peter. *Leisure and Class in Victorian England: Rational Recreation and the Contest for Control, 1830–1885*. London: Routledge and Kegan Paul; Toronto: University of Toronto Press, 1978.

———. "Ally Sloper's Half-Holiday: Comic Art in the 1880s." *History Workshop Journal* 16 (Autumn 1983): 4–31.

———. "Parasexuality and Glamour: The Victorian Barmaid as Cultural Prototype." *Gender and History* 2, no. 2 (Summer 1990): 148–72.

———. " 'Naughty but Nice': Musical Comedy and the Rhetoric of the Girl." In *The Edwardian Theatre: Essays on Performance and the Stage*, edited by Michael R. Booth and Joel H. Kaplan. Cambridge: Cambridge University Press, 1996.

———., ed. *Music Hall: The Business of Pleasure*. Milton Keynes and Philadelphia: Open University Press, 1986.

Baker, T. F. T. *A History of the County of Middlesex*. Vol. 9 *Hampstead and Paddington Parishes*. Oxford: Oxford University Press, 1989.

Bakhtin, Mikhail. *Rabelais and His World*. Translated by Hélène Iswolsky. Bloomington: Indiana University Press, 1984.

Ballaster, Ros, Margaret Beetham, and Sandra Hebron. *Women's Worlds: Ideology, Femininity, and the Woman's Magazine*. London: Macmillan, 1991.

Banks, J. A. *Prosperity and Parenthood: A Study of Family Planning among the Victorian Middle Classes*. London: Routledge and Kegan Paul, 1954.

Banks, Olive. *Faces of Feminism: A Study of Feminism as a Social Movement*. New York: St. Martin's Press, 1981.

Barker, T. C., and Michael Robbins. *A History of London Transport: Passenger Travel and The Development of the Metropolis*. 2 Vols. London: George Allen and Unwin, 1974.

Barker-Benfield, G. J. *The Culture of Sensibility: Sex and Society in Eighteenth-Century Britain*. Chicago: University of Chicago Press, 1992.

Barmen, Christian. *The Man Who Built London Transport: A Biography of Frank Pick*. London: David and Charles, 1979.

Barret-Ducrocq, François. *Love in the Time of Victoria: Sexuality, Class, and Gender in Nineteenth-Century London*. Translated by John Howe. London: Verso, 1991.

Barth, Gunther. *City People: The Rise of Modern City Culture in Nineteenth-Century America*. Oxford: Oxford University Press, 1980.

Barthes, Roland. *The Fashion System*. Translated by Matthew Ward and Richard Howard. New York: Hill and Wang, 1983.

Basch, Norma. *In the Eyes of the Law: Women, Marriage, and Property in Nineteenth-Century New York*. Ithaca: Cornell University Press, 1982.

Bataille, Georges. *The Accursed Share: An Essay on General Economy*. Vol. 1. *Consumption*. Translated by Robert Hurley. New York: Zone Books, 1988.

Baudrillard, Jean. *Selected Writings*. Edited by Mark Poster. Stanford, Calif.: Stanford University Press, 1988.

Beals, Polly. "Fabian Feminism: Gender, Politics and Culture in London, 1880–1930." Ph.D. diss. Rutgers University, 1989.

Beckson, Karl. *London in the 1890s: A Cultural History*. New York: W. W. Norton, 1992.

Beetham, Margaret. *A Magazine of Her Own? Domesticity and Desire in the Woman's Magazine, 1800–1914*. London: Routledge, 1996.

Benhabib, Seyla. "Models of Public Space: Hannah Arendt, the Liberal Tradition, and Jürgen Habermas." In *Habermas and the Public Sphere*, edited by Craig Calhoun. Cambridge: MIT Press, 1992.

Benjamin, Walter. *Illuminations*. Edited with an introduction by Hannah Arendt, translated by Harry Zohn. New York: Schocken Books, 1969.

———. *Reflections: Essays, Aphorisms, Autobiographical Writings*. Edited by Peter Demetz, translated by Edmund Jephcott. New York: Harcourt, Brace, Jovanovich, 1978.

———. *Charles Baudelaire: A Lyric Poet in the Era of High Capitalism*. Translated by Harry Zohn. London: Verso, 1983.

———. "Central Park." Translated by Lloyd Spencer. *New German Critique* 34 (Winter 1985): 32–58.

Bennett, Tony. "A Thousand and One Troubles: Blackpool Pleasure Beach." In *Formations of Pleasure*, edited by Frederic Jameson. London: Routledge and Kegan Paul, 1983.

———. "The Exhibitionary Complex." *New Formations* 4 (Spring 1988): 73–102.

Benson, John. *The Rise of Consumer Society in Britain, 1880–1980*. London: Longman, 1994.

Benson, John, and Gareth Shaw, eds. *The Evolution of Retail Systems, ca. 1800–1914*. Leicester: Leicester University Press, 1992.

Benson, Susan Porter. *Counter Cultures: Saleswomen, Managers, and Customers in American Department Stores, 1890–1940*. Urbana: University of Illinois Press, 1988.

Berger, John. *Ways of Seeing*. Harmondsworth: Penguin, 1972.

Berman, Marshall. *All That Is Solid Melts into Air: The Experience of Modernity*. London: Verso, 1982.

Bermingham, Ann, and John Brewer, eds. *The Consumption of Culture, 1600–1800: Image, Object, Text*. London: Routledge, 1995.

Betterton, Rosemary, ed. *Looking On: Images of Femininity in the Visual Arts and the Media*. London: Pandora, 1987.

Biagini, Eugenio F. *Liberty, Retrenchment, and Reform: Popular Liberalism in the Age of Gladstone, 1860–1880*. Cambridge: Cambridge University Press, 1992.

Birken, Lawrence. *Consuming Desire: Sexual Science and the Emergence of a Culture of Abundance, 1871–1914*. Ithaca: Cornell University Press, 1988.

Black, Gerry. *Living Up West: Jewish Life in London's West End*. London. London Museum of Jewish Life, 1994.

Blair, Karen J. *The Clubwoman as Feminist: True Womanhood Redefined, 1868–1914*. New York: Holmes and Meier, 1980.

Blumin, Stuart M. *The Emergence of the Middle Class: Social Experience in the American City, 1760–1900*. Cambridge: Cambridge University Press, 1989.

Booth, Michael R. "East End and West End: Class and Audience in Victorian London." *Theatre Research International* 2, no. 2 (February 1977): 98–103.

———. "The Metropolis on Stage." In *The Victorian City: Images and Realities*, vol. 1, edited by H. J. Dyos and Michael Wolff. London: Routledge and Kegan Paul, 1978.

———. *Victorian Spectacular Theatre, 1850–1910*. London: Routledge and Kegan Paul, 1981.

———. *Theatre in the Victorian Age*. Cambridge: Cambridge University Press, 1991.

Booth, Michael R., and Joel H. Kaplan, eds. *The Edwardian Theatre: Essays on Performance and Style*. Cambridge: Cambridge University Press, 1996.

Borsay, Peter. *The English Urban Renaissance: Culture and Society in the Provincial Town, 1660–1760*. Oxford: Clarendon Press; New York: Oxford University Press, 1989.

Bostick, Theodora, "The Press and the Launching of the Woman's Suffrage Movement, 1866–1867." *Victorian Periodicals Review* 13, no. 4 (Winter 1980): 125–31.

Bourdieu, Pierre. *Outline of a Theory of Practice*. Translated by Richard Nice. Cambridge: Cambridge University Press, 1977.

———. *Distinction: A Social Critique of the Judgment of Taste*. Translated by Richard Nice. Cambridge: Harvard University Press, 1984.

Bowlby, Rachel. *Just Looking: Consumer Culture in Dreiser, Gissing, and Zola*. London: Methuen, 1985.

———. *Shopping with Freud*. London: Routledge, 1993.

———. "Soft Sell: Marketing Rhetoric in Feminist Criticism." In *The Sex of Things: Gender and Consumption in Historical Perspective*, edited by Victoria de Grazia with Ellen Furlough. Berkeley: University of California Press, 1996.

Boyer, M. Christine. "Cities For Sale: Merchandising History at South Street Seaport." In *Variations on a Theme Park: The New American City and the End of Public Space*, edited by Michael Sorkin. New York: Noonday Press, 1992.

Braithwaite, Brian. *Women's Magazines: The First 300 Years*. London: Peter Owen, 1995.

Brake, Laurel. *Subjugated Knowledges: Journalism, Gender, and Literature in the Nineteenth Century.* New York: New York University Press, 1994.

Brake, Laurel, Aled Jones, and Lionel Madden, eds. *Investigating Victorian Journalism.* New York: St. Martin's Press, 1990.

Branca, Patricia. *Silent Sisterhood: Middle-Class Women in the Victorian Home.* London: Croom Helm, 1975.

Brand, Dana. *The Spectator and the City in Nineteenth-Century American Literature.* Cambridge: Cambridge University Press, 1991.

Brandon, Ruth. *The New Woman and the Old Men: Love, Sex and the Woman Question.* New York: W. W. Norton, 1990.

Bratton, J. S. "Beating the Bounds: Gender Play and Role Reversal in the Edwardian Music Hall." In *The Edwardian Theatre: Essays on Performance and Style*, edited by Michael R. Booth and Joel H. Kaplan. Cambridge: Cambridge University Press, 1996.

Breen, T. H. " 'Baubles of Britain': The American and Consumer Revolutions of the Eighteenth Century." *Past and Present* 119 (May 1988): 73–104.

Breward, Christopher. "Femininity and Consumption: The Problem of the Late-Nineteenth-Century Fashion Journal." *Journal of Design History* 7, no. 2 (1994): 71–89.

———. *The Culture of Fashion: A New History of Fashionable Dress.* Manchester: Manchester University Press, 1995.

Brewer, John. *The Pleasures of the Imagination: English Culture in the Eighteenth Century.* London: HarperCollins, 1997.

Brewer, John, and Roy Porter, eds. *Consumption and the World of Goods.* London: Routledge, 1993.

Brewer, John, and Susan Staves, eds. *Early Modern Conceptions of Property.* London: Routledge, 1995.

Briggs, Asa. *Friends of the People: The Centenary History of Lewis's.* London: B. T. Batsford, 1956.

———. *Victorian People: A Reassessment of Persons and Themes, 1851–1867.* Rev. ed. Chicago: University of Chicago Press, 1975.

———. *Victorian Cities.* 1963. Reprint, Berkeley: University of California Press, 1993.

———. "The Human Aggregate." In *The Victorian City: Images and Realities.* Vol. 1. London: Routledge and Kegan Paul, 1973.

———. *Victorian Things.* Chicago: University of Chicago Press, 1988.

Bronner, Simon J. "Reading Consumer Culture." In *Consuming Visions: Accumulation and Display of Goods in America, 1880–1920*, edited by Simon J. Bronner. New York: W. W. Norton for the Henry Francis du Pont Winterthur Museum, 1989.

Brooks, Peter. *The Melodramatic Imagination: Balzac, Henry James, Melodrama, and the Mode of Excess.* New York: Columbia University Press, 1985.

Brown, Lucy. *Victorian News and Newspapers.* Oxford: Clarendon Press, 1985.

Buci-Glucksmann, Christine. "Catastrophic Utopia: The Feminine as Allegory of the Modern." *Representations* 14 (Spring 1986): 220–29.

Buck-Morss, Susan. "The Flâneur, the Sandwichman, and the Whore: The Politics of Loitering." *New German Critique* 39 (Fall 1986): 99–140.

———. *The Dialectics of Seeing: Walter Benjamin and the Arcades Project.* Cambridge: MIT Press, 1989.

Burke, Timothy. *Lifebuoy Men, Lux Women: Commodification, Consumption, and Cleanliness in Modern Zimbabwe.* Durham, N.C.: Duke University Press, 1996.

Burman, Sandra, ed. *Fit Work for Women.* London: Croom Helm, 1979.

Burn, W. L. *The Age of Equipoise: A Study of the Mid-Victorian Generation.* London: George Allen and Unwin, 1964.

Burnett, John. *Plenty and Want: A Social History of Diet in England from 1815 to the Present Day.* London: Thomas Nelson and Sons, 1966.

———., ed. *Destiny Obscure: Autobiographies of Childhood, Education, and Family from the 1820s to the 1920s.* London: Routledge, 1994.

Burton, Antoinette. *Burdens of History: British Feminists, Indian Women, and Imperial Culture, 1865–1915.* Chapel Hill: University of North Carolina Press, 1994.

Bush, David, and Derek Taylor. *The Golden Age of British Hotels.* London: Northwood, 1974.

Butler, Judith P. *Gender Trouble: Feminism and the Subversion of Identity.* New York: Routledge, 1990.

Butsch, Richard. "Bowery B'hoys and Matinee Ladies: The Re-Gendering of Nineteenth-Century American Theatre Audiences." *American Quarterly* 46, no. 3 (September 1994): 374–405.

Buzard, James. *The Beaten Track: European Tourism, Literature, and the Ways to Culture, 1800–1918.* Oxford: Clarendon Press, 1993.

Byrd, Max. *London Transformed: Images of the City in the Eighteenth Century.* New Haven: Yale University Press, 1978.

Caine, Barbara. *Victorian Feminists.* Oxford: Oxford University Press, 1992.

Calhoun, Craig, ed. *Habermas and the Public Sphere.* Cambridge: MIT Press, 1992.

Callaway, Helen, and Dorothy O. Helly. "Crusader for Empire: Flora Shaw/Lady Lugard." In *Western Women and Imperialism: Complicity and Resistance,* edited by Napur Chaudhuri and Margaret Strobel. Bloomington: Indiana University Press, 1992.

Campbell, Beatrix. *The Iron Ladies: Why Do Women Vote Tory?* London: Virago, 1987.

Campbell, Colin. *The Romantic Ethic and the Spirit of Modern Consumerism.* Oxford: Basil Blackwell, 1987.

Camplin, Jamie. *The Rise of the Plutocrats: Wealth and Power in Edwardian England.* London: Constable, 1978.

Cannadine, David. *Lords and Landlords: The Aristocracy and the Towns, 1774–1967.* Leicester: Leicester University Press, 1980.

———. "Victorian Cities: How Different?" In *The Victorian City: A Reader in British Urban History, 1820–1914,* edited by R. J. Morris and Richard Rodger. London: Longman, 1993.

Carter, Erica. "Alice in the Consumer Wonderland: West German Case Studies in Gender and Consumer Culture." In *Gender and Generation,* edited by Angela McRobbie and Mica Nava. London: Macmillan, 1984.

Castells, Manuel. *The Urban Question: A Marxist Approach.* 2d ed. Translated by Alan Sheridan. Cambridge: MIT Press, 1977.

Casteras, Susan P., and Colleen Denny, ed. *The Grosvenor Gallery: A Palace of Art in Victorian England.* New Haven: Yale University Press, 1996.

Centre for Urban Studies. *London: Aspects of Change.* London: MacGibbon and Kee, 1964.

Chaney, David. "The Department Store as a Cultural Form." *Theory, Culture, and Society* 1, no. 3 (1983): 22–31.

Charney, Leo, and Vanessa R. Schwartz, eds. *Cinema and the Invention of Modern Life.* Berkeley: University of California Press, 1995.

Clapham, John. *An Economic History of Modern Britain: Machines and National Rivalries, 1887–1914.* 1938. Reprint, Cambridge: Cambridge University Press, 1968.

Clark, Anna. *The Struggle for the Breeches: Gender and the Making of the British Working Class.* Berkeley: University of California Press, 1990.

Clarke, John, and Chas Critcher. *The Devil Makes Work: Leisure in Capitalist Britain.* Urbana: University of Illinois Press, 1985.

Clinton-Baddeley, V. C. *The Burlesque Tradition in the English Theater after 1660.* New York: Benjamin Blom, 1971.

Coffin, Judith G. *The Politics of Women's Work: The Paris Garment Trades, 1750–1915.* Princeton: Princeton University Press, 1996.

Cohen, Daniel A. "The Murder of Maria Bickford: Fashion, Passion and the Birth of a Consumer Culture." *American Studies* 31, no. 2 (Fall 1990): 5–30.

Cohen, Erik. "The Tourist Guide: The Origins, Structure, and Dynamics of a Role." *Annals of Tourism Research* 12, no. 1 (1985): 5–29.

———. "Authenticity and Commoditization in Tourism." *Annals of Tourism Research* 15 (1988): 371–86.

Cohen, Lizabeth. *Making a New Deal: Industrial Workers in Chicago, 1919–1939.* Cambridge: Cambridge University Press, 1990.

Cohen, Margaret. "Panoramic Literature and the Invention of Everyday Genres." In *Cinema and the Invention of Modern Life,* edited by Leo Charney and Vanessa R. Schwartz. Berkeley: University of California Press, 1995.

Cohen, Patricia Cline. "Safety and Danger: Women on American Public Transport." In *Gendered Domains: Rethinking the Public and Private in Women's History. Essays from the Seventh Berkshire Conference on the History of Women,* edited by Dorothy O. Helly and Susan M. Reverby. Ithaca: Cornell University Press, 1992.

Colby, Reginald. *Mayfair: A Town within London.* London: County Life, 1966.

Cooper, Nicholas. *The Opulent Eye: Late Victorian and Edwardian Taste in Interior Design.* London: Architectural Press, 1976.

Copelman, Dina M. *London's Women Teachers: Gender, Class, and Feminism, 1870–1930.* New York: Routledge, 1996.

Coppock, J. T., and Hugh C. Prince. *Greater London.* London: Faber and Faber, 1964.

Corina, Maurice. *Fine Silks and Oak Counters: Debenhams, 1778–1978.* London: Hutchinson, 1978.

Corley, T. A. B. "Consumer Marketing in Britain, 1914–1960." *Business History* 29, no. 4 (October 1987): 65–83.

Cornish, W. R., and G. de N. Clark. *Law and Society in England, 1750–1950.* London: Sweet and Maxwell, 1989.

Cott, Nancy. *The Grounding of Modern Feminism.* New Haven: Yale University Press, 1987.

Cowan, Ruth Schwartz. *More Work for Mother: The Ironies of Household Technology from the Open Hearth to the Microwave*. New York: Basic Books, 1983.

Coward, Rosalind. *Female Desire: Women's Sexuality Today*. London: Paladin Books, 1984.

Crary, Johnathan. *Techniques of the Observer: On Vision and Modernity in the Nineteenth Century*. Cambridge: MIT Press, 1990.

Cross, Gary S. *A Quest for Time: The Reduction of Work in Britain and France, 1840–1940*. Berkeley: University of California Press, 1989.

———. *Time and Money: The Making of Consumer Culture*. London: Routledge, 1993.

Crossick, Geoffrey. "The Emergence of the Lower-Middle Class in Britain: A Discussion." In *The Lower Middle Class in Britain, 1870–1914*, edited by Geoffrey Crossick. New York: St. Martin's Press, 1977.

———. *An Artisan Elite in Victorian Society: Kentish London, 1840–1880*. London: Croom Helm, 1978.

———. "The Petite Bourgeoisie in Nineteenth-Century Britain." In *Shopkeepers and Master Artisans in Nineteenth Century Europe*. Edited by Geoffrey Crossick and Heinz-Gerhard Haupt. London: Methuen, 1984.

———. "Shopkeepers and the State in Britain, 1870–1914." In *Shopkeepers and Master Artisans in Nineteenth-Century Europe*, edited by Geoffrey Crossick and Heinz-Gerhard Haupt. London: Methuen, 1984.

———. "The Organization of Space." In *A New Economic and Social History of Modern Europe*, edited by Heinz-Gerhard Haupt and Albert Carreras. London: Routledge, forthcoming.

Crossick, Geoffrey, and Heinz-Gerhard Haupt. *The Petite Bourgeoisie in Europe, 1780–1914: Enterprise, Family, and Independence*. London: Routledge, 1995.

Crossick, Geoffrey, and Serge Jaumain, eds. *Cathedrals of Consumption: The European Department Store, 1850–1939*. Aldershot: Ashgate, 1999.

Culver, Stuart. "What Manikins Want: *The Wonderful Wizard of Oz* and *The Art of Dry Goods Windows*." *Representations* 21 (Winter 1988): 97–116.

Cunningham, Gail. *The New Woman and the Victorian Novel*. London: Macmillan, 1978.

Cunningham, Hugh. *Leisure in the Industrial Revolution, ca. 1780–1880*. New York: St. Martin's Press, 1980.

Dale, Tim. *Harrod's: The Store and the Legend*. London: Pan Books, 1981.

Damon-Moore, Helen. *Magazines for the Millions: Gender and Commerce in the "Ladies Home Journal" and the "Saturday Evening Post."* Albany: State University of New York Press, 1994.

Dangerfield, George. *The Strange Death of Liberal England, 1910–1914*. 1935. Reprint, New York: Perigree Books, 1980.

Darwin, Bernard. *British Clubs*. London: Collins, 1947.

Davidoff, Leonore. *The Best Circles: Women and Society in Victorian England*. Totowa, N.J.: Rowman and Littlefield, 1973.

———. "Regarding Some 'Old Husbands' Tales': Public and Private in Feminist History." In *Worlds Between: Historical Perspectives on Gender and Class*. New York: Routledge, 1995.

Davidoff, Leonore, and Catherine Hall. *Family Fortunes: Men and Women of the English Middle Class, 1780–1850*. Chicago: University of Chicago Press, 1987.

Davies, Tony. "Transports of Pleasure: Fiction and Its Audiences in the Later-Nineteenth Century" In *Formations of Pleasure*, edited by Frederic Jameson. London: Routledge and Kegan Paul, 1983.

Davis, Belinda. "Home Fires Burning: Politics, Identity, and Food in World War I Berlin." Ph.D. diss., University of Michigan, 1992.

Davis, Dorothy. *Fairs, Shops, and Supermarkets: A History of English Shopping*. Toronto: University of Toronto Press, 1966.

Davis, Jessica Milner. *Farce*. London: Methuen, 1978.

Davis, John. *Reforming London: The London Government Problem, 1855–1900*. Oxford: Clarendon Press, 1988.

———. "Radical Clubs and London Politics, 1870–1900." In *Metropolis London: Histories and Representations since 1800*, edited by David Feldman and Gareth Stedman Jones. London: Routledge, 1989.

Davis, Natalie Zemon. *Society and Culture in Early Modern France*. Stanford, Calif.: Stanford University Press, 1975.

Davis, Susan G. *Parades and Power: Street Theatre in Nineteenth-Century Philadelphia*. Philadelphia: Temple University Press, 1986.

Davis, Tracy C. *Actresses as Working Women: Their Social Identity in Victorian Culture*. London: Routledge, 1991.

———. "Indecency and Vigilance in the Music Halls." In *British Theatre in the 1890s: Essays on Drama and the Stage*, edited by Richard Foulkes. Cambridge: Cambridge University Press, 1992.

———. "Edwardian Management and the Structures of Industrial Capitalism." In *The*

Edwardian Theatre: Essays on Performance and Style, edited by Michael R. Booth and Joel H. Kaplan. Cambridge: Cambridge University Press, 1996.

Debord, Guy. *Society of the Spectacle*. Rev. ed. Detroit: Black and Red, 1983.

de Certeau, Michel. *The Practice of Everyday Life*. Translated by Steven F. Rendall. Berkeley: University of California Press, 1984.

Deghy, Guy. *Paradise in the Strand: The Story of Romano's*. London Press: Richards, 1958.

de Grazia, Victoria. *How Fascism Ruled Women: Italy, 1922–1945*. Berkeley: University of California Press, 1992.

de Grazia, Victoria, with Ellen Furlough, eds. *The Sex of Things: Gender and Consumption in Historical Perspective*. Berkeley: University of California Press, 1996.

de Lauretis, Theresa. *Alice Doesn't: Feminism, Semiotics, Cinema*. Bloomington: Indiana University Press, 1984.

———. *Technologies of Gender: Essays on Theory, Film, and Fiction*. Bloomington: Indiana University Press, 1987.

de Maré, Eric. *The London Doré Saw: A Victorian Evocation*. New York: St. Martin's, 1973.

Deutsch, Sarah. "Reconceiving the City: Women, Space, and Power in Boston, 1870–1910." *Gender and History* 6, no. 2 (August 1994): 202–23.

Diamond, B. I. "A Precursor of the New Journalism: Frederick Greenwood of the *Pall Mall Gazette*." In *Papers for the Millions: The New Journalism in Britain, 1850s to 1914*, edited by Joel H. Wiener. Westport, Conn.: Greenwood Press, 1988.

Doane, Mary Ann. "Film and the Masquerade: Theorising the Female Spectator." *Screen* 23, nos. 3–4 (September–October 1982): 74–87.

———. "The Economy of Desire: The Commodity Form in/of the Cinema." *Quarterly Review of Film and Video Studies* 11 (1988–89): 23–33.

Dolin, Tim. "*Cranford* and the Victorian Collection." *Victorian Studies* 36, no. 2 (Winter 1993): 179–206.

Domosh, Mona. "Shaping the Commercial City: Retail Districts in Nineteenth-Century New York and Boston." *Annals of the Association of American Geographers* 80, no. 2 (June 1990): 268–84.

Donahue, Joseph, ed. "The Empire Theatre of Varieties Licensing Controversy of 1894: Testimony of Laura Ormiston Chant before the Theatres and Music Halls Licensing Committee of the London County Council, Sessions House, Clerkenwell, 10 October 1894." In *Nineteenth Century Theatre* 15, no. 1 (Summer 1987): 50–60.

Donajgrodzki, A. P., ed. *Social Control in Nineteenth-Century Britain*. London: Croom Helm, 1977.

Doughan, David. *Feminist Periodicals, 1855–1984*. New York: New York University Press, 1987.

Douglas, Mary, and Baron Isherwood. *The World of Goods*. New York: Basic Books, 1979.

Drawbell, James W. "How the Press Caters for Women's Interests." In *The Press, 1898–1948*. London: Newspaper World, 1948.

Dudden, Faye E. *Women in the American Theatre: Actresses and Audiences, 1790–1870*. New Haven: Yale University Press, 1994.

Duncan, Hugh Dalziel. *Culture and Democracy: The Struggle for Form in Society and Architecture in Chicago and the Middle West during the Life and Times of Louis H. Sullivan*. Totowa, N.J.: Bedminster Press, 1965.

Dunlop, C. R. B. "Debtors and Creditors in Dickens' Fiction." *Dickens Studies Annual: Essays on Victorian Fiction* 19 (1990): 25–47.

Dyer, Gary R. " 'The Vanity Fair' of Nineteenth-Century England: Commerce, Women, and the East in the Ladies Bazaar." *Nineteenth Century Literature* 46, no. 2 (September 1991): 196–222.

Dyhouse, Carol. "Mothers and Daughters in the Middle-Class Home, ca. 1870–1914." In *Labour and Love: Women's Experience of Home and Family, 1850–1940*, edited by Jane Lewis. Oxford: Basil Blackwell, 1986.

———. *Feminism and the Family in England, 1880–1939*. Oxford: Basil Blackwell, 1989.

Dyos, H. J. *Victorian Suburb: A Study of the Growth of Camberwell*. 2d ed. Leicester: Leicester University Press, 1977.

Dyos, H. J., and Michael Wolff, eds. *The Victorian City: Images and Realities*. 2 vols. London: Routledge and Kegan Paul, 1973.

Dyos, H. J. and D. A. Reeder. "Slums and Suburbs." In *The Victorian City: Images and Realities*. Vol. 1. London: Routledge and Kegan Paul, 1973.

Earle, Peter. *The Making of the English Middle Classes: Business, Society, and Family Life in London, 1660–1730*. Berkeley: University of California Press, 1989.

Eckert, Charles. "The Carol Lombard in Macy's Window." *Quarterly Review of Film Studies* 3, no. 1 (Winter 1978): 1–22.

Elbaum, Bernard, and William Lazonick, eds. *The Decline of the British Economy: An Institutional Approach*. Oxford: Clarendon Press, 1986.

Eley, Geoff. "Nations, Publics, and Political Cultures: Placing Habermas in the Nineteenth Century." In *Habermas and the Public Sphere*, edited by Craig Calhoun. Cambridge: MIT Press, 1992.

Ellenberger, Nancy W. "The Transformation of London 'Society' at the End of Victoria's Reign: Evidence from the Court Presentation Records." *Albion* 22, no. 4 (Winter 1990): 633–53.

Elliott, Blanche B. *A History of English Advertising*. London: B. T. Batsford, 1962.

Elliott, Bridget. "New and Not So 'New Women' on the London Stage: Aubrey Beardsley's *Yellow Book* Images of Mrs. Patrick Campbell and Réjane." *Victorian Studies* 31, no. 1 (Autumn 1987): 33–57.

Elshtain, Jean Bethke. *Public Man, Private Woman: Women in Social and Political Thought*. Princeton: Princeton University Press, 1981.

Erenberg, Lewis A. *Steppin' Out: New York Nightlife and the Transformation of American Culture, 1890–1930*. Westport, Conn.: Greenwood, 1981.

———. "Impresarios of Broadway Nightlife." In *Inventing Times Square: Commerce and Culture at the Crossroads of the World*, edited by William Taylor. New York: Russell Sage Foundation, 1991.

Erickson, Amy Louise. *Women and Property in Early Modern England*. London: Routledge, 1993.

Etherington-Smith, Meredith, and Jeremy Pilcher. *The "It" Girls: Lucy, Lady Duff Gordon, the Couturière "Lucile"; and Elinor Glynn, Romantic Novelist*. London: Harcourt Brace Jovanovich, 1986.

Ethington, Philip P. *The Public City: The Political Construction of Urban Life in San Francisco, 1850–1900*. Cambridge: Cambridge University Press, 1994.

Ewen, Stuart. *Captains of Consciousness: Advertising and the Social Roots of Consumer Culture*. New York: McGraw-Hill, 1976.

Ewen, Stuart, and Elizabeth Ewen. *Channels of Desire: Mass Images and the Shaping of American Consciousness*. New York: McGraw Hill, 1982.

Faderman, Lilian. *Surpassing the Love of Men: Romantic Friendship and Love between Women from the Renaissance to the Present*. New York: Morrow, 1981.

Featherstone, Mike. "Perspectives on Consumer Culture." *Sociology* 24, no. 1 (February 1990): 5–22.

———. *Consumer Culture and Postmodernism*. London: Sage, 1991.

Feinstein, Charles. "A New Look at the Cost of Living, 1870–1914." In *New Perspectives on the Late Victorian Economy: Essays in Quantitative Economic History, 1860–1914*, edited by James Forman-Peck. Cambridge: Cambridge University Press, 1991.

Feldman, David, and Gareth Stedman Jones, eds. *Metropolis London: Histories and Representations since 1800*. London: Routledge, 1989.

Ferguson, Marjorie. *Forever Feminine: Women's Magazines and the Cult of Femininity*. London. Heinemann, 1983.

Ferguson, Priscilla Parkhurst. "The Flâneur: Urbanization and Its Discontents." In *Home and Its Dislocations in Nineteenth-Century France*, edited by Suzanne Nash. Albany: State University of New York Press, 1993.

Ferguson, R. B. "The Adjudication of Commercial Disputes and the Legal System in Modern England." *British Journal of Law and Society* 7, no. 2 (Winter 1980): 141–57.

———. "Commercial Expectations and the Guarantee of the Law: Sales Transactions in Mid-Nineteenth-Century England." In *Law, Economy, and Society, 1750–1914: Essays in the History of English Law*, edited by G. R. Rubin and David Sugarman. Abingdon, Oxon.: Professional Books, 1988.

Ferry, John William. *A History of the Department Store*. New York: Macmillan, 1960.

Fielding, Daphne. *The Duchess of Jermyn Street: The Life and Good Times of Rosa Lewis and the Cavendish Hotel*. Harmondsworth: Penguin, 1978.

Fine, Ben. "Modernity, Urbanism, and Modern Consumption: A Comment." *Environment and Planning* D.: *Society and Space* 11, no. 5 (October 1993): 599–601.

Fine, Ben, and Ellen Leopold. "Consumerism and the Industrial Revolution." *Social History* 15, no. 2 (May 1990): 151–79.

———. *The World of Consumption*. London: Routledge, 1993.

Fine, Elizabeth C., and Jean Haskell Speer. "Tour Guide Performances as Sight Sacralization." *Annals of Tourism Research* 12, no. 1 (1985): 73–95.

Finkelstein, Joanne. *Dining Out: A Sociology of Modern Manners*. Oxford: Polity Press in association with Basil Blackwell, 1989.

———. *The Fashioned Self*. Philadelphia: Temple University Press, 1991.

Finn, Margot. "Debt and Credit in Bath's Court of Requests, 1829–1839." *Urban History* 21, pt. 2 (October 1994): 211–36.

———. "Women, Consumption, and Coverture in England, ca. 1760–1860." *Historical Journal* 39, no. 3 (September 1996): 703–22.

Fisher, F. J. "The Development of London as a Center of Conspicuous Consumption in the Sixteenth and Seventeenth Centuries." In *Essays in Economic History*, vol. 2, edited by E. M. Carus Wilson. London: Edward Arnold, 1962.

Fisher, Judith L., and Stephen Watt, eds. *When They Weren't Doing Shakespeare: Essays on Nineteenth-Century British and American Theatre.* Athens: University of Georgia Press, 1989.

Fiske, John. *Reading the Popular.* Boston: Unwin Hyman, 1989.

Fitzgerald, Robert. *Rowntree and the Marketing Revolution, 1862–1962.* Cambridge: Cambridge University Press, 1995.

Flint, Kate. *The Woman Reader, 1837–1914.* Oxford: Clarendon Press, 1993.

Ford, P. "Excessive Competition in the Retail Trades: Changes in the Number of Shops, 1901–1931." *Economic Journal: The Journal of the Royal Economic Society* 45 (September 1935): 501–8.

Forty, Adrian. *Objects of Desire.* New York: Pantheon, 1986.

Foucault, Michel. *Discipline and Punish: The Birth of the Prison.* Translated by Alan Sheridan. New York: Pantheon, 1977.

———. *The History of Sexuality*, Vol. 1, *An Introduction*, translated by Robert Hurley. New York: Vintage Books, 1980.

———. "Of Other Spaces." Translated by Jay Miskowiec. *Diacritics* 16, no. 1 (Spring 1986): 22–27.

Foulkes, Richard, ed. *British Theatre in the 1890s: Essays on Drama and the Stage.* Cambridge: Cambridge University Press, 1992.

Fox, Richard Wrightman, and T. J. Jackson Lears, eds. *The Culture of Consumption: Critical Essays in American History, 1880–1980.* New York: Pantheon Books, 1983.

Frank, Dana. *Purchasing Power: Consumer Organizing, Gender, and the Seattle Labor Movement.* Cambridge: Cambridge University Press, 1994.

Fraser, Derek. "The Edwardian City." In *Edwardian England*, edited by Donald Read. New Brunswick, N.J.: Rutgers University Press, 1982.

Fraser, Derek, and Anthony Sutcliffe, eds. *The Pursuit of Urban History.* London: Edward Arnold, 1983.

Fraser, Hamish. *The Coming of the Mass Market, 1850–1914.* Hamden, Conn.: Archon, 1981.

Fraser, Nancy. "Rethinking the Public Sphere: A Contribution to the Critique of Actually Existing Democracy." *Social Text* 25/26 (1990): 56–80.

Friedberg, Anne. *Window Shopping: Cinema and the Postmodern.* Berkeley: University of California Press, 1993.

Fulford, Roger. *Votes for Women: The Story of a Struggle.* London: Faber and Faber, 1957.

Furlough, Ellen. *Consumer Cooperation in France: The Politics of Consumption, 1834–1930.* Ithaca: Cornell University Press, 1991.

———. "Packaging Pleasures: Club Méditerranée and French Consumer Culture, 1950–1968." *French Historical Studies* 18, no. 1 (Spring 1993): 65–81.

Gagnier, Regina. *Idylls of the Marketplace: Oscar Wilde and the Victorian Public.* Stanford, Calif.: Stanford University Press, 1986.

Gaines, Jane. "The Queen Christina Tie-Ups: Convergence of Show Window and Screen." *Quarterly Review of Film and Video Studies* 11 (1988–89): 35–60.

Gaines, Jane, and Charlotte Herzog, eds. *Fabrications: Costume and the Female Body.* New York: Routledge, 1990.

Gallagher, Catherine, and Thomas Laqueur, eds. *The Making of the Modern Body: Sexuality and Society in the Nineteenth Century.* Berkeley: University of California Press, 1987.

Garber, Marjorie. *Vested Interests: Cross-Dressing and Cultural Anxiety.* New York: Routledge, 1992.

Gardiner, James. *Gaby Deslys: A Fatal Attraction.* London: Sidgwick and Jackson, 1986.

Garside, Patricia. "West End, East End: London, 1890–1914." In *Metropolis, 1890–1920*, edited by Anthony Sutcliffe. Chicago: University of Chicago Press, 1984.

———. "Representing the Metropolis: The Changing Relationship between London and the Press, 1870–1939." *London Journal* 16, no. 2 (1991): 156–73.

Garvey, Ellen Gruber. *The Adman in the Parlor: Magazines and the Gendering of Consumer Culture, 1880s to 1910s.* New York: Oxford University Press, 1996.

Geist, Johann Friedrich. *Arcades: The History of a Building Type.* Cambridge: MIT Press, 1983.

Gernsheim, Alison. *Victorian and Edwardian Fashion.* New York: Dover, 1963.

Gillis, John R. *For Better or Worse: British Marriages, 1600 to the Present.* New York: Oxford University Press, 1985.

Girouard, Mark. *The Return to Camelot: Chivalry and the English Gentleman.* New Haven: Yale University Press, 1981.

———. *Victorian Pubs.* New Haven: Yale University Press, 1984.

———. *Cities and People: A Social and Architectural History.* New Haven: Yale University Press, 1985.

Glasstone, Victor. *Victorian and Edwardian Theatres: An Architectural and Social Survey.* Cambridge: Harvard University Press, 1975.

Glennie, P. D., and N. J. Thrift. "Modernity, Urbanism, and Modern Consumption." *Environment and Planning D: Society and Space* 10, no. 4 (August 1992): 423–43.

Goheen, P. G. "The Ritual of the Streets in Mid-Nineteenth-Century Toronto." *Environment and Planning D: Society and Space* 11, no. 2 (April 1993): 127–45.

Goodall, Francis. "Marketing Consumer Products before 1914: Rowntrees and Elect Cocoa." In *Markets and Bagmen: Studies in the History of Marketing and Industrial Performance, 1830–1939,* edited by R. P. T. Davenport-Hines. Aldershot, Hants: Gower, 1986.

Goodway, David. *London Chartism, 1838–1848.* Cambridge: Cambridge University Press, 1982.

Gottdiener, Mark. *The Social Production of Urban Space.* Austin: University of Texas Press, 1985.

———. "Recapturing the Center: A Semiotic Analysis of Shopping Malls." In *The City and the Sign: An Introduction to Urban Semiotics,* edited by Mark Gottdiener and Alexander Ph. Lagopoulos. New York: Columbia University Press, 1986.

Gourvish, T. R. "The Standard of Living, 1890–1914." In *The Edwardian Age: Conflict and Stability, 1900–1914,* edited by Alan O'Day. Hamden, Conn.: Archon Books, 1979.

Graveson, Ronald Harry. *A Century of Family Law, 1857–1957.* London: Sweet and Maxwell, 1957.

Gray, Robert. *A History of London.* London: Hutchinson, 1978.

Green, David R. "The Metropolitan Economy: Continuity and Change, 1800–1939." In *London: A New Metropolitan Geography,* edited by Keith Hoggart and David Green. London: Edward Arnold, 1991.

Green, Oliver. *Underground Art: London Transport Posters, 1908 to the Present.* London: Studio Vista, 1990.

Greenhalgh, Paul. *Ephemeral Vistas: The Expositions Universelles, Great Exhibitions, and World's Fairs, 1851–1939.* Manchester: Manchester University Press, 1988.

Grossman, Peter. *American Express: The Unofficial History of the People Who Built the Great Financial Empire.* New York: Crown, 1987.

Gurney, Peter. *Co-operative Culture and the Politics of Consumption in England, 1870–1939.* Manchester: Manchester University Press, 1996.

Haagen, Paul. "Eighteenth-Century English Society and the Debt Law." In *Social Control and the State: Historical and Comparative Studies,* edited by Stanley Cohen and Andrew Scull. Oxford: Basil Blackwell, 1983.

Habakkuk, John. *Marriage, Debt, and the Estates System: English Landownership, 1650–1950.* Oxford: Clarendon Press, 1994.

Habermas, Jürgen. *The Structural Transformation of the Public Sphere: An Inquiry into a Category of Bourgeois Society.* Translated by Thomas Burger. Cambridge: MIT Press, 1991.

———. "Further Reflections on the Public Sphere." In *Habermas and the Public Sphere,* edited by Craig Calhoun. Cambridge: MIT Press, 1992.

Hall, P. G. *The Industries of London since 1861.* London: Hutchinson, 1962.

Hall, Stuart, and Tony Jefferson. *Resistance through Rituals: Youth Subcultures in Post-War Britain.* London: Hutchinson, 1976.

Halttunen, Karen. *Confidence Men and Painted Women: A Study of Middle-Class Culture in America, 1830–1870.* New Haven: Yale University Press, 1982.

Hammerton, A. James. "Victorian Marriage and the Law of Matrimonial Cruelty." *Victorian Studies* 33, no. 2 (Winter 1990): 268–92.

———. *Cruelty and Companionship: Conflict in Nineteenth-Century Married Life.* London: Routledge, 1992.

Hansen, Miriam. *Babel and Babylon: Spectatorship in American Silent Film.* Cambridge: Harvard University Press. 1991.

Harris, Neil. "Museums, Merchandising, and Popular Taste: The Struggle for Influence." In *Material Culture and the Struggle for Influence,* edited by Ian Quimby. New York: W. W. Norton, 1978.

———. "The Drama of Consumer Desire." In *Yankee Enterprise: The Rise of the American System of Manufactures,* edited by Otto Mayr and Robert C. Post. Washington, D.C.: Smithsonian Institution Press, 1981.

———. *Cultural Excursions: Marketing Appetites and Cultural Tastes in Modern America.* Chicago: University of Chicago Press, 1990.

———. "Urban Tourism and the Commercial City." In *Inventing Times Square: Commerce and Culture at the Crossroads of the World,* edited by William Taylor. New York: Russell Sage Foundation, 1991.

Harrison, Brian. *Drink and the Victorians: The Temperance Question in England, 1815–1872.* Pittsburgh: University of Pittsburgh Press, 1971.

———. "Pubs." In *The Victorian City: Images and Reality.* Vol. 1. London: Routledge and Kegan Paul, 1973.

———. *Separate Spheres: The Opposition to Women's Suffrage in Britain.* London: Croom Helm, 1978.

Harrison, Molly. *People and Shopping: A Social Background.* London: Ernest Benn, 1975.

Hartwell, R. M. "The Service Revolution: The Growth of Services in the Modern Economy." In *Fontana Economic History of Europe*, vol. 3, *The Industrial Revolution*, edited by C. M. Cipolla. London: Collins, 1973.

Harvey, David. *Consciousness and the Urban Experience: Studies in the History and Theory of Capitalist Urbanization.* Baltimore: Johns Hopkins University Press, 1985.

———. *The Condition of Postmodernity: An Enquiry into the Origins of Cultural Change.* Oxford: Basil Blackwell. 1989.

Hatch, Alden. *American Express: A Century of Service, 1850–1950.* New York: Doubleday, 1950.

Haug, Wolfgang, F. *Critique of Commodity Aesthetics: Appearance, Sexuality, and Advertising in Capitalist Society.* 8th ed. Minneapolis: University of Minnesota Press, 1986.

Hayden, Dolores. *The Grand Domestic Revolution: A History of Feminist Designs for American Homes, Neighborhoods, and Cities.* Cambridge: MIT Press, 1985.

Hebdige, Dick. *Subculture: The Meaning of Style.* London: Methuen 1979.

Heller, Agnes, and Ferenc Fehér. *The Postmodern Political Condition.* Oxford: Polity Press in association with Basil Blackwell, 1988.

Helly, Dorothy O., and Susan M. Reverby, eds. *Gendered Domains: Rethinking the Public and Private in Women's History. Essays from the Seventh Berkshire Conference on the History of Women.* Ithaca: Cornell University Press, 1992.

Hendrickson, Robert. *The Grand Emporiums: The Illustrated History of America's Great Department Stores.* New York: Stein and Day, 1979.

Hennock, E. P. "The Social Composition of Borough Councils in Two Large Cities." In *The Study of Urban History*, edited by H. J. Dyos. New York: St. Martin's Press, 1968.

Herstein, Sheila R. "The *English Woman's Journal* and the Langham Place Circle: A Feminist Forum and Its Women Editors." In *Innovators and Preachers: The Role of the Editor in Victorian England*, edited by Joel H. Wiener. Westport, Conn.: Greenwood, 1985.

———. *A Mid-Victorian Feminist: Barbara Leigh Smith Bodichon.* New Haven: Yale University Press, 1985.

Herzog, Charlotte. " 'Powder Puff' Promotion: The Fashion Show-in-the-Film." In *Fabrications: Costume and the Female Body*, edited by Jane Gaines and Charlotte Herzog. London: Routledge, 1990.

Hibbert, Christopher. *London: The Biography of a City.* London: Longmans, 1969.

Hinchcliffe, T. F. M. "Highbury New Park: A Nineteenth-Century Middle-Class Suburb." *London Journal* 7, no. 1 (1981): 29–44.

Hindley, Diana, and Geoffrey Hindley. *Advertising in Victorian England, 1837–1901.* London: Wayland Publishers 1972.

Hirschman, Albert O. *The Passions and the Interests: Political Arguments for Capitalism before Its Triumph.* Princeton: Princeton University Press, 1977.

Hobhouse, Hermione. *Thomas Cubitt: Master Builder.* New York: Universe Books, 1971.

———. *A History of Regent Street.* London: Macdonald and Jane's in association with Queen Anne Press, 1975.

Hobsbawm, E. J. *Industry and Empire, from 1750 to the Present Day.* Harmondsworth: Penguin, 1987.

Hobsbawm, E. J., and Terence Ranger, eds. *The Invention of Tradition.* Cambridge: Cambridge University Press, 1983.

Hohendahl, Peter Uwe. *The Institution of Criticism.* Ithaca: Cornell University Press, 1982.

Höher, Dagmar. "The Composition of Music Hall Audiences, 1850–1914." In *Music Hall: The Business of Pleasure*, edited by Peter Bailey. Milton Keynes and Philadelphia: Open University Press, 1986.

Holcombe, Lee. *Victorian Ladies at Work: Middle-Class Working Women in England and Wales, 1850–1914.* Hamden, Conn.: Archon Books, 1973.

———. *Wives and Property: Reform of the Married Women's Property Law in Nineteenth-Century England.* Toronto: University of Toronto Press, 1983.

Holder, Heidi J. " 'The Drama Discouraged': Judgment and Ambivalence in *The Madras House.*" *University of Toronto Quarterly* 58, no. 2 (Winter 1988–89): 275–94.

Holderness, B. A. "Credit in English Rural Society before the Nineteenth Century, with Special Reference to the Period 1650–

1720." *Agricultural History Review* 24, pt. 2 (1976): 97–109.

Hollis, Patricia. *Ladies Elect: Women in English Local Government, 1865–1914.* Oxford: Clarendon Press, 1987.

Hollister, Robert M., and Lloyd Rodwin, eds. *Cities of the Mind: Images and Themes of the City in the Social Sciences.* New York: Plenum, 1984.

Honeycombe, Gordon. *Selfridges, Seventy-Five Years: The Story of the Store, 1909–1984.* London: Park Lane Press, 1984.

Hont, Istvan, and Michael Ignatieff. "Needs and Justice in *The Wealth of Nations*: An Introductory Essay." In *Wealth and Virtue: The Shaping of Political Economy in the Scottish Enlightenment.* Cambridge: Cambridge University Press, 1983.

Hood, J., and B. S. Yamey. "Middle-Class Co-operative Retailing Societies in London, 1864–1900." In *Economics of Retailing*, edited by K. A. Tucker and B. S. Yamey. London: Penguin, 1973.

Hoppit, Julian. *Risk and Failure in English Business, 1700–1800.* Cambridge: Cambridge University Press, 1987.

Horn, Pamela. *Ladies of the Manor: Wives and Daughters in Country House Society.* Gloucestershire: Alan Sutton, 1991.

Hosgood, Christopher. "The 'Pigmies of Commerce' and the Working-Class Community: Small Shopkeepers in England, 1870–1914." *Journal of Social History* 22, no. 3 (Spring 1989): 439–60.

———. " 'A Brave and Daring Folk': Shopkeepers and Associational Life in Victorian and Edwardian England." *Journal of Social History* 26, no. 2 (Winter 1992): 258–308.

———. "The Shopkeeper's 'Friend': The Retail Trade Press in Late-Victorian and Edwardian Britain." *Victorian Periodicals Review* 25, no. 4 (Winter 1992): 164–72.

Howard, Diana. *London Theatres and Music Halls, 1850–1950.* London: Library Association, 1970.

Huberman, Jeffrey. *Late Victorian Farce.* Ann Arbor, Mich.: UMI Research Press, 1986.

Humpherys, Anne. *Henry Mayhew.* Boston: Twayne, 1984.

Hunt, Margaret. *The Middling Sort: Commerce, Gender, and the Family in England, 1680–1780.* Berkeley: University of California, 1996.

Huyssen, Andreas. "Mass Culture as Woman, Modernism's Other." In *Studies in Entertainment: Critical Approaches to Mass Culture*, edited by Tania Modleski. Bloomington: Indiana University Press, 1986.

Hynes, Samuel. *The Edwardian Turn of Mind.* Princeton: Princeton University Press, 1968.

Irigaray, Luce. *The Sex Which Is Not One.* Translated by Catherine Porter with Carolyn Burke. Ithaca: Cornell University Press, 1985.

Jackson, Alan A. *Semi-Detached London: Suburban Development, Life, and Transport, 1900–1939.* London: Allen and Unwin, 1973.

Jackson, Stanley. *The Savoy: The Romance of a Great Hotel.* New York: Dutton, 1964.

Jahn, Michael, "Suburban Development in Outer West London." In *The Rise of Suburbia*, edited by F. M. L. Thompson. Leicester: Leicester University Press, 1982.

Jalland, Patricia. *Women, Marriage, and Politics, 1860–1914.* Oxford: Clarendon Press, 1986.

Jameson, Frederic. "Pleasure: A Political Issue." In *Formations of Pleasure*, edited by Frederic Jameson. London: Routledge and Kegan Paul, 1983.

———. "Postmodernism and Consumer Society." In *Postmodern Culture*, edited by H. Foster. London: Pluto Press, 1985.

Jefferys, James B. *Retail Trading in Britain, 1850–1950.* Cambridge: Cambridge University Press, 1954.

Jhally, Sut. *The Codes of Advertising: Fetishism and the Political Economy of Meaning in the Consumer Society.* London: Frances Pinter, 1987.

Jhally, Sut, Stephen Kline, and William Leiss, eds. *Social Communication in Advertising: Persons, Products, and Images of Well-Being.* New York: Routledge, 1986.

Johnson, James H., and Colin G. Pooley. "The Internal Structure of Nineteenth-Century British Cities—An Overview." In *The Structure of Nineteenth-Century Cities*, edited by James H. Johnson and Colin G. Pooley. London: Croom Helm; New York: St. Martin's Press, 1982.

Johnson, Paul. "Credit and Thrift and the British Working Class, 1870–1914." In *The Working Class in Modern British History: Essays in Honour of Henry Pelling*, edited by Jay Winter. Cambridge: Cambridge University Press, 1983.

———. *Saving and Spending: The Working-Class Economy in Britain, 1870–1939.* Oxford: Clarendon Press, 1985.

———. "Conspicuous Consumption and Working-Class Culture in Late Victorian and Edwardian Britain." *Transactions of the Royal Historical Society* 38 (1988): 27–42.

———. "Small Debts and Economic Distress in England and Wales, 1857–1913." *Eco-*

nomic History Review 46, no. 1 (February 1993): 65–87.

Johnson, Paul. "Class Law in Victorian England." *Past and Present* 141 (November 1993): 147–69.

Jones, Gareth Stedman. "Working-Class Culture and Working-Class Politics in London, 1870–1900: Notes on the Remaking of a Working Class." In *Languages of Class: Studies in English Working Class History, 1832–1982*. Cambridge: Cambridge University Press, 1983.

———. *Outcast London: A Study in the Relationship between Classes in Victorian Society.* Rev. ed. New York: Pantheon, 1984.

Jones, Jennifer. "*Coquettes* and *Grisettes*: Women Buying and Selling in Ancien Régime Paris." In *The Sex of Things: Gender and Consumption in Historical Perspective*, edited by Victoria de Grazia with Ellen Furlough. Berkeley: University of California Press, 1996.

Jordan, Ellen. "The Lady Clerks at the Prudential: The Beginning of Vertical Segregation by Sex in Clerical Work in Nineteenth-Century Britain." *Gender and History* 8, no. 1 (April 1996): 65–81.

Jordan, William Chester. *Women and Credit in Pre-industrial and Developing Societies.* Philadelphia: University of Pennsylvania Press, 1993.

Jorgensen-Earp, Cheryl R. *"The Transfiguring Sword": The Just War of the Women's Social and Political Movement.* Tuscaloosa: University of Alabama Press, 1997.

Jump, John D. *Burlesque.* London: Methuen, 1971.

Kaplan, Cora. "Wild Nights: Pleasure/Sexuality/Feminism." In *Formations of Pleasure*, edited by Frederic Jameson. London: Routledge and Kegan Paul, 1983.

Kaplan, E. Ann. "Is the Gaze Male?" In *Powers of Desire: The Politics of Sexuality*, edited by Ann Snitow, Christine Stansell, and Sharon Thompson. New York: Monthly Review Press, 1983.

Kaplan, Joel H., and Sheila Stowell. *Theatre and Fashion: Oscar Wilde to the Suffragettes.* Cambridge: Cambridge University Press, 1994.

Kasson, John F. *Amusing the Million: Coney Island at the Turn of the Century.* New York: Hill and Wang, 1978.

Kearns, Gerry, and Chris Philo. *Selling Places: The City as Cultural Capital, Past and Present.* Oxford: Pergamon, 1993.

Keller, Alexandra. "Disseminations of Modernity: Representation and Consumer Desire in Early Mail-Order Catalogs." In *Cinema and the Invention of Modern Life*, edited by Leo Charney and Vanessa R. Schwartz. Berkeley: University of California Press, 1995.

Kellner, Douglas. "Critical Theory, Commodities, and the Consumer Society." *Theory, Culture, and Society* 1, no. 3 (1983): 66–83.

Kenin, Richard. *Return to Albion: Americans in England, 1760–1940.* New York: Holt, Rinehart, and Winston, 1979.

Kennedy, Carol. *Mayfair: A Social History.* London: Hutchinson, 1986.

Kennedy, Dennis. *Granville Barker and the Dream of Theatre.* Cambridge: Cambridge University Press, 1985.

———. "The New Drama and the New Audience." In *The Edwardian Theatre: Essays on Performance and Style*, edited by Michael R. Booth and Joel H. Kaplan. Cambridge: Cambridge University Press, 1996.

Kent, Susan. *Sex and Suffrage in Britain, 1860–1914.* Princeton: Princeton University Press, 1987.

Kerber, Linda. "Separate Spheres, Female Worlds, Woman's Place: The Rhetoric of Women's History." *Journal of American History* 75, no. 1 (June 1988): 9–39.

Kift, Dagmar Höher. *The Victorian Music Hall: Culture, Class, and Conflict.* Translated by Roy Kift. Cambridge: Cambridge University Press, 1996.

Kinchin, Perilla. *Tea and Taste: The Glasgow Tea Rooms, 1875–1975.* Wendlebury: White Cockade, 1991.

Knopp, L. "Sexuality and the Spatial Dynamics of Capitalism." *Environment and Planning D.: Society and Space* 10, no. 6 (December 1992): 651–69.

Koditschek, Theodore. *Class Formation and Urban Industrial Society: Bradford, 1750–1850.* Cambridge: Cambridge University Press, 1990.

Kogan, Herman, and Lloyd Wendt. *Give the Lady What She Wants! The Story of Marshall Field and Company.* Chicago: Rand McNally, 1952.

Koss, Stephen. *The Rise and Fall of the Political Press in Britain: The Nineteenth Century.* Chapel Hill: University of North Carolina Press, 1981.

Kowaleski-Wallace, Elizabeth. *Consuming Subjects: Women, Shopping, and Business in the Eighteenth Century.* New York: Columbia University Press, 1997.

Kuchta, David. "The Making of the Self-Made Man: Class, Clothing and English Masculinity." In *The Sex of Things: Gender and Consumption in Historical Perspective*, edited by Victoria de Grazia with Ellen

Furlough. Berkeley: University of California Press, 1996.

Kusamitsu, Toshio. "Great Exhibitions before 1851." *History Workshop Journal* 9 (Spring 1980): 70–89.

Kynaston, David. *The City of London*, Vol. 1, *A World of Its Own*. London: Chatto and Windus, 1994.

Lacey, Candida Ann. *Barbara Leigh Smith Bodichon and the Langham Place Group*. New York: Routledge and Kegan Paul, 1987.

Laermans, Rudi. "Learning to Consume: Early Department Stores and the Shaping of Modern Consumer Culture, 1860–1914." *Theory, Culture, and Society* 10, no. 4 (November 1993): 79–102.

Lambert, Richard S. *The Universal Provider: A Study of William Whiteley and the Rise of the London Department Store*. London: George G. Harrap, 1938.

Lancaster, William. *The Department Store: A Social History*. London: Leicester University Press, 1995.

Landes, Joan B. *Women and the Public Sphere in the Age of the French Revolution*. Ithaca: Cornell University Press, 1988.

Langland, Elizabeth. *Nobody's Angels: Middle-Class Women and Domestic Ideology in Victorian Culture*. Ithaca: Cornell University Press, 1995.

Lansdell, Avril. *Fashion à la Carte, 1860–1900: A Study of Fashion through Cartes-de-Visite*. Aylesbury: Shire Publications, 1985.

Laver, James. *Edwardian Promenade*. London: Edward Hulton, 1958.

Lawrence, Jeanne Catherine. "Steel Frame Architecture versus the London Building Regulations: Selfridges, the Ritz, and American Technology." *Construction History* 6 (1990): 23–46.

———. "Geographical Space, Social Space, and the Realm of the Department Store." *Urban History* 19, no. 1 (April 1992): 64–84,

Lazere, Donald, ed. *American Media and Mass Culture: Left Perspectives*. Berkeley: University of California Press, 1987.

Leach, William. *True Love and Perfect Union: The Feminist Reform of Sex and Society*. New York: Basic Books, 1980.

———. "Transformations in a Culture of Consumption: Women and Department Stores, 1890–1925." *Journal of American History* 71, no. 2 (September 1984): 319–42.

———. *Land of Desire: Merchants, Power, and the Rise of a New American Culture*. New York: Pantheon, 1993.

Lears, T. J. Jackson. *No Place of Grace: Antimodernism and the Transformation of American Culture, 1880–1920*. New York: Pantheon, 1981.

———. "Beyond Veblen: Rethinking Consumer Culture in America." In *Consuming Visions: Accumulation and Display of Goods in America, 1880–1920*, edited by Simon J. Bronner. New York: W. W. Norton, 1989.

———. *Fables of Abundance: A Cultural History of Advertising in America*. New York: Basic Books, 1994.

Lee, Alan J. *The Origins of the Popular Press in England, 1855–1914*. London: Croom Helm, 1976.

Lee, Martyn J. *Consumer Culture Reborn: The Cultural Politics of Consumption*. London: Routledge, 1992.

Lees, Andrew. *Cities Perceived: Urban Society in European and American Thought, 1820–1940*. New York: Columbia University Press, 1985.

Lefebvre, Henri. *The Production of Space*. Translated by Donald Nicholson-Smith. Oxford: Basil Blackwell, 1984.

Leiss, William. *The Limits to Satisfaction: An Essay on the Problem of Needs and Commodities*. Toronto: University of Toronto Press, 1976.

Lejeune, Anthony, and Malcolm Lewis. *The Gentlemen's Clubs of London*. London: Dorset Press, 1979.

Lemire, Beverly. "Consumerism in Preindustrial and Early Industrial England: The Trade in Secondhand Clothes." *Journal of British Studies* 27, no. 1 (January 1988): 1–24.

———. *Fashion's Favorite: The Cotton Trade and the Consumer in Britain, 1660–1800*. Oxford: Oxford University Press, 1992.

Lester, V. Markham. *Victorian Insolvency: Bankruptcy, Imprisonment for Debt, and Company Winding-Up in Nineteenth-Century England*. Oxford: Clarendon Press, 1995.

Levine, George. "From 'Know-Not-Where' to 'Nowhere': The City in Carlyle, Ruskin, and Morris." In *The Victorian City: Images and Realities*, vol. 2, edited by H. J. Dyos and Michael Wolff. London: Routledge and Kegan Paul, 1973.

Levine, Philippa. *Victorian Feminism, 1850–1900*. London: Hutchinson, 1987.

———. *Feminist Lives in Victorian England: Private Roles and Public Commitment*. Oxford: Basil Blackwell, 1990.

———. "The Humanising Influences of Five O'Clock Tea: Victorian Feminist Periodicals." *Victorian Studies* 33, no. 2 (Winter 1990): 293–306.

Levy, Herman. *The Shops of Britain: A Study of Retail Distribution*. London: Kegan Paul, 1947.

Lewis, Jane. *Women in England, 1870–1950: Sexual Divisions and Social Change*. Sussex: Wheatsheaf Books; Bloomington: Indiana University Press, 1984.

———., ed. *Labour and Love: Women's Experience of Home and Family, 1850–1940*. Oxford: Basil Blackwell, 1986.

Little, Jo, Linda Peake, and Pat Richardson, eds. *Women in Cities: Gender and the Urban Environment*. New York: New York University Press, 1988.

Loeb, Lori Anne. *Consuming Angels: Advertising and Victorian Women*. New York: Oxford University Press, 1994.

Longhurst, Derek. "Sherlock Holmes: Adventures of an English Gentleman, 1887–1894." In *Gender, Genre, and Narrative Pleasure*, edited by Derek Longhurst. London: Unwin Hyman, 1989.

Lyons, J., and Co. *The Tea Diary*. Greenford, Middlesex: J. Lyons and Co., 1989.

MacCannell, Dean. *The Tourist: A New Theory of the Leisure Class*. New York: Schocken Books, 1976.

Mackenzie, Compton. *The Savoy of London*. London: George G. Harrap, 1953.

Mackenzie, Gordon. *Marylebone: Great City North of Oxford Street*. London: St. Martin's and Macmillan, 1972.

Macqueen-Pope, W. *Carriages at Eleven: The Story of The Edwardian Theatre*. London: Hutchinson, 1947.

———. *Twenty-Shillings in the Pound*. London: Hutchinson, 1948.

———. *Gaiety: Theatre of Enchantment*. London: W. H. Allen, 1949.

———. *Goodbye Piccadilly*. New York: Drake Publishers, 1972.

Mander, Raymond, and Joe Mitchenson. *Musical Comedy: A Story in Pictures*. New York: Taplinger, 1970.

Marchand, Roland. *Advertising the American Dream: Making Way for Modernity, 1920–1940*. Berkeley: University of California Press, 1985.

Marcus, Jane, ed. *Suffrage and the Pankhursts*. London: Routledge and Kegan Paul, 1987.

Marcus, Leonard. *The American Store Window*. London: Architectural Press, 1978.

Marcus, Steven. "Reading the Illegible." In *The Victorian City: Images and Realities*, vol. 1, edited by H. J. Dyos and Michael Wolff. London: Routledge and Kegan Paul, 1973.

Margetson, Stella. *Leisure and Pleasure in the Nineteenth Century*. New York: Coward-McCann, 1969.

Marks, Patricia. *Bicycles, Bangs, and Bloomers: The New Woman in the Popular Press*. Lexington: University of Kentucky Press, 1990.

Martin, Theodora Penny. *The Sound of Our Own Voices: Women's Study Clubs, 1860–1910*. Boston: Beacon, 1987.

Mathias, Peter. *Retailing Revolution: A History of Multiple Retailing in the Food Trades Based upon the Allied Suppliers Group of Companies*. London: Longmans, 1967.

Matthews, Glenna. *"Just a Housewife": The Rise and Fall of Domesticity in America*. New York: Oxford University Press, 1987.

May, Lary. *Screening Out the Past: The Birth of Mass Culture and the Motion Picture Industry*. Chicago: University of Chicago Press, 1980.

McBride, Theresa. "A Woman's World: Department Stores and the Evolution of Women's Employment, 1870–1920." *French Historical Studies* 10, no. 4 (Fall 1978): 664–83.

McCauley, Elizabeth Ann. *A. A. Disdéri and the Cartes de Visite Portrait Photograph*. New Haven: Yale University Press, 1985.

McCracken, Grant. *Culture and Consumption: New Approaches to the Symbolic Character of Consumer Goods and Activities*. Bloomington: Indiana University Press, 1988.

McDonald, Jan. *The "New Drama," 1900–1914*. New York: Grove Press, 1986.

McDowell, L. "Towards an Understanding of the Gender Division of Urban Space." *Environment and Planning D: Society and Space* 1, no. 1 (March 1983): 59–72.

McGregor, O. R. *Social History and Law Reform*. London: Stevens and Sons, 1981.

McKendrick, Neil. "Home Demand and Economic Growth: A New View of the Role of Women and Children in the Industrial Revolution." In *Historical Perspectives: Studies in English Thought and Society*, edited by Neil McKendrick. London: Europa Press, 1974.

McKendrick, Neil, John Brewer, and J. H. Plumb, eds. *The Birth of a Consumer Society: The Commercialization of Eighteenth-Century England*. Bloomington: Indiana University Press, 1982.

Meisel, Martin. *Realizations: Narrative, Pictorial, and Theatrical Arts in Nineteenth-Century England*. Princeton: Princeton University Press, 1983.

Meller, Hellen. *Leisure and the Changing City, 1870–1914*. London: Routledge and Kegan Paul, 1976.

———. "Planning Theory and Women's Role in the City." *Urban History Yearbook* 17 (1990): 85–98.

Mendelson, Edward. "Baedeker's Universe." *Yale Review* 74, no. 3 (Spring 1985): 386–403.

Mercer, Colin. "A Poverty of Desire: Pleasure and Popular Politics." In *Formations of Pleasure*, edited by Frederic Jameson. London: Routledge and Kegan Paul, 1983.

Miller, Daniel. *Material Culture and Mass Consumption*. Oxford: Basil Blackwell, 1987.

———., ed. *Acknowledging Consumption: A Review of New Studies*. London: Routledge, 1995.

Miller, Michael. *The Bon Marché: Bourgeois Culture and the Department Store, 1869–1920*. Princeton: Princeton University Press, 1981.

Miller, Roger. "Selling Mrs. Consumer: Advertising and the Creation of Suburban Socio-Spatial Relations, 1910–1930." *Antipode* 23, no. 3 (July 1991): 263–301.

Minney, R. J. *The Edwardian Age*. Boston: Little, Brown, 1964.

Mitchell, Sally. *The Fallen Angel: Chastity, Class, and Women's Reading, 1835–1880*. Bowling Green, Ohio: Bowling Green University, Poplar Press, 1981.

———. *The New Girl: Girls' Culture in England, 1880–1915*. New York: Columbia University Press, 1995.

Mitchell, Timothy. *Colonising Egypt*. Berkeley: University of California Press, 1991.

Morgan, Brian. *Express Journey, 1864–1964*. London: Newman Neame, 1964.

Morgan, David. *Suffragists and Liberals: The Politics of Women's Suffrage in Britain*. Oxford: Basil Blackwell, 1975.

Morris, Meaghan. "Things to Do with Shopping Centres." In *Grafts: Feminist Cultural Criticism*, edited by Susan Sheridan. London: Verso, 1988.

Morris, R. J. "Voluntary Societies and British Urban Elites, 1780–1850: An Analysis." *Historical Journal* 26, no. 1 (1983): 95–118.

———. *Class, Sect, and Party: The Making of the British Middle Class, Leeds, 1820–1850*. Manchester: Manchester University Press, 1990.

———. "Men, Women, and Property: The Reform of the Married Women's Property Act, 1870." In *Landlords, Capitalists, and Entrepreneurs: Essays for Sir John Habakkuk*, edited by F. M. L. Thompson (Oxford: Clarendon, 1994).

Morris, R. J., and Richard Rodger. "An Introduction to British Urban History, 1820–1914." In *The Victorian City: A Reader in British Urban History*. London: Longman, 1993.

Morrison, C. A. "Contract." In *A Century of Family Law, 1857–1957*, edited by R. H. Graveson and F. R. Crane. London: Sweet and Maxwell, 1957.

Mort, Frank. "Archaeologies of City Life: Commercial Culture, Masculinity, and Spatial Relations in 1980s London." *Environment and Planning D: Society and Space* 13 (1995): 573–90.

———. *Cultures of Consumption: Masculinities and Social Space in Late-Twentieth-Century-Britain*. London: Routledge, 1996.

Mort, Frank, and Peter Thompson. "Retailing, Commercial Culture, and Masculinity in 1950s Britain: The Case of Montague Burton, the 'Tailor of Taste.' " *History Workshop Journal* 38 (Autumn 1994): 106–28.

Moss, Michael, and Alison Turton. *A Legend of Retailing: The House of Fraser*. London: Weidenfeld and Nicholson, 1989.

Mui, Hoh-Cheung, and Lorna Mui. *Shops and Shopkeeping in Eighteenth-Century England*. Kingston: McGill-Queen's University Press and Routledge, 1989.

Mukerji, Chandra. *From Graven Images: Patterns of Modern Materialism*. New York: Columbia University Press, 1983.

Muldrew, Craig. "Interpreting the Market: The Ethics of Credit and Community Relations in Early Modern England." *Social History* 18, no. 2 (May 1993): 163–83.

Mulvey, Laura. "Visual Pleasure and Narrative Cinema." *Screen* 16, no. 3 (Autumn 1975): 6–18.

Musson, A. E. "Newspaper Printing in the Industrial Revolution." *Economic History Review* 2d ser. 10, no. 3 (1958): 411–26.

Myers, Kathy. *Understains: The Sense and Seduction of Advertising*. London: Comedia, 1986.

Nasaw, David. *Going Out: The Rise and Fall of Public Amusements*. New York: Basic Books, 1993.

Nava, Mica. "Consumerism and Its Contradictions." *Cultural Studies* 1, no. 2 (May 1987): 204–10.

———. *Changing Cultures: Feminism, Youth, and Consumers*. London: Sage, 1992.

———. "Modernity's Disavowal: Women, the City, and the Department Store." In *Modern Times: Reflections on a Century of Modernity*, edited by Mica Nava and Alan O'Shea. London: Routledge, 1996.

Nead, Lynda. *Myths of Sexuality: Representations of Women in Victorian Britain*. Oxford: Basil Blackwell, 1988.

Nevett, T. R. *Advertising in Britain: A History.* London: Heinemann, on behalf of the History of Advertising Trust, 1982.

———. "Advertising and Editorial Integrity in the Nineteenth Century." In *The Press in English Society from the Seventeenth to the Nineteenth Centuries*, edited by Michael Harris and Alan Lee. London: Fairleigh Dickinson University Press, 1986.

Nixon, Sean. "Have You Got the Look? Masculinities and Shopping Spectacle." In *Lifestyle Shopping: The Subject of Consumption.* London: Routledge, 1992.

Nord, Deborah Epstein. "The Social Explorer as Anthropologist: Victorian Travellers among the Urban Poor." In *Visions of the Modern City: Essays in History, Art, and Literature*, edited by William Sharpe and Leonard Wallock. New York: Columbia University Press, 1983.

———. "The City as Theater: From Georgian to Victorian London." *Victorian Studies* 31, no. 2 (Winter 1988): 159–88.

———. *Walking the Victorian Streets: Women, Representation, and the City.* Ithaca: Cornell University Press, 1995.

Nord, Philip G. *Paris Shopkeepers and the Politics of Resentment.* Princeton: Princeton University Press, 1986.

Norton, Theodore Mills. "The Public Sphere: A Workshop." *New Political Science* 11 (Spring 1983): 75–84.

Nunokawa, Jeff. "*Tess*, Tourism, and the Spectacle of Women." In *Rewriting the Victorians: Theory, History, and the Politics of Gender*, edited by Linda M. Shires. New York: Routledge, 1992.

O'Brien, Patricia. "The Kleptomania Diagnosis: Bourgeois Women and Theft in Late-Nineteenth-Century France." *Journal of Social History* 17 (Fall 1983): 65–77.

O'Day, Alan, ed. *The Edwardian Age: Conflict and Stability, 1900–1914.* Hamden, Conn.: Archon Books, 1979.

Offen, Karen. "Defining Feminism: A Comparative Historical Approach." *Signs* 14, no. 1 (Autumn 1988): 119–57.

Offer, Avner. *Property and Politics, 1870–1914: Landownership, Law, Ideology, and Urban Development in England.* Cambridge: Cambridge University Press, 1981.

Olney, Martha L. *Buy Now, Pay Later: Advertising, Credit, and Consumer Durables in the 1920s.* Chapel Hill: University of North Carolina Press, 1991.

Olsen, Donald. J. *The Growth of Victorian London.* London: B. T. Batsford, 1976.

———. *Town Planning in London: The Eighteenth and Nineteenth Centuries.* 2d ed. New Haven: Yale University Press, 1982.

———. *The City as a Work of Art: London, Paris, Vienna.* New Haven: Yale University Press, 1986.

Ousby, Ian. *The Englishman's England: Taste, Travel, and the Rise of Tourism.* Cambridge: Cambridge University Press, 1990.

Owen, David. *The Government of Victorian London, 1855–1889: The Metropolitan Board of Works, the Vestries, and the City Corporation.* Edited by Roy MacLeod. Cambridge: Harvard University Press, Belknap Press, 1982.

Palmer, Arnold. *Movable Feasts.* Oxford: Oxford University Press, 1952.

Parker, Derek, and Julia Parker. *The Natural History of the Chorus Girl.* London: David and Charles, 1975.

Pasdermadjian, Hrant. *The Department Store: Its Origins, Evolution, and Economics.* London: Newman Books, 1954.

Peel, Derek W. *A Garden in the Sky: The Story of Barkers of Kensington, 1870–1957.* London: W. H. Allen, 1960.

Peiss, Kathy. *Cheap Amusements: Working Women and Leisure in Turn-of-the-Century New York.* Philadelphia: Temple University Press, 1986.

———. "Making Faces: The Cosmetics Industry and the Cultural Construction of Gender, 1890–1930." *Genders* 7 (Spring 1990): 143–69.

———. "Making Up, Making Over: Cosmetics, Consumer Culture, and Women's Identity." In *The Sex of Things: Gender and Consumption in Historical Perspective*, edited by Victoria de Grazia with Ellen Furlough. Berkeley: University of California Press, 1996.

Pennybacker, Susan D. *A Vision for London, 1889–1914: Labour, Everyday Life, and the LCC Experiment.* New York: Routledge, 1995.

Perkin, Harold. *The Origins of Modern English Society, 1780–1880.* London: Routledge and Kegan Paul, 1969.

Perkin, Joan. *Women and Marriage in Nineteenth-Century England.* London: Routledge, 1989.

Perrot, Michelle, ed. *A History of Private Life.* Vol. 4, *From the Fires of Revolution to the Great War.* Translated by Arthur Goldhammer. Cambridge: Harvard University Press, Belknap Press, 1990.

Perrot, Philippe. *Fashioning the Bourgeoisie: A History of Clothing in the Nineteenth Century.* Translated by Richard Bienvenu. Princeton: Princeton University Press, 1994.

Peterson, M. Jeanne. "The Victorian Governess: Status Incongruence in Family and Society." In *Suffer and Be Still: Women in the Victorian Age*, edited by Martha Vicinus. Bloomington: Indiana University Press, 1972.

Petrie, Charles. *The Edwardians*. New York: W. W. Norton, 1965.

Petro, Patrice. *Joyless Streets: Women and Melodramatic Representation in Weimar Germany.* Princeton: Princeton University Press, 1989.

Phillips, Martin. "The Evolution of Markets and Shops in Britain." In *The Evolution of Retail Systems, ca. 1800–1914*, edited by John Benson and Gareth Shaw. Leicester: Leicester University Press, 1992.

Pick, John. *The West End: Mismanagement and Snobbery.* Sussex: John Offord, 1983.

Pimlott, J. A. R. *The Englishman's Holiday: A Social History.* London: Faber and Faber, 1947.

Pollard, Sidney. *Britain's Prime and Britain's Decline: The British Economy, 1870–1914.* London: Edward Arnold, 1989.

Pollock, Griselda. *Vision and Difference: Femininity, Feminism, and Histories of Art.* London: Routledge, 1988.

———. "Vicarious Excitements: *London: A Pilgrimage*, by Gustave Doré and Blanchard Jerrold, 1872." *New Formations* 2 (Spring 1988): 25–50.

Poovey, Mary. *Uneven Developments: The Ideological Work of Gender in Mid-Victorian England.* Chicago: University of Chicago Press, 1988.

———. *Making a Social Body: British Cultural Formation, 1830–1864.* Chicago: University of Chicago Press, 1995.

Port, M. H. *Imperial London: Civic Government Building in London, 1850–1915.* New Haven: Yale University Press, 1995.

Porter, J. H. "The Development of a Provincial Department Store, 1870–1939." *Business History* 18, no. 1 (January 1971): 64–71.

Porter, Roy. *London: A Social History.* Cambridge: Harvard University Press, 1995.

Pottinger, G. *The Winning Counter: Hugh Fraser and Harrod's.* London: Hutchinson, 1971.

Pound, Reginald. *Selfridge: A Biography.* London: Heinemann, 1960.

Powell, David. *The Edwardian Crisis: Britain, 1901–1914.* New York: St. Martin's Press, 1996.

Power, E. J. "The East and West in Early-Modern London." In *Wealth and Power in Tudor England: Essays Presented to S. T. Bindoff.* Edited by E. W. Ives, R. J. Knecht, and J. J. Scarisbrick. London: University of London Press, 1978.

Prince, Hugh C. "North-West London, 1814–1863." In *Greater London*, edited by J. T. Coppock and Hugh C. Prince. London: Faber and Faber, 1964.

———. "North-West London, 1864–1914." In *Greater London*, edited by J. T. Coppock and Hugh C. Prince. London: Faber and Faber, 1964.

Prochaska, F. K. *Women and Philanthropy in Nineteenth-Century England.* Oxford: Clarendon Press, 1980.

Pugh, Martin. *The Tories and the People, 1880–1914.* Oxford: Basil Blackwell, 1985.

Purvis, Martin. "Co-operative Retailing in Britain." In *The Evolution of Retail Systems, ca. 1800–1914*, edited by John Benson and Gareth Shaw. Leicester: Leicester University Press, 1992.

Raban, Jonathan. *Soft City.* 1974. Reprint, London: Collins Harvill, 1988.

Rabinovitz, Lauren. "Temptations of Pleasure: Nickelodeons, Amusement Parks, and the Sights of Female Sexuality." *Camera Obscura* 23 (May 1990): 71–89.

Raeburn, Antonia. *The Militant Suffragettes.* London: Michael Joseph, 1973.

Rapp, Rayna, and Ellen Ross. "The Twenties Backlash: Compulsory Heterosexuality, the Consumer Family, and the Waning of Feminism." In *Class, Race, and Sex: The Dynamics of Control*, edited by Amy Swerdlow and K. Lessinger. Boston: G. K. Hall, 1982.

Rappaport, Erika. "The West End and Women's Pleasure: Gender and Commercial Culture in London, 1860–1914." Ph.D. Diss., Rutgers University, 1993.

———. " 'A New Era of Shopping': The Promotion of Women's Pleasure in London's West End." In *Cinema and the Invention of Modern Life*, edited by Leo Charney and Vanessa R. Schwartz. Berkeley: University of California Press, 1995.

———. " 'The Halls of Temptation': Gender, Politics, and the Construction of the Department Store in Late Victorian London." *Journal of British Studies* 35, no. 1 (January 1996): 58–83.

———. " 'A Husband and His Wife's Dresses': Consumer Credit and the Debtor Family in England, 1864–1914." In *The Sex of Things: Gender and Consumption in Historical Perspective*, edited by Victoria de Grazia with Ellen Furlough. Berkeley: University of California Press, 1996.

Rasmussen, Steen Eiler. *London: The Unique City.* Rev. ed. Cambridge: MIT Press, 1982.

Raven, James. "Viewpoint: British History and Enterprise Culture." *Past and Present* 123 (May 1989): 178–204.

Read, Donald. *The Age of Urban Democracy: England, 1868–1914*. Rev. ed. London: Longman, 1994.

Reeder, D. A. "A Theatre of Suburbs: Some Patterns of Development in West London, 1801–1911." In *The Study of Urban History*, edited by H. J. Dyos. New York: St. Martin's Press, 1968.

Reekie, Gail. "Changes in the Adamless Eden: The Spatial and Sexual Transformation of a Brisbane Department Store, 1930–1990." In *Lifestyle Shopping: The Subject of Consumption*. London: Routledge, 1992.

———. *Temptations: Sex, Selling, and the Department Store*. St. Leonards, Australia: Allen and Unwin, 1993.

Rendall, Jane. " 'A Moral Engine'? Feminism, Liberalism, and the *English Woman's Journal*. In *Equal or Different: Women's Politics, 1800–1914*, edited by Jane Rendall. Oxford: Basil Blackwell, 1987.

———. "Friendship and Politics: Barbara Leigh Smith Bodichon (1827–1891) and Bessie Rayner Parkes (1829–1925)." In *Sexuality and Subordination: Interdisciplinary Studies of Gender in the Nineteenth Century*, edited by Susan Mendus and Jane Rendall. London: Routledge, 1989.

———., ed. *Equal or Different: Women's Politics, 1800–1914*. Oxford: Basil Blackwell, 1987.

Richards, Thomas. "The Image of Victoria in the Year of Jubilee." *Victorian Studies* 31, no. 1 (Autumn 1987): 7–32.

———. *The Commodity Culture of Victorian England: Advertising and Spectacle, 1851–1914*. Stanford, Calif.: Stanford University Press, 1990.

Richardson, D. J. "J. Lyons and Co., Ltd.: Caterers and Food Manufacturers, 1894–1939." In *The Making of the Modern British Diet*, edited by Derek Oddy and Derek Miller. London: Croom Helm, 1976.

Richter, Donald. *Riotous Victorians*. Athens: Ohio University Press, 1981.

Ritchie, Harry M. "Harley Granville Barker's *The Madras House* and the Sexual Revolution." *Modern Drama* 15, no. 2 (September 1972): 150–58.

Robb, George. *White-Collar Crime in Modern England: Financial Fraud and Business Morality, 1845–1929*. Cambridge: Cambridge University Press, 1992.

Rose, Jacqueline. *Sexuality in the Field of Vision*. London: Verso, 1986.

Rose, Jonathan. *The Edwardian Temperament, 1895–1919*. Athens: Ohio University Press, 1986.

Rosen, Andrew. *Rise Up, Women! The Militant Campaign of the Women's Social and Political Union, 1903–1914*. London: Routledge and Kegan Paul, 1974.

Ross, Ellen. " 'Fierce Questions and Taunts': Married Life in Working-Class London, 1870–1914." *Feminist Studies* 8, no. 3 (Fall 1982): 575–602.

———. *Love and Toil: Motherhood in Outcast London, 1870–1918*. Oxford: Oxford University Press, 1993.

Rowell, George. *The Victorian Theatre, 1792–1914*. Cambridge: Cambridge University Press, 1978.

Ruane, Christine. "Clothes Shopping in Imperial Russia: The Development of a Consumer Culture." *Journal of Social History* 28, no. 4 (Summer 1995): 765–82.

Rubin, Gerry R. "From Packman, Tallymen and 'Perambulating Scotchmen' to Credit Drapers' Associations, ca. 1840–1914." *Business History* 28, no. 2 (April 1986): 206–25.

———. "The County Courts and the Tally Trade, 1846–1914." In *Law, Economy and Society, 1750–1914: Essays in the History of English Law*, edited by G. R. Rubin and David Sugarman. Abingdon: Professional Books, 1988.

———. "Law, Poverty, and Imprisonment for Debt." In *Law, Economy, and Society, 1750–1914: Essays in the History of English Law*, edited by G. R. Rubin and David Sugarman. Abingdon: Professional Books, 1988.

Rubinstein, David. *Before the Suffragettes: Women's Emancipation in the 1890s*. New York: St. Martin's Press, 1986.

———. *A Different World for Women: The Life of Millicent Garret Fawcett*. New York: Wheatsheaf, 1991.

Rubinstein, W. D. *Elites and Wealthy in Modern British History: Essays in Social and Economic History*. Sussex: Harvester; New York: St. Martin's Press, 1987.

———. *Capitalism, Culture, and Decline in Britain, 1750–1990*. London: Routledge, 1993.

Rudé, George. *Hanoverian London, 1714–1808*. Berkeley: University of California Press, 1971.

Ryan, Mary P. *Women in Public: Between Banners and Ballots, 1825–1880*. Baltimore: Johns Hopkins University Press, 1990.

———. "Gender and Public Access: Women's Politics in the Nineteenth Century." In *Ha-*

bermas and the Public Sphere, edited by Craig Calhoun. Cambridge: MIT Press, 1992.

Rydell, Robert. "The Culture of Imperial Abundance: World's Fairs in the Making of American Culture. In *Consuming Visions: Accumulation and Display of Goods in America, 1880–1920*, edited by Simon J. Bronner, 191–216. New York: W. W. Norton, 1989. 191–216.

Sack, Robert D. "The Consumer's World: Place as Context." *Annals of the Association of American Geographers* 78, no. 4 (December 1988): 642–64.

Saint, Andrew. *Richard Norman Shaw.* New Haven: Yale University Press, 1976.

Sandage, Scott. " 'Small Man, Small Means, Doing Small Business': Credit Reporting and the Commodification of Character." Paper presented at the Warren I. Susman Memorial Graduate History Conference, Rutgers University, New Brunswick, N.J., April 1993.

Santink, Joy L. *Timothy Eaton and the Rise of His Department Store.* Toronto: University of Toronto Press, 1990.

Saul, S. B. "The American Impact on British Industry, 1895–1914." *Business History* 3 (December 1960): 19–38.

Scanlon, Jennifer R. *Inarticulate Longings: The "Ladies Home Journal," Gender, and the Promises of Consumer Culture.* New York: Routledge, 1995.

Scharff, Virginia. *Taking the Wheel: Women and the Coming of the Motor Age.* Albuquerque: University of New Mexico Press, 1992.

Schivelbusch, Wolfgang. *The Railway Journey: The Industrialization of Time and Space in the Nineteenth Century.* Berkeley: University of California Press, 1986.

———. *Disenchanted Night: The Industrialization of Light in the Nineteenth Century.* Translated by Angela Davies. Berkeley: University of California Press, 1988.

Schudson, Michael. *Advertising, the Uneasy Persuasion: Its Dubious Impact on American Society.* New York: Basic Books, 1984.

Schwartz, Vanessa R. "Cinematic Spectatorship before the Apparatus: The Public Taste for Reality in *Fin-de-Siècle* Paris." In *Cinema and the Invention of Modern Life*, edited by Leo Charney and Vanessa R. Schwartz. Berkeley: University of California Press, 1995.

Schwarz, L. D. "Social Class and Social Geography: The Middle Classes in London at the End of the Eighteenth Century." *Social History* 7, no. 2 (May 1982): 167–85.

———. *London in the Age of Industrialization: Entrepreneurs, Labour Force, and Living Conditions, 1700–1850.* Cambridge: Cambridge University Press, 1992.

Scobey, David. "Anatomy of the Promenade: The Politics of Bourgeois Sociability in Nineteenth-Century New York." *Social History* 17, no. 2 (May 1992): 203–27.

Scola, Roger. *Feeding the Victorian City: The Food Supply of Manchester, 1770–1870*, edited by W. A. Armstrong and Pauline Scola. Manchester: Manchester University Press, 1992.

Scott, Anne Firor. *Natural Allies: Women's Associations in American History.* Urbana: University of Illinois Press, 1991.

Scott, Joan Wallach. *Gender and the Politics of History.* New York: Columbia University Press, 1988.

Seigel, Jerrold E. *Bohemian Paris: Culture, Politics, and the Boundaries of Bourgeois Life, 1830–1930.* New York: Viking, 1986.

Sekora, John. *Luxury: The Concept in Western Thought, Eden to Smollett.* Baltimore: Johns Hopkins University Press, 1977.

Sennett, Richard. *The Fall of Public Man: On the Social Psychology of Capitalism.* New York: Vintage, 1978.

———. *Flesh and Stone: The Body and the City in Western Civilization.* New York: W. W. Norton, 1994.

———., ed. *Classic Essays on the Culture of Cities.* Englewood Cliffs, N.J.: Prentice-Hall, 1969.

Service, Alistair. *London, 1900.* London: Granada, 1979.

Shammas, Carole. "Re-assessing the Married Women's Property Acts." *Journal of Women's History* 6, no. 1 (Spring 1994): 9–30.

Shanley, Mary Lyndon. *Feminism, Marriage, and the Law in Victorian England.* Princeton: Princeton University Press, 1989.

Sharpe, William, and Leondard Wallock, eds. *Visions of the Modern City: Essays in History, Art, and Literature.* Baltimore: Johns Hopkins University Press, 1987.

Shaw, Gareth. "The Role of Retailing in the Urban Economy." In *The Structure of Nineteenth-Century Cities*, edited by James H. Johnson and Colin G. Pooley. London: Croom Helm; New York: St. Martin's Press, 1982.

———. "The European Scene: Britain and Germany." In *The Evolution of Retail Systems, ca. 1800–1914*, edited by John Benson and Gareth Shaw. Leicester: Leicester University Press, 1992.

———. "The Evolution and Impact of Large-Scale Retailing in Britain." In *The Evolu-*

tion of Retail Systems, ca. 1800–1914, edited by John Benson and Gareth Shaw. Leicester: Leicester University Press, 1992.

Shaw, Gareth. "The Study of Retail Development." In *The Evolution of Retail Systems, ca. 1800–1914*, edited by John Benson and Gareth Shaw. Leicester: Leicester University Press, 1992.

Shaw, Gareth, and M. T. Wild. "Retail Patterns in the Victorian City." *Transactions of the Institute of British Geographers* 4 (1979): 278–91.

Sheppard, F. H. W. *Local Government in St. Marylebone, 1688–1835*. London: University of London, Athlone Press, 1958.

———. *London, 1808–1870: The Infernal Wen*. Berkeley: University of California Press, 1971.

Shevelow, Kathryn, *Women and Print Culture: The Construction of Femininity in the Early Periodical*. London: Routledge, 1989.

Shires, Linda M., ed. *Rewriting the Victorians: Theory, History, and Politics of Gender*. New York: Routledge, 1992.

Showalter, Elaine. *Sexual Anarchy: Gender and Culture at the Fin-de-Siècle*. London: Penguin, 1990.

Silverman, Deborah. "The 1889 Exhibition: The Crisis of Bourgeois Individualism." *Oppositions* 8 (Spring 1979): 71–91.

———. *Art Nouveau in Fin-de-Siècle France: Politics, Psychology, and Style*. Berkeley: University of California Press, 1989.

Simmons, Jack. "Railways, Hotels, and Tourism in Great Britain, 1839–1914." *Journal of Contemporary History* 19, no. 2 (April 1984): 201–22.

Singer, Ben. "Modernity, Hyperstimulus, and the Rise of Popular Sensationalism." In *Cinema and the Invention of Modern Life*, edited by Leo Charney and Vanessa R. Schwartz. Berkeley: University of California Press, 1995.

Sizemore, Christine Wick. *A Female Vision of the City: London in the Novels of Five British Women*. Knoxville: University of Tennessee Press, 1989.

Slater, Don. *Consumer Culture and Modernity*. Cambridge: Polity, 1997.

Smith, Victoria. "Constructing Victoria: The Representation of Queen Victoria in England, India, and Canada, 1897–1914." Ph.D. diss., Rutgers University, 1998.

Smith-Rosenberg, Caroll. "The Female World of Love and Ritual: Relations between Women in Nineteenth-Century America." *Signs* 1, no. 1 (Autumn 1975): 1–29.

Smuts, R. Malcolm. "The Court and Its Neighborhood: Royal Policy and Urban Growth in the Early Stuart West End." *Journal of British Studies* 30, no. 2 (April 1991): 117–49.

Solomon-Godeau, Abigail. "The Other Side of Venus: The Visual Economy of Feminine Display." In *The Sex of Things: Gender and Consumption in Historical Perspective*, edited by Victoria de Grazia with Ellen Furlough. Berkeley: University of California Press, 1996.

Sorkin, Michael, ed. *Variations on a Theme Park: The New American City and the End of Public Space*. New York: Hill and Wang, 1992.

Squier, Susan Merrill. *Virginia Woolf and London: The Sexual Politics of the City*. Chapel Hill: University of North Carolina Press, 1984.

———., ed. *Women Writers and the City: Essays in Feminist Literary Criticism*. Knoxville: University of Tennessee Press, 1985.

Stallybrass, Peter, and White, Allon. *The Politics and Poetics of Transgression*. Ithaca: Cornell University Press, 1986.

Stanley, Jackson. *The Savoy: A Century of Taste*. 3d ed., rev. London: Frederick Muller, 1989.

Stansell, Christine. *City of Women: Sex and Class in New York, 1789–1860*. Urbana: University of Illinois Press, 1987.

Staves, Susan. *Married Women's Separate Property in England, 1660–1833*. Cambridge: Harvard University Press, 1990.

Steele, Valerie. *Fashion and Eroticism: Ideals of Feminine Beauty from the Victorian Era to the Jazz Age*. New York: Oxford University Press, 1985.

Stevens, D. F. "The Central Area." In *Greater London*, edited by J. T. Coppock and Hugh C. Prince. London: Faber and Faber, 1964.

Stokes, John. *In the Nineties*. Chicago: University of Chicago Press, 1989.

Stone, Lawrence. "The Residential Development of the West End of London in the Seventeenth Century." In *After the Reformation: Essays in Honor of J. H. Hexter*, edited by Barbara Malament. Philadelphia: University of Pennsylvania Press, 1980.

Storch, Robert D. " 'Please to Remember the Fifth of November': Conflict, Solidarity, and Public Order in Southern England, 1815–1900." In *Popular Culture and Custom in Nineteenth-Century England*, edited by Robert D. Storch. London: Croom Helm, 1982.

Stowell, Sheila. *A Stage of Their Own: Feminist Playwrights of the Suffrage Era*. Ann Arbor: University of Michigan Press, 1992.

Strasser, Susan. *Satisfaction Guaranteed: The Making of the American Mass Market*. New York: Pantheon, 1989.

Sugarman, David, and Gerry R. Rubin. "Towards a New History of Law and Material Society in England, 1750–1914." In *Law, Economy and Society, 1750–1914: Essays in the History of English Law*, edited by David Sugarman and Gerry R. Rubin. Abdingden: Professional Books, 1984.

Summerson, John. *Georgian London*. 3d ed. Cambridge: MIT Press, 1978.

Susman, Warren I. "Personality and the Making of Twentieth-Century Culture." In *Culture as History: The Transformation of American Society in the Twentieth Century.* New York: Pantheon Books, 1984.

Taylor, A. J. P. "Prologue." In *Edwardian England*, edited by Donald Read. New Brunswick, N.J.: Rutgers University Press, 1982.

Taylor, Lou. "Marguerite Shoobert, London Fashion Model, 1906–1917." *Costume: The Journal of the Costume Society* 17 (1983): 105–10.

Taylor, William R. "The Evolution of Public Space in New York City: The Commercial Showcase of America." In *Consuming Visions: Accumulation and Display of Goods in America, 1880–1920*, edited by Simon J. Bronner. New York: W. W. Norton, 1989.

———., ed. *Inventing Times Square: Commerce and Culture at the Crossroads of the World.* New York: Russell Sage Foundation, 1991.

Teal, Laurie. "The Hollow Women: Modernism, the Prostitute, and Commodity Aesthetics." *Differences: A Journal of Feminist Cultural Studies* 7, no. 3 (Fall 1995): 80–108.

Tebbutt, Melanie. *Making Ends Meet: Pawnbroking and Working Class Credit*. New York: St. Martin's Press; Leicester: Leicester University Press, 1983.

Thale, Mary. "Women in London Debating Societies in 1780." *Gender and History* 7, no. 1 (April 1995): 5–24.

Thane, Pat. "Late-Victorian Women." In *Late-Victorian Britain*, edited by T. Gourvish and A. O'Day. London: Macmillan, 1987.

Thirsk, Joan. *Economic Policy and Projects: The Development of Consumer Society in Early Modern England.* Oxford: Clarendon Press, 1978.

Thompson, Dorothy. "Women and Radical Politics: A Lost Dimension." In *The Rights and Wrongs of Women*, edited by Juliet Mitchell and Ann Oakley. Harmondsworth: Penguin, 1976.

Thompson, E. P. "The Moral Economy of the English Crowd" and "The Moral Economy Reviewed." In *Customs in Common: Studies in Traditional Popular Culture*. New York: New Press, 1991.

———. "Rough Music." In *Customs in Common: Studies in Traditional Popular Culture.* New York: New Press, 1991.

Thompson, F. M. L. *Hampstead: Building a Borough, 1650–1964*. London: Routledge and Kegan Paul, 1974.

———., ed. *The Rise of Suburbia*. Leicester: Leicester University Press, 1982.

Thompson, Paul. *The Edwardians: The Remaking of British Society.* London: Granada, 1977.

Thorne, Robert. "Places of Refreshment in the Nineteenth-Century City." In *Buildings and Society: Essays on the Social Development of the Built Environment*, edited by Anthony D. King. London: Routledge and Kegan Paul, 1980.

Thrift, Nigel, and Peter Williams, eds. *Class and Space: The Making of Urban Society*, London: Routledge and Kegan Paul, 1987.

Tickner, Lisa. *The Spectacle of Women: Imagery of the Suffrage Campaign, 1907–1914*. Chicago: University of Chicago Press, 1988.

Tiersten, Lisa. "Redefining Consumer Culture: Recent Literature on Consumption and the Bourgeoisie in Western Europe." *Radical History Review* 57 (Fall 1993): 116–59.

———. "Marianne in the Department Store: Gender and the Politics of Consumption in Turn-of-the-Century Paris." In *Cathedrals of Consumption: The European Department Store, 1850–1939*, edited by Geoffrey Crossick and Serge Jaumain (Aldershot: Ashgate, 1999).

Todd, Ellen Wiley. *The "New Woman" Revised: Painting and Gender Politics on Fourteenth Street*. Berkeley: University of California Press, 1993.

Trewin, J. C. *The Edwardian Theatre*. Oxford: Basil Blackwell, 1976.

Trussler, Simon. *The Cambridge Illustrated History of the British Theatre*. Cambridge: Cambridge University Press, 1994.

Turner, E. S. *The Shocking History of Advertising!* New York: E. P. Dutton, 1953.

Underdown, D. E. "The Taming of the Scold: The Enforcement of Patriarchal Authority in Early Modern England." In *Order and Disorder in Early Modern England*, edited by Anthony Fletcher and John Stevenson. Cambridge: Cambridge University Press, 1985.

Urry, John. *The Tourist Gaze: Leisure and Travel in Contemporary Societies*. London: Sage, 1990.

Valverde, Mariana. "The Love of Finery: Fashion and the Fallen Woman in Nineteenth-Century Social Discourse."

Victorian Studies 32, no. 2 (Winter 1989): 169–88.

Van Arsdel, Rosemary T. "Women's Periodicals and the New Journalism: The Personal Interview." In *Papers for the Millions: The New Journalism in Britain, 1850s to 1914*, edited by Joel H. Weiner. Westport, Conn.: Greenwood Press, 1988.

Van Den Abbeele, Georges. "Sightseers: The Tourist as Theorist." *Diacritics* 10, no. 4 (December 1980): 2–14.

Van Thal, Herbert. *Eliza Lynn Linton, the Girl of the Period: A Biography.* London: Allen and Unwin, 1979.

Vardac, Nicholas A. *Stage to Screen: Theatrical Method from Garrick to Griffith.* 1949. Reprint, New York: Benjamin Blom, 1968.

Vicinus, Martha. *Independent Women: Work and Community for Single Women, 1850–1920.* Chicago: University of Chicago Press, 1985.

———. "Lesbian Perversity and Victorian Marriage: The 1864 Codrington Divorce Trial." *Journal of British Studies* 36, no. 1 (January 1997): 70–98.

———. ed. *A Widening Sphere: Changing Roles of Victorian Women.* Bloomington: Indiana University Press, 1977.

Vickery, Amanda. "Golden Age to Separate Spheres? A Review of the Categories and Chronology of English Women's History." *Historical Journal* 36, no. 2 (June 1993): 383–414.

Vidler, Anthony, "The Scenes of the Street: Transformations in Ideal and Reality, 1750–1870." In *On Streets*, edited by Stanford Anderson. Cambridge: MIT Press, 1978.

Vigne, Thea, and Allen Hawkins. "The Small Shopkeeper in Industrial and Market Towns." In *The Lower Middle Class in Britain, 1870–1914*, edited by Geoffrey Crossick. New York: St. Martin's Press, 1977.

Wainwright, E. D. *Army and Navy Stores Limited Centenary Year.* London: The Stores, 1971.

Walker, Linda. "Party Political Women: A Comparative Study of Liberal Women and the Primrose League, 1880–1914." In *Equal or Different: Women's Politics, 1800–1914*, edited by Jane Rendall. Oxford: Basil Blackwell, 1987.

Walker, Lynn. "Vistas of Pleasure: Women Consumers of Urban Space in the West End of London, 1850–1900." In *Women in the Victorian Art World*, edited by Clarissa Campbell Orr. Manchester: Manchester University Press, 1995.

Walkley, Christina. *The Ghost in the Looking Glass: The Victorian Seamstress.* London: Peter Owen, 1981.

Walkowitz, Judith R. *Prostitution and Victorian Society: Women, Class, and the State.* Cambridge: Cambridge University Press, 1980.

———. *City of Dreadful Delight: Narratives of Sexual Danger in Late-Victorian London.* Chicago: University of Chicago Press, 1992.

———. "Going Public: Shopping, Street Harassment, and Streetwalking in Late Victorian London." *Representations.* no. 62 (Spring 1998): 1–30.

Waller, P. J. *Town, City, and Nation: England, 1850–1914.* Oxford: Oxford University Press, 1983.

Walsh, Claire. "The Newness of the Department Store: A View from the Eighteenth Century." In *Cathedrals of Consumption: The European Department Store, 1850–1939*, edited by Geoffrey Crossick and Serge Jaumain. Aldershot: Ashgate, 1999.

Walton, John K. *The English Seaside Resort: A Social History, 1750–1914.* Leicester: Leicester University Press, 1983.

Walton, John K., and James Walvin, eds. *Leisure in Britain, 1780–1939.* Manchester: Manchester University Press, 1983.

Walton, Whitney. *France at the Crystal Palace: Bourgeois Taste and Artisan Manufacture in the Nineteenth Century.* Berkeley: University of California Press, 1992.

Warner, Marina. *Monuments and Maidens: The Allegory of the Female Form.* New York: Atheneum, 1985.

Watkins, Charlotte C. "Editing a 'Class Journal': Four Decades of the *Queen.*" In *Innovators and Preachers: The Role of the Editor in Victorian England*, edited by Joel H. Wiener. Westport, Conn.: Greenwood Press, 1985.

Wearing, J. P. "Edwardian London West End Christmas Entertainments, 1900–1914." In *When They Weren't Doing Shakespeare: Essays on Nineteenth-Century British and American Theatre*, edited by Judith L. Fisher and Stephen Watt. Athens: University of Georgia Press, 1989.

Weatherill, Lorna. "A Possession of One's Own: Women and Consumer Behavior in England, 1660–1740." *Journal of British Studies* 25, no. 2 (April 1986): 131–56.

———. *Consumer Behaviour and Material Culture in Britain, 1660–1760.* London: Routledge, 1988.

Weightman, Gavin, and Steve Humphries. *The Making of Modern London, 1815–*

1914. London: Sidgwick and Jackson, 1983.

Whitaker, Wilfred B. *Victorian and Edwardian Shopworkers: The Struggle to Obtain Better Conditions and a Half-Holiday.* Totowa, N.J.: Rowman and Littlefield, 1973.

White, Cynthia L. *Women's Magazines, 1693–1968*. London: Michael and Joseph, 1970.

Wiener, Joel H. "Edmund Yates: The Gossip as Editor." In *Innovators and Preachers: The Role of the Editor in Victorian England*, edited by Joel H. Wiener. Westport, Conn.: Greenwood, 1985.

———. "How New Was the New Journalism?" In *Papers for the Millions: The New Journalism in Britain, 1850s to 1914*, edited by Joel H. Weiner. Westport, Conn.: Greenwood Press, 1988.

———. "Sources for the Study of Newspapers." In *Investigating Victorian Journalism*, edited by Laurel Brake, Aled Jones, and Lionel Madden. New York: St. Martin's Press, 1990.

Wiener, Martin J. *English Culture and the Decline of the Industrial Spirit, 1850–1981.* Cambridge: Cambridge University Press, 1981.

Williams, Alfred H. *No Name on the Door: A Memoir of Gordon Selfridge*. London: W. H. Allen, 1956.

Williams, Raymond. *The Long Revolution.* London: Chatto and Windus, 1961.

———. *The Country and the City.* New York: Oxford University Press, 1973.

———. "Advertising: The Magic System." In *Problems in Materialism and Culture*. London: Verso, 1980.

Williams, Rosalind. *Dream Worlds: Mass Consumption in Late-Nineteenth-Century France*. Berkeley: University of California Press, 1982.

Williamson, Judith. *Decoding Advertisements: Ideology and Meaning in Advertising*. London: Marion Boyars, 1978.

———. *Consuming Passions: The Dynamics of Popular Culture*. London: Marion Boyars, 1986.

Wilson, Charles. *Economic History and the Historian: Collected Essays*. New York: Frederick A. Praeger, 1969.

Wilson, Christopher P. "The Rhetoric of Consumption: Mass-Market Magazines and the Demise of the Gentle Reader, 1880–1920." In *The Culture of Consumption: Cultural Essays in American History, 1880–1980*, edited by Richard Wightman Fox and T. J. Jackson Lears. New York: Pantheon, 1983.

Wilson, Elizabeth. *Adorned in Dreams: Fashion and Modernity.* London: Virago, 1985.

———. "All That Rage." In *Fabrications: Costume and the Female Body*, edited by Jane Gaines and Charlotte Herzog. London: Routledge, 1990.

———. *The Sphinx in the City: Urban Life, the Control of Disorder, and Women*. Berkeley: University of California Press, 1991.

———. "The Invisible Flâneur." *New Left Review* 191 (January–February 1992): 90–110.

Winship, Janice. *Inside Women's Magazines*. London: Pandora, 1987.

Winstanley, Michael J. *The Shopkeeper's World, 1830–1914*. Manchester: Manchester University Press, 1983.

Winter, James. *London's Teeming Streets, 1830–1914*. London: Routledge, 1993.

Wolff, Janet. "The Invisible Flâneuse: Women and the Literature of Modernity." *Theory, Culture, and Society* 2, no. 3 (1985): 37–48.

———. "The Culture of Separate Spheres: The Role of Culture in Nineteenth-Century Public and Private Life." In *The Culture of Capital: Art, Power, and the Nineteenth-Century Middle Class*, edited by John Seed and Janet Wolff. Manchester: Manchester University Press; New York: St. Martin's Press, 1988.

Wollen, Peter. "Fashion/Orientalism/The Body." *New Formations* 1 (Spring 1987): 5–33.

Women and the Built Environment 12 (1990). Special issue on shopping.

Yeo, Eileen, and Stephen Yeo, eds. *Popular Culture and Class Conflict, 1590–1914: Explorations in the History of Labour and Leisure*. Sussex: Harvester Press; Atlantic Highlands, N.J.: The Humanities Press, 1981.

Young, Ken, and Patricia L. Garside. *Metropolitan London: Politics and Urban Change, 1837–1981*. London: Edward Arnold, 1982.

Zelizer, Viviana A. "The Social Meaning of Money: 'Special Monies.'" *Journal of American Sociology* 95, no. 2 (September 1989): 342–77.

Zimmeck, Meta. "Jobs for Girls: The Expansion of Clerical Work for Women, 1850–1914." In *Unequal Opportunities: Women's Employment in England, 1800–1918*, edited by Angela John. Oxford: Basil Blackwell, 1986.

• INDEX •